LITIGATION AND TRIAL PRACTICE FOR THE LEGAL ASSISTANT

LITIGATION AND TRIAL PRACTICE FOR THE LEGAL ASSISTANT

FOURTH EDITION

Roderick D. Blanchard

WEST PUBLISHING

an International Thomson Publishing company I(T)P®

Albany • Bonn • Boston • Cincinnati • Detroit • London • Madrid
Melbourne • Mexico City • Minneapolis/St. Paul • New York • Pacific Grove
Paris • San Francisco • Singapore • Tokyo • Toronto • Washington

NOTICE TO THE READER

Copyedit: Cheryl Drivdahl
Interior and Cover Design: Roslyn M. Stendahl, Dapper Design

COPYRIGHT © 1976,1982,1990,1995
By West Publishing
an imprint of Delmar Publishers
a division of International Thomson Publishing

The ITP logo is a trademark under license.

Printed in the United States of America

For more information, contact:

Delmar Publishers
3 Columbia Circle , Box 15015
Albany, New York 12212-5015

International Thomson Publishing – Europe
Berkshire House
168-173 High Holborn
London, WC1V 7AA
England

Thomas Nelson Australia
102 Dodds Street
South Melbourne, 3205
Victoria, Australia

Nelson Canada
1120 Birchmount Road
Scarborough, Ontario
Canada M1K 5G4

International Thomson Editores
Campos Eliseos 385, Piso 7
Col Polanco
11560 Mexico D F Mexico

International Thomson Publishing GmbH
Königswinterer Strasse 418
53227 Bonn
Germany

International Thomson Publishing – Asia
221 Henderson Road
#05 -10 Henderson Building
Singapore 0315

International Thomson Publishing – Japan
Hirakawacho Kyowa Building, 3F
2-2-1 Hirakawacho
Chiyoda-ku, Tokyo 102 Japan

5 6 7 8 9 10 XXX 03 02 01 00 99

Library of Congress Cataloging-in-Publication Data

Blanchard, Roderick D.
    Litigation and trial practice for the legal assistant/Roderick D. Blanchard.—4th ed.
        p. cm.
    Includes index.
    ISBN 0-314-04446-9 (hard)
    1. Civil procedure—United States.   2. Trial practice—United States.   3. Legal
    assistants—United States—Handbooks, manuals, etc.   I. Title.
KF8840.B53   1995
346.7304'86—dc20
[347.306486]

94-40807
CIP

To my wife, Mary

CONTENTS

4   AFFIRMATIVE DEFENSES 87

5   COURT ORGANIZATION 103

6   INTRODUCTION TO FEDERAL PROCEDURE 117

11 EXPERT WITNESSES   259

12 ORAL DEPOSITIONS   276

13 PREPARATION OF CLIENT FOR AN ORAL DEPOSITION   321

14 MEDICAL EXAMINATIONS AND RECORDS   350

INSPECTION OF PROPERTY, DOCUMENTS, AND THINGS   385

15

REQUESTS FOR ADMISSIONS   395

16

FACT BRIEF   414

17

FINAL TRIAL PREPARATION   424

18

19 JURIES AND VERDICTS 447

20 STRUCTURE OF A CIVIL TRIAL 470

21 POSTTRIAL MOTIONS 491

22 JUDGMENTS 502

EXHIBITS

PREFACE

■ DEVELOPMENT OF THIS BOOK

During the past thirty years I have seen many changes in the practice of law and in civil litigation in particular. Most of the changes have been good. One of the best developments has been lawyers' acceptance of paralegals in the field of civil litigation. Paralegals now have a great opportunity to develop personal pride and satisfaction in doing important work well. In civil litigation, each case is a new challenge. Each case provides a new opportunity to learn about the kinds of activities and problems that caused the dispute. The variety of problems encountered by lawyers and paralegals makes civil litigation a fascinating area of the law.

My entire career has been spent handling all aspects of all types of civil cases, including appeals. Twenty years ago I was asked to teach a course in civil litigation for paralegal students at the University of Minnesota. It was a new course in a new college program. At that time my law firm employed some highly skilled investigators and very experienced legal secretaries, but no paralegals. The idea of giving paralegals responsibility for handling any aspect of a civil action was somewhat controversial. But the concept made sense to me, and I decided to become involved.

No textbooks, or even an established format, were available for a civil litigation course. After a good deal of consultation and consideration, I concluded that my course should focus on the Federal Rules of Civil Procedure because those Rules control nearly every aspect of civil actions in the federal courts. Moreover, the Federal Rules are similar to the rules of civil procedure followed in most states, so their precepts have general application. However, paralegal students could not possibly grasp the Rules' applications unless they had some background in the substantive law and principles upon which the civil justice system operates. Paralegals who work in civil litigation must have a basic understanding of the civil justice system as a whole, so that they can see how their work augments the lawyers' work and will benefit the client. *Litigation and Trial Practice for the Legal Assistant* begins by explaining the reasons for having a civil justice system, the principles that drive its operation, and the responsibility lawyers have in handling civil cases.

Litigation and Trial Practice is predicated upon the belief that the more understanding paralegals have about the legal system and the functions of lawyers, the better they can help clients and lawyers. Paralegals who understand the civil justice system and procedures can readily apply this information in an office setting, preparing legal documents and using them. It is not enough to hear about the documents used in civil litigation; students must see them and work with them. Therefore, this book contains examples of most of the documents used in civil litigation.

The paralegal field is growing. Lawyers who have the assistance of paralegals can provide quicker and more thorough attention to their clients' problems. The entire legal system benefits from the help of well-educated, competent paralegals. Certified paralegals are taking major roles in interviewing clients, locating and interviewing witnesses, analyzing and preserving evidence, and preparing litigation documents. Paralegals are involved in almost all phases of trial preparation. Paralegals who understand the civil litigation process may assume major responsibility in handling matters in arbitration. A person does not need to be a lawyer to represent another person or company before an arbitration tribunal. Some casualty insurance companies are asking laypersons to handle intercompany arbitrations in an effort to adjust losses efficiently and economically. The construction industry is turning to arbitration to resolve disputes between owners and contractors, between contractors, and between contractors and suppliers. For several decades, many labor disputes have been resolved in arbitration and mediation by persons who are not lawyers. This book goes a long way in preparing paralegals for such responsibilities.

■ DESIGN OF THIS BOOK

Litigation and Trial Practice introduces civil litigation by explaining why a civilized society must have a civil justice system. The text develops the subject in a logical progression starting with the basic principles that guide civil litigation. It describes the structure of the civil justice system and the organization of the court system. It profiles lawyers' work in civil litigation, the attorney-client relationship, and lawyers' responsibilities to the courts.

A paralegal cannot perform assignments well by functioning in a superficial, mechanical manner. Most lawyers, businesses, and governmental organizations that hire paralegals want paralegals to appreciate the civil justice system's operation and understand the technical aspects of litigation. A paralegal who understands why the system functions as it does can avoid making mistakes. Therefore, this book discusses the law, what it is, and how it applies to resolve disputes.

A paralegal is not expected to try civil lawsuits; the ultimate responsibility for presenting a case in court must remain with the lawyers. Nevertheless, lawyers may delegate to paralegals many of the functions that lawyers traditionally performed in preparing cases for trial. Although paralegals may not have to know *everything* about court jurisdiction, causes of actions, preparing pleadings, or making motions, the better they understand these things, the better they can handle civil litigation responsibilities. Paralegals who understand how their efforts apply to a client's overall representation can provide initiatives and creative solutions to litigation problems. Similarly, although paralegals may not have to know all about legal analysis and trial strategy, those who understand the basis for legal analysis and a method for developing trial strategy for each case will do a better job of gathering and organizing evidence. To these ends, this book identifies and explains the rules of law and the rules of civil procedure that make the system function. But this is not a mere how-to-do-it book. It may be used as a text for learning or a reference book to complement a civil procedure rule book. Although it focuses on the Federal Rules of Civil Procedure, it discusses variations commonly found in state court procedures.

Litigation and Trial Practice deals with many aspects of the rules of law that determine the parties' legal rights and obligations, but primarily with civil litigation procedures that control the parties' preparation and court presentation. It emphasizes the areas in which paralegals can have major responsibility. Specifically, the text explains the methods and the means for gathering and preserving evidence for use at trial. Since many of the procedures are codified in the Federal Rules of Civil Procedure for the district courts, the discussion centers around those Rules. A vast majority of the state courts use similar, if not identical, rules; therefore, studying the Federal Rules has a double value. Lawyers must scrupulously follow the rules of civil procedure. Paralegals must understand what the Rules require in order to avoid embarrassing the lawyers with whom they work and avoid harming clients.

The book's core concerns are investigation and discovery procedures. Paralegals who work in civil litigation are expected to help gather evidence, preserve it, and organize it for use. The text explains each discovery procedure with sample discovery documents. It discusses the different civil litigation procedures, how to use them, and their limits. It compares the relative value of the discovery procedures for various situations, depending upon the purpose of the discovery effort. For example, paralegals may schedule an independent medical examination; this book not only explains the scope and limitations on such examinations, but provides suggestions for preparing letters to clients and physicians. Each discussion is comprehensive and complemented with examples to illustrate the operation of the rules.

This book also explains how a civil trial is structured and conducted, to show how a paralegal's work product is used and why matters are handled the way they are. Civil litigation does not end with the trial: posttrial motions may be made, judgments may need to be enforced, and sometimes appeals must be processed. The entire process is outlined and explained. A student who carefully studies the entire text should be well prepared to assume major responsibilities in civil litigation.

Ethics

Lawyers are officers of the courts in which they practice. They must honor and protect those courts. At the same time, lawyers are advisers and representatives of their clients. Therefore, lawyers must serve both the courts and their clients. Paralegals must understand how and on what basis lawyers balance these sometimes conflicting interests. Ethical considerations apply to every procedure employed by a lawyer. Therefore, paralegals must become familiar with the professional standards and ethical considerations by which lawyers are bound. *Litigation and Trial Practice* discusses legal ethics problems that may confront paralegals in handling their assignments, and makes suggestions for avoiding difficulties. The book explains what lawyers' legitimate objectives are when prosecuting and defending cases, and what lawyers may and may not do when handling civil cases.

Chapter Format

Students beginning their study of civil litigation must learn to deal with new concepts and terminology. Each chapter of this text is designed to reinforce and aid this learning process.

- A chapter opening outline and numerous subheads guide students through the material.
- Key terms and phrases are bold-faced and explained in the text, listed at the end of the chapter, and defined in a glossary at the back of the book.

- Example documents and forms are included with discussions in the text.
- A chapter summary reiterates the important learning points.
- Chapter review questions help students determine whether they have grasped the material and can apply it.

Text Organization

Chapters 1 through 6 provide background information about the civil justice system, its organization, and how and why it operates the way it does. Chapters 5 and 6 introduce court organization and civil procedure. Chapter 7 explains what evidence is and how it is used to prove disputed facts. Chapters 8 and 9 build on the preceding chapters to explain how evidence is gathered and preserved through investigation and discovery procedures.

Chapters 10 through 17 provide detailed instructions about discovery rules and procedures. Specifically, these chapters describe interrogatories, depositions, document inspections, and independent medical examinations. In addition, they explain how paralegals may expect to be involved in discovery procedures—what they may do and not do. Each procedure is illustrated with examples and forms.

Chapter 17 is unique for a paralegal book. It shows the structure of legal analysis applicable to dealing with cases destined for trial. Most lawyers go through the described analysis intuitively. This chapter explains how the analysis is conducted, beginning with the pleadings. The analysis made in the fact brief helps lawyers to anticipate problems in proving cases and how to deal with the problems. A fact brief identifies the evidence that is needed, the evidence that is available, the sources for the evidence, how best to use the evidence, and how to meet the opponent's evidence. The teaching points of this chapter may be applied to the hypothetical case or to any case the instructor finds useful.

Chapter 18 describes how lawyers and paralegals prepare for trial on the basis of all the information and evidence they have obtained through the investigation and discovery procedures. They must organize the evidence to make it admissible and persuasive. They must prepare witnesses and clients to testify before a judge and jury. The discussion leads into chapter 19, which tells about juries, including how they are selected, what role they play in the trial, and how they affect the presentation of evidence. Chapter 20 explains, step by step, the procedures followed in a civil trial. Chapter 21 explains what the losing party can do if errors in the proceedings prevented him or her from having a fair trial. Paralegals may be directly involved in gathering information and preparing documents to support or oppose posttrial motions.

The concept of judgments is the basis for understanding how a party's claim is converted into a right that the party may have enforced against another person. Chapter 22 discusses what judgments are and how they are enforced.

Chapters 23 and 24 deal with facets of civil litigation in which some lawyers neglect to use the skills of paralegals. Chapter 23 discusses summary judgments. A party is not entitled to a summary judgment if any dispute exists on the material facts. This limitation creates a challenge to assemble and present the facts to show that there is no such dispute. This means reviewing relevant documents to determine whether they contain material facts, and preparing exhibits to support the motion. It may also mean preparing affidavits. Chapter 24 describes the appellate process. Paralegals may review transcripts, find transcript citations, proofread, review documents for content and understandability, check case citations, prepare exhibits for use in the appeal, and more.

Chapter 25 describes various types of settlements and settlement agreements. Paralegals may assist with the consummation of settlements.

Chapter 26 is new. Under the common law, arbitration and mediation were disfavored; today, courts encourage these alternative methods of dispute resolution. Unless a court is involved in the mediation-arbitration process, paralegals can handle major, even primary, responsibility. Paralegals who are trained in civil litigation will do a better job in these areas.

■ CHANGES IN THIS EDITION

The fourth edition of *Litigation and Trial Practice* is a major revision of the text to reflect changes in the field and to enhance the teaching and learning format. The principal changes include the following:

- The December 1993 changes in the Federal Rules of Civil Procedure have been incorporated, along with explanations concerning their effect.
- Many more examples of pleadings, motions, and deposition summaries are included. The forms may be used for study and as a reference source.
- An entirely new chapter has been added that discusses arbitration and mediation and how paralegals may be involved in those processes.
- Perhaps the biggest improvement is the reduction of repetition and wordiness. In fact, the entire text has been rewritten to make it more succinct and yet present the same content.
- Evidence and its use are discussed before investigation and discovery.
- The discussion of summary judgment procedures has been moved toward the end of the book, to follow trials.
- The third edition's chapters 6, 7, and 8, on federal procedure, pleadings, and joinder of claims and parties, have been combined into one chapter.

■ HYPOTHETICAL CASE

The appendix and study guide for this text contain a hypothetical case that gives students an opportunity to apply the rules of law and procedure as their studies progress. The hypothetical case has a basis in fact and was chosen because it has many interrelated facets. It arises from a routine automobile accident with the claim of a wrongful death. The case raises basic questions about negligence, damages, contracts, the right to indemnity, the appointment of a trustee, and commencement of a civil action. The surviving driver did not have an insurance policy. The person from whom he had purchased the automobile had promised in writing to provide coverage under another insurance policy, but the seller's insurance policy had lapsed. The seller contended that his insurance agent was negligent for not informing him that his policy had terminated. These circumstances give rise to a malpractice claim against the agent. Various affirmative defenses may be used. The entire scenario gives ample opportunity to consider and analyze the applicable rules of civil procedure and strategies common to civil litigation.

The hypothetical case has some relevancy to nearly every chapter in this text. It may be used as an ongoing story that has evolving problems and subplots. It may also be used as the basis for independent work and tests.

■ TEACHING AND LEARNING SUPPLEMENTS

Litigation and Trial Practice is supported with a comprehensive **student study guide,** which students may use to enhance their understanding of the material. The study guide covers the material with short-answer, true-or-false, multiple-choice, and essay questions. Every question has a complete, understandable answer. The study guide also defines the key terms identified in the text. An instructor has the option of making reading the study guide mandatory or optional. Instructors may use the study guide to promote classroom discussions and as a source for assignments.

The **instructor's manual** for *Litigation and Trial Practice* highlights the teaching points in each chapter. It provides a discussion of each review question and additional questions relevant to the chapter, including true-or-false, short-answer, and multiple-choice questions, all with answers. The instructor's manual discusses the book's hypothetical case as the case develops with the course material. The Instructor's Manual and Test Bank are also available on disk.

The pamphlet *Strategies and Tips for Paralegal Educators,* by Anita Tebbe, of Johnson County Community College, covers the *who, what,* and *how* of paralegal education. One copy is available to qualified adopters. Additional copies may be purchased for faculty.

Qualified adopters can select and exchange videotapes from West Publishing Company's Paralegal Video Library. They may choose from *The Drama of the Law II: Paralegal Issues, I Never Said I Was a Lawyer, The Making of a Case, West's Legal Research, Arguments to the United States Supreme Court,* and the ABA mock trial videos *Business Litigation* and *Trial Techniques: Products Liability Case.*

Westmate Tutorial for DOS and Windows and ten free hours of Westlaw are also available to qualified adoptors of this text.

■ ACKNOWLEDGMENTS

It has been a great pleasure to work with the highly skilled, professional people at West Publishing Company. I have developed a great appreciation for the hard work a book publisher's staff performs to make sure a book is the best it can be. In particular, I wish to acknowledge the invaluable help of the copyeditor, Ms. Cheryl Drivdahl, who reviewed every word of every page to ensure understandability; Ms. Elizabeth Hannan, editor, and Ms. Patty Bryant, development editor, who formulated the revision plan and supervised the project; and Mr. Steven Yaeger, production editor, who coordinated the writing and production activities at every step. Each made invaluable contributions to the fourth edition in substance as well as form.

Catherine Dolan, who is a certified paralegal, and my daughter, had to study from the third edition. She has helped me to make the fourth edition much more focused. My son Scott Blanchard, who is a law graduate and who co-authored the Study Guide, made significant contributions to the book as well.

I thank my wife Mary for her thoughtful assistance, advice and understanding. She has read and edited every page, helping me to communicate legal concepts to nonlawyers. Her support has been invaluable.

I wish also to thank the reviewers who made excellent suggestions for improving this fourth edition:

Mary Cain, Esq.
Barry University, FL

John W. Howay
Tampa College, FL

Roberta L. Comer
Kansas City, Kansas,
Community College, KS

Michael Johnson
Iowa Lakes Community
    College, IA

Robert R. Cummins, Esq.
Southern College, FL

Marion E. MacIntyre
Harrisburg Area Community
    College, PA

Denise A. Hill
College of St. Mary, NE

Roger E. Stone
Hilbert College, NY

I hope this book will contribute to a greater appreciation of the judicial system and the legal profession that helps make it work as well as it does.

PRINCIPLES OF LITIGATION

The civil justice system exists to resolve disputes between persons, businesses, and governments. A party who brings a civil lawsuit invokes the power of the government to force the other person to respond to the claim. Claims that result in litigation usually arise from an alleged unlawful act or omission concerning an occurrence or a transaction between the parties. Such disputes have various bases. The parties may disagree about whether the transaction or occurrence actually took place; whether a wrongful act was committed; who committed the act; whether the defendant caused the alleged harm; whether the claimant sustained any harm; what remedy would be adequate, or what would be fair compensation. Civil courts are equipped to deal with these kinds of questions. The purpose of the system is to enable the parties to ferret out the truth and fully resolve their dispute according to the objective standards of the law.

The judicial system provides a forum in which parties may assert their claims and defenses. Each party is required to gather his or her own evidence and present it. The government does not assist the parties in proving their claims and defenses. The parties must present their evidence according to rules that are calculated to keep the evidence reliable and the presentation fair. A court conducts a trial to resolve disputes over the underlying facts. If there is no dispute over the material facts, there is no need for a trial. When the facts have been established, usually in a jury's verdict, the court applies the law to those facts and determines the parties' legal

rights and obligations. Questions of law, whether substantive or procedural, are always decided by a court.

Occasionally, courts must create new laws to resolve controversies for which there are no established laws or precedents. Court-made law is often referred to as **common law.** A court declares the parties' legal rights and obligations in a judgment that is recorded in a public record called the judgment book. If a party fails or refuses to comply with a court's judgment, the prevailing party may invoke the court's help to enforce the judgment.

If governments did not provide citizens with the means to compel a resolution of their disputes, people who believe they have valid claims might resort to self-help and violence to obtain justice. The civil justice system has proven effective for peaceably resolving private controversies. The judicial system is based upon reason, but it is successful largely because it takes the strengths and weaknesses of human nature into consideration. The system contains checks and balances and safeguards to ensure that justice is achieved according to law. The system may not work perfectly, but it works very well. As a paralegal, you will have the opportunity to play an important part in the administration of justice and to serve clients who need your help.

Civil litigation involves many areas of the law, each of which melds into the others. A lawyer must call upon all his or her education, training, and experience to handle civil litigation. Litigation involves the whole field of law: substantive law, procedural law, and the law of evidence. The **substantive law** determines what the parties' rights and obligations are. The substantive law has three main categories: contracts, property, and torts, and each of these has many subcategories. Lawyers must follow the **procedural law** of the court to establish the client's substantive legal rights. The **law of evidence** determines what may be considered by a jury or judge in determining the facts material to the case.

This chapter provides an overview of the principles, objectives, and limitations of the civil litigation system. Many of the principles, such as jurisdiction, are discussed in greater detail in other chapters.

When a person's legal rights have been violated, causing injury or loss, litigation provides a means for identifying the rights, proving the violations, establishing the nature and extent of the loss, and providing a remedy. In most cases, the remedy is an award of money to provide compensation. Money awarded as compensation is usually referred to as money damages or simply **damages.**

When a person believes that another person has wrongfully caused him or her to suffer a loss, that person should not feel forced to resort to violence or self-help to obtain recompense. If the judicial system were too complicated, too expensive, or too unpredictable in administering justice, parties would avoid using the system and would resort to self-help. Therefore, the procedures for instituting a lawsuit and prosecuting it have been kept relatively simple. The cost of litigation to the parties is only a fraction of its actual cost. For example, the current filing fee for the plaintiff in a federal district court is one hundred dollars. There is no filing fee for the defendant. If parties were forced to bear the entire cost of their litigation, such as the cost of the courtroom and court personnel, they might be forced to forgo valuable rights or consent to obligations that, in truth, they do not owe. Courts should be available to everyone who needs them, and generally they are.

Considering the number of courts and the enormous amount of important litigation they handle, it is amazing that they work so well. Most lawyers who regularly appear in court have the utmost respect for the system and confidence in the ability of courts to make just determinations.

■ THE AUTHORITY OF THE COURTS

When a controversy is put into suit, the parties call upon the government to use its personnel, facilities, and power to bring about a resolution of the problem. A court provides the forum in which parties state their claims and present their evidence in an orderly manner. Through the court's **subpoena** power, parties may require witnesses to appear in court to testify and produce any tangible evidence in their possession. Parties to a pending lawsuit may be compelled to comply with court orders and procedures through the court's power to impose sanctions and penalties. The prevailing party is awarded a judgment in his or her favor, which is enforceable against the losing party through the power of the executive branch of the government. Courts have power to litigate controversies between individuals, corporations, governmental agencies, states, the federal government, and other legal entities.

■ JURISDICTION

Jurisdiction may be thought of as the authority or power of a court. A court's power comes from the government that created the court. Therefore, federal courts depend upon the federal government's authority as the basis for their jurisdiction, and state courts depend upon the state's authority. The United States Supreme Court was created by the United States Constitution; therefore, the Constitution is the source of its power. Similarly, the highest court in each state is limited by the state's constitution. The federal district courts and the federal courts of appeal were created by federal statutes enacted by Congress, so the statutes describe the scope and extent of the courts' jurisdiction. In other words, the statutes prescribe what kind of cases those courts handle, whose cases the courts may decide, where the courts may operate, and what kinds of awards they may make.

To decide a case, the court must have personal jurisdiction over the parties, territorial jurisdiction, and subject matter jurisdiction. If a court fails to obtain total jurisdiction, the court's judgment is void and unenforceable.

Obtaining jurisdiction over the plaintiff is seldom a problem, because the plaintiff submits to the court's jurisdiction by filing the complaint with the court for the purpose of commencing the action. A court obtains jurisdiction over the defendant when the plaintiff causes a summons and complaint to be served upon the defendant. A defendant may voluntarily submit to a court's jurisdiction by agreement or by failing to make a timely objection to the court's exercise of jurisdiction. Once a defendant submits to the court's jurisdiction—even if inadvertently—the defendant cannot avoid the court's authority. A court obtains limited jurisdiction over a person who is not a party when the court's subpoena is duly served upon him or her. A subpoena requires the person to appear (come before the court) for purposes of the particular case at the time specified in the subpoena.

The term "service of process" includes service of a summons or service of a subpoena.

Jurisdiction is subject to a territorial or geographical limitation. The usual territorial limit is a state. A court may obtain jurisdiction over a defendant only if the defendant is duly served with a summons and complaint within the state in which the court functions. However, a defendant may be served outside the state if the lawsuit arises out of the defendant's activity within the state, such as doing business there, or if the defendant was involved in an occurrence in the state, or is a citizen of the state.

The territorial limitation on a court's jurisdiction may also relate to the subject matter. In particular, a court may not be able to decide issues affecting the legal rights of parties and property located in another state. For example, a court could not determine the voting rights of citizens in another state or legal title to real estate located in another state or the constitutional rights afforded by the constitution of another state. The parties cannot, by agreement between them, give a court jurisdiction over the subject matter. As soon as a court becomes aware of any jurisdictional defect, the case must be dismissed.

A judgment obtained in one jurisdiction is readily enforceable in another jurisdiction. The procedure is quite simple. The foreign judgment is made the subject of a lawsuit in the new jurisdiction. An allegation is made that the judgment was duly obtained in the other court, and an authenticated or exemplified copy of the judgment is filed with the new court. The only basis for the defendant (judgment debtor) to avoid the judgment is to prove that the court that rendered the judgment lacked jurisdiction over the defendant or lacked jurisdiction over the subject matter. Since state courts must give full faith and credit to other states' judgments, the burden of proof is on the judgment debtor to prove a lack of jurisdiction. Assuming the judgment debtor fails to prove a lack of jurisdiction, the local court renders its own judgment, which may be enforced like any other judgment within that jurisdiction.

■ CAUSE OF ACTION

The cause-of-action principle is fundamental to the civil law and civil procedures. Nonetheless, it is a difficult, esoteric concept to grasp and difficult to define. A **cause of action** is a claim upon which a court will grant some form of relief. Courts devised the cause-of-action concept as a basis for identifying and limiting the types of controversies that courts are willing to handle. Obviously, the federal and state courts cannot use their power and resources to resolve every kind of dispute that can arise between persons. Some of the issues the courts consider in determining whether a claim amounts to a cause of action is whether the claim has substance, whether the plaintiff should be protected, whether the defendant's conduct should be prohibited, and whether the courts can provide a remedy for the harm. A plaintiff's claim must have all the elements of one or more causes of action before a court will consider the claim.

Many causes of actions (types of claims) are recognized by the courts. All have three predicates:

1. The person against whom the claim has been made (defendant) must have breached a **legal duty** owed to the claimant (plaintiff).

2. The breach of legal duty must have been a **proximate cause** (direct cause) of the plaintiff's harm or loss.

3. The claimant must have sustained an actual loss or harm to her or his person or property.

Causes of action always arise from a transaction or an occurrence. Some common causes of action are discussed in detail in chapter 3.

A legal duty may arise from a contract between the parties, a statute, or a common-law tort rule. When two or more people enter into a contract, they voluntarily make commitments to each other, and each has the right to rely upon the other to keep that commitment. The duty to fulfill the commitment is a legal duty.

If a claim is brought under a statute, it must appear to the court that the legislature intended the statute to protect people in the plaintiff's position and to prohibit persons in the defendant's position from engaging in the allegedly wrongful conduct. For example, each state has a highway code that provides in great detail what each driver and pedestrian must do and not do while using the public roads. The highway code creates legal duties for the protection of those who are on or near the highways. The statutory duties are legal duties which, if violated, give rise to a cause of action.

A legal duty may come from the common law propounded by the courts. In the process of resolving disputes and controversies, the courts have found, declared, and defined legal duties that people owe to each other. A legal duty may require the defendant to do something or not do something. The duties imposed by the common law usually express the minimum care that people must accord to each other and each other's property to make it possible for people to live in communities and be joined in a society. For example, long ago the common law determined that a person who owned land had a right to keep others from entering upon that land. Out of that principle, the common law developed a cause of action called trespass, which permits the owner or occupant of land to make a claim for harm to the land caused by an intruder. In another instance, courts recognized that people should be protected from the harm caused by justified reliance upon false representations. From that principle came the cause of action called fraud. In yet another instance, courts recognized that people should be protected from the harm caused by culpable careless conduct of others. From that principle came the cause of action called negligence. When a person negligently injures another person or another's property, he is liable to pay compensation (damages) for the harm.

Sometimes the courts' common-law rules of law do not work well and need to be changed because society has changed. Courts may overrule their own rules of law and make new ones to accommodate society's needs. When the minimum standards of the common-law rules prove to be inadequate, governments may change the common-law rules through legislation. Insofar as a statute is inconsistent with a common-law rule, the common-law rule is abrogated. If a statute is abolished for some reason, the common-law rule arises to fill the void.

■ SPLITTING A CAUSE OF ACTION

Courts require the plaintiff to assert his or her claim as a whole, not in a piecemeal fashion. For example, suppose the defendant drives his car into the plaintiff's car and injures the plaintiff and damages the plaintiff's car. If the plaintiff starts a lawsuit to recover compensation, the lawsuit must include all the claims that arose from the occurrence. Any claim that is not asserted in the one lawsuit is lost or barred. Therefore, if the plaintiff makes a claim only for the personal injury, the plaintiff cannot subsequently make a claim for the damage to the car. The courts refuse to handle two or three lawsuits where one will do. This principle has been formulated into a rule of law. The rule prohibits parties from **splitting causes of action.** The same rule precludes a party from prosecuting a breach-of-contract claim in a piecemeal fashion. Whatever losses were caused by the breach must be claimed in the one lawsuit. The same principle prevents the plaintiff from asserting a claim pursuant to one legal theory and subsequently making the claim by asserting a different legal theory.

■ COMBINING CAUSES OF ACTION

A defendant's wrongful conduct may give rise to more than one cause of action even though the loss comes from a single transaction or occurrence. For example, if the plaintiff bought a hunting rifle from a sporting goods store and the rifle exploded in his hands, the plaintiff may have a cause of action against the vendor and the manufacturer for negligence, breach of warranty, and strict liability in tort. All three causes of action arise from the same occurrence. The plaintiff must assert all three causes of action in one lawsuit. The plaintiff is not allowed to sue three times on three separate legal theories. Any cause of action not asserted in the first action is waived. Similarly, the defendant loses any defense not duly asserted. A defendant cannot obtain a new trial or a second trial on the ground that he or she inadvertently overlooked a defense that might have been effective.

■ STARE DECISIS

The law must be consistent and predictable, otherwise, parties could only guess at what their legal rights and obligations are. When a rule of law is propounded by statute, all we have to do is read the statute to determine the law. However, much of our law comes from the common law, which is court-made law. If court-made law is to be fair and predictable, courts must be consistent in applying it. The common law derives consistency through application of the **stare decisis** doctrine. The doctrine provides that once an appellate court propounds a rule of law, that court and all lower courts in the jurisdiction must continue to apply that rule in all similar cases. That rule of law controls unless and until the legislature changes it or until that appellate court or a higher appellate court in that jurisdiction overrules the decision.

A court cannot **overrule** or change the law propounded by the legislature in a statute. On the other hand, courts are charged with the responsibility of interpreting statutes and determining whether statutes are constitutional. If a statute is found to be unconstitutional, a court having jurisdiction in the matter may declare the statute void as unconstitutional.

A court may overrule its own decisions, and a higher appellate court may overrule a rule of law made by a lower court. For example, the United States Supreme Court may overrule a rule of law propounded by any federal district court (trial court) or any circuit court of appeals (intermediate appellate court).

The common law has a certain amount of fluidity: it is always changing to meet the changing needs of society and the community. The changeability of the common law is both its strength and its weakness.

Suppose a state trial judge concludes that in wrongful death cases there should be a rebuttable presumption that the decedent was not negligent, because the decedent is not available to testify, and the jury should be told about the presumption even if some evidence indicates that the decedent was negligent and caused the accident or death. The trial judge has produced a new common law rule. Other trial judges in the same jurisdiction do not have to follow that judge's holding. Now suppose the defendant appeals on the grounds that the rule of law is discriminatory against defendants. If the court of appeals affirms, the new common law rule becomes binding upon all trial courts in the state. Other trial judges must apply the same rule in similar cases. Finally, suppose the defendant appeals to the highest appellate court in the state. The defendant persuades the higher appellate court that the new rule of law is unfair because the case is supposed to be decided on the basis of the facts as proved by evidence. A party's difficulty or failure to obtain necessary evidence to support a claim has never been a basis for awarding a verdict. The higher appellate court may overrule the lower courts' decisions and state a different rule of law. The highest appellate court always has the right to change the rule in a later case. In other words, an appellate court may overrule its own prior decisions. But when the court does overrule a prior decision, the prior case is unaffected. The parties to the prior case remain bound by the final decision in that case.

REMEDIES

Sometimes courts are able to restore to a party the very thing she or he lost through the wrongful conduct of another person. Included in such things may be real estate, personal property, documents, and, to a certain extent, intangibles such as a job or a reputation. Where restoration is not feasible, the law attempts to provide fair compensation for injury, damage, and losses through an award of money damages. Money seems to be the best common denominator.

Through a civil suit, a party may be able to prevent (enjoin) an individual, government, or corporation from pursuing a course of conduct that is harmful to a person or the person's property. Courts have the power to issue restraining orders and injunctions to prohibit wrongful conduct, but are seldom able to compel a party to perform services. Regardless of the specific remedy sought, the procedures used for preparing and presenting a claim and a defense are much the same.

■ MULTIPLICITY OF SUITS

More than one court may have jurisdiction over the parties and cause of action. However, the plaintiff may not maintain a civil action in more than one court. If the plaintiff does commence a suit in two courts and the suits arise from the same transaction or occurrence, the defendant is entitled to make a motion for dismissal of one of the cases. When the defendant schedules a motion for dismissal on the grounds of multiplicity of suits, the plaintiff should decide which forum he or she prefers and voluntarily dismiss one of the actions. Multiplicity of litigation wastes the courts' time and imposes an economic hardship on the parties.

One might wonder why the plaintiff's lawyer would ever start more than one suit. The answer is that on occasion, the plaintiff may experience difficulty obtaining personal jurisdiction over one or more of the defendants in one territorial jurisdiction, so he or she starts as many lawsuits as necessary, wherever necessary. Also, the plaintiff may start a lawsuit in one jurisdiction to keep the statute of limitations from running out while trying to obtain service on defendants in another, more convenient jurisdiction.

■ RES JUDICATA

A controversy may be litigated only once. When the parties have had their dispute determined by a court of competent jurisdiction, they cannot relitigate the matter. If the loser attempts to raise the same issues in a new case, the prevailing party has a complete defense by merely showing that the issues were already determined. The second court will not litigate the same issues a second time. The second court will not even litigate issues that should have been determined in the first trial but were not. This principle is referred to as **res judicata,** which means "the subject has been adjudicated." Neither party may go to another court and contend that the first court reached the wrong result, except through established appellate procedures. However, if the first determination was made by a court that lacked jurisdiction, that court's judgment or decree is a nullity. For a court's judgment to be effective and binding, the court must have jurisdiction over the parties and the subject matter. Therefore, the judgment debtor may contest the first court's jurisdiction when the judgment creditor tries to enforce the judgment in a new (foreign) jurisdiction. If jurisdiction was lacking, the judgment cannot be enforced.

■ COLLATERAL ESTOPPEL

An occurrence may give rise to a cause of action in favor of the plaintiff against two or more persons. If the plaintiff sues only one person and the court determines that the plaintiff did not sustain a loss or that the loss was caused solely by the plaintiff's own wrongful conduct, that determination may be a bar to any claim the plaintiff may have against other persons not sued in the first case. This principle is called **collateral estoppel** or estoppel by verdict. The rationale is that the plaintiff presumably tried the original case as well as she or he could and presented all the available evidence. The adverse result should be the same in a second trial against a different defendant. Courts should not be bothered by piecemeal litigation. The plaintiff should join, in one action, all persons who are liable to him or her. But suppose the jury in the first trial finds that nonparties were responsible. Collateral estoppel would not prevent the plaintiff from bringing a new action against those other persons, because such an action is not inconsistent with the determinations made in the first trial.

Suppose the plaintiff was a passenger in an automobile that collided with another automobile, and was injured. Suppose further that the plaintiff sued one driver to obtain money damages for his injuries. If the jury found that the driver was negligent and fully responsible for the accident, that finding would not collaterally estop the plaintiff from suing the other driver in another lawsuit to obtain more compensation. However, the defendant driver in the second suit could adopt the jury's verdict from the first suit and allege that the plaintiff is estopped from claiming additional damages. The rationale is that the plaintiff had the opportunity and incentive to prove all his damages in the first suit, and the courts should not be bothered with having to litigate that issue twice. On the other hand, if the defendant in the second suit wanted to litigate the damages issue, he would have a right to do so. The second defendant cannot be denied the right to present evidence on a material issue. Consequently, if the plaintiff chooses to bring separate suits against two defendants, both of whom may be liable for the accident, the plaintiff runs the risk of incurring a bad result in the first suit and being bound by that result in the second suit, at the second defendant's election. The second defendant has the option of asserting collateral estoppel against the plaintiff or trying to obtain a better result in the second suit.

■ REAL CONTROVERSY

Fundamental limitations restrict the kinds of controversies that courts may handle. A controversy must be real, as opposed to hypothetical. It must arise from an actual transaction or occurrence. Parties could conjure up all kinds of interesting fact situations for which they would like a court's "advisory opinion." But people are not permitted to use the courts to resolve their hypothetical questions. This principle of jurisprudence has some very practical applications. For example, if one party to a contract believes that the other party is going to breach the contract, it might be nice to have the issue litigated before the breach actually occurs. But there is at this point no controversy between them that will permit either party to invoke the power of the courts. For another illustration, suppose that during the course of a trial the parties are able to reach a settlement so that their controversy is, in fact, resolved. It would be considered a fraud upon the court for the parties to continue with the case just to see how it would have been decided. Their settlement ended the dispute; they cannot impose upon the courts.

■ REAL PARTY IN INTEREST

A lawsuit must be brought in the name of the **real party in interest**. As stated in Rule 17 of the Federal Rules of Civil Procedure, "Every action shall be prosecuted in the name of the real party in interest." The defendant has an absolute right to deal with the party who owns the cause of action. If it appears that the plaintiff is not the real party in interest, the action must be dismissed by the court. Suppose Johnson loans Richards five hundred dollars on a promissory note, and Richards defaults. Johnson considers the note to be almost worthless because Richards has no ability to pay at the present time. But O'Callahan decides to buy the promissory note from Johnson for fifty dollars on the basis that someday Richards will pay or can be compelled to pay. Who owns the cause of action? O'Callahan is the real party in interest in an action on the note, since contract claims are assignable.

As a general rule, personal injury claims cannot be assigned or transferred. This principle tends to discourage intermeddlers from fomenting personal injury litigation. However, there is a growing list of exceptions to the prohibition against assignment of injury claims. For example, if a medical insurance policy has paid an accident victim's medical bills, the insurer may have a right of **subrogation** against the **tortfeasor**. Subrogation is the process by which a person who pays another's obligation acquires the right to proceed against the person who in truth or law is primarily liable for the obligation, and recover from that person the amount paid. A tortfeasor is someone who commits a tort—a civil wrong that causes injury to another person or damage to another's property. A tort is the result of a violation of a legal duty imposed by the common law or statute. Some courts have indicated a willingness to permit the insurer to pursue its subrogation claim even though it is part of the insured's personal injury claim.

■ NECESSARY PARTIES

Court procedures encourage, and even require, joinder of all claims into one lawsuit to facilitate the ends of justice and to minimize the number of cases and trials. The plaintiff should join as parties to the case all persons whose presence is necessary to fully resolve the dispute. Example 1: If the plaintiff is one of several owners of a building that was destroyed by a fire, and the plaintiff brought the action against the defendant to recover money damages for loss of the building, the rights of the other owners should be determined in the same action. Example 2: If the tenant in an apartment building claims an injury because of a premises defect and sues only one of the two persons who own the building, a judgment against the one owner would be unfair to her. She is entitled to contribution from the co-owner. Unless the co-owner is made a party, the court cannot provide complete relief. If a person has not been joined who should be joined, the court may order that person joined through proper service of process. The person joined in the action may be made an involuntary plaintiff or defendant. Of course, the court must have jurisdiction over the person to be joined (Rule 19(a)).

Suppose an "indispensable" party is outside the jurisdiction of the court and refuses to join as a party. The court must consider the "equities" of the situation and decide whether it is more fair to let the action proceed without that party, or to dismiss. Rule 19(b) states:

> The factors to be considered by the court include: first, to what extent a judgment rendered in the person's absence might be prejudicial to the person or those already parties; second, the extent to which, by protective provisions in the judgment, by the shaping of relief, or other measures, the prejudice can be

lessened or avoided; third, whether a judgment rendered in the person's absence will be adequate; fourth, whether the plaintiff will have an adequate remedy if the action is dismissed for nonjoinder.

The factors the court must consider are whether the court's judgment will prejudice the rights of persons who are already parties to the action. In example 2, the defendant owner might be held liable and unable to obtain contribution from the other owner. However, if the plaintiff agrees to limit the damages to one-half of the total entitlement, the defendant owner would not be prejudiced. If the plaintiff could pursue the claim in another court and obtain full relief from all persons who should be joined, the court would likely dismiss the plaintiff's claim. If the defendant will voluntarily agree to submit to the jurisdiction of another court where the action can be brought against all persons who should be defendants, the court would probably dismiss the action.

■ JUDGES AND JURIES

The trial judge determines all questions of law and procedure that arise during the course of a trial. He or she controls the courtroom and the people in it. Lawyers, witnesses, parties, and even spectators may be held in contempt of court for disruptive conduct and be summarily punished. Judges must have this plenary authority to ensure respect for their courts and for the justice system.

Federal and state courts have extensive power that is limited, primarily, by self-discipline. The physical features of the typical courtroom promote the dignity of the courtroom and proceedings. Invariably, the judge's robes set the judge apart from everyone else and provide an air of classic dignity. The robes are always black, emphasizing the solemnity of the proceedings. Professional ethics require lawyers to underscore the dignity of the court by always being respectful, even during moments of acute disagreement.

With experience, a judge acquires knowledge and understanding helpful to the handling of his or her responsibilities. But experience may also cause a judge to acquire prejudices for or against certain lawyers, parties, and types of litigation. Even though a judge endeavors to keep personal feelings from affecting decisions, the potential for bias exists. Since jurors are exposed to only a few cases during their term of service, they are not likely to develop strong, fixed attitudes about a particular lawyer or a party or certain types of cases. Trial by jury provides the civil justice system with an important check that promotes the appearance of fairness and gives the parties confidence in the system.

■ APPELLATE COURTS

Appellate courts, such as the United States Supreme Court, are primarily concerned with determining questions of law. Only after a controversy has been fully presented to a trial court and a determination made by the trial court does an appellate court become involved. Appellate courts depend upon the trial courts to resolve disputed issues of fact so that the law can be applied to established facts. Appellate courts are concerned with matters of both substantive law, which determines the parties' rights, and procedural law, which determines how the case must be prosecuted.

Appellate courts have inherent power to change court-made rules of law. On occasion, an appellate court determines that an old, established rule of law must be set aside. This is done by issuing a decision and written opinion that expressly overrules all prior decisions that are inconsistent with the new holding. Usually the new rule is made effective prospectively only. In that event, all causes of action arising from transactions or occurrences before the date of the new decision are governed by the old rule of law, but all causes of action arising thereafter are governed by the new rule of law. If an appellate decision does not expressly state that the new rule is to be given prospective effect only, its effect is retroactive as well. Then the new rule applies even to pending cases, but not to cases already adjudicated or settled.

■ COURTS AS NEUTRALS IN AN ADVERSARY SYSTEM

Civil litigation is an adversary proceeding. Each party is required to gather and present her or his own evidence. The trial court remains entirely neutral. Judges are permitted to ask clarifying questions of witnesses during the course of a trial, but when this is done, the judge usually explains to the jury that it should not give any greater or lesser weight to the testimony elicited through those questions. In federal courts, a trial judge may comment on the evidence after instructing the jury concerning the applicable law. Most state court judges avoid doing that. If the judge's comments are adverse to the party who subsequently loses, it makes the party feel that she or he did not have a fair trial.

When a judge elects to comment on the evidence at the end of the trial, he or she should remind the jurors that they are the exclusive judges of the facts. They must determine the truth solely from the evidence presented during the trial. They should not be influenced by what they think the judge wants the verdict to be. A judge usually instructs the jury that his or her comments are not intended to indicate what he or she thinks the outcome of the case ought to be. A judge usually tells the jury, at the end of the trial, that if he or she has said anything or done anything that would seem to indicate such an opinion, the jury is to disregard it.

There are a few situations in which a judge may affirmatively act to protect one party. For example, judges do intercede on behalf of minors and incompetent persons to make sure their rights are protected. Courts always make sure that guardians are appointed to represent minors who are involved in civil litigation whether as plaintiffs or defendants. If the plaintiff is a minor who wishes to settle the claim, the proposed settlement cannot be binding upon the minor unless it is approved by a court. The court must inquire into the circumstances of the occurrence or transaction that gave rise to the defendant's liability as well as into the nature and extent of the minor's injuries or other losses. The defendant's ability to pay may be a consideration. The judge must evaluate all the facts to determine whether the settlement is prudent from the minor's standpoint. Only if the judge decides that the settlement is truly in the minor's best interests should the judge give approval. If the judge refuses to approve the settlement and the defendant is unwilling to pay more, the case must go to trial. If the jury finds in favor of the defendant, the minor plaintiff has no recourse against the judge for not approving the proposed settlement; she or he must abide by the verdict.

■ REPRESENTATIVES

In cases involving a person who is incompetent to manage his or her own matters, such as a minor, the court must see to it that a guardian is or has been appointed for the purpose of protecting that person's interests in the litigation. This is true whether the incompetent person is a plaintiff or a defendant. A guardian who is specially appointed to represent a litigant is called a **guardian ad litem.** The guardian will be discharged by the court upon conclusion of the litigation. Her or his duty in the litigation is to protect the incompetent party's interests and carry out the court's orders. If a guardian has already been appointed by a probate court, ordinarily that person is a proper representative to handle the incompetent party's litigation. Then a guardian ad litem is not necessary.

The parties' statuses in the case are indicated in the title of the action (see exhibit 1.1). The complaint usually contains a separate paragraph alleging that the representative was duly appointed to act in a representative capacity. Rule 9(a) specifically states, however, that such an allegation is not essential.

■ ASSIGNMENT OF CLAIMS

The owner of a claim (cause of action) for money damages has the right to prosecute the claim in court. The purpose of proving or establishing the claim in court is to have the mere claim adjudged to be an absolute right that is enforceable against the party who is liable. This absolute right is established by a judgment that declares the parties' rights and obligations. A cause of action that is subject to **assignment,** or transfer, to another person is sometimes referred to as a chose in action. This phrase means that it is an unperfected right. Though unperfected, the right is identifiable and has value. Though it is not property, as such, a chose in action can be bought, and sold or assigned. For example, if a dispute arises between a seller and a buyer of goods, and the buyer refuses to pay for the goods, the seller's alleged right to payment could be assigned or sold to another person or company, which could bring suit to recover on the claim. As part of the cause of action, the assignee would have to prove a valid assignment.

■ **EXHIBIT 1.1**
Action Title

John Jones, as guardian ad litem of
Mary Jones, a minor,
                                        plaintiff,
                vs.
Robert M. Smith, and
Michael M. Smith,
                        defendants.

A trespass to real estate could cause damage. The owner of the damaged property may want to sell the property before he or she can bring suit against the trespasser. The buyer may be willing to take an assignment of the cause of action against the trespasser. The value of the assignment is quite subjective and is usually negotiable between the assignor and the assignee. The assignee's recovery is often limited to the amount paid for the assignment, but not always. The law discourages people from buying assignments of causes of action with the expectation of making a profit on the assignment.

As a general rule, personal injury claims cannot be bought and sold, or assigned. There is no commercial necessity for such assignments. This rule effectively prevents lawyers and others from speculating in personal injury claims. Suppose Wu sustains injuries owing to the tortious conduct of the defendant. Wu is the only person who is permitted to sue the defendant to recover money damages for those injuries. If the law were otherwise, Wu might be inclined to sell his cause of action to another person. It is not too difficult to imagine some well-to-do individual or company speculating in personal injury lawsuits. Some injured parties would be willing to sell their claims for an inadequate sum of money to obtain payment immediately. The buyer might be able to turn a handsome profit on a subsequent settlement or jury verdict. But profit making is contrary to the objectives of civil litigation. Also, such dealings tend to shortchange injury victims who are in need. The plaintiff's lawyer must not permit the plaintiff to become a party to such a scheme.

Indemnification for a loss by the plaintiff's own insurance company may complicate ownership of the claim. For example, if an automobile is damaged by the defendant in an accidental collision, the automobile's owner may elect to receive payment for the loss under the collision coverage of her or his own automobile insurance policy. The insurance company has a right to an assignment of the automobile owner's claim against the tortfeasor. Most automobile insurance policies provide that the insured must bear the first one hundred dollars of the loss. If the insured retains a partial interest in the claim because of a deductible clause, she or he remains owner of the cause of action and is the real party in interest to bring the claim. If the insured makes a recovery against the tortfeasor, the insured's contract with the insurer requires a reimbursement to the insurer out of the recovery. The insured holds the funds in trust for the insurer.

If an insurer pays the full amount of its insured's loss pursuant to the terms of a direct-loss (not liability) insurance policy, the insurer becomes the real party in interest to bring an action against the tortfeasor who caused the loss. The insurer owns the cause of action; the action must be brought in the insurer's name. For example, suppose the insured's automobile was destroyed by a fire caused by the defendant's negligence. The insured may elect to obtain payment for the loss under the automobile policy. The loss comes under the comprehensive coverage, which does not require the insured to pay any portion of the loss, or any deductible. In that event, when the insurer pays its own insured for the loss, the insurer is subrogated to the claim against the defendant. The insurer becomes the owner of the cause of the action and is the real party in interest. Suits against the defendant tortfeasor must be brought in the name of the insurance company. The insured has no right to control the litigation. The insured's contract with the insurance company requires the insured to cooperate in the prosecution of the lawsuit.

Whenever a cause of action is properly assigned, it must be prosecuted in the name of the assignee. The maximum amount of money damages that the assignee can recover is, ordinarily, the amount paid for the assignment. Proof that the assignment was duly consummated is part of the cause of action. The assignee must plead and prove the assignment as part of the case.

■ COMMENCEMENT OF LAWSUIT

A lawsuit is very easy to start. The first step is to prepare a document called a complaint, which sets forth the plaintiff's claim against the defendant. The complaint presents the basic facts and alleges that the defendant breached one or more legal duties owed to the plaintiff. In federal court, **commencement of action** occurs when the complaint is filed with the clerk of court. The clerk then prepares a summons directed to the defendant. The summons instructs the defendant that he or she must answer the complaint or be held liable by default.

Several methods may be used to serve the summons and complaint upon defendants. The traditional method is to have the United States marshal serve them by delivering a copy of each to the defendant personally or by delivering the copies to the defendant's residence and leaving them with a person who resides there also. The person with whom the summons and complaint are left need not be related to the defendant, but must be of suitable age to understand the importance of the event. Many states now authorize service of the summons and complaint by mail. However, the service is not effective until the defendant decides to accept it by signing an acknowledgment, which the defendant then returns to the plaintiff's lawyer. Some types of cases, such as automobile accident cases, allow service of the summons and complaint upon a state official, such as the secretary of state. Under some circumstances, service of process may be made by publication in a legal newspaper. These methods of service are discussed in greater detail in chapter 6.

■ COUNTERCLAIMS AND CROSS-CLAIMS

A defendant is required to assert, by way of **counterclaim,** all claims that she or he has against the plaintiff arising from the same transaction or occurrence. If the defendant fails to assert any claims against the plaintiff, the claims are waived and the defendant is barred from bringing them in another lawsuit at another time. The entire controversy should be determined once, in one proceeding. It is more economical for the parties and the court to resolve the entire matter in one trial.

Where there are two or more defendants, they may assert **cross-claims,** which will be litigated in the same action as the plaintiff's claim against the defendants. The cross-claims may be served by mail upon a defendant's lawyer once the defendant has appeared in the action by answering the complaint. A cross-claim may seek compensation for the defendant's own loss caused by the transaction or occurrence on which the plaintiff's action is based, or it may seek contribution toward the plaintiff's claim, or both.

The presence of a cross-claim establishes **adversity** between defendants. When there is adversity between parties, they may cross-examine each other and each other's witnesses. In addition, they will not have to share peremptory challenges when selecting the jury (see chapter 19). The use of cross-claims is another example of courts trying to resolve as many issues as possible in one proceeding.

■ THIRD-PARTY CLAIMS

If a defendant determines that he or she has a right to indemnity or contribution from a person who is not yet a party to the case, the defendant may commence a **third-party action** to obtain indemnity or contribution. A claim for indemnity is a claim for complete reimbursement. For example, in accident cases, defendants who have liability insurance are entitled to indemnification by their liability insurer for any obligation the defendants have to a plaintiff. An action for indemnity is sometimes necessary when a dispute arises between the defendant and his or her own liability insurer as to whether the plaintiff's claim is covered by the insurance policy. A third-party claim is limited to the claims arising from the plaintiff's alleged loss. The defendant cannot use a third-party action as a basis for obtaining compensation for the defendant's own loss.

A claim for contribution looks for a sharing of liability and responsibility. For example, if two automobile drivers are negligent so as to cause injury to the plaintiff, but the plaintiff brings action against only one of the drivers, the driver who was sued could bring a third-party action against the driver who was not sued, to obtain contribution for any award the plaintiff may obtain.

■ DECLARATORY JUDGMENT ACTIONS

Courts may resolve controversies requiring the interpretation of statutes and documents. A lawsuit brought for this purpose is called a **declaratory judgment** action. The court judgment determines the meaning and effect of the statute or documents in dispute. For example, if two parties have a disagreement over the meaning of a contract between them, either party may start a declaratory judgment action to have a court interpret the contract for them even though the contract has not been breached and no loss has been sustained. The court declares the parties' rights and obligations. The controversy must be real or the action will be dismissed. Declaratory judgment actions are given special treatment by Rule 57. Through declaratory judgments, parties are also able to establish legal status concerning employment, marriage, property ownership, and right to government benefits.

■ CIVIL PENALTIES

Rarely is civil litigation concerned with penalizing a wrongdoer. That is the role of the criminal justice system. An award of money damages is for the purpose of making the plaintiff whole. The financial obligation that the defendant incurs as a result of her or his liability is merely incidental or a consequence of compensating the plaintiff. Courts are not usually concerned with whether the defendant can afford to pay or whether the plaintiff can afford to absorb the loss or whether the defendant could really afford to pay more. A few exceptions do exist, though. Many states have legislation imposing a civil penalty recoverable by a plaintiff employee if a defendant employer wrongfully withholds the employee's wages. A court may award an employee treble the amount of wages wrongfully withheld. In addition, the employee may be allowed interest from the date the wages were due. Similarly, in some states a trespasser who takes crops or lumber from the land of another is subject to paying three times the value of the property taken. Obviously, the purpose of treble damages is to deter the wrongful conduct.

Another exception is that many states allow plaintiffs to recover punitive damages—a penalty assessed against the defendant in addition to compensatory damages in cases where the defendant intentionally inflicted injury. For example, an intentional battery with a knife, gun, or even fist may be the basis for imposing punitive damages. Punitive damages are recoverable regardless of the degree of injury or other harm—as long as some harm was incurred. The measure of punitive damages depends upon the character of the wrongful conduct and the financial worth of the defendant. The term *exemplary damages* is sometimes used for punitive damages because the award is held out as an example to others to discourage wrongful conduct. If the award is really going to penalize the defendant, its size must take into consideration the defendant's ability to pay—at least, that is the rationale. Consequently, in cases where punitive damages are allowable, the defendant's financial worth may become part of the evidence.

Opposition to allowing punitive damages in civil actions is considerable and growing. Members of this opposition argue that punitive damage awards subject the defendant to double jeopardy—in other words, the defendant pays twice (or more) for one mistake. Civil procedures lack the safeguards of criminal cases. For example, the burden of proof is less in civil cases. Opponents argue that only the state should impose fines for criminal conduct. Where more than one claim may result from a tortious act, the imposition of multiple penalties can have ruinous consequences for the defendant. A claim of punitive damages injects the defendant's financial worth into the case, which could adversely influence the jury on other issues and be a personal embarrassment to the defendant.

■ LITIGATION EXPENSES

Each party to a civil lawsuit must bear most of his or her own expenses, including investigation costs, most witness fees, and lawyers' fees. The few exceptions to this general rule usually involve special remedies provided by statute where the monetary loss may be relatively small, but the principle at issue is important. Such legislation makes the courts more readily available to those who have been the victim of some form of official harassment or discrimination. The prevailing parties in such lawsuits are usually allowed to recover all their expenses, including lawyers' fees. In most cases, however, taxable costs are limited to the filing fee, subpoena fees, United States marshal's fees, and some small portion of expert witness fees.

Taxable costs are the costs of the litigation that may be added to the parties' recovery of money damages.

SETTLEMENTS

When parties negotiate a **settlement** of a claim, they may take into consideration many issues that have no actual relevancy to their legal rights and obligations—such as the effect of the dispute on friends, business associates, or relatives. A defendant's lack of insurance or lack of financial responsibility may be an important element inducing the plaintiff to accept a compromise or reduced settlement. A party might be constrained to settle because of the cost of litigation or the unavailability of witnesses. But legal rights and duties do not turn on the availability or unavailability of insurance or on the effect of litigation on personal relationships. If the parties are unable to reach a settlement, they have to set aside all collateral considerations and rely solely upon the issues that are material to an action at law. The parties must evaluate the strengths and weaknesses of their respective positions in light of rules of law and the procedures by which courts apply those rules.

In various ways, the judicial system encourages parties to settle their own disputes. But when the parties cannot reach an accord or agree upon a settlement, the person who wants to force a determination may obtain a judicial determination and a judicial remedy through litigation. However, the controversy must be one that creates a cause of action. This is another way of saying that the controversy must be one over which courts have jurisdiction, one that can be determined by law, and one for which the law provides a remedy.

PROFESSIONAL ETHICS

Lawyers are subject to a strict Code of Professional Responsibility. The Code controls all aspects of lawyers' work and specifically dictates how lawyers are to conduct themselves when handling civil litigation. A lawyer's violation of the Code subjects the lawyer to disciplinary action, which may result in a loss of license to practice law. The Code dictates the obligations that lawyers owe to their clients, to the courts, to opposing lawyers, and even to persons with whom they do not have any direct contact or relationship. A lawyer who violates the Code is subject to disciplinary action even if the violation does not cause any actual harm to anyone, whereas, with very few exceptions, claims upon which courts can provide relief in civil actions require proof of actual harm or injury to be actionable. The Code also helps lawyers deal with obligations and loyalties where there are apparent conflicts in their duties. Ethical considerations that govern lawyers' conduct are discussed throughout this book.

An unethical act committed by a paralegal is the ethical responsibility of the lawyers who employ the paralegal. In other words, a lawyer could probably be censured for the mistakes or misconduct of a paralegal who has acted within the course of her or his employment. It's doubtful that paralegals could be censured and punished in the same way that lawyers can be sanctioned by the courts and by the boards of professional responsibility. Nevertheless, paralegals must avoid being involved in any conduct that violates the Code, and any violation of the Code by a paralegal must be considered to be a matter of grave concern.

Courts control the unlawful practice of law. Anyone who tries to practice law without a license may be disciplined by a court. The practice of law consists of giving legal advice to another person or representing another person in a court proceeding. As will be discussed in Chapter 26, a paralegal may fully participate in an arbitration and not be guilty of practicing law.

SUMMARY

Civil litigation is a highly structured means for resolving disputes between persons. A court that has jurisdiction over the subject matter and parties has the power to force the parties to participate in the process. A court provides the forum in which parties state their claims and present their evidence in an orderly manner. The purpose of a trial is to determine the truth about the facts that gave rise to the parties' dispute. The court applies the law to the facts to determine the parties' legal rights and obligations. The parties' legal rights and obligations are stated in the court's judgment. A court has the power to enforce its judgment against the parties. When the plaintiff is entitled to a remedy, the most common type of relief that courts provide is money damages. The award of money damages is intended to compensate the plaintiff for the loss he or she sustained.

A court's jurisdiction is its authority or power. A court must have jurisdiction over the parties, the subject matter, and the territory to be able to decide a case. If a court decides a case without having complete jurisdiction, its judgment is a nullity and may be attacked in a subsequent action. Even though a court may not have jurisdiction over a party, that party may submit to the court's jurisdiction voluntarily or even inadvertently. Once the court obtains jurisdiction, it does not lose it.

A plaintiff must be able to state her or his claim in the form of a cause of action, which is a type of claim for which the courts will provide a remedy. The plaintiff must present evidence to prove each element to the cause of action alleged. Each cause of action has certain elements and requisites. Regardless of the particular type of claim, a plaintiff must show that the defendant breached a legal duty that the defendant owed to the plaintiff, and that the breach directly caused the plaintiff's loss or harm.

A plaintiff may not split a cause of action. All claims that arise from a single transaction or occurrence must be included in one lawsuit; otherwise, the claim is barred. If the defendant fails to assert a defense to the plaintiff's claim or claims, the defense is lost.

Stare decisis requires courts to follow established rules of law, at least until the rules are expressly overruled. A court may overrule its own decisions. A higher court may overrule a lower court's decisions. A legislature may change a court-made rule of law.

The plaintiff must assert all claims against the defendant that arose from the transaction or occurrence, or give up the claims. In other words, if the plaintiff omits any claim for damages or omits any legal theory for recovery, the plaintiff is barred from trying to assert the claim in a subsequent action. Similarly, the defendant must assert all defenses to the claim and waives any defenses not duly asserted.

Courts are restricted in the kind of remedies or relief they can provide. The most common relief courts provide is money damages. Where the parties have a dispute over ownership of certain property, a court may determine who is the real owner. Where a party is engaged in a course of wrongful, harmful conduct, a court may enjoin that conduct by issuing an injunction. In rare circumstances, a court may actually order a party to take some affirmative action, but courts are reluctant to do that because it is difficult to enforce the order.

The plaintiff may not maintain a civil action in more than one court. If the plaintiff does commence the same suit in two courts, the defendant may move for a dismissal of one of the cases. The motion should be granted. Therefore, the plaintiff may want to dismiss one of the suits before the motion is heard, to keep the court the plaintiff prefers.

Res judicata precludes a party from bringing the same claim against the same person a second time. It also precludes a party from bringing a claim against a person who is in **privity** with a former party. The doctrine requires the plaintiff to include in one action all claims that arise from a single transaction or occurrence. Res judicata complements the rule against splitting a cause of action.

Collateral estoppel precludes a party from litigating the same issue more than once where the issue was decided adversely to that party. The doctrine differs from res judicata in that it applies to a subsequent action even though the later action involves a different party.

A lawsuit must involve a real dispute, not a hypothetical problem. As a general rule, the plaintiff must show that the defendant has breached a legal duty owed to the plaintiff and has caused actual harm. This rule has one exception: a party may bring a declaratory judgment action to have the court interpret a contract or statute where the parties have an actual dispute concerning the application of the contract or statute but neither has yet breached a legal duty.

A declaratory judgment action is authorized by statute but is prosecuted like any other civil action. Where fact issues exist, the parties have a right to have a jury determine those facts. However, the interpretation of a contract or statute is strictly the responsibility of the judge.

A lawsuit must be prosecuted by the real party in interest. The plaintiff cannot be a mere "front" for someone else. When a party duly assigns a claim to another person, the assignee becomes the real party in interest. The assignee must prove the validity of the assignment as part of his or her claim.

When a person is under a legal disability, such as being too young to bring a lawsuit, the action may be brought by a representative. A natural guardian may act on behalf of a child in a lawsuit by being the child's representative. All other "representative" plaintiffs must be appointed by court order. A representative may be required to post a bond to guarantee due and proper performance.

The plaintiff commences a civil lawsuit by preparing a complaint. The complaint must state a claim upon which a court may grant relief against the defendant. The plaintiff must file the complaint with the clerk of court.

The clerk issues a summons with the title of the action and a court file number. The plaintiff must arrange to serve the summons and complaint upon the defendant. The plaintiff may pay a U.S. marshal to serve the summons and complaint, or arrange to have an adult who is not a party to the suit serve them. The action was commenced at the time of the filing.

A defendant may assert a claim against the plaintiff by making a counterclaim. If the counterclaim arises from the same transaction or occurrence, it is mandatory; that is to say, if the claim is not brought in the same suit, the defendant loses it. Defendants may assert claims against each other in a cross-claim. A cross-claim may seek compensation for the defendant's own loss or it may seek contribution toward the plaintiff's claim or both.

A defendant may join another person in a lawsuit as a third-party defendant to obtain indemnity or contribution toward the claim made by the plaintiff. The defendant may not bring a third-party action to obtain compensation for the defendant's own loss.

Courts allow the plaintiff to recover punitive damages from the defendant when the defendant has intentionally committed a wrongful act in willful disregard of the rights or safety of the plaintiff. Punitive damages are awarded in addition to compensatory damages. The customary issues that the jury may consider in determining how much money to award include the degree of the defendant's culpability, the extent of the defendant's financial resources, and the nature of the harm to which the defendant exposed the plaintiff.

The prevailing party is entitled to recover some of the costs of the litigation as provided by statute. Usually, the recoverable costs include the filing fee, subpoena fees, witness fees, and some portion of the expert witness fees. As a general rule, each party must bear his or her own attorney's fees.

Courts favor settlements. Parties settle their dispute by entering into a contract that provides that the claimant releases the defendant from any liability for the transaction or occurrence. To be valid, the settlement must have all the elements of a valid contract. Most settlements are the result of compromise. A valid settlement provides a complete defense to the settled claim.

KEY TERMS

common law	real party in interest
substantive law	subrogation
procedural law	tortfeasor
damages	appellate courts
subpoena	guardian ad litem
jurisdiction	assignment
cause of action	commencement of action
legal duty	counterclaim
proximate cause	cross-claims
splitting causes of action	adversity
stare decisis	third-party action
overrule	declaratory judgment
res judicata	settlement
collateral estoppel	privity

REVIEW QUESTIONS

1. What is the source of a court's authority? *pg 3*

2. How does a court obtain personal jurisdiction over the plaintiff and the defendant? *pg 3*

3. How does a cause of action differ from a claim? *pg 4–5*

4. How may an established rule of law be overruled? *pg 8*

5. What issues must be considered in determining whether a court has jurisdiction in a particular case? *pg 19*

6. Why will a court preclude the plaintiff from splitting a cause of action? *pg 19*

7. What are the essential elements to every cause of action? *pg 5*

8. Who benefits from the application of the res judicata doctrine? *pg 8+20*

9. What is the purpose of an appellate court? *pg 11*

10. How do declaratory judgment actions differ from other civil actions? *pg 16+20*

2

LAWYER AND CLIENT RELATIONSHIP AND ETHICS

■ QUALIFICATIONS TO PRACTICE LAW

Lawyers are officers of the courts in which they practice. They are committed by oath to serve the courts honorably, to adhere to the courts' rules, and to support the laws of the land. Their highest duty and obligation is to those courts. At the same time, lawyers ordinarily derive their income from advising and representing clients. On the surface, it appears that lawyers have an inherent conflict of interest between representing clients and serving the courts. However, the civil justice system has thoughtfully and positively resolved the potential for conflicts.

Lawyers must have the education, knowledge, experience, and skill to handle whatever case or other legal matter they undertake. Of course, they must not only possess such abilities, but must also exercise the abilities with due diligence and care. Lawyers must not assume responsibilities beyond their experience and competence. These requirements present a significant dilemma for the neophyte, because it is difficult to obtain experience in the absence of the necessary underlying experience. Many lawyers deal with this problem by working under the supervision of established, experienced lawyers or as judges' clerks until they obtain sufficient experience to act independently.

The highest court in each state establishes the criteria that individuals must meet to be able to practice law in that state. Most states require applicants to be graduated from an accredited law school, and a college degree is a prerequisite to enter most accredited law schools. In addition, most states require each applicant to pass a state bar examination. The examination tests applicants on their knowledge of substantive law, procedural law, and ethics. A person who is not licensed to practice law may handle her or his own legal matters but cannot advise or represent others in legal matters. No one has a constitutional right to practice law.

An applicant for a license to practice law is screened to determine whether there is any evidence the applicant lacks good moral character. A criminal conviction involving some minor crime usually requires a detailed explanation but will not preclude admission to the state's bar. Conviction of a crime involving moral turpitude should preclude licensure.

After a lawyer has been admitted to practice in the courts of a state, the lawyer may petition to practice in the federal district court for that state. Federal district courts do not require petitioners to take any test; they presume that the state courts have adequately screened the petitioners for competency. The lawyer's petition must be supported by affidavits of two other lawyers who are admitted to practice in the federal court. The sponsors must affirm that they know the petitioner; that the petitioner is a competent lawyer and has good moral character. Each federal district court periodically has a swearing in ceremony. The petitioners must appear in person with one of the sponsors. The ceremony is usually a memorable experience, especially for the younger lawyers. A lawyer's admission to practice in one federal district court does not give the lawyer a right to practice in other federal courts. If a lawyer wants to try a case in another district, the lawyer may obtain special leave from that court to appear in the one case. The lawyer does not have to file a petition; however, a local lawyer must move the applicant's admission.

A lawyer obtains leave to practice in a federal circuit court of appeals by filing a petition with the court. The petitioner does not have to appear before the court for a swearing in ceremony. Similarly, a lawyer may obtain leave to practice in the United States Supreme Court merely by filing a written petition.

A lawyer is subject to disbarment for any conduct that constitutes moral turpitude. Of course, this does not mean that misdemeanors or ordinance violations would necessarily result in disbarment. The privilege of practicing law is valuable and cannot be taken away at the "pleasure" of the court. A lawyer is entitled to have a hearing to controvert any charges which may affect his or her privilege to practice law.

In states that have an **integrated bar,** a person cannot practice law without belonging to the bar association. The bar association is clothed with an official status and is given the initial responsibility for determining whether an applicant may be admitted to practice. An integrated bar association also has responsibility for conducting disciplinary proceedings against lawyers who are found guilty of unethical conduct. In states that do not have integrated bars, the highest court in the state has the authority to discipline and disbar errant lawyers. The court ordinarily appoints personnel to perform the investigation and prosecution functions. Nevertheless, the authority and responsibility remain with the court, and it must make the final decisions on admissions, disciplinary action, and disbarment.

Any individual who attempts to practice law without a license is subject to disciplinary proceedings by the court having jurisdiction of the matter, just as though the individual were a lawyer. Furthermore, an individual

who unlawfully attempts to practice law is subject to criminal prosecution. Paralegals are not authorized to practice law. A paralegal must not advise other persons about legal matters or represent another person in court. Paralegals may do many of the things lawyers do in the handling of litigation, but the work must be performed under the direction of a lawyer. The lawyer must assume ultimate responsibility for whatever advice is given to a client and whatever legal services are provided. A paralegal's work in civil litigation must be done under a lawyer's supervision. In that way, courts retain their authority over the process, because lawyers are subject to control of the courts in which they are licensed.

Parties and lawyers increasingly tend to look to **mediation** and **arbitration** as alternatives to civil litigation. Paralegals may handle any aspect of these dispute resolution methods because they are not judicial procedures and thus do not require a license to practice law. Most of the skills that paralegals develop in handling civil litigation are basic to handling mediation and arbitration. Of course, paralegals may not render legal advice while handling a matter in arbitration.

■ PROFESSIONAL RESPONSIBILITY

Lawyers are advisers to and representatives of their clients. Lawyers are authorized to give clients advice about the law and its application to the clients' problems and concerns. As advisers, lawyers may prepare legal documents for clients, such as deeds, contracts, wills, and so on. Such documents may be prepared by anyone for his or her own use, but only a lawyer is authorized by law to prepare them for another person or for a company. If a layperson were to prepare such documents for another person, that would constitute the unauthorized practice of law and would be punishable. The layperson would be subject to criminal prosecution and to civil sanctions by the courts.

As representatives of their clients, lawyers have authority to act and speak on behalf of their clients for the purpose and to the extent authorized by the clients. In addition, lawyers have implied authority to perform any act or make representations relevant to the handling of the clients' litigation. Lawyers regularly represent clients in state and federal courts as well as in many situations not involving courtrooms and trials. They represent clients in legislative hearings, business transactions, arbitration hearings, mediations, and business negotiations. They also represent clients before official bodies that conduct hearings affecting legal rights, such as at city council meetings and regulatory agency hearings. Professional people such as physicians, ministers, teachers, and lawyers need lawyers to represent them in peer review hearings where the client has been charged with "unprofessional conduct." The accusation may not have any criminal or civil ramifications but could cause the professional to lose his or her license. Sometimes a fine line separates the functions performed by lawyers and the activities of real estate brokers, tax advisers, and certified public accountants—indeed, certain accountants are authorized to appear on behalf of clients in tax courts.

A lawyer must follow the client's wishes and directives. In civil litigation, this means that even though a lawyer may believe the client should pursue a claim or is entitled to demand a larger settlement, the client has

the right to reject the lawyer's advice. If the client wants to settle a claim on terms less favorable than those the lawyer honestly believes are fair and obtainable, the lawyer must accede to the client's preference. This is true even when the lawyer's fee is determined by the amount of the recovery. By the same token, if the client wishes to forgo a valid claim or dismiss a meritorious claim, regardless of the reason, the lawyer must comply, even if the lawyer is handling the case on a contingent fee and will lose that fee. Civil litigation and claims are not the same as merchandise and commercial services. A lawyer must accept the client's decision concerning the objectives of the litigation and the manner in which the litigation is prosecuted. On the other hand, a lawyer should not try to prosecute a claim when the lawyer believes that the claim lacks merit in the law or on the facts. And, of course, a client cannot require a lawyer to commit an unlawful act.

When a client hires a lawyer to handle civil litigation, the lawyer has implied authority to do whatever is necessary to prosecute the claim through to a judgment. In other words, a lawyer may assume that he or she is authorized to follow the customary practices and procedures for prosecuting or defending against a civil claim without consulting the client about each step. However, a lawyer is not authorized to commence or dismiss a suit without the client's express permission. Furthermore, a lawyer must abide by the client's decisions concerning time, expenses, and costs. Subject to the client's approval, a lawyer handling civil litigation has responsibility for choosing the procedures and means for obtaining the client's objectives. Although parties must follow certain procedures when prosecuting or defending a civil action, there is a fair amount of latitude with regard to when and how the various procedures may be used. But the lawyer must always keep in mind the client's best interests and lawful objectives when deciding how to proceed.

■ CONFLICT OF INTEREST

A lawyer is not allowed to represent one client against another client. If a lawyer has two clients who have a dispute between them, the lawyer may not represent either of them. Each client must obtain legal advice or representation from another lawyer. Similarly, if a lawyer has represented a client in the past and is currently representing another client who has a dispute with that former client, professional ethics preclude the lawyer from advising or representing either party concerning their dispute. There is a presumption that the former client had disclosed to the lawyer important information of a personal nature and that the lawyer may have gained an understanding of how the client handles legal matters, so it would be unfair to use that information and knowledge against the former client. In a sense, the relationship between a client and a lawyer lasts forever.

This rule concerning **conflict of interest** has a very important exception. The two clients may agree to allow the one lawyer to represent both of them. Or a former client may waive the right to object to the lawyer's representing a new client against him or her. But the burden is on the lawyer to inform both clients about the conflict. The lawyer must explain that either of the clients has a right to object to the lawyer's being involved in their matter. Although the clients' permission does not have to be in

writing, a lawyer would be foolish not to record her or his disclosures and the clients' consent.

If a lawyer undertakes to represent two clients who have adverse interests and either one of those clients *subsequently* objects to the joint representation, the lawyer has to withdraw from the entire matter. The lawyer then loses both clients. The lawyer's contract for fees is not enforceable against either client. At most the lawyer can obtain payment for the value of the services already rendered to the clients and reimbursement of necessary costs already incurred. The measure of the lawyer's claim is the value of the services to the clients, which is not necessarily the value of the lawyer's time.

A lawyer might be asked to represent the injured driver and passenger of one automobile against the driver of another automobile with which they collided. A potential conflict of interests exists between the passenger and his driver, because the passenger may have a claim against both drivers. But suppose the passenger and his driver are married and the passenger does not want to obtain any money damages from his wife. The lawyer could undertake to represent both if the lawyer fully explains that the passenger is forgoing a valid claim and may, consequently, recover no damages. The lawyer's explanation and the clients' consent should be reduced to writing for the purpose of showing that the matter was fully discussed and clearly communicated, and to create evidence of the clients' informed consent. As a further precaution against criticism, the lawyer could advise one or both of the potential clients to talk with another lawyer about the desirability of separate representation.

This hypothetical situation can have numerous variations, so there is no one best course of action. For example, if the passenger's injuries are very minor and the driver's very serious, it would make a lot of sense for the lawyer to represent the driver and handle the spouse-passenger's claim as an "add-on." On the other hand, if the passenger's injury is very serious and the driver's claim is nominal, the lawyer would be foolish (not unethical) to handle both claims with the risk of having to give up both in the event either client changed her or his mind about the joint representation.

A lawyer's representation of several clients who are making claims as a result of the same transaction or occurrence presents a problem where the parties have an opportunity to settle the case for an aggregate amount. A lawyer is in a very awkward position to recommend how the settlement proceeds should be allocated between clients. Using the preceding example where a husband and wife are injured and both have a claim against the other driver, suppose that the other driver has a twenty-five-thousand-dollar liability insurance policy that the insurer is willing to pay to settle *both* claims. The insurer may not care how the claimants divide the money, but no additional money is available. If the clients agree on the allocation, there is no problem. But if they are unable to agree, their lawyer may counsel them but should not insist upon a particular allocation. Each client may need to consult another lawyer concerning the acceptability of the offer and a fair division.

■ FIDUCIARY RESPONSIBILITY

A lawyer is considered a **fiduciary** of the client's properties and monies. A fiduciary voluntarily assumes a legal duty to act for another person for a particular undertaking in a position of trust and confidence. A fiduciary must put the interests of the beneficiary ahead of the fiduciary's own interests. As a fiduciary, the lawyer must exercise the highest degree of care in handling the client's monies, properties, papers, and confidential communications. If a loss occurs, the lawyer has the burden of showing that it was for reasons beyond his or her control. The fiduciary relationship lasts as long as the lawyer continues to possess or control the client's property. A lawyer's fiduciary duties are limited to protecting and maintaining the client's property. A lawyer does not have the higher obligations of a fiduciary when giving legal advice or representing a client in a legal proceeding.

■ AGENT

An **agent** is a person who is authorized by a principal to act on behalf of the principal. The acts of an agent are binding upon the principal just as if the principal had performed them. However, an agent can bind the principal only to the extent that the agent acts within the scope of his or her authority.

The relationship between a lawyer and a client is basically that of an agent and a principal. It does not matter whether the client hires the lawyer on a full-time basis for a salary or retains the lawyer to handle only one legal matter for a fee. In either arrangement, the lawyer is an agent of the client and subject to the client's control.

Usually, the client looks to the lawyer for advice and recommendations concerning how the legal problem should be handled. The lawyer is considered the expert, and the client expects the lawyer to do whatever is necessary and appropriate to obtain a favorable resolution. In addition, the lawyer is expected to act for and speak on behalf of the client concerning matters that are within the scope of the engagement.

As in any agency relationship, the extent of a lawyer's authority to bind the client and to make representations on behalf of the client is subject to limitations that the client imposes. As a general rule, the scope of an agent's authority is determined by the principal, and that is also true for lawyers who handle civil litigation. A lawyer acts on behalf of the client when preparing legal documents and representing a client in a legal proceeding. Parties may deal with the lawyer on the basis that the lawyer has authority to act for and make commitments on behalf of the client. Notices directed to a lawyer as a representative of a client are binding upon the client. However, a lawyer's actual authority is limited to the particular matter for which he or she has been retained.

Some very important limitations restrict what a lawyer may do in handling a client's litigation. A lawyer must not start a lawsuit for the client without the client's authorization. The client has the ultimate right to decide whether or not to sue. The client may insist that the lawyer pursue a claim in some other manner such as through negotiations or mediation or arbitration, or abandon the matter. In settlement negotiations, the client ordinarily looks upon the lawyer as the expert to decide when and how to proceed. Nevertheless, the lawyer is not allowed to accept or reject a proposed settlement without first obtaining the client's authority to do so—even if the settlement is clearly in the client's best interest. Similarly, the lawyer must not dismiss a lawsuit without the client's authority and direction to do so. If the lawyer believes or even knows that the client's claim lacks merit and will be subject to dismissal by a court and that the court may impose penalties upon the client and lawyer for bringing the claim, the lawyer cannot dismiss the claim without the client's permission. The lawyer can exonerate herself or himself by obtaining the court's leave to withdraw from the case. Under such circumstances, the sooner the lawyer withdraws, the better for the lawyer.

Despite these limitations, a lawyer's authority and responsibility to a client go beyond those of an ordinary agency. A lawyer has implicit authority to do whatever is reasonably necessary for the preparation and management of a trial. A lawyer may prepare interrogatories, schedule depositions, prepare requests for admissions, issue demands for documents, attend calendar calls, attend pretrial conferences, and make representations to the court about the case's state of the readiness, all without first obtaining the client's permission. Many of these responsibilities may be performed by a paralegal.

A lawyer may also enter into stipulations with opposing parties concerning the evidence and trial procedures. The lawyer's implicit authority includes the right to object or not object to the admissibility of certain evidence. This does not mean that the lawyer's decisions concerning the handling of evidence are immune from criticism or a claim of malpractice. It merely means that the lawyer does not have to consult the client in making those decisions in the first instance. The lawyer may consult the client about such matters but is not required to do so. The lawyer has the *responsibility* for handling the litigation, but he or she is always subject to the client's ultimate *authority*.

◼ DUTIES AS AN OFFICER OF THE COURT

Lawyers have dual roles in the judicial system. They are officers of the courts in which they practice, but they are also representatives of their clients. Lawyers are required to act in their clients' best interests and to give advice that will benefit their clients in the conduct of their legal matters. But lawyers are also required to protect the courts from fraud and abuse. The success of the judicial system is absolutely dependent upon the ability of lawyers to serve their clients' legitimate needs and the courts' interests without compromise. Consequently, a very stringent code of professional ethics has been established to guide lawyers. Any violation of the code of ethics hurts the legal profession and contaminates the entire judicial system.

The Code of Professional Responsibility was adopted by the American Bar Association in 1969. The Code provides guidelines for the resolution of various ethical problems. Many states have adopted the Code and the Disciplinary Rules as standards of conduct that if violated, provide the basis for imposing sanctions—including disbarment.

The preamble to the Code of Professional Responsibility states the importance of the ethical considerations (see exhibit 2.1).

Although the Code of Professional Conduct is directed to lawyers, it applies, at least by implication, to any person who assists lawyers, whether as an investigator, a secretary, or a certified legal assistant.

■ **EXHIBIT 2.1**

Preamble to the Code of Professional Responsibility

PREAMBLE

The continued existence of a free and democratic society depends upon recognition of the concept that justice is based upon the rule of law grounded in respect for the dignity of the individual and his capacity through reason for enlightened self-government. Law so grounded makes justice possible, for only through such law does the dignity of the individual attain respect and protection. Without it, individual rights become subject to unrestrained power, respect for law is destroyed, and rational self-government is impossible.

Lawyers, as guardians of the law, play a vital role in the preservation of society. The fulfillment of this role requires an understanding by lawyers of their relationship with and function in our legal system. A consequent obligation of lawyers is to maintain the highest standards of ethical conduct.

In fulfilling his professional responsibilities, a lawyer necessarily assumes various roles that require the performance of many difficult tasks. Not every situation which he may encounter can be foreseen, but fundamental ethical principles are always present to guide him. Within the framework of these principles, a lawyer must with courage and foresight be able and ready to shape the body of the law to the ever-changing relationships of society.

The Code of Professional Responsibility points the way to the aspiring and provides standards by which to judge the transgressor. Each lawyer must find within his own conscience the touchstone against which to test the extent to which his actions should rise above minimum standards. But in the last analysis it is the desire for the respect and confidence of the members of his profession and of the society which he serves that should provide to a lawyer the incentive for the highest possible degree of ethical conduct. The possible loss of that respect and confidence is the ultimate sanction. So long as its practitioners are guided by these principles, the law will continue to be a noble profession. This is its greatness and its strength, which permit of no compromise.

The Disciplinary Rules were developed from ethical considerations. They help to define those considerations and specify their application to problem areas. If accused of a violation of professional ethics, a lawyer is entitled to a hearing that meets all the requirements of due process of law. A lawyer has a right to know the charges against her or him, to present evidence in defense, and to be heard by an impartial tribunal.

A lawyer must not direct or encourage a client to engage in conduct that is unethical for the lawyer. In other words, a lawyer may not do indirectly through a client that which the lawyer is forbidden to do. He or she must not let the client violate the lawyer's oath by making false answers to interrogatories or testifying falsely or procuring the absence of witnesses or suborning perjury. If a lawyer discovers that a client is guilty of some such impropriety, he or she must take affirmative action to correct the wrong.

Lawyers are forbidden to engage in activities that foment litigation. It is not difficult to imagine that a lawyer whose business is a little slow may be tempted to examine public records to find a problem with the title to a parcel of real estate for the purpose of obtaining a client. Similarly, unscrupulous lawyers could research newspapers and magazines to find potential libel suits. By such conduct, lawyers create problems solely for their own financial gain. Similarly, lawyers are in a good position to encourage accident victims to pursue litigation rather than drop a claim or settle out of court. Such practices are degrading to the profession and could flood the courts with petty, unnecessary, and unwanted litigation. Any lawyer who creates that kind of business should not be practicing law. Society's interests should be served, not damaged, by lawyers and civil litigation.

A lawyer who incites litigation is subject to disciplinary proceedings and possible disbarment. Paralegals, too, must avoid instigating litigation. That is not to say that a paralegal must avoid recommending a good lawyer when and where one is needed, but a paralegal should not create a controversy where none exists.

■ CHAMPERTY AND MAINTENANCE

A lawyer is not permitted to provide financial support for a client by paying the client's living expenses during the pendency of litigation. The practice of advancing monies to a litigant on the basis that the "loan" will be paid out of the verdict or settlement is known as **maintenance,** and it is unethical. At first blush, it would appear to be considerate, even charitable, for a lawyer to provide a means of support for a client until the case is concluded, especially if the client is disabled and unable to work because of injuries. If a lawyer were to become financially involved in the client's case, then, before the case is over, the client could end up "assigning" the claim to the lawyer. If lawyers were to provide financial aid to clients with the expectation of being repaid through the court award or settlement, they would soon find themselves personally involved in the clients' financial affairs and personally interested in the outcome of the case. The danger is much too great that a lawyer's professional judgment could be affected by personal interest in the litigation. The lawyer might be inclined to recommend for or against a settlement in light of her or his own needs rather than those of the client. Good advice is rarely rendered by a person who is personally involved in the matter. In addition, financing clients could become an expected practice—and most lawyers would find that an impossible burden. The lending of money is better left to banks and other financial institutions. A lawyer is permitted to advance, on behalf of the client, various expenses incurred in connection with the litigation. But this may be done only on the basis that ultimately the expenses will be paid by the client, regardless of the outcome of the case.

A lawyer may not invest in a client's lawsuit by buying an interest in the expected recovery. The law frowns upon speculation in litigation for profit. The same principle was an obstacle to the use of contingent fees in civil litigation. Even today, contingent fees are unethical in criminal cases. When the owner of a claim enters into an agreement with a third person to share the recovery, the arrangement is called **champerty.** Champerty is unethical and may be illegal. Champerty differs from maintenance in that the third person, whether or not a lawyer, tries to buy an interest in the expected recovery. Maintenance is concerned with financing a litigant's costs during the pendency of litigation regardless of the litigant's recovery. On the other hand, certain causes of action may be assigned. The difference is that an assignee of a cause of action may prosecute the action in her or his own name, and the arrangement is not made for profit. It is permissible to assign causes of action arising from transactions such as claims on contracts. However, assignment of personal injury claims is contrary to public policy. The law distinguishes between such assignments because there is a real danger of champerty in the personal injury field. When an assignee prosecutes a claim, the assignee is the named party, so the assignee's interest in the outcome of the case is fully disclosed.

■ SOLICITATION AND ADVERTISING

Historically, lawyers were forbidden to advertise their services. They could not even permit others to advertise on their behalf. This prohibition was based, in part, on the concern that advertising would foment litigation and lawyers would unduly impose themselves on prospective clients at unpropitious times. The legal profession is currently in a dilemma over advertising. Advertising is considered to be degrading, but perhaps necessary if the public is going to be fully informed about the availability of lawyers' various services and the charges for services. Many people are not personally acquainted with any lawyer and are unaware of the types of services lawyers can provide.

Today advertising is permitted on a limited basis. The limitations are concerned not with the amount of advertising, but with the methods of advertising. Advertising is justified on the basis that the public benefits from dissemination of information about the kinds of services lawyers provide, the cost of legal services, the background and experience of lawyers, and where and how to locate lawyers.

Lawyers may advertise in public media, including newspapers, television, billboards, radio, and directories. Lawyers may not advertise by direct solicitation, whether in person or by telephone. Lawyers may not pay or reward other persons for recommending them to handle legal matters. Lawyers may include in their public advertisements information about themselves, such as age, date admitted to practice, law school attended, offices held in bar associations, teaching positions held, and certification in any specialties in the law. The information must be accurate and factual. For example, it would be unethical for a lawyer to advertise that he or she graduated from Harvard if the lawyer did not obtain a law degree from Harvard. The advertisement would be considered misleading.

A public advertisement may state the lawyer's address and telephone number and describe the basis for charges. For example, it may state flat rates for certain types of representations such as adoptions and uncontested divorces, or hourly rates for defending against a drunk driving citation. An advertisement may state that the lawyer handles civil litigation claims on a contingent fee and that the lawyer will advance court costs. An advertisement must be so worded that it does not create unjustified expectations about the results the lawyer will obtain. For example, it would be unethical for a lawyer to advertise that the lawyer "wins most" of the cases he or she tries.

Lawyers may permit their name to be listed in professional directories. These directories are particularly useful to lawyers who need to refer clients to other lawyers in other communities. The principal such directory is *Martindale-Hubbell,* which is published in several large volumes each year.

■ LAWYER-CLIENT PRIVILEGE

The relationship between a lawyer and a client is very personal and confidential. A client must feel free to disclose her or his most personal secrets to the lawyer. Otherwise, a client might hold back information the lawyer needs in order to provide good advice and effective representation. Lawyers have an ethical obligation not to disclose to other people anything a client has said or written in confidence when seeking legal advice. A lawyer cannot even disclose such communications or information to a judge. Furthermore, a court may not compel a lawyer to make such a disclosure. This rule of **privileged communication** does have a few exceptions. A client cannot claim a privilege to discuss with his or her lawyer how to commit a crime or how to evade the law. A client has no privilege to consult a lawyer about how to defraud the court.

Paralegals may expect to participate in lawyer-client conferences. These conferences may concern a client's wish to obtain a divorce, buy some land, bring a personal injury lawsuit, obtain workers' compensation benefits, and so on. Regardless of the purpose, the communication is privileged. Paralegals have the same obligation as the lawyer to guard against any improper disclosure.

The lawyer-client relationship is established whenever a lawyer permits a client to seek her or his professional advice. If the client discloses information, believing it to be under the protection of the attorney-client privilege, that is sufficient to establish the relationship. A lawyer is forever precluded from using such information to the detriment of the client and from disclosing it to others. The communication is privileged whether written or oral. Only the client may waive the privilege. The same proscriptions that apply to lawyers apply to paralegals.

A lawyer's records prepared from communications with a client are similarly privileged. The privilege belongs to the client, not to the lawyer, and applies to written communications as well as oral communications. The client may waive the privilege either intentionally or inadvertently. All that is needed for a waiver to occur is for the client to relate to some third person the substance of an otherwise privileged communication. In other words, the privilege must be carefully protected.

Confidential communications are substantially different from privileged communications. A matter that is kept secret between two or more persons would be considered confidential. Most businesses wish to keep their customers' matters confidential. Banks, lending institutions, credit card companies, and department stores all strive to keep their records from getting into the hands of the curious. They avoid publicizing information in their possession about their customers. Nevertheless, a court of law could compel a company to produce its records if the records were relevant to a civil action. But if a communication is privileged, no person and no court can legally compel its disclosure for any purpose.

A client's statements to a lawyer are privileged because the client is able to obtain good, competent legal advice only by "telling all" to the lawyer. If the client labored under the fear that statements to the lawyer could be used against him or her as admissions, the client might be inclined to hold back vital information. The privilege applies whether the client discusses marital problems, business problems, past criminal conduct, preparation of tax returns, or whatever. It does not matter what the subject is as long as the client is seeking professional legal help or advice that is not for the purpose of committing an unlawful act.

The law makes an important distinction between legal advice sought by the client for the purpose of determining legal rights and advice sought for the purpose of evading the law, in either a current or a future activity. For example, if a client were to consult a lawyer for the purpose of working out a plan to illegally evade taxes, the communication would not come within the privilege. Indeed, under those circumstances, the lawyer would be duty bound to try to persuade the client to comply with the law. If that fails, the lawyer could be required to inform the proper authorities of the client's scheme. The lawyer could even be compelled to testify against the client concerning the scheme.

For a long time, the privileged status of a communication was lost if the subject matter was voluntarily disclosed to any third person, even the lawyer's secretary. Most courts now recognize that lawyers must act through others, such as private secretaries and legal assistants. Consequently, the privilege has been extended in most jurisdictions to include lawyers' agents. Courts should recognize that it is desirable and necessary for lawyers to disclose privileged information to paralegals assisting them. Of course, if the privilege is enlarged in this manner, paralegals must be subject to the same close controls that courts have over lawyers and to the same rigid professional ethics.

In several recent cases reporters have attempted to establish a rule that their "confidential" news sources should have privileged status. In the past, reporters could be punished through contempt-of-court proceedings for their failure or refusal to divulge sources, assuming there was a good and sufficient reason for litigants to know the identity of the sources. The issue presented to the courts in the recent cases is whether the need for privileged news sources outweighs the need for identification of witnesses who have important evidence relevant to criminal and civil lawsuits. A second question is whether any story is newsworthy if the identity of the source is not subject to disclosure. Some reporters who have challenged the law in order to bring about a change have been forced to spend time in jail for refusing to comply with court orders directing them to testify. Their incarceration was punishment for being in contempt of court.

If a client files an ethics complaint against a lawyer or commences a negligence action for malpractice, the client cannot claim the attorney-client privilege in an effort to keep the former lawyer from using records and communications to defend herself or himself. The privilege is intended to be used as a shield for the client, never as a sword. A lawyer may use all the client's records and communications, whether written or oral, to defend herself or himself.

■ DUTY TO THE COURT

A lawyer is an officer of the court and must conduct himself or herself in a professional manner at all times, showing respect to the court even when seriously disagreeing with the presiding judge. A lawyer's zeal and desire to serve a client must not lead to misuse or abuse of the court. If a lawyer believes that a judge has acted improperly in any matter, the lawyer has the right and duty to bring that concern to the attention of the proper authorities. The lawyer must not insult or cast aspersions on the court in public.

Though a lawyer owes complete fidelity to a client and ordinary care in the handling of the client's litigation, a lawyer's highest obligation is to the courts. Therefore, a lawyer must not perpetrate a fraud upon a court by producing false testimony, or otherwise abuse the judicial process for any purpose. If a lawyer learns that a client has attempted to bribe a witness or juror or the like, the lawyer's first effort should be to urge the client to confess the wrongdoing to the other party in the action, with the hope that the matter can be resolved. If the client refuses to do so, the lawyer's only recourse may be to inform the court of the wrongful act. Some authorities argue that under such circumstances, a lawyer may withdraw from further representation of the client and should make no disclosure to the court. This position is based on the premise that the criminal act—the fraud—has already occurred without the lawyer's knowledge. At this point, the client is in need of legal advice because of the problem, just as for any other crime. Most courts have rejected this argument.

There should never be a direct conflict between a lawyer's duty to a client and duty to the court. The Code of Professional Conduct helps lawyers to determine where their primary obligations lie and how to avoid or resolve apparent conflicts.

■ COLLATERAL PROFITS

If a lawyer handles a client's legal matters in such a way as to realize a profit, aside from a proper legal fee for services, there is a presumption that the profit was obtained by undue influence or fraud. This is particularly possible in the fields of estate planning, business planning, and real estate transactions. If the client or client's representative (such as a guardian or administrator) brings a claim against the lawyer, the lawyer has the burden of showing that the transaction was fair and otherwise proper. For example, if a lawyer prepared a will for a client and included herself or himself as a beneficiary, the heirs would be in a good position to challenge the bequest. The lawyer would have the burden of proving that the bequest is in accord with the testator's wishes, that the testator was competent, and that the testator was not subjected to any undue influence.

■ TERMINATION OF RELATIONSHIP

A client may discharge a lawyer at will. The relationship is considered to be so personal and so dependent upon the client's trust that the client cannot be compelled to continue using a lawyer she or he does not want. A client does not even need a good reason for terminating the relationship. A lawyer, on the other hand, may have a little more difficulty ending the relationship. For example, if a lawyer is handling a case that is very near trial, the lawyer's withdrawal from the case could impose a hardship not only on the client, but also upon the court. Consequently, some courts have special rules and procedures that lawyers must follow to withdraw from a case. Some courts have determined that a client's inability to pay a fee for legal services is not grounds for a lawyer to withdraw. This is especially true in criminal cases. Consequently, lawyers may feel constrained to obtain a substantial retainer at the outset.

A lawyer is permitted to withdraw from a case if the client refuses to follow court orders or other legal requirements. If a lawyer comes to believe that the client is using the lawyer's services to perpetuate a fraud, the lawyer is under a duty to withdraw. Lawyers must be careful not to prejudice their clients' rights or interests by withdrawing. This means that a lawyer must provide reasonable notice to the client so that the client can obtain a replacement lawyer and meet all deadlines.

■ MALPRACTICE

A lawyer is required to exercise due diligence and ordinary skill in handling a client's legal matters. If a lawyer is negligent and fails to measure up to the standards of the profession, she or he is liable to the client for any loss proximately caused by the negligence. Negligence in rendering professional service is commonly called legal **malpractice.** The due care requirement does not mean that lawyers handling litigation must win their clients' cases. Theoretically, lawyers are going to "lose" half the cases they try. The standard of ordinary care or due care does mean that trial lawyers must possess the knowledge and skill ordinarily possessed by lawyers handling civil litigation. (However, if a lawyer advertises as a specialist, the lawyer is held to the standards of specialists which may be significantly higher.) Lawyers must use due care in gathering the evidence. They must exercise ordinary ability in trying cases. The same skill and knowledge must be applied in the preparation of legal documents and in giving legal advice. The largest problem that lawyers, as a group, seem to have is not being diligent. It is all too easy to wait too long before giving necessary notices, commencing an action, or otherwise actively pursuing matters—especially if a matter seems to lack substance or merit. With the help of conscientious paralegals, lawyers can do a better job of keeping current. Paralegals may initiate action on files by preparing pertinent documents for the lawyers' approval.

If a lawyer withdraws from a case, the lawyer should document the withdrawal. A letter should be sent to the client by registered mail, and a copy should be filed with the court if an action is pending. Otherwise, if problems develop with the case, the client may try to excuse himself or herself on the basis that the lawyer was still acting on his or her behalf. The lawyer would then be in trouble with the court and might face a malpractice action. A letter or formal notice of withdrawal helps to protect against such problems. If a lawyer is handling litigation that is actually pending in court, a formal **notice of withdrawal** must be filed with the court. In some states, a lawyer may have to obtain permission from the court in order to withdraw.

Occasionally, a would-be client discusses with a lawyer the merits of a claim she or he wants to make, but the lawyer advises that the claim has no merit or for other reasons refuses to take the case. Before the would-be client gets around to talking to another lawyer, the statute of limitations runs against the claim. The client decides to pursue the claim but cannot because it is barred. The would-be client may contend that she or he thought the lawyer was working on the case and that the lawyer should not have let the statute of limitations run out. To protect against this kind of scenario, the lawyer should make sure that the would-be client is told and understands (1) that the lawyer is not going to handle the case and (2) the date on which the statute of limitations will run against the alleged cause of action. The best procedure is to provide this information in a letter to the would-be client to reduce the possibility of a misunderstanding. It is also a good idea to establish proof of delivery of the letter.

■ LAWYERS' FEES

A lawyer's compensation for services is a matter of negotiation between the lawyer and the client. Fees may be an agreed sum for a particular undertaking, or based upon an hourly rate. A lawyer's hourly rate is usually based upon his or her experience and the complexity of the particular legal problems. When a lawyer represents the plaintiff in civil litigation to recover money damages, the lawyer's fee may be based upon a percentage of the monies recovered. When the fee is based upon a percentage of monies recovered, it is contingent upon an actual recovery, which means the lawyer receives payment only if the lawyer actually collects compensation for the client. Contingent fee percentages range between 20 percent and 50 percent. The percentage ordinarily depends upon the size of the case, the possibilities of an appeal, and the likelihood of obtaining a recovery. Historically, contingent fees were considered to be unethical, because they tended to foment litigation. Today, contingent fees are common. Disciplinary Rule 2-106 prohibits "clearly excessive" fees. Therefore, lawyers must keep accurate records of the time they actually put in to a matter. A client is always free to choose another lawyer if the proposed fee arrangement is unacceptable.

When a lawyer undertakes to represent a client, she or he may be precluded from representing certain other persons or companies and, consequently, from obtaining other business. The kind of limiting effect on a lawyer's business opportunities is another consideration in setting fees. In some types of cases, the amount of the fee or the contingency percentage may be limited by statute or court rule. For example, court rules may prohibit a lawyer from charging over a certain percentage when representing a minor. In class actions, the lawyer's fee is subject to court approval for reasonableness.

If discharged, a lawyer is entitled to be paid for services rendered. Payment may be based on the value of the services received by the client. The lawyer may not necessarily be entitled to recover fees on the basis of the original retainer agreement, although that agreement is one indicator of the value of such services. If the client refuses to pay, the lawyer may file a lien with the court in which the action is pending. The lien gives the lawyer a claim upon any recovery of money obtained by the client. The priority of the lawyer's claim depends upon state law. The amount of the lien is subject to determination by litigation if the parties are unable to agree upon that amount. A lawyer always has the right to bring an action in court for payment of a fee. Otherwise, lawyers would be at the mercy of unscrupulous clients.

■ ATTORNEY PRO SE

A person may choose to represent himself or herself in a civil action; the law does not require individuals to hire lawyers. A person who elects to represent himself or herself is referred to as an **attorney pro se.** Usually, judges try to discourage laypersons from representing themselves, because laypersons can become lost in the maze of procedural rules and substantive law. An attorney pro se has probably consulted with several lawyers who have advised that the claim or defense is not valid, but wants to proceed anyway. If a claim is too large for the small claims court, the cost of having a lawyer's help is well justified. If a person determines that a lawyer's proposed charges are too much, that person should simply shop around for a better price.

SUMMARY

The practice of law entails giving legal advice and representing another person in a court of law. Only a person duly licensed to practice law may do these things. A lawyer is a counselor (adviser) concerning the law and its application to a client's concerns. She or he must generally have and exercise ordinary ability in giving advice and handling the client's legal matters. However, if a lawyer presents herself or himself as a civil litigation specialist, the lawyer is held to the higher standard of a specialist.

Communications between a lawyer and a client are privileged, whether oral or written. Records of communications are also privileged. The privilege extends to members of the lawyer's staff. The privilege belongs to the client, not to the lawyer. The client may elect to waive the privilege and disclose a communication. A lawyer cannot object to the client's disclosure. If a client makes a claim against the lawyer, the lawyer may disclose privileged communications to the extent necessary to defend himself or herself.

A lawyer must avoid any conflict of interest with a client. Therefore, a lawyer must not try to serve two clients where those clients may have conflicting interests. This rule even precludes a lawyer from representing a client against a former client. However, if the lawyer makes a full disclosure of the conflict of interest, the client may elect to waive the right to object. The burden lies with the lawyer to show that a full disclosure was made and that the client made an informed choice to waive the conflict. When a lawyer is faced with an ethical question, the lawyer may seek the advice of a board of professional responsibility for guidance.

A lawyer owes the duty of a fiduciary to protect any property and money the lawyer holds for a client. A fiduciary must put the client's interests ahead of his or her own. If property is lost or damaged while under the control of a fiduciary, the fiduciary has the burden of proving that the loss was not his or her fault.

A lawyer is the client's agent when handling civil litigation. When a lawyer acts within the scope of her or his authority, the lawyer binds the client the same as if the client had acted. A client has the right to control her or his civil litigation. A client may refuse to commence an action. A client may refuse to settle a claim or may insist that a claim be settled. A client may insist that a lawyer dismiss a claim. A client may insist that a lawyer withdraw a defense. A client may discharge a lawyer at any stage of the proceeding. However, if a case is in progress, a court does not have to grant a continuance or delay because of the discharge. Otherwise, a lawyer might feel constrained to have a client "discharge" her or him to stop a trial where the case is obviously going badly.

Champerty is an agreement between a plaintiff and a lawyer by which the lawyer acquires an interest in the outcome of the case for purposes of profit. The practice is unethical. Nevertheless, contingent fees are permissible and common in personal injury litigation.

Historically, lawyers were strictly forbidden to solicit business, and they could not advertise. Today, advertising is permitted within certain prescribed limits. Those limits vary from state to state.

When a lawyer handles a civil action on behalf of a client, the lawyer must serve the client, but the lawyer's highest duty is to the court. This principle requires lawyers to actively prevent a client from perpetrating a fraud upon the court. The matter of duty should not be confused with the matter of privileged communications. A court cannot require a lawyer to disclose a client's privileged communications.

If a lawyer handles a client's legal matters in such a way as to realize a profit, aside from a proper legal fee for services, the law presumes that the profit was obtained by undue influence or fraud. A lawyer has the burden of proving that any financial benefit he or she derived from the relationship, aside from reasonable fees, was not the result of undue influence.

A client may discharge her or his lawyer at will. A client does not need a reason for terminating the relationship. A lawyer may terminate the relationship but not under circumstances that leave the client's litigation in a precarious position. Courts have special rules and procedures that lawyers must follow to be able to withdraw from a case. Some courts have determined that a client's inability to pay a fee for legal services is not grounds for a lawyer to withdraw. This is especially true in criminal cases. A lawyer may withdraw from a case if the client refuses to follow court orders or other legal requirements. If a lawyer believes that the client is using the lawyer's services to perpetrate a fraud, the lawyer is under a duty to withdraw. Lawyers must not prejudice clients' rights or interests by withdrawing. This means that the lawyer must provide reasonable notice to the client so that the client can obtain a replacement lawyer and meet all deadlines. A lawyer should document her or his withdrawal to protect against a subsequent claim by the client that the withdrawal was without notice and was prejudicial.

The amount of a lawyer's fee and the basis for the fee are a matter of contract between the lawyer and the client. However, if a fee is unconscionable, a court may modify it. It is unethical for a lawyer to charge an unconscionable fee. Historically, contingent fees were considered unethical. Today such fees are very common, especially in personal injury cases. Lawyers are not allowed to share fees with nonlawyers.

When a person represents herself or himself in court, the person acts as attorney pro se. An attorney pro se does not need a license to practice law or permission from the court to act on his or her own behalf.

KEY TERMS

integrated bar	maintenance
mediation	champerty
arbitration	privileged communication
conflict of interest	malpractice
fiduciary	notice of withdrawal
agent	attorney pro se

REVIEW QUESTIONS

1. What is the difference between confidential information and privileged information? P3
2. Is a paralegal subject to the direct control of the court system? pg 25
3. What constitutes legal malpractice? pg 36
4. How does the legal relationship between a lawyer and a client differ from that between an agent and a principal? pg 28
5. If a court orders parties to a civil suit to arbitrate their dispute, may a paralegal handle the examination of witnesses in the arbitration hearing? pg 25
6. What are the considerations for establishing a lawyer's fee? pg 39
7. What does a lawyer have to do before withdrawing from a civil case? pg 36
8. Why does a lawyer owe her or his highest duty to the court? pg 23-29

3

CAUSES OF ACTION AND REMEDIES

People are social beings. We live in communities. Our communities are connected through a social structure and several levels of government. Our interaction inevitably leads to disputes between individuals, between individuals and organizations, and between individuals and governments. The disputes arise from transactions, such as making and performing contracts, and occurrences involving wrongful acts or omissions that cause harm. Most of our disputes are inconsequential and are best resolved by forgiving and forgetting, but some are serious and have serious consequences. Since no one has devised a means of preventing disputes, our society has developed a method for resolving them through our civil justice system. Without this system, citizens would engage in self-help and, perhaps, violence to resolve their disputes. Disputes would then inevitably lead to conflicts that would threaten the foundations of our society and government.

Peace among the citizens would not be possible if the courts merely decided who is right and who is wrong. In addition, government must provide remedies that satisfy most litigants. The remedies must be in proportion to the loss and comport with a generally accepted sense of reason and fairness. The means of obtaining a remedy must be economical, fair, and calculated to bring about a just result based upon the truth. The obligations imposed by law must be consistent with what an obligor reasonably can do or can afford to pay. Furthermore, the obligations must comport with what society can afford. The need to maintain order justifies civil courts. The need to enforce the courts' decisions justifies government operation of the civil courts.

Civil litigation operates alongside criminal law but is quite separate from it. The basic objectives are different. Criminal law is concerned with identifying criminals and criminal acts and punishing the guilty. Civil law is concerned with resolving disputes on an orderly basis and providing compensation for injuries and other types of losses. The most common remedy that courts provide in civil actions is an award of **compensatory damages.** Compensatory damages are intended to make up for the loss a party sustained as a direct consequence of another party's breach of a legal duty. A trend in criminal law is to require a convicted criminal to provide **restitution** to the victim, where that is possible, as part of a criminal's punishment. Restitution is similar to compensation in that the purpose is to restore to the victim that which was taken or lost. And a trend in civil law is to allow the plaintiff to obtain **punitive damages** as a civil penalty for willful wrongful conduct that caused harm to another's person or property.

The civil justice system strives to provide a suitable remedy to every person who has suffered an injury, damage, or loss as a consequence of another person's unlawful conduct.[1] The task is monumental. It seems there is no limit to the kinds of controversies that develop between people. Courts cannot undo every wrong. Nor can they provide a remedy for every perceived loss or inconvenience. Based upon several centuries of experience, the courts have determined that only certain types of wrongful conduct that cause certain kinds of losses are actionable. Courts are able to redress only certain kinds of losses. Courts have a limited number of remedies to redress those losses. If a person's claim is one that courts consider to be actionable, for which a remedy can be provided and the loss can be compensated, the claim may be the basis for a *cause of action.* The term *action* is synonymous with *lawsuit.* The term *cause of action* refers to the basis for the lawsuit.

In every action the plaintiff must prove that (1) the defendant breached a legal duty owed to the plaintiff; (2) the plaintiff sustained an injury to person or a property loss recognized by law; and (3) the defendant's breach of duty was the proximate cause of the plaintiff's injury or property loss. There are many kinds of causes of action. Each cause of action is predicated upon a particular legal duty protecting persons and/or property. Each cause of action affords the plaintiff a particular remedy. Much of a lawyer's education and training is devoted to learning about the many causes of actions recognized by courts, their elements, their applications, and their limitations. There are many, many causes of action. Establishing a cause of action is a prerequisite to obtaining a judicial remedy.

1. Lawyers usually use the term *illegal* to describe conduct that is criminal in nature. The term *unlawful* may include conduct that is illegal, but tends to be used more broadly to include any conduct that is contrary to the civil law or criminal law. The word *unlawful* is used here to describe conduct that is in violation of common-law standards or standards established by statutes.

When a lawyer undertakes to handle a case for a plaintiff, the first thing the lawyer must do is obtain the material facts about the transaction or occurrence. Next, the lawyer must determine whether those facts support all the elements of a cause of action. If one or more of the elements necessary to a cause of action are missing, the courts cannot provide a remedy. If the lawyer did commence a lawsuit, the court would be constrained to dismiss the case as soon as the court determined that one or more of the elements were missing. Rule 12(b) of the Federal Rules of Civil Procedure provides that the case must be dismissed if the complaint fails to state a claim upon which relief can be granted. Another way of saying this is that the case must be dismissed if the complaint fails to state a cause of action. Whatever time, effort, and money are spent to prove a defective claim are simply wasted. If the plaintiff does not have a cause of action, he or she should be told that as soon as possible.

Claims arise from transactions or occurrences or both. When parties enter into a legally binding transaction, whether a contract, lease, promissory note, or whatever, they create legal duties that they owe to each other. Courts will enforce those duties by providing a remedy against the party who breaches his or her legal duty. We have a general duty not to harm other persons or their property. But that general duty is subject to many exceptions and qualifications. For example, a person may injure another when he or she acts in self-defense. Two professional boxers have a license to injure each other because they have consented to be injured, and the law approves of the limited consent. A baseball player may hit another player with a batted ball and cause a serious injury, but the injured player has assumed the risk of such an injury. If a person drives a truck on another person's property and damages a tree, the driver is liable for damages for trespassing on another's property. But suppose an airplane is inadvertently forced to land on the property and damages the tree; has the pilot breached a legal duty? Should he be liable for making a forced landing to save his life and that of his passengers?

Those are the kinds of considerations that have shaped causes of actions and help courts decide the kinds of remedies to provide. The important point to understand is that particular kinds of transactions and occurrences give rise to particular legal duties. Courts take cognizance only of claims that involve breaches of legal duties. In determining whether the alleged facts show the existence of a legal duty and identifying the type of duty, lawyers and judges look at the alleged facts to see whether, if proved, they establish all the elements of a particular cause of action. The plaintiff will have to provide evidence to prove all the elements of the cause of action. The facts that relate to the elements of the cause of action are the material facts.

A party's investigation, discovery procedures, and trial preparation are controlled by the legal issues, and the legal issues are largely determined by the elements of the plaintiff's cause of action. For example, if the plaintiff's claim is based upon common-law negligence, the plaintiff must present evidence to prove that (1) the defendant failed to exercise due (reasonable) care considering the foreseeability of harm to the plaintiff; (2) the defendant's negligent act or omission breached a legal duty owed to the plaintiff; (3) the plaintiff sustained a compensable injury or property damage; and (4) the negligent act or omission was a proximate cause of the plaintiff's injury or property damage. If any one of these elements is missing, the plaintiff's claim does not meet the requirements for a cause of action in negligence.

If the plaintiff's claim is based on breach of contract, the plaintiff's lawyer must present evidence to prove that (1) the parties were competent to enter into a contractual relationship; (2) a contract was made through a valid offer and acceptance; (3) the parties exchanged legal consideration for their mutual undertakings; (4) if the alleged contract is of the type that must be in writing and signed, the formalities were met; and (5) the defendant's breach of the contract caused the plaintiff to suffer an actual loss. If the plaintiff's evidence fails to prove any of these elements, the cause of action for breach of contract must fail.

The defendant can defeat the claim, whether in tort or contract, by disproving any one of the elements necessary to the plaintiff's cause of action. But the burden of proof is upon the plaintiff to establish all the elements of the cause of action; the burden is not upon the defendant to disprove the claim. The customary burden of proof is to establish the cause of action by a fair **preponderance of the evidence.** The evidence preponderates in favor of a particular fact when all the evidence, taken as a whole, shows that the fact is more likely true than not true.

The **measure of damages** is the basis for assessing or evaluating the amount of money that should be awarded to compensate a party for a particular loss. The law has various bases for evaluating losses and converting them into monetary awards as compensation. Each cause of action has its own measure of damages. Consequently, the amount of compensation provided for a loss may differ depending upon the legal theory (cause of action) the plaintiff pursues. A client may feel that she or he has a claim for breach of contract, but on analysis, the lawyer may determine that the only cause of action is for fraud, which involves different elements and a different measure of damages. Or a client may want to sue for an alleged trespass to real estate in order to recover money damages, but upon reducing the facts to their basic elements, the lawyer may determine that the proper claim—or only claim—is for an injunction to abate a nuisance created by the defendant's conduct. A nuisance, in this context, is any wrongful conduct that substantially interferes with or disturbs the occupant's lawful use and enjoyment of her or his real property. Nuisance is a cause of action and gives a court the basis for providing a remedy.

For each cause of action, certain **affirmative defenses** may be available. An affirmative defense usually arises from some wrongful conduct on the part of the plaintiff—but not always. Each affirmative defense has certain elements that the defendant must prove. Proof of an affirmative defense totally defeats the plaintiff's cause of action or, in certain cases, reduces the amount of the plaintiff's recovery of money damages. The defendant must prove an affirmative defense or the defense is disallowed. Ordinarily, the burden of proof is by a fair preponderance of the evidence.

A paralegal is not expected to know all about all causes of action and all affirmative defenses. But when working on a particular case, a paralegal should become familiar with the elements applicable to the particular cause of action and the affirmative defenses. Lawyers are anxious to have paralegals indicate an interest in the technical aspects of a case. The more knowledgeable a paralegal is about the law and legal procedures, the more effectively he or she can handle assignments in litigation. A paralegal should have a basic understanding about causes of action and their elements. This chapter provides an introduction to nineteen of the more common causes of action.

■ BREACH OF CONTRACT

In its most simple form, a contract is a legally enforceable promise. The parties ordinarily enter into a contract voluntarily, expecting that each will benefit from their mutual commitments. The benefits may be monetary profit or the acquisition of something desired, such as land, personal property, or even an idea. If the defendant violates the contract, she or he is subject to an action for **breach of contract.** The type of remedy afforded by law depends, in part, on the purpose of the contract, the parties' objectives, and their reasonable expectations. The most common remedy is the award of money damages compensating for loss of the benefit of the bargain.

When undertaking a case involving an alleged breach of contract, a lawyer's first effort must be to determine whether a contract exists. An action for breach of contract presupposes a valid, enforceable agreement. Contracts may take many forms and may come about in numerous ways. Some contracts are in writing, signed by both parties; some are entirely oral; some are implied by the parties' conduct; and some are implied by operation of law. Despite the variety of types of contracts, certain elements are essential to all contracts. An enforceable contract requires (1) that the parties be legally competent to enter into a contract; (2) a valid offer and acceptance that results in a meeting of the parties' minds concerning the subject of the contract; (3) the exchange of legal consideration; and (4) compliance with particular formalities imposed by statute for certain types of contracts. A purported contract is not enforceable if the object of the contract is unlawful.

The parties must have the capacity to contract. Otherwise, the contract is void or voidable at the election of the party who lacked capacity. A person is not capable of making a contract if, at the time the purported contract is made, he or she is a minor, under a guardianship, insane, or intoxicated. A company that is not incorporated has no separate legal existence and cannot contract for itself. An unincorporated company may contract only through its owners as individuals. Partnerships are legal entities that may contract through one or more partners. In effect, the partners are each other's agents.

The contract offer ordinarily contains the substance, terms, and conditions of the contract. Acceptance of the offer must be effectively communicated to the offeror in compliance with any conditions imposed by the offeror. If the acceptance is qualified, or changes one or more of the essential terms of the offer, the acceptance may actually be a counteroffer, which does not create a contract unless duly accepted by the original offeror.

A contract is made only if the parties reach a meeting of minds concerning the subject matter. For example, if the seller offers to sell an automobile to the buyer, they must have in mind the same automobile or a valid contract cannot result from their negotiations.

A contract requires the exchange of consideration. A simple promise—even if made under oath—is not a contract and cannot be enforced at law. Unless a consideration is given for the promise, no contract exists. The most common consideration is the payment of money. But even a mere promise exchanged for another promise may be legal consideration that will support a contract. If a contract recites that a consideration has been paid, but in fact it was not, the alleged contract is defective and unenforceable.

The pleadings in exhibits 3.1 and 3.2 illustrate those for a typical breach-of-contract case. They are based upon hypothetical disputes but are true to life. (Note that a complaint should set forth the allegations and particular facts separately, in numbered paragraphs, making it easy for the defendant to admit the allegations that are true.)

Certain contracts must be in writing and signed in order to be enforceable. The state statute that identifies such contracts is commonly referred to as the **statute of frauds.** The statute specifies what kinds of contracts must be in writing and the necessary elements to each written contract. If a contract is required to be in writing but is not, the contract is not enforceable. The statute of frauds provides the defendant with a complete defense.

The plaintiff who sues on a contract has the burden of proving that the contract was made, that all technical requirements were met, that she or he has performed all conditions precedent, and that all conditions of the contract have occurred.[2] The plaintiff must prove that the defendant breached the contract. There is no need to show that the breach was willful or the result of fault. Culpability is not a consideration or an issue. The plaintiff must prove the nature and extent of the loss resulting from the defendant's breach of the contract. The proof on all elements must be by a fair preponderance of the evidence.

The defendant may have a basis to avoid a contract that was duly made. If the plaintiff also breached the contract, that breach provides the defendant with a complete defense, but the defendant has the burden of proving that the plaintiff also breached the contract. If the contract was obtained through fraud by the plaintiff, the contract is voidable by the defendant, but the defendant must allege and prove the fraud. If the parties made a new agreement to replace an old one and fully performed the new agreement, the old one is a nullity and unenforceable. The new agreement and its performance, called an accord and satisfaction, are a complete defense. The defendant has the burden of proving the defense. A plaintiff's failure to sue within the time provided by the statute of limitations provides

---

2. A condition precedent must occur before the contract becomes effective even though all the terms and conditions have been agreed upon. A common example of a condition precedent is when the buyer agrees to purchase a new house on condition that he can sell his.

COMPLAINT

Comes now plaintiff and for its cause of action against defendant alleges:

1. [Jurisdictional allegations.]

2. On August 2, 1994, defendant contracted to sell and deliver to plaintiff ten tons of newsprint-quality rolled paper.

3. The terms and conditions of said contract between the parties were reduced to writing; a copy of said written contract is attached hereto and incorporated by reference as exhibit A.

4. Said written contract was duly signed by defendant's representative at the time and place specified in the contract.

5. Plaintiff paid to defendant the sum of three thousand dollars as the initial partial payment as recited in the written contract.

6. All conditions precedent of said contract have been performed or have occurred.

7. Defendant did not deliver said newsprint paper to plaintiff as required by the terms of said contract, and defendant is in default.

8. Plaintiff has necessarily sought and obtained other newsprint paper to meet its needs and requirements.

9. As a direct consequence of defendant's failure to perform on said contract, plaintiff has suffered damages as follows:

   a. Plaintiff is entitled to recover the three thousand dollars initially paid to defendant as a down payment, together with interest at the rate specified in the written contract [or the legal rate provided by law].

   b. Plaintiff's printing business was necessarily interrupted for a period of ten working days, causing plaintiff to suffer a loss of profit in the amount of ten thousand dollars.

   c. Plaintiff was required to purchase similar newsprint from another supplier at an additional cost of six thousand dollars.

Wherefore, plaintiff prays for judgment against defendant in the sum of nineteen thousand dollars, together with plaintiff's costs and disbursements herein.

[date]

_____
Attorney for Plaintiff

---

the defendant with an affirmative defense. The defendant must prove the facts making the statute of limitations applicable. The defense must be raised in the defendant's answer, or it is waived. Once in a while, after a contract is made, circumstances develop making performance of the contract impossible. Impossibility is a defense.

When a breach of contract occurs, the parties may elect to continue performance of the remainder of the contract. That may be the only realistic choice in some cases. If a party elects to proceed with the contract knowing that the other party has breached one of its terms or conditions, the election to proceed may constitute a waiver of the breach. It would be unfair for the plaintiff to sue on the contract after waiving a breach. The parties may formalize the waiver by preparing a writing in which the extent of the waiver is described and the consequences of the waiver stated. Ordinarily,

ANSWER

Comes now defendant and for its answer to plaintiff's complaint:

1. Denies each and every allegation, statement, and matter in plaintiff's complaint, except as hereinafter expressly admitted or alleged:

2. Admits the allegation of paragraphs 1 through 8 of the complaint.

3. Admits that defendant is liable to plaintiff in the amount of three thousand dollars for money had and received, but denies defendant is liable for interest thereon.

Defense 1

Alleges that paragraph 9(b) of the complaint fails to state a claim upon which relief can be granted.

Defense 2

Alleges that on August 7, 1994, defendant's entire plant and warehouse were destroyed by fire through no fault of defendant, and that the loss of the plant and warehouse made impossible defendant's performance of the contract

Wherefore, defendant prays that plaintiff take nothing by reason of its alleged cause of action and that defendant have judgment for its costs and disbursements.

[date]   _____
                                     Attorney for Defendant

a waiver is a complete defense that the defendant must allege in the answer and prove.

Other affirmative defenses may be available in contract actions. A partial list of them appears in Rule 8(c).

■ SPECIFIC PERFORMANCE

In some breach-of-contract actions, the award of money damages is clearly an insufficient remedy. In those cases, a court of general jurisdiction has the authority to require a party to perform the contract. The remedy is called **specific performance.** Courts are frequently asked to decree specific performance of contracts involving the sale of land. The law views each parcel of land as unique. Therefore, money damages are not adequate to replace land. That is not to say that every breached contract for the sale of land is enforced by an action for specific performance. The law turns to the same remedy in a breach of contract for the sale of a piece of art that is unique. The buyer may use an action for specific performance to force the seller to deliver the artwork and title.

Courts may enjoin (command) parties to perform or not perform certain activities. For example, a court may order a union not to strike or not to picket. A court may order a corporation to undertake negotiations to settle a labor dispute. Actions to enjoin conduct may involve use of restraining orders, temporary injunctions, and permanent injunctions. On the other hand, courts cannot order an individual to perform personal services, for that would constitute involuntary servitude and would be unconstitutional.

A sample complaint for specific performance and its answer appear in exhibits 3.3 and 3.4, respectively.

■ FRAUD AND MISREPRESENTATION

Some kinds of **misrepresentations** give rise to an action in tort against the persons who made them. Misrepresentations that are actionable fall into either of two categories: **fraud** or **negligent misrepresentation.** Fraud is an intentional misrepresentation of a fact to induce another person to rely upon the misrepresentation. This kind of fraud is also called deceit. A person makes a negligent misrepresentation when she or he misstates a fact as true and should have known that the other person would properly rely upon the statement as being true. For example, a real estate agent might tell a prospective buyer that the seller's house never had a wet basement without having first confirmed the fact with the seller. The agent did not know his statement was false, but his statement was negligently made. He expected the seller to rely upon the statement.

The law recognizes that many people make many statements, both written and oral, that are not true or are only half-true but for which no legal liability should result. If a person regularly understates her age by five years, should that misrepresentation create a cause of action? Of course not.

■ EXHIBIT 3.3

Complaint for Specific Performance

COMPLAINT

Comes now plaintiff and for his cause of action against defendant alleges:

1. [Jurisdictional allegations.]
2. On or about August 3, 1994, plaintiff and defendant, through his duly appointed agent, entered into a written contract by which defendant agreed to sell and plaintiff agreed to buy certain specific real estate. A copy of said contract is attached hereto as Exhibit A.
3. As provided by said written contract plaintiff duly tendered to defendant the purchase price for the land as provided for in exhibit A.
4. Defendant wrongfully refused to accept tender of the purchase price.
5. Defendant wrongfully refused to convey title of said land to plaintiff.
6. Plaintiff is ready, willing, and able to perform on the contract and hereby offers the full purchase price to defendant.
7. Plaintiff cannot obtain similar land, similarly situated, that would meet plaintiff's requirements.
8. All conditions precedent have been performed or have occurred.

Wherefore, plaintiff prays that court issue its decree ordering defendant to perform the contract by providing plaintiff with a warranty deed to said land.

If specific performance is not granted, plaintiff prays for judgment against defendant in the sum of fifty thousand dollars as damages for defendant's breach of contract.

Plaintiff further prays for his costs and disbursement herein.

[date]   _____
                                Attorney for Plaintiff

■ **EXHIBIT 3.4**

Answer to Complaint for
Specific Performance

ANSWER

Comes now defendant and for his answer to plaintiff's complaint:

1. Denies each and every allegation, statement, and matter in said complaint contained, except as hereinafter expressly admitted or alleged.
2. Admits that he is the owner of the land described in exhibit A.
3. Denies that he executed the contract identified as exhibit A attached to the complaint.
4. Denies that any person had authority to sign said contract for him or to act on his behalf concerning said land.
5. Denies that he received any consideration for the alleged contract.

Wherefore, defendant prays that plaintiff take nothing by reason of his pretended cause of action and that defendant have judgment for his costs and disbursements herein.

[date]

_____
Attorney for Defendant

But if a person misrepresents her age on an application for a life insurance policy, and the insurer relies upon the misrepresentation to its detriment, the misrepresentation may be actionable as a fraud. If the owner of an automobile claims he has an automobile that gives thirty miles per gallon of gasoline, but it actually delivers only fifteen miles per gallon, the misrepresentation is reprehensible, but it is not actionable. In contrast, if the seller of an automobile makes a similar misrepresentation to a buyer, a cause of action for fraud may accrue in favor of the buyer.

Suppose the seller of a house misrepresents to his buyer that the neighbors are very nice people, when he knows that the neighbors are cantankerous, difficult people. Does this misrepresentation create a cause of action for fraud in favor of the buyer against the seller? Suppose the seller of a house represents that he has never had a wet basement, but soon after the buyer acquires possession, she discovers water that was unknown to the seller, in the heating ducts under the basement floor. Does the sellers' statement constitute a misrepresentation? No, since there never was any water in the basement. Did the statement create a duty on the part of the seller to know that there was no water in the heating ducts? Answer: No. Was the seller's statement only a representation of the seller's own knowledge and experience with the property? Answer: Yes. If the seller has not misrepresented his actual knowledge, should that be grounds for finding a fraud? Answer: No. However, if the buyer asked the seller whether there had ever been water in the heat ducts, the seller must respond that he does not know. If he says "No," without knowing, and is wrong, he has negligently misrepresented a material fact.

Suppose an art dealer misrepresents a certain painting to be an original, and the painting is purchased by a knowledgeable collector who knows that it is not an original. Does the collector have a claim for fraud? Should the party who claims damage because of a misrepresentation have to show that he or she in fact relied upon the misrepresentation? Answer: Reliance is essential to an action based upon fraud or negligent misrepresentation.

Does it make a difference whether the misrepresentation is made in good faith? Answer: To be actionable for fraud, the misrepresentation must be made with the intent or expectation that the other party will rely upon it. For a misrepresentation to be actionable in negligence, the declarant must make the statement as based upon his or her actual knowledge without actually knowing the truth.

Fraud is a tort. A tort is wrongful conduct that violates another person's rights, causing harm to that person or to that person's property. The law provides a remedy to the victim of tortious conduct. The objective of the law of torts is to compensate a party for her or his loss without providing profit. However, in contract law, the parties voluntarily enter into an agreement for the purpose of profit. If one party breaches the contract, the loss of the anticipated profit flows naturally from the breach. The law does allow a recovery of loss of profits in contract actions. The loss of profit is often referred to as a loss of the bargain.

At common law, certain elements must be present before a misrepresentation becomes tortious and, therefore, actionable as a fraud. The elements have been listed in various ways by courts and legal scholars. The following list has been used by more than one court and provides a rather detailed analysis of the elements relevant to actions for fraud and misrepresentation.

1. There must be a representation.
2. The representation must be false.
3. The misrepresentation must have to do with a past or present fact.
4. The misrepresented fact must be material to the contract or transaction.
5. The representation must be susceptible of knowledge.
6. The representer must know the representation to be false or, in the alternative, must assert the fact as of his or her own knowledge without knowing whether it is true or false.
7. The representer must intend to have the other person induced to act, or the other person must be justified in acting upon the misrepresentation.
8. The other person must justifiably act in reliance upon the misrepresentation.
9. The other person must suffer damage by reason of reliance upon the misrepresentation.

A statement of mere opinion is not usually actionable. However, if the opinion is rendered by an expert concerning a matter within the scope of her or his expertise, an erroneous opinion may be actionable on the basis of fraud or negligent misrepresentation. For example, a statement of opinion about the law and its application could possibly be actionable against a lawyer but not against a layperson. Ordinarily, a representation concerning future events is not actionable as fraud—but there are exceptions. By way of illustration, if the seller of a parcel of land knows that an aircraft flight pattern is going to be established over the land in the near future, a representation to the contrary may constitute a fraud. The fraud occurs because the defendant has present knowledge of established plans for action. Otherwise, prognostication is similar to rendering a mere opinion—not actionable as a fraud.

The defendant must intend or expect that the plaintiff will rely upon the misrepresentation, and the plaintiff must, in fact, rely upon it. If the vendor of a parcel of land represents that the parcel is 200 feet deep, but before the sale, the buyer measures the length and determines it is only 190 feet deep, the buyer cannot later sue for fraud, because he did not rely upon the alleged misrepresentation. Reliance is essential to any action for fraud or misrepresentation.

The plaintiff must prove that the misrepresentation that was relied upon caused him or her to suffer actual damage or a loss. Suppose that the seller of a used automobile misrepresents that it is a 1988 model, knowing that it is a 1987 model; suppose that 1988 models have an average value that is three hundred dollars more than that for comparable 1987 models; suppose further that the buyer ends up paying no more for the automobile than she would have paid for a known 1987 model. In other words, suppose the buyer received full value for what was paid but believed she was getting a better bargain. Has the buyer really sustained a loss because of the misrepresentation? By contract standards, the answer would be yes. Certainly there was a breach of contract, and maybe a breach of warranty. The buyer received less than she bargained for. But by tort standards, most courts would say that the buyer did not sustain a loss. The answer to whether or not a loss occurred depends upon whether the parties are in a state that follows the **loss-of-the-bargain measure of damages** or the **out-of-pocket measure of damages** for fraud. In this example, the buyer is not out of pocket any money; she has not lost any actual thing, but has merely lost an expectation. If the state allows damages for a loss of the bargain, the buyer's damages are three hundred dollars.

In most states, an action for negligent misrepresentation lies if a person makes a statement as a positive assertion, not knowing whether it is true, and, nevertheless, intends the statement to be relied upon. For example, suppose a real estate agent shows a house for the owner, and a prospective buyer asks the agent whether there are any liens against the property. The agent, without knowing one way or the other, says no. If there is a lien against the property, and the buyer relied upon the agent's statement, an action for negligent misrepresentation may be brought against the agent.

Rule 9(b) requires that the plaintiff plead fraud and misrepresentation with particularity. This means that, unlike most cases of action, fraud and misrepresentation must be alleged with the specific facts supporting each element of the cause of action set forth in the complaint. Exhibit 3.5 and 3.6 are examples of a complaint and answer in fraud.

The answer in exhibit 3.6 does not undertake to raise all possible defenses to an action in fraud. It merely purports to illustrate a proper way of alleging denials and defenses.

■ TRESPASS

A person who is in possession of real property has a right to the quiet, peaceful possession of the property. The right to possession may be based upon ownership, lease, easement, or adverse possession. Any unauthorized

COMPLAINT

Comes now the plaintiff and for her cause of action against defendant alleges:

1. [Jurisdictional allegations.]

2. On or about June 1, 1994, plaintiff and defendant entered into an agreement by which defendant agreed to sell to plaintiff a certain 1985 Buick automobile, and plaintiff agreed to buy said automobile.

3. The parties' agreement was reduced to writing, and a copy thereof is attached hereto as exhibit A and is incorporated herein by reference.

4. Defendant represented to plaintiff that said automobile had a "new" engine, as appears more fully in exhibit A.

5. Defendant intended plaintiff to rely upon said representation, and plaintiff did so rely.

6. Plaintiff's said representation was false; the engine is not new, and the original engine was never replaced or overhauled before the sale.

7. Plaintiff paid to defendant the sum of seventy-five hundred dollars for said automobile in reliance upon defendant's false representation.

8. The cost of a new engine for said automobile is fifteen hundred dollars, and the fair market value of the automobile without a new engine is not more than seven thousand dollars.

9. Plaintiff has sustained a loss due to defendant's fraudulent misrepresentations in the amount of fifteen hundred dollars.

Wherefore, plaintiff prays for judgment against defendant in the sum of fifteen hundred dollars, together with her costs and disbursements herein.

[date]

_____
Attorney for Plaintiff

---

entry on the premises constitutes a **trespass.** The occupant may sue for damages resulting from the wrongful entry. For example, suppose the lessee of a farm has remained in possession of the property after the lease expired. If a stranger enters upon the land without permission, the stranger is a trespasser, and the tenant may bring an action in trespass against the stranger for any damage the stranger caused. If the trespasser did not cause any discernible damage, he is still liable for nominal money damages and, possibly, punitive damages—depending upon the purpose for which he entered upon the premises. The law presumes some damage, such as a bending of the grass. On that basis, the law is able to affirm the possessor's right to exclusive, peaceful occupancy. The occupant is able to protect those rights by bringing a civil action against anyone who violated the occupant's right to exclusive occupancy.

A trespass occurs whenever the entry is made without consent of the possessor or without legal authority. In the preceding example, even though the farmer-tenant is in possession, her possessory rights are subject to the owner's higher or superior right to recover possession upon expiration of the lease. The holdover tenant cannot sue the landlord who enters the land to take back possession in accordance with the requirements of local law. Historically, the common law permitted a landlord to use reasonable force to eject a holdover tenant. Many states have enacted laws against self-help and now require the landlord to use the services of the state by bringing an action for unlawful detainer or an action in ejectment against the holdover tenant. A person unlawfully detains land when he or she retains possession after the lease has expired. The owner has a right to have an expedited hearing to have the former tenant removed from the premises. Ejectment is a cause of action used by a person who has rights to the immediate use of the land to have the courts, through the sheriff, remove another person who wrongfully took possession of or wrongfully remains upon the property. Such actions enable the landlord to obtain possession within thirty days or less.

A trespasser may acquire ownership and title to real estate by wrongfully occupying it for a number of years specified by statute, such as ten or fifteen years. The occupancy must be open, notorious, and contrary to anyone else's rights in the property. This is commonly referred to as adverse possession. A tenant cannot acquire title from the landlord through occupancy because a tenant's occupancy is not hostile to the rights of the landlord.

The trespasser is liable for the damage caused by her or his entry. The wrongful entrance may be involuntary, as where a ship is forced ashore or into a dock by a storm or where an airplane crashes on the land. A trespass may be intentional for the purpose of using the property or of removing from the premises material such as water, trees, crops, or minerals. Or a trespass may result from negligent conduct on the part of the defendant. For example, suppose a drunken person drives a car off the road and into the plaintiff's house. The unpermitted entry is a trespass. An involuntary

■ **EXHIBIT 3.6**

Answer to Complaint in Fraud

ANSWER

Comes now defendant and for her answer to plaintiff's complaint:

1. Denies each and every statement, matter, and thing in said complaint contained, except as hereinafter expressly admitted or alleged.

2. Denies that the court has jurisdiction over the subject matter of plaintiff's claim and that the controversy exceeds the threshold requirement of ten thousand dollars.

3. Admits that the parties did enter into a sales agreement for the sale of an automobile about the time and place specified in the complaint.

4. Specifically denies that the automobile engine, referred to in the complaint, was misrepresented and puts plaintiff to her strict proof of the alleged misrepresentation.

5. Denies that plaintiff did not receive full value for the purchase price of said automobile.

6. Alleges that exhibit A, attached to the complaint, is incomplete and does not set forth the full agreement of the parties.

Wherefore, defendant prays that plaintiff take nothing by reason of plaintiff's pretended cause of action, and that defendant have judgment for her costs and disbursements herein.

[date]

_____

Attorney for Defendant

entry caused by the wrongful conduct of another person is not a trespass. For example, if the alleged trespasser was driving an automobile that was struck by another vehicle, forcing it off the road onto the plaintiff's property, the entrant is not a trespasser. However, the negligent motorist who caused the accident and entrance may be treated as a trespasser. A trespass may be committed by throwing articles upon the plaintiff's land or across the land. For example, the wrongful placement of utility lines over property may constitute a trespass.

If a person enters upon real estate without legal right, and without the occupant's consent, the entry is wrongful and is a trespass. The trespasser is absolutely liable for any damage to the property—even if the entry was unavoidable. If an airplane accidentally crashes upon the plaintiff's land, causing damage to the land, the airplane's entry is a trespass. The pilot is liable for the damage caused by the trespass even though he was not negligent and could not have prevented the accident.

If the trespasser enters for the purpose of stealing crops, trees, or minerals, he or she is liable for the value of the materials taken or for the resulting diminution in the value of the real estate. For example, if a trespasser cuts down an ornamental tree for the wood or as a matter of spite, the damage to the land (diminution in value) may exceed the worth of the tree or the cost of a similar tree. On the other hand, if the trespasser wrongfully removes a mineral such as gravel, the gravel may be worth more than the land's diminution in value. In this instance, the occupant may elect to recover the value of the gravel. In many states, the occupant is allowed by statute to recover three times the value of the trees, crops, or minerals taken by the trespasser. Treble damages in such cases are a civil penalty for the benefit of the victim. The penalty is to act as a deterrent. A penalty is necessary because if trespassers had to pay only for the value of the property taken, the trespasser could, in effect, force the property owner to make a sale of the trees, minerals, or crops. That would be intolerable.

At common law, the occupant of property is allowed to use such force as is reasonably necessary to eject a trespasser from the premises. The occupant owes the trespasser a duty not to intentionally injure or kill her or him. The law places a higher value on "life and limb" than on the protection of real estate. Therefore, a trespasser does not subject herself or himself to being intentionally shot or injured just because she or he is trespassing. Nor may the occupant set a "trap" for trespassers without being liable in tort for compensation for personal injuries the trespasser sustains. Of course, the occupant of land does have a common-law right to self-defense. The occupant's best alternative, when practicable, is to call upon the local authorities to remove trespassers.

The occupant's consent to an entry upon the premises and the authority to enter that is implied by law are complete defenses to an action in trespass. The defendant has the burden of proving consent or authority. These defenses must be pleaded in the answer. Consent may be expressed orally or in writing or implied by the circumstances. Authority is implied by law when the entrant has a legal duty to enter. Police officers or firefighters who enter upon the property in the line of official duty have implied authority to enter. They are not trespassers.

Exhibit 3.7 and 3.8 illustrate the documents that are filed to open a trespass suit.

■ **EXHIBIT 3.7**

Complaint in Trespass

COMPLAINT

Comes now plaintiff and for his cause of action against defendant alleges:

1. [Jurisdictional allegations.]

2. At all times material herein plaintiff was and is the owner and in possession of lots 1–5, block 4, Townsend Addition, Clay County, State of Iowa.

3. On August 4, 1994, defendant wrongfully entered and trespassed upon said premises and damaged plaintiff's buildings, removed gravel from the premises, and destroyed three trees, all to plaintiff's damage in the sum of twenty-six thousand dollars.

Wherefore, plaintiff prays for judgment against defendant in the sum of twenty-six thousand dollars, together with his costs and disbursements herein.

[date]

_____
Attorney for Plaintiff

■ ASSAULT

An **assault** is any intentional threat of bodily harm or death that puts the victim in fear of physical harm. An assault gives rise to an action for compensatory damages in favor of the person who has been put in fear. The threat of injury or death may come from a mere physical gesture with or without words. The tortfeasor need not use a weapon to threaten the victim. The wrongful conduct must cause the victim to be in fear of immediate bodily harm, or there is no assault. An assault does not require any physical contact. If a contact does occur, then there is a battery in addition to the assault.

The defendant perpetrator must have a specific intent to cause the victim to be fearful or apprehend immediate harm. The defendant commits an assault if he or she puts the victim in fear while unsuccessfully trying to commit a battery. For example, if the defendant intentionally shoots a gun at the plaintiff but misses, an assault has occurred if the defendant was put in fear of being shot. The apprehension of injury must occur while the defendant is in a position to cause harm, not subsequently. If the plaintiff did not know that the defendant tried to shoot her with a gun but found out about the event later, no cause of action will lie for assault.

Some people are fearful of even innocuous or ordinary conduct. But the victim's apprehension of injury is judged on the basis of whether an ordinary, reasonable person would feel threatened. Stated another way, the plaintiff must have been put in fear, and the fear must have been reasonably justified. Mere swearwords or foul language uttered in the presence of the victim or uttered at the victim do not constitute an assault. The words must convey a threat of harm with an apparent ability to do harm. An assault may be by a gesture, such as a "cocked fist" held close to the victim's face.

A cause of action for assault accrues when the victim experiences apprehension. Consent to an assault is an affirmative defense. When people voluntarily enter into some games and athletic contests, they impliedly consent to conduct that under other circumstances would constitute an assault. Another defense would be that the perpetrator has a privilege to conduct

ANSWER

Comes now defendant and for his answer to plaintiff's complaint:

1. Denies each and every allegation, statement, and matter in said complaint contained, except as hereinafter expressly admitted or alleged.

2. Admits the allegations contained in paragraph 2 of the complaint.

3. Admits that defendant entered upon said premises on August 4, 1994, but specifically denies that the entry was wrongful or a trespass.

4. Denies that defendants caused any damage to plaintiff's buildings and puts plaintiff to his strict proof of same.

5. Admits that defendant cut down three trees that had been located upon the premises, but denies that said trees had any value to the premises.

6. Alleges that defendant entered the premises with consent of the owner and/or possessor of the premises, and that he was duly authorized and directed to remove the trees from the premises.

Wherefore, defendant prays that plaintiff take nothing by reason of his pretended cause of action and that defendant have judgment for his costs and disbursements herein.

[date]   _____
                                          Attorney for Defendant

herself or himself as an authority figure, as where a parent disciplines her or his own child or a police officer makes an arrest.

■ BATTERY

A **battery** involves an impermissible physical contact of an injurious nature or a physical contact that is offensive to ordinary sensibilities. Ordinary physical contacts incidental to living in a society are considered permissible and not actionable. Common batteries include an intentional punch in the face, an intentional shooting, intentional tripping, spanking, rape, a tackle in the course of a basketball game, and a surgeon's operating on the wrong part of the body. The contract must be intentional to be actionable as a battery.

Some contacts are batteries not because they are harmful, but because they are offensive to most people. An allegedly obnoxious contact is not actionable unless the plaintiff actually experiences emotional distress. Mental suffering is not presumed. An obvious example of a battery without any actual physical harm is contact that is sexually oriented, such as an unwanted kiss. Merely touching a person with a knife in a threatening manner would constitute a battery. Maliciously throwing a pail of water on the plaintiff could give rise to an action for a battery. All too often, practical jokes end up being batteries.

A cause of action for battery requires proof (1) of a contact; (2) that the contact was without actual or implied consent; and (3) that the contact was intentional. The intent to make contact may be implied from the nature of the contact and surrounding circumstances. Compensatory money damages are allowed for any physical injury and emotional distress resulting from a battery. Punitive damages are allowed in many states where the battery is malicious, that is, where there is an intent to cause harm as a result of the impermissible contact.

A complaint and answer for assault and battery appear in exhibits 3.9 and 3.10.

■ NEGLIGENCE

Negligence is failure to use reasonable care where some consequential harm is foreseeable. Reasonable care is care that a reasonable person would use under like circumstances. Negligence involves doing something a reasonable person would not do, or failing to do something a reasonable person would do, under like circumstances. In the case of a child, reasonable care is care that a reasonable child of the same age, intelligence, training, and experience would use under like circumstances. A cause of action in negligence lies against a person who causes damages or destruction of property or injury to a person through negligent conduct.

Some states recognize degrees of negligence such as ordinary negligence, gross negligence, and willful and wanton negligence. But these characterizations have lost their original significance in most states. In the hierarchy of culpability, the next level above negligence is reckless misconduct, which is conduct intentionally perpetrated in the face of substantial

■ **EXHIBIT 3.9**

Complaint for Assault and Battery

COMPLAINT

Comes now plaintiff and for her cause of action against defendant alleges:

1. [Jurisdictional allegations.]

2. On August 6, 1994, in the city of Smithville, Ohio, defendant assaulted plaintiff by pointing a rifle (weapon) at plaintiff, and defendant verbally threatened to shoot plaintiff.

3. Plaintiff was put in great fear for her life and was fearful of severe bodily injury.

4. Defendant struck plaintiff with a blunt portion of her rifle, thereby breaking plaintiff's jaw and rendering plaintiff unconscious.

5. As a direct consequence of the battery, plaintiff suffered severe and painful injuries that may be permanent in nature.

6. Plaintiff incurred medical expenses, will incur future medical expenses, has suffered a loss of income, and will suffer a loss of earning capacity as a direct consequence of the battery.

7. The assault and battery perpetrated by defendant upon plaintiff was intentional and malicious.

8. Plaintiff is entitled to recover punitive (exemplary) damages from defendant.

Wherefore, plaintiff demands judgment against defendant in the sum of fifty thousand dollars for compensatory damages and ten thousand dollars as punitive damages, together with plaintiff's costs and disbursements herein.

[date]

_____
Attorney for Plaintiff

■ **EXHIBIT 3.10**

Answer to Complaint for
Assault and Battery

ANSWER

Comes now defendant and for her answer to plaintiff's complaint:

1. Denies each and every allegation, statement, and matter in the complaint, except as hereinafter expressly admitted or alleged.

2. Admits the allegations of paragraphs 1, 2, 3, and 4 of the complaint.

3. Alleges that defendant is without sufficient knowledge or information upon which to form a belief concerning plaintiff's claims of injuries and damages and, therefore, puts plaintiff to her strict proof of same.

4. Alleges that plaintiff trespassed upon defendant's premises and entered defendant's dwelling for the purpose of burglarizing the dwelling.

5. Alleges that when defendant discovered plaintiff in defendant's home, plaintiff was armed with a knife and carrying off personal property belonging to defendant.

6. Alleges that defendant then and there arrested plaintiff and held plaintiff until the police could be summoned.

7. Specifically denies that defendant used more force than appeared necessary to protect herself and her property and to effectuate the arrest.

Wherefore, defendant prays that plaintiff take nothing by reason of her pretended cause of action and that defendant have judgment for her costs and disbursements herein.

    [date]   _____
                                              Attorney for Defendant

and obvious danger to other persons or property without specific intent to injure anyone. For example, driving on a crowded city street at a speed slightly over the speed limit is negligence, but driving on a city street at eighty miles per hour is reckless misconduct.

Legal Duty

To understand the basis for a negligence action, it is necessary to understand the underlying legal duty of due, or reasonable, care. Every person owes a duty of reasonable care not to injure others or damage others' property. The duty is to act reasonably considering the foreseeability of harm to others. The law does not demand perfection. What is reasonable care depends upon existing circumstances that are known or should be known. The test is whether the act or omission in question is reasonable in light of the foreseeable harm. A person's conduct is not judged on the basis of hindsight. Adults are charged with knowledge ordinarily possessed by members of the community and knowledge of natural laws such as gravity. A higher duty is imposed upon common carriers such as airlines, railroads, and bus companies. They must exercise the highest degree of care for the protection of their passengers.

Legal Duty Based on Relationships. The relationship between persons may be critical in determining whether a duty of care exists. The following examples illustrate the concept of a duty and the basis for a duty:

1. Suppose a person sees a neighbor using a metal ladder very near an uninsulated electric power line and recognizes that the neighbor is in danger of being electrocuted. Does he have a legal duty to warn or stop the neighbor? No. Failure to warn or stop the neighbor would not result in legal liability if injury did occur. The law does not require ordinary individuals to act to protect fellow citizens, whether or not neighbors, from injuring themselves. But if a homeowner has an acquaintance on the premises helping with some house-painting and sees her on a metal ladder near a power line, the homeowner has a duty to stop the dangerous activity and will be considered negligent if she violates the duty. The duty arises from the special relationship between the owner of the property and the invitee.

2. Suppose a pedestrian comes upon a trench in the road and realizes that motorists may not be so fortunate to discover and avoid it; that if a vehicle were to run into the trench, it would be damaged and its occupants injured. Does the pedestrian have a legal duty to warn approaching motorists of the danger or to stop motorists or to fill the trench? Is there negligence toward the motoring public for a failure to take these precautions? Well, yes, but there is no breach of a legal duty. Therefore, no action in negligence will lie against the defendant. However, the person who excavated the trench or failed to erect barricades is negligent. By creating the "trap" in the public highway, he breached a legal duty to members of the public using the highway. Suppose the trench exists in an area of highway that is under the control of a construction contractor. He may have a duty to protect the public from the trench, even though he did not create the trench. The contractor's duty arises from his contractual relationship with the government to protect the public in the construction zone. The state may be negligent for failing to discover the danger and for failing to eliminate it.

3. Suppose a woman invites people to her home for a social gathering. She knows that most of the guests will use the front sidewalk but is unaware that several bricks in the sidewalk are dangerously loose. One of the guests trips on a loose brick, falls, and is injured. A negligence action may lie against the hostess as the occupant of the premises. She owes a legal duty of reasonable care to make the premises reasonably safe. In some states, the duty of reasonable care includes an obligation to conduct reasonable inspections to discover potential dangers to her guests and to take preventive action such as to give warnings or correct the danger. Conversely, the laws of some states provide that the occupant of a house does not owe a legal duty of inspection and preparation to mere social guests. The occupant's only duty is to correct *known* defects or hazardous conditions or to warn social guests of *known* dangers. So if this hostess was unaware of the loose bricks, she would not be liable in negligence to the injured social guest because she did not have a legal duty to inspect and prepare the premises for her guests. In all states, however, the law imposes a legal duty on the part of a business to inspect and prepare the premises for business invitees.

4. Suppose a man dug a hole in his backyard for planting a tree. During the night a thief entered the premises to steal an outboard motorboat engine. As he was leaving the premises with the engine, he fell in the hole and was injured. Is the property owner liable to the thief for negligently leaving the hole unguarded? Does the thief's malevolent purpose insulate the property owner from liability? In most states, thieves are treated as trespassers. They have no right to be on the premises; the property owner owes them no duty of care. However, the property owner must not use more force than is reasonably necessary to eject a trespasser. Nor may the property owner set traps for the purpose of catching or injuring trespassers. If the property owner dug the hole to catch a thief, the property owner might have liability for creating a trap.

In some negligence actions it is necessary to determine whether there is a relationship between the injured plaintiff and the proposed defendant. This determines whether there is a legal relationship that creates a legal duty on the part of the defendant to avoid injuring the plaintiff or to actively protect the plaintiff from injury.

So-called **malpractice** cases are really just actions in negligence. They are claims against professional people based upon their alleged failure to comply with the standards of their profession. Of course, the substandard performance or conduct must have caused some harm to the plaintiff for an action to lie. Malpractice actions may be brought against physicians, lawyers, nurses, accountants, pharmacists, engineers, architects, and so on. The gravamen of the claim is that the professional failed to have the necessary education or skill to practice in the profession or to perform the particular function in question. Or the professional may be negligent for failing to exercise due care in the performance of the service or function. In either event, the standard of the profession dictates the minimum standard of care and performance.

Laypersons are presumed to be unfamiliar with professional duties and standards. Consequently, the law requires other professionals, who are familiar with professional standards, to establish the applicable standards in court. This is done through expert testimony. Expert testimony may also be necessary to determine whether the standards have been violated. An untoward or disappointing result from the professional's services is not, in itself, a sufficient basis for maintaining or proving a malpractice action in court. For this reason, a patient who sues his or her physician usually must find another physician who will testify that the treating physician's conduct deviated from acceptable professional standards. Otherwise, the patient's case must be dismissed for failure to prove a prima facie case. (A prima facie case is one that has sufficient facts to support all the elements to the cause of action. There must be sufficient evidence to establish the material [necessary] facts. When determining whether a prima facie case has been established, there is no consideration given to the persuasiveness of the evidence.)

The preceding examples illustrate that even though the concept of negligence is simple, its application is often very complex. To make the whole subject more difficult, the law of negligence is constantly changing. The study of negligence involves a study of the interrelationships between people, public institutions, and governments. Each special relationship creates a different duty. For example, a bus driver must exercise the highest degree of care for the protection of passengers, but only reasonable care for the protection of other motorists or pedestrians using the roadways. The difference in the duty of care is based upon the difference in the relationships.

Legal Duty Established by Statute. Many legal duties are established by statute. A violation of a statutory duty is negligence. There can be no excuse or justification for noncompliance with a statute enacted to protect a particular person or class of people or properties. A violation of a statute is commonly referred to as **negligence per se,** which means that the violation is, in itself, negligence. For example, a statute forbids merchants to sell guns to minors. A gun is sold to a minor who accidentally shoots another person. The vendor's illegal sale is negligence per se. The statute was enacted to prevent exactly that kind of an occurrence.

Some statutes, by their terms, provide that a violation is not negligence per se, but merely **prima facie evidence of negligence,** or merely evidence of negligence. The application of such a statute is illustrated in the following typical jury instruction: If the statute was violated, the violation is negligence unless the jury finds evidence tending to show reasonable excuse or justification or evidence from which a reasonable person, under the circumstances, could believe that the violation would not endanger any person entitled to the protection of the statute. If the statutory violation were not limited to prima facie negligence, the violator would not be permitted to show excuse or justification.

Most state highway codes provide that traffic violations are merely prima facie evidence of negligence and not negligence per se. A technical violation may be excused or justified. A violation is to be judged on the basis of all the other circumstances surrounding the accident, including the known risks and the risks that reasonably should have been anticipated and the reasons for the violation. A jury has the task of weighing the reasons for the violation against the gravity of the violation and the foreseeability of harm resulting from the violation. In the absence of any reasonable excuse or justification, a judge would have to determine that the violation was a negligent act or omission. Could a jury be justified in excusing a father's unlawful speed if he is driving his seriously injured child to a hospital to obtain medical care? Perhaps. Suppose he collides with a car that violated a stop sign—the father being on a through street. The jury would be entitled to weigh the reasons for the violation against the reasons for the statute.

Causation

In a negligence action, the plaintiff must prove that the defendant's conduct was negligent and that the negligence was a proximate cause of the occurrence or accident. If the defendant's negligence was not a proximate cause of the accident, the defendant is not liable for the accident. The term *direct cause* is sometimes used instead of **proximate cause.**

The subject of causation is just as esoteric as the concept of negligence. A proximate cause is a cause that has a substantial part in bringing about the accident either immediately or through happenings that naturally follow one after another. For example, suppose a motorist parks an automobile two feet from the curb when local law requires her to park within one foot, and another motorist runs into the back of the parked automobile. It is unlikely that the technical violation of parking two feet from the curb was the actual cause of the accident. Or suppose a motorist is traveling ten miles per hour over the posted speed limit and is struck by another vehicle that went through a stop sign. The excessive speed is merely coincidental and not a proximate cause. The cause of the accident was the stop sign violation because that violation would have resulted in a collision even if the other motorist had been traveling within the speed limit. Speed did not cause this accident or induce negligence on the part of the driver who ran the stop sign. But suppose the motorist is traveling twenty-five miles per hour over the speed limit. It is reasonable to believe that a passenger's injuries will be greater because of the excessive speed. Speed limits are established to reduce the severity of injuries as well as to prevent accidents. Again the question arises, Did the excessive speed cause the accident or consequential injury? Usually, the issue of proximate cause is a question of fact for a jury to decide.

An accident may have more than one proximate cause. When the effects of the negligent conduct of two or more persons actively work at substantially the same time to cause the accident, the conduct of each may be a proximate cause of the accident. If two defendants contribute toward a plaintiff's loss, they are jointly and severally liable for the entire loss. For example, if two motorists collide in an intersection because both failed to keep a proper lookout, their concurrent negligence makes both of them liable for their passengers' injuries. Each motorist is individually liable to the passenger for all of the passenger's injuries, but either motorist has the right to contribution from the other. If one of the negligent motorists has no insurance and no money, the entire loss could fall on the motorist who is financially responsible.

Another facet of the law of causation is the concept of the **efficient intervening cause,** or **superseding cause.** A superseding cause relieves a person from his or her liability for all prior negligent conduct. The requirements of a superseding cause are very specific. For a cause to be a superseding cause, its harmful effects must have occurred after the original negligence, and the superseding cause must not have been brought about by the original negligence. For example, if the driver of an automobile sees a truck unlawfully stopped on the highway ahead and has sufficient time in which to avoid a collision but negligently fails to do so, the automobile driver's negligence is a superseding cause of the collision. The superseding negligence of the driver insulates the owner of the stopped truck from legal liability for the collision, though he created the dangerous condition.

A party who claims that another party was negligent must prove negligence by a fair preponderance of the evidence; or, said another way, negligence must be established by the greater weight of the evidence. The mere fact that an accident occurs does not, in itself, necessarily mean that someone was negligent. If there is a deficiency in the evidence so that negligence is not proved, the court must direct a verdict against the party who has the burden of proof. A direct verdict means that the claim or defense is disallowed by the judge because there are insufficient facts to support the alleged cause of action.

Affirmative Defenses

Historically, two affirmative defenses were frequently asserted in negligence actions: **contributory negligence** and **assumption of risk.** Contributory negligence is *not* a special kind of negligence or a special quality of negligence. It is simply negligence on the part of the plaintiff. The old rule was that if the defendant was able to prove by a fair preponderance of the evidence that the plaintiff was negligent, that negligence defeated the plaintiff's claim. Similarly, if the defendant could prove by a fair preponderance of the evidence that the plaintiff assumed the risk of his or her injury, the plaintiff's assumption of risk constituted a complete defense. Where these affirmative defenses were established, the defendant would prevail even though the plaintiff was able to show that the defendant was negligent.

Historically, the law was not at all concerned with any comparisons of fault between the parties. Negligence and causation were considered absolutes. Any causal negligence was sufficient to create a claim or a defense. Similarly, the plaintiff's assumption of the risk provided the defendant with a complete defense. The plaintiff assumed the risk if she or he voluntarily placed herself or himself in a position to chance a known hazard. To prove assumption of risk, the defendant had to prove that the plaintiff had actual knowledge of the specific risk; that the plaintiff appreciated the risk; that the plaintiff had a choice or opportunity to avoid the risk; that the plaintiff voluntarily chose to incur the risk; and that the assumed risk materialized to cause the plaintiff's injury or harm.

As an example of an assumption of risk, suppose a cook in a restaurant negligently permits the sink to overflow and a lot of soapy water spills on the floor, making it slippery. The janitor is summoned to clean up the water. She begins the task but then slips in the soapy water and falls on the floor. She knew the risk and appreciated the danger of the slippery floor, but it is her job to deal with such conditions. By proceeding with the cleanup work, she voluntarily chose to incur the risk. She has no claim against the cook or the cook's employer because of the assumed risk. Before the days of workers' compensation, employers were able to use the assumption-of-risk defense very effectively in many of the personal injury cases brought by employees.

The law of contributory negligence and assumption of risk has evolved in most states into the law of **comparative negligence.** The law of comparative negligence is a so-called equitable approach to tort litigation. Its proponents justify the doctrines as more fair. The objective is to obtain some compensation for the plaintiff even though he or she was also negligent and contributed to the loss. When a case is tried pursuant to the law of comparative negligence, the jury is required to evaluate each party's casual negligence and apportion the parties' negligence on a percentage basis.

There are two principal forms of comparative negligence. In states adopting **pure comparative negligence,** the plaintiff's recovery of money damages is reduced by the amount or percentage of her or his causal negligence. For example, if the plaintiff is found to be 20 percent causally negligent, the damages award is reduced to 80 percent of the amount awarded by the jury. If the plaintiff's causal negligence is 75 percent of the total negligence causing the accident, the damages award is reduced to 25 percent of the amount awarded by the jury.

States having **ordinary comparative negligence** similarly reduce the plaintiff's award by his or her percentage of causal negligence, but if the plaintiff's causal negligence is greater than the defendant's causal negligence, the plaintiff is not permitted to recover any damages against the defendant. Where ordinary comparative negligence applies, a plaintiff who is 51 percent at fault cannot recover any compensation. In states having ordinary comparative negligence, the defense of assumption of risk is treated as a form of comparative negligence.

In states that apply the law of contributory negligence, each defendant who is liable for the plaintiff's injury or loss is liable jointly and individually for the whole loss and the entire award of compensatory damages. If the action involves two defendants, they are equally liable to each other for one-half of the award made to the plaintiff. In states having comparative negligence, the codefendants are also jointly and individually liable for the amount of damages recoverable by plaintiff. But among the codefendants, each is liable only for her or his percentage of causal negligence. For example, if the jury determines that the plaintiff was 20 percent at fault, defendant A was 10 percent at fault, defendant B was 30 percent at fault, and defendant C was 40 percent at fault, and the amount of money damages awarded to the plaintiff is $10,000.00, the plaintiff's recovery will be $8,000.00. The plaintiff cannot recover any damages from defendant A, who was less negligent than the plaintiff. Defendants B and C are together liable to the plaintiff for the entire $8,000.00. Between defendant B (30 percent) and defendant C (40 percent), their obligation for the $8,000.00 award is in proportion. Defendant B is obligated for $3,428.57, and defendant C is obligated for $4,571.43. The proportionate amounts are easily calculated by converting the 30 percent to $30/70$, or $3/7$, and converting the 40 percent to $40/70$, or $4/7$.

$$3/7 \times \$8,000.00 = \$3,428.57$$
$$4/7 \times \$8,000.00 = \$4,571.43$$

Sample Complaint and Answer

The documents in exhibits 3.11 and 3.12 are typical of those filed for an action in negligence.

The answer in exhibit 3.12 admits the occurrence of the accident, but denies liability by denying negligence. Plaintiffs are put to their proof to establish their damages. The answer raises two affirmative defenses: contributory negligence and assumption of risk. Maria Gallegos's claim is based upon a derivative cause of action. Therefore, her claim is defeated by any affirmative defense that defeats her husband's claim.

■ PRODUCTS LIABILITY

Products liability law includes a number of causes of action that are available to persons who are injured by defective products. Historically, the injured consumer had to prove an action in negligence against the product manufacturer or vendor to recover money damages for any injury caused by a defective product. The consumer had to prove that the product was defective; that the defect was the result of some negligent conduct on the part of the vendor against whom the claim was made; and that the defect

■ **EXHIBIT 3.11**

Complaint in Negligence

COMPLAINT

Come now the plaintiffs and for their cause of action against defendants allege:

1. [Jurisdictional allegations.]

2. Plaintiffs are and at all times material herein have been husband and wife, and they reside in the state of Wisconsin.

3. Defendant Shawn and Associates, Inc., is and at all times material herein was a Wisconsin corporation having its office and principal place of business in Spencer, Wisconsin.

4. Defendant Drake Apartments, Inc., is and at all times material herein was a Wisconsin corporation having its office and principal place of business in Spencer, Wisconsin.

5. Defendant Barton and Associates, Inc., is and at all times material herein was a Minnesota corporation having its office and principal place of business in Madison, Minnesota.

6. On or about July 19, 1992, Shawn and Associates contracted with Drake Apartments, the owner of premises located at 724 South Fifth Street, Spencer, Wisconsin (hereinafter the job site), to act as general contractor for the construction of an addition to said premises, and in connection therewith Shawn and Associates agreed to assume responsibility for providing a safe place to work for all persons working at the job site, including all subcontractors and their employees.

7. On or about October 26, 1992, Drake Apartments entered into a contract with Barton and Associates whereby Barton and Associates agreed to provide certain services, including architectural services, to Drake Apartments. On or about the 28th day of July, 1992, Shawn and Associates, as general contractor, entered into a contract, attached as exhibit A, with Johnson Construction, a subcontractor, for erection by Johnson Construction of the structural steel frame for the addition to said premises. In connection therewith Shawn and Associates agreed to assume responsibility for providing a safe place to work for Johnson Construction and all Johnson Construction employees at the job site, and Johnson Construction agreed to indemnify Shawn and Associates from all claims for damages and injury in connection with the work.

8. Plaintiff Juan Gallegos at all times material herein was employed by Johnson Construction as a steelworker.

9. Drake Apartments negligently and in violation of its legal obligations failed to employ a competent and careful contractor to do the work and to perform the duties that Drake Apartments owed to third persons, including the plaintiffs, and to take precautions against the risk of physical harm to persons on the premises.

10. Prior to and on February 7, 1993, defendants negligently and in violation of federal and state OSHA standards and in breach of their contractual obligations, failed to provide plaintiff Juan Gallegos with a safe place to work at the job site; failed to use proper construction procedures and failed to properly supervise the work at the job site; failed to properly inspect the job site and failed to correct unsafe conditions; failed to erect proper barricading to protect plaintiff at the job site; failed to adequately warn plaintiff of unsafe conditions and hazards existing at the job site; and failed to fulfill its nondelegable contractual and legal responsibilities with respect to working conditions at the job site.

—Continued

—Continued

11. Defendant Barton and Associates negligently and in breach of contractual duties to plaintiff failed to provide general administration of the construction contract; failed to properly represent the owner; failed to determine, in general, if the work was proceeding properly and in accordance with contract documents; and failed to advise and consult with Drake Apartments regarding safety on the job site.

12. On February 7, 1993, as a direct consequence of the negligence of the defendants, and each of them, plaintiff Juan Gallegos, while working at the job site, fell in a stairwell at the job site and suffered permanent injuries and permanent disability.

13. Because of his injuries, plaintiff Juan Gallegos has been prevented from transacting his business and has lost wages in the approximate amount of fifty thousand dollars; he has incurred expenses and obligations for medical attention, hospitalization and related care, and miscellaneous items in the approximate amount of one hundred thousand dollars; he has been and will in the future be totally physically disabled and totally dependent upon others for his care; he has lost all future earning capacity and will lose all future wages; he will incur substantial medical expenses, and additional living and miscellaneous expenses in the future; and he has suffered and will in the future suffer great pain of body and mind.

14. Owning to the injuries sustained by Juan Gallegos, plaintiff Maria Gallegos has been and in the future will be required to provide care for her husband; she has permanently lost the services of her husband; and her comfort and happiness in his society and companionship have been permanently impaired.

Wherefore, the plaintiffs, and each of them, demand judgment in their favor and against the defendants, and each of them, jointly and severally, as follows:

1. Money damages for plaintiff Juan Gallegos in the sum of $150,000.

2. Money damages for plaintiff Maria Gallegos in the sum of $50,000.

3. Reimbursement for plaintiffs' costs and disbursements herein.

[date]   _____
                          Attorneys for Plaintiffs

was the proximate cause of the plaintiff's injury. A product is considered to be defective if it is unreasonably dangerous for use in the ordinary manner. A product may be unreasonably dangerous because of its design, the materials used, poor fabrication or assembly, failure to provide adequate instructions for its use, or failure to provide adequate warnings about dangers in its use. In a negligence action the manufacturer is not liable for defects if the manufacturer acted with reasonable care. Often it is difficult for the plaintiff to prove a prima facie case of negligence against the vendor.

The next step in the evolution of products liability law was the creation of implied warranties, which arose from the contract between the seller and the buyer. The law had long recognized the right of the parties to create

■ **EXHIBIT 3.12**

Answer to Complaint
in Negligence

ANSWER

Comes now defendant Drake Apartments, Inc., and for its answer to plaintiffs' complaint:

1. Denies each and every allegation, statement, matter, and thing in said complaint contained, except as hereinafter expressly admitted or otherwise alleged.

2. Admits that plaintiff Juan Gallegos sustained injuries about the time and place mentioned in the complaint, but specifically denies that Drake Apartments was negligent.

3. Alleges that this answering defendant does not have sufficient knowledge or information upon which to form a belief concerning plaintiffs' claims of injuries and damages; therefore, plaintiffs are put to their strict proof of same.

4. Alleges that plaintiff Juan Gallegos was negligent so as to cause his alleged injuries and damages.

5. Alleges that plaintiff Juan Gallegos assumed the risk of his alleged injuries.

Wherefore, defendant Drake Apartments prays that plaintiffs take nothing by reason of their pretended cause of action, and that this answering defendant have judgment for its costs and disbursements herein.

[date]

_____
Attorney for Defendant

express warranties concerning the quality and fitness of goods sold. As the marketplace became more structured, the law came to impose implied warranties that products were of merchantable quality and reasonably fit for the purpose for which they were sold. Even so, implied warranties benefited only the immediate buyer because the cause of action is predicated upon the contract between the buyer and the seller. The law made privity of contract a condition to maintenance of the action. In other words, only persons who were parties to the sales contract could assert a claim that arose from the sales transaction. The warranty claim was a creature of the transaction, not a creature of the product failure and injury. Therefore the retail purchaser could not bring an implied warranty action directly against the manufacturer, since they had no contract between them. The purchaser could only make the warranty claim directly against the retail vendor. In turn, the retailer could seek indemnity from the wholesaler from whom the retailer had purchased the product and the wholesaler could seek indemnity from the manufacturer. Also, the purchaser's claim could be barred by failure to notify the seller of the defect and injury within a "reasonable" period of time.

Gradually some of the restriction on implied warranty actions were abrogated by court decision and statute. For example, the privity-of-contract condition was relaxed so that members of the purchaser's family could sue on the contract for breach of implied warranty. Nevertheless, vendors were often able to avoid liability by including warranty disclaimers as part of the sales contract. Also, the common law recognized various common-law affirmative defenses to the implied warranty actions, such as contributory negligence and/or assumption of risk on the part of the user.

Legal scholars and writers began to feel that the law should make compensation for the harm caused by defective products a cost of doing business. They reasoned that most products in modern society are manufactured and marketed by large, well-established companies that could easily spread the cost of damage claims by simply increasing the cost of their products.

This rationale led to the creation of a relatively new cause of action commonly known as **strict liability in tort.** Now all states have adopted this cause of action in one form or another as an additional means of providing compensation to persons injured by defective products whether or not the injured person was a purchaser of the particular product. All the injured person has to prove is that the product was defective at the time it left the vendor's possession and the defect was the proximate cause of the plaintiff's injury. A cause of action for strict liability in tort lies against manufacturers, distributors, wholesalers, and retailers. But no action will lie against a seller of a product who is not in the business of selling that kind of product. In other words, implied warranty actions and strict liability actions can be maintained only against merchants of the particular product.

Privity of contact is not necessary to strict liability actions. As originally conceived, contributory negligence and assumption of risk, and comparative negligence were not supposed to be defenses to strict liability tort actions. Nevertheless, the current trend is to allow **comparative fault** as a basis for reducing the plaintiff's recovery of damages, just as in ordinary comparative negligence actions. Comparative fault is a concept by which the courts attempt to apportion the causal fault of each party, and then allocate the recovery of damages between the parties on the basis of their comparative fault. Comparative fault is similar to comparative negligence; however, it is broader and applies to any tort action and tort defense that do not involve wrongful intent to harm. The need for such an approach became manifest from a whole line of cases that showed consumers grossly abusing products—using them in ways that were totally improper. The defendant vendor had to prove that the product was not being used for its intended purpose or was being used in a dangerous manner that could not reasonably have been foreseen by the vendor. Once the courts recognized product abuse as a defense to strict liability claims, it was relatively easy to move to the comparative fault concept for allocating damages in product cases. Note that strict liability became a cause of action before comparative fault came into vogue as a basis for obtaining compensation for personal injuries. The concept is now being carried into product litigation.

Nowadays, the plaintiff's claim may be based upon negligence or breach of warranty or strict liability in tort. Sometimes the facts permit the plaintiff to pursue all three legal theories (causes of action) at the same time. The theory upon which recovery is sought determines what facts must be proved, what evidence is necessary, and even what damages are recoverable. Defenses applicable to a negligence action may not apply to a warranty action or to a strict liability action, and defenses that apply to a warranty action may not apply to a negligence action. The amount of damages recoverable under one theory may be significantly more than those recoverable under another theory. Therefore, the plaintiff's lawyer must choose the cause or causes of action carefully. In many cases, all three causes of action will be pleaded against the vendor. In some states, the plaintiff is required to elect between a negligence claim and a strict liability claim before the case is submitted to the jury. This development has occurred because, on occasion, some states have found that the submission of both theories in the same case leads to inconsistent verdicts.

With regard to negligence actions, manufacturers owe to purchasers and users a duty to use reasonable care to make their products reasonably safe for ordinary use. Said another way, manufacturers must use due care to make their products so that they are not unreasonably dangerous when used in the ordinary manner for a proper purpose. But a manufacturer is not liable for the consequences of a product's failure if the manufacturer used ordinary care in making the product. For example, if a manufacturer builds an automobile that has a defective axle and the defect could not have been prevented or discovered by the exercise of reasonable care, the manufacturer is not liable to the purchaser or occupants who are injured in an accident caused by the broken axle. The retail vendor of the automobile is also not liable. Very often, reasonable care is looked upon as the care that other manufacturers use in making similar products.

The same example may be used to illustrate a breach of implied warranty theory for recovery. An automobile with a defective axle is not of merchantable quality and certainly is not fit for use as a motor vehicle. Therefore, a recovery in favor of the purchaser and members of his family may be possible under the breach-of-implied-warranty theory. But passengers who are not members of the purchaser's family could not maintain a warranty action—at least not in some states. The law permits the vendor to qualify and limit implied warranties. Indeed, the contract of sale may exclude all warranties by making the sale "with all faults" or "as is." Furthermore, contracts often limit the time during which a warranty may be claimed. Assume, for purposes of this example, that the axle broke twenty-five months after the automobile was purchased and the contract eliminated all warranties after twenty-four months. The sales contract effectively negated the implied warranties.

The owner and occupants of the automobile in this example could maintain an action in strict liability in tort for their personal injuries caused by the defective axle. They would need to prove that the axle was defective when it left the manufacturer's hands. One might wonder why a negligence action is ever pursued in a products case, since a strict liability case is easier to prove. In certain cases a jury has determined that the product in question was not defective, but the vendor's negligence caused the accident behind the suit. See *Bigham v. J. C. Penney Co.,* 268 N.W.2d 802 (Minn. 1978).

Each vendor in the chain of sale is liable to the plaintiff consumer for the full amount of the plaintiff's damages. But each vendor whose liability is based upon mere warranty or strict liability in tort is entitled to obtain indemnity from the preceding vendor or vendors in the chain. Therefore, a negligent vendor is precluded from obtaining indemnity but may be allowed to obtain contribution from other negligent vendors in the chain of sale.

Sample documents for initiating an action in strict liability in tort appear in exhibits 3.13 and 3.14.

■ LIQUOR VENDOR'S LIABILITY

It is a well-known and accepted fact that the use of intoxicating liquors often causes or contributes significantly to accidental injuries and property

COMPLAINT

Comes now the plaintiff and for her cause of action against defendant alleges:

1. [Jurisdictional allegations.]

Count 1

2. At the times herein mentioned, defendant Dawn Company, Inc., was engaged in the manufacture of a chemical oven cleaner called Sparkle. Said cleaner was manufactured for sale to the general public.

3. During the month of February 1994, plaintiff purchased a can of defendant's oven cleaner identified by the marking 5M142D, which was manufactured and sold by defendant for retail sales to the general public.

4. At all times following the purchase of the oven cleaner, plaintiff reasonably and properly handled the product.

5. Defendant sold and delivered the oven cleaner to retailers knowing that in the regular course of business it would be resold to a customer for use as an oven cleaner.

6. Defendant failed to provide plaintiff with a warning concerning the hazards of using the oven cleaner.

7. The oven cleaner was negligently designed, manufactured, tested, and inspected by defendant, and the oven cleaner was dangerous to the physical health of users when it left defendant's control or possession.

8. Defendant was negligent in failing to provide adequate instructions for the oven cleaner's use and failing to warn of the product's dangers.

9. On March 12, 1994, plaintiff used the oven cleaner for the first time and in accordance with the printed instructions on the can, for the purpose of cleaning her oven in her home located at 5606 Lawndale Lane, Spencer, Illinois.

10. Defendant's negligence directly caused plaintiff to suffer severe itching, swelling, dizziness, restricted breathing, and an anaphylactic reaction, all to plaintiff's general damage in the sum of thirty thousand dollars.

11. Plaintiff incurred expenses for medical attention, hospital care, and medicines in the sum of five hundred dollars.

Count 2

12. Plaintiff realleges paragraphs 1 through 10 of count 1 as if those allegations were set forth in full in this count.

13. In marketing the oven cleaner product, defendant impliedly warranted that the product was of merchantable quality and was fit for the purpose for which it was intended.

14. In fact, the product was not of merchantable quality and was unsafe and unfit for the purpose for which it was sold, purchased, and used.

15. Defendants breach of said implied warranties caused plaintiff to suffer serious bodily injuries.

Count 3

16. Plaintiff realleges paragraphs 1 through 14 of counts 1 and 2 as if those allegations were set forth in full.

—Continued

—Continued

17. Defendant expressly warranted that the oven cleaner contained no caustic or choking fumes or chemicals to irritate eyes or nose.

18. The oven cleaner did not conform to the express warranties made by defendant and printed on the product container.

19. As a result of defendant's breach of the express warranties, plaintiff suffered serious bodily injuries.

Count 4

20. Plaintiff realleges paragraphs 1 through 18 of counts 1 through 3 as if those allegations were set forth in full.

21. The oven cleaner manufactured and sold by defendant was unreasonably dangerous for use in the ordinary manner and, therefore, was a defective product.

22. Plaintiff used the product in the intended manner for the proper purpose.

23. As a result of the defective and injurious character of the oven cleaner, plaintiff suffered injuries as described above.

24. As a result of the defective condition of the oven cleaner, defendant is strictly liable in tort to plaintiff for the injuries sustained and losses suffered as described above.

Wherefore, plaintiff prays for judgment against defendant in the sum of twenty-five thousand dollars and her costs and disbursements herein.

[date]

_____
Attorney for Plaintiff

damage. Historically, vendors of intoxicating liquors were not liable for the accidents caused by inebriated customers, because an inebriated person's wrongful conduct was considered the sole proximate cause of a resulting accident. The consumer was held responsible to know when he or she had enough alcohol; the vendor was not the consumer's guardian. In recent decades, a concern grew that vendors ought to be responsible if they made an illegal sale of intoxicants and the illegal use contributed to cause harm to others. Most or all states have now adopted dramshop legislation, which creates a civil action against liquor vendors and in favor of persons, other than the inebriate, who suffer harm as the result of an illegal sale of intoxicants.

In these **dramshop actions,** an illegal sale or barter does not have to be a proximate cause of the accident. The law only requires that the illegal sale contribute to the occurrence of the accident. For example, if it is determined that an illegal sale of intoxicants may have contributed to a man's suicide, the vendor could be liable to the man's surviving spouse and children for loss of support. Even if courts have acknowledged that intoxication probably did not cause the intoxicated person to commit suicide, the jury could properly find that the intoxication contributed to the suicide.

The plaintiff must prove that the defendant vendor made a sale prohibited by law. The two most common types of illegal sales resulting in liability are sales to minors and sales to persons who are already **obviously**

ANSWER

Comes now defendant and for its answer to plaintiff's complaint:

1. Denies each and every allegation, statement, matter, and thing in said complaint contained, except as hereinafter expressly admitted or alleged.

2. Admits the allegations of paragraphs 1 and 2 of the complaint.

3. Alleges that defendant is without sufficient knowledge or information upon which to form a belief concerning plaintiff's claims of injuries and damages and, therefore, puts plaintiff to her strict proof of same.

4. Alleges that if plaintiff sustained injuries and damages as alleged in the complaint, they were caused by the negligence of plaintiff.

5. Alleges that plaintiff did not serve defendant with notice of breach of warranty as required by law.

6. Alleges that plaintiff assumed the risk of injury.[1]

Wherefore, defendant prays that plaintiff take nothing by reason of her pretended cause of action and that defendant have judgment for its costs and disbursements herein.

[date]   _____
                                                  Attorney for Defendant

1. It is not necessary to allege that plaintiff misused the product, and that was the cause of injury, because misuse is not an affirmative defense even though misuse by plaintiff would prevent plaintiff from recovering money damages. Plaintiff has the burden of proving that plaintiff used the product in the ordinary, intended manner.

intoxicated. A person is obviously intoxicated when he or she manifests outward symptoms of intoxication such as loss of coordination, slurred speech, incoherence in thinking, loss of balance, emotional volatility, and so on. The determination is made on an objective basis.

The alleged intoxicated person does not have any claim against the vendor for injuring herself or himself. Nevertheless, if the intoxicated person is injured and becomes disabled for a period of time, the spouse and children of the intoxicated person have a claim against the vendor for loss of support. If the intoxicated person dies, the claim for loss of support may be substantial.

Most states recognize **complicity** as an affirmative defense. Complicity describes the victim's conduct if the victim participated in the illegal sale or effectively brought about the inebriant's intoxication. Complicity is an affirmative defense that the liquor vendor must allege and prove. It is a complete defense even in states that have comparative fault statutes. For example, suppose two men spend several hours in a liquor establishment buying each other intoxicants and become obviously intoxicated. An illegal sale of liquor is made to them, and one of the intoxicated men attempts to drive his car with the other as a passenger. They have an accident that was contributed to by the driver's intoxication. The passenger's complicity in the illegal sale is a bar to his claim against the liquor vendor who illegally sold liquor to the driver. Similarly, if a person acts with complicity in the sale of intoxicants to a minor and is injured as a result of the minor's intoxication, that person cannot recover compensation from the liquor vendor who made the illegal sale. Some states may not recognize complicity as a defense.

Dramshop statutes require the plaintiff to give notice of the illegal sale, occurrence, loss, and intent to make a claim. The notice must be given to the liquor vendor within a specified number of days after the occurrence, typically 120 days. Failure to give the statutorily mandated notice bars any action against the vendor. The reason for the notice requirements is to give the vendor an opportunity to investigate and evaluate the claim before the evidence disappears. If a notice is required by state law, the plaintiff must allege in the complaint that he or she complied with the notice requirement. If the allegation is denied, the burden is on the plaintiff to prove that notice was duly given or served. The plaintiff's lawyer must be careful to establish and preserve proof of service of the notice.

Unless specified in the dramshop statute, negligence on the part of the injured plaintiff is not a defense to the liquor vendor. On the other hand, the law seems to be moving toward application of comparative fault principles to these cases. If comparative fault or negligence is applicable, the plaintiff's recovery of money damages is reduced by her or his percentage of causal negligence.

Exhibits 3.15 and 3.16 are a typical complaint and answer in a dramshop action.

■ NUISANCE

The owner and occupants of real estate are entitled to the comfortable use and enjoyment of the property without being subjected to disturbing odors, noises, or activities. The law protects occupants against the loss of use and enjoyment of real property by allowing them to bring an action for **nuisance** to recover money damages as compensation for interference with their use and enjoyment of the property. The interference must be substantial in nature and duration. If the nuisance is likely to continue, courts have the power to enjoin a nuisance, that is, order abatement of the nuisance.

Courts must weigh the value of the activity complained of and the character of the area, against the effects on the plaintiff's use of her or his premises. For example, if the defendant sets up a creosote plant near an established residential area, the smell and fumes may be too much for the residents. They may have a cause of action for damages in nuisance and grounds for obtaining an injunction to abate operation of the plant. But suppose the plaintiff buys a house near a commercial airport and in the path of aircraft landing and taking off. Excessive noise may constitute a nuisance that is actionable. But the necessity of having the airport where it is and the utility of the activity justify some impairment of plaintiff's use and quiet enjoyment of her property. Also, the courts tend to protect the existing character of an area, so if an airport or railroad or sanitary landfill or paint factory was in the area first, fairness suggests that the newcomer

COMPLAINT

Come now the plaintiffs and for their cause of action against defendants, and each of them, allege:

Count 1

1. [Jurisdictional allegations.]

2. Joy Peterson is the personal representative for the estate of James William Peterson.

3. On June 1, 1994, defendant Kenneth Roberts was operating his motor vehicle on Constance Boulevard at or near the intersection of Highway 65 in Tampa, Florida.

4. At said time and place, James Anderson was operating his motor vehicle on Highway 65 at or near the intersection with Constance Boulevard in Tampa, Florida.

5. Plaintiffs Christine Peterson and James Peterson were passengers in the automobile owned and operated by James Anderson.

6. At the above time and place, defendant Kenneth Roberts and the intestate James Anderson operated their respective vehicles in such a negligent, careless, and unlawful manner that they caused their vehicles to come into violent collision.

7. As a direct result of said collision, Christine Peterson and James Peterson suffered serious and permanent injuries and were prevented from transacting their business, sustained great pain of body and mind, and have incurred and will in the future incur expenses for medical attention and hospitalization in a sum not presently known but believed to exceed fifty thousand dollars.

8. As a direct and proximate result of defendants' negligence, plaintiffs Christine Peterson and James Peterson have each sustained and will sustain in the future a loss of earnings and loss of earning capacity in a sum not presently capable of determination.

Count 2

Plaintiffs reallege all paragraphs set out in count 1 as if fully set forth herein.

9. On May 31 and June 1, 1994, defendant Happy Hour Tavern illegal sold, furnished, and/or bartered intoxicating liquors to Kenneth Roberts in violation of [statute] and by this violation of statute and by the illegal sale, furnishing, or bartering caused and/or contributed to the intoxication of Kenneth Roberts.

10. On May 31 and June 1, 1994, defendant Happy Hour Tavern illegally supplied, furnished, or gave alcoholic beverages to defendant Kenneth Roberts, thereby causing or adding to the intoxication of said Kenneth Roberts. [In most states an allegation of a negligent sale of intoxicants would not state a cause of action.]

11. As a direct and proximate result of the illegal selling, furnishing, bartering [or negligence in supplying] on May 31 and June 1, 1994, Kenneth Roberts collided with a motor vehicle owned and negligently operated by James Anderson, in which plaintiffs Christine Peterson and James Peterson were passengers, thereby causing severe and permanent injuries to Christine Peterson and James Peterson as alleged above.

—Continued

■ **EXHIBIT 3.15**

Complaint in Dramshop,
Continued

—Continued

12. As a direct and proximate consequence of said collision, plaintiffs Christine Peterson and James Peterson suffered injuries of which they herein complain.

13. As a further direct and proximate consequence of said collision, plaintiffs Christine Peterson and James Peterson have incurred hospital expenses and medical expenses and will require medical attention in the future.

14. Plaintiffs Christine Peterson and James Peterson have been damaged in their ability to earn income and will suffer and inability into the future.

Wherefore, plaintiffs, and each of them, pray for judgment against defendants, and each of them, in the sum of fifty thousand dollars, together with their costs and disbursements herein.

[date]   _____
                         Attorney for Plaintiffs

should expect to put up with the status quo. Nevertheless, being there first is no guaranty of prevailing in a nuisance action.

An action to recover damages caused by a nuisance does not require proof of fault or of wrongful conduct. The plaintiff must prove that the alleged nuisance has created a substantial interference in the use and enjoyment of the property and that the utility of the nuisance does not justify its continuance. A distinction between an action for trespass and an action for nuisance is that the former concerns an act against the property whereas the latter concerns an act against the use and enjoyment of the property. In both instances, the person in possession ordinarily has the real

■ **EXHIBIT 3.16**

Answer to Complaint
in Dramshop

ANSWER

Comes now defendant, Happy Hour Tavern, and for its separate answer to plaintiffs' complaint.

1. Denies each and every allegation, statement, matter, anything in said complaint contained, except as hereinafter expressly admitted or alleged.

2. Alleges defendant is without sufficient knowledge or information upon which to form a belief concerning plaintiffs' claims of injuries and damages and, therefore, puts plaintiffs to their strict proof of same.

3. Alleges that plaintiffs failed to serve notice of claim upon defendant as required by law.

Wherefore, defendant prays that plaintiffs take nothing by reason of their pretended cause of action and that it have judgment for its costs and disbursements herein.

[date]   _____
                         Attorney for defendant

interest, as opposed to the interest that an owner or holder of the remainder may have.

A nuisance complaint may take the form illustrated in exhibit 3.17, and its answer the form in exhibit 3.18.

■ REPLEVIN

If a person wrongfully obtains or retains possession of personal property, the rightful owner may bring an action in **replevin** to recover possession of the property. Courts use their power to restore the property to its rightful owner or custodian. The gravamen of the action is the right to immediate possession.

COMPLAINT

Comes now plaintiff and for his cause of action against defendant alleges:

1. [Jurisdictional allegations.]
2. At all times material herein plaintiff was the owner and in possession of the premises commonly known as 3908 East Ninth Street, Bakersville, Ohio.
3. Plaintiff occupied said premises as his homestead with his family.
4. During the period of June 1, 1994, to the date of the commencement of the above entitled action, defendant has occupied and used the premises at 4000 East Ninth Street, Bakersville, Ohio, as a meat-cutting plant and for the preparation of various meats for sale in commerce.
5. During said period of time defendant has allowed meat products, meat by-products, and various chemicals to create toxic and offensive-smelling fumes and odors.
6. Said fumes and odors significantly reduce the plaintiff's use, comfort, enjoyment, and value of plaintiff's said property.
7. Before commencement of this action, plaintiff notified defendant of the adverse effect that defendant's activities have had on plaintiff's premises.
8. Defendant's activities could be conducted in a manner so as not to endanger and impair the use of other properties in the area.
9. Defendant's present activities create and permit the noxious and toxic odors and fumes that damage plaintiff's property and impair its use.
10. Plaintiff has suffered damages in the amount of fifteen thousand dollars for the loss of enjoyment and impaired use of his property.
11. Unless defendant is enjoined from continuing to create the noxious fumes and odors, plaintiff's property will continue to suffer damage.

Wherefore, plaintiff prays for judgment against defendant permanently enjoining defendant from creating toxic and noxious fumes and odors that escape from defendant's premises to adjoining properties, and further prays for damages in the sum of fifteen thousand dollars, together with plaintiff's costs and disbursements herein.

    [date]   _____
                                           Attorney for Plaintiff

■ **EXHIBIT 3.17**
Complaint for Nuisance

■ **EXHIBIT 3.18**

Answer to Complaint
for Nuisance

ANSWER

Comes now defendant and for its answer to plaintiff's complaint:

1. Denies each and every allegation, statement, and matter in the complaint contained, except as hereinafter expressly admitted or alleged.

2. Admits the allegations of paragraphs 1, 2, 3, 4, and 7.

3. Specifically denies that defendant's use of defendant's land has created a nuisance.

4. Alleges that defendant is without sufficient knowledge and information upon which to form a belief concerning plaintiff's alleged damages and puts plaintiff to his strict proof of same.

5. Alleges that defendant's plant and operations have been conducted in essentially the same manner for twenty-five years and that plaintiff acquired his premises knowing the existence of defendant's facilities.

6. Alleges that defendant purchased an easement from plaintiff's predecessors in interest, which easement[1] and covenant[2] runs with the land and binds plaintiff, precluding plaintiff from suing defendant for the alleged nuisance.

7. Alleges that plaintiff's pretended cause of action is barred by laches.[3]

8. Alleges that plaintiff's pretended cause of action is barred by the easement and covenant, a copy of which is attached hereto as exhibit A and incorporated by reference.

9. Alleges that plaintiff's cause of action is barred by the applicable Ohio statute of limitations.

Wherefore, defendant prays that plaintiff take nothing by reason of his pretended cause of action and that defendant have judgment for its costs and disbursements herein.

[date]   _____
                                     Attorney for Defendant

1. An easement is a right created by an agreement, express or implied, to use a certain area of land for some specified purpose. The purpose may be general or limited. An easement is considered a right to use, rather than an interest in the land.
2. A covenant is an agreement or promise to do or not to do something and is commonly made part of a real estate transaction that affects or limits the buyer's use of the land. For example, the buyer could covenant not to sell liquor on the premises.
3. Laches is a doctrine that precludes a person from asserting a right where that party has let the claim become stale with the passage of time. It is analogous to a statute-of-limitations defense.

Sometimes the plaintiff can obtain possession with commencement of the action through use of an **order to show cause.** This order requires the defendant possessor to demonstrate, if he or she can, why custody of the property should not be given to the plaintiff or kept by the court while the action is pending. A party obtains an order to show cause by making a motion to the court with supporting affidavits that show that the moving party has a right to immediate possession of the property. Upon a prima facie showing of the right to immediate possession, the court usually issues an order compelling the defendant possessor to appear before the court and show good cause why the property should not be turned over to the moving party. The plaintiff may be required to post a bond that will protect the defendant in the event the case is decided in favor of the defendant.

The bond is intended to compensate the defendant for loss of use of the property and even for the value of the property.

ULTRAHAZARDOUS ACTIVITIES

A person who engages in **ultrahazardous activity** is strictly liable for damage caused by the activity. An activity is ultrahazardous if it is incapable of being conducted without a significant likelihood of damage to property or injury to persons. A person engaged in an ultrahazardous activity is liable even though he or she conducts the activity with great care. Culpability is not an issue. Nor is the utility or necessity of the activity an issue. The only real question is whether the activity is appropriate for the area in which it is conducted.

Two examples of ultrahazardous activity are pile driving and dynamiting. Very often, heavy construction work requires pile driving in urban areas where vibrations in the earth caused by that activity may cause substantial damage to nearby structures. Even though the pile driving is necessary, the contractor is liable for its consequential effects on surrounding properties. Similarly, a contractor using dynamite is absolutely liable for damage caused by the vibrations and debris that damage surrounding properties. The flying debris might also be grounds for an action in trespass.

Activities do not have to be as inherently dangerous as dynamiting and pile driving to be ultrahazardous. For example, construction of a dam that stores a large quantity of water may be an ultrahazardous activity. The owner of the dam could be absolutely liable to other properties damaged by percolation of water through the soil. If the dam should break, the owner could be absolutely liable for harm to persons and property caused by the escaping water. Keeping a wild animal, as opposed to domestic animals, is another ultrahazardous activity. The owner is absolutely liable for any injury caused by a wild animal that escapes her premises. Crop spraying is yet another ultrahazardous activity. If some of the chemical escapes onto neighboring properties and causes damage, the person applying the chemical is absolutely liable for the damage caused. Conversely, the crop sprayer is not absolutely liable to the contracting customer for damage to "other" foliage on the customer's property. Liability to the customer will depend upon the contract or an action in negligence.

In each of the preceding examples, the defendant acted reasonably to promote his or her own business or other legitimate interest. In each instance, the party to be held liable acted for a proper purpose. But because the activity is considered to be ultrahazardous, the actor is strictly liable for harm caused to others.

INTENTIONAL INFLICTION OF MENTAL SUFFERING

Most states now recognize a cause of action in tort for the intentional infliction of mental suffering. The cause of action requires a specific, subjective intent on the part of the defendant to inflict suffering upon the plaintiff. Mere negligence, or failure to use due care, does not support this cause of action. The mental suffering may be inflicted by words or by conduct or by a combination of words and conduct. (It is difficult to imagine a situation where the cause of action would lie and words were not used.) Not only must the defendant intend the plaintiff to experience mental suffering, the defendant's conduct to accomplish it must be outrageous in character. The conduct must be the type that is utterly intolerable in a civilized society. Mere insults, swearing, foul language, even verbal threats do not give rise to the cause of action. The jury must find an actual, wrongful intent on the part of the defendant to cause the plaintiff to suffer. It is not enough for the jury to find that the defendant should have known that her or his conduct could cause mental suffering. The plaintiff must prove that the wrongful conduct was the proximate cause of her or his suffering. It is not necessary for the plaintiff to show physical symptoms manifesting the mental suffering. Nor is medical treatment a necessary element to the damages.

This cause of action may be available in situations where actions for assault and defamation would not lie—although the actions certainly could overlap. For example, suppose the defendant maliciously tells the plaintiff that the plaintiff's spouse has just been killed in an accident at work. In fact, the statement is not true. The sole motive for uttering this false statement is to upset the plaintiff, and the plaintiff does suffer a severe emotional breakdown because of the statement. These facts would give rise to an action for intentional infliction of mental suffering. An action for defamation would not lie because the statement, even though false, is not damaging to the plaintiff's reputation. An action for assault would not lie because the plaintiff was not put in fear of bodily harm. A cause of action for invasion of privacy would not lie because the statement has not been made public and because other elements are also missing.

The cause of action accrues when the plaintiff experiences the mental suffering. In the preceding example, the cause of action accrued when the statement was made to the plaintiff.

■ NEGLIGENT INFLICTION OF MENTAL SUFFERING

Courts allow plaintiffs to recover compensatory damages where the defendant has negligently inflicted mental suffering without inflicting any bodily injury, *if* the defendant subjected the plaintiff to a bodily injury and the plaintiff developed appreciable physical manifestations of mental suffering. Negligent infliction of mental suffering is a very narrow and limited cause of action. As social beings who live in communities, we are going to "bother" each other a lot. That is the kind of discomfort the courts simply cannot concern themselves about. On the other hand, where the defendant's negligence subjects the plaintiff to a grievous bodily harm and the plaintiff suffers a serious emotional reaction, the law permits the plaintiff to prosecute a claim for money damages.

In this action, the plaintiff must prove that he or she was in a zone of danger of grievous bodily harm. For example, suppose the plaintiff is a tenant in an apartment building that explodes because the local utility negligently failed to turn off the supply of gas. A fire ensues, and many people are burned and killed. The plaintiff manages to escape without physical injury, but after the fire the plaintiff develops an ulcer because of the experience. The plaintiff has the basis for making a claim for negligent infliction of mental suffering.

Courts have held that mere headaches, sleeplessness, and loss of weight are not appreciable physical manifestations of mental suffering. Furthermore, it appears that an aggravation of preexisting physical problem does not support the cause of action. Courts require a physical manifestation of the emotional upset in order to provide some independent corroboration of the injury, and a mere aggravation does not suffice.

■ FALSE IMPRISONMENT

False imprisonment involves the intentional confinement of the plaintiff to a specific area without authority in law to do so. The confinement must be real and significant. The plaintiff must be aware of the confinement. It is not sufficient for the plaintiff to discover, after the alleged confinement, that she or he would not have been permitted to leave the premises had she or he wanted or attempted to. On the other hand, the cause of action does not require physical restraints such as walls or a fence. The defendant can effectively confine the plaintiff through mere threats of force or false assertions of authority. The defendant may be liable for a false imprisonment where the defendant forces the plaintiff to accompany the defendant. There is a fundamental difference between confining a person and preventing a person from entering a restricted area. For example, a cause of action for false imprisonment will not lie against a theater for not allowing certain customers to enter.

The defendant must intend to *confine* the plaintiff by limiting or controlling the plaintiff's freedom of movement. Parents have legal authority to limit their children's freedom of movement. A parent may delegate such authority to a baby-sitter or neighbor under some circumstances and for some purposes. The confinement must be intentional and not merely inadvertent or even negligent. For example, if a storeowner closes and locks the store for the night and a customer is accidentally locked in the store, the customer does not have an action against the storekeeper for false imprisonment. But that would not necessarily preclude an action in negligence.

The restriction on the plaintiff's movement must be complete and not voluntary. If the plaintiff remains in a certain area because merely requested to do so, no cause of action will lie. The confinement must be against the plaintiff's will. The cause of action accrues as soon as the plaintiff becomes aware that his or her freedom of movement has been wrongfully restricted. No actual mental or physical injury is required. The plaintiff could recover damages for consequential damages, such as pain and suffering, that might result from such wrongful conduct.

The defendant can defeat a claim of false imprisonment by proving that she or he had actual authority to confine or restrain the plaintiff or that the plaintiff consented.

■ MALICIOUS PROSECUTION

The tort of **malicious prosecution** involves the improper use of criminal court proceedings, without justification, for an improper purpose. For example, a person becomes subject to an action for malicious prosecution by filing a criminal complaint against another person to damage the other's reputation or to cause the other to experience the inconvenience of being arrested or to cause the other to experience an emotional upset. To be liable for malicious prosecution, the defendant must have instituted the criminal proceedings against the plaintiff or wrongfully caused the proceedings to continue. The criminal proceedings must be resolved in the plaintiff's favor by dismissal or verdict. As part of the plaintiff's cause of action, the plaintiff must show that the defendant lacked probable cause to believe that the criminal proceedings were justified. In other words, it must be proved that the defendant acted out of malice against the plaintiff and not to serve the ends of justice.

The plaintiff is entitled to recover money damages for loss of time spent in defending against the criminal proceedings, expenses incurred in the defense, loss of income, damaged reputation, and mental suffering. A cause of action for malicious prosecution accrues when the criminal proceedings have been terminated in the plaintiff's favor. No special affirmative defenses are applicable to this cause of action. The defense is usually based upon the defendant's reasonable belief that the plaintiff committed a particular crime or upon the defendant's lack of malice.

■ ABUSE OF JUDICIAL PROCESS

The cause of action called **abuse of process** is somewhat similar to malicious prosecution, but it involves the unjustified use of civil procedures for a wrongful purpose. The plaintiff must prove that the defendant was motivated by an improper purpose. Again, the cause of action does not accrue until the plaintiff obtains a dismissal of the underlying action. Therefore, the defendant cannot file a counterclaim against the plaintiff to obtain money damages for abuse of process. An abuse of process claim must be brought as a separate, new action. The burden of proof is difficult, and the plaintiff must prove actual damages.

■ DEFAMATION

An action for **defamation** arises from an utterance and publication of a false, defamatory statement. A statement is defamatory if it would cause the plaintiff to suffer a loss of esteem in the eyes of those who know him or her. In other words, the cause of action is concerned with protecting the plaintiff's reputation. The law gives the plaintiff the opportunity to hold the defendant accountable for publishing defamatory statements, and a remedy in the form of money damages for the harm to the plaintiff's reputation.

A defamatory statement is uttered when it is spoken or written; it is published when it is communicated to some third person, that is, someone other than the plaintiff. Unless there is a publication to a third person, there is no cause of action, but publication to only one other person is sufficient. Therefore, an action will not lie where the defendant tells the plaintiff that the plaintiff is a crook—no matter how much the plaintiff's feelings are hurt by the statement—unless the statement is heard by another person. Furthermore, the plaintiff cannot create a cause of action by telling other persons what the defendant said to him or her. However, the defendant is liable for any republications.

Several types of statements are commonly looked upon as being obviously defamatory. They include allegations of criminal conduct, sexual misconduct, professional incompetence, and affliction with a loathsome disease. But any statement may be considered defamatory if it would tend to cause other people to lose confidence in the plaintiff's abilities, trustworthiness, or reliability.

Some statements may be defamatory only because of the plaintiff's particular circumstances, position, or relationships. For example, it could be defamatory to say that the plaintiff is inclined to have an alcoholic drink on occasion if the plaintiff is a leader in a church that has abstinence as one of its tenets.

Statements that merely reflect the defendant's *opinion* about the plaintiff are not considered to be defamatory. Such statements are understood to reflect upon the defendant as much as, or more than, upon the plaintiff. The distinction between fact and opinion is sometimes very difficult to ascertain. Nevertheless, it is clearly defamatory to call someone a crook. A person could not avoid being liable for defamation by qualifying the statement by saying, "In my opinion, the plaintiff is a crook."

In determining whether a statement is defamatory, the words are to be given their ordinary meaning. However, the plaintiff has the right to prove that the words used by the defendant contain an innuendo that, when taken in context, is understood by others to be defamatory.

An action for defamation cannot be brought on behalf of a deceased person for the benefit of the decedent's reputation or to assuage the feelings of the survivors. A corporation can be defamed, but only if the defamatory statements reflect adversely upon the corporation's honesty, integrity, or credit. A corporation is not defamed by a statement that its products or services are bad.

The plaintiff has the burden of proving the utterance, publication to another person, and consequential harm. However, in libel actions and certain slander actions, the law infers *some* harm even if no specific damage can be shown.

No matter how derogatory the statement is, truth is a complete defense. For example, if the defendant stated that the plaintiff is a crook, the statement is obviously defamatory. If the defendant can prove that the defendant committed the crime, the defendant's proof defeats the cause of action. The defendant's proof need only be by a fair preponderance of the evidence. Even if the plaintiff was previously tried in a criminal action and found innocent, the defendant in the libel action has the right to try to prove that the plaintiff is, in fact, a crook.

The law of defamation has two primary subdivisions: libel and slander. **Libel** concerns the publication of defamatory statements through any kind of documentation such as a letter, memorandum, article, photograph, motion picture, or painting. **Slander** involves the publication of defamatory statements through oral communication. The dichotomy exists because the different methods of publication have different consequences. In the eyes of the law, libel is somewhat more serious because of the tendency of people to believe statements that are in writing. Furthermore, defamatory statements in documents appear more calculated and have potential for greater distribution. Generally speaking, damages are easier to obtain and larger in actions for libel.

The defendant may avoid liability for defamation by showing that the publication was subject to a privilege or a qualified privilege. Statements made by officers of the court and by parties in pursuit of proper legal proceedings are clothed with a privilege. Therefore, statements made in pleadings or testimony in depositions, testimony at trial, and legal opinions are clothed with a privilege. Legislators acting in their official capacity are clothed with an immunity. Newspapers and other publishers are given a qualified privilege that allows them to print information about public persons when that information is newsworthy, provided the publisher acts in good faith. The plaintiff must prove that the newspaper, television station, and so on acted out of malice; otherwise, the cause of action will fail. A member of the news media may mitigate damages by printing a retraction.

■ INVASION OF PRIVACY

An unauthorized intrusion into the plaintiff's privacy made by disclosing private matters to public scrutiny without social justification gives rise to a cause of action for **invasion of privacy.** The intrusion must be to a significant degree. The publication must be to many people, not just one or two. This is one of the features that distinguish the action from defamation. Courts look to the reason or purpose for the publication. If the publication was motivated by malice or by a desire for commercial profit, a breach of duty is more readily found.

Truth is not a defense. It is not even necessary for the plaintiff to show that the plaintiff's reputation was damaged by the publication. Indeed, the publication that constitutes an invasion of privacy might actually engender sympathy for the plaintiff. Only living individuals may bring an action for an invasion of privacy. The plaintiff does not have to prove any monetary loss in order to be able to recover money damages for mental suffering, embarrassment, and humiliation.

The defendant may avoid liability by proving that the plaintiff is a public figure and that the matters publicized are not private or should not remain private. For example, suppose a woman is running for high office, and a newspaper reporter discovers that the candidate is involved in an extramarital affair and publishes the facts. The candidate's right to privacy has probably been invaded. But by becoming a candidate for public office, she has opened up her private life to public scrutiny. The defendant may also avoid liability by showing that the plaintiff consented to the publication. For example, if a person posed for a photograph for commercial use, there is a presumption that the person consented to its publication. In this instance, the best evidence and defense would be to have a contract reflecting the person's consent.

■ OTHER CAUSES

Many, many other causes of action provide various forms of relief. They include actions for dissolution of marriage, dissolution of a partnership, damages caused by domestic animals, damages for United States patent infringements, damages for unfair competition and violation of civil rights. Each action has its own specific requirements or elements and is subject to certain affirmative defenses. You may wish to increase your understanding of the law by studying causes of action. *Corpus Juris Secundum* and *American Jurisprudence Second* are treatises on the law that provide concise statements about causes of action, their application, and their limitations.

■ SUMMARY

A court cannot decide a dispute unless the plaintiff's complaint states a claim upon which a court may grant relief. A court can provide a remedy only when the claim can be stated as a cause of action. There are many different causes of action. Some causes of action come from the common law, some have been created by statute, some arise from contracts. The plaintiff has the burden of proving each element to the alleged cause of action. All causes of action have certain basic requirements. For a cause of action to exist, (1) the defendant must owe a legal duty to the plaintiff; (2) the defendant must have breached the legal duty; and (3) the defendant's breach of the legal duty must be the proximate cause of the plaintiff's injury, loss, or other harm. The harm must be a type of loss that courts recognize as real and substantial. Finally, the court must be able to provide an appropriate remedy.

The plaintiff must allege the cause of action in a complaint. The allegations must show that the court has jurisdiction over the claim and that the claim is of the type for which the court can grant relief. The complaint must identify the transaction or occurrence that gave rise to the claim and the time and place of the defendant's alleged breach of a legal duty. Some causes of action, such as fraud, must be pleaded with particularity. In other words, the facts supporting each element of the claim must be stated. A complaint should set forth allegations and facts in convenient, numbered paragraphs. The plaintiff's lawyer or paralegal should draft the complaint in such a manner as to encourage the defendant's lawyer to admit by paragraphs facts that are not really contested.

The elements of the cause of action are the skeleton of the civil action that must be pleaded and proved. The plaintiff must prove facts to establish each contested element. The material facts determine what evidence is necessary. When assisting the plaintiff, the paralegal must focus on gathering evidence to prove the material (controlling) facts. When assisting the defendant, the paralegal must focus on gathering evidence to show that the facts do not support the alleged cause of action.

Each cause of action is subject to a particular standard of proof, such as a fair preponderance of the evidence or clear and convincing evidence. Each cause of action permits certain remedies. Each remedy has its own measure of damages. In a contract case, the usual measure of damages is the loss of the bargain, which may include a loss of expected profits. In a fraud case, the usual measure of damages is the out-of-pocket loss. In most tort cases, the usual measure of damages is an amount of money that fully, fairly compensates the plaintiff for the loss. Consequently, the paralegal and the lawyer must make sure that they have found the best cause of action for the client.

A transaction or occurrence may give rise to more than one cause of action. A plaintiff may pursue two or more causes of action at the same time against the defendant. On occasion, the law requires a party to choose between causes of action. That decision must be made by a lawyer. When more than one cause of action is alleged in the complaint, each cause of action should be set forth as a separate count.

Rule 11 requires lawyers and parties to believe there is good basis in law and fact for any cause of action asserted in a complaint. A party or lawyer who alleges a claim that does not have merit is subject to disciplinary action by the court.

KEY TERMS

compensatory damages	efficient intervening cause
restitution	superseding cause
punitive damages	contributory negligence
preponderance of the evidence	assumption of risk
measure of damages	comparative negligence
affirmative defenses	pure comparative negligence
breach of contract	ordinary comparative negligence
statute of frauds	products liability
specific performance	strict liability in tort
misrepresentation	comparative fault
fraud	dramshop actions
negligent misrepresentation	obviously intoxicated
loss-of-the-bargain measure of	complicity
damages	nuisance
out-of-pocket measure of damages	replevin
trespass	order to show cause
assault	ultrahazardous activity
battery	malicious prosecution
negligence	abuse of process
malpractice	defamation
negligence per se	libel
prima facie evidence of negligence	slander
proximate cause	invasion of privacy

REVIEW QUESTIONS

1. How does a common-law civil battery differ from a civil assault?
2. How does a nuisance differ from a trespass?
3. What elements give rise to the legal duty to act with reasonable care?
4. What elements give rise to a dramshop action?
5. When is specific performance awarded, rather than money damages?
6. How does fraud (deceit) differ from negligent misrepresentation?
7. How does an action for invasion of privacy differ from an action for defamation?
8. How does a cause of action for malicious prosecution differ from a cause of action for abuse of process?

AFFIRMATIVE DEFENSES

There are two approaches to defending against a civil action. In one approach, the defendant denies that the plaintiff's claim has any merit. The defendant forces the plaintiff to prove the claim and challenges the plaintiff's evidence. The objective is to prevent the plaintiff from proving a cause of action. Simply stated, the plaintiff claims, "You did it," and the defendant replies, "No, I didn't."

The defense strategy is simple. If the plaintiff has some evidence with which to prove a disputed fact, the defendant may make appropriate objections to try to keep the court from considering the evidence. If the evidence is admissible, the defendant may try to impeach or discredit it. If the evidence is admissible and cannot be impeached, the defendant may try to negate its persuasiveness by offering other evidence to explain or qualify it. For example, in a breach-of-contract action, the plaintiff must prove that a contract existed, that the defendant breached the contract, and that the breach of contract caused the plaintiff to sustain a loss. At trial, the defendant would try to keep the plaintiff from proving that a contract existed or that the defendant breached the contract or that the plaintiff sustained any loss. The defendant can try to do this by keeping the plaintiff's evidence about the facts from being heard or if it is heard, from being believed. If the court receives the plaintiff's evidence, the defendant may try to discredit it by showing that it is unreliable because of its type or because it comes from an unreliable source. If the plaintiff cannot prove a valid contract or prove a breach of the contract or prove that the plaintiff sustained a loss because of the breach, the plaintiff's claim for money damages necessarily fails, and the defendant wins.

Rule 8(b) of the Federal Rules of Civil Procedure provides that the defendant's answer shall admit allegations in the complaint that the defendant knows are true. If an allegation in the complaint is not denied, it is deemed admitted. Any admission precludes the defendant from disputing the truth of facts admitted in the answer. An admitted fact is taken out of contention. Therefore, it is common for a defendant to begin the answer by stating, "The defendant denies each and every allegation, statement, matter, and thing in the complaint, except as expressly admitted or alleged in the answer." Then the answer admits specific allegations in the complaint. The admission may be made by reiterating the facts the defendant believes are true or by simply identifying the paragraphs of the complaint that state those facts. The plaintiff should encourage the defendant's admissions by keeping controversial allegations separate from noncontroversial statements of fact in the complaint. The defendant may deny, in a general fashion, facts that the defendant does not know to be true. Rule 8(b) is very specific: "Denials shall fairly meet the substance of the averments denied." In other words, denials must be made in good faith.

The second approach to defending against any civil action is to allege and prove an affirmative defense that avoids or defeats a plaintiff claim. An affirmative defense overcomes the claim even though the claim is true and fully proven. Simply sated, the plaintiff says, "You did it," and the defendant replies, "Even if I did do it, your claim is not good because you did something too." The "something too" is the affirmative defense.

All causes of action (claims) are subject to one or more affirmative defenses. The Rules require the defendant to allege all affirmative defenses in the answer. A defendant has the same burden to prove an affirmative defense that the plaintiff has to prove a cause of action.

Most affirmative defenses must be proved by a fair preponderance of the evidence. In other words, the jury must believe that the affirmative defense is more likely true than not true. A few affirmative defenses, like some causes of action, require proof by evidence that is clear and convincing. For example, proof of a **mutual mistake,** which is grounds for reforming a written contract, must be established by evidence that is clear and convincing. Even then, the burden of proof is less than "beyond a reasonable doubt," which is the government's burden of proof in prosecuting criminal actions.

Pleading an affirmative defense is much like pleading a cause of action. The defendant's answer must contain a short, plain statement of the facts upon which the affirmative defense is based. Each affirmative defense should be pleaded in a separate paragraph for clarity and convenience of the parties. The time and place of the events that give rise to each affirmative defense must be stated, as provided by Rule 9(f). The defendant's failure to plead an affirmative defense in the answer results in a waiver of the defense. Sometimes it is sufficient for the defendant to simply allege the defense as a legal conclusion. For example, a defendant's answer may allege, "Plaintiff's cause of action is barred by plaintiff's assumption of risk." The material time and place were sufficiently stated in the plaintiff's complaint, so those allegations need not be reiterated in the defendant's answer. However, if the affirmative defense relates to a new transaction or occurrence, it must be fully identified by time and place. For example, if the defendant pleads a release as an affirmative defense, she or he must allege the time and place at which the release was made, along with the terms of the release. (A release is a contract in which a claimant agrees to give up his or her claim against another person.)

The Rules assume that the plaintiff denies the defendant's affirmative defense allegations, and the plaintiff is not required to answer the affirmative defense allegations. However, if the plaintiff has an affirmative defense to the defendant's affirmative defense, the plaintiff must plead it in a reply to answer (see Rule 7(a)). For example, if the plaintiff alleged an action in negligence to recover money damages for personal injuries sustained in an automobile accident, and the defendant alleged a release as a defense to the claim, the plaintiff could allege fraud as an affirmative defense to the release. Since the allegation of fraud raises a new legal theory and new fact issues, the claim of fraud must be fully pleaded.

Rule 8(c) provides a partial list of affirmative defenses that are raised most often. Some of the more common ones are discussed in the following sections.

▣ RELEASE

A **release** is a type of contract by which some claim or right is voluntarily relinquished. A release ends the right of the plaintiff to sue on the claim in question. It is usually reduced to a writing, but no rule of law requires this. The parties to a release must have a meeting of minds concerning the essential terms and conditions. As in any contract, an exchange of consideration must take place between the parties. Therefore, the party who obtains a release of a claim must give something in return. Sometimes both parties agree to give up claims or rights against each other. In that event, the release is commonly called a mutual release.

If release is claimed as an affirmative defense, the terms and conditions of the release must be pleaded in the answer. If the release was put into writing, a copy may be attached to the answer and incorporated into the answer by reference. If the release is valid and pertains to the plaintiff's claim, it provides a complete defense even though, at one time, the plaintiff had a valid claim. The plaintiff may dispute the validity or application of the release. Affirmative defenses to the claim of release include mutual mistake, lack of consideration, duress, and fraud. (See chapter 25 for a more detailed discussion of releases.)

▣ ACCORD AND SATISFACTION

The first affirmative defense mentioned in Rule 8(c) is **accord and satisfaction.** This defense may be thought of as a type of release. It arises from the parties' decision to replace their former agreement (contract) with a new agreement, called an accord, which, if fully performed by the defendant, is a satisfaction. An accord and satisfaction provides a complete defense to an action on the original contract. The defendant must offer evidence to prove that the parties had a bona fide dispute over the terms or application of their original agreement and that the new agreement was consciously made as a compromise on both sides. The existence of the bona fide dispute and compromise provide the necessary consideration to make the accord an enforceable contract. Proof of the satisfaction, such as a payment, is essential to the defense. If the defendant has defaulted on both the old agreement and the new accord, the plaintiff may elect to sue on either.

When a dispute arises from a transaction, it is common for a person to tender a check in a reduced amount as "payment in full." If it is made clear that the check is offered to resolve a disputed claim—not as a partial payment of a disputed obligation—and if the check is accepted by the payee, the disputed obligation is fully discharged. The payee must accept the check on the terms and conditions tendered or return the check uncashed. The payee accepts the check by cashing it. The payee may be deemed to have accepted the check as tendered if the payee retains the check for an unreasonable length of time even though she or he does not cash it. However, the payer's purpose to create an accord and satisfaction must be manifest to the payee.

■ ARBITRATION AND AWARD

If the parties to a dispute agree to submit their controversy to a third person or tribunal for a determination and resolution, and the matter is duly decided by the arbitrator, the disappointed party cannot subsequently litigate the controversy in court. The arbitrator's determination is binding as an **arbitration and award.** The award may be enforced through a court by being confirmed by the court. This is a relatively simple and inexpensive procedure. Only if fraud or some other defect occurred in the arbitration procedure could the losing party dispute the award.

Arbitration is frequently used to settle disputes that arise from insurance policies, construction contracts, and labor agreements, and there is a growing interest in using it to resolve medical malpractice claims. The arbitration procedure may be determined by the statute that requires the parties to arbitrate or propounded by the parties' agreement. For example, the parties' agreement may specify that the matter is to be decided by one arbitrator or three, and it may specify how the arbitrators are to be chosen. The parties may elect to follow the provisions of the Uniform Arbitration Act, which has been adopted by most state legislatures, and incorporate its provisions by reference. The parties must agree on the scope of the submission to arbitration. The scope of submission is the parties' description of the problem that they have agreed to submit to the tribunal for resolution. The tribunal may not go beyond the scope of submission. It should be reduced to writing. As part of the scope of submission, the parties may agree to arbitrate questions of fact and/or questions of law. The scope of submission determines and limits the arbitrator's authority. The more specific it is, the better.

On occasion a dispute develops over the extent of the arbitrator's authority. Similarly, a dispute may arise concerning what issues are to be decided in the arbitration. When a dispute arises concerning the scope of submission, the parties may take it to a court for resolution, or enter into a new agreement to have the scope of submission arbitrated as well. Absent a specific agreement to the contrary, an arbitration tribunal is not authorized to determine disputes concerning the scope of its power. A court of general jurisdiction that has jurisdiction over the parties would have to determine the scope of the parties' submission to arbitration.

Arbitration is increasing in popularity as an alternative means of resolving disputes. It often provides a quicker, less expensive resolution than does litigation in the courts. It provides a determination that is final. Public policy and courts favor arbitration, just as courts favor voluntary settlements. However, arbitration has fewer safeguards to ensure fairness to the parties, and sometimes it neglects strict application of the law. Therefore, where the parties are interested in a quick, commonsense, fair resolution, as opposed to a decision according to law, arbitration is an attractive alternative to litigation.

Paralegals may enjoy an expanded role in arbitration because no rule of law prohibits nonlawyers from handling arbitration procedures. A layperson may be an arbitrator, unless the parties' scope of submission provides otherwise. The parties' representatives (advocates) may be laypersons who present the evidence. Nevertheless, the procedures are patterned after civil litigation, so a good understanding of civil litigation procedures makes learning arbitration procedures very easy. See Chapter 26 for a more detailed discussion of arbitration.

■ STATUTES OF LIMITATIONS

A **statute of limitations** establishes the time within which a plaintiff must commence action on a claim. If the claim is not brought within the specified time period, the claim is barred. The statute of limitations defeats the claim.

The purpose of a statute of limitations is to disallow old, stale claims. If a claim has been overlooked or disregarded for an excessively long time, the plaintiff should not disturb the status quo. The mere passage of time directly affects and even creates legal rights, because there is value in maintaining the status quo. For example, if two motorists were involved in what seemed to be a minor accident, it would be unfair for one to sue the other ten years afterward, claiming that the accident actually caused grievous bodily harm. In all probability, the passage of time would impair (prejudice) the defendant's ability to gather evidence with which to defend against the claim. The same is true for contract actions. So state and federal legislatures have established various time periods in which claims must be sued.

Congress determines what time limitations are applicable to rights created by federal statutes. State legislatures determine what time limitations should be imposed on various causes of action. Each state has several general statutes of limitations that apply to various common-law types of actions, such as breach of contracts, defamation, trespass, and assault. Each cause of action is subject to a separate time limitation. For example, a statute of limitations may require breach-of-contract actions to be brought within four years from the date of the alleged breach; another statute of limitations may require that an action in trespass be brought within two years from the date of the alleged trespass. In addition, certain statutes, such as dramshop statutes and wrongful death statutes, may contain their own time limitations. Each state has a compendium of statutes of limitations. All causes of action are subject to being barred by an applicable statute of limitations.

In some states, the applicable statute may be as short as one year for a particular cause of action. In other states, the same cause of action may be subject to a much longer statutory period, maybe as long as six years. Typically, medical malpractice actions have relatively short statutes of limitations. These cases often present unique problems in preserving evidence, so there is good reason for treating them specially.

The general rule is that the statute of limitations begins to run against a claim when the injury or loss occurs. The rule has a simple, clear application in automobile accident cases, where the cause of action accrues the day of the accident. Whatever injury was caused by the accident had its origin at the time of the accident. The time period allowed by the statute of limitations begins to run the same day; the day of the event is counted. In this regard, the computation of time differs from Rule 6. In a defamation case, the statute begins to run from the day after the defamatory statement is published, even though the actual harm to the plaintiff's reputation may not occur until later; the law presumes that some harm occurred at the time of publication. The same is true in most tort actions, where the plaintiff seeks money damages for personal injury or property damage. An action for breach of contract accrues the day the breach occurs and the statute of limitations begins to run the same day.

It is not always easy to determine when a cause of action accrued. For example, suppose the plaintiff alleges that a medical doctor was negligent for exposing the plaintiff to an excessive amount of radiation over a period of weeks. It may be difficult to determine just when the treatment became injurious and when the cause of action accrued. Consequently, in medical malpractice actions the statute begins to run when treatment ceases or, in some states, when the injury is discoverable. Some torts are continuous, such as some trespasses and the maintenance of a nuisance. For example, if the defendant has a manufacturing process that continuously introduces a toxic chemical into a body of water or onto another's land, the statute of limitations does not begin to run until the tortious activity stops.

If the plaintiff's cause of action is based upon fraud, the cause of action does not accrue until the fraud is discovered or reasonably should have been discovered. If the defendant acts to conceal the fact that the plaintiff has a claim, the statute does not begin to run until the plaintiff discovers that he or she has a claim. In other words, the defendant's fraud keeps the statute of limitations from running, but once the fraud is discovered, the statute does begin to run. Some courts have come to view medical malpractice cases in this category.

States differ in their use of the statute of limitations in medical malpractice cases. In these cases, the cause of action accrues when the injury occurs. However, the statute of limitations does not begin to run until treatment for the condition in question terminates. In some states, the statute does not begin to run until the patient discovers the malpractice and consequential injury. States that take that approach have what is commonly called the discovery rule. For example, if the surgeon inadvertently leaves a surgical sponge in the patient, the patient's claim for injury does not begin to run until the harm becomes apparent to the patient. Postponement of the running of the statute of limitations in medical malpractice cases is justified on the basis that the time limitation is relatively short and the physician has a fiduciary relationship to the patient that allows an inference of fraud or concealment if the patient is not told about the problem when it occurs.

A statute of limitations does not run against a minor during her or his minority. A minor plaintiff is always allowed the time designated by the statute. If that time runs out during the plaintiff's minority, the plaintiff is allowed another year after reaching legal age, in which to bring the action. For example, if a six-year statute of limitations applies to a negligence action, and the plaintiff is age sixteen at the time the cause of action accrues and will attain majority at age eighteen, the statute runs against the plaintiff's claim when the six-year period expires, or during the plaintiff's twenty-second year. If the minor plaintiff is only ten years old when the cause of action accrues, the six-year period would end during the plaintiff's sixteenth year. However, the law provides that the statute of limitations is "tolled" during the plaintiff's minority. (To toll the statute of limitations is to stop the statute from running against the cause of action.) Furthermore, a minor has one more year after reaching majority, in which to assert the claim. In this example, the statute runs against the minor's claim when the minor attains the age of nineteen.

A statute of limitations is also tolled by legal disabilities such as insanity.

LACHES

Laches is a court-made doctrine that resembles a statute of limitations. It applies only to actions in equity, such as an action to reform a written instrument or an action to enjoin the defendant's conduct. Courts created laches as a defense to these equitable actions because ordinarily no statute of limitations applies to them. At some point a claim must be deemed stale and time-barred. When applying laches, courts determine whether the defendant has been prejudiced by the delay. The defendant may have been prejudiced because he or she no longer has access to witnesses and evidence that would have been available if the claim has been timely. In addition, a defendant may be prejudiced because the defendant has somehow changed his or her legal position assuming that there was no claim or dispute. Laches is an affirmative defense that is similar to a statute of limitations defense, but applies only when there is no applicable statute of limitations.

STATUTES OF REPOSE

A **statute of repose** bars a claim because the act that gave rise to the claim took place many years ago and, even if the injury is recent, the actor should not be held accountable at such a late date. For example, a statute of repose may protect a contractor from liability for an injury caused by a defect in a building that was constructed twenty-five years ago. Similarly, a statute of repose may protect the manufacturer of a product that is defective where the product performed satisfactorily for twenty years before the defect caused any injury. Industrial punch presses are one product that may first cause an injury many years after being put into service.

ASSUMPTION OF RISK

Assumption of risk is an affirmative defense that applies to actions in negligence and to some breach-of-warranty claims in products liability cases.

The defendant must prove that the plaintiff's injury or property damage was the result of a danger that was open and apparent to the plaintiff; that the plaintiff appreciated the risk of harm created by the condition; that the plaintiff voluntarily chose to incur the risk; and that the injury resulted from the risk assumed. For example, suppose the defendant negligently spills some slippery liquid on the floor, making the floor dangerous. If the plaintiff sees the liquid and understands that the floor is slippery but voluntarily walks on the floor, the plaintiff has assumed the risk of slipping, falling, and being injured. But suppose the defendant has a duty to maintain a sidewalk that the plaintiff must use, and the sidewalk is dangerously slippery. Even though the plaintiff uses the sidewalk knowing the danger, the plaintiff does not assume the risk of injury if the sidewalk is the only practicable means of ingress or egress. Under the circumstances, the plaintiff does not *voluntarily* incur the risk.

Spectators at baseball games should know that some baseballs will likely be hit into the stands. That is a normal occurrence, and one that some spectators hope for. If a spectator has the opportunity to sit in a protected area but voluntarily chooses to sit in an open area, the spectator can hardly complain about getting hit by a home run ball. The spectator has chosen to be where the action is. Even though the ballpark could have provided more protection for more spectators, it is not liable if a spectator assumes the risk of being hit by a ball. Similarly, a football player assumes the risk of injury from a hard but fair tackle. However, a football player does not assume the risk of being assaulted by a disgruntled opponent.

If someone chooses to ride with a drunk driver, that person must know and appreciate that the driver is not competent to control the vehicle and is likely to have an accident. The same is true if someone elects to ride in an automobile that is driven by another in a race on the public streets. Both passengers assume the risk of injury that arises from a danger that is apprehended and voluntarily incurred. In determining the availability of the defense, courts weigh the utility of the parties' conduct and the necessities of the situation.

One more example: Suppose a man has purchased a new electric appliance. After using it a couple of times, he discovers that it has an apparent short. If he nevertheless continues to use the appliance, he assumes the risk of injury or loss that results from the electrical short. He is also negligent. Often the defense of contributory negligence or comparative fault overlaps that of assumption of risk.

With the advent of comparative fault, some states have abolished assumption of risk as a defense that is separate from contributory negligence or comparative fault. In those states, assumption of risk is looked upon as being merged with negligence. In other words, a plaintiff who assumes the risk of an obvious danger is negligent, but the plaintiff's causal negligence must be weighed against the defendant's causal negligence.

■ CONTRIBUTORY NEGLIGENCE

Contributory negligence is negligence attributable to the plaintiff. The common-law rule is that contributory negligence is a complete defense to the plaintiff's claim. For example, if the plaintiff's vehicle and the defendant's vehicle collide in an intersection, and the jury determines that both were negligent, the plaintiff cannot recover damages from the defendant. It does not matter that the plaintiff may have been less negligent than the defendant; any causal negligence on the part of the plaintiff is sufficient to bar the plaintiff's claim. Contributory negligence is not a defense to other tort actions such as trespass, assault, battery, strict liability in tort, and dramshop claims.

The defense of contributory negligence has been abolished by states that have adopted the comparative fault doctrine.

■ COMPARATIVE FAULT

The comparative fault doctrine provides a method of allocating legal responsibility between parties to an occurrence and assigning their financial responsibility in proportion to their legal responsibility. Comparative fault is a modern day concept for dealing with tort claims and liability; the common law we derived from England did not allow for any allocation of fault. Many states have adopted the comparative fault doctrine by legislation. Some state supreme courts have adopted the doctrine through judicial decisions and thereby modified the states' common-law rule. The comparative fault doctrine encompasses almost any type of wrongful act or omission that is actionable but not intentional. It is specifically applicable to negligence cases.

Three types of comparative fault are recognized; in all types, the fault is measured in percentages. (1) Pure comparative fault allocates fault between parties on the basis of their respective causal negligence. The plaintiff's recovery of money damages is limited to the amount of the causal negligence that is *not* attributable to the plaintiff. For example, if the plaintiff is 90 percent at fault for the accident and the defendant is 10 percent at fault, the plaintiff is limited to recovering 10 percent of his or her damages. In other words, if the plaintiff's money damages total $20,000, the defendant is liable for only $2,000. (2) The comparative fault doctrine in some states provides that the plaintiff cannot recover any damages if the plaintiff was as much at fault as the defendant. For example, the plaintiff cannot recover any money damages if the jury determines that the plaintiff and the defendant were each 50 percent causally negligent. (3) The comparative fault doctrine adopted by some states provides that the plaintiff may recover money damages if the plaintiff was no more at fault than the defendant. If the plaintiff and defendant are equally at fault, the plaintiff is entitled to recover one-half of his or her damages. If three motorists collide and a jury determine that each was $33^1/_3$ percent negligent, then each party may recover two-thirds of her damages from the other two motorists.

The comparative fault doctrine becomes fairly complex and difficult to apply where several parties are involved. It is further complicated by the doctrine of joint liability between co-tortfeasors. Joint tortfeasors are each liable for the entire amount of the victim's damages. In the last example, each motorist was negligent. Each is a claimant and each is a defendant. Each is liable for two-thirds of the other's damages. Each is entitled to contributions from the joint tortfeasor in proportion to the joint tortfeasor's percentage of causal fault.

■ DISCHARGE IN BANKRUPTCY

Federal laws provide that individuals and corporations may voluntarily declare bankruptcy if they cannot meet their current obligations. Three creditors can force an individual or corporation into involuntary bankruptcy. The effect of the court's determination that the petitioner is bankrupt is to discharge the petitioner from all declared debts as of the date of the petition. The creditors must be given notice of the petition for bankruptcy so that they have an opportunity to challenge the petition and to share in the debtor's existing assets. Defects in the proceedings, such as a failure to give a creditor notice, preclude the debtor from being discharged.

Certain kinds of debts are not dischargeable in bankruptcy. These include debts created by the petitioner's fraud, willful conversion (theft) of property, and intentional tortious acts that cause injury to persons or damage to property such as assault, battery, murder and fraud.

■ DURESS

A promise that would be legally enforceable is not binding if it was exacted through duress. **Duress** is the threat of death, bodily harm, or damage to property. The defendant must actually believe that he or she was subject to some harm if he or she did not make the promise.

■ ESTOPPEL

Estoppel is an esoteric concept that has a variety of applications to actions in tort and to actions in contract. It originated in equity, but it is now firmly recognized as a legal defense. The defense of estoppel precludes the plaintiff from recovering money damages for a loss that resulted from the defendant's mistake where that mistake was induced by the plaintiff's wrongful conduct in the first place. For example, suppose a corporation replaces its outstanding stock certificates with new certificates but fails to collect the old certificates from one shareholder. If that shareholder subsequently sells the old certificates to a bona fide purchaser, the corporation could be estopped from denying their validity. The purchaser would be entitled to dividends and to having her ownership recorded on the stockholders' register. Also for example, where an insurance company holds out an agent as authorized to sell its insurance policies, it cannot subsequently avoid a policy on the grounds that the agent was not properly licensed. The insurer could be estopped from denying the agent's qualifications.

If the plaintiff were to represent to the defendant that the plaintiff's camera was owned by another person, who had possession of the camera, and the possessor sold the camera to the defendant, the plaintiff could be estopped from denying that the possessor was the owner. The law would give effect to the sale because of the plaintiff's misrepresentation on which the defendant reasonably relied.

■ WAIVER

Waiver is an affirmative defense that has application to actions in contract and in tort. Waiver is the intentional relinquishment of a known legal right under circumstances where the defendant would be prejudiced if the plaintiff were allowed to reassert the right. For example, suppose an automobile insurance application and policy provide that the policy shall be void if the applicant has had an accident within the year preceding the application. An applicant misrepresents in the application that he has not had any accidents, but the insurer learns about the misrepresentation within a month after the policy is issued and does nothing about canceling the policy. The insurer's failure to take steps to revoke or cancel the policy in good season after discovering the misrepresentation could result in a waiver of the right to cancel.

Suppose a store lease provides that the landlord may terminate the lease if the tenant sells liquor on the premises, and to the landlord's knowledge, the tenant does sell liquor for a couple of years. The landlord's acquiescence in the tenant's violation may constitute a waiver of the right to cancel the lease on the basis of the violation.

◼ FRAUD

Fraud and its elements are discussed in chapter 3 as a cause of action in tort that gives rise to a claim for money damages. The same elements will give rise to an affirmative defense to actions in contract and in tort.

◼ CONSENT

Consent is an affirmative defense to actions for battery, trespass to real estate, and conversion of personal property. For example, if the plaintiff sues the defendant in battery to obtain money damages for personal injuries caused by a punch in the nose, the defendant may avoid civil liability by proving that the plaintiff agreed to fight. When boxers enter the ring, they consent to be battered. Consent is not the same as assumption of risk. Consent requires actual agreement to the defendant's conduct and the bodily contact. If the plaintiff sues the defendant for trespassing upon the plaintiff's property and cutting down a tree, consent will be an affirmative defense. The defendant will have the burden of proving that the plaintiff duly consented. A civil action to obtain money damages for rape is an action for a battery. Other than the statute of limitations, the only viable defense to such an action is consent. Consent must be proved by a fair preponderance of the evidence.

Consent does not have to be express to be effective; it may be implied from the circumstances. For example, if the defendant asks the plaintiff for permission to use the plaintiff's automobile, and the plaintiff responds by pointing to the keys lying on the table, and the defendant picks up the keys and enters the automobile and drives away, permission to use the car will be implied from the circumstances. Suppose that while the defendant is using the automobile, the defendant is involved in a collision that totally destroys the automobile. Suppose further that the defendant is not negligent in operating the automobile. The plaintiff will not be able to sue the defendant in negligence for loss of the automobile. However, if the defendant wrongfully *converted*[1] (appropriated) the automobile, the plaintiff

---

1. In civil litigation the word "convert" means to misappropriate or steal. It is a theft.

would have a right to obtain damages from the defendant. The plaintiff's cause of action for conversion of the automobile may be defeated by the defendant's proof that the plaintiff actually consented to its use. Perhaps the plaintiff expected that the defendant would just drive a few blocks away, but the accident occurred two hundred miles away. Now is there a conversion? Is there consent to the use of the automobile? The consent to use must encompass the time and place of use.

■ PROCEDURAL AFFIRMATIVE DEFENSES

Some affirmative defenses arise because the plaintiff failed to comply with court rules or follow civil litigation procedures. When such an error prevents the court from obtaining personal jurisdiction over the defendant or impairs the defendant's ability to have a fair trial, the defendant may assert the error as a defense. The defendant must assert the defense in a motion or in the defendant's answer. If the defendant fails to raise the defense, it is waived. The defendant has the burden of proving the plaintiff's procedural error. When a court dismisses the plaintiff's action because of a procedural error, the dismissal usually is without prejudice, so the plaintiff may bring the action again.

Insufficiency of Process

If the plaintiff fails to follow the prescribed procedures upon commencing an action, the defendant may allege that the court lacks jurisdiction over her or him owing an **insufficiency of process** or of service. The defendant may raise the defense in a motion or in the answer. For example, if the plaintiff served a complaint without a summons attached, the service would be defective, and the defendant would be entitled to a dismissal. Believe it or not, this has happened many times.

Absence of Necessary Party

If the plaintiff fails to include a necessary party to the lawsuit, the defendant is entitled to a dismissal. The absence-of-necessary-party defense may be raised by motion or in the answer. For example, if the plaintiff brings an action to establish that he or she is the owner of certain property that is being held by two owners in common, the plaintiff must join both persons to obtain a full adjudication of the matter.

Res Judicata

The plaintiff may prosecute the claim only once. If the plaintiff brought the same claim in a prior action, perhaps as part of another claim, the result in the first action is binding and prevents the suit from being brought again. *Res judicata* means "the matter has been adjudicated." It is an affirmative defense that must be pleaded in the answer or it is waived.

Collateral Estoppel

If the plaintiff has litigated a claim through to a judgment against another party and obtained an adverse result, the defendant in a later case may raise the prior determination as a matter adjudicated by and against the plaintiff. Suppose the plaintiff was a passenger in a two-car collision and brought a lawsuit against one driver to recover money damages for her alleged injuries, and the jury determined that the plaintiff did not sustain any injury. If the plaintiff then brings a lawsuit against the other driver, the latter could show that the plaintiff litigated the injury issue in the first lawsuit and that determination is an adjudicated fact that she cannot relitigate. In other words, the plaintiff is collaterally estopped from avoiding the fact of no injury duly established *against* her in her first lawsuit.

■ ETHICAL CONSIDERATION

Lawyers are subject to disciplinary action for asserting a claim or defense that is frivolous. A claim or defense is frivolous if it has no apparent basis in fact or law. This is another important difference between criminal law and civil law. In criminal law, a defendant and the defendant's lawyer may put the state to its burden of proving every element of the crime, even though they know the defendant did what she or he is accused of doing. They know that no defense exists; nevertheless, they may put the state to its proof.

In addition to professional ethics, Rule 11 provides that a lawyer's signature on a pleading is the lawyer's certification that the lawyer has made reasonable inquiry into the matter and believes that the claims and defenses alleged in the pleading have basis in fact. A lawyer also certifies that the claim or defense is not being asserted for an improper purpose, such as harassment or delay.

SUMMARY

An affirmative defense defeats the plaintiff's claim even though the claim is true and has a basis in law. Every cause of action is subject to some type of affirmative defense. On the other hand, only certain affirmative defenses are available to certain causes of action.

The defendant must allege his or her affirmative defenses in the answer. Procedural affirmative defenses may sometimes be raised by motion. Any defense not alleged is waived. The defendant may have more than one affirmative defense to a claim. The plaintiff does not have to serve a reply to the defendant's affirmative defense allegations, because an affirmative defense is not a counterclaim.

The defendant has the burden of proving all the facts upon which an alleged affirmative defense is based. Whenever possible, the defendant's defense strategy is to attack the plaintiff's claim and to prove whatever affirmative defenses are available, because the two approaches are not inconsistent. Most affirmative defenses must be proved by a fair preponderance of the evidence.

The defendant's answer must assert his or her affirmative defenses by providing a short, plain statement of the facts upon which each defense is based. Each affirmative defense should be pleaded in a separate paragraph for the clarity and convenience of the parties. The time and place of the events that give rise to each affirmative defense must be stated, as provided by Rule 9(f).

Rule 8(c) contains a partial list of affirmative defenses. The list is not complete. Some of the more common affirmative defenses are discussed in this chapter.

A release is a type of contract by which some claim or legal right is voluntarily relinquished. It ends the right of the plaintiff to sue on the claim that is released. A release is usually reduced to a writing, but no law requires this.

An accord and satisfaction is an agreement to replace a prior contract with a new agreement, which, if fully performed by the defendant, precludes enforcement of the prior agreement. An accord and satisfaction is a complete defense to an action on the original contract.

An arbitration and award resolves a dispute and precludes litigation of the same dispute. An arbitrator's award is binding, and a court may enforce it by confirming it. Only if there were fraud or some other defect in the arbitration procedure could the losing party dispute the award. The arbitration procedure may be established in the parties' agreement to arbitrate, or the parties may adopt a procedure provided by statute. The parties must agree on the scope of the submission to arbitration, and the scope should be reduced to writing. No rule of law prohibits nonlawyers from handling arbitration procedures.

A statute of limitations establishes the time within which a plaintiff must commence action on the claim; otherwise, the claim is time barred. The statute of limitations begins to run against a claim when the cause of action accrues, and that is usually, but not always, when the injury or other loss occurs. However, if the plaintiff's cause of action is based upon fraud, the cause of action does not accrue until the fraud is discovered or reasonably should have been discovered. States differ in their use of the statute of limitations. In some states, a statute of limitations does not begin to run until the plaintiff discovers the tortious act or injury, or reasonably should have discovered it. States that take that approach have what is commonly called the discovery rule. A statute of limitations does not run against a minor during his or her minority. A statute of limitations is also tolled by legal disabilities such as insanity.

Laches applies only to actions in equity, such as an action to reform a written instrument or to enjoin the defendant's conduct. Courts created laches as a defense to these equitable actions because ordinarily no statute of limitations applies to them. When applying laches, courts look to see if the defendant has been prejudiced by the delay.

A statute of repose bars a claim because the act that gave rise to the claim took place many years ago and, even if the injury is recent, the actor should not be held accountable at such a late date. Statutes of repose apply most commonly to actions against building contractors and manufacturers of products.

Assumption of risk applies to actions in negligence and some products cases. The defendant must prove that the plaintiff's injury or property damage was the result of a danger that was open and apparent to the plaintiff; that the plaintiff appreciated the risk of harm created by the condition; that the plaintiff voluntarily chose to incur the risk; and that the injury resulted from the risk assumed. With the evolution of comparative fault, some states have abolished assumption of risk as a defense that is separate from contributory negligence or comparative fault. In those states, assumption of risk is looked upon as merged with negligence.

Contributory negligence is negligence attributable to the plaintiff. The common-law rule is that contributory negligence is a complete defense to the plaintiff's claim. Contributory negligence is not a defense to other tort actions such as trespass, assault, battery, strict liability in tort, and dramshop claims. The defense of contributory negligence has been abolished by states that have adopted the comparative fault doctrine.

The comparative fault doctrine allocates legal responsibility between parties to an occurrence and apportions their financial responsibility in proportion to their legal responsibility. Comparative fault is specifically applicable to negligence cases. Comparative fault is always measured in percentages. There are three types of comparative fault: (1) pure comparative fault, which allocates fault and financial responsibility between parties on the basis of their respective causal negligence; (2) a modified comparative fault doctrine that precludes the plaintiff from recovering any damages if the plaintiff was equally as or more at fault than the defendant; and (3) a modified comparative fault doctrine that allows the plaintiff to recover money damages provided the plaintiff was not more at fault than the defendant; if the plaintiff and the defendant were equally at fault, the plaintiff is entitled to recover one-half the plaintiff's damages.

Discharge in bankruptcy eliminates the legal obligation upon which a claim is based, whether in contract or in tort. Certain kinds of debts are not dischargeable in bankruptcy, including debts based upon fraud, willful conversion (theft) of property, and intentional tortious acts that cause injury to persons or damage to property.

Duress is a defense to any contractual obligation. It is the threat of death, bodily harm, or damage to property. The defendant must actually believe that she or he was subject to some harm if she or he did not make the promise.

Estoppel precludes the plaintiff from recovering money damages for a loss that resulted from the defendant's mistake where that mistake was induced by the plaintiff's wrongful conduct in the first place. The wrongful conduct may be verbal or behavioral.

Waiver is the intentional relinquishment of a known legal right under circumstances where the defendant would be prejudiced if the plaintiff were allowed to reassert the right. Waiver applies to actions in contract and in tort.

The same elements that give rise to a cause of action for fraud will give rise to an affirmative defense based on fraud in contract and in tort.

Consent is an affirmative defense to actions for battery, trespass to real estate, and conversion of personal property. It must be provided by a fair preponderance of the evidence. The defendant must show that the plaintiff knew exactly to what he or she was consenting. Consent does not have to be express to be effective; it may be implied from the circumstances.

Some affirmative defenses are procedural in nature. That is, they arise from the prosecution of the litigation. These include insufficiency of process, where the plaintiff fails to follow the prescribed procedures for commencing an action; absence of necessary party, where the plaintiff fails to include a necessary party to the lawsuit; res judicata, which precludes the plaintiff from prosecuting the claim more than once; and collateral estoppel, which precludes the plaintiff from prosecuting the same issue a second time, even against another party, where that issue has been decided against the plaintiff.

KEY TERMS

mutual mistake	duress
release	estoppel
accord and satisfaction	waiver
arbitration and award	consent
statute of limitations	insufficiency of process
statutes of repose	

REVIEW QUESTIONS

1. How does an affirmative defense affect the plaintiff's cause of action?
2. How many affirmative defenses may a defendant raise?
3. How may the defendant raise (assert) an affirmative defense?
4. Does Rule 8(c) contain a complete list of all affirmative defenses?
5. There are three different bases for applying the comparative fault doctrine. Describe each type.
6. Which type of comparative fault is used in your state?
7. Which type of comparative fault is applied by the federal district courts?
8. How does collateral estoppel differ from res judicata?
9. How does consent differ from assumption of risk as an affirmative defense?

5

COURT ORGANIZATION

The focus of this discussion is on the federal judicial system because it functions in all states and because many states pattern their court system after the federal system. The civil justice system functions at two levels. A case may begin and be tried in a district court, but the case may end in an appellate court.

◼ TRIAL COURTS

Trial courts are courts of **original jurisdiction.** This means that cases begin in these courts. Trial courts provide a forum in which the parties make their claims, assert their defenses, and present their evidence. Trial courts resolve fact issues and apply the law to the facts. The disputed facts may be tried to a jury, or to a judge without a jury. When a case is tried without a jury, the proceeding is commonly called a court trial or bench trial. A trial court enters a judgment that determines the parties' legal rights and obligations concerning the transaction or occurrence in question. The trial court's entry of a judgment is the trial court's last act in the case. The trial court's judgment is final, unless one or both of the parties appeal from the judgment to an appellate court.

A fair judicial system must have trial courts and appellate courts. If a trial court were not subject to the control of an appellate court, the trial court would have absolute, dictatorial power. An appellate court obtains jurisdiction over a case only if a party duly appeals from the judgment or from an appealable order. Most trial court orders are not appealable, because appellate courts do not want to review cases on a piecemeal basis. Therefore, even when a party (lawyer) knows that the trial court has made a serious error and objects to the error, the trial must proceed to a conclusion. Only after the trial has been completed and a judgment entered in the judgment book may the complaining party appeal.

■ APPELLATE COURTS

A trial court must be given an opportunity to correct mistakes. Therefore, the parties have the right to make post-trial motions for the purpose of reconsidering possible errors and the effect of the errors on the outcome. A party (appellant) may appeal on the grounds that the trial court committed one or more errors of law. In addition, the appellant must show that the error adversely affected the outcome of the trial. Less than 10 percent of the cases that are tried to a conclusion are appealed to an appellate court.

Appellate courts do not have original jurisdiction of lawsuits; that is, cases are not commenced in these courts. The function of an appellate court is to supervise the trial courts and make sure that trial courts act within the law, follow prescribed procedures, and do not abuse their discretionary powers. Although appellate courts make the final determination of all questions of law when a case is appealed, the trial courts still have primary responsibility for resolving disputed facts. For that reason, appellate courts do not "second-guess" a trial court's determination of the facts, as long as some evidence supports the trial court's findings. Appellate courts never take testimony to resolve issues before them—in other words, witnesses are never allowed to testify.

Appellate courts reverse trial judges for an abuse of discretion only when the abuse is significant and prejudicial to the outcome of the case. For example, trial judges have broad discretion in determining whether a person qualifies as an expert witness. If a trial court's ruling is challenged on appeal, the appellate court commonly states in its published opinion that the appellate court might have ruled differently than the trial court did, but the holding is affirmed because the trial court's ruling was not clearly wrong. The same is true where an appellate court is asked to pass judgment on a trial court's order that affirms or disallows the amount of money damages awarded by a jury.

When an issue of law is duly raised in an appellate court, the parties submit briefs that discuss the legal issue. The format for briefs is strictly structured. The parties' briefs must contain a clear statement of each legal issue, a concise statement of the facts that gave rise to the issues, and an argument on the law. The appellant's argument tries to show that the trial court used the wrong rule of law or misapplied the law. The respondent's brief tries to support the trial court's holding by arguing that the trial court was correct or that the error did not affect the outcome of the case. An appellate court's rules may or may not provide for oral argument to supplement the written briefs. An oral argument provides an opportunity for the appellate judges to have a dialogue with the attorneys. Parties' motions made to an appellate court are always in writing.

Appellate procedures are quite technical and discourage laypersons from attempting to prosecute their own appeals. Appellate court decisions are published so that other litigants may obtain guidance from the precedent they establish. The publishing of appellate court decisions, called opinions, is another check within the judicial system to keep courts responsible to the parties and to all citizens.

■ JURISDICTION

A court's authority to determine legal rights and to enforce its decrees is limited to the court's jurisdiction. In civil litigation, the term *jurisdiction* is synonymous with the terms *authority* and *power*. Every court in the United States is subject to some jurisdictional limitations. When a court acts beyond its jurisdiction, its judgments are void and not enforceable. The government that created a court may modify the court's jurisdiction and functions through subsequent legislation. Courts are subject to various legislative controls.

The government that created the court determines the scope of the court's jurisdiction. The United States Constitution created the United States Supreme Court and established that Court's jurisdiction. Congress cannot abridge the Supreme Court's jurisdiction. Congress created all other federal courts, so it determined what authority those courts should have. State legislatures created state courts and thus may change the structure and functions of state courts through legislation. For example, a state legislature may add more judges, may redefine judicial districts, may abolish courts, and may establish new courts—such as a new intermediate appellate court. In most states, the highest appellate court was created by the state's constitution, and therefore the state legislature cannot modify the powers of that court. The "constitutional" court has the authority to supervise the lower courts in its state.

One of the first considerations a plaintiff's lawyer has when starting a lawsuit is to determine which courts have jurisdiction. Then the lawyer must select the "best court" for the case. Frequently, more than one court could take jurisdiction. The defendant's lawyer must decide whether the court chosen by the plaintiff does have jurisdiction and if it does not, whether to challenge the court's jurisdiction or to waive the jurisdictional defect. Some jurisdictional defects cannot be waived. Waiver of jurisdictional defects is discussed below.

Jurisdiction may be divided into three categories: geography or territory, person, and subject matter. A court does not have jurisdiction over a case unless the court has jurisdiction in all three respects.

Territorial Jurisdiction

Territorial jurisdiction refers to the geographic limits on a court's authority. With some few exceptions, courts have no authority beyond their territorial limits. Some very practical considerations preclude courts from having jurisdiction beyond their territories. By way of example, if a judgment debtor and his property are within the territorial limits of the court, enforcement of the judgment is a relatively straightforward procedure. However, one can imagine the difficulty that a court in Massachusetts would have enforcing its judgment in Texas. Texas probably would not look kindly upon Massachusetts's officious conduct. And the Massachusetts court simply could not have enough personnel to handle extrastate activities. Similarly, a Massachusetts court would have practical difficulties trying to determine title to real estate located in Texas, and even more difficulty trying to enforce a judgment affecting title to property in another state. State courts do not have authority to determine ownership of real estate located in another state. A state district court cannot subpoena a witness who is located in another state.

The territorial limitation on a court's jurisdiction becomes a little vague in accident cases. For example, suppose two acquaintances from California are traveling in an automobile through Minnesota when they are involved in a collision, and the passenger desires to bring a lawsuit action against the driver to obtain money damages for personal injuries. Must the lawsuit be brought in Minnesota? Suppose the driver and the passenger return to their native California. Do they have to travel back to Minnesota to litigate their dispute? Causes of action arising from occurrences (torts) usually are transitory. This means that they arise in the territory where the accident occurred, but also follow the defendant. Consequently, the plaintiff can sue the defendant driver in any state where the defendant can be found.

In this situation, the action could be brought in Minnesota, whether or not the defendant driver can be found in Minnesota. The Minnesota court's authority exists under the state's nonresident motorist statute, which provides that a nonresident motorist impliedly appoints the Minnesota commissioner of highways as the motorist's agent to receive service of process for any motor vehicle accident in which he or she is involved within the state. All states have such statutes. The plaintiff passenger may serve the summons and complaint upon the Minnesota commissioner of highways. The plaintiff must also mail a copy of the summons and complaint to the nonresident motorist at that person's last known address. Through this procedure, the Minnesota courts obtain jurisdiction over a nonresident driver.

Personal Jurisdiction

Personal jurisdiction refers to jurisdiction over a party, whether the party is an individual, corporation, governmental subdivision, or any other legal entity. By commencing a civil action, the plaintiff necessarily submits her or his person to the court's jurisdiction for the remainder of the litigation. Consequently, the defendant may prosecute a counterclaim against the plaintiff even though the court could not otherwise have obtained jurisdiction over the plaintiff.

The court obtains jurisdiction over the person of the defendant through service of process upon the defendant. This is a procedure by which the defendant is given notice that an action has been brought against the defendant in a particular court. The defendant must appear in the action and defend himself or herself; otherwise, the plaintiff may take a default judgment against the defendant. The most common form of service of process is the delivery of a summons to the defendant, with a copy of the civil complaint. Depending upon circumstances, process may be duly served using other methods (see chapter 6).

If, for some reason, a court has not obtained jurisdiction over the defendant, the defendant may challenge the court's jurisdiction or may voluntarily submit to the court's jurisdiction. The absence of personal jurisdiction is an affirmative defense that may be waived. The waiver may be intentional or inadvertent. To challenge the court's jurisdiction over his or her person, the defendant must raise the issue in the answer or by motion. Otherwise, the defendant submits to the court's jurisdiction merely by appearing in the case. Personal jurisdiction defects are often waived because the technicality that impaired jurisdiction could be easily cured and there is no sense in putting off the litigation.

A personal injury cause of action accrues in the state where the injury occurs. The manufacturer of a defective product that is shipped into another state for resale or use submits to the jurisdiction of the courts in the state where the product is sold. A few decades ago it would have been necessary for the consumer to bring the lawsuit in the state where the manufacturer was incorporated or where it had physical presence. In recent years, the concept of due process of law has been expanded to permit states to enact so-called long-arm statutes for protection of their citizens in cases such as this. The court obtains personal jurisdiction over manufacturers and vendors because they do business in the state, even though they are not physically in the state.

Process may be served upon a foreign corporation by serving the secretary of the state in which the product was sold. The plaintiff must promptly mail copies of the summons and complaint to the foreign corporation at its registered office or principal place of business. The foreign corporation will have to defend itself in the state where the consumer's injury occurred. If the plaintiff consumer moves to another state, the cause of action does *not* follow. The suit must be brought in the state where the product was sold or the state where the defendant manufacturer conducts its business as of the time of service.

A corporation is subject to personal jurisdiction in the state where it is incorporated whether or not it does business in that state. A cause of action in tort or for breach of contract follows the defendant to another jurisdiction but does not follow the plaintiff. However, if the plaintiff follows the defendant to another state and brings the action there, the defendant can counterclaim against the plaintiff for any claim the defendant has that arises from the same transaction or occurrence. Whenever the plaintiff elects to sue in a particular court, she or he submits to the jurisdiction of that court while the suit is pending.

Subject Matter Jurisdiction

Subject matter jurisdiction refers to the type of case and the subject of the case. Not all courts can try all kinds of cases. For example, federal courts do not have jurisdiction over divorce cases, adoptions, registration of real estate, or probate of wills. State courts do not have jurisdiction over the United States government or any of its agencies. All civil actions involving the United States must be brought in a federal court, usually a district court. A state court does not have jurisdiction over a civil action against another state. One state may obtain jurisdiction over another state only in a federal court. A defendant cannot do anything to give a court jurisdiction over the subject matter of the case. Subject matter jurisdiction may be challenged at any time, even after entry of judgment.

The amount of money damages claimed in the complaint determines whether certain courts have jurisdiction to handle the case. Small claims courts usually cannot award money damages for more than a few thousand dollars—the exact amount varies from state to state. If a plaintiff has a claim for $350 but the jurisdictional limit of the small claims court is only $300, the plaintiff must give up $50 of the claim in order to use the small claims court. On the other hand, in **diversity-of-citizenship** cases, all federal district courts have a jurisdictional requirement that the amount in controversy must *exceed* $50,000. (Diversity suits authorize a citizen of one state to sue in federal court if the plaintiff and defendant are residents of different states.) Federal district courts do not have jurisdiction to handle diversity cases involving amounts of $50,000 or less. The parties cannot avoid the jurisdictional requirement by agreement or otherwise. If the amount in controversy is $50,000 or less, it would be a fraud on the court to feign a larger amount for the purpose of trying to give the federal court jurisdiction.

A court of **general jurisdiction** has authority to grant all remedies available in law and equity. In addition to awarding money damages in unlimited amounts, it can issue decrees for adoption, divorce, injunctions, specific performance, change of name, and judgments determining title to real estate. (Some of these remedies are discussed in chapter 3.) Courts of limited jurisdiction are unable to provide some of these remedies.

■ FEDERAL COURT ORGANIZATION

The federal judicial system has three levels of courts. The United States Supreme Court is the dominant court. Its genesis is in the United States Constitution, which establishes and defines its authority. Article III provides that the judicial power of the United States is vested in the Supreme Court and in such lower courts as Congress establishes through the legislative process. The Court's powers cannot be abridged or changed by Congress.

Pursuant to Article III, Congress has created two levels of lower courts. The first level is the district courts. Congress created a district court for each state and for each United States territorial possession. Congress provided for the organization of the Federal district courts, the extent of their jurisdiction, and the manner in which they may function. Each district court may have several divisions, and each division is located in a separate city and has its own courthouse. Almost all cases originate in the district courts. The district courts conduct trials, and the trials lead to entry of a judgment that determines the parties' ultimate rights and obligations. Most cases terminate at the district court level.

The second level of courts created by Congress consists of eleven circuit courts of appeal. Each circuit court serves as an intermediate appellate court for several district courts. By way of example, the Ninth Circuit serves the federal district courts in Alaska, Arizona, California, Hawaii, Idaho, Montana, Nevada, Oregon, and Washington. The circuit courts of appeal handle appellate matters; they do not handle trials. A party who believes that the district court committed error may appeal from the district court judgment to the circuit court of appeals that serves that locality. The appendix contains a map that shows the geographic territories of the eleven circuit courts of appeal.

Federal Jurisdiction

The federal judicial system has the power to hear and decide civil lawsuits that arise under the United States Constitution, and some treaties and federal laws. Furthermore, federal courts have the power to adjudicate cases between two or more states, and between a citizen of one state and the citizen of another state if the amount in controversy exceeds fifty thousand dollars. The fifty thousand dollar plus requirement is to limit the number of cases federal courts are required to handle. Congress does not want the federal system to replace or interfere with the states' judicial systems. The federal system does not oversee state judicial systems and does not supplant state courts. For the most part, the federal system and the state systems operate independently of each other.

Federal courts have authority to interpret the meaning and scope of federal laws, including the United States Constitution. In particular, federal courts have authority to determine whether a statute is constitutional and whether the manner in which a statute has been applied is constitutional. The Supreme Court has ultimate authority to determine what federal statutes mean and how federal laws are to be applied. The Supreme Court may even determine whether a statute was properly enacted so that it may become law. Congress determined that the Supreme Court should participate in establishing the Rules of Civil Procedure by which the lower courts conduct their business. Congress therefore enacted enabling legislation authorizing the Supreme Court to promulgate the Federal Rules of Civil Procedure.

Federal law provides that certain types of cases must be brought in federal court, such as cases involving patent infringements, regardless of the amount of money in controversy. Any action against the United States government or any of its agencies must be brought in a federal district court. In addition, federal district courts may be used to bring actions against foreign governments, against the government of another state, or against a corporation incorporated in a foreign country. If the case is not subject to federal jurisdiction, the plaintiff must resort to a state court.

Federal District Courts

Federal district courts are courts of original jurisdiction. Cases are tried and the initial decisions are made in these courts. The federal district courts are also courts of limited jurisdiction. They are limited to certain types of cases, and only certain persons may bring actions in them. For example, two Texans who are involved in an automobile accident in Texas and who decide to sue each other for personal injuries cannot bring their actions against each other in the Federal District Court for Texas. However, if one of the Texans moved to another state, even after the automobile accident, then there would be diversity of citizenship, which would permit an action in federal district court, assuming the amount in controversy exceeds fifty thousand dollars. Even though a diversity of citizenship exists, if the claim is for the sum of fifty thousand dollars or less, a federal district court does not have jurisdiction. This limitation is imposed by federal statue, not by the Constitution.

A large body of law has developed concerning diversity of residency, or diversity of citizenship, as a prerequisite to federal jurisdiction. In cases arising from transactions, such as an action on a contract or promissory note, there is no problem determining whether the controversy involves more than fifty thousand dollars. However, cases that arise from personal injury and property damage claims are more difficult to evaluate for purposes of jurisdiction. As a rule of thumb, courts and parties look to the amount of special damages and the "apparent" seriousness of the injuries. (Special damages are out-of-pocket expenses that the claimant incurs because of the alleged wrongful conduct of the defendant.) If there is evidence of a significant permanent disability caused by a personal injury, federal courts usually accept jurisdiction. However, individual federal judges may differ on how stringently they apply this limitation on jurisdiction. If a case goes through trial and the jury determines that full compensation should be less than fifty thousand dollars, federal district courts allow entry of judgment for the amount of the verdict, even though the award is below the jurisdictional amount. The monetary limitation does not cause the court to lose jurisdiction retroactively.

At times, two or more federal district courts, each in a different state or territory, have jurisdiction. In that event, the case should be commenced in the court that is most convenient for everyone involved. A number of rules determine which court provides the proper **venue.** The term *venue* is often used interchangeably with the term *forum*, which designates the place where the case is pending or set for trial. The term *venue* may relate to the district (state or territory) or to a particular division within a district. Generally speaking, the proper venue is the one where the cause of action accrued or the place that is most convenient to the parties and witnesses.

Federal district courts are **courts of record.** That means they keep a complete, verbatim record of everything that is said in the course of all hearings and all trials. The record is made by a reporter who makes stenographic notes (courts have not yet come to rely upon electronic recordings). However, a person who wants a transcript of the notes must pay a reasonable fee for the transcript. Transcripts are usually necessary to support a party's appeal. The court reporter's notes are available to the public. They may be obtained by persons who are not parties to the action. A person may want a transcript of testimony another person gave in a trial when that person has a related case.

Federal Circuit Courts

If a party concludes that some error occurred during the course of the trial and the error prejudiced the outcome of the case, the party may appeal the trial court's judgment to a circuit court of appeals. The supposed error may involve the application of a rule of substantive law or an error in the manner in which the trial was conducted. An error is considered prejudicial if it could have adversely affected the outcome of the case. An error must be prejudicial to be appealable. The appeal is taken to the circuit court of appeals that serves the area in which the trial court is located. A federal district court case cannot be appealed to a state court. However, on occasion a federal court may certify to a state supreme court a question concerning state law.

United States Supreme Court

The Supreme Court acts to keep the eleven circuit courts from developing separate and inconsistent bodies of law. It is an appellate court, not a court of original jurisdiction.[1] Relatively few cases are appealed to the Supreme Court. Most of the cases that do reach the Court are accepted pursuant to an appellant's petition for a **writ of certiorari.** This procedure requires the appellant to file a brief that explains to the Court why the lower court was wrong and why the Supreme Court should be concerned about the effect of the holding. If the Supreme Court deems the issue to be significant to society or to the law in general, it may grant the application by ordering the lower court to send up its file for review. There are very few cases in which a party has a right to have the United States Supreme Court take the appeal.

■ STATE COURT ORGANIZATION

State District Courts

Each state has a system of courts that have general jurisdiction, usually described as district courts. Each district court has power to hear almost any kind of case involving any sum of money and to grant all forms of judicial remedies. Each district court has statewide jurisdiction; that is, its subpoenas, orders, and decrees may be enforced anywhere within the state and even against its citizens who are outside the state. Nevertheless, each district court operates within a specified territory, usually a county or group of counties.

As a general rule, a cause of action should be brought in the district court located in the county in which the cause of action accrues. Other courts may have jurisdiction, but usually only one court is the proper venue. The rules that determine the proper venue take into consideration which venue is most convenient for the action to be tried. By way of example, one consideration is, In which venue does a majority of the defendants reside? Venue also refers to the geographic area from which the jury is selected. Considerations that determine jurisdiction and the proper venue may be similar, but the two terms involve quite different concepts. The basic difference is that *jurisdiction* relates to the court's authority, and *venue* relates to matters of convenience for trial of the action.

One rule for determining the proper venue for a tort action is that the venue in which the cause of action accrues is the proper venue. A tort action accrues at the place where the wrongful act and injury occur. However, if the tortious conduct occurs in one venue and the plaintiff's injury occurs in another venue, the cause of action accrues where the injury occurred. In a contract case, the cause of action accrues where the contract was to be performed and the breach occurred. If the contract was not performed at all, the cause of action may accrue where the contract was made. Also,

---

1. Article III provides, in part: "In all cases affecting ambassadors, other public ministers and consuls, and those in which a State shall be party, the Supreme Court shall have original jurisdiction. In all other cases before mentioned, the Supreme Court shall have appellate jurisdiction, both as to law and fact, with such exceptions, and under such regulations as the Congress shall make."

contracts may anticipate the possibility of litigation and designate what state's laws shall apply and where the action shall be brought. In cases involving title or possession of real estate, the cause of action accrues in the venue in which the real estate is located.

The plaintiff selects a venue when he or she commences the action by filing the complaint. If the defendant believes the plaintiff selected the wrong venue, he or she must make a demand for a change of venue within the time specified by law—usually before the answer is due. Otherwise, the defendant waives the right to have the case heard in the proper venue.

Small Claims Courts

Most cities have a small claims court. These courts exist for the speedy, inexpensive handling of small claims that involve nothing more than an award of money damages. They handle a tremendous volume of claims for property damage, wages, breached contracts, collection of rent, collection of delinquent accounts, and even small personal injury amounts. The jurisdiction of small claims courts may be as large as six thousand dollars or more, depending upon the needs of the community. The rules of some small claims courts preclude parties from using lawyers to represent them, because the object is to keep the trial short and inexpensive. The rules of evidence are not followed closely. The parties are encouraged to simply tell their story in their own words with as few interruptions as possible. The judge or referee asks such questions as she or he deems necessary. Of course, companies and corporations cannot appear in person, so they often send lawyers to appear on their behalf, along with the necessary witnesses. Small claims courts have subpoena power, but subpoenas are seldom used.

Service of process in small claims courts is kept very simple and inexpensive. The usual procedure is to have the plaintiff prepare a sworn complaint in the clerk of court's office. The complaint is supposed to contain a short narrative of the plaintiff's version of the facts. The clerk often helps the plaintiff frame the allegations. In particular, the complaint must state the time and place of the occurrence or transaction. The filing fee is nominal, generally one to ten dollars. The clerk of court mails a copy of the complaint to the defendant at his or her last known address. A notice is sent with the complaint directing the defendant to appear in court at a specified time to defend against the allegations. The notice states that if the defendant fails to appear and defend, the plaintiff may take a default judgment against the defendant in the amount specified in the complaint. If the last known address proves to be incorrect, that would be grounds for setting aside a default judgment obtained against the defendant. The defendant is not required to prepare and serve an answer to the complaint.

Cases in a small claims court are usually heard within six weeks from the date of filing. Twenty or more cases may be scheduled for hearing in the course of morning or afternoon session. As soon as the judge has heard the parties' evidence, the judge makes a decision and notes the decision in the judge's record. The judge must make a decision right away because it would not be possible to keep all the cases in mind for very long. However, the judge tells the parties that the matter has been taken under advisement, and the decision is sent to the parties by mail a few days later. The delay in rendering a decision prevents other litigants, who are waiting for their case to be heard, from figuring out what the judge is looking for in the evidence and changing their story to fit the judge's pronouncements. The delay also allows for a cooling-off period. If the judge were to announce the decision in open court, that might lead to a courtroom altercation. For the same reason, a judge never comments on the credibility of the witnesses. Judges are acutely aware of the importance of making litigants feel that the system is working properly. This is especially true in small claims courts because parties do not have lawyers to explain the problems to them.

Notwithstanding the informality of small claims courts, a judge's decision should be made according to the law rather than the judge's personal sense of equity. For example, if the plaintiff has sued on an oral contract that is invalid because the law requires such contracts to be in writing and signed to be enforceable, the decision should be for the defendant. The judge may explain to the parties that the decision will be controlled by rules of law and why a particular rule may apply in the case. The explanation can be given without pronouncing the court's decision in open court. Using this approach, the court helps a party to understand why he or she may lose even though the court did not disbelieve the party's evidence. When the case is handled in that manner, a party may not be quite as angry against the system upon receiving the decision in the mail.

Small claims courts are not courts of record. The only documentation of the trial is the court's order for judgment. If a litigant is disappointed in the outcome, she or he cannot appeal directly to an appellate court. Usually, the procedure is to appeal to the next higher court of original jurisdiction—perhaps a municipal court or a county court. The appeal does not examine what took place in the small claims court. Instead, the parties receive a new trial, described as a trial de novo. This time, the case is tried with all the usual court formalities. The appeal must be taken within the designated period of time and in the manner prescribed by the small claims court's rules. The notice of the decision and entry of judgment usually contains the information necessary for the losing party to appeal and obtain a trial de novo.

Justice Courts

In some communities, certain "smaller" civil cases are tried by a local justice of the peace. A justice of the peace may not be a lawyer and may not have formal training in the law. His or her income probably depends directly upon the litigation handled. "Justice courts" lack some of the safeguards that characterize courts of law. Consequently, they seem to be disappearing.

Municipal and County Courts

Municipal courts and county courts handle a large volume of litigation even though they are courts of limited jurisdiction. They cannot render judgments in excess of a specified amount, such as twenty thousand dollars. They are courts of original jurisdiction. They are also courts of record, so a transcript of the proceedings is kept and available. An appeal may be taken directly to an appellate court from a municipal or county court judgment. The parties have a right to trial by jury, as in courts of general jurisdiction. Usually, the rules of procedure for municipal and county courts are very similar to those for district courts. There is considerable value in keeping the rules of procedure uniform in all courts throughout the state. For the same reason, many states have adopted rules of civil procedure that mirror the Federal Rules of Civil Procedure. The limitations on municipal courts' jurisdiction prevent them from handling suits for divorce or determining title to real estate or granting injunctions or rendering other types of equitable relief.

Courts of General Jurisdiction

Courts of general jurisdiction can handle any type of civil lawsuit. They are courts of record. No maximum amount limits the money damages they can award; no minimum amount is required for jurisdiction. Their judgments and decrees may be enforced anywhere within the territorial limits of the state. The losing party may appeal directly to an appellate court. A state court of general jurisdiction has authority that the state legislature cannot abridge. For example, the legislature could not provide by statute that district courts shall not have jurisdiction to determine whether a statute is unconstitutional. Some district court rules provide that if the plaintiff is the prevailing party but recovers a judgment for an amount within the monetary jurisdiction of a small claims court or a county court, the *losing* party may recover her or his costs against the prevailing party. The purpose of such rules is to encourage parties to use the lower courts when possible, and to save the courts of general jurisdiction for the more significant cases. Taxable costs may include the filing fee, witness fees, and charges for service of process.

Specialized Courts

Each state has a variety of specialized courts, including a tax court, probate court, family court (for divorces and adoptions), workers' compensation court, and municipal courts. Each of these courts handles only one type of case. A state's rules may provide for an appeal from those courts to a district court. The specialized courts do not authorize jury trials and may provide for only limited discovery. Otherwise, the proceedings in them are conducted much like the proceedings in a district court.

SUMMARY

The parties must assert and prove their claims and defenses in the trial court. The parties must offer evidence in the trial court to prove the facts upon which they rely. An appellate court does not receive new evidence. An appellant may obtain relief in an appellate court only if the appellant can show that the trial court committed an error of law that prejudiced the outcome of the case.

A court must have jurisdiction to decide a case; if it lacks jurisdiction, its judgment is a nullity. A court must have jurisdiction over the subject matter, and over the parties. Parties may grant jurisdiction over their person voluntarily or inadvertently. Where the subject matter has a physical location, the subject matter must be within the territory served by the court, that is, territorial jurisdiction. Parties cannot waive or grant the subject matter jurisdiction. A judge must dismiss a case when the judge learns or realizes that his or her court does not have jurisdiction.

Each state has one federal district court. Each federal district has several divisions. Federal district courts have original jurisdiction. They are not appellate courts. They hear cases that involve federal questions. Federal district courts have original jurisdiction of cases involving disputes between residents of different states even though no federal question is involved. However, the amount in controversy must *exceed* fifty thousand dollars.

The term *venue* refers to the forum in which a case is set for trial. The defendant has a right to have the case prosecuted in a reasonably convenient venue. If the case was brought in the wrong venue, the burden lies with the defendant to take some affirmative action to have the case transferred to the correct venue. Venue statutes state the considerations that determine which venue should be used. The case may be in the wrong venue even though the court has jurisdiction.

In addition to the district courts, the federal court system has two levels of appellate courts. A disappointed litigant has the right to appeal from a federal district court to the circuit court of appeals that serves that area. The appeal may be based upon errors that affected how the case was tried, or errors concerning the law that governed the parties' substantive rights. The appeal must be prosecuted within the time and in the manner prescribed by the Federal Rules of Appellate Procedure.

A litigant who is disappointed with a decision made by a federal circuit court of appeals may petition the United States Supreme Court for review of the circuit court's decision. To obtain review by the United States Supreme Court, a party must show that the lower court's decision is probably wrong, that the decision has broad application, and that it is likely to recur. A good basis for obtaining review is to show that the circuit courts of appeal are divided on the issue—in other words, that the circuit courts have made conflicting decisions and reached inconsistent results.

State district courts have general jurisdiction. States also have small claims courts, justice courts, municipal and county courts. Only the district courts are courts of general jurisdiction. The jurisdiction of a small claims court is usually limited to the county in which the court is situated. The only remedy a small claims court may provide is money damages. The awards are limited to only a few thousand dollars. The other specialized courts handle only one kind of case, the kind for which the court was created, such as probate, family court and bankruptcy court.

KEY TERMS

original jurisdiction	general jurisdiction
territorial jurisdiction	venue
personal jurisdiction	courts of record
subject matter jurisdiction	writ of certiorari
diversity of citizenship	trial de novo

REVIEW QUESTIONS

1. What happens if the defendant fails to object to the court's lack of jurisdiction?

2. When may the parties waive a jurisdictional defect?

3. What is the difference between venue and jurisdiction?

4. If a party loses a case in a federal district court, to what court may that party appeal?

5. In what federal circuit is your federal district court located?

6. Does a party have a right to prosecute an appeal to a federal circuit court of appeals? If so, under what conditions? If not, why not?

7. Does a party have a right to appeal to the United States Supreme Court? If so, under what conditions? If not, why not?

6

INTRODUCTION TO FEDERAL PROCEDURE

A paralegal needs to understand what lawyers do in the handling of civil litigation, how they do it, and why. Since the Federal Rules of Civil Procedure govern every aspect of civil litigation, a good place to begin is with an examination of the Rules. Rule 1 explains that the objectives of the Rules are to promote justice and economies and to facilitate a resolution of each case. In that spirit, the Rules prescribe the methods for commencing lawsuits, serving process, conducting discovery, making motions, preparing for trial, conducting trials, and perfecting appeals. The Rules are interrelated. Therefore, they must be read and applied together.

It is relatively easy to start a lawsuit, and it should be. Parties who have claims between them should be encouraged to use the courts to resolve their disputes. People would be discouraged from using the courts if litigation were cumbersome, too expensive, or too slow. The very first step in bringing a lawsuit is to prepare a complaint. In federal court, the clerk prepares a summons when the complaint is filed. The lawsuit is commenced when the complaint is filed with the clerk of court, but the named defendant does not become a party or subject to the suit until the summons and complaint are served upon him or her. The defendant is required to respond by serving and filing an answer to the complaint. The plaintiff's complaint and the defendant's answer frame the fact issues and the legal issues to be determined by the court.

A paralegal may prepare pleadings. However, the Rules require that a lawyer who is licensed to practice in the court where the case is venued sign a pleading, or where a party represents herself or himself as attorney pro se, that person may sign a pleading. The lawyer's signature certifies that the lawyer has read the pleading, and the lawyer is responsible for the pleading's content as though the lawyer had actually drafted it. A lawyer may not justify any omission or improper allegation by contending that she or he did not actually draft it or that she or he was in a hurry when reviewing it.

■ COMPLAINT

Before the Federal Rules of Civil Procedure were adopted, a complaint had to set forth, in detail, all the facts constituting the plaintiff's cause of action. For example, in a trespass action, the plaintiff had to set forth in detail all the facts that proved that he or she occupied the particular parcel of land as owner or lessee; that the defendant entered upon the land on a particular date; that the entry was made in a particular manner; that the entry was without the plaintiff's consent; that the defendant lacked authority to enter the land at the specified time and place; that the entry resulted in specified damage to the land. From these allegations, the defendant's lawyer knew that the plaintiff was claiming that the defendant had committed a trespass, knew the harm caused, and knew the amount of the claim. Those were the facts the plaintiff would have to prove at trial. The plaintiff was not allowed to prove additional or different facts. The defendant's only source of information about the plaintiff's claim was the complaint and the defendant's independent investigation. If the complaint failed to state sufficient facts to establish the cause of action being claimed, the complaint was disallowed by the court. The action was dismissed.

Though still essential to civil litigation procedures, the complaint has lost the function to inform the defendant about the facts upon which the claim is based. Now the complaint may omit the factual details of the alleged wrong. However, the complaint still must identify the plaintiff's cause of action, the occurrence or transaction and the alleged breach of *legal* duty. Modern rules of procedure minimize the old technical requirements for drafting pleadings. The criteria for the complaint are well stated in Rule 8(a):

> A pleading which sets forth a claim for relief, whether an original claim, counterclaim, cross-claim, or third-party claim, shall contain (1) a short and plain statement of the grounds upon which the court's jurisdiction depends, unless the court already has jurisdiction and the claim needs no new grounds of jurisdiction to support it; (2) a short and plain statement of the claim showing that the pleader is entitled to relief; and (3) a demand for judgment for the relief the pleader seeks. Relief in the alternative or of several different types may be demanded.

A complaint has several practical functions. The plaintiff commences the civil action by filing the complaint with the clerk of district court. The time at which an action is commenced determines whether the action is timely and starts a timetable that leads the case to trial. The caption of the complaint identifies the court chosen by the plaintiff's lawyer. The clerk of court assigns a court file number to the caption. The complaint's title identifies the plaintiff or plaintiffs and the person or persons who are expected to be defendants. However, a person does not actually become a defendant until served with a summons and a copy of the complaint—or, under certain circumstances, until service is made by publication (Rule 4(e)). The complaint must allege facts that show that the court has jurisdiction over the subject matter and the basis for jurisdiction over the named defendant or defendants. The plaintiff automatically submits to the court's jurisdiction when she or he commences the lawsuit by filing the complaint.

Elements of a Complaint

The complaint must identify the transaction or occurrence by its type, date, and place (Rule 9(f)). The complaint must describe the plaintiff's legal theory, such as trespass, defamation, breach of contract, negligence, and so forth. It may have exhibits attached. The complaint must state the type of injury or loss and list the plaintiff's special damages. The complaint must specify the type of relief the plaintiff wants the court to provide. If the relief sought is money damages, the complaint must state the amount. Finally, it must be signed.

Time and Place.   Whether the claim is founded upon a transaction or an occurrence, the complaint must state the material time and place. Time is important not only to identify the occurrence, but also to determine whether the statute of limitations has run against the claim and whether the parties have complied with all notice requirements. Since laws change from time to time, the allegation may be material in determining what law applies. The place of the occurrence may determine which court has jurisdiction. It may also determine which state's laws apply in determining the parties' substantive rights.

Cause of Action.   The element of causation is fundamental to all tort litigation. This means the plaintiff must prove that the defendant committed a tortious act *and* that the tortious act was a direct and immediate cause of the harm for which the plaintiff seeks money damages. Historically, courts used the term *proximate cause*; now many courts use the term *direct cause*. The meaning is the same; the rule of law has not changed, just the terminology. If no causal connection exists between the defendant's wrongful conduct and the plaintiff's loss, the plaintiff is not entitled to any compensation from the defendant. Therefore, the complaint must specifically allege that the defendant's alleged tortious conduct was the direct, or proximate, cause of the plaintiff's loss.

The Rules do not require the allegations to be stated in a legalistic manner. Nevertheless, the complaint must show that all the elements of a cause of action (a claim upon which the court can grant relief) exist. This may be done by simply naming the cause of action. A lawyer must have the substantive law well in mind when drawing a complaint, making sure that the allegations state a claim upon which relief may be granted and the legal theory the lawyer intends to pursue.

Not every wrong or controversy gives rise to a claim that can be litigated. A man may call his neighbor stupid or say the neighbor is a jerk. As unflattering as these remarks are, they do not give rise to a cause of action for defamation. A saleswoman may spend many hours helping a customer with the selection of a car, and then lose the sale to another sales-woman who spent only a few minutes with the customer. The first sales-woman may feel that she has been wronged, her time and help abused, but she does not have a cause of action for breach of contract.

If a complaint fails to state a cause of action, the complaint is subject to being stricken on motion (application to the court for an order) (Rule 12(b)). A motion may be made in writing, or orally when the parties are before the court and a record is being made of the proceedings. Most motions are concerned with procedural issues. They are made to obtain the court's help, direction, clarification. The court acts upon a party's motion by issuing an order to the parties (Rule 7(b)).

A complaint should state each important allegation separately in a short paragraph (Rule 8(a)). By limiting each paragraph to a single set of circumstances or to a single idea, the plaintiff makes it easier for the defendant to admit allegations contained in the paragraph. If a paragraph contains several subjects, it is likely that the defendant will feel justified in denying some of the matters alleged and will, consequently, deny the entire paragraph. On the other hand, a defendant will feel constrained to admit the allegations contained in a paragraph if all of the allegations in the paragraph are true. For example, where the plaintiff's complaint sets forth indisputable facts in paragraphs 1, 2, and 5 of the complaint, the defendant's answer may state, "Defendant admits the truth of the allegations contained in paragraphs 1, 2, and 5 of the complaint." A plaintiff wants the defendant to admit as many of the allegations as possible, because the plaintiff does not have to prove the facts the defendant admits in the answer. Facts admitted in the answer are not subject to dispute. The defendant would have to amend the answer to the complaint to be able to contest facts previously admitted in the answer. Similarly, the plaintiff cannot deny facts that he or she alleges in the complaint. For example, suppose a plaintiff's complaint alleges that she was employed by the defendant at the time of an accident, but as the case develops she concludes that her case would be better if she were not considered to be an employee of the defendant.[1] She may not deny her status as an employee for purposes of the lawsuit without amending her complaint.

If the complaint includes more than one transaction or occurrence, each should be set forth in a separate count. A **count** is a separate section or part of the complaint that is independent of other counts of the complaint. When two or more plaintiffs have claims arising from the same transaction or occurrence, they may join as coplaintiffs in a single action (Rule 20). The complaint should clearly segregate the plaintiffs' claims. That may be done by using separate counts. A separate count is like a separate division or section or part of the complaint.

Exhibits. If a document such as a contract or a promissory note is the subject of the claim, a copy of the document may be attached to the complaint. The complaint may incorporate the exhibit into the complaint by reference. The complaint gives a good picture of the claims against the defendant so that he or she is able to admit the legal obligation or begin

---

1. An employee's right to recover money damages for work-related injuries may be severely limited by a state's workers' compensation laws.

preparation of defenses against the claims. The complaint, then, establishes the scope of the plaintiff's claims.

Type and Extent of Injury or Loss.   The complaint must describe, in general terms, the type and extent of the loss or injury the plaintiff sustained. When two or more plaintiffs are named in the complaint and each has a separate loss, the losses must be stated separately. The loss may take various forms such as a loss of profits, expenses, damage to property, a total loss of property, physical pain, mental anguish, disfigurement, embarrassment, disability, loss of good reputation, loss of use of money, loss of support—the list is almost without limit. The claim may be for future losses, such as future pain, future loss of income, or loss of future profits.

Relief or Recovery Sought.   The complaint must contain an **ad damnum clause**—the "Wherefore" clause—in which the plaintiff specifies the relief or recovery wanted from the defendant. The ad damnum clause tells the defendant just how much money damages the plaintiff is claiming. **Special damages** must be specifically stated, and items of special damages must be specifically stated (Rule 9(g)). Special damages are the out-of-pocket expenses the plaintiff has incurred because of the defendant's wrongful conduct. In a personal injury action, the plaintiff's medical expenses, loss of past income, and property damage are items of special damages. A monetary value need not be given for each item—though it frequently is. In a breach-of-contract action, the amount of the lost profits and consequential expenses should be stated. The defendant needs to know this information at the outset; the other pertinent facts can be obtained by the defendant through discovery procedures.

Nothing but a sense of professional responsibility prevents the plaintiff's counsel from asking for an excessively large amount of money. The news media is unduly impressed by large demands stated in civil complaints. Consequently, a few jurisdictions have enacted laws or rules that provide that the complaint shall state an amount not more than fifty thousand dollars. If the claim is for more than fifty thousand dollars, the complaint simply states that the amount demanded is "in excess of" fifty thousand dollars.

The amount stated in the ad damnum is particularly important in courts where jurisdiction is affected by the amount in controversy. If the ad damnum is too much, a county or municipal court cannot have jurisdiction over the case. Courts such as the United States district courts may not have jurisdiction in certain types of cases unless the plaintiff, in good faith, is able to demand judgment for an amount in excess of fifty thousand dollars, exclusive of costs and interest.

If the defendant fails to serve an answer to the complaint within the time specified, she or he is considered to be in default. The plaintiff is able to obtain judgment against the defendant by application to the court (Rule 55). The plaintiff's recovery is limited to the amount of the ad damnum even though she or he is able to show more damages when "proving up" the default judgment. (A plaintiff "proves up" a default judgment by presenting in an uncontested hearing evidence of the default, a prima facie case of liability, and damages.) By duly appearing and defending against the claim, the defendant's obligation could be determined to be more than the amount demanded in the complaint. In that event, the plaintiff could obtain a judgment for the entire amount. Nevertheless, if the defendant defaults, the plaintiff's recovery is limited to the amount stated in the ad damnum clause.

Occasionally, a case seems to be minor when sued but develops into a very serious one commanding a much higher award than originally presumed. The plaintiff's lawyer may move the court for an order increasing the ad damnum to the correct, higher amount. The motion must be supported by one or more affidavits setting forth the change in circumstances. The plaintiff must show the court that the amendment will not prejudice the defendant's preparation for trial. For purposes of illustration, if a defendant has let his liability insurance company defend him against a claim, and the amendment permits a recovery of money damages in excess of the insurance policy limits, the court must afford the defendant sufficient time in which to consult with another lawyer about the personal exposure. In addition, the insured's personal lawyer must be given enough time to become fully acquainted with the case so that she can make appropriate recommendation concerning the handling of the case.

Ordinarily, the plaintiff would not be allowed to increase the ad damnum clause to an amount in excess of the defendant's liability insurance policy limits once the case reached trial. When the ad damnum exceeds the coverage provided by the defendant's insurance policy, a significant conflict of interests may develop between the defendant and the defendant's liability insurance company. The defendant may need the advice and services of a lawyer whom the defendant must retain at his or her own expense. One problem they must address is whether the insurance company should try to pay the full amount of the insurance policy limits to settle the case, considering the possibility or likelihood that if the case does not settle there may be a recovery against the defendant for an amount in excess of the insurance policy limits. If there is time for everyone to further evaluate the case and prepare for trial, the plaintiff would usually be allowed to increase the ad damnum, notwithstanding the lack of insurance to cover the higher amount. This assumes that the plaintiff is able to convince the court there is good cause for the increase.

Signature.   If the plaintiff has not hired a lawyer to handle the claim, the plaintiff must sign the complaint as attorney pro se. If the plaintiff *has* hired a lawyer, the lawyer must sign the complaint; the plaintiff does not have to sign it. The lawyer's signature is her or his verification that the claim has a basis in fact and in law and that the action has not been brought for the purpose of harassment, embarrassment, or delay. The complaint does not have to be notarized.

The complaint must be filed for the purpose of making a claim and not for some ulterior or collateral purpose (Rule 11). A lawyer does not have to intimidate the client to determine whether the claim has merit. On the other hand, a lawyer may have to subject the client to some searching questions to make sure the claim is not fraudulent and not groundless. Litigants are expected to comply with the letter and spirit of Rule 11. If either a lawyer or a client violates Rule 11 by starting a groundless lawsuit, he or she is subject to court sanctions. A lawyer should explain to the client the seriousness of Rule 11 and its application. This is just one reason to emphasize to clients that they must be forthright.

Sample Complaint

The complaint in exhibit 6.1 identifies the contract, the place of its performance, the time and place of the breach, the nature of the breach, and the nature and extent of the loss claimed. The contract document is fully identified by attaching a photocopy to the complaint. The use of photocopies eliminates the possibility of introducing error into documents where the wording may be critical. This complaint provides the defendant with enough information to determine whether to deny the claim or admit liability.

Procedure for a Complaint

The date the complaint is filed establishes the date on which the action is commenced. The clerk of court assigns a file number to the action. The number may be similar to this: 94 Civ. 532. The 94 means the case was filed during the year 1994. *Civ.* means it is a civil action. The last number indicates the case's chronology. All subsequent pleadings, motions, orders, affidavits, and depositions must use that file number.

When the complaint is duly filed and the filing fee paid, the clerk of court prepares a summons (a document directing the defendant to appear and defend), which the lawyer must attach to a copy of the complaint. A separate summons must be issued for each defendant. The clerk gives the summons to the plaintiff's lawyer, who is then responsible for promptly serving the summons and a copy of the complaint upon the defendant (Rules 4(a) and (d)). The plaintiff's lawyer may arrange for the United States marshal to serve the summons and complaint upon the named defendant or defendants. The plaintiff's lawyer must give the marshall a defendant's last known address. It is helpful to also give to the marshall the defendant's employment address.

The summons is not a pleading. A summons directs the defendant to serve an answer to the complaint within twenty days after the date on which the summons and complaint were served. The twenty-day period begins to run on the next day after service. If the summons and complaint are served on Tuesday, the twenty-day period begins to run on Wednesday.

A defendant who has liability insurance that might apply to the claim should deliver the complaint to the insurance company right away. Unfortunately, sometimes defendants delay contacting the agent. The insurance company may have difficulty determining whether claims are covered by the insurance policy and whether to accept defense of the case. The insurer may need extra time in which to make that corporate decision. More often than not, the plaintiff's lawyer agrees to grant additional time for answering. Both sides should try to avoid the unnecessary time and expense of procedural motions. An attitude of goodwill and cooperation benefits all parties and the court. Laypersons are often surprised at how much and how often lawyers who are adverse in a case accommodate each other. Cooperation and accommodation are good.

All pleadings filed with the court are public records for anyone to read. They are thus subject to engendering publicity that could be very harmful to a party or even third persons. Therefore, a pleading must be signed by a lawyer or by the party who acts as her or his own lawyer. The signature is a certification that the signer has read the pleading; that she or he believes

For his cause of action against defendant, plaintiff alleges:

1. Plaintiff is a resident of the state of New York, and defendant is a resident of the state of New Jersey; the amount in controversy exceeds ten thousand dollars, not including costs and interest.

2. On May 10, 1994, plaintiff and defendant entered into a written contract in which plaintiff agreed to purchase from defendant and defendant agreed to sell a certain XYZ electronic computer bearing manufacturer's serial number 54321 and then located at defendant's plant at 33 Hart Street, Newark, New Jersey.

3. The agreed purchase price for the computer to be delivered at defendant's said plant was thirty thousand dollars.

4. A copy of said contract is attached hereto as exhibit A and incorporated herein by reference.

5. Defendant promised to deliver said computer to plaintiff at defendant's plant in Newark, New Jersey, on June 15, 1994.

6. Defendant failed to deliver said computer to plaintiff at said time and place, although plaintiff has made demand upon defendant to do so.

7. Plaintiff tendered to defendant the agreed purchase price of thirty thousand dollars, and all other conditions precedent have occurred or have been performed by plaintiff.

8. By reason of defendant's breach of contract, plaintiff has been required to purchase another electronic computer, similar in type, at a cost of fifty thousand dollars; therefore, defendant's breach of contract has caused plaintiff to sustain a loss in the amount of twenty thousand dollars, plus interest thereon at the legal rate of 8 percent per annum.

Wherefore, plaintiff prays for judgment against defendant in the sum of twenty thousand dollars, together with interest thereon at the legal rate of 8 percent per annum from the date of defendant's breach, together with plaintiff's costs and disbursements herein.

Plaintiff demands trial by jury.

_____

Attorney for Plaintiff

[date]

good grounds support the allegations in the pleading; and that the pleading has not been filed for the purpose of delaying a claim or for some other secondary purpose. Any allegation that is scandalous, impertinent, or immaterial to the cause of action or defenses may be stricken by order of the court. Parties must not use a pleading as a vehicle to malign another party or person (Rules 11 and 12(f)). Any allegation that is redundant, incompetent, or insufficient to state a claim or defense is subject to being stricken by court order (Rule 12(f)).

State Practice for a Complaint

The rules of civil procedure for some state courts provide that the plaintiff's lawyer shall prepare and sign the summons as well as the complaint. The lawyer may arrange for service of the summons and complaint on the defendant before filing the summons and complaint with the court. In those states, the cause of action is commenced either (1) when the summons and complaint are delivered to a proper public officer, such as a sheriff, for service or (2) when the summons and complaint are actually served upon the defendant. If the second procedure is followed, the action may be commenced against multiple defendants on different days. In states that have such a procedure, there is no rule that the summons and complaint ever be filed. However, as soon as either party wants the court to become involved for purpose of motions or trial, that party must file a pleading (complaint or answer) with the clerk of court, and matters then proceed as they would in federal court.

Determination of the exact time an action is commenced may be critical to maintenance of the lawsuit. For example, a question may arise as to whether the action was commenced before the statute of limitations ran against the cause of action. Some contracts, especially insurance policies, provide that an action on the contract must be brought within a specified period of time after the occurrence in question. Failure to comply constitutes a breach of a condition that bars an action on the contract. A single day's delay can make, and has made, the difference.

■ AMENDED COMPLAINT

The plaintiff may amend the complaint as a matter of right, and without leave of the court if the plaintiff serves the amended complaint within twenty days after service of the original complaint or before the defendant serves the answer (Rule 15(a)). Otherwise, the plaintiff must obtain leave of the court to serve and file an amended complaint. The defendant may agree (stipulate) to accept service of an amended complaint after expiration of the time provided by Rule 15(a). Usually the admission of service is made on the original amended complaint, but it may be made in a separate document. The admission statement may be worded as follows:

> Due and proper service of the amended complaint is admitted this first day of April, 1994.

> _____
> Attorney for Defendant

An amended pleading is usually identified by the word "amended." If another amendment becomes necessary, it may be designated second amended complaint.

For a number of reasons, a party may agree to accept an amended pleading without forcing the opponent to make a motion to the court. The amendment may simply correct a technical defect or clerical error that does not affect the parties' substantive rights. Or the amendment may contain corrections or allegations that the adverse party considers beneficial or true. Furthermore, courts liberally permit amendments.

A party who opposes an amendment must show that he or she would be prejudiced by the amendment (Rule 15). A party is prejudiced by an amendment only if the party can show that if the allegation had been made earlier, he or she could have effectively defended against the claim, but the delay has interfered with that ability. Although the amendment may significantly help the plaintiff to prove a claim against the defendant, that does not constitute prejudice to the defendant.

Most lawyers choose not to waste time and money resisting a motion to amend when it is clear that the court should allow the amendment. Ordinarily, the party seeking to amend volunteers to permit his or her opponent to conduct whatever additional discovery procedures need to be prepared on the new issues raised by the amendment.

The defendant has at least ten days in which to answer an amended complaint. But if the amended complaint was served within just a few days after the original complaint was served, the defendant must answer within the same period of time as that established by service of the original complaint. In other words, the defendant's answer to the amended complaint is due at the same time as it would be to the original complaint or within ten days after service of the amended complaint, whichever time period is longer.

Amendments relate back to the date of the original pleading. For example, suppose the plaintiff brings an action to recover compensation for damage to real estate; the original complaint alleged only a cause of action in negligence; and after the suit was started, the statute of limitations ran on all tort claims. If the plaintiff is allowed to amend the complaint to allege a cause of action in trespass too, the amendment is deemed to relate back to the date on which the action was originally commenced. By amending the original complaint, the plaintiff has successfully avoided having the statute of limitations bar the claim.

If, for some cogent reason, a party needs additional time to prepare and serve any pleading and the opposition will not agree to an extension of time, the needy party may apply to the court for an order granting an extension. The application (motion) may be made with or without notice to the opposing party if it is made before the prescribed time period expires (Rule 6(b)). The moving party must show the court that she or he has good reason (grounds) for making the request. The reasons ordinarily are set forth in an affidavit that must be filed with the motion.

■ SUPPLEMENTAL COMPLAINT

The plaintiff has a right to serve and file a **supplemental complaint** to state a new cause of action against the defendant where a new claim has accrued in favor of the plaintiff since the original complaint was served. The supplemental complaint uses the same title and court number as the original complaint, assuming the plaintiff wants to have the new action heard with the first action. If the second claim is totally unrelated to the first, it may be preferable to keep the matters separate.

■ ANSWER

Procedure for an Answer

The defendant defends against the plaintiff's lawsuit by serving and filing an answer to the complaint. The defendant must serve the answer twenty days after service of the complaint. The defendant determines the date the answer is due by counting twenty days beginning with the next day after the summons and complaint were served. All the time periods prescribed by the Rules exclude the day of the act or event, so it makes no difference whether the defendant was served at 10:00 A.M. or 8:00 P.M. The answer is due *on* the twentieth day, not after twenty days. If the twentieth day falls on a Saturday, Sunday, or legal holiday, the time period is automatically extended to the next day that is not a Saturday, Sunday, or legal holiday.

If more time is required, the defendant may request an extension. Customarily, the defendant's lawyer simply telephones the plaintiff's lawyer and asks for an additional few days in which to serve the answer. If an informal extension is granted, it should be confirmed by a letter stating the date on which the answer is due. The confirmation helps to avoid any misunderstanding and provides good evidence of the lawyers' intent if a disagreement subsequently develops.

Usually, a formal **stipulation** is not essential, but one could be used. (A stipulation is a written, dated agreement signed by the lawyers by which the parties make a commitment concerning the case.) If the plaintiff will not or cannot voluntarily accommodate the defendant, the defendant may move the court for an order extending the time for answering (Rule 6(b)). If the application is made within twenty days after service of the complaint, the motion to the court may be made ex parte (Rule 6(b). An ex parte motion is a motion made by one party without notice to other parties. Motions to enlarge the time in which to act are routinely granted if made before expiration of the original time period. On the other hand, if the time period for acting has expired, the party in default must show the court that the failure to act is the result of excusable neglect. A party's failure to comply with the Rules, a court order, or time limitation may be excused if there is some justification for the failure and the consequences would be out of proportion to the neglect. Courts have broad discretion to grant or disallow such motions. They consider the moving party's excuse, the effect upon the moving party if the motion were denied, the merits of the parties' claims and defenses, the prejudice to the nonmoving party, and the costs the nonmoving party has incurred by reason of the moving party's delay.

The defendant **appears** in the case by serving an answer, or by serving and filing a motion challenging jurisdiction, or by moving the court for an order striking the complaint, or by moving the court for judgment on the pleadings, or by moving the court for an order compelling a more definite statement of the allegations in the complaint (Rule 12(a)). If the defendant elects to appear in the case by serving a motion, an answer need not be served while a Rule 12 motion is pending. After the court rules on the motion, the answer is due within ten days of the ruling—unless the court dismisses the complaint or sets a different time for answering (Rule 12(a)).

If the defendant fails to appear in the action by serving a motion or serving an answer to the complaint within the time specified by the summons, the plaintiff may have judgment entered by default (Rule 55(a)). The defendant may move the court to set aside the default judgment (Rule 55(c)), but the defendant must show the court that the default was the result of excusable neglect or inadvertence (Rule 60(b)).

The term **excusable neglect** covers a lot of territory. The Rules do not attempt to define circumstances that constitute valid excuses. A court considers the defendant's explanation, whether the defendant has a meritorious defense, whether the defendant is merely stalling, and whether the plaintiff will be prejudiced by setting aside the judgment. The defendant who succeeds in setting aside a default judgment usually has to pay the costs the plaintiff incurred in properly obtaining the judgment. These costs may include reasonable attorneys' fees.

If the complaint is vague or ambiguous, so that the defendant's lawyer is uncertain about the nature or scope of the plaintiff's claim, the lawyer may move the court for an order compelling the plaintiff to state the allegations with more particularity or more specifically or more definitely (Rule 12(e)).

Elements of an Answer

Title.   The answer uses the same title as the complaint, even if the defendant's name is misspelled or some other technical problem exists with the title. Later on, the title may be amended by court order. The correct spelling of the parties' names may be set forth as a separate allegation in the answer, but the original title as set forth in the complaint must be used until it is amended by court order. If the case involves two or more plaintiffs or two or more defendants, the answer and all subsequent pleadings may omit all names except those of the first plaintiff and the first defendant. The abbreviation *et al.* is used on these documents to indicate that the case involves additional parties who have not been specifically named, but the summons and complaint must list all the parties.

Response to Allegations.   The defendant's answer must admit the truth of the allegations in the complaint that are known to be true. Formal admissions in the answer establish conclusively that the specified facts and allegations are not disputed. The plaintiff will not have to prove the admitted facts. The court will inform the jury that the admitted facts are not in issue. The answer must also specifically deny the allegations that the defendant believes are not true. Any allegation in the complaint that is not denied is presumed to be admitted (Rule 8(d)). Consequently, an answer usually begins with a general denial such as "Defendant denies each and every allegation, statement, matter, and thing contained in the complaint, except as hereinafter expressly admitted or alleged."

If the defendant does not have sufficient knowledge upon which to form a belief concerning an allegation in the complaint, he or she may so state. The statement has the same effect as a denial. The plaintiff is put to his or her proof on the matter. The language typically used is "Defendant alleges that defendant does not have sufficient knowledge or information upon which to form a belief concerning plaintiff's claims of injuries and damages and, therefore, puts plaintiff to his strict proof of same." A general denial, standing alone, is insufficient and contrary to the spirit of the Rules of Civil Procedure, unless the defendant disputes that he or she was even involved in the transaction or occurrence in question.

The answer uses numbered paragraphs, just as the complaint does, to separate each set of circumstances and each affirmative defense. It is common practice to use one paragraph to set forth all admissions. For example,

> 2. Defendant admits the allegations contained in paragraphs 1, 2, and 3 of the complaint, and further admits that the motor vehicle accident occurred about the time and place specified in the complaint.

An admission that the accident occurred is not an admission of fault or legal responsibility for the accident. Nevertheless, some lawyers are constrained to add a statement such as "specifically denies that the defendant was negligent," after admitting that the defendant was involved in the accident or other occurrence. When the defendant admits an alleged fact that is part of a paragraph that contains many facts, the defendant must be careful to clearly delineate the scope of the admission.

Allegations and denials in the answer do not have to be consistent with one another (Rule 8(e)). For example, the answer may deny that the plaintiff and the defendant entered into a contract, and therefore the plaintiff cannot maintain an action on the alleged contract for its breach. At the same time, the answer may allege that the plaintiff's claim on the contract is barred by affirmative defenses such as accord and satisfaction, release, fraud, and waiver, which assume that the contract was made.

See Rules Appendix of Forms, forms 20 and 21, for examples of answers and their responses to allegations.

Affirmative Defenses.   The answer must allege all the affirmative defenses that the defendant has (Rule 8(c)). Any affirmative defense not asserted in the answer is waived. An affirmative defense is a fact or set of circumstances that defeats the plaintiff's claim even though the plaintiff is able to prove the cause of action. Rule 8(c) provides a partial list of affirmative defenses.

The defendant has the burden of proving her or his affirmative defenses. The plaintiff is not obligated to serve and file a responsive pleading to the answer for the purpose of admitting or denying the defendant's affirmative defenses. The affirmative defenses are presumed to be denied. Each affirmative defense should be set forth in a separate, numbered paragraph for convenience of the parties and the court (see Rules Appendix of Forms, form 20).

Request for Relief.   An answer concludes with a "Wherefore" clause in which the defendant states his or her request for relief. The following is a typical concluding paragraph:

> Wherefore, defendant prays that plaintiff take nothing by reason of her alleged cause of action, and that defendant have judgment for her costs and disbursements herein.

■ AMENDED ANSWER

The defendant has twenty days after serving the answer in which to amend the answer, as a matter of right. After the twenty-day period has expired, the answer may be amended only by agreement (stipulation) of the plaintiff or by court order (Rule 15(a)). An answer may be amended to correct mistakes made in the original answer, to allege new facts, or to allege a new affirmative defense. The defendant could amend the answer simply to admit facts that the defendant has come to accept as true and should have admitted in the first answer. An admission that is corrected or withdrawn by an amended answer cannot be used against the defendant.

Again, courts liberally grant amendments unless the late amendment causes prejudice. The plaintiff is prejudiced by a late amendment only if the delay impairs the plaintiff's ability to deal with the new matter raised. For example, the plaintiff is not prejudiced if the defendant amends the answer to allege the statute of limitations as an additional defense, even though the new defense will defeat the claim. On the other hand, if the defendant admitted in the answer that the defendant's stairway was unlighted at the time of the accident and the defendant wants to amend the answer to withdraw the admission, and the scene of the accident has been altered so that the evidence the plaintiff needs to prove the absence of lighting is not now available, the plaintiff could be prejudiced by the proposed amendment (Rule 15(b)).

■ COUNTERCLAIM

If a defendant has a claim against the plaintiff, the defendant may assert it in a counterclaim. The counterclaim must be served with the answer. Usually, the two documents are combined. If the defendant's claim against the plaintiff arises from the same transaction or occurrence as the plaintiff's claim, it is a **compulsory counterclaim.** That means it must be asserted with the defendant's answer or it is waived (Rule 13(a)). On the other hand, if the claim arises from a separate transaction or occurrence, the defendant may decide whether or not to pursue it as a counterclaim. It is then a **permissive counterclaim** (Rule 13(b)).

A counterclaim is the defendant's complaint against the plaintiff. All the requirements of a complaint apply to a counterclaim, except that many of the essential allegations are already provided by the complaint and the answer. Allegations in the complaint and answer may be incorporated into the counterclaim by reference. Counterclaims commonly contain a paragraph similar to the following:

> Defendant hereby incorporates the allegations of paragraph 1 of the complaint and all the allegations of defendant's answer as though fully set forth herein.

The defendant may not assert a counterclaim concerning a matter over which the court does not have jurisdiction. But in federal courts, a counterclaim may seek relief that is more or different in kind than what is claimed in the complaint (Rule 13(c)). On the other hand, this difference may preclude jurisdiction over some counterclaims in state courts that have limited jurisdiction. For example, if the plaintiff's claim was brought in a municipal court and that court's jurisdiction is limited to twenty thousand dollars, and the defendant's counterclaim is higher than that amount, the usual procedure is to transfer the whole case to a court of general jurisdiction.

It would be unfair to require the defendant to assert her or his cause of action in a counterclaim if it is already the subject of another pending lawsuit, whether in the same court or in another court; therefore, this is not required (Rule 13(a)). For example, suppose four motorists were involved in a single accident consisting of multiple rear-end collisions, and motorist A sued motorist E for damages, and motorist C sued motorist A in a separate action. If A decided to make a claim against C, he could include C in the first action as a direct defendant or he could counterclaim in the action brought by C. If the cases were all in the same court, they probably would be consolidated for purposes of discovery and trial anyway (Rule 42). But if the two cases were in different courts, A could have some difficulty deciding which procedure to follow.

A counterclaim based upon a cause of action that accrues after the answer was served may be brought by a supplemental counterclaim (Rule 13(e)). Supplemental pleadings are permitted only by order of the court upon a showing that the cause of action accrued after service of the original pleading (Rule 15(d)). The court order allowing the supplemental pleading should specify whether a responsive pleading is necessary—that is, an answer, answer to cross-claim or reply to counterclaim.

If a counterclaim requires the presence of a third person who is not subject to the court's jurisdiction, it need not be asserted; it is not then compulsory. For example, if a plaintiff sues for breach of contract, and the defendant claims that the plaintiff and the plaintiff's partner caused the defendant to be defrauded in the same transaction, and that the partner is not subject to this court's jurisdiction, the counterclaim is not compulsory. The defendant may assert her claim for fraud against both persons in another action in another court that does have jurisdiction over both persons.

The form of a counterclaim is similar to that of a complaint. If the counterclaim is added to the answer, the combined documents are usually identified as answer and counterclaim. The counterclaim may be separately stated but must be served with the answer. If the defendant inadvertently fails to serve the counterclaim with the answer, the defendant may move the court for an order allowing service of the counterclaim. The grounds for the motion include oversight, inadvertence, and excusable neglect (Rule 13(f)). The defendant must obtain permission to serve a counterclaim separately because the late pleading may cause a delay in the normal progression of the case to trial. Since a counterclaim will inevitably raise new issues of fact and the law, the parties may need additional time to investigate and conduct additional discovery.

Most courts liberally permit amendments to pleadings, additional pleadings, and supplemental pleadings in the absence of prejudice to the party to be served. A party is prejudiced only if the delay adversely affected the party's ability to present his or her claim or defense on the merits (Rule 15(b)). Generally, the courts allow late pleadings and/or amendments to pleadings so as to avoid prejudicing a meritorious claim or defense. But courts often place a heavy burden on the delinquent party to expedite the necessary discovery procedures and all other trial preparation. The court may impose costs and other sanctions as a condition precedent to allowing a late counterclaim. If the court refuses to allow the late counterclaim, the defendant is precluded from asserting the claim at a later date if the claim arose from the same occurrence or transaction as the plaintiff's claim (Rule 13(a)). Some lawyers believe that a counterclaim may be served anytime within twenty days after service of the answer, because the answer may be amended without a court order during the first twenty days (Rule 15(a)).

A counterclaim has obvious application where the defendant in an automobile accident case sues for his own injury and/or property damage—claiming that the plaintiff is liable. A counterclaim may also be used by the defendant to make a claim against one plaintiff for contribution to the claim of another plaintiff. For example, suppose the two plaintiffs are husband and wife. They sustained injuries when their automobile was struck by the defendant's truck. If the plaintiff husband was driving, and he was partially at fault, the defendant could counterclaim against the plaintiff husband for contribution to the wife's claim—assuming that the lawsuit is brought in a state that does not recognize interspousal immunity. (Interspousal immunity means spouses cannot sue each other for money damages for torts. Most states have done away with interspousal immunity.)

As a general rule, the courts favor consolidating claims so that they can be determined in a single trial. Consolidation usually leads to a speedier, more economical determination by avoiding duplication of effort. But if trial of a counterclaim along with the main action would unduly complicate the proceedings, the court may order a severance of the claims for purpose of trial (Rules 13(i) and 42(b)).

■ REPLY TO COUNTERCLAIM

Since a counterclaim is for the purpose of making a claim against the plaintiff, the plaintiff must be given the opportunity to deny the defendant's allegations and plead affirmative defenses. A plaintiff responds to a counterclaim by serving and filing a reply to counterclaim (Rule 7(a)). The reply is tantamount to an answer, so the requirements are the same as those for the defendant's answer. A reply to counterclaim must be served within twenty days after service of the counterclaim. When the counterclaim is served by mail, as it usually is, three days are added to the time period (Rules 12(a) and 6(e)).

■ CROSS-CLAIM AND ANSWER TO CROSS-CLAIM

Two or more persons who are liable to the plaintiff for injury or property damage may be joined as codefendants (Rule 20). The codefendants may have claims to make against each other for injuries or losses they sustained for contribution to the plaintiff's claim. A defendant may make a claim against a codefendant by serving and filing a cross-claim. A cross-claim is, in effect, a complaint that states one or more causes of action against a codefendant. The rules and guidelines for drafting complaints apply to preparing cross-claims.

Exhibit 6.2 is typical of allegations found in cross-claims.

A cross-claim is usually served as a separate document. If a defendant has appeared in the case by serving an answer or a Rule 12 motion, the cross-claim may be served upon the defendant's lawyer by mail (Rule 5(b)). Usually, the cross-claim cannot be served with the answer because the iden-

Comes now defendant and for her cross-claim against defendant C alleges:

1. Plaintiff has commenced the above entitled action against each defendant above named and alleges that defendants are jointly and severally liable to plaintiff for money damages, as more fully set forth in the complaint, a copy of which has been duly served upon each defendant.

2. Defendant B has denied liability to plaintiff as set forth more fully in her answer, which has been served on all parties and filed with the court (attached hereto as exhibit A).

3. Defendant C's negligence was the proximate cause of the accident described in the complaint.

4. If defendant B is determined to be liable to plaintiff as alleged in the complaint, or otherwise, defendant B is entitled to contribution from defendant C on the grounds that C's negligence was a proximate cause of the accident and concurred with defendant B's alleged negligence to cause plaintiff's alleged loss.

Wherefore, defendant B prays for judgment of contribution from defendant C to any sums awarded in favor of plaintiff against defendant B, together with her costs and disbursements herein.

tity of the codefendant's lawyer is not yet known. If a named codefendant has not yet been served with summons and complaint, a cross-claim may be served in the manner provided by Rule 4, like an original summons and complaint.

The rules do not express a time limit for serving and filing cross-claims. Nevertheless, an inherent principle requires that service of a cross-claim shall not be so late as to unduly delay the trial of the main action, that is, the plaintiff's case.

A defendant who has been served with a cross-claim must respond by serving and filing an answer to cross-claim (Rule 12(a)). The codefendant has twenty days in which to answer the cross-claim. If the cross-claim was served by mail, three days are added (Rule 6(e)). The answer to cross-claim serves the same function as an answer to complaint, and the same general rules apply.

Usually a defendant's lawyer may readily obtain the identity of a lawyer representing a codefendant by contacting the plaintiff's lawyer. Otherwise, it may be necessary to contact the codefendant directly, but the facts of the case must not be discussed with the codefendant if she or he is represented by a lawyer. A note of issue, which is used in most state courts to place an action on the active trial calendar, must identify all the parties and their lawyers, including the lawyers' addresses and telephone numbers, and it must be served upon all the lawyers in order to be effective. Consequently, the note of issue is a convenient vehicle for informing each lawyer about the identity of all the other lawyers who have appeared in the case.

The use of cross-claims establishes technical adversity between the defendants. This may be important at trial in determining whether one defendant's lawyer has the right to cross-examine another defendant and whether the defendants are required to share peremptory challenges in the jury selection (see chapter 20).

■ THIRD-PARTY PRACTICE

The defendant may bring a third-party action against another person, called a third-party defendant, to obtain indemnity or contribution from that person for the liability that the defendant has to the plaintiff. The claim for indemnity or contribution must be asserted in a third-party complaint. A third-party complaint must be served upon the third-party defendant in the same manner that Rule 4 provides for service of the original complaint. A third-party complaint can be used only to obtain indemnity or contribution. It cannot be used to assert a new, unrelated claim. Third-party actions are not compulsory.

Third-party actions are very common because the same facts that give rise to the plaintiff's cause of action against the defendant may also create rights in favor of the defendant against some third person who has not been sued. For example, if a plaintiff consumer was injured owing to a defect in a product she purchased, the consumer has a cause of action against the retailer and against the manufacturer. If the plaintiff chooses to sue only the retailer, the retailer may commence a third-party action against the manufacturer to obtain indemnity and/or contribution. Frequently, the manufacturer has the ultimate responsibility for the injury. If the retailer shows that the manufacturer was responsible for the defect and injury, the retailer may obtain full reimbursement (indemnity) from the manufacturer for any money damages the retailer is obligated to pay to the plaintiff consumer. Another example: When an employee acts within the scope of his employment to carry out his employer's business purposes, the employer is vicariously liable to any person injured by reason of the negligent acts of the employee. This is true whether the employer is an individual or a corporation. If an injured person brings an action against the employer, the employer may have a cause of action against the employee for indemnity. So if the employer is held liable to the plaintiff, the employer may be able to recover the same amount of money damages from the negligent employee, together with the employer's costs incurred in defending against the plaintiff's action. The employer may bring a third-party action against the employee to obtain indemnity if the employee was not sued directly by the plaintiff.

A third-party action may be brought by one joint tortfeasor against another for contribution. Joint tortfeasors are entitled to contribution between them. For example, if two negligent motorists collide, causing injury to a passenger, and the passenger sues only one driver, that defendant driver may bring a third-party action to sue the other driver for contribution. This situation occasionally arises when a wife is injured in an automobile accident while her husband is driving. She may elect to sue only the other driver. The defendant may bring a third-party action against the husband for contribution, assuming no family immunity exists in the state where the accident occurred.

Third-Party Complaint

The defendant commences a third-party action by serving a summons and third-party complaint upon the third-party defendant in the manner prescribed for serving a complaint upon the defendant (Rule 4). The defendant is thereafter identified as defendant and third-party plaintiff or as third-party plaintiff. The defendant has a right to commence a third-party action, without leave of the court, anytime within ten days after serving his or her answer to the complaint (Rule 14(a)). Otherwise, the defendant must apply to the court for leave to commence the third-party action. Again, the time is limited because the defendant must not cause the plaintiff's case to be unduly delayed, and the act of bringing in an additional party has the potential for causing some delay. A substantial delay may seriously prejudice the plaintiff's right to a speedy trial.

A third-party action unavoidably complicates the litigation. Nevertheless, it is highly preferable to consolidate the action for indemnity or contribution with the plaintiff's case. A consolidation conserves the court's time and resources. It also prevents inconsistent determinations between the parties. For example, if the defendant had to bring an entirely separate lawsuit against a joint tortfeasor in order to obtain contribution, the jury's determination of the amount of the plaintiff's damages might be more in the first action than in the second action, and that would reduce the amount of contribution that the defendant could obtain. In a third-party action, the defendant can force the joint tortfeasor to participate in the case brought by the plaintiff, and they are both bound by the result obtained by the plaintiff.

The third-party complaint should be drafted with the same considerations in mind that apply to the original complaint and to cross-claims. A third-party complaint alleges that the plaintiff commenced the action by service of a summons and complaint upon defendant, includes the date of service, and has attached a copy of the plaintiff's complaint as an exhibit. A third-party complaint alleges the gist of the plaintiff's claim and that the defendant denies liability for that claim; that the defendant duly interposed an answer on a specified date; that a copy of the answer is attached as an exhibit; that the third-party plaintiff is entitled to indemnity or contribution, as the case may be, from the third-party defendant for any sums that may be awarded to the plaintiff against the third-party plaintiff. The third-party complaint uses an ad damnum clause to specify the relief sought.

The ten-day period for starting a third-party action begins to run the day after service of the defendant's answer. The defendant may move the court for an extension of time. If the motion for an extension of time is made within the ten-day period, notice of the motion need not be given to the plaintiff (Rule 6(b))—that is to say, the motion may be made and heard ex parte. But if the ten-day period has expired, the defendant must make the motion by giving due notice to the plaintiff (Rule 6(d)). A motion made after expiration of the ten-day period should show that there was excusable neglect for failing to act within the ten-day period prescribed by Rule 14; that the plaintiff will not be prejudiced by the late joinder; and that there is reason to believe that the proposed third-party defendant is liable to the defendant for indemnity or contribution. Frequently, the defendant includes a copy of the proposed third-party complaint that states the cause of action for indemnity or contribution. If the plaintiff does not oppose the defendant's motion, the court usually grants the motion as a matter of course.

Third-Party Answer

The third-party defendant has twenty days in which to serve her or his answer to third-party complaint. The third-party answer must be served upon the plaintiff *and* upon the third-party plaintiff. In turn, the third-party defendant may commence a fourth-party action for indemnity or contribution against anyone who is liable to her or him because of the transaction or occurrence in question. The third-party defendant then has the additional title of *fourth-party plaintiff.* Theoretically, any number of parties may be joined in a lawsuit in this manner.

The third-party defendant's answer must assert whatever defenses the third-party defendant has to the third-party plaintiff's claim. In addition, the third-party defendant may allege defenses that the third-party plaintiff has against the plaintiff's claim. For example, if the defendant has a defense to the plaintiff's claim—such as contributory negligence, assumption of risk, release, immunity, or statute of limitations—the third-party defendant may raise that defense in his or her answer, even if the third-party plaintiff failed to raise the defense in his or her answer to the complaint. This is important because the third-party action is, by its nature, predicated entirely upon the defendant's liability to the plaintiff. If the third-party plaintiff is not liable to the plaintiff, the third-party defendant cannot have any liability to the third-party plaintiff for indemnity or contribution. In other words, if the third-party defendant keeps the plaintiff from recovering against the original defendant, the third-party defendant automatically wins too.

Severance

Any party may move the court to sever the third-party action from the main action. Numerous reasons and grounds exist for obtaining a severance (Rule 42). Nevertheless, consolidation of claims and parties is generally favored. If the defendant is unsuccessful in a belated effort to obtain leave to commence a third-party action, the defendant may, nevertheless, start a separate lawsuit for the same purpose of obtaining contribution or indemnity. But by having a separate lawsuit, the defendant runs the risk that she or he may be found liable to the plaintiff and yet will be unsuccessful in proving a right to indemnity or contribution in the second action. Furthermore, the defendant who seeks indemnity or contribution in a separate action has the burden of proving the plaintiff's damages, and that can be a little awkward. A second trial also increases the expense of the litigation.

Third-Party Actions

A third-party defendant may serve a claim against the plaintiff if that claim arises from the same transaction or occurrence. The plaintiff may also serve a claim upon the third-party defendant. When that is done, the third-party defendant is then treated as a direct defendant. The two or more defendants are referred to as codefendants.

■ CROSS-CLAIMS

If there is more than one third-party defendant, each third-party defendant may serve a cross-claim against the others, just as codefendants may (Rules 13(g) and 14(a)). A third-party cross-claim requires an answer to cross-claim.

■ JOINDER OF CLAIMS AND CONSOLIDATION OF CASES

One objective of the Rules of Civil Procedure is to keep civil litigation as inexpensive as possible (see Rule 1). The joinder of two or more claims into one lawsuit may make the overall handling of several disputes between the same parties more efficient and less expensive. Similarly, the consolidation of two or more lawsuits into one trial may provide a significant savings for the parties and the court. On the other hand, there are circumstances that mitigate against consolidation of claims and cases, including untoward delay, added complexity, and potential confusion over the issues and evidence. Therefore, courts have broad discretion in determining whether or not to join claims and whether to consolidate cases for trial. The variations on consolidation and joinder are nearly endless, and the ramifications are many. Not every party always benefits. Some parties may be harmed in presenting their claims or defenses by a consolidation. Therefore, courts must give serious consideration to any party's objection to a consolidation or joinder.

Joinder of Claims

A plaintiff may include in one lawsuit all the claims he or she has against the defendant, even if some of the claims arose from unrelated transactions or unrelated occurrences. Rule 18(a) provides for this:

> A party asserting a claim to relief as an original claim, counterclaim, cross-claim, or third-party claim may join, either as independent or as alternate claims, as many claims, legal, equitable, or maritime, as he has against an opposing party.

Each separate claim should be stated in the complaint as a separate count.

The possibility of a party having several claims against a defendant may seem remote, but it is not. By way of example, suppose the plaintiff company has been purchasing bolts of cloth from the defendant company for many years, but for the last three years the defendant's deliveries have been late, frequently causing the plaintiff to experience downtime; that the bolts of cloth are increasingly defective; and that orders are being misplaced. Finally, the defendant company makes a major error that causes the plaintiff to suffer a large loss. Their business relationship is at an end. Once the plaintiff company has decided to sue, it might as well sue for all the breaches of contract and warranties that occurred over the past several years, although the statute of limitations will act as a bar to older claims. All the claims may be included in the one lawsuit. Each transaction should be pleaded as a separate count.

The preceding example involves a series of transactions between two parties. A series of occurrences that gives rise to multiple claims in a favor of a plaintiff is a little more difficult to envision. Nevertheless, it can happen. Suppose the defendant is a large contractor who has overall responsibility for the construction of a large interstate freeway interchange next to a large shopping center owned by the plaintiff. The highway construction work may cause damage to the plaintiff's property at various times by use of explosives, pile driving, and trespasses by large machinery. The contractor may have blocked access to the shopping center, causing a loss of business. Dust and noise from the project might have created an actionable nuisance. Each of these untoward events may be the basis for a separate cause of action against the unfortunate contractor. Again, each claim and/or cause of action should be stated in the complaint as a separate count. The time and place of each event is material to properly stating a cause of action (Rule 9).

Suppose the defendant offers his house for sale, the plaintiff likes the house, and the two enter into a purchase agreement. The plaintiff returns to the house to inspect it and is injured by a defect on the premises. As a result of the plaintiff's accident, the defendant refuses to sell the house. The plaintiff could sue for the breach of contract and the bodily injury in the same lawsuit, even though one claim is based upon a transaction and the other upon an unrelated occurrence. It might be quicker and more economical for the parties to have just one trial. However, the defendant may want to have the claims tried separately because his liability for one claim might adversely affect his defense of the second claim.

Suppose the plaintiff was injured in two automobile accidents that occurred one year apart. The plaintiff may not want the cases consolidated for trial, especially if one of the accidents was her fault. The defendants may try to show that most of the plaintiff's injury was caused by the accident that was her fault. On the other hand, if neither accident was the plaintiff's fault, the plaintiff may want the two cases consolidated to avoid having the first jury conclude that her injuries were caused by the second accident and the second jury conclude that her injuries were caused by the first accident. If the two cases are tried together, the plaintiff can let the defendants worry about how the jury will allocate the injuries between the two accidents.

The defendant also has the right to join two or more claims into one lawsuit. The defendant may assert multiple claims in the counterclaim (Rule 18(a)). Or the defendant can start a separate lawsuit, as a plaintiff, against the original plaintiff, and then seek a court order consolidating that action with the action brought by the original plaintiff. The two cases can be tried as one (Rule 42(a)).

When two claims accrue in the same jurisdiction and the same venue, consolidation is a relatively simple process. But consolidation is not possible when a party's venue rights are impaired or the court lacks jurisdiction over one or more of the claims or parties.

Severance of Claims

Even though the plaintiff may elect to consolidate into one lawsuit all claims against the defendant, the court may order certain claims to be tried separately (Rule 42(b)). The defendant may make a motion for severance, or the court may order a severance on its own motion (Rule 42). A severance of claims is desirable when consolidated claims make a trial too complicated, too long, or too cumbersome. Consolidation might even make the proceedings more expensive for one or more parties. Even the plaintiff may decide, when the case reaches trial, that a trial of two or more claims before the same jury would be inconvenient or more expensive, and move for a severance. If a resolution of one of the claims may lead to a settlement or to a summary disposition of the other claims, a severance should be ordered and the pivotal case tried.

Severance of Issues

Rule 42 allows the court to order a severance of issues as well as a severance of claims. For example, a negligence action in which the plaintiff seeks money damages for a personal injury involves at least three major issues: negligence, proximate cause, and damages. Pursuant to Rule 42, a trial court could order that the issues of negligence and causation be tried together and that the damages issue be tried separately. The damages issue is material only if the plaintiff prevails on the negligence and causation issues. Severing the issues allows the opportunity for saving everyone a good deal of time and expense.

Lawyers representing plaintiffs in personal injury cases usually want the injury (damages) issue presented at the same time as the liability issues because there is a belief that the sympathy engendered by the plaintiff's injuries helps to carry the liability portion of the case.

Consolidation of Cases

Federal district courts have authority to consolidate cases for trial whenever cases involve common questions of law or common questions of fact (Rule 42(a)). This is true even though the cases involve different parties. Cases are never consolidated for trial merely because they coincidentally involve common questions of fact or law. For example, the fact that two automobile accident cases happen to involve stop sign violations is no reason to consolidate those cases. Even if the two automobile accidents involved the same intersection and the same stop sign, a trial judge would not consolidate the cases. Some underlying unifying circumstance must make a consolidation convenient for the court without unduly complicating or prolonging the trial for the parties.

Suppose five people sustain injuries in the crash of a small airplane. Each injured person decides to sue the pilot, the manufacturer, and the airplane maintenance company. Legal responsibility is quite unclear. The court may elect to consolidate the five cases for trial, at least to determine the liability issues. The five cases may take twice as long to prove as one case but only two-fifths as long as each case separately. If the plaintiffs are able to establish liability, some of them could settle the damages issue. The defendants gain by having to defend only once rather than five times. The basis for consolidation is the common question of the facts surrounding the single accident.

Another example of a case involving common questions of fact is where the plaintiff has been injured in two separate accidents and has two separate claims. Each defendant is likely to contend that the plaintiff's injuries occurred in "the other" accident. The parties may determine that they would prefer to consolidate both cases because they involve a common question of fact, that is, What injuries were sustained in which accident?

Consolidation is useful in cases involving business transactions as well as in accident cases. Suppose a corporation sells franchises for fast-food stores, and a problem develops with ten of the franchisees. Their contracts with the franchisor are all the same. The parties may want to have the cases consolidated for one trial. Everyone will save time and expense.

Many cases have common questions of law but would not be eased or helped by consolidation. For example, assume that during three months, five pedestrians fell on city sidewalks at separate locations, sustained injuries, and sued the city. These five cases involve common questions of law. The questions of law are not a major consideration; they are pretty well settled. Could the cases be consolidated? Perhaps. Should they be consolidated? No. A consolidation of the cases for trial will be of no value if no genuine dispute exists about the application of legal principles common to the several cases. But suppose a statute requires plaintiffs to give the city notice of an accident within thirty days after the accident, as a condition precedent to bringing a lawsuit against the city. In each of the five cases, a legal question exists as to whether the plaintiffs gave due notice of their claim to the defendant city. The plaintiffs each challenge the constitutionality of the statute. The legal issue is important and common to all. The cases may be consolidated for the purpose of determining the issue. If the legal issue were resolved in the plaintiffs' favor, the cases subsequently would be separated (severed) for individual jury trials.

In another example, property owners near an airport sued the airport commission, claiming that the noise from airplanes landing and taking off constituted an involuntary, partial condemnation or taking of their property for which they should be compensated. The legal theory was novel. Consolidation of those cases would permit the property owners to participate in a trial of the legal issue—that is, whether a cause of action existed for damages for condemnation. The property owners would be able to minimize their legal expenses by hiring one lawyer for all cases. If the legal issue were resolved in favor of the plaintiffs, clearing the way for an award of money damages to each property owner, each plaintiff could prove her or his damage in a separate hearing or trial (Rule 42).

Intervention

A procedure called **intervention** permits a person to join in a pending lawsuit by applying to the court for leave to become a party (Rule 24). He or she may apply to be a defendant or a plaintiff. The criteria are the same as for consolidating cases pursuant to Rule 42—that is, common questions of law or fact. The intervenor must show the court that he or she has an interest in the outcome of the case. The original parties have a right to object to the motion to intervene. Intervention could be opposed on the grounds that the intervenor does not have an actual interest in the outcome of the case or that the intervention would unduly delay or complicate the case.

A motion for leave to intervene must show the court that the applicant's claim or defense does involve an important common question of law or fact and that the intervention will conserve the court's time, save the parties' expense, and not prejudice anyone. Some statutes expressly encourage consolidation and direct the courts to order consolidations. Certain federal civil rights actions are typical of those encouraging consolidation and intervention. In those instances, a party may intervene as a matter of right (Rule 24(a)). This means the party does not have to convince the court of the desirability of the intervention. In that event, the motion for leave to intervene is not addressed to the court's discretion.

A person may intervene as a matter of right if his or her interests in the subject matter may be affected by the outcome of the litigation (Rule 24(a)). For example, suppose the defendant caused damage to real estate by creating a nuisance, and the real estate is owned by three joint tenants, and two of the joint tenants sue for damages. The third joint tenant will be allowed to intervene in the case as a matter of right (Rule 24(a)). If a trustee sues or is sued, the beneficiary may elect to intervene to protect his or her interest in the trust res. (*Res* is a Latin word meaning "thing" or "matter"; a trust res is the subject of the trust.) If an agent is sued for a wrongful act committed in the course and scope of the agency, the principal, who is vicariously liable for the agent's acts, may intervene to make sure the defense is adequately presented (Rule 24). The right to intervene is granted whenever a person could properly be joined as a party or his or her claim or defense could be consolidated as involving common questions of law or fact.

The procedure for intervening is clearly described in Rule 24(d). A motion must be served upon all parties, stating the grounds for the consolidation—that is, the moving party's interest in the subject matter. Or the moving party must show that she or he has a special relationship to the parties to the action. Or the motion must show the common questions of law or fact that permit the intervenor's matter to be joined with the pending action. The motion must include a proposed pleading (complaint or answer), with the proposed new title. The pleading must fully set forth the claim or defense (Rule 24(c)). The motion must give the parties at least five days' notice of the hearing (Rule 5). The original parties may appear in opposition to the motion.

Class Actions

The most ambitious consolidation of claims, defenses, and parties is the use of class actions as authorized by Rule 23. The subject of class actions is complex, presenting problems that paralegals seldom are required to handle. It is enough to understand that on occasion, an entire class or group of persons may be plaintiffs or defendants in an action in which the class or group is represented by just one or a few litigants. Class actions are not generally favored because the procedure limits the parties' actual participation. Courts have to exercise close supervision over the representatives of the class to make sure the class is adequately represented. The prerequisites for a class action are difficult to meet.

An example will illustrate the use and prerequisites of class actions. Suppose a large commercial bank contracted to pay interest on money it collects from mortgagors to hold in escrow to pay real estate taxes as the taxes come due. A dispute arises as to whether the bank has calculated the interest properly or has made questionable charges against the escrow accounts. The number of mortgagors may be several thousand, but they can be easily identified. If an action is brought by one or several mortgagors to recover their alleged losses due to overcharges by the bank, it would be best for the class (all mortgagors) and for the bank to have a resolution of the problem in one lawsuit and one trial. The active participation of each and every mortgagor should not be necessary if the class is adequately represented. If liability exists, the damages for each mortgagor should be easy to calculate. The bank will avoid the expense of multiple lawsuits. The amount in dispute may be fairly small for each member of the class, so having a large number of claimants may help justify the cost of the litigation. The total recovery could be substantial. If the case were not certified as a class action, the bank's successful defense against the initial plaintiff could not be binding upon other plaintiff mortgagors. The decision would be binding only upon the parties to the action. As to them, the decision would be res judicata. The decision in the first case would have some value as precedent, but that would not make it binding upon nonparties. Theoretically, if the prerequisites of Rule 23 are met so that a class action is permissible, everyone would tend to benefit.

It may be to the defendant's very real advantage to keep a case from beginning a class action. If the potential recovery by each plaintiff in the proposed class would be very small, the plaintiffs, as individuals, might have no interest in pursuing the claim. If the defendant can keep the court from certifying the case as a class action, the claims may go away.

The promoters of a class action usually get to be the representatives of the class. They may be entitled to substantial compensation for their services to the class. Class actions are often very lucrative for the lawyers who handle them.

If a party wants to move the court for an order certifying the case as a class action, the party must show the court that all the following elements are present:

1. The class is so large that it is not practical for its members to sue or defend as individual parties in a consolidation of cases or as a joinder of parties in a single action.

2. Common questions of law or fact have the same effect on the rights or obligations of all members of the class.

3. The party or parties applying for class certification are truly representative of the proposed class.

4. Separate suits by or against individual members of the proposed class might result in varying or inconsistent determinations for the members.

5. A class action can effectively dispose of all the legal and fact issues that exist between members of the proposed class and the adverse party.

6. The individual members of the proposed class do not have a superior interest in controlling the handling of the litigation.

7. No other pending litigation would be adversely affected by certifying the class action.

8. Commencement of a class action would not unduly burden the court and would not cause prejudice to persons who might choose to have their case presented in another forum.

If a class action is allowed, the court exercises control over the case to make sure that the members of the class are given notice about the case and that their rights are protected and that they are informed about their obligations in the action. A class action cannot be compromised or dismissed without court approval (Rule 23(e)).

One type of class action has been given special treatment by the Rules: a shareholders' derivative action to enforce rights of their corporation against a party when the board of directors wrongfully refuses or neglects to do so (Rule 23). Since the board of directors—not the shareholders—is charged with the responsibility for running the business, the shareholders may institute actions on behalf of the corporation only in extreme circumstances. The shareholders must show the court that an effort has been made to have the directors take the appropriate action and that the directors have refused. The shareholder who seeks to institute a derivative action must show that he or she was a shareholder at the time the transaction or occurrence in question took place and that he or she adequately represents the other shareholders. As in other class actions, a shareholders' derivative action cannot be compromised or dismissed without court approval.

■ SUBSTITUTION OF PARTIES

A civil lawsuit is between parties. Two or more parties must be involved for a lawsuit to have any basis. Therefore, when a party dies, someone must arrange to have the decedent's representative substituted as the party, assuming that the cause of action did not die with the party. Any party may move the court for an order directing the substitution. If a representative has been appointed in a probate proceeding, that representative may move the court for an order substituting herself or himself for the deceased party. If a party makes the motion for a substitution, and a probate court has already appointed a representative to handle the estate, that representative must be served with the motion and notice of hearing. The motion must be served in the manner provided in Rule 4 for service of a summons. The motion may not be served by mail upon a nonparty.

Once the parties and the court receive notice of a party's death, the remaining parties have just ninety days in which to act to obtain a substitution for the deceased party. Otherwise, the action against the decedent will be dismissed (Rule 25(a)). The rule implies that the court shall order the dismissal upon its own motion. Suppose the defendant dies one week before trial of a personal injury action. The defendant's lawyer should give notice to the court. The trial will have to be postponed. If the plaintiff fails to take steps to have the decedent's personal representative substituted as the defendant, the court will have to dismiss the action ninety days after receiving notice of the defendant's death. Under these circumstances, the burden does not lie with the defendant's lawyer to obtain the substitution, or with the decedent's estate.

If a party becomes legally incompetent to handle his or her business, a representative party must be appointed and substituted. For example, if a party becomes senile, a guardian should be appointed by a probate court having jurisdiction. The guardian must replace the senile party in the manner discussed previously.

If an action is brought by joint tenants of some real estate and one tenant dies before a determination is reached, the action will continue in the name of the survivor. One characteristic of joint ownership of property is that title inures to the survivor. (Tenants in common do not have a similar right of survivorship.) The title of the action may be amended by an order of the court showing that the surviving joint tenant plaintiff is the only plaintiff (Rule 25(c)).

■ SERVICE OF PROCESS

An action is commenced in federal court when the plaintiff files a complaint with the clerk of court. However, the defendant is not a party and is not subject to the court's jurisdiction until she or he receives an effective notice of the action by service of a summons and complaint. Principles of due process (fairness) require that the defendant have actual notice whenever possible and to the extent possible. Furthermore, the procedure must tell the defendant what she or he must do about the lawsuit. Rule 4 addresses these concerns and provides various methods for serving the defendant with legal process.

Procedure for Service

As soon as the plaintiff files the complaint, the clerk of court must give the case a file number and then prepare a **summons** (see Rules Appendix of Forms, form 1). The summons uses the full title of the action and the court's file number. The clerk must sign and date the summons at the bottom. The body of the summons directs that the defendant must appear in the case and defend against the claim, or judgment will be taken against the defendant for the relief demanded in the complaint. The summons directs the defendant to appear by serving an answer to the complaint upon the plaintiff's attorney or, if none, upon the plaintiff. The summons gives the proper address to which the answer may be mailed or otherwise delivered. The summons directs the defendant to serve the answer within twenty days or such longer time as the plaintiff may allow. Invariably, the time is limited to twenty days, unless the United States is the defendant. In that case, the United States has sixty days in which to answer. The twenty-day period does not necessarily begin to run on the same day that the action is commenced.

When the clerk of court issues the summons, the clerk gives it to the plaintiff's lawyer, who is then responsible for arranging prompt service on the defendant. The summons and a copy of the complaint shall be served together (Rule 4(d)). Service shall be made by a United States marshal, unless the court designates someone else to do the job (Rule 4(c)). Courts are directed to "freely" grant the appointment of other persons to make service (Rule 4(c)(3)). The plaintiff's attorney must provide the defendant's last known address to the marshal. If the plaintiff obtains an order allowing someone else to serve the summons and complaint, the person appointed must be at least eighteen years of age (Rule 4(c)(2)(A)). Under no circumstance may a plaintiff serve the summons and complaint upon the defendant. This is because the law wants to keep the parties separated, at least at the outset. Initial separation reduces the possibilities of violence and fraud. If the plaintiff served the summons and complaint, some defendants might react physically against the plaintiff or might falsify the affidavit of service to obtain a default judgment against the defendant. For these reasons, the United States marshal is the first choice for serving the summons and complaint in a civil action.

The summons informs the defendant that he or she has 20 days in which to appear and defend against the plaintiff's action. The defendant does not have to actually appear in court. All the defendant has to do is serve an answer to the complaint, or file a Rule 12 motion, or move the court for an extension of time in which to do these things. The clerk of court gives the summons to the plaintiff's attorney or, if there is no attorney, to the plaintiff. The attorney is required to arrange for service on the defendant as soon as practical. If a copy of the summons and complaint is not served upon the defendant within 120 days after the complaint is filed with the clerk of court, the action is subject to dismissal without prejudice. A dismissal without prejudice may nevertheless prevent the case from being sued again if the statute of limitations runs against the claim.

The defendant has twenty days in which to appear and defend (Rule 4(b)). She or he may appear in the action, within the meaning of the Rules, by serving and filing an answer or motion contesting the sufficiency of the complaint or of the service of process (Rule 12). If the defendant needs more than twenty days to prepare the answer or to decide what to do about defending the action, the defendant may make a motion to the court for an order enlarging the time. The motion must state the reasons more time is needed. Courts are quite willing to grant reasonable extensions of time. More commonly, the defendant simply contacts the plaintiff's lawyer and asks for more time in which to answer.

Many circumstances justify granting the defendant additional time in which to answer the complaint. For example, once a defendant's lawyer receives a complaint, he or she may need a few extra days to meet with the defendant, digest the factual information, and analyze the case so that the answer will adequately state the issues. An informal extension of time for answering helps everyone. The plaintiff's lawyer knows that the defendant can probably obtain an extension from the court, so the request is usually granted. The plaintiff's lawyer actually retains a little more control over the situation by stipulating to enlarge the time for answering. The lawyer decides how much time to give the defendant, rather than the court. If the defendant acts promptly to consult a lawyer or to deliver the summons and complaint to the defendant's liability insurer, the twenty-day period provided by the Rules should be sufficient.

Methods of Service

The summons and complaint may be served upon the defendant by personal service or in several other ways. These other methods are simple, fairly inexpensive, and reasonably effective for notifying the defendant of the suit.

Personal Service.   Personal service is the traditional and most sure method of serving the summons and complaint upon the defendant. Personal service may be made by handing a copy of the summons and complaint to the defendant, or by leaving the summons and complaint at the defendant's usual place of abode with a person of suitable age and discretion who also lives there. The summons and complaint may not be left at a place where the defendant is staying only temporarily, such as a vacation spot or a hotel room where the defendant is staying on business. The summons and complaint must be handed to some person. The Rules purposely do not require that the person who receives the summons and complaint be an adult. Historically, anyone fourteen years of age or older is presumed to meet the age requirements. A younger person may qualify, but if any question should later arise as to whether service was valid, the burden is upon the plaintiff to show that the recipient was of suitable age and discretion.

Suppose the defendant's adult sister is staying at the defendant's home for only a few days. Could the summons and complaint be effectively served upon the defendant by leaving the papers with her? No, because she is not a resident of the household.

When the process server is handing the summons and complaint to the defendant, if the defendant decides to be uncooperative and "turns her or his back" on the server, the server may simply leave the summons and complaint in the defendant's presence. There is no need to touch the defendant as if playing a game of tag.

The law does not require that service of process be made at any particular time of the day, but service must be made at a reasonable hour considering the circumstances. Service may be in the dead of the night if the defendant ordinarily works nights and sleeps days. There is no prohibition against service on Sundays or legal holidays.

Proof of service must be filed with the clerk of court before the time for answering expires (Rule 4(g)). If the server was a United States marshal, the marshal makes a record of the service of process in a document called the marshal's return. If a person other than a United States marshal serves the summons and complaint, he or she prepares an **affidavit** (sworn statement) that shows when, where, and how service was made. Specifically, the marshal's return and the process server's affidavit must show the date, the time, the place, the manner of service, and the identify of the person to whom the papers were delivered.

Service to an Agent. Some companies are frequently involved in litigation, so it is convenient for them to appoint a particular person or agent to receive service of process for them. Service on the company may be made by delivering the summons and complaint to the managing agent or office (Rule 4(d)(3)). A company cannot restrict the method of service by limiting its officers' authority. But a company may appoint a nonofficer, or even a nonemployee, to be an agent to receive service of legal process.

Also, an agent may be appointed by law to receive service of process for certain defendants. When service is made upon an agent who is appointed by law, the plaintiff must provide the agent with at least one additional copy of the papers, which the agent may send to the defendant's last known address or registered address. In addition, the plaintiff may be required to mail a copy of the summons and complaint to the defendant's last known address. Ordinary first-class mail will suffice, unless registered mail is specified by state law. The plaintiff or plaintiff's lawyer must file an affidavit of compliance showing that the mailing requirements have been met. The affidavit is prima facie evidence of compliance and must be filed with the clerk of court. Nothing prevents an individual from appointing another person such as a lawyer to act as a personal agent to receive service of process. This is a convenience for some entrepreneurs.

Most, if not all, states provide for service of process on the secretary of state as an agent for domestic and foreign corporations. By state statute, the commissioner of highways or the secretary of state is appointed to be an agent to receive service of process for nonresident motorists who have had motor vehicle accidents within the state. The commissioner of insurance is appointed by statute to receive service of process on behalf of any insurance company doing business within the state where the insured lives or does business. A copy of the summons and complaint are actually delivered to the official's office. The official stamps the original summons and complaint, thereby acknowledging receipt and admitting service. The office makes a record of the time of service and then sends the papers to the defendant.

Service by Mail. The summons and complaint may be served upon an adult individual by mailing a copy to him or her with two copies of a notice and acknowledgment of service. The notice must explain the service-by-mail procedure (Rule 4(c)(2)(C), form 18-A). The papers must be sent by first-class mail. The letter must contain a return envelope, self-addressed and postage paid. The defendant may elect to accept service by mail in this manner, by signing and returning to the sender one copy of the notice and acknowledgment. The notice informs the defendant to return the acknowledgment within twenty days; otherwise, the service by mail is without effect. The consequence is that the plaintiff will have to ask the United States marshal or a process server to make service. The cost of service may be taxed to the defendant if the defendant loses the case (Rule 4(c)(2)(D)). When service is made by mail, as described here, the date of service is the date of the acknowledgment signed by the defendant. The defendant is required to appear and defend within twenty days after the acknowledgment is signed.

The person who places the document in the mail must make an affidavit of service by mail. The affidavit does not have to include the title of the case. For an example, see exhibit 6.3. The original copy of the affidavit must be attached to the original document, which is filed with the court. It is highly desirable, if not essential, to attach a copy of the affidavit to the file copy of the original document, for future reference.

The notice of service states that once the defendant acknowledges service, the defendant must appear by serving an answer or motion within twenty days after acknowledging service; otherwise, the plaintiff may take a default judgment against the defendant. If service upon a corporation or partnership is made by mail, the officer of the defendant who accepts service must state her or his authority to accept service of process.

■ **Exhibit 6.3**

Form for Affidavit of Service by Mail

AFFIDAVIT OF SERVICE BY MAIL

STATE OF _____
COUNTY OF _____
_____ , being first duly sworn, deposes and says that on the __ day of _____ , 19___ , she served the attached _____ , upon _____ , the attorney representing the _____ , by depositing a true and correct copy thereof in the United States mail in the city of _____ , state of _____ , with postage prepaid, in an envelope directed and addressed to said attorney at _____ .

/s/ _____

Subscribed and sworn to
before me this _____
day of _____ , 1994.

In some state courts, the action is not commenced until the summons and complaint are actually served upon the defendant. In those states, if the plaintiff chooses to serve the summons and complaint by mail, the statute of limitations is not tolled while the defendant decides whether or not to acknowledge service. Therefore, the defendant's delay could cause the plaintiff's cause of action to become time barred. For this reason, if time is running short and the statute of limitations could possibly run out, the plaintiff should not rely upon service by mail; the plaintiff should use personal service. In federal court, the action is commenced by filing the complaint with the clerk of court, so there is no danger of running into a statute of limitations problem. But if the action is not perfected by service within 120 days after the complaint is filed, the action is subject to dismissal after service is made upon the defendant.

Service to a Guardian. If the defendant is a minor, service must be made in the manner prescribed by the laws of the estate in which she or he resides. Usually, service must be made upon one of the minor's parents or upon a legal guardian. The plaintiff may cause a guardian to be appointed if the child does not have one. A guardian who is appointed for the sole purpose of the lawsuit is called a guardian ad litem. Some states authorize service directly upon a minor at least fourteen years of age. A guardian ad litem may later be appointed for the minor.

Age is only one type of legal disability that may affect service of process. If a defendant has been adjudged mentally incompetent to handle his or her own legal matters, the plaintiff must serve a copy of the summons and complaint on the defendant's guardian. The guardian must act to protect the ward's legal interests. The guardian does not actually conduct the litigation. The guardian's responsibility is to select and hire a lawyer to represent the defendant ward, and to make decisions that are ordinarily reserved to the ward, such as whether or not to settle the claim. Some states require a guardian to be bonded so as to guaranty faithful performance on behalf of the ward.

Service on the Government. Service on the United States government requires at least two steps. The summons and complaint must be served upon the United States district attorney or assistant district attorney for the particular district in which the action is commenced. Also, copies must be sent to the United States attorney general in Washington, D.C., by registered mail or certified mail. In addition, copies of the papers must be mailed to all United States offices or agencies affected by the litigation. Again, registered or certified mail must be used. Service is not complete (effective) until all the requirements are met. Nevertheless, the action is effectively *commenced* by filing the complaint with the clerk of court.

The local United States district attorney may designate a nonlawyer to accept service for him or her at the district attorney's office. When that is done, a letter or notice must be filed with the clerk of court, naming the administrative employee who has been so designated.

A plaintiff cannot sue the United States government per se, but only its agencies as authorized by law. The various statutes creating the agencies designate the manner for service of process upon an agency and specify the proper person to receive service within the agency.

When a municipality is a defendant, service can be made upon the chief executive officer or in any other manner prescribed by local law.

Service by Publication.   The summons and complaint may be served by the United States marshal anywhere within the state of her or his jurisdiction, but not outside the state. If the defendant has left the state to evade service of process or is in the state but is hiding to avoid service, another method of service must be available to the plaintiff. In such cases, service may be made by publishing the summons in a newspaper having substantial circulation in the area. The methods prescribed are intended to give the defendant actual notice, especially if she or he is more or less expecting to be sued. Most state laws require the summons to be published for three weeks. As part of the publication procedure, the complaint must be filed with the clerk of court and be available for inspection. The plaintiff is still required to mail a copy of the summons and complaint to the defendant's last known address. The plaintiff's lawyer and the publisher must each file an affidavit proving that the notice was duly published and mailed. The plaintiff must file copies of the notice that was published. If the defendant can be found in another state, delivery in the other state may be tantamount to service by publication and may give the local court personal jurisdiction. In divorce actions, where the defendant is not a resident of the state, service of process may be made by publication. Recall that federal courts do not handle divorce actions or other domestic relations cases.

Service for an Action in Rem.   On occasion, the subject of litigation is land or other tangible things within the state. In such cases, the local court has jurisdiction over the subject matter, and anyone claiming an interest in the property, even nonresidents, can be compelled to submit to the court's jurisdiction or forfeit their interest in the property. A lawsuit against the property is called an action in rem. Service of a summons and complaint must be made on each person known to claim an interest in the subject matter. Furthermore, the "world" must be given notice through publication of a notice of the action. In these cases, no person is designated as a defendant. Nonetheless, anyone who claims an interest in the property must assert his or her claim by filing an answer, or the interest will be forfeited.

Service to a Lawyer.   Once a party is represented by a lawyer, all pleadings, orders, motions, and so forth must be served directly upon the lawyer. This is the most convenient arrangement for the parties and the lawyers. Service is made by simply mailing the documents to the lawyer at his or her last known address (Rule 5(h)). Service by mail is complete when the document is deposited at a post office or put in a United States mailbox. The date of mailing is the date of service. Whenever a pleading, motion, or notice is served by mail, the addressee is given an extra three days in which to respond—that is, three extra days from the date of mailing (Rule 6(e)).

On occasion, it is desirable, even necessary, to serve motions, interrogatories, demands for documents, orders, and other documents by personal service upon the opposing lawyer. Personal service is complete when the papers are delivered to the lawyer, wherever she or he may be. If the lawyer cannot be found, personal service may, nevertheless, be made by handing the papers to the lawyer's clerk or secretary or to a person who is in charge of the lawyer's office. Otherwise, the papers may simply be left in a conspicuous place at the lawyer's office during regular business hours. Alternatively, personal service may be made by leaving the papers at the lawyer's home with a resident therein who is of suitable age and discretion (Rule 5(b)). The person to whom the papers are given must be old enough to realize the importance of the matter and not inclined to forget to bring the papers to the lawyer's attention. Personal service on a lawyer may be ordered by the court whenever time is critical and short. The process server must make an affidavit describing the manner, time, and place of service.

Service to the Clerk of Court.   If neither the opposing party nor his or her lawyer can be found so that service can be made by mail or personally, service may be made by leaving the documents with the clerk of court. An affidavit must be prepared stating that the party and his or her lawyer could not be found. The affidavit should contain a brief description of the efforts made to locate them (Rule 5(b)).

■ DEMAND FOR JURY TRIAL

The plaintiff may demand a jury trial by "endorsing" a **jury demand** on the complaint (see exhibit 6.1, page 124). This simply means that the plaintiff may state on the complaint, in some conspicuous place, that "plaintiff demands trial by jury." If the plaintiff fails to make the demand in the complaint, she or he may still make the demand anytime within ten days after service of the last pleading directed to the issues to be tried. The defendant may demand a jury trial during the same ten-day period. For example, the plaintiff's demand may be made ten days after the defendant serves the answer. The demand may be made in a separate document, but the time requirements must be met. If the defendant demands a jury trial in her or his answer, the plaintiff need not make a separate or additional demand. A third-party defendant may demand a jury trial by endorsing the demand on her or his third-party answer, or in a separate document served within ten days after the third-party answer was served. Failure to demand a jury trial in the manner prescribed by Rule 38(b) results in a waiver of the right to a jury trial, and all the issues shall be tried to a judge without a jury (Rule 38(b)).

■ STATE COURT NOTE OF ISSUE

In federal court, the case is automatically placed on the trial calendar when the summons and complaint are filed. But in many courts, the case is not put on the trial calendar until one of the parties serves and files a **note of issue** (see exhibit 6.4). The note of issue informs the clerk of court that the party who files it is ready for trial. A note of issue identifies all the parties and their respective lawyers, so the clerk is able to send notices to the lawyers. The party who serves and files the note of issue may demand "trial by jury" or "trial by court." Trial by court precludes having a jury.

If the first party to serve a note of issue demands a jury trial, no other party needs to file a note of issue. A demand for a jury trial takes priority over the opposing party's preference for a trial by judge without a jury. If

■ **EXHIBIT 6.4**

Note of Issue

NOTE OF ISSUE

[Title of Cause]

To Defendant Sally Smith and _____ , her attorney,

   Please take notice that the above entitled action will be placed upon the trial calendar for the next general term of court for trial by <u>jury</u> at the district courthouse in and for said county in the city of _____ [state], beginning on the _____ day of _____ , 19___ .

_____

Attorney for Plaintiff

---

the first note of issue demands trial by court, any other party who wants a jury trial must serve a *counter–note of issue,* usually within ten days after the first note of issue, specifically demanding trial by jury.

   If the state court has terms of court, the state rules of procedure usually require service of the note of issue at least thirty days before the opening of the term, or the case will have to wait until the next term. This is not a consideration in courts that have a continuous general term of court, that is, where jury cases are tried year-round.

   If a party fails to demand a jury trial in the proper manner, it is still possible to move the court for an order setting the case for trial by jury. However, the *right* to a jury trial is lost. A court has discretion whether to grant the motion. The adverse parties may oppose the motion. The trial court could deny a motion that seeks a jury trial even if the parties reach an agreement that they want the case to be tried by a jury. This illustration points up the importance of making a seasonable demand for a trial by jury.

■ CONTINUANCE

In some instances, a case simply cannot be ready for trial at the time scheduled. Personal injury actions involving serious injuries or the probability of permanent disability usually cannot be evaluated until twelve to eighteen months after the injury was sustained. It may take that long before the attending physician can make a reasonably accurate prognosis. A trial at an earlier date might result in an unjust verdict for either side because of the difficulty in evaluating the medical evidence. The defendant may not want to obtain a Rule 35 independent medical examination until the plaintiff's injuries have stabilized and a prognosis can be made. If a continuance (delay) of the trial is necessary, the parties may stipulate to a continuance or show the court good cause why the court should order a continuance. A motion to delay a trial is not always granted, even when the adverse party does not oppose the motion. The ruling is discretionary with the court. One consideration is whether the moving party has already had one continuance of the trial. Time may be a natural healer, but the passage of time can only detract from a good cause of action or a good defense.

■ MOTIONS

Parties to an action may apply to the court for assistance or guidance concerning almost any aspect of the case. The application for an order is called a **motion.** Rule 7(b) states guidelines for making a motion:

(1) An application to the court for an order shall be by motion which, unless made during a hearing or trial, shall be made in writing, shall state with particularity the grounds therefore, and shall set forth the relief or order sought. The requirement of writing is fulfilled if the motion is stated in written notice of the hearing of the motion.

(2) The rules applicable to captions and other matters of form of pleadings apply to all motions and other papers provided for by these rules.

(3) All motions shall be signed in accordance with Rule 11.

Motions made during the course of the trial are usually made orally and "on the record." Motions made before or after the trial are usually made in writing. A routine written procedural or discovery motion must be served at least five days before it is to be heard (Rule 6(d)). A motion for summary judgment must be served at least ten days before it is heard.

A **notice of motion** must be served with every written motion, unless the motion may be heard ex parte. The notice tells the nonmoving party when and where the motion will be heard. A motion may be scheduled as provided by the local court's rules or by special arrangements made directly with the judge or the judge's clerk.

Paralegals may help prepare motions and supporting documentation. Rule 11 requires that the lawyer who is handling the case read, approve, and sign every motion, but that does not mean the lawyer has to draft the motion. Whoever drafts the motion should keep in mind that there must be a good basis for a motion. A motion must not be made for an improper, ulterior purpose.

Parts of a Motion

A written motion ordinarily has four parts, which may not be separated into numbered paragraphs as is customary with pleadings. The first part of the motion is the application, which tells the court what assistance and what order the moving party wants. The second part of the motion should identify the authority by which the motion is made, such as one of the Rules of Civil Procedure. The third part of the motion should state the grounds for the motion. The grounds are the underlying issues that cause the moving party to need the court's assistance or direction and the court's authority to provide that assistance. In the fourth part of the motion the party identifies the supporting documents upon which the motion is based, such as records, affidavits, and exhibits. The special rules of some courts require parties to serve and file memorandums of law before the hearing. A memorandum of law is a type of legal brief used to assist a trial court in dealing with an issue of law. Lawyers use memorandums of law to educate and persuade the court as to what the law is concerning a particular matter or how the law applies to the particular facts of the case. Most memorandums of law follow the same format or structure: the first section succinctly states the material facts; the second section is a clear statement of the legal issue or proposition; the third section is an argument that usually begins by referring to a legal authority, such as a written court opinion or a statute, and then provides an analysis for the court; finally a memorandum of law should end with a conclusion that states exactly what the author wants the court to hold or to do. In the absence of a special rule requiring memorandums, the responding party does not have to serve or file anything to oppose a motion.

Exhibit 6.5 illustrates the structure of a properly drawn motion.

Any documents that the moving party relies upon to support the motion must be served with the motion unless previously served and filed. If a document was previously served and filed, it is sufficient to merely identify it in the motion. If the nonmoving party wants to bring additional documents to the court's attention, to oppose the motion, the additional documents must be served and filed no later than one day before the motion is heard (Rule 6(d)).

Kinds of Motions

There is no apparent limit to the kinds of motions that can be made. Nevertheless, a few motions deserve special mention.

Motion for Judgment on the Pleadings—Rule 12(c). If a complaint, answer, or other pleading is insufficient to state a claim or defense, the opposing party may make a motion for judgment on the pleading, that is, may move the court to strike the pleading. For example, an answer that merely alleges that the parties' contract is unfair does not allege a defense. The answer would be subject to being stricken as insufficient. If the answer were stricken as insufficient, the defendant would be left in default. In this example, the damages claimed by the plaintiff may still pose an issue.

Motion for More Definite Statement. The pleadings tend to be very general in routine cases. Sometimes they are too general, and that leads to ambiguities and uncertainties. The parties have a right to know what is being claimed against them. One way of forcing an opponent to be specific and descriptive is to make a **motion for more definite statement.** For example, a complaint that attempts to allege a cause of action for defamation and merely alleges that the defendant has made various false statements about the plaintiff over an unspecified period of time is not technically adequate. The time and place of each defamatory publication must be stated

■ **EXHIBIT 6.5**
Motion for Order of Dismissal

MOTION

Defendant moves the court for an order dismissing plaintiff's complaint.

This motion is made pursuant to Rule 12 of the Federal Rules of Civil Procedure.

The grounds for this motion are that the complaint fails to state a claim upon which relief can be granted. The complaint fails to allege the claim of fraud with particularity as required by Rule 9(b).

This motion is based upon the allegations of plaintiff's complaint, which is on file with the court; the allegations and denials set forth in defendant's answer, which is on file with the court; a copy of the parties' contract upon which plaintiff's claim is based; and the affidavit of John Sutherland, which is attached hereto.

_____
Attorney for Moving Party

[date]

in the complaint (Rule 9(f)). The defendant is entitled to move the court for an order directing the plaintiff to specify each defamatory statement: what was said, when it was said, where it was said, and to whom it was published. Each publication is a separate tort. The court should order a more definite statement of the tort if asked to do so. The court should not leave the defendant to obtain the information through answers to interrogatories, because the missing information is fundamental to the cause of action. A motion for a more definite statement may be made as an alternative to a motion for judgment on the pleadings.

Motion to Strike—Rule 12(f).   It does not happen very often, but on occasion, a lawyer or party pro se may use a pleading to make a derogatory, impertinent, or scandalous remark about the opposing party. If a pleading contains such allegations, the pleading or the allegation is subject to being stricken upon motion. Because such allegations are subject to a motion to strike, lawyers are deterred from abusing pleadings in that manner.

Ex Parte Motion.   Making a motion is part of the adversary process. Consequently, most motions must be served upon all other parties in the case. The few motions that may be made to a court without notice to other parties are called **ex parte motions.** The most common ex parte motion is a motion to obtain an extension of time in which to comply with a court rule or court order. If the time allowed has not already expired, such a motion may be made. The motion must be in writing and must conform generally with the four-part format required for all motions. The grounds for the ex parte motion include an excuse and justification for being unable to comply and an expectation of compliance within a reasonable period of time, and the absence of prejudice to the opposing party.

The ex parte motion in exhibit 6.6 is illustrative.

■ **EXHIBIT 6.6**

Ex Parte Motion for Extension of Time to Answer

EX PARTE MOTION

Plaintiff hereby moves the court for an order extending the time in which plaintiff may answer defendant's interrogatories, which were served upon plaintiff on [date].

This motion is made pursuant to Rule 6(b).

The grounds for this motion are that plaintiff was out of the country on business from October 6, 1994, to October 21, 1994, and has not been able to gather the evidence requested by defendant's interrogatories. Plaintiff believes that an additional ten days would provide sufficient time in which to prepare the necessary answers. The case is currently one year away from trial. Therefore, defendant will not be prejudiced by a ten-day extension.

This motion is supported by plaintiff's affidavit, which is attached hereto, explaining that plaintiff was unable to attend to the preparation of answers to interrogatories while on his business trip.

A proposed order extending the period of time for answering is attached hereto.

_____
                                                              Attorney for Plaintiff

[date]

A copy of the ex parte motion could be sent to the opposing party as a courtesy. An ex parte motion is addressed to the judge's sound discretion. The motion may be granted subject to terms and conditions that the judge believes are appropriate.

■ SUBPOENAS

The Federal Rules of Civil Procedure provide for issuance of subpoenas in civil actions to compel any witness or party to appear at a specified time and place to testify. *Subpoena* means "under penalty." A subpoena is a command to appear subject to the penalties provided by law. A subpoena is used to give the court jurisdiction over a person who is not a party: generally, it is not necessary to subpoena a party, because parties are already under the jurisdiction and authority of the court. A subpoena may be used to compel a person to appear for a deposition or for trial. A subpoena may be used to compel a witness to produce records, books, papers, documents, or tangible things for use at trial or in a deposition (Rules 45(b) and 45(d)(1)). A subpoena must state the time and place for the witness to appear and testify.

Parties obtain subpoenas from the clerk of court. No motion is required. If a subpoena is to be used to compel a witness or party to appear for a deposition, it is necessary to provide the clerk of court with a copy of the notice of taking deposition along with proof of service of the notice (Rule 45(d)(1)).

The United States marshal or any person who is eighteen years of age or older and who is not a party to the action may serve a subpoena. A subpoena is served by delivering a copy of the subpoena to the person named in the subpoena. A subpoena may not be served by leaving the subpoena at that person's usual place of abode. It must be tendered to the person along with a witness fee and mileage. The amount for these is established by statute and changes from time to time. A subpoena may be served anywhere within the territorial jurisdiction of the court. In addition, a subpoena to testify at trial may be served upon a witness outside the judicial district, provided the witness is not required to travel more than one hundred miles from the place where he or she resides, works, or was actually served with the subpoena (Rule 45(e)). A subpoena that is used to compel a witness to give deposition testimony cannot be served outside the jurisdictional limits of the court that issues the subpoena. Furthermore, a deposition witness cannot be compelled to travel more than one hundred miles from his or her home, his or her place of employment, or the place at which he or she was served with the subpoena.

A couple of examples may help illustrate the application and limitations of Rule 45. Suppose the plaintiff needs to have the witness testify *at trial* in New York City, but the witness resides in Newark, New Jersey. Since Newark is less than one hundred miles from the federal district court in New York City, the New York federal court could issue a subpoena to be served in Newark. However, the New York federal court could not issue a subpoena to require the witness to travel from Newark to New York City for a deposition. The party who wants to depose the witness would have to travel to New Jersey to take the deposition there, and if a subpoena were necessary, the party would have to obtain the subpoena from the Federal District Court for the State of New Jersey.

A subpoena could be used to require a witness to travel from Rochester, New York, to New York City to testify at a trial, a distance of 369 miles. However, a witness could not be compelled to travel that distance for a deposition, even though the Federal District Court for the State of New York has jurisdiction covering the entire state of New York. Depositions are supposed to be taken at a place that is reasonably convenient for the witness, not the litigants. But if the resident of Rochester is found in New York City, while on a shopping trip, and served with a subpoena to appear in New York City for a deposition, the service would be valid and effective.

The person who is named in a subpoena has the right to move the court to quash the subpoena if it has been used for an improper purpose. If a subpoena requests production of documents or other things that the person named in the subpoena wants to protect, that person may send to the lawyer who had the subpoena issued an objection to inspection. The objection precludes the lawyer from enforcing the subpoena. Instead, the lawyer must obtain a court order requiring the person to produce the documents or things for inspection. The person who objects must serve the notice of objection within ten days after service of the subpoena, unless a shorter time has been allowed by the subpoena (Rule 45(d)). If the party still wants the opportunity to inspect the documents in question, that party must make a motion to the court for an order for production. The moving party must give notice of the motion to the person who served the objection to inspection.

Any person who wrongfully disobeys a subpoena may be held in contempt of court (Rule 45(f)). Only the court that issued the subpoena may make the necessary determination and impose sanctions.

SUMMARY

A lawsuit is commenced in federal court when the plaintiff files the complaint. The filing starts running the time during which certain things must be done. Furthermore, the time at which a suit is filed determines whether the suit was commenced before the statute of limitations has barred the claim.

A complaint must contain a short and plain statement of the claim, showing that the pleader is entitled to relief. It must state a cause of action. It must describe the occurrence or transaction and the time and place when the cause of action accrued. The complaint must state the type of relief the plaintiff wants and if the relief sought is money damages, the amount. The complaint must show that the court has jurisdiction. When the action centers upon a contract or promissory note or other document, it is desirable to attach the document or a photocopy of the document to the complaint and to incorporate the document into the complaint by reference. A lawyer must sign the complaint. If the plaintiff is acting as her or his own attorney, the plaintiff must sign it. The lawyer's signature is a certification to the court that the lawyer has made due inquiry and believes that good grounds exist for the action.

The plaintiff may amend the complaint as a matter of right during the first twenty days following service of the complaint. Thereafter, the complaint may be amended only by leave of the court or by stipulation of the defendant. The plaintiff may serve a supplemental complaint to allege new facts or claims that accrued after service of the original complaint.

The defendant must serve his or her answer within twenty days after service of the complaint, unless the plaintiff grants more time or the defendant obtains a court order for an extension of time. If the defendant fails to serve an answer in a timely manner, the plaintiff may take a default judgment against the defendant. The defendant's answer must admit the allegations in the complaint that are true, and may deny the rest. It must allege all the defendant's affirmative defenses. It must specify the relief claimed by the defendant. The defendant has a right to amend the answer within twenty days after serving the initial answer.

The defendant may assert her or his claim against the plaintiff in a counterclaim. If the counterclaim arises from the same transaction or occurrence that produced the main action, it is compulsory; in other words, it must be asserted with the answer or it is waived. If the defendant has a claim against the plaintiff that arose from another transaction or occurrence, the counterclaim is permissive—it can be brought in a separate suit. The plaintiff must respond to a counterclaim by serving and filing a reply to the counterclaim. The replay must assert the plaintiff's affirmative defenses to the counterclaim.

One defendant may assert claims against another defendant by serving a cross-claim upon the defendant. The defendant who receives a cross-claim must serve an answer to the cross-claim. The answer to cross-claim must assert the defendant's affirmative defenses to the cross-claim. The cross-claim must arise from the transaction or occurrence that is the subject of the action alleged in the complaint. A cross-claim may seek a remedy for a loss that the defendant sustained, unrelated to the loss or losses claimed by the plaintiff.

A defendant may bring a third-party action against another person to obtain indemnity or contribution toward the claim that the plaintiff has asserted against the defendant. A third-party claim cannot be used to assert a new, unrelated claim against a third person.

A plaintiff may include two or more claims in the complaint even though the claims arise from separate transactions or occurrences. The purpose of joining claims is to reduce costs and increase efficiency. Alternately, either party may move the court for an order joining two or more claims between the parties into one lawsuit. Separate lawsuits may be consolidated for purposes of discovery and/or trial if they involve common questions of fact or law. The purpose of consolidating lawsuits is to promote economy and efficiency for the parties and the court. Various factors may mitigate against consolidating cases, including untoward delay, added complexity, and potential confusion over the issues and evidence. Therefore, courts have broad discretion in determining whether to join claims and whether to consolidate cases for trial. Not every party always benefits from the joinder or consolidation—some parties may be harmed in presenting their claims or defenses by a joinder or consolidation.

Class actions are not generally favored because the procedure limits the parties' actual participation. Courts have to exercise close supervision over the representatives of the class to make sure the class is adequately represented. The prerequisites for a class action are difficult to meet. If a party wants to move the court for an order certifying the case as a class action, the party must show the court: the class is so large it is not practical for the separate parties to sue or defend individually; common questions of law or fact exist that affect the rights or obligations of all members of the class the same; the party that applies for certification is truly representative of the proposed class; separate suits involving individual members of the proposed class might produce varying or inconsistent results; a class action can dispose of all the legal and fact issues that exist between members of the proposed class and the adverse party; individual members of the proposed class do not have a superior interest in controlling the handling of the litigation; no other pending litigation would be adversely affected by certifying the class action; commencement of a class action would not unduly burden the court and would not cause prejudice to persons who might choose to have their case presented in another forum. When a class action is allowed, the court makes sure that the members of the class are given notice about the case, that their rights are protected, and that they are informed of their obligations. A class action cannot be compromised or dismissed without court approval (Rule 23(e)).

When a party dies, someone must arrange to have the decedent's personal representative substituted as the party, assuming that the cause of action didn't die with the party. Once the parties and the court receive notice of a party's death, the remaining parties have just ninety days in which to act to obtain a substitution for the deceased party. Otherwise, the action against the decedent will be dismissed (Rule 24(a)). Any party may move the court for an order for making the substitution. If a personal representative has been appointed in a probate proceeding, the representative may seek the substitution. If a party becomes legally incompetent to handle his or her business, a representative party must be appointed and substituted.

The plaintiff may serve the summons and complaint upon the defendant by having them delivered to the defendant or by leaving them at the defendant's residence with a person of suitable age. Any person who is eighteen years of age or older, except the plaintiff may deliver the summons and complaint. The person who serves the papers must make an affidavit of service.

The plaintiff may try to serve the defendant by mail. However, the service is not complete or effective unless and until the defendant acknowledges service. If the defendant refuses to acknowledge service by mail, the plaintiff's only remedy is to arrange for personal service. The plaintiff is entitled to recover the cost of serving the papers if he or she prevails on the claim.

The party who wants a jury trial must make a timely demand. In federal court, the demand may be made as part of a party's pleading. In state court, the demand is usually made by serving and filing a note of issue.

A party may invoke the aid of the court at any stage of the proceedings by making a motion. Unless the parties are before the court, in trial, the motion must be made in writing and scheduled for hearing at a time that gives the opposing party an opportunity to prepare for the hearing. A routine procedural or discovery motion requires at least five days' notice. A summary judgment motion requires at least ten days' notice. A written motion should state the relief or help that the moving party wants; the rule or authority by which the motion is made; the grounds for the motion; and the supporting documentation that the moving party relies upon. The special rules of some courts require parties to serve and file memorandums of law before the hearing. A memorandum of law is a type of legal brief used to assist a trial court in dealing with an issue of law. The key parts of a memorandum of law are: a summary of the material facts; a statement of the legal issue; an argument with reference to the controlling law; and a conclusion. In the absence of a special rule requiring memorandums, the responding party does not have to serve or file anything to oppose a motion. A party may make an ex parte motion to obtain an extension of time under the rules. An ex parte motion is any motion that is made without giving the opposing side notice.

A party may compel a nonparty to appear in the case and provide evidence by serving a subpoena upon the nonparty. A subpoena may be served by any adult other than a party. The subpoena must be delivered to the nonparty, or delivered to the nonparty's residence and left with a person of suitable age. No rule or statute defines "suitable age"; a person under eighteen years of age may qualify. A person who does not comply with the mandates of the subpoena is subject to being found in contempt of court.

KEY TERMS

count	intervention
ad damnum clause	summons
special damages	affidavit
supplemental complaint	jury demand
stipulation	note of issue
appears	motion
excusable neglect	notice of motion
compulsory counterclaim	motion for more definite statement
permissive counterclaim	ex parte motions

REVIEW QUESTIONS

1. What functions does the complaint serve?
2. Why must the amendment to a pleading relate back to the date of the original pleading?
3. What is the difference between a supplemental complaint and an amended complaint?
4. How does a defendant appear in a civil action?
5. What is the effect of a waiver of a legal right?
6. When is a counterclaim compulsory?
7. In what way is a third-party claim tied to the plaintiff's claim?
8. May a cross-claim be based upon a transaction or occurrence unrelated to the plaintiff's claim?
9. Who may serve a subpoena?
10. How are a summons and complaint served?

CHAPTER

7

EVIDENCE

Most civil lawsuits involve a dispute about some of the facts concerning the transaction or occurrence. In other words, the parties disagree about what happened, how it happened, or why it happened. A trial provides a forum in which each party has an opportunity to prove the facts by presenting evidence. The Federal Rules of Evidence require the parties to focus on the facts that are disputed and material to the case.

A fact is not the same as evidence of a fact. However, the difference is not always clear. A **fact** is a truth, something that happened, something that exists or did exist. A fact is an absolute, but the existence of a fact may be far from clear. Some facts can be determined with certainty, such as your present height and weight. However, most of the time, the facts material to a civil lawsuit cannot be demonstrated with such certainty. The best the parties can do is to bring to court evidence that tends to prove the facts. For example, how can you prove what your weight was three years ago? You may make an estimate; your medical records may indicate your past weight; your driver's license may be evidence of your past weight. These sources are evidence of the fact.

Evidence is anything that tends to prove a fact. To illustrate, though skid marks are not now available to be measured, their existence and length sometimes can be established by police records of their measurements or by photographs of them or by someone's memory of their measurement or by someone's estimate of their length. These forms of proof are evidence of the skid marks and their length.

The parties may offer evidence to prove or disprove any **material fact.** Historically, facts were classified as material or immaterial to the issues in the case. Some writers and courts now use the term *relevant fact* instead. A fact is material if it controls or at least affects an issue in the case. A fact is immaterial when it has no relationship to the issues in the case. For example, when two automobiles crash at an intersection controlled by a traffic light, a dispute may arise concerning which driver had the green light and which had the red light. The condition of the light is a fact. The fact is material in determining who had the right-of-way (had a legal right to the immediate use of the intersection) and who was required to stop. Is it material that the defendant was involved in two other automobile accidents that same month? Or is it material that the defendant received a speeding ticket two days earlier? These other facts probably are not material. They are not facts the plaintiff could try to prove.

Every civil lawsuit involves at least one ultimate question of fact that a **fact finder** must decide. An **ultimate fact,** such as negligence or proximate cause, is the fact finder's conclusion drawn from underlying, proven facts. An ultimate fact is a fact that in itself may determine the parties' legal rights and obligations. For example, if the evidence shows that one of the motorists in the preceding example drove over the speed limit and did not have control of his vehicle, those two facts would be the basis for finding, as an ultimate fact, that the motorist was negligent in the operation of the vehicle. The fact finder may also determine that the excessive speed and lack of control were the direct cause of the parties' accident. A determination that the motorist was negligent and that the motorist's negligence caused the accident is a basis for concluding that the motorist is legally liable (responsible) for the accident.

The evidence a party offers must be relevant. Evidence is relevant if it *tends* to make the existence of a fact more probable or less probable. Irrelevant evidence is not admissible at trial. **Relevant evidence** is admissible at trial, unless the evidence conflicts with an exclusionary rule of evidence. The exclusionary rules that prevent courts from considering certain evidence exist to promote truth, fairness, and various public policies. There is a good reason for each of the exclusionary rules, and often more than one reason. Their purpose is to help the court and parties (lawyers) determine when relevant evidence should be kept out of the trial.

The admissibility and use of evidence are highly technical subjects, but also very interesting. Certain kinds of evidence may be used in some cases but not in other cases. Some evidence must be presented in a particular manner. Some kinds of evidence are more persuasive than other kinds and, therefore, are preferable. A lawyer must carefully consider what evidence is available, its admissibility, and its probative value, when evaluating the client's legal rights and obligations. When the client's rights depend upon a resolution of disputed facts, the client cannot prevail unless the lawyer can obtain and present persuasive evidence to establish the facts upon which the client's case depends. The primary purpose for evidence is to prove a fact. The evidence should cause reasonable minds to believe that the alleged fact is true. But lawyers have in mind several collateral purposes when they present evidence. A lawyer hopes not only to prove the controverted facts, but to educate the jury about her or his client's claim or defense and to persuade the jury that the client's position is deserving.

Once the fact finder determines the facts (truth) from the evidence, the judge or jury must apply the law to those facts to determine the parties' legal rights and obligations. When a jury does this, its determination is called a verdict. The word translates to mean "to speak the truth."

■ CREDIBILITY AND PERSUASIVENESS

Suppose that the plaintiff's lawyer needs to prove that the defendant went through a stop light and caused the parties' intersection collision. Suppose four people witnessed the occurrence. The most emphatic witness happens to be the plaintiff's best friend, who was riding in the plaintiff's car and who also has a claim against the defendant. The police determined at the accident scene that this witness was intoxicated. A second witness was a pedestrian who was not looking at the traffic lights when the collision occurred but did see that the light was red for the defendant immediately *after* the accident. He does not know any of the parties but is easily confused and has difficulty expressing himself. A third witness was driving another automobile that was approaching the intersection from the direction opposite that of the defendant. This witness does not specifically remember the color of the light at the time the vehicles entered the intersection or when they collided, but she recalls that she was intending to stop. The fourth witness is the defendant. He was charged with a traffic violation but pleaded not guilty to the charge in traffic court. The problem is What witnesses should the plaintiff's lawyer have testify at trial? Who will the jury believe? Will the witnesses present conflicting versions? Will the witness enlighten or confuse the jury?

A lawyer must decide how much time and money should be spent to gather and present the evidence. Should the client have the benefit of one expert witness, or three? If the case involves a machine, should the trial lawyer ask an operator, an engineer, the vendor, or the manufacturer to explain its operation? Should a matter be illustrated on a blackboard or with an engineer's scale drawing or by photographs or by a simple model or by a working model or by all the above? Should the "thing in question" be brought to the courtroom? Should the jury be transported to the situs of the occurrence so that the jury can view it? Facts can be proved with any of the listed forms of evidence. Probably, not all the forms of evidence could be used together. The choice comes down to a judgment call that considers several factors, especially time, expense, admissibility, and persuasiveness. Besides technical considerations, a lawyer must be concerned with the likely effect the presentation will have on the judge and jury. Will too much evidence bore the jury? Will the jury feel that the evidence is trustworthy? What is the best order for presenting the evidence? Can a weak witness be "sandwiched" between two strong witnesses? The evidence should be presented so that it is understandable, interesting, and appealing. A lawyer must make many judgment calls concerning what evidence to use, when to use it, and how to use it.

■ FACT FINDER'S USE OF EVIDENCE

Courts instruct juries to consider the evidence as a whole in determining the truth, regardless of who brought the evidence to court. The jury may draw inferences from established facts, but the jury may not speculate about facts not proved by the evidence. The jury must not supply missing evidence by speculation and conjecture. Jurors may not, through their own independent knowledge, supply any apparent missing facts. For example, if the witnesses to an accident cannot remember whether the roadway in question had a painted centerline, jurors who are familiar with the roadway may not use their independent knowledge of the roadway to make that determination. However, jurors may use their experience in life to evaluate the parties' evidence. Jurors are not witnesses. They are not subject to cross-examination. For this reason, parties are inclined to strike jurors who profess familiarity with facts material to the case.

The reliability and, ultimately, the acceptability of courts' judgments are directly dependent upon the quality of the evidence the courts receive. Courts must have a rational basis for allowing and disallowing evidence, and they do. The facts must be material to the parties' dispute. The evidence must be relevant to the facts—it must tend to prove or disprove the fact for which it is offered. The evidence must have some guarantees of trustworthiness. Therefore, only competent witnesses are allowed to testify. Most evidence is presented under oath and is subject to cross-examination. The evidence must not be unduly repetitious and cumulative. Evidence must not be disruptive to the proceedings. It must not create "unfair" prejudice. Courts must be practical about what evidence is reasonably available to parties. It would be unfair to the parties to allow only the very "best" evidence.

■ RULES OF EVIDENCE

The procedures for proving facts and the rules of evidence exist to promote the truth, be founded in fairness, and be practical. The common law developed a battery of exclusionary rules of evidence to promote justice between the parties by making evidence more reliable. Congress promulgated the Federal Rules of Evidence on July 1, 1975. They are a codification of the common-law exclusionary rules of evidence. The Federal Rules of Evidence apply to all judicial proceedings in our federal courts. Many states have adopted a similar codification following the federal rules, in order to keep laws and procedures uniform throughout the nation.

The presumption is that evidence is admissible at trial unless the evidence violates an exclusionary rule. The burden to show that an exclusionary rules applies rests upon the party desiring to exclude evidence. A party must object to evidence in a timely manner. If a party fails to interpose an objection or if the objection is untimely, the trial judge usually receives the evidence. For example, if a party offers evidence that is hearsay and therefore subject to exclusion, the evidence will nevertheless be received unless a timely objection is made. A jury may base a verdict on any evidence the court receives, that is, allows them to hear.

The exclusionary rules preclude a court from receiving evidence offered by a party in the following instances:

1. The witness is **incompetent** or is disqualified from testifying because he or she

   a. has not taken the oath;

   b. is not mentally competent;

   c. lacks knowledge about the matter;

   d. cannot qualify as an expert.

2. The testimony lacks probative value and is therefore **irrelevant** because

   a. it is logically too weak;

   b. it is too remote in time;

   c. it is too remote in location;

   d. it concerns a collateral matter that could cause more confusion than assistance.

3. The testimony is **hearsay** because it is based not upon what the witness observed, but rather upon what someone told the witness. The testimony or documents contain unsworn statements that are not subject to cross-examination.

4. The testimony is **parol evidence** because it contradicted or changes the terms of a legally enforceable, fully integrated written agreement. Parol evidence is objectionable because it impairs the validity of written agreements that are intended to embody the full agreement.

5. The testimony would require the disclosure of privileged communications or privileged records. The privilege must be duly asserted by the person who owns it, or it is waived. The exclusion of privileged communications applies to oral and written communications. Matters to which a privilege may apply include

   a. communications between lawyer and client;

   b. communications between husband and wife during their marriage;

   c. communications between physician and patient about the patient's medical condition, and the physician's treatment records;

   d. communications between a person and her or his priest or minister for spiritual guidance;

   e. statements that require a witness to incriminate herself or himself.

6. The testimony lacks **foundation.** Before a witness may testify about a fact, it must be shown that the witness was able to make reasonably reliable observations concerning the fact. If the witness is to testify as an expert, it must be shown that he or she has adequate training and experience to render expert opinions concerning the subject matter.

7. Testimony is subject to objection and exclusion because a statute forbids the court to allow the evidence. A legislature or other rule-making body may establish a public policy against the use of certain evidence.

This brief description of the exclusionary rules is not all-inclusive. It indicates the areas of concern and some of the considerations that led to the exclusionary rules of evidence. A more detailed discussion of the application of these rules begins on page 179.

CATEGORIES OF EVIDENCE

Evidence may be categorized on the basis of its source, character, purpose, and other factors. The categories do not, in themselves, affect the admissibility of evidence at trial. The categories merely help lawyers and judges to communicate about evidence and issues concerning evidence.

■ TESTIMONY

The most common form of evidence is testimony. Testimony is a statement, oral or written, made under oath, subject to the right of cross-examination. A witness's statement that is not under oath or not subject to cross-examination might be received into evidence under some exception to the rules of evidence, but such statements are not testimony.

Ordinarily, only persons who observed or experienced a fact may testify about the fact. In other words, testimony is usually based upon personal knowledge. In an accident case, the speed of a party's automobile immediately before the collision may be a controverted, material fact. A witness's testimony concerning the speed of the automobile is evidence of that fact. The existence and length of skid marks may be a fact issue. A witness's testimony concerning his or her observations about the skid marks is evidence of that fact. In addition, the existence and length of skid marks may be circumstantial evidence of the automobile's speed, because they may make a certain speed more or less probable. Therefore, the skid marks may be evidence of speed and evidence that the motorist applied the brakes and of where the vehicle was when the brakes were applied.

Ordinarily, a witness who observed the automobiles immediately before an accident will be allowed to estimate the automobiles' speeds, because speed is a fact that the witness observed. However, witnesses who saw the collision would not be allowed to testify to the ultimate fact of negligence even though they saw the accident occur. The jury must make that determination in light of all the underlying facts proved by the evidence. In deciding the issue, the jury must determine whether the speed, as shown by the evidence, was a reasonable speed in light of all the other facts and circumstances. Similarly, the jury would decide, as an ultimate fact, whether the driver's negligence was a direct cause of the accident.

Of course, every rule has an exception. In certain types of cases, expert witnesses are allowed to give expert witness opinions that are the same as ultimate facts. For example, in a professional malpractice action, whether medical, legal, or engineering, an expert may be allowed to testify that the defendant professional did or did not act in accord with the standards of the profession, and that is the ultimate question of fact in a malpractice action. Similarly, in a products liability case, an expert may testify that, in her or his opinion, the product was unreasonably dangerous or defective. Again, these are ultimate questions of fact that the jury decides.

The oath a witness takes serves several purposes. It emphasizes the court's commitment to the truth and the witness's duty to tell the whole truth. When a witness is put under oath, the witness knows that she or he is not just having a conversation with the jury. An oath adds to the solemnity of the proceedings. A witness who makes a false statement under oath is subject to criminal prosecution for perjury, which is a felony. If a judge believes that a witness has testified falsely, the judge may ask the prosecuting attorney to investigate and bring charges against the witness.

A witness may testify to almost anything the witness observed through his or her senses. The witness must establish that he or she was able to perceive and comprehend the matters to which he or she will testify. Even a child of tender years may qualify to testify to facts she or he observed if the court is satisfied that the child appreciates the duty to tell the truth, had an opportunity to make a reasonably reliable observation, and did comprehend the fact. In addition, the witness must be able to describe what he or she observed.

A witness must be mentally competent to testify. The witness must not be under the influence of intoxicants or drugs when in court. But a witness who was intoxicated at the time of an occurrence may, nevertheless, be permitted to testify concerning his or her observations about the occurrence or transaction. The witness's state of intoxication goes to the witness's credibility (believability) but not to the admissibility of the witness's testimony.

A witness testifies by answering questions asked by the parties' lawyers. The lawyer who calls the witness to the witness stand asks the witness a series of questions, and the witness must answer the questions. The process continues until the witness has covered all the matters that the lawyer wants to cover. The lawyer controls the testimony through the selection of questions. The lawyer is supposed to keep the witness from interjecting statements that are irrelevant, unfairly prejudicial, or otherwise inadmissible. The witness only has to listen to the question and respond to the question. The witness has no responsibility for knowing what to talk about. The procedure for examining witnesses allows for the full development of a witness's testimony and prevents the witness from interposing improper evidence.

Witness examination takes two forms: direct examination and cross-examination. The rules of evidence apply somewhat differently to each form. A **direct examination** is conducted by the lawyer who calls the witness for her or his side of the case. A **cross-examination** is the examination of an adverse party, a hostile witness, or a witness who is aligned with the opposing party. A witness is considered to be aligned with an adverse party if she or he is related to that party by blood, marriage, or employment or has some other close association with the party. Merely disagreeing with a party does not make a witness a hostile witness or one who is aligned with the other side. As a general rule, a lawyer may cross-examine any independent witness who is called to testify by the opposing side. Furthermore, a lawyer may call an adverse party to the stand and cross-examine that party. Similarly, a lawyer may cross-examine a witness who is clearly aligned with the adverse party even though the lawyer called the witness to the stand.

A direct examination is suppose to be conducted without using leading questions. A **leading question** is one that suggests the answer desired by the interrogator. On direct examination, the testimony is supposed to come from the witness, not from the lawyer. Consequently, leading questions on direct examination are subject to objection. However, leading questions are often used to expedite a witness's testimony concerning necessary, but non-controverted, matters. For example, a lawyer may lead a witness by asking: "You are 25 years of age? You live at 425 Rose Street? You witnessed an accident on January 1, 1995? You are appearing in court today at my request?"

A leading question does not make the answer less acceptable as evidence. Consequently, in the absence of an objection, the answer to a leading question will be received into evidence, and the possible objection is waived. Though a leading question does not make the answer incompetent, experienced trial lawyers know that leading questions used in a direct examination of a friendly witness tend to overprotect the witness and reduce the authority, effectiveness, and credibility of the witness. If a lawyer leads his or her own witnesses, the presentation lacks persuasiveness. Most students of trial strategy believe that the jury wants to hear the witnesses, not the lawyers.

Leading questions are not only proper but necessary on cross-examination. Although witnesses have a tendency to simply agree with answers suggested by an interrogator, the law presumes that an adverse witness or adverse party will not permit herself or himself to be led by the opposing lawyer. Therefore, on cross-examiantion, leading questions are not subject to objection. By asking carefully phrased leading questions, a lawyer can effectively circumscribe a hostile witness's responses, because a witness is not allowed to answer more than the question before her or him. There is general agreement that this limitation on witnesses is a good one. It keeps the proceedings from becoming a debate or shouting match. On redirect examination, the witness usually has an opportunity to give any explanation that is really necessary in light of the cross-examination. The re-direct examination is the follow-up examination by the lawyer who called the witness to testify.

■ DEMONSTRATIVE EVIDENCE

Demonstrative evidence shows facts, in contrast to verbalizing facts. Any tangible evidence (exhibit) is considered to be demonstrative evidence. Demonstrative evidence may involve the very heart of the controversy, such as the product in a products liability case. For example, an allegedly defective tire may be the subject of the lawsuit. The tire in question is demonstrative evidence. If a similar tire is offered into evidence to make comparisons, it also is an item of demonstrative evidence. Photographs, diagrams, sketches, and models are common types of demonstrative evidence.

Tangible evidence that is directly related to the case is ordinarily received into evidence as exhibits. The jury may take those exhibits with them into their deliberations. Then jurors have the opportunity to examine the exhibits without the lawyers there to point out things or offer explanations.

In the preceding example, the defective tire would be an exhibit that the jury could examine during its deliberations. If the jurors found something from the exhibit that the lawyers and witnesses had not noticed or mentioned, the jurors could, nevertheless, consider it. The alleged defective tire is, in itself, evidence that proves facts. Not all demonstrative evidence (not all exhibits) proves facts.

Not all tangible evidence is allowed to go to the jury. Some exhibits are received into evidence and used during the trial solely for **illustrative purposes.** This means that the exhibit, by itself, does not tend to prove any fact relevant to the case, but it helps a witness to explain his or her testimony. Exhibits commonly used for illustrative purposes include photographs taken after the scene of the accident has changed, products that are similar to the one in question but have some differences, a freehand drawing that is not made to scale. A physician may use a model of the human spine to illustrate an injury to a vertebra or intervertebral disc, or use a model to show how a nerve injury occurred.

Illustrative exhibits need not be examined by the jury during its deliberations, because they are not evidence of anything. Indeed, they might actually mislead jurors who might come to think of them as evidence of some fact. In some cases, though, some judges allow illustrative exhibits to be used by the jury in its deliberations. For example, a photograph taken well after the scene of the accident has changed may show a particular feature of the scene that is relevant to the case, although other matters shown in the photograph may not pertain to the accident. The photograph would be received and not limited to an illustrative role. However, the jury would be instructed and cautioned about its limited application.

Suppose a large machine has been made the subject of a lawsuit. It is much too large to bring into the courtroom. The plaintiff claims that the machine is defective in design because it is top-heavy and dangerously unstable. Photographs that fairly depict the machine are evidence of what the machine looks like. A motion picture or videotape could be used to show its operation. A model of the machine may show physical characteristics, including the alleged built-in instability. All these items could be received into evidence as exhibits the jury could examine during its deliberations.

Photographs may be used to show the facts in issue such as, at an accident scene, the vehicles in their at-rest positions, skid marks, and vehicle damage. A motion picture of an airplane crashing would be graphic evidence. However, unless the motion picture tended to establish controverted facts, its effect would be to incite passion and prejudice in the jury without having any probative value. In such a case, the judge must decide whether the exhibit's prejudicial effect outweighs its probative value. A similar problem exists with the use of photographs taken to show the plaintiff's injuries in their acute state or photographs of the plaintiff while undergoing surgery. If the prejudicial effect of the photographs outweighs their probative value, they should be kept from the jury's view and consideration.

Engineers' scale drawings may be very helpful at trial to show sizes, relationships, and even functions. Often, the drawings are used by several different witnesses to illustrate each witness's observations. The jury could not possibly absorb and remember all the detail shown in the drawings.

Consequently, more often than not, such drawings become evidence that goes to the jury for consideration during deliberations.

Forms of demonstrative evidence that are encouraged by courts as time-savers are summaries, charts, and graphs for the purpose of reducing voluminous documents down to the essentials (Rule 1006[1]). The preparation of such summaries requires a thorough knowledge of the subject and the purpose of the evidence. Paralegals are often asked to prepare such documents.

Demonstrative evidence has the obvious value of psychological impact. Jurors are more likely to understand and remember the facts and a party's theory of the facts when it is used. Lawyers are always looking for new and better ways of using demonstrative evidence. Paralegals who have a good appreciation for the role of evidence and who understand the client's case can be very helpful in locating and preparing demonstrative evidence.

■ FACTS AND OPINIONS

Generally, courts require evidence to be factual rather than someone's **opinion** or belief about the facts. It is the jury's responsibility to draw **conclusions** from the facts observed by the witnesses. However, courts make some very important exceptions to this principle.

In everyday situations, people act and react more on the basis of their opinions or conclusions than on the basis of established facts. Many situations and conditions cannot be described factually in a meaningful way. For example, an experienced driver observes that an automobile ahead of her has stopped, so she knows she must stop before she reaches the other automobile. Most drivers would be able to bring their automobile to a smooth, complete stop at a reasonable distance behind the other vehicle without *knowing* the measured distance or the measured braking force. Similarly, a driver stopping in an intersection to make a left-hand turn knows he must yield to oncoming traffic that is close enough to constitute a hazard. A motorist in this situation must make a judgment concerning the oncoming vehicle's distance and speed. These judgments are usually quite reliable even though the motorist might not be able to estimate the number of feet or yards involved. But should a jury make a finding on the basis that a driver believed he or she had enough time to turn safely? If the driver cannot measure the distance or estimate the distance, should the driver lose the case even though he or she was right?

How does a person measure, factually, the slipperiness of a floor or the condition of lighting at a certain place at dusk? How can an eyewitness ever know, factually, whether another person is intoxicated or the speed of a passing vehicle? At best, the witness can have an opinion about the facts. The law was established by people to deal with human situations and institutions. It must, therefore, deal with human problems on human terms. When a condition or situation can best be described in the form of an opinion that is meaningful, opinion evidence is generally permitted. So, ordinarily, a witness who has personal knowledge about the condition of a sidewalk is permitted to express an opinion that it was or was not slippery.

1. The Federal Rules of Evidence use numbers in the hundreds, whereas the Federal Rules of Civil Procedure use numbers under one hundred.

In addition, the witness would have to be able to describe the conditions or circumstances that caused the slipperiness. Lighting conditions may be described in common terms such as *pitch-black* or *fairly dark* or *fairly light* or *bright.* These terms are probably more meaningful to a jury than would be scientific measurements. A lay witness who admits to some "worldliness" usually qualifies to express an opinion as to whether a person she or he observed was or was not intoxicated.

Eyewitness Views

Fact	Opinion
sixty miles per hour	fast
one mile	far or close
ten thousand candelas	bright
a specific color	dark or light
no variation	smooth
many variations	rough
ten inches, feet, yards, meters	a block (as unit of measurement)
ten inches, feet, yards, meters	wide or narrow
ten inches, feet, yards, meters	high, long, close, far
twenty decibels	loud or soft
crying	sad, depressed, unhappy, hurting
grimace, muscle spasm	pain
able to lift or move one hundred pounds	weak or strong
sixty watts	dim or bright
disfigured	ugly
in compliance	sufficient, adequate
out of compliance	wrong, mistaken

A witness cannot have a valid opinion unless he or she had an adequate opportunity to observe the occurrence, condition, or person in question. Only after the witness has shown that he or she is capable of observing, did observe, and is able to recall the observations may the witness go on to render an opinion about what was observed. In other words, opinion evidence requires a foundation. A witness would not qualify to give an opinion that a sidewalk was slippery owing to ice if he or she merely observed it at a distance or had not used it for over a week. A witness would not qualify to give an opinion that another person was intoxicated unless he or she observed signs of intoxication such as slurred speech, unsteady gait, loud and inappropriate conduct, loss of inhibitions, flushed appearance, odor of alcohol, or red eyes. A witness may express an opinion about the speed of a passing vehicle only if he or she observed it long enough and has sufficient experience to form a valid opinion about speed in miles per hour. In automobile accident cases, witnesses are *not* allowed to express opinions of speed in relative terms such as *fast, slow,* or *normal.* Nevertheless, if a party *admits* to going "too fast," the admission would be received into evidence against him or her.

The following typical jury instructions contain guidelines for evaluating testimony:

> You are the sole judges of whether a witness is to be believed and of the weight to be given to her or his testimony. There are no hard and fast rules to guide you in this respect. In determining believability and weight, take into consideration the following:
>
> 1. interest or lack of interest in the outcome of the case
> 2. relationship to the parties
> 3. ability and opportunity to know, remember, and relate the facts
> 4. manner and appearance
> 5. age and experience
> 6. frankness and sincerity, or lack thereof
> 7. reasonableness or unreasonableness of the testimony in light of all the other evidence in the case
> 8. any impeachment of the testimony
> 9. any other circumstances that bear on believability and weight
>
> In the last analysis, rely upon your own experience, good judgment, and common sense.

■ EXPERT WITNESS TESTIMONY

A person who has special education, training, knowledge, and experience in a particular subject or field *may* qualify to give expert opinion testimony. A physician's diagnosis of an injury may be the determination of a fact, or an opinion based upon apparent facts. A physician's determination of the cause of an injury or disability is almost always a matter of opinion. The preferred method of treatment is frequently a matter of opinion. A professional baseball manager, Billy Martin, testified as an expert that even when a batter uses due care in gripping the bat, it might inadvertently fly out of the batter's hands.[2] The types of cases in which expert witnesses may be called are practically without limit. There are also many kinds of experts, including scientists, accountants, farmers, carpenters, electricians, engineers, architects, physicians, mechanics, and machine operators.

Again, expert opinion evidence requires a foundation to establish that the witness has the necessary background and is sufficiently knowledgeable about the subject in question to have a reasonably reliable opinion. The judge must decide, in each case, whether the foundation is adequate. Competent expert witnesses often reach different conclusions. This difference of opinion is not a concern to the judge. If a sufficient foundation supports an opinion, the jury must weigh the opinion along with the other evidence.

---

2. The expert testimony was sufficient to overcome the permissible inference of a res ipsa loquitur case presented by the plaintiff. (A res ipsa loquitur case involves an occurrence that ordinarily would not happen unless someone was negligent. The term *res ipsa loquitur* means "the thing speaks for itself.") The claim was that the bat slipped out of the defendant's hands, so the jury should infer that the batter was negligent in controlling the bat.

Even though jurors are not experts, they may have to evaluate two or more experts' opinions and choose between experts. Jurors may conclude that none of the expert witnesses are believable. That has happened.

Cases involving claims of professional malpractice—medical or otherwise—usually depend upon expert testimony in at least three or four areas. First, experts must determine the underlying facts concerning the nature of the injury, loss, or failure. Second, experts must determine what caused the injury, loss, or failure. Third, experts must determine whether the injury, loss, or failure was due to negligence on the part of the professional. The expert witness must be familiar with the standards and practices of the defendant's profession. *Negligence* is synonymous with *malpractice* in such cases. A professional person is liable for the harm proximately caused by his or her negligence.

In some cases, it is necessary to go another step with the proof and show that a deviation from the applicable professional standards cannot be justified on the basis of professional judgment. When an expert gives such testimony, she or he is actually giving an opinion on the ultimate question of fact—telling the jury how she or he would decide the case based upon the information assumed by her or him. Historically, a witness was not permitted to invade the province of the jury by testifying to the ultimate question of fact. However, the law has changed. Rule 704 expressly authorizes such opinion testimony—even by laypersons. Perhaps a lay witness is now permitted to testify not only that the sidewalk was slippery, but that it was too slippery to walk upon. The courts have not yet established the parameters of this relatively new and somewhat controversial rule.

The following is a typical jury instruction that contains guidelines on how to evaluate an expert witness and his or her opinion testimony:

> A witness who has special training, education, or experience in a particular science, profession, or calling is an expert and, in addition to giving testimony as to facts, may be allowed to express an expert opinion. In determining the believability and the weight to be given such opinion evidence, you may consider, among other things
>
> 1. the education, training, experience, knowledge, and ability of the expert;
> 2. the reasons given for the expert's opinion;
> 3. the sources of information;
> 4. considerations already given for evaluating the testimony of a witness.

■ DIRECT AND CIRCUMSTANTIAL EVIDENCE

A fact may be proved by direct evidence or circumstantial evidence or both. The law does not prefer one form over the other. **Direct evidence** is testimony from witnesses who observed the facts to which they testify. Direct evidence also includes exhibits that, in themselves, establish facts. A witness's testimony that she saw certain automobile skid marks is direct evidence proving the existence of the skid marks. A photograph showing skid marks is direct evidence proving the existence of the skid marks.

Circumstantial evidence is *indirect* proof that depends upon principles of logic and common experience. The process depends upon deductive reasoning. Where one or more facts are established through direct evidence, it is *permissible* to infer, from them, the existence of other facts. For example, by proving through direct evidence the existence of skid marks, a party may prove through circumstantial evidence the location of the vehicles before impact and at impact. The skid marks also permit an inference that the driver applied her brakes at a certain point and, further, that the driver observed the danger at some point before applying her brakes. Or suppose a construction worker spent two weeks working near an electric power line and then sustained an electrical burn by contacting the wire. The circumstantial evidence permits an inference that he knew the wire was there and considered it to be dangerous, since he successfully avoided it for two weeks. The inference is permissible and valid, even though the construction worker denies that he was aware of the power line. Circumstantial evidence is really a matter of using common sense.

■ SUBSTANTIVE EVIDENCE

Substantive evidence is *any* evidence the jury is allowed to consider that is capable of supporting a verdict. It is distinguished from impeachment evidence and illustrative evidence.

■ IMPEACHMENT EVIDENCE

Impeachment evidence is received by a court for the purpose of testing the credibility of a witness. It is evidence that the witness has said something or written something or conducted herself or himself in a manner inconsistent with what the witness testified to in court. For example, if a witness testified that he observed the defendant enter the intersection without stopping for a red light, he would be impeached by the testimony of another witness who heard him say that he did not notice the color of the traffic lights at the time of the accident or that the *plaintiff* was the one who went through the red light. The second witness's testimony is not substantive evidence, but merely impeachment evidence, because the first witness's out-of-court statement was not sworn testimony subject to cross-examination. The second witness's testimony is sworn testimony subject to cross-examination, but not as to the truth of the first witness's observations— only about what the first witness said. If the jury chooses to believe the sworn testimony of the first witness, it could determine that the defendant did violate the traffic light. But if the jury believes the second witness, the jury is left with no substantive evidence from these two witnesses about the color of the traffic light. Only the first witness claimed to see the color of the light, and he cannot be believed, so these two witnesses have provided no evidence on the point.

A prior inconsistent statement of a party may be received into evidence to impeach the party. In addition, the prior inconsistent statement may be considered by the fact finder as substantive evidence. For example, if a witness heard the plaintiff admit that he went through a stop sign, but the plaintiff testifies at trial that he stopped, the *party admission* would be received as impeachment and as substantive evidence that the plaintiff did go through the stop sign.

■ HYPOTHETICAL QUESTIONS

An expert witness must base an opinion on facts that he or she has observed or on facts that have been proved through other witnesses and exhibits. Proved, in this sense, does not mean that the jury necessarily accepted those facts; it means that the facts have been received into evidence and the jury is allowed to consider them. Since an expert witness usually does not have personal knowledge about the occurrence and many other important facts, the question arises, how can he or she qualify to render an opinion based upon those facts? The answer is through the device of the **hypothetical question.**

A hypothetical question permits the expert to *assume* the facts are true, just as though the expert had personally observed the facts. The lawyer relies heavily upon the jury to find those facts from the evidence. Otherwise, the hypothetical question is without relevance.

Sometimes, the hypothetical question is very long, involving many paragraphs. The longer the hypothetical question, the greater the risk that it might fail—either because it is technically defective, not entirely supported by the evidence, or because it lacks persuasiveness. The jury is instructed, at the end of the trial, that the expert's opinion assumes and depends upon the truth of *all* the facts contained in the hypothetical question. If the jury should determine that any one or more of the assumed facts is not true or not established, the expert's opinion based upon the hypothetical question should be rejected. The cross-examination of an expert whose opinion is based upon a hypothetical question is often designed to show that the hypothetical question is incomplete, or that with the addition of other facts, the answer would have to be different. A cross-examination may also try to show that the expert is assuming each fact in the hypothetical question to be true, and the cross-examiner may be able to show later that one or more of those assumed facts were false. Sometimes, the cross-examiner is able to show that the hypothetical question contains facts that are contrary to the expert's own records or inconsistent with calculations or observations the expert has made. To some extent, the cross-examiner is also permitted to test the expert with additional hypothetical questions.

Hypothetical questions are almost always reduced to writing and previewed with the expert before she or he takes the stand. An experienced paralegal may help prepare the hypothetical questions. Each lawyer develops her or his own form and approach. As a general rule, the shorter the hypothetical question is, the more reliable and effective it is.

■ EXHIBITS

Any tangible item that a party offers into evidence for the jury to consider must first become an exhibit and part of the record. It becomes an exhibit only after a witness has identified it and has shown that it is relevant to the case. Once it has been given an exhibit identification mark, the lawyers refer to it by the marking, usually a number or a letter.

The following dialogue is representative of the necessary foundation establishing identity, authenticity, and relevancy of an exhibit. In this scenario, the lawyer is questioning a personnel manager of a company to lay foundation for personnel records. The lawyer has had the exhibit marked by the court reporter for identification.

Q: I am now showing you what has been marked as plaintiff's exhibit A. Can you identify that for us?

A: Yes, that is Mr. Albin Moyers's personnel file with the XYZ Corporation.

Q: Who has custody of these records?

A: As personnel manager of the XYZ Corporation I have custody of these records.

Q: How long have you been the personnel manager?

A: For the past ten years.

Q: Did you bring these records with you to court pursuant to a subpoena served upon you yesterday?

A: Yes.

Q: Have you brought with you all of Mr. Moyers's personnel records that are kept in your custody and control?

A: Yes.

Q: Are these records kept in the ordinary course of the business of the XYZ Corporation?

A: They are.

Counsel to the court: Plaintiff offers plaintiff's exhibit A into evidence.

Court to defendant's counsel: Is there any objection to the exhibit?

If the relevancy of the records is not apparent, it must be shown by indicating how the documents tend to prove controverted facts. When a party offers a record into evidence, he or she must have the entire record available so that any portions omitted from the offer can be examined, and perhaps offered, by the cross-examiner. Otherwise, facts might be taken out of context.

Once the original records are made available for examination, the parties commonly stipulate that photocopies may be received into evidence in lieu of the originals. The originals are then returned to their custodian.

In the following scenario, the plaintiff's lawyer is questioning the plaintiff to lay a foundation for a photograph the plaintiff took of his automobile after the accident in question:

Q: I am now showing you a photograph marked as plaintiff's exhibit A. Can you identify it for us?

A: Yes, it is a photograph that I took of my automobile.

Q: When was the photograph taken?

A: On June 7, 1994.

Q: Where was it taken?

A: At the Anderson Chevrolet garage.

Q: What portion of your vehicle is depicted in the photograph?

A: The rear portion of my automobile.

Q: Does the picture fairly show the condition of your automobile as it appeared after the accident?

A: Yes.

Q: Is the damage that appears in the photograph entirely a result of the automobile accident on June 4, 1994?

A: No.

Q: What damage is shown in the photograph that, to your knowledge, did not occur in the accident?

A: The photograph shows the rear bumper pulled back on the right side. That happened at the garage—maybe when the car was towed in.

Q: Otherwise, does the photograph fairly show and represent the damage that the rear portion of the car sustained in the accident?

A: Yes.

Counsel to the court: Plaintiff offers plaintiff's exhibit A into evidence.

Court to defendant's counsel: Is there any objection?

At this point, the defendant's lawyer is allowed to ask questions only about the foundation for the exhibit, that is, questions concerning the admissibility of the exhibit. Any questions about its probative value will have to wait until the plaintiff's lawyer has finished direct examination.

When a photograph is offered into evidence, it is desirable to have the photographer available to explain the method of making the photograph as well as its subject matter. It is well-known that the type of lens used in a camera can significantly change the subject matter's appearance, especially its depth and apparent width. Distances between two points can be made to look quite different depending upon the type of lens used. However, it is often sufficient, for purposes of laying foundation, to have a witness or party to the suit who is acquainted with the subject matter testify that the photograph accurately portrays the subject. Note that the photograph does not establish itself. It is just an extension of the testimony of the witness. The extent of the foundation that is required depends upon the purposes for which the photograph is offered and whether any actual dispute over it exists. As often as not, both sides want the photograph in evidence.

■ JUDICIAL NOTICE

A trial judge may take **judicial notice** of certain facts, and those facts are binding upon the parties and the jury. As stated in Rule 201(b),

> A judicially noticed fact must be one not subject to reasonable dispute in that it is either (1) generally known within the territorial jurisdiction of the trial court or (2) capable of accurate and ready determination by resorting to sources whose accuracy cannot reasonably be questioned.

For example, a judge may determine that December 25, 1994, fell on a Sunday or that a mile contains 5,280 feet. When the judge takes judicial notice of a fact, the parties do not have to present evidence to establish the fact. The judge simply tells the jury that it is an established fact that they must accept as true.

Suppose the plaintiff brought a negligence action for damage to certain property, and it becomes material to the case whether the accident occurred within the corporate limits of a municipality. If the precise location of the accident is not in controversy, the trial judge could take judicial notice of the fact that the conduct occurred inside or outside the corporate limits. However, any controversy over the location of the accident would have to be resolved by the jury from the evidence.

A court may take judicial notice of scientific fact. Examples: an object traveling at sixty miles per hour moves eighty-eight feet per second, water boils at 212 degrees Fahrenheit, Los Angeles is in the Pacific time zone. By statute, in some states, a trial judge is authorized to take judicial notice of a person's normal life expectancy as established by approved actuarial tables.

According to Rule 201, the court may take judicial notice of such facts whether or not the parties ask it to do so. In civil litigation, judicially noticed facts are to be accepted by the jury as conclusive. The judge may conduct a hearing in the absence of the jury to determine whether the fact in question is true and whether to take judicial notice of it.

■ SUMMARIES

Occasionally, litigation involves thousands of records and documents, the contents of which are essential to proving a claim or defense. More often than not, the parties do not have any real dispute about the contents, but they do differ on the effect of the documents or conclusions to be drawn from them. The discovery rules provide a means for reviewing and copying the documents in advance of trial. Rule 1006 authorizes a party to prepare a summary of the records or charts that may be received into evidence, in lieu of the original documents. The rule encourages the parties to conduct a thorough review of all the relevant documentation *before* the trial and thereby reduce the amount of time needed for presentation of the essential evidence from the documents. The rule authorizes the following:

> The contents of voluminous writings, recordings, or photographs which cannot conveniently be examined in court may be presented in the form of a chart, summary, or calculation. The originals, or duplicates, shall be made available for examination or copying, or both, by other parties at a reasonable time and place. The court may order that they be produced in court.

Summaries that are prepared for use as provided in Rule 1006 are not part of a lawyer's work product. They are discoverable and should be seasonably disclosed to all other parties to avoid unnecessary delay at trial. The original documents must be available for inspection and comparison. Paralegals may prepare summaries of evidence to be used at trial.

■ PRESUMPTIONS

Some facts may be established at trial by presumptions in law. The presumptions, unlike judicially noticed facts, are not binding upon the parties and the jury. A jury may find for or against a presumed fact.

Suppose the plaintiff has the burden of proving that a certain written notice was delivered to the defendant. The plaintiff may prove it by showing that the notice was sent to the defendant by United States mail in an envelope that was properly addressed, had the proper postage, and was deposited in a United States mailbox or delivered to a post office. Proving these facts and that the envelope was not returned raises a presumption in law that the letter was delivered to the defendant addressee. This is true even though the defendant denies receiving the letter. The underlying facts concerning addressing and mailing the notice must be established by a witness who has personal knowledge, or through business records. A post office receipt is not necessary but is helpful. The jury must decide whether the presumption of delivery is more convincing or less convincing than the defendant's sworn denial. The presumption exists because of the necessity of such proof and the probability that it is true.

As described by Rule 301:

> In all civil actions and proceedings not otherwise provided for by statute or by these rules, a presumption imposes on the party against whom it is directed the burden of going forward with evidence to rebut or meet the presumption, but does not shift to such party the burden of proof in the sense of the risk of nonpersuasion, which remains throughout the trial upon the party on whom it was originally cast.

In cases involving death, the law presumes that the decedent did not commit suicide. In cases where the plaintiff delivers personal property to the defendant's custody and it is returned in a damaged condition, the law presumes that the damage was caused by negligence on the part of the defendant. If the defendant fails to present any evidence explaining how the damage occurred, so as to negate any negligence on her or his part, the plaintiff is entitled to a verdict against the defendant. If the defendant does offer an explanation, it must be weighed by the jury against the presumption in law that the loss was caused by the defendant's negligence.

There are many other presumptions in law. Some have been created by the courts as part of the common law; others have been created by statute.

■ RES IPSA LOQUITUR

In a negligence action the plaintiff has the burden of proving that the defendant was negligent and that the defendant's negligence caused the accident which resulted in the plaintiff's injury or other loss. Ordinarily, the burden of proof is met by showing how the accident occurred. But once in a while, no evidence is available to the plaintiff to show how or why the accident occurred, because the instrumentality was solely under the control of the defendant at the time of the accident. The plaintiff's problem of proving negligence in such cases has been given special treatment by the courts.

Where the accident is of the type that, in itself, speaks of negligence on the part of the defendant, the plaintiff is given the benefit of the **res ipsa loquitur** doctrine. The doctrine creates a permissible inference of negligence on the part of the defendant. *Res ipsa loquitur* means "the thing (accident) *speaks for itself* of negligence."

For example, if a passenger train derails and crashes, the inference is that railroad employees were negligent because trains do not ordinarily leave the tracks in the absence of negligence. The railroad has the right to try to explain why it denies it was negligent. The doctrine has its origin and justification in the probability that the accident was due solely to the defendant's negligence and the evidence concerning the occurrence is more readily available to the defendant, so the defendant should come forward with an explanation. In most states, the doctrine does not shift the burden of proof. The permissible inference, however, is sufficient in itself to carry the burden of proof even if the defendant has an explanation that exonerates him or her from fault.

The following jury instruction on res ipsa loquitur is typical:

When an accident is such that ordinarily it would not have happened unless someone had been negligent, and if the instrumentality that caused the injury is shown to have been under the exclusive control of the defendant, you are permitted to infer from the accident itself and the circumstances surrounding it that the defendant was negligent. Before you are permitted to make this inference, you must find all the following:

1. The accident is of the type that does not ordinarily occur in the absence of negligence.

2. The defendant was in *exclusive* control of the instrumentality that caused the injury or property damage claimed;

3. The accident did not result from any voluntary act or negligence on the part of the plaintiff or some third person for whom the defendant would not be responsible.

The doctrine has applicability where a restaurant customer is injured by a foreign object in her food; an airplane passenger is injured or killed owing to an unexplained crash; a passenger on a railroad train is injured when the train derails or crashes into another train operated by the same railroad; a patient undergoes surgery and sustains injury to another part of his body during the operation; a passenger is injured when an automobile leaves the highway and crashes for some unknown reason; an elevator falls; city gas escapes from utility pipes; electricity escapes from an appliance under the defendant's control; a dentist's drill slips and causes injury to the patient's mouth; a surgeon leaves a surgical instrument or sponge in the patient; a baseball player lets the bat fly out of her hands, so the bat strikes another player. In the example involving the surgeon who left an instrument or sponge in the patient, a jury would be allowed to infer that the surgeon was negligent even though no physician testified on behalf of the plaintiff patient that a professional medical standard was violated. Most courts have concluded that laypersons are capable of making that decision without expert testimony.

The doctrine may have applicability in numerous other situations. In all cases, it must be shown that the defendant was in exclusive control of the instrumentality at the time the alleged negligence occurred. For example, if the defendant's building collapsed, damaging the plaintiff's property, and the defendant could show that the building was occupied by trespassing vandals at the time, the plaintiff would fail to establish the requisite of exclusive control by the defendant and, therefore, would not have the benefit of the doctrine. The doctrine may work in favor of the defendant against the plaintiff where the plaintiff has exclusive control of the instrumentality.

APPLICATION OF THE FEDERAL RULES OF EVIDENCE

The ultimate objective of the Federal Rules of Civil Procedure is the determination of each case on a just basis. Justice is accomplished when the truth is ascertained and the law is correctly applied to those facts (Rule 102).

Most of the exclusionary rules of evidence are merely commonsense rules that help to ensure that the jury's verdict is based on evidence that is factual, probative, the best available, and not fabricated for purposes of the lawsuit. The exclusionary rules are premised in logic, practicality, human experience, and human nature. The exclusionary rules cannot be applied with mathematical precision or certainty. Trial judges have a great deal of latitude or discretion in determining whether or not evidence should be excluded. When a judge has acted within her or his discretion, the judge will not be reversed. The trial judge may be reversed only for a clear abuse of discretion. The tendency is to rule in favor of admissibility, letting the jury decide what weight to give to the evidence.

If a party fails to object or neglects to move the court to strike evidence improperly received, he or she waives the right to complain. The party is not permitted to use the error as a basis for seeking a new trial or reversal upon appeal. An exception to the general rule is that if the error is manifest and extremely likely to have brought about an unjust result, the trial court or appellate court may take notice of plain error and grant relief by ordering a new trial or reversal (Rule 103(d).

If a lawyer believes that the court has erroneously excluded evidence that would be helpful to a client, she or he has a right to make an offer or proof outside the hearing of the jury. The **offer of proof** is nothing more than a statement by the lawyer or testimony of a witness showing the facts that would have been established if the evidence had been allowed. The lawyer's statement or witness's testimony is made part of the trial record and, therefore, may be considered by the appellate court in the event of a subsequent appeal (Rule 102(a)(2).

Objections to evidence are supposed to be stated in a concise technical form without argument. For example, a lawyer may state, "The question is objected to on the grounds of hearsay." A lawyer is subject to criticism by the court and possibly receives a counter objection if he or she argues, "The question is objected to because this witness doesn't have any personal knowledge about the subject matter and is only relying upon some highly questionable statement she heard or read." The objection is an argument. Lawyers are not supposed to argue the value, weight, or effect of the evidence until the final arguments (Rule 103(c)). They may seek leave of the court to argue their positions on the evidence outside the hearing of the jury.

■ MATERIALITY

Probably the most fundamental requirement of evidence is that it be material. Evidence is material if it has a bearing on the issues in the lawsuit. If one party attempts to inject into the case facts that do not relate to the issues as raised by the pleadings, the opposing lawyer should object on the grounds that the facts are immaterial. If no objection is made, that evidence may amend the pleadings by implication and change the issues. The pleadings are then construed to conform to the evidence, rather than vice versa (Rule 15(b)). A judge may exclude immaterial evidence on his or her own motion to keep the parties from digressing and to avoid abuses of the court's time.

■ RELEVANCY

To be admissible, evidence must be relevant. This means the evidence must be material *and* have probative value. Rule 401 defines relevant evidence as "evidence having any tendency to make the existence of any fact that is of consequence to the determination of the action more probable or less probable than it would be without the evidence." If the evidence does not tend to prove or disprove a controverted fact, the evidence is subject to exclusion on the grounds that it is irrelevant.

Relevance may be determined by such factors as time and distance. For example, if a witness observed a motor vehicle traveling at a high rate of speed when it was ten miles away from the point where it was subsequently involved in an accident, the question arises whether this evidence would logically tend to prove excessive speed at the time of the accident or how the accident occurred. The answer is not always easy. If the observation was made on a freeway, so the driver had no occasion to change speeds during the ten miles, maybe the evidence would be relevant. But if the driver had traffic and traffic controls to deal with while traveling the ten miles, as in a typical urban area, the prior excessive speed is probably irrelevant.

The law presumes that parties involved in an accident were sober. A claim of intoxication must be proved. Evidence that proves that the defendant motorist is a drunkard and that he was drunk during the day preceding the accident in question would not tend to prove that the defendant was drunk at the time of the accident. The evidence is too remote in time. The prejudicial effect of the evidence would outweigh its probative value. However, if other competent evidence proved that the defendant was drunk at the time of the accident and the defendant controverted that evidence, perhaps the defendant's habit of drinking and recent intoxication would be relevant (Rule 406—Habit; Routine Practice).

Evidence that the defendant was involved in a similar accident at the same place three years earlier does not tend to prove how or why the accident in question occurred. However, where the alleged cause of the accident, such as a defective step, has caused other accidents, proof of the prior accidents is relevant to prove that the conditions were dangerous, were known to the defendant, and have the capacity to cause an accident of the type in question. The courts usually distinguish between animate and inanimate causes of accidents when determining relevancy.

The absence of prior accidents may be relevant. Suppose a visitor in an apartment building falls on a common stairway and contents that the accident was due to inadequate lighting. The landlord will be allowed to present evidence that the stairway was frequently used; the lights in use at the time of the accident had been in use for ten years; and no one else ever reported a fall due to insufficient lighting. This example assumes that all the lights for the stairway were working at the time of the accident.

Proof that the defendant was found liable on other contracts, which she contested, does not prove she is liable on the one in question. Evidence that shows that the defendant had one beer before the accident should be excluded unless it can be shown that the party's conduct was actually affected by the alcohol. Irrelevant evidence tends to cloud and confuse the issues. Too often, it has a prejudicial effect because it raises innuendos of wrongdoing without any factual basis. If the evidence does not adversely affect the opposing party, it probably should not even be offered; it is probably immaterial. So courts must balance the probative value against the prejudicial effect of evidence when determining relevancy.

■ BEST EVIDENCE

Courts require the parties to present the best evidence reasonably available. This means that a copy of a document should not be used if the original document is reasonably available (Rule 1002—Requirement of Original). Otherwise, copies of documents are subject to the objection that they are not the best evidence. If the absence of the original can be explained, then a copy is the best evidence and may be used. For example, if it can be shown that the opponent was the last to have custody of the original or that the original is needed elsewhere, a copy may be used. Parties may stipulate to the use of copies, and that is often done in cases involving hospital and business records.

■ HEARSAY

Hearsay evidence is any out-of-court statement, oral or written, that is offered to prove the truth of matters referred to in the out-of-court statement. The rule excluding hearsay is logical and goes to the very heart of the adversary system. Facts should be established through witnesses who have first-hand knowledge about them. Juries should assess the powers of observation, memory, and truthfulness of those witnesses, not of another person who heard the observer's description of the facts. Hearsay evidence deprives the parties of the *right* of cross-examination.

The basic rule against hearsay and its application is fairly simple. The numerous important exceptions to the hearsay rule are what create the difficulties for lawyers and the courts. The exceptions are based upon the usual reliability of some kinds of hearsay evidence and the convenience of using it.

Historically any statement made by an adverse party could be received into evidence against that party as an admission. Admissions were received into evidence as an exception to the hearsay rule. Rule 108(d)(2) provides that such admissions shall be received into evidence on the basis that they are not hearsay. An admission may be made by the party or by the party's agent who had authority to make such statements. The admission by an agent must be made during the agency relationship. Rule 801(d)(1) provides that prior out-of-court statements made by a witness may be received into evidence as substantive evidence, not merely impeachment, if they were under oath and subject to cross-examination. Such prior statements would have to be part of a deposition or testimony at a hearing or a trial. Again, the rule declares such statements not to be hearsay.

■ PAROL EVIDENCE

When the parties enter into a written contract that purports to contain the entire agreement, it would be unfair to have either party attempt, at trial, to change the terms of that agreement by oral testimony. Consequently, an exclusionary rule of evidence has evolved, known as the parol evidence rule, that precludes any evidence that attempts to vary or contradict the clear language of a writing that the parties have used to formalize their agreement. The rule applies to contracts, promissory notes, mortgages, deeds, wills, and so forth.

One exception to the rule is that parol evidence may be received to clarify ambiguities in the writing. But a judge must first determine that the writing is ambiguous, that is, reasonably subject to more than one meaning. Also, parol evidence may be used to prove that the written document was induced or procured by fraud by the other party. A contract may be set aside (rescinded) where there is a mutual mistake by the parties, if the mutual mistake goes to the very heart of the contract. Proof of a mutual mistake must be established by clear and convincing evidence—not by a mere preponderance of the evidence. Parol evidence may be received to establish a subsequent change in the contract mutually agreed to by the parties. However, most formal written agreements or undertakings expressly provide that any modification must be in writing and signed by all parties.

■ DEAD MAN STATUTE

Some states have the so-called dead man statute, which provides that a party to a lawsuit may not testify concerning any oral statement she or he heard another person make if, at the time of trial, the person who made the utterance is deceased. The statute is intended to reduce the possibility that parties may fabricate evidence. If a party fails to object to such testimony when it is presented, the evidence will be received, and a verdict may be based upon it. In other words, the exclusionary rule created by the statute must be asserted in a timely manner at trial, or the statutory prohibition is waived. Note that the exclusionary rule applies only to prevent *parties* from testifying. It does not prevent independent witnesses from testifying about oral statements made by persons who died before trial. The dead man statute has no application to writings; it applies only to oral statements.

The Federal Rules of Evidence do not recognize the dead man statute.

■ SETTLEMENT NEGOTIATIONS

Some evidence is excluded because it would be contrary to public policy to allow its use at trial. A primary example is evidence of another party's statements made in the course of settlement negotiations (Rule 408—Compromise and Offers to Compromise). The courts want parties to discuss their differences and to settle their controversies without having to go through a trial, if possible. Settlement negotiations are good. If parties had to labor under the fear that their efforts to compromise would be used against them, negotiations would be sharply curtailed, if not impossible. Therefore, a jury is never told about the parties' negotiations. The danger is much too great that a jury would be unduly influenced by such knowledge.

Rule 409 goes on to provide that a party's offer to pay another's medical expenses may not be used against the offeror as an admission of liability for the accident in question. A typical situation is where a person falls down on premises where he or she is visiting. The owner of the premises may suggest, even urge, the guest to have a medical checkup, which the owner will pay for. The suggestion cannot be used against the offeror as an admission of fault. It may, however, be proved for the purpose of holding the offeror to his or her promise.

■ REMEDIAL MEASURES

In a personal injury action involving a dangerous condition of a building, such as a poorly lit stairway, the plaintiff would undoubtedly benefit from evidence showing that immediately after the accident, the defendant remedied the condition. Such evidence would help to show that the defendant considered the condition to be dangerous; otherwise, no repairs would have been needed. The inference is that a reasonable person would have repaired the condition *before* the accident. The evidence would help the plaintiff to meet her or his burden of proving that the condition was unreasonably dangerous.

On the other hand, if the courts were to allow evidence of remedial measures, defendants would be discouraged from making changes that may provide greater safety in the future. Furthermore, it is human nature to be extra careful about conditions once an accident has occurred. Remedial measures are often taken not because they are really necessary, but because they are some kind of insurance against the accident's happening again. Furthermore, a party's standard of care should not be judged on the basis of hindsight. Public policy considerations have led the courts to exclude evidence of *most* remedial measures (Rule 407—Subsequent Remedial Measures).

Where changes have been made after an accident, the defendant's lawyer usually brings that fact to the attention of the court at the very beginning of the trial and asks the court to order the plaintiff and the plaintiff's witnesses to avoid any reference to the changes. Evidence of the changes could be so prejudicial as to require a mistrial. Proof that the condition was dangerous will have to come from some other source or be accomplished in some other manner.

In cases where a dispute develops as to whether a product is unreasonably dangerous, one consideration may be the cost of changes to make the product safe. If the cost is prohibitive, the manufacturer may be excused for not eliminating the hazard. Evidence of subsequent improvements in products liability cases is allowed where the defendant claims that the changes, which would have prevented the plaintiff's accident, would have been too expensive to be justifiable. Proof that the defendant made changes after the accident is very persuasive evidence that the expense was not prohibitive. The remedial measures evidence is received, in those cases, to impeach the defendant's claim that the cost was prohibitive. This exception to the remedial measures exclusionary rules does not come into effect unless invoked by the defendant. The defendant can avoid any evidence of the changes in the product simply by not claiming that the cost of the changes would have been prohibitive before the accident.

Evidence of remedial measures is permissible whenever the defendant contends that it was not feasible to make the product or premises safe. For example, suppose the manufacturer of a drill press claims, by way of defense, that it was not feasible to install the type of guard that the plaintiff's expert says was needed and without which the drill press was a defective product. The plaintiff could offer into evidence proof that the defendant modified the product after the accident by installing that type of guard. Again, the evidence of remedial measures is received on the basis that it impeaches the defendant's claim that the guard was not feasible.

Evidence that the defendant made subsequent changes to the property involved in the plaintiff's accident may be admissible to prove that the defendant was an owner of the property. The evidence is admissible to prove ownership only if the defendant who made the repairs or changes after the accident denies that he or she was the owner of the property (Rule 407).

■ EVIDENCE OF CONDUCT

Admissions may be made by conduct or silence. These are sometimes called verbal acts. For example, immediately following an automobile accident, one driver might accuse the other of failing to signal or failing to stop for a stop sign. If the person accused of wrongdoing fails to respond by denying the accusation, her or his silence, under some circumstances, may be considered to be an admission that the accusation was true. The test is whether under the circumstances, one would ordinarily expect a denial if the accusation were false. Perhaps the party was hard of hearing or incapacitated due to injuries—then silence could not be considered to be an admission of fault.

If a party's "admission" is offered into evidence against him or her and came from a written statement, deposition, oral conversation, and so forth, the party who made the admission has a right to introduce into evidence the entire conversation or entire statement insofar as it relates to the "admission" in dispute. The Rules of Evidence do not allow parties to take alleged admissions out of context.

■ HEARSAY EXCEPTIONS

Rules 803 and 804 undertake to codify many of the exceptions to the hearsay rule. The hearsay definitions, rules, and exceptions are quoted here for convenient reference.

Definitions

RULE 801

The following definitions apply under this article:

- **(a) Statement.** A "statement" is (1) an oral or written assertion or (2) nonverbal conduct of a person, if it is intended by him as an assertion.
- **(b) Declarant.** A "declarant" is a person who makes a statement.
- **(c) Hearsay.** "Hearsay" is a statement, other than one made by the defendant while testifying at the trial or hearing, offered into evidence to prove the truth of the matter asserted.
- **(d) Statements which are not hearsay.** A statement is not hearsay if:
  - **(1) Prior statement by witness.** The declarant testifies at the trial or hearing and is subject to cross-examination concerning the statement, and the statement is (A) inconsistent with his testimony, and was given under oath subject to the penalty of perjury at a trial, hearing, or other proceeding, or in a deposition, or (B) consistent with his testimony and is offered to rebut an express or implied charge against him of recent fabrication or improper influence or motive, or

(2) **Admission by party-witness.** The statement is offered against a party and is (A) his own statement, in either his individual or a representative capacity or, (B) a statement of which he has manifested his adoption or belief in its truth, or (C) a statement by a person authorized by him to make a statement concerning the subject, or (D) a statement by his agent or servant concerning a matter within the scope of his agency or employment, made during the existence of the relationship, or (E) a statement by a co-conspirator of a party during the course and in furtherance of the conspiracy.

RULE 802

Hearsay Rule

Hearsay is not admissible except as provided by these rules or by other rules prescribed by the Supreme Court pursuant to statutory authority or by Act of Congress.

RULE 803

Hearsay Exceptions; Availability of Declarant Immaterial

The following are not excluded by the hearsay rule, even though the declarant is available as a witness:

(1) **Present sense impression.** A statement describing or explaining an event or condition made while the declarant was perceiving the event or condition, or immediately thereafter.

(2) **Excited utterance.** A statement relating to a startling event or condition made while the declarant was under the stress of excitement caused by the event or condition.

(3) **Then existing mental, emotional, or physical condition.** A statement of the declarant's then existing state of mind, emotion, sensation, or physical condition (such as intent, plan, motive, design, mental feeling, pain, and bodily health), but not including a statement of memory or belief to prove the fact remembered or believed unless it relates to the execution, revocation, identification, or terms of declarant's will.

(4) **Statements for purposes of medical diagnosis or treatment.** Statements made for purposes of medical diagnosis or treatment and describing medical history, or past or present symptoms, pain, or sensations, or the inception or general character of the cause or external source thereof insofar as reasonably pertinent to diagnosis or treatment.

(5) **Recorded recollection.** A memorandum or record concerning a matter about which a witness once had knowledge but now has insufficient recollection to enable him to testify fully and accurately, shown to have been made or adopted by the witness when the matter was fresh in his or her memory and to reflect that knowledge correctly. If admitted, the memorandum or record may be read into evidence but may not itself be received as an exhibit unless offered by an adverse party.

(6) **Records of regularly conducted activity.** A memorandum, report, record, or data compilation, in any form, of acts, events, conditions, opinions, or diagnoses, made at or near the time by, or from information transmitted by, a person with knowledge, if kept in the course of a regularly conducted business activity, and if it was the regular practice of that business activity

to make the memorandum, report, record, or data compilation, all as shown by the testimony of the custodian or other qualified witness, unless the source of information or the method or circumstances of preparation indicate lack of trustworthiness. The term "business" as used in this paragraph includes business, institution, association, profession, occupation, and calling of every kind, whether or not conducted for profit.

(7) **Absence of entry in records kept in accordance with the provisions of paragraph (6).** Evidence that a matter is not included in the memoranda, reports, records, or data compilations, in any form, kept in accordance with the provisions of paragraph (6), to prove the nonoccurrence or nonexistence of the matter, if the matter was of a kind of which a memorandum, report, record, or data compilation was regularly made and preserved, unless the sources of information or other circumstances indicate lack of trustworthiness.

(8) **Public records and reports.** Records, reports, statements, or data compilations, in any form, of public offices or agencies, setting forth (A) the activities of the office or agency, or (B) matters observed pursuant to duty imposed by law as to which matters there was a duty to report, excluding, however, in criminal cases matters observed by police officers and other law enforcement personnel, or (C) in civil actions and proceedings and against the government in criminal cases, factual findings resulting from an investigation made pursuant to authority granted by law, unless the sources of information or other circumstances indicate lack of trustworthiness.

(9) **Records of vital statistics.** Records or data compilations, in any form, of births, fetal deaths, deaths, or marriages, if the report thereof was made to a public office pursuant to requirements of law.

(10) **Absence of public record or entry.** To prove the absence of a record, report, statement, or data compilation, in any form, or the nonoccurrence or nonexistence of a matter of which a record, report, statement, or data compilation, in any form, was regularly made and preserved by a public office or agency, evidence in the form of a certification in accordance with Rule 902, or testimony, that diligent search failed to disclose the record, report, statement, or data compilation, or entry.

(11) **Records of religious organizations.** Statements of births, marriages, divorces, deaths, legitimacy, ancestry, relationship by blood or marriage, or other similar facts of personal or family history, contained in a regularly kept record of a religious organization.

(12) **Marriage, baptismal, and similar certificates.** Statements of fact contained in a certificate that the maker performed a marriage or other ceremony or administered a sacrament, made by a clergyman, public official, or other person authorized by the rules or practices of a religious organization or by law to perform the act certified, and purporting to have been issued at the time of the act or within a reasonable time thereafter.

(13) **Family records.** Statements of fact concerning personal or family history contained in family Bibles, genealogies, charts, engravings on rings, inscriptions on family portraits, engravings on urns, crypts, or tombstones, or the like.

(14) **Records of documents affecting an interest in property.** The record of a document purporting to establish or affect an interest in property, as proof of the content of the original recorded document and its execution and delivery by each person by whom it purports to have been executed, if the

record is a record of a public office and an applicable statute authorizes the recording of documents of that kind in that office.

(15) Statements in documents affecting an interest in property. A statement contained in a document purporting to establish or affect an interest in property if the matter stated was relevant to the purpose of the document, unless dealings with the property since the document was made have been inconsistent with the truth of the statement or the purport of the document.

(16) Statements in ancient documents. Statements in a document in existence twenty years or more the authenticity of which is established.

(17) Market reports, commercial publications. Market quotations, tabulations, lists, directories, or other published compilations, generally used and relied upon by the public or by persons in particular occupations.

(18) Learned treatises. To the extent called to the attention of an expert witness upon cross-examination or relied upon by him in direct examination, statements contained in published treatises, periodicals, or pamphlets on a subject of history, medicine, or other science or art, established as a reliable authority by the testimony or admission of the witness or by other expert testimony or by judicial notice. If admitted, the statements may be read into evidence but may not be received as exhibits.

(19) Reputation concerning personal or family history. Reputation among members of his family by blood, adoption, or marriage, or among his associates, or in the community, concerning a person's birth, adoption, marriage, divorce, death, legitimacy, relationship by blood, adoption, or marriage, ancestry, or other similar fact of his personal or family history.

(20) Reputation concerning boundaries or general history. Reputation in a community, arising before the controversy, as to boundaries of or customs affecting lands in the community, and reputation as to events of general history important to the community or state or nation in which located.

(21) Reputation as to character. Reputation of a person's character among his associates or in the community.

(22) Judgment of previous conviction. Evidence of a final judgment, entered after a trial or upon a plea of guilty (but not upon a plea of nolo contendere), adjudging a person guilty of crime punishable by death or imprisonment in excess of one year, to prove any fact essential to sustain the judgment, but not including, when offered by the government in a criminal prosecution for purposes other than impeachment, judgments against persons other than the accused. The pendency of an appeal may be shown but does not affect admissibility.

(23) Judgment as to personal family or general history, or boundaries. Judgments as proof of matters of personal, family or general history, or boundaries, essential to the judgment, if the same would be provable by evidence of reputation.

(24) Other exceptions. A statement not specifically covered by any of the foregoing exceptions but having equivalent circumstantial guarantees of trustworthiness, if the court determines that: (A) the statement is offered as evidence of a material fact; (B) the statement is more probative on the point for which it is offered than any other evidence which the proponent can procure through reasonable efforts; and (C) the general purposes of these rules and interests of justice will best be served by admission of the statement into evidence. However, a statement may not be admitted under this exception unless the proponent of it makes known to the adverse party sufficiently in advance of the trial or hearing to provide the adverse party with a fair opportunity to prepare to meet it, his intention to offer the statement and the particulars of it, including the name and address of the declarant.

Hearsay Exceptions: Declarant Unavailable

RULE 804

(a) **Definition of unavailability.** "Unavailability as a witness" includes situations in which the declarant:

   (1) is exempted by ruling of the court on the ground of privilege from testifying concerning the subject matter of his statement; or

   (2) persists in refusing to testify concerning the subject matter of his statement despite an order of the court to do so; or

   (3) testifies to a lack of memory of the subject matter of his statement; or

   (4) is unable to be present or to testify at the hearing because of death or then existing physical or mental illness or infirmity; or

   (5) is absent from the hearing and the proponent of his statement has been unable to procure his attendance (or in the case of a hearsay exception under subdivision (b) (2), (3), or (4), his attendance or testimony) by process or other reasonable means.

   A declarant is not unavailable as a witness if his exemption, refusal, claim of lack of memory, inability, or absence is due to the procurement or wrongdoing of the proponent of his statement for the purpose of preventing the witness from attending or testifying.

(b) **Hearsay exceptions.** The following are not excluded by the hearsay rule if the declarant is unavailable as a witness:

   (1) **Former testimony.** Testimony given as a witness at another hearing of the same or a different proceeding, or in a deposition taken in compliance with law in the course of the same or another proceeding, if the party against whom the testimony is now offered, or, in a civil action or proceeding, a predecessor in interest, had an opportunity and similar motive to develop the testimony by direct, cross, or redirect examination.

   (2) **Statement under belief of impending death.** In a prosecution for homicide or in a civil action or proceeding, a statement made by a declarant while believing that his death was imminent, concerning the cause or circumstances of what he believed to be his impending death.

   (3) **Statement against interest.** A statement which was at the time of its making so far contrary to the declarant's pecuniary or proprietary interest, or so far tended to subject him or her to civil or criminal liability, or to render invalid a claim by him or her against another, that a reasonable man in his position would not have made the statement unless he believed it to be true. A statement tending to expose the declarant to criminal liability and offered to exculpate the accused is not admissible unless corroborating circumstances clearly indicate the trustworthiness of the statement.

   (4) **Statement of personal or family history.** (A) A statement concerning the declarant's own birth, adoption, marriage, divorce, legitimacy,

relationship by blood, adoption, or marriage, ancestry, or other similar fact of personal or family history, even though declarant had no means of acquiring personal knowledge of the matter stated; or (B) a statement concerning the foregoing matters, and death also, of another person, if the declarant was related to the other by blood, adoption, or marriage or was so intimately associated with the other's family as to be likely to have accurate information concerning the matter declared.

(5) **Other exceptions.** A statement not specifically covered by any of the foregoing exceptions but having equivalent circumstantial guarantees of trustworthiness, if the court determines that (A) the statement is offered as evidence of a material fact; (B) the statement is more probative on the point for which it is offered than any other evidence which the proponent can procure through reasonable efforts; (C) the general purposes of these rules and the interests of justice will best be served by admission of the statement into evidence. However, a statement may not be admitted under this exception unless the proponent of it makes known to the adverse party sufficiently in advance of the trial or hearing to provide the adverse party with a fair opportunity to prepare to meet it, his intention to offer the statement and the particulars of it, including the name and address of the declarant.

RULE 805

Hearsay within Hearsay

Hearsay included within hearsay is not excluded under the hearsay rule if each part of the combined statements conforms with an exception to the hearsay rule provided in these rules.

SUMMARY

The parties' pleadings define the legal issues. The legal issues determine which facts are material to the case. For evidence to be admissible (usable) at trial, it must be relevant to a material fact. A fact is immaterial when it has no relationship to the issues in the case. A court will not receive evidence concerning an immaterial fact. A court will receive only evidence that is relevant. Evidence is relevant if it makes the existence of a fact more probable or less probable. The burden to seasonably object to improper evidence and to show why the evidence is objectionable lies with the party who wants to exclude the evidence.

Every civil lawsuits involves at least one ultimate question of fact that a fact finder must determine. An ultimate fact is a conclusion drawn from the collage of facts that gave rise to the parties' dispute. A determination that a party was negligent or breached a contract or breached a warranty or trespassed or assumed a risk or was defamed or was defrauded is an ultimate question of fact. The fact finder determines the ultimate fact by applying the law to the established facts. For example, in determining whether a party was negligent, the fact finder must determine what the party did and did not do. Then the fact finder must decide whether the party's conduct was consistent with due care or showed a lack of due care.

In addition to being admissible, the evidence should be understandable, interesting and persuasive. A lawyer must make judgments concerning what evidence to use, when to use it, and how to use it. A lawyer must decide how much time and money to spend preparing and presenting an item of evidence. Many factors affect the persuasiveness of the evidence and a lawyer must consider such things as the relationship of the witness to the parties and motives the witness may have. Evidence gains credibility when it is presented by a witness who appears sincere and authoritative. There is sometimes a danger that offering certain evidence will adversely affect some other item of evidence. Ethics preclude a lawyer from offering false evidence, and good trial strategy says that a lawyer should guard against presenting evidence he or she believes is not reliable.

A jury may draw inferences from established facts, but the jury may not speculate about facts not proved by the evidence. The jury must not supply missing evidence by speculation and conjecture or on the basis of information the jurors obtained outside the trial. Jurors may not, through their own independent knowledge, supply any missing facts.

The most common form of evidence is testimony. Testimony is a statement, oral or written, made under oath, subject to the right of cross-examination. Ordinarily, only a person who observed or experienced a fact may testify about the fact. In other words, testimony is usually based upon personal knowledge. A lawyer controls a witness's testimony through the selection of questions. A lawyer is supposed to keep the witness from interjecting statements that are irrelevant, unfairly prejudicial, or otherwise inadmissible. The procedure for examining witnesses allows for the full development of a witness's testimony and, at the same time, prevents the witness from injecting improper evidence.

Through demonstrative evidence, a party may show facts, in contrast to talking about them. Any tangible evidence is considered to be demonstrative evidence. An exhibit that is received into evidence for illustrative purposes is not, by itself, evidence of a fact. Illustrative exhibits are used to help a witness explain her or his testimony. A jury (fact finder) may not use an illustrative exhibit as substantive evidence. For that reason, courts usually do not allow the jury to take illustrative exhibits with it to its deliberations.

Generally, courts require evidence to be factual, rather than someone's opinion or belief about the facts. It is the jury's responsibility to draw conclusions from the facts observed by the witnesses. However, courts make some very important exceptions to this principle. When a layperson cannot possibly describe a set of circumstances on a factual basis, the law allows opinion evidence. For example, a layperson could describe a floor as slippery or not slippery, because the condition cannot be described in any other way. Experts are allowed to state their opinions to the jury when it appears the opinion evidence will help the jury to understand a material fact or to understand other evidence.

A person who has special education, training, knowledge, and experience in a particular subject or field *may* qualify to give expert opinion testimony about the subject. Expert opinion evidence requires a foundation to establish that the witness has the necessary background and is sufficiently knowledgeable about the subject in question to have a reasonably reliable opinion.

A fact may be proved by direct evidence or circumstantial evidence or both. The law does not prefer one form over the other. Direct evidence is the testimony from witnesses who observed the facts to which they testify. Circumstantial evidence is indirect proof that depends upon principles of logic and common experience. The process depends upon deductive reasoning.

Substantive evidence is any evidence the jury is allowed to consider that is capable of supporting a verdict. The form of the evidence makes no difference.

Impeachment evidence is considered for the purpose of testing the credibility of a witness. It is evidence that the witness has said something or written something or conducted himself or herself in a manner inconsistent with what was testified to in court.

A hypothetical question assumes facts that the evidence tends to establish and an expert may give an opinion based upon those assumed facts just as though the expert had personally observed them. The jury is instructed, at the end of the trial, that the expert's opinion assumes and depends upon the truth of all the facts contained in the hypothetical question. If the jury determines that any one or more of the assumed facts is not true or not established, the expert's opinion based upon the hypothetical question should be rejected. An experienced paralegal may help with the preparation of hypothetical questions. As a general rule, the shorter a hypothetical question is, the more reliable and effective it is.

An exhibit is any document or item that the court allows the jury to consider in determining a material fact. An exhibit may be evidence of the fact, as when a written contract is evidence of the parties' agreement. An exhibit may be merely illustrative and offered for the purpose of helping a witness to explain or describe a fact. Exhibits are a form of demonstrable evidence, something jurors may examine in their quest for the truth.

"A judicially noticed fact must be one not subject to reasonable dispute in that it is either (1) generally known within the territorial jurisdiction of the trial court or (2) capable of accurate and ready determination by resorting to sources whose accuracy cannot reasonably be questioned" (Rule 201(b)).

The rules of evidence authorize a party to prepare a summary of detailed or lengthy records or charts, and the summary may be received into evidence in lieu of the original documents. The rule encourages the parties to conduct a thorough review of all the relevant documentation before the trial and thereby reduce the amount of time needed for presentation of the essential evidence from the documents. Paralegals may prepare summaries of evidence to be used at trial.

Some facts may be established at trial by presumptions in law. The presumptions, unlike judicially noticed facts, are not binding upon the parties and jury. A jury may find for or against a presumed fact. In cases involving death, there is a presumption that the decedent did not commit suicide. In cases where the plaintiff delivers personal property to the defendant's custody and it is returned in a damaged condition, there is a presumption that the damage was caused by negligence on the part of the defendant. If the defendant fails to present any evidence explaining how the damage occurred, the plaintiff is entitled to a verdict against the defendant.

When an accident in itself speaks of negligence on the part of the defendant, the plaintiff is given the benefit of the res ipsa loquitur doctrine, which creates a permissible inference of negligence on the part of the defendant. Res ipsa loquitur means that "the thing (accident) speaks for itself" of negligence. The defendant has the opportunity to explain why he or she denies the negligence. In most states, the doctrine does not shift the burden of proof. The permissible inference, however, is sufficient to carry the burden of proof even if the defendant presents an explanation that exonerates him or her from any fault. Before a jury is permitted to infer negligence on the part of the defendant, the jury must find that (1) the accident is of a type that would not ordinarily occur in the absence of negligence; (2) the defendant was in exclusive control of the instrumentality that caused the injury or claimed; and (3) the accident did not result from any voluntary act or negligence on the part of the plaintiff or some third person for whom the defendant would not be responsible.

A fact is material when it relates to the parties' dispute, that is, to an issue in the case. Evidence is relevant when it tends to prove or disprove a material fact. Courts prefer that the parties present the best evidence available concerning any relevant fact. The best evidence is the evidence that is most directly related to the fact. For example, the original of a document is better than a photocopy, and a photocopy is better than a person's summary of the document.

Hearsay evidence is any out-of-court statement, oral or written, that is offered to prove the truth of matters referred to in the out-of-court statement. Facts should be established through witnesses who have first-hand knowledge about them. When hearsay evidence is offered, the opposing side has no opportunity to cross-examine the source.

The parol evidence rule excludes any evidence that attempts to vary or contradict the clear language of a writing that the parties have used to formalize their agreement. The rule does not apply unless the writing fully integrates the parties' agreement. Parol evidence is admissible to explain ambiguities in the written agreement.

A party may not offer evidence about settlement discussions in an effort to show the jury that the opposing party made concessions or admissions. This exclusionary rule is based upon the public policy that favors settlement and settlement negotiations.

In accident cases, the plaintiff is not allowed to prove that the defendant had or caused an unreasonably dangerous condition by offering evidence that after the plaintiff's accident, the defendant made repairs that made the condition less dangerous. The remedial measures rule arises from a public policy to encourage safety. Besides, if the property was truly unreasonably dangerous, the defect can be proved by other means.

KEY TERMS

fact	relevant evidence
evidence	incompetent
material fact	irrelevant
fact finder	hearsay
ultimate fact	parol evidence

foundation
direct examination
cross examination
leading question
demonstrative evidence
illustrative evidence
opinion
conclusions
expert witness

direct evidence
circumstantial evidence
substantive evidence
impeachment evidence
hypothetical question
judicial notice
res ipsa loquitur
offer of proof
remedial measures

REVIEW QUESTIONS

1. How does a fact differ from a material fact?

2. When is evidence relevant?

3. How does illustrative evidence differ from demonstrative evidence?

4. Why is evidence of a remedial measure inadmissible at trial?

5. Describe an accident that would permit the plaintiff to use the res ipsa loquitur doctrine.

6. May a paralegal prepare an evidence summary for use at trial?

7. Give an example of circumstantial evidence.

8. What circumstances determine whether a person qualifies as an expert witness?

9. When may a witness testify to an ultimate question of fact?

10. When a lawyer attacks a witness's credibility, is the lawyer challenging the ability of the witness to testify? Explain.

8

GATHERING THE EVIDENCE

The civil justice system exists to resolve disputes according to law. Courts resolve disputes by applying the law to the parties' facts. If the parties do not dispute the facts, the court may resolve the case without a trial. Rule 56 prescribes the procedure for the parties to use in such cases. The procedure is called a summary judgment. The parties can submit the matter to the court on a motion with supporting documentation. No trial is necessary.

Controversies that result in litigation usually involve some disagreement about the underlying facts. Each party sees or remembers or interprets the facts concerning the transaction or occurrence somewhat differently. Courts conduct trials for the purpose of ascertaining the truth about the material facts. After the truth has been found, the court may apply the law to those facts to determine the parties' legal rights and obligations. Then the court may declare the parties' rights and obligations by entering a **judgment** in the court's records.

A trial gives the parties the opportunity to prove the facts upon which they base their claims and defenses. The parties prove facts by presenting evidence. Unless a party has evidence that is admissible in the trial, the party will not be able to prove his or her version of the facts. Unless the party has evidence that is more persuasive than the opponent's evidence on disputed points, the party will not prevail on the disputed facts. Parties need to gather their evidence before the trial. Indeed, they should begin gathering the evidence as soon as they realize they have a dispute that might result in litigation.

The process of gathering evidence may be divided into two phases: investigation and discovery. The investigation phase is the search for information and evidence that a party conducts without using court procedures. The discovery phase uses various procedures prescribed by court rules. A person may begin an investigation as soon as the person realizes he or she is involved in a dispute. A person's own investigation is the most basic and most economical means of obtaining information and evidence. Anyone may conduct an investigation. No license or certification is required. On the other hand, with some few exceptions, a party may not use discovery procedures until a lawsuit has been commenced. Discovery procedures usually require the participation of the other parties and are conducted subject to some supervision by the court. The discovery procedures are described in Rules 26 through 37 of the Federal Rules of Civil Procedure. Investigation procedures and discovery procedures should be used together for effectiveness and economy.

Neither the government nor the court will help a party to develop and present her or his case. Each party is required to prove his or her version of the disputed facts with evidence. Each party must gather and present her or his own evidence. It is that feature that makes our civil justice system an adversary system. The term *adversary* does not mean "contentious" or "mean-spirited." It means simply that the parties have opposing positions. Each party is responsible for proving his or her position. Trials are structured to give each party an opportunity to present evidence supporting her or his claims and defenses and to present evidence to refute the other party's evidence. When a party retains a lawyer to represent her or him in a civil action, the lawyer assumes responsibility for gathering and presenting the evidence for the party. No party is under an obligation to present all the evidence she or he has or to help the opposing party present evidence, but the adversary nature of civil litigation does not permit a party to conceal or misrepresent evidence.

Most people who work with the civil justice system believe that the system works well. Trials bring out the truth, and cases are usually decided on the basis of the truth. Since each party must develop his or her own case, lawyers act on the premise that the party who does the best job of collecting, preserving, and presenting the evidence will prevail. Probably a more realistic view is that if each party presents his or her own case well, the case will be correctly decided according to its merits. On the other hand, a party who fails to prepare and present a good case will lose. Consequently, poor preparation can doom a meritorious case. The more information and evidence a party obtains through investigation and discovery, the better he or she can prepare for trial, evaluate the case, and present a convincing case. Having a strong position on the law is no good without having the facts upon which to base the legal theory. Even the most skilled advocate cannot expect to win a case where all the evidence favors the opponent.

The pleadings frame the legal issues and the fact issues. The plaintiff's complaint must state the basic facts and the legal theories upon which the plaintiff relies. The defendant's answer must admit the facts that the defendant knows are true, deny the facts that the defendant disputes, and allege additional facts upon which the defendant's theory is based. The facts that the plaintiff alleges in the complaint and that the defendant admits in the answer need not be proved at trial. Therefore, neither party has to present evidence on those "established" facts. They are conclusively established for all purposes of the case.

With only a few exceptions, the discovery procedures authorized by the Federal Rules of Civil Procedure are designed to give both parties equal access to all the relevant evidence—even evidence that is under the control of the opposing party and of persons who are not parties. A party may be compelled by the Rules to disclose evidence that is adverse to that party's position. Gathering the evidence includes determining what evidence is needed, locating the evidence, and preserving the evidence. Paralegals perform all these functions for clients.

■ INFORMATION AND INADMISSIBLE EVIDENCE

The term *information* describes knowledge that a witness or investigator has obtained about facts or about evidence but which, in itself, is not capable of proving or disproving a fact. The search for evidence may uncover information that cannot be used at trial but that may lead to evidence that can be used at trial. Courts and lawyers often use the term *inadmissible evidence* to describe something that would tend to prove or disprove a relevant fact but for some reason is not allowed into evidence. There is no technical distinction between mere information and inadmissible evidence; nevertheless, a party ordinarily knows that information could not be received by a court as evidence, but may believe that an item labeled as inadmissible should have been received by the court as evidence.

An investigation should be broad in scope. A good investigation builds upon information as the information is obtained. As a person gathers information and evidence about the case, she or he should gain a better understanding about the merits of the case and be able to evaluate the parties' respective legal positions more accurately. This is important, because at some point each party must decide whether to proceed with the case, drop a claim, drop a defense, settle the case, or go to trial. The sooner those decisions are made, the better for everyone. However, the primary purpose for gathering evidence is to prove or disprove the claims and defenses at trial.

■ INVESTIGATION PARAMETERS

An investigation is a search for information and evidence. The three primary sources are the client, witnesses, and the situs of the occurrence. Investigators (lawyers and legal assistants) should begin the search and inquiry as soon as possible and with as little involvement of the other side as possible. The party who starts the investigation first generally obtains the greatest volume of evidence, the most reliable evidence, and the most cooperation from independent sources. A superior investigation is exemplified by attention to the details.

A profound jurisprudential principle guides an investigation: "The early bird catches the worm." The effectiveness of an investigation is directly dependent upon its timeliness and thoroughness. Like vapor, evidence tends to vanish quickly. Physical evidence gets lost. The authority and reliability of evidence tends to lessen with the passage of time. For example, photographs of skid marks taken at the scene of a motor vehicle accident, while the vehicles are in their at-rest position, are much more authoritative than photographs taken three days later. A timely investigation does not just happen; the investigator must make it happen.

An investigator is not usually in a position to force other people to cooperate. Therefore, the investigator must learn how to engender cooperation and maintain contacts. Witnesses who are "independent" or "nonaligned" tend to develop an empathy with the party whose representative contacts them first. This does not always happen, but it occurs often enough to be a reason to try to be the first to meet and interview nonaligned witnesses.

Witnesses to an accident usually have an acute interest in the accident and its consequences during the next few days, but then their interest begins to diminish. Furthermore, too often witnesses quickly forget the facts they observed. They lose their notes, and records get misplaced. Some witnesses try to forget. If a witness has been contacted by the other side and treated poorly, he or she may try to avoid being contacted by anyone else. Witnesses start thinking about not wanting to be involved in someone else's litigation.

There is no set formula for conducting an investigation. The nature of the occurrence, the type of claim, and the potential defenses determine the direction and scope of the investigation. The investigation usually begins with an interview of the client. In most cases, the client can provide a good description of the transaction or occurrence, and significant background information. Usually, the client can identify important witnesses who have information and/or evidence. All too often, clients fail to appreciate the value of some of the evidence they already have. Consequently, it is necessary to ask clients searching questions about the information they should possess but have not volunteered. An investigator should never assume that the information the client volunteers is all the information she or he has.

An investigator should not assume the truth of "apparent" facts, not even the facts claimed by the client, because the assumption might deter the investigator from seeking out evidence. On the other hand, an investigator should start with a *theory* about the facts—about what happened, how it happened, and why it happened in the manner that it did. This theory will point the investigator in the direction to find more evidence and help the investigator to evaluate the facts. An investigator must remain flexible. The theory must be subject to modification when the evidence collected conflicts with the theory. An investigator must pay strict attention to the details, look for patterns, and watch for inconsistencies. As information is obtained, it must be examined objectively, and recorded accurately or otherwise preserved.

■ DISCOVERY PARAMETERS

The philosophy underlying the Federal Rules of Civil Procedure is that each party shall have the opportunity to determine before trial what facts are in dispute and to discover all the evidence that tends to prove or disprove the disputed facts. To implement the policy of full access to the evidence, the Rules require each party to fully disclose the evidence he or she knows about, when properly asked. The Rules provide the means for asking other parties and witnesses pertinent questions about the case.

The discovery procedures are available to the parties as soon as the action has been commenced, and in some situations they may be utilized even before an action has been started (Rule 27(a)). In most cases, the Rules of Civil Procedure provide sufficient direction and guidance to the parties to conduct discovery without any involvement of the courts. However, sometimes a court or a party may want a formal plan for discovery. Upon motion or by an order **sua sponte,** the court in which the action is pending may order a discovery conference for the purpose of establishing a discovery plan. (A court acts sua sponte when it acts on its own initiative, without any motion or request by a party.) If a party moves the court for an order scheduling a discovery conference, the moving party must state that the parties have tried and failed to establish their own discovery plan. In that event, the party seeking a formal discovery plan must have prepared and submitted a proposed plan to the other parties. (The new Federal Rules require each party to submit a proposed discovery plan. See the section ''Recent Changes to Federal Discovery Rules'' in this chapter.)

A discovery plan must identify the legal and fact issues to which discovery will be directed and, perhaps, limited. It should establish a timetable or schedule for completing discovery or phases of discovery. The plan may be subject to constraints such as a limit on the number of interrogatories that may be served, the number of witnesses who may be deposed, the number of inspections of the subject matter that may be allowed, and the number of expert witnesses that may be used. A discovery plan may provide for the allocation of expenses, such as expert witness fees. Whether prepared by the parties or by the court, the plan may be modified from time to time as circumstances require, but once established, it should be assiduously followed.

A party's investigation is not limited by a discovery plan. Nevertheless, since parties should use both investigation and discovery in gathering evidence, so that each approach complements the other, a discovery plan may indirectly affect a party's investigation.

Although the discovery procedures are well-defined and well understood, on occasion they must be modified to protect a party against untoward consequences. Therefore, Rule 26(c) provides that a party against whom discovery is sought may apply to the court for a protective order. A protective order may be issued to avoid unnecessary ''annoyance, embarrassment, oppression or expense.'' For example, a plaintiff who has a personal injury claim may be asked about her general medical history. Her history may include an elective abortion that is not relevant to the case. The plaintiff could seek an order excluding evidence about the abortion and relevant records from further discovery, or impose limits on the use to which the medical information could be put. The burden rests upon the party from whom discovery is being sought to move the court for a protective order.

If a party wrongfully fails to comply with discovery demands, the party seeking discovery may move the court for an order to compel that party to comply with the demands (Rule 37). If the court orders a party to answer questions put to her or him in interrogatories or an oral deposition, the court may order the culpable party to pay the costs that the moving party incurred to obtain the order (Rule 37(a)(4)). On the other hand, if the court determines that the deponent was correct in refusing to respond to discovery demands, it may require the moving party to pay the costs that the deponent incurred in defending against the motion. (A deponent is a person who makes a statement under oath.) Rule 37 motions to compel discovery do not always result in an award of costs. A court may determine that both parties had reasonable grounds for their respective positions and acted in good faith. On that basis, the court could decide to let each party bear her or his own costs.

If a party fails to comply with an order compelling discovery, the next step for the party seeking discovery is to move the court for **sanctions** (Rule 37(b)). A Rule 37 sanction is a penalty. District courts have a broad range of power to impose various sanctions upon remiss parties. A court may strike all or part of the remiss party's pleading. For example, suppose the plaintiff in a personal injury action refuses to name his past and present employers. This refusal would significantly interfere with the defendant's ability to evaluate and meet the plaintiff's claim for loss of income. The court could strike the plaintiff's complaint or strike the portion that seeks damages for loss of income and loss of earning capacity.

Where a party refuses to disclose evidence about a particular subject, the court may order that the determinative facts are resolved against the remiss party (Rule 37(b)(A)). A case in point would be where the plaintiff claims damage to personal property but will not permit the defendant to examine the property. The court could issue an order that provides, for purposes of the pending action, that the property was not damaged.

A court may issue an order that precludes the disobedient party from asserting a claim or defense or offering evidence of a particular nature (Rule 37(b)(B)). A court may find a party to be in contempt of court for failing to comply with a discovery order (Rule 37(b)(D)). The right to discovery includes the right to have one or more **independent medical examinations** of a party who has put his or her physical, mental, or blood condition in issue; however, a party who refuses to submit to an independent medical examination cannot be held in contempt of court even though ordered to submit. Some other sanction must be utilized. The most severe penalty that a court may impose is to enter judgment against the disobedient party (Rule 37(b)(C)).

■ OVERVIEW OF THE DISCOVERY RULES

Discovery includes all the pretrial court procedures by which parties are able to obtain information and evidence from other parties and from non-parties. These are called court procedures only because they are authorized by court rules and subject to court supervision; they are not conducted in a courtroom or even at a court.

Each discovery procedure has been designed to meet a particular need. Each procedure may be used independently of the others. Nevertheless, to be most effective and economical, the discovery procedures should be used in concert and combined with a party's own investigation. Each party decides what discovery procedures to use and, within limits, when to use them.

Discovery Rules 26 through 37 provide the framework within which the parties may conduct discovery. Rule 26 specifies the purpose, scope, and limits concerning the use of discovery procedures:

> Parties may obtain discovery by one or more of the following methods: depositions upon oral examination or written questions; written interrogatories; production of documents or things or permission to enter upon land or other property, for inspection and other purposes; physical and mental examination [of a party]; and requests for admissions.

Although a request for admission is commonly referred to as a discovery tool, it is not. A party who serves one upon another party presumably knows the truth of the fact that is the subject of the request, and the purpose of the request is to commit the other party to that fact. A party does not obtain new information or evidence through a request for admission. Indeed, it might be considered an abuse of the request procedure to use it to obtain new information or new evidence or to find new facts.

Rule 26 also prescribes the scope of discovery and specifies certain limits:

> Parties may obtain discovery regarding any matter, not privileged, which is relevant to the subject matter involved in the pending action, whether it relates to the claim or defense of the party seeking discovery or to the claim or defense of any other party, including the existence, description, nature, custody, condition and location of any books, documents, or other tangible things and the identity and location of persons having knowledge of any discoverable matter. It is not ground for objection that the information sought will be inadmissible at the trial if the information sought appears reasonably calculated to lead to the discovery of admissible evidence.

Rule 27 authorizes the use of some discovery procedures even before an action has been commenced, where a special need exists and that need can be shown by petition to a district court that has jurisdiction over the subject matter. Rules 28 and 29 authorize parties to conduct discovery by taking **oral depositions** of other parties and of nonparty witnesses. The term *deposition* means "testimony under oath." Rule 30 provides detailed instructions concerning the procedures for taking oral depositions of parties and witnesses. Rule 31 provides instructions for taking a person's deposition through the submission of written questions. Rule 32 describes how the parties may use **deposition transcripts** at trial. A deposition transcript is the typed, verbatim record of the questions and answers. Rule 33 authorizes a party to serve **interrogatories,** or written questions, upon another party. The responding party (deponent) must provide written answers to the interrogatories. The written answers must be under oath. Rule 34 enables each party to require another party to produce for inspection any real estate, personal property, document, or "thing" that is in another party's custody or under another party's control. As part of the inspection, the party may take photographs and photocopy documents. Rule 35 provides a means for obtaining an independent medical examination of a party who is making a claim for personal injury.

Discovery procedures have been created to help parties obtain access to information and evidence that is under the control of another party or under the control of a person who is not cooperative. Parties have the power of the court behind them when they use discovery procedures in a proper manner for a proper purpose. If a party or witness refuses to co-operate with a proper discovery request, that person is subject to the penalties provided by law.

■ SCOPE OF DISCOVERY

The philosophy behind the discovery rules is that all parties should have equal access to all the information and evidence that is reasonably necessary to the case. The premise is that if the parties have equal access to all the evidence, they will know and understand the material facts before the case reaches trial, and that knowledge will lead to a settlement of most cases. Therefore, discovery is favored; concealment is disfavored.

The primary limitation to discovery is that the inquiry, whether in an oral deposition, a written interrogatory, or another form, must seek information or evidence that is relevant to the case. The information sought need not be directly admissible as evidence. An inquiry is properly within the scope of discovery if it "appears" calculated to "lead" to discovery of admissible evidence. Remember, evidence is relevant if it tends to prove or disprove a fact that is material to a claim or defense asserted in the pleadings. Therefore, the main consideration in determining whether an inquiry is within the scope of discovery is whether the inquiry is calculated to lead to the discovery of admissible evidence. The "relevancy rule" prevents parties from using discovery procedures for ulterior purposes. Thus, where a customer slips and falls in a store and brings a negligence action to recover money damages for bodily injuries, the customer is not permitted to conduct discovery about the store's financial condition, business operations, trade secrets, or the like. The scope of the customer's discovery is limited to determining whether the store was negligent in the manner in which it maintained the premises. Discovery procedures may not be used to harass another party.

Notice that discovery procedures are not limited to obtaining just evidence; they may also be used to obtain information. Again, the limitation is that the inquiry must be calculated to lead to admissible evidence. A party may use discovery to obtain evidence that is not admissible at trial. Using the preceding example, the customer's inquiry about the size of the store's bank account might be interesting but has nothing to do with the negligence action and could not lead to the discovery of admissible evidence. Therefore, the inquiry would be disallowed.

There seems to be an ongoing conflict between the purpose of providing parties with the information and evidence they need to develop their case and the need to protect parties from harassment and undue expense. Rule 26(b)(1) addresses these concerns:

> The frequency or extent of use of the discovery methods set forth in subdivision (a) shall be limited by the court if it determines that: (i) the discovery sought is unreasonably cumulative or duplicative, or is obtainable from some other source that is more convenient, less burdensome, or less expensive; (ii) the discovery is unduly burdensome or expensive, taking into account the needs of the case, the amount in controversy, limitations on the parties' resources, and the importance of the issues at stake in the litigation. The court may act upon its own initiative after reasonable notice or pursuant to a motion under subdivision (c).

Rule 26 recognizes that discovery procedures operate as in an adversary environment. Therefore, whenever a party uses a discovery procedure, that party must give reasonable notice to all other parties about the inquiry or intent to make inquiry. Whenever a party serves a discovery request upon one other party, a copy of the request must be served upon all other parties to keep them apprised. Similarly, when a party responds to a discovery request, a copy of the response must be sent to all parties.

Technically, the availability of a defendant's liability insurance to pay the claim against her or him is irrelevant in most civil lawsuits. However, the availability of liability insurance may be a very important consideration in determining whether a case can be settled or should be settled and for how much. The amount and availability of that insurance may be very significant to the plaintiff's evaluation of the claim and may directly affect the plaintiff's willingness to settle. Consequently, Rule 26(b)(2) allows parties to discover the existence of liability insurance, the scope of coverage, and the amount of coverage provided by the insurance. In a proper case, a party even has a right to obtain a copy of the other party's insurance policy. On occasion, a difficult situation develops between the defendant and her or his liability insurer because they may not agree on whether the claim is covered. The plaintiff may want to intervene, but needs a copy of the policy to determine who is correct.

Rule 26(b)(2) appears to refer only to liability insurance, which is insurance that will be available to pay a judgment or otherwise indemnify a party for liability. Nevertheless, there is general agreement that the defendant may discover whether the plaintiff has direct-loss insurance that covers all or part of the loss in question. One reason for this is that a direct-loss insurer who has made payments to the insured plaintiff may have subrogation rights. The insurer may even be the real party in interest. The defendant is entitled to know all the circumstances affecting an insurer's interest in the case, and such information is most conveniently obtained through interrogatories. Furthermore, the direct-loss insurer may have relevant information about the amount of the loss and the measure of damages. A defendant should be able to discover whether the plaintiff in a personal injury action has medical insurance to cover some of the expenses.

■ SEQUENCE AND TIMING

Rules 26 through 36 very clearly state when the various methods of discovery may be initiated. Generally, the plaintiff may not compel the defendant to respond to discovery until after the defendant has had an opportunity to interpose the answer and, in addition, has the usual minimum amount of time provided by the Rules. No party has a right to go first or second. No party may delay discovery or delay responding to discovery on the basis that the other party has been dilatory or uncooperative or obstructive. In other words, each party is responsible for conducting and responding to discovery in the manner provided by the Rules, regardless of the other party's conduct. The parties may stipulate, as provided by Rule 29, to different time parameters. But they may not stipulate to extend the time for discovery as limited by Rules 33 (Interrogatories to a Party), 34 (Demand for Production of Documents or Things), and 36 (Request for Admissions) if doing so would change a formal discovery plan or conflict with a discovery cutoff established by the court.

■ SUPPLEMENTATION OF DISCOVERY RESPONSES

A party is under a continuing duty to supplement and correct his or her discovery responses, regardless of the mode of discovery. The duty to supplement includes the duty to disclose new information that has been acquired since the original disclosure. It also includes the duty to make the answer or response "complete," not just technically correct (Rule 26(e)).

■ LIMITATIONS ON DISCOVERY

Discovery inquiries, whether in a deposition or in interrogatories, must be calculated to lead to admissible evidence. Discovery procedures may not be used to obtain information about the opposing party's trial preparation, such as the attorney's mental impressions, conclusions, opinions, or theories about the case (Rule 26(b)(3)). This limitation on discovery is commonly referred to as the **attorneys' work product rule.** However, it applies to discovery of the work product of a party's employees, agents, and other representatives, including insurance representatives. For example, a party may not use a discovery procedure to ask an opposing party how that party will conduct her or his investigation or what significance the opposing lawyer places on certain evidence or what facts the lawyer believes the evidence tends to prove. A party may not use discovery to find out what the opposing party has done to prepare for trial. For example, a party may inquire about the names and addresses of all witnesses, but a party cannot use discovery to find out what the witnesses told the party's investigator. On the other hand, Rule 26(a)(1)(A) requires parties to disclose the subject matter to which any known witness will testify.

A party may demand and obtain a recorded statement he or she made and gave to another party. The statement is not protected by the work product rule. Similarly, a person who is not a party has a right to obtain a copy of the statement that person has given to a litigant. Nevertheless, the Federal Rules do not authorize a party to demand that an opposing party give up the recorded statements obtained from other persons. Those witness statements are considered to be the work product of the party who obtained them. Many states, however, have adopted a different approach by requiring parties to disclose all witness statements that they have obtained. There is considerable controversy over the discoverability of a recorded statement obtained from a party by that party's own insurance company. The general rule is that the statement is not discoverable if it was prepared in anticipation of litigation.

Discovery procedures may not be used to obtain privileged information, communications, or documents. The matter of what is privileged is determined primarily by state law and also by federal statute. Ordinarily, privileged matters include communications between a physician and a patient, and the patient's medical records; communications between a lawyer or paralegal and a client, and related records; communications between a cleric and a penitent concerning matters of religious counseling; and communications between a husband and a wife. However, the privilege is forfeited if the party lets someone hear the communication or tells someone else about the subject of the communication. A party must preserve and protect the privilege, or it is lost.

■ RECENT CHANGES TO FEDERAL DISCOVERY RULES

Effective December 1, 1993, the federal district court rules of civil procedure were amended to express a new philosophy concerning discovery. The new federal approach has met with a good deal of resistance. The federal district courts have been granted authority to modify the new rules through the adoption of local rules. After the new approach has been tried for a while, we may see a movement to combine the new and the old in an effort to promote the objectives of Rule 1: a just, speedy, economical resolution of civil actions. It is likely that some states will adopt the amended rules or some version of them. Lawyers and paralegals must understand the new approach and be prepared to apply the new Rules 27 through 37 in courts where the new approach has been implemented.

In the past, discovery was conducted as an adversary process. Each party had the burden of gathering the evidence needed to establish the facts she or he relied upon. Each party had the right to demand that the other parties make disclosures about the evidence they had obtained and even make that evidence available for inspection and copying. However, the burden remained with each party to seek and obtain the evidence. A party did not have to voluntarily disclose evidence or otherwise proactively help another party to obtain evidence. The new federal court philosophy is that each party must voluntarily disclose and produce to the other parties the evidence she or he believes the other parties might need, even though the other parties have not asked for it. This is called the initial disclosure requirement.

Rules 26(a) and (f) provide that as soon as practicable after commencement of the action, the parties and their lawyers shall meet to discuss the "nature" and "basis" of their claims and defenses and to discuss settlement. The meeting is mandatory. The rule does not take into consideration that the parties may have had extensive negotiations, or even mediation, before the suit was commenced. If the parties have not already engaged in mediation, it is an alternative that should be explored at that time—even though once a civil action has been commenced, parties seem reluctant to engage in alternative dispute resolution.

If the parties do not settle the case, they must develop a formal plan for discovery. The plan must be reduced to writing and submitted to the court. The plan is subject to modification by the court. It must take into consideration each party's obligation to voluntarily disclose to the other parties the information and evidence concerning all facts that are alleged with particularity in the pleadings. The disclosures must include all evidence and information that is then reasonably available to the party. In other words, lawyers and paralegals have an obligation to actively seek out and collect the evidence that is in the client's possession, under the client's control, and within the client's knowledge. A party cannot justify a failure to disclose on the basis that he or she has not yet completed the investigation or that the other party has not complied with the disclosure requirements. Withholding information or being late in making disclosures subjects a party to sanctions provided by Rule 37, but does not allow an opposing party to avoid or delay making the required disclosures.

After receiving the plan for discovery, the court then prepares a discovery scheduling order that directs what discovery may be conducted, when it must be finished, and the limits on the methods of discovery.

Parties, lawyers, and paralegals are going to find some of the mandated disclosures and procedures in the amended rules to be overburdensome and unfair. The authors of the changes anticipated that the new philosophy and approach will not work in every case, and left a couple of safety valves. Amended Rule 29 provides that the parties may stipulate to some modifications of the procedures. Such a stipulation must be made in writing and signed by the parties or their lawyers. The stipulation may modify the time parameters and even the procedures. However, the parties may not stipulate to extend the time for responding to interrogatories or conducting inspections or providing responses to requests for admissions, if doing so would impair the court's scheduling. For example, if the court has ordered the parties to complete discovery by a particular date, the parties may not avoid that order through a stipulation. If the court has scheduled a dispositive motion for a particular date, the parties cannot make a discovery stipulation that would interfere with the court's hearing the motion as scheduled. The parties may make their stipulation and then seek the court's approval. In practice, courts generally allow the parties to do whatever the parties reasonably want or feel they need to do.

Initial Disclosure

Witnesses.   The initial disclosure must identify every witness by name, address, and telephone number, including expert witnesses. The disclosure must describe the subject about which each witness has knowledge. For example, a treating physician has knowledge about the plaintiff's injuries and medical expenses. An auto mechanic has knowledge about the condition of the defendant's automobile. An eyewitness to the accident has knowledge about the facts and circumstances of the accident. Police who investigated the accident have knowledge about the facts and circumstances of the accident, and the plaintiff's injuries. The disclosure need not go beyond the subject matter; it need not be a summary of the expected testimony of the witness. Rule 26(a)(1)(B) requires the plaintiff to include in his or her initial disclosure all documents and compilations relevant to the facts that must be alleged in the complaint with particularity, such as special damages, mistake, and fraud. (See Rule 9(b).)

Documents.   The disclosure must identify by category and location every document and other tangible thing that is relevant to the disputed facts that are pleaded with particularity. The disclosure must provide a meaningful description by which the recipient could reasonably know what is included and what is excluded. It need not summarize the contents of the documents or even describe why the documents have probative value. For example, a party may disclose the existence of witness statements, including the name of each witness, the date of each statement, and the custodian of each statement, but she need not include a summary of each statement. The disclosure must provide enough information so that the recipient can decide whether to include the documents and tangible things in the discovery plan and determine how they can be obtained through the discovery procedures. A party must disclose the identity of documents and things that are relevant even though they are privileged or work product. The privilege and work product doctrines are retained, and the material is not made subject to discovery, but the new rule requires disclosure of the nature of the material so that the opposing party can decide whether or not to challenge the claim of privilege or work product (Rule 26(b)(5)).

Computation of damages.   The plaintiff must provide to the defendant a compilation of the damages that the plaintiff is claiming (Rule 26(a)(1)(C)). If the defendant makes a counterclaim, the defendant must provide a similar compilation. The rule does not distinguish between general damages and special damages; therefore, it appears to apply to all damages claims. The rule implies that for each item for which damages may be separately awarded, the party must provide a statement of the amount of those damages and, where feasible, an explanation of how those damages were computed. The compilation is suppose to be by category. A party must identify any supporting documents. In personal injury cases, the supporting documentation must include the materials "bearing on the nature and extent of the injuries suffered." The required initial disclosures are part of the discovery process; they are not solely for the purpose of settlement negotiations. Therefore, the compilation (statement of damages) might well be used by the opposing party as an admission against the party who provides it if, subsequently, the damages seem to be significantly more. Lawyers and paralegals will probably find a way of hedging and making disclaimers in their required computations and compilations of damages. Remember, amended Rule 29 allows the parties to make stipulations concerning the discovery procedures, including how the disclosures may be used.

Insurance Contracts.   A defendant's initial disclosure is supposed to identify any insurance policy that may be available to respond to the claim for money damages (Rule 26(a)(1)(D)). The rule primarily applies to defendants' liability insurance policies. However, most lawyers and parties do not want to spend time examining insurance policies unless they have a particular reason. In the past, most plaintiffs' lawyers have been well satisfied to have the defendant disclose the name of the insurer, the amount of coverage, and the identifying contract number. If the defendant's lawyer assured the plaintiff's lawyer that the insurer did not deny coverage, the plaintiff had no reason to obtain the policy. The parties may still agree to this kind of a limited disclosure.

Usually, all the information the plaintiff needs is contained in the declarations page of the insurance contract. This page shows the types of coverage provided, the amount of coverage for each type of coverage, and the period of time the policy covers. The body of the contract contains the terms of coverage, exclusions, and conditions.

The defendant has as much interest in establishing coverage as does the plaintiff. Therefore, if the defendant's lawyer is sure she or he has the correct information, the plaintiff's lawyer should be comfortable relying upon her or his disclosure. If the defendant provided the wrong information about insurance coverage, and the plaintiff relied upon that information, the plaintiff would have good grounds for setting aside any settlement or payment accepted on the basis of the disclosure.

Discovery Conferences

The Rules require federal district courts to conduct a scheduling conference. Ordinarily, this conference is held several months after commencement of the action. Rule 26(f) requires the parties to meet and prepare a discovery plan that they can submit to the court for approval at the scheduling conference. The parties' meeting is supposed to be held as soon as feasible, but it must be held at least fourteen days before the scheduling conference. The parties must arrange to fully comply with the initial disclosures requirement. They may stipulate to modifications of Rule 26's requirements, but they cannot avoid those requirements. In addition, they must prepare a discovery plan for submission to the court at the scheduling conference. Hopefully, they can agree and stipulate to the entire plan. To the extent that they cannot agree, they must submit their respective proposals in the plan, and the court will finalize the plan.

Meeting to Plan for Discovery

Rule 26(f) provides:

> Except in actions exempted by local rule or when otherwise ordered, the parties shall, as soon as practicable and in any event at least 14 days before a scheduling conference is held or a scheduling order is due under Rule 16(b), meet to discuss the nature and basis of their claims and defenses and the possibilities for a prompt settlement or resolution of the case, to make or arrange for the disclosures required by [Rule 26] subdivision (a)(1), and to develop a proposed discovery plan.

The parties' discovery plan must state their views and proposals concerning the timing for discovery. The first order of business is to agree when the initial disclosures must be completed, if they are not already done. The parties must decide when the various aspects of discovery will be completed, such as exchanging interrogatories, conducting independent medical examinations, and inspecting property and things. The parties may choose to conduct discovery in phases. For example, the first phase may be to exchange interrogatories and documents; the next to take depositions of independent witnesses; the next to take depositions of the parties; the next to obtain an independent medical examination. The parties must choose the forms of discovery they will use, including how many interrogatories may be served, how many depositions each party may take. If a party has a concern about the scope of inquiry, the plan requires the parties to discuss the problem and state any limitations upon which they can agree. If they have a disagreement on the scope of discovery, the written discovery plan must note it, and the court will decide the issue when it finalizes the plan. For example, a party may claim that certain information is a trade secret. The trade secret may not be discoverable, or certain limitations may be imposed upon the parties' use of it when it is disclosed. As an assist to the court, the discovery plan must identify (list) the subjects on which discovery is needed.

The limitations on discovery imposed by the rules apply unless the parties stipulate to a change or the court finds a good reason for deviating. For example, Rule 33(a) limits to twenty-five the number of interrogatories a party may serve upon another party. Absent a stipulation or court order, that is all one party may serve upon another. Rule 30 allows one a party to take the deposition of not more than ten persons, inclusive of parties and independent witnesses. Absent a stipulation or court order, a party may not take more.

The lawyers and all unrepresented parties are jointly responsible for arranging for the meeting to plan discovery (Rule 26(f)). Each party is required to be present or to have a representative at the meeting. The rule requires "good faith" participation. In other words, the parties must conduct themselves in a reasonable manner and have justification for their positions when they fail to agree upon a required item. The rule will probably be construed to allow paralegals to handle the planning meeting. However, the party and the attorney of record remain ultimately responsible to the court for the timely preparation of the written plan as well as its content and execution. The written plan must be submitted to the court within ten days after the meeting. According to Rule 6,

> When the period of time prescribed or allowed is less than 11 days, intermediate Saturdays, Sundays, and legal holidays shall be excluded in the computation.

Since the meeting must be conducted (concluded) no less than fourteen days before the scheduling conference, the court has at least four days to examine the plan before the conference.

Discovery Plan

The lawyers and unrepresented parties have joint responsibility for preparing the discovery plan. Presumably one or the other will volunteer to initiate a written proposal for the other's consideration. Undoubtedly, paralegals will play a major role in the document's preparation and in working out its details. The written plan must be filed with the court; therefore, it must contain the caption of the case and use the title "Report of Parties' Planning Meeting." It must state the time and place of the meeting and who attended. Exhibit 8.1 is a sample of a written plan.

Requests for Admissions

Rule 36 authorizes the parties to serve requests for admissions upon another party. The procedure assumes that the proponent knows the fact or facts in question. The purpose is to force the opposing party to admit that a fact is true, so that neither party will have to offer evidence at trial to prove the fact. Requests for admissions may be used to establish that a document is genuine (is what it purports to be). No limit is placed on the number of requests that a party may serve, because they are useful for narrowing the areas of controversy.

Although the procedure for making requests for admissions is grouped with discovery procedures, it is not a discovery device. A party should know the fact or know the document is genuine before asking another party to admit it. Consequently, the best time to serve requests for admissions is when discovery has been completed. The more admissions the parties make, the shorter and simpler the trial will be. For this reason, courts should encourage parties to make requests for admissions. There is no limit on the number of requests for admissions that a party may serve. Unfortunately, some judges treat requests for admissions as though they are part of a party's discovery. Therefore, it is a good idea to find out whether a scheduling order that cuts off discovery on a particular date applies to requests for admissions. Even if there is no cut-off date for requests for admissions, to be effective a request must be served more than 30 days before the trial is to begin.

If a party wrongfully refuses to make admissions pursuant to Rule 36, the only penalty a court may impose is an award of costs in favor of the proponent of the request for admissions. The costs recoverable are those the proponent incurred to prove the facts that should have been admitted by the respondent. On the other hand, a court may disallow the costs of proving the fact where it appears that the respondent had reasonable grounds to believe that the request for admission was not true or justifiable (Rule 37(c)).

Discovery Sanctions

All discovery demands and disclosures must be signed by a lawyer or by a party. A person who signs a disclosure that is not "complete and correct as of the time it is made" is subject to court sanctions (Rule 26(g)(1)). In addition, a party has an obligation to correct and supplement previous disclosures in a timely manner (Rule 37). A party or lawyer may seek to justify a nondisclosure only with a showing of "substantial justification" and "harmless" error. In the language of Rule 37(c)(1):

■ **EXHIBIT 8.1**

Written Discovery Plan

REPORT OF PARTIES' PLANNING MEETING

1. Pursuant to Fed. R. Civ. P. 26(f), a meeting was held on March 8, 1995, at 45575 East White Aster Street, Phoenix, Arizona. The meeting was attended by
   Attorney Ms. Hanh Nguyen for the plaintiff;
   Attorney Mr. Robert Barr for the defendant.

2. Prediscovery Disclosures. The parties will exchange by May 1, 1995, the information required by Fed. R. Civ. P. 26(a)(1) and local Rule 44.

3. Discovery Plan. The parties jointly propose to the court the following discovery plan:

   Discovery will be needed on the following subjects: liability, damages, ownership of the defendant's vehicle.

   All discovery will be commenced in time to be completed by August 1, 1995.

   A maximum of fifty interrogatories may be served by each party. Responses shall be due forty-five days after receipt of the interrogatories.

   A party may serve any number of requests for admissions.

   The plaintiff shall take a maximum of three discovery depositions and one evidentiary deposition; the defendant shall take a maximum of four discovery depositions and intends to take no evidentiary depositions.

   The discovery deposition of the plaintiff shall not exceed four hours. The discovery deposition of the defendant shall not exceed two hours, unless extended by agreement. The other planned depositions are under no time limit.

   Reports from the parties' retained experts [for example, accident reconstructionists] shall be due
   from the plaintiff by June 1, 1995;
   from the defendant by July 1, 1995.

   Supplementation under Rule 26(e) shall be due August 1, 1995.

   —Continued

—*Continued*

4. The parties have not been able to agree upon the discoverability of the plaintiff's hospital records concerning a prior accident and injury.

The parties request a conference with the court before entry of the scheduling order, because of the plaintiff's claim of privilege concerning the hospital records.

The parties request a pretrial conference to be held in September or October 1995.

The parties wish to reserve the right to amend pleadings until the time of the pretrial conference.

The parties do not expect or intend to add parties to the action.

All potentially dispositive motions should be filed by the date of the pretrial conference.

Settlement cannot be evaluated before August 1, 1995.

Alternative dispute resolution in the form of mediation could enhance the possibilities of settlement.

Final lists of witnesses and exhibits under Rule 26(a)(3) should be due
      from the plaintiff by the date of the pretrial conference;
      from the defendant by the date of the pretrial conference.

The parties should have thirty days after service of the final lists of witnesses and exhibits, to list objections under Rule 26(a)(3).

The case should be ready for trial by November 1, 1995. The parties expect the trial will take four full days.

Dated: _____ /s/ _____

                        /s/ _____

> A party that without substantial justification fails to disclose information required by Rule 26(a) or 26(e)(1) shall not, unless such failure is harmless, be permitted to use as evidence at a trial, at a hearing, or on a motion any witness or information not so disclosed. In addition, . . . on motion and after affording an opportunity to be heard, [the court] may impose other appropriate sanctions.

The sanctions include payment of costs and attorneys' fees, and the court may tell the jury about the party's (lawyer's) failure to make the proper disclosure. The court's statement could adversely affect the credibility of a party's entire case. In addition, the court may order that the particular facts shall be deemed to be established, or prohibit the delinquent party from denying the opponent's claim or defense, or preclude the disobedient party from presenting certain evidence at trial. The court may even strike the disobedient party's pleading, leaving that party in default.

■ AVOIDING DISCOVERY PITFALLS

If a party has any doubt about the scope of information and evidence that must be provided in the initial disclosure, that party should consider moving the court for an order requiring the opposing party to state the claim with greater clarity or particularity. The moving party may assert as a grounds for the motion that the pleading is too vague and prevents a response to the Rule 26 initial disclosure requirements. The motion is authorized by Rule 12(e). Perhaps the party can meet with the opposing lawyer and make a stipulation, pursuant to Rule 29, that defines what information and evidence must be disclosed and specifically includes or excludes the matters of concern. The party may move the court for an order that qualifies his or her obligation to make disclosures until the underlying issues have been resolved. For example, suppose the plaintiff brings an action seeking damages for breach of two separate contracts, but one of those claims has been settled and the defendant has a release to prove it. The defendant may move for a protective order that allows him to test and enforce the release before making voluntary initial disclosures concerning the claim of breach of contract and damages. The motion for a protective order could be combined with a motion to sever the two claims.

Lawyers and paralegals must keep in mind that any communication they have with a witness, except a client, may be discovered and disclosed by the opposition. Therefore, a paralegal should never say anything to a witness that could cause embarrassment to anyone. Witnesses should be assured that it is proper for them to meet and talk with paralegals. A witness should feel free to acknowledge such a meeting and discussion. If handled properly, an interview should make the interviewee feel comfortable with the interviewer and the process.

■ ENSURING ACCURACY AND CONSISTENCY

Where parties have established certain facts through judicial admissions, as in the pleadings or in responses to requests for admissions, the parties are absolutely committed to those facts unless and until a court releases them from the commitment. The rest of the case and evidence should be consistent with the facts that the parties have admitted or that are otherwise irrefutable. Similarly, a lawyer's trial preparation must make certain that the client's version of the transaction or occurrence is consistent with physical facts or scientific facts. The physical facts may include time, place, size, measurements, color, and so forth. In automobile accident cases, the physical facts include point of impact on the roadway, point of impact on each vehicle, amount of damage caused by the impact, lighting conditions, road surface, weather, and so on. If photographs show that both cars were red, a lawyer does not want the client and witnesses describing them as brown and black. The witnesses should be shown the photographs. They should be confronted with the physical facts.

Part of the trial preparation includes helping witnesses and the client to fully understand what they observed, refreshing the witnesses' recollections, and helping them appreciate all the facts that are relevant to their testimony. In other words, witnesses should be given the opportunity to see how each witness's testimony fits into the case as a whole. However, lawyers and paralegals must not try to tell witnesses what to say. A witness's testimony must be based upon what the witness knows from his or her own observations and knowledge, not upon what the witness knows from listening to others. Nevertheless, sometimes a witness's observations must be put into perspective. For example, a witness may have a valid estimate of the width of an intersection by reason of the witness's own observations, but it is not wrong to tell the witness what the exact measurement is, to assure the witness that her estimate is reasonable. If the witness's estimate is not reasonable, the witness ought to examine the roadway again and measure the distance in question, assuming that nothing has changed since the time of the accident. If the witness changes her estimate as a result of a subsequent measurement, the reason for the change is a matter that is subject to cross-examination. It is perfectly proper to help a witness to be accurate with estimates and recollections. It is never improper to help a witness to find the truth and understand why it is the truth.

Documentary evidence, such as business records, should comport with the judicial admissions, physical facts, and anticipated testimony. If they do not, the reason for any inconsistency must be determined so that evidence can be reconciled and/or a proper explanation provided.

■ PRESERVING AND ORGANIZING EVIDENCE

A party must organize the evidence and prepare to present it in a manner to make it authoritative, interesting, and persuasive. The first step is to revisit the legal issues. The pleadings establish the basic legal issues and should contain the basic facts; therefore, a good place to begin the trial preparation is to review the pleadings. The legal issues determine what facts are material to the case. The fact issues determine what evidence is relevant to the parties' claims and defenses. Some lawyers begin their preparation for trial by considering where they want to be when the trial concludes. More specifically, they determine what they want to say to the jury in their final arguments. Final arguments often focus on the persuasiveness of the parties' evidence and the application of the evidence to the disputed facts. When a lawyer determines what she or he wants to tell the jury about the case, the lawyer has necessarily determined what evidence must be presented to support the argument.

Parties often do not present all the evidence that is available and relevant to the case, but offer only the evidence that is reasonably necessary to prove the claim or defense at issue. A party does not have any legal or ethical duty to present all the evidence. On the other hand, a party must not take evidence out of context or use it to present a false picture. Furthermore, a lawyer must not conceal evidence or suppress evidence or tamper with evidence or procure false testimony. If lawyers could disregard these proscriptions, the judicial system as we know it would collapse overnight. Lawyers must look upon the truth as sacred.

Before parties can use evidence effectively, they must sort through it, analyze it, evaluate it, and organize it. The process may be very simple when dealing with a small, routine case, or very complex in a large, involved case. While gathering the evidence, it is a good idea to think about how it is going to be preserved, organized, and used.

■ ROLE OF PARALEGALS IN GATHERING EVIDENCE

Paralegals enjoy a major role in gathering the evidence. They may handle any aspect of an investigation. They may handle most aspects of discovery procedures, subject to a lawyer's supervision. Court rules require that a lawyer sign discovery requests and discovery answers, but paralegals may prepare those documents. About the only discovery function that a paralegal may not handle is taking a discovery deposition.

Paralegals perform a vital function in helping to prepare the evidence for use at trial. Sometime before the trial begins, the trial lawyer and paralegals working on the case must carefully analyze all the evidence they have collected, and organize it. They need to make sure they have the evidence they need to prove the client's version of the disputed facts. They must assess what their evidence proves and whether the evidence is going to be admissible at trial, evaluate the persuasiveness of the evidence, determine what facts cannot be proved with the evidence that is available, and decide how best to present the evidence. The evidence must be admissible, understandable, and persuasive. Therefore, a legal assistant needs to have a good understanding about how evidence may be used and the limitations on certain kinds of evidence. The evidence has minimal value unless it can be used in the trial.

SUMMARY

The parties to a civil suit must gather their own evidence. They may obtain evidence through their own investigation efforts and through discovery procedures. These methods of gathering evidence should be used in such a way that they complement each other.

The elements of the plaintiff's causes of action and the defendant's affirmative defenses determine what facts are material (controlling). The evidence that tends to prove a material fact is relevant evidence. Most relevant evidence is admissible in a civil trial.

The advantages of obtaining evidence through investigation are that a party need not wait or depend upon the cooperation of the opposing side. Obtaining evidence and information through an investigation is usually more economical than doing so through discovery. A party need not share the investigation with another party. However, the products of a party's investigation may be subject to disclosure under the court's discovery rules. A party (lawyer) has more control over the development of the evidence when conducting her or his own investigation. A party may begin an investigation even before the suit has been commenced.

The Federal Rules of Civil Procedure have created several methods for conducting discovery to obtain information and evidence. As discovery should be used to complement a party's own investigation efforts, the various methods of discovery should be used to complement each other. Discovery procedures are useful when trying to obtain information from an opposing party and from uncooperative persons who are not parties. They may be used to inquire about any relevant (material) fact or relevant evidence or to obtain information that may lead to the discovery of admissible evidence.

A party may initiate discovery after the suit has been commenced. Each discovery procedure provides a specified period of time in which the respondent must comply with the proponent's discovery request. A party may not resist discovery on the grounds that the opposing party has been delinquent or uncooperative in conducting discovery. A party must keep his or her discovery disclosures current and must supplement the discovery responses as new information becomes available. A party cannot use discovery to obtain privileged information or documents. A party cannot use discovery to obtain the work product of another party or of the other party's lawyer.

The new Federal Rules of Civil Procedure have significantly changed the philosophy and methods of conducting discovery. Under the new rules, a party must volunteer basic discovery information to the opponent at the very beginning of the case. The parties must formulate a discovery plan that they can propose to the court. Then the court prepares a discovery scheduling order that directs what discovery may be conducted, when it must be finished, and the limits on methods of discovery. The parties are limited to ten depositions and twenty-five interrogatories and one independent medical examination, unless the parties stipulate to more and broader discovery. If the parties cannot agree on discovery parameters, the court will establish the parameters for them. It remains to be seen whether those parameters will be liberal or will force discovery economies.

Although the procedure for making requests for admissions is grouped with discovery procedures, it is not a discovery device. Obtaining admissions is a means for narrowing the disputed facts and establishing the genuineness of evidence to facilitate the trial. Consequently, very few limitations are placed on the use of requests for admissions. Unfortunately, some courts actually cut off the use of requests for admissions when discovery is ended. However, that is the point at which a party should prepare and serve requests for admissions, because that is when the facts are known and the admissions should be made.

If a party wrongfully refuses to make admissions pursuant to Rule 36, the only penalty that a court may impose against that party is an award of costs in favor of the proponent of the request for admissions. The costs recoverable are the costs which the proponent incurred to prove the facts which should have been admitted by the respondent.

All discovery demands and disclosures must be signed by a lawyer or by a party. A person who signs a disclosure that is not complete and correct when made is subject to court-imposed penalties. A party who fails to disclose information required by Rule 26 is precluded from using the evidence at a trial, unless the nondisclosure was harmless to the opposing party. The court may impose additional penalties such as payment of the other party's costs and attorney's fees. The court may even tell the jury about the lawyer's failure to make disclosures required by law. Such a statement to the jury could be devastating to the client's case. A court may instruct the jury that the particular facts are deemed established, or prohibit the delinquent party from denying the opponent's claim or defense affected by the nondisclosure. A court could even strike the disobedient party's pleading, leaving that party in default.

If a party has any doubt about the scope of information and evidence that must be provided, the party should consider moving the court for an order requiring the opposing party to state the claim with greater clarity or particularity. The moving party may discuss the question with the opposing party and make a stipulation, pursuant to Rule 29, defining the information and evidence that must be disclosed and specifically including or excluding the matters that are ambiguous. The party may ask the court for an order that allows him or her to delay making an disclosure until the underlying issue has been resolved.

Paralegals must keep in mind that any communication they have with a witness, except a client, may be discovered and used by the opposition. Therefore, a paralegal should never say anything to a witness that could lead to embarrassment for anyone. Witnesses should be assured that it is proper for them to meet and talk with paralegals. A witness should feel free to acknowledge meeting with a paralegal and having discussed the case with him or her. An interview should make the interviewee feel comfortable with the interviewer and the process.

Trial preparation includes helping the client and the witnesses to fully understand what they observed, to refresh witnesses' recollections and to help them appreciate all the facts that are relevant to the witnesses' testimony. Witnesses should be given "the big picture." However, lawyers and paralegals must not try to tell witnesses what to say. It is perfectly proper to help a witness to be accurate with estimates and recollections. It is not improper to help a witness to find the truth and understand why it is the truth.

Documentary evidence, such as business records, should comport with the judicial admissions, physical facts, and anticipated testimony. If they do not, the reason for any inconsistency must be determined so that evidence can be reconciled and/or a proper explanation provided.

The legal issues determine what facts are material to the case. The fact issues determine what evidence is relevant to the parties' claims and defenses. A party must organize and "package" his or her evidence to make it authoritative, instructive, interesting, and persuasive. Parties often do not present all of the evidence that is relevant to the case, but only that evidence that is necessary to prove the claim or defense at issue. A party has no legal or ethical duty to present all of the evidence, but a party must not take evidence out of context or use the evidence to present a false picture. Lawyers must look upon the truth as sacred. A party's evidence should be consistent with facts established by the pleadings and responses to requests for admissions and physical facts.

KEY TERMS

judgment	oral depositions
sua sponte	deposition transcripts
protective order	interrogatories
sanctions	attorneys' work product rule
independent medical examinations	scheduling conference

REVIEW QUESTIONS

1. Why does an investigator need to have a theory about the accident or claim?

2. What is the one discovery function that a paralegal may not handle?

3. Name three advantages that an investigation has over discovery procedures.

4. When does the task of gathering the evidence end?

5. What are the principal limits on the scope of discovery?

6. When is a party required to supplement discovery responses?

7. When is evidence or information relevant for the purpose of discovery procedures?

8. What is a discovery plan?

9. How do requests for admissions differ from discovery procedures?

10. What sanction may be imposed upon a party who wrongly fails to admit a fact pursuant to a Rule 36 request for admission?

CONDUCTING AN INVESTIGATION

Most people who work with the civil litigation system believe that trials bring out the truth, and cases are usually decided on the basis of the truth. But the truth must be found, and lawyers act on the premise that the party who does the best job of collecting, preserving, and presenting the evidence will prevail. The civil justice system requires each party to gather and present his or her own evidence. The more information and evidence an investigator obtains, the better his or her client can evaluate the case and prepare for trial. A superior investigation is exemplified by attention to the details. The information and evidence a party obtains in the course of the initial investigation provide the basis for developing the party's theory of the case. Everything builds on the investigation.

An investigation is an active, hands-on procedure. No amount of education and experience will enable an investigator to sit in the office and gather information and locate evidence. Indeed, like a news reporter, an investigator must try to be at the right place at the right time. An investigation must be conducted aggressively but not obnoxiously. It should be conducted according to a plan—not necessarily a written plan, although that would be fine. A plan helps to avoid wasteful false starts and unnecessary duplication. Making a plan forces the investigator to use forethought, to be deliberate and focused. With forethought, an investigator can determine what information *ought* to exist and where it ought to be found. The plan may be as simple as a list of things to do, or as complete as an outline.

A reason should exist for each step and for the order in which the steps are taken. An investigation plan should (1) identify the facts in dispute; (2) establish a logical sequence for locating evidence and sources of evidence; (3) provide for collecting, organizing, and preserving of evidence; (4) establish the ability to take possession of evidence that is not otherwise protected; (5) coordinate the investigation with discovery procedures (see chapter 8); and (6) determine what witnesses to contact, the order in which to contact the witnesses, and from whom statements should be obtained. The investigator must also decide what kind of a statement to obtain from each witness. The options include an electronic recording, stenographer's verbatim recording, handwritten statement signed by the witness, or typed statement signed by the witness. Sometimes the investigator is better off merely making a memorandum of interview, which is not verified by the witness. The investigation is not complete until the investigator knows what happened, how it happened, and has the means for proving the facts to the court.

The investigation should build in a natural progression. For example, suppose the investigator has to investigate an automobile accident, and information may be available from the client driver, one independent eye-witness, and a police officer. The most common approach would be to interview the client driver first. The client should be readily available, and the investigator needs to know what he claims happened. The client should also provide whatever authorization might be needed to obtain a copy of the police report. Then the investigator makes an appointment to see the police officer. She probably cannot interview the officer while the officer is on duty, and officers usually have a preference about when and where they will meet lawyers and investigators. Before the meeting, the investigator obtains a copy of the police accident report, which should have been filed the same day as the accident and thus should be available. The report will provide the basic information and will be helpful when examining the accident location. Next the investigator inspects the location of the accident. She takes photographs. She makes diagrams to reinforce her memory. Now she is in a good position to interview the independent witness. She does not need an appointment. She finds the witness at her work or at her home, and talks with her. The investigator can communicate effectively about the accident because she has seen the accident situs. She has not wasted any time. Finally, she can keep her appointment with the police officer. She can conduct an efficient and effective interview with the officer because she is fully prepared for it.

■ INTERVIEWING THE CLIENT

An investigator usually begins by obtaining the client's version of the transaction or occurrence. After all, in most cases, the client was directly involved in whatever gave rise to the dispute. Clients generally do not want to have their initial interview with the lawyer or paralegal recorded, but they usually do not object to note taking. The investigator must establish a dialogue by encouraging the client to narrate the transaction or occurrence. The investigator must press gently for the details. The investigator must be patient and must encourage the client to be open, reflective, and candid. All too often, clients have more information than they realize, and the investigator must explore subjects with questions that encourage the client to talk rather than to be reticent. The investigator should avoid stopping or correcting the client until the investigator is confident that she or he *knows* what happened and how it happened. At that point, and not before, the investigator may begin pointing out mistakes, inconsistencies, and "holes" in the client's version of the matter and assumptions.

If the investigation concerns a transaction, it is best to review the documents and circumstances with the client and obtain the client's perspective. If the investigation concerns an accident, it is best to view the scene or location with the client as soon as possible. (The site of the accident is called the **accident scene** when the circumstances relevant to the accident are still the same; if circumstances have changed from the way they were at the time of the accident, the site of the accident is called the accident location.) Hopefully, the client can provide an authoritative explanation about what happened and how it happened. By examining the accident situs together, the investigator and the client can develop a mutual frame of reference that will help them to communicate more effectively about the accident and the evidence and investigation. The investigator could ask the client to demonstrate what the client did leading up to the accident and what happened at the time of the accident. Where that is not feasible, perhaps the client can illustrate what he or she did. If the accident can be simulated, the relevant speed, time, and distance can be calculated and analyzed. If the client was involved in a slip-and-fall accident, the client can show the investigator exactly where the accident happened and how it happened. Some types of accidents, such as airplane crashes, fires in large buildings, and the collapse of large structures, are subject to being re-created through computer models. Some accidents simply cannot be duplicated, demonstrated or illustrated.

If the client did not actually see the accident, it is still useful for the investigator and the client to visit the accident situs together, so they have the same frame of reference. Again, that will make their communications easier and more effective. It is even a good idea for the investigator to find out what the client *believes* probably happened, even though the client really does not know the facts. By obtaining the client's ideas about the event, the investigator will have a better understanding of the client's expectations and assumptions about the case. Later on, it may be necessary to explain to the client why her or his assumptions are wrong. As the investigation progresses, the investigator should try to form a mental picture, perhaps even motion picture, of the critical events in the transaction or occurrence. The mental picture should be constructed from the evidence obtained. Voids in the mental picture point to the need for more evidence.

The physical features of the accident situs may have a good deal to do with how and why the accident happened. These features should be measured, photographed, and diagrammed. In the typical automobile accident case, the investigator should record directions, widths of the roadways, location of traffic controls, landmarks, obstructions to the parties' views, and the apparent points of impact. The investigator should position himself or herself to obtain the perspective that each party and witness had. The measurements and related information can be kept on a diagram and/or on a data sheet. Diagrams are useful even if they are not to scale. The mere act of preparing a diagram helps most people to orient their thinking and reinforces the investigator's memory about the conditions. An investigator who has been to the situs cannot help but feel more authoritative when speaking with witnesses, and can better understand the photographs and diagrams made by others.

■ INTERVIEWING WITNESSES

The investigation plan must consider how to locate and deal with witnesses. Being at the right place at the right time is especially important, and the sooner a witness is contacted the better. There is usually a logical order for interviewing the witnesses that allows an investigator to build on the evidence as it is obtained. Consideration should be given to determining the interview parameters. For example, should the witness be contacted at home or at work or during lunch or at some other time? The investigator is not usually in a position to force other people to cooperate. Therefore, the investigator must do her or his work when and where convenient for the person whose cooperation is needed. Would the witness consider meeting at the scene of the accident? Is it going to be necessary to compensate the witness for her or his time? Should the client attend the witness interview? If the witness is particularly friendly to the client, it may be very useful to have the client attend the interview. If the witness is neutral or somewhat hostile, it might be counterproductive.

The investigator must approach the witness in a manner that is comfortable for the investigator and for the witness. The investigator must appear to be forthright, sincere, and concerned about discovering the truth. To some extent, the approach depends upon the investigator's own personality. If the investigator approaches the witness on a basis that is not comfortable for the investigator, the investigator will appear to lack sincerity and make the witness uncomfortable. Witnesses also differ in how they react to investigators. Each investigator may operate somewhat differently. The manner in which the investigator approaches the witness often depends upon the witness's relationship to the parties. If a witness is known to be friendly to the client, the interview should be relatively easy. On the other hand, if the witness is aligned with the opposing party, he or she may be evasive, contrary, and even belligerent. Consequently, there is no one best way for all investigators to approach all witness.

Although there is no set formula for dealing with witnesses, some guidelines and issues should be considered. An investigator, like a lawyer, is a representative of the client. Whatever the investigator does or does not do will reflect upon the client. It follows that the investigator's manner should gain the witness's respect and trust. The investigator should be polite and respectful, almost to the point of being solicitous. The investigator's approach should develop the witness's interest in the client's case and encourage the witness's cooperation. The interview should be conducted in a relaxed, not pushy, manner. The investigator should never conceal his or her identity from the witness. On the other hand, the investigator may in some instances choose not to identify the client for whom the investigation is being conducted. The interview may begin with an explanation about the purpose of the meeting, that is, to obtain information about the occurrence or transaction. An investigator should always emphasize that he or she is seeking the truth. At the outset, the witness should be assured that it is proper to discuss the event with the investigator. Indeed, the meeting is essential so that the truth can be ascertained. That perspective is vital when dealing with witnesses who are known to be aligned with the opposing side.

It is always nice to work with a witness who has some empathy for the client. The witness may identify with the client because of what the witness observed or otherwise knows about the event, or because of the witness's relationship to the client. On the other hand, these same elements may cause the witness to feel antagonistic toward the client. As part of the investigation plan, an investigator should determine whether something can be said or brought to the witness's attention to cause the witness to develop some concern for the client or the client's problem. It may be useful to explain to the witness how serious the accident was or how serious the injury is. When representing the defendant, it may be useful to explain the defendant's position and that without the witness's help, a serious injustice may result. It may be useful to tell the witness just how important his or her evidence is to the client or to the case as a whole.

The witness should be made to feel that her or his role is truly important to the investigation, to the case, and to the investigator. A witness who believes that his or her contribution is really important and unique will likely be interested and motivated to help. Most witnesses derive a feeling of satisfaction from being part of the civil justice system and doing their duty. Some witnesses do not want to become involved merely because they do not understand the process and they fear some personal involvement. An investigator needs to be able to answer witnesses' questions (concerns) about the process and assure them that their cooperation will not lead to undue personal involvement. If a witness's reluctance to cooperate has some other basis, the investigator's task may be more difficult. For example, a witness who has a criminal record may shy away from interviews and refuse to give statements. Witnesses who have been involved in litigation of their own that did not go well for them may be reluctant to cooperate in someone else's case. They will avoid investigators, refuse to give witness statements, and generally be evasive when they do talk.

Sometimes an investigator can set the stage for a productive interview by informing the witness about the event and the evidence already obtained. An overview may help the witness to understand where and how his or her own evidence fits into the case. It may help the investigator to catch the witness's interest and cooperation. An overview may also help the witness to recall additional facts that the witness might otherwise forget or consider to be unimportant and not mention. If the witness believes the investigator has been candid and the investigator's overview is correct, the witness may be reluctant to contradict the investigator's statements and descriptions. This may be good for the client if the witness had some misinformation or misconceptions about the event. However, the witness may be deterred from discussing his or her version with the investigator because the witness does not want to get into an argument over the facts. So the "overview approach" has potential ramifications that must be gauged before the witness is interviewed. When the investigator wants to lead the witness without cutting off a source of information, the investigator can make brief statements about a fact and ask the witness about his or her version before moving on.

Knowing something about the witness's background and position in the community can help the investigator evaluate the witness's evidence. Therefore, it is useful to find out about the witness's age, address, employment, education, and experience with courts. It is also useful to find out whether the witness has had similar relevant experiences. For example, if the case arises from an industrial accident, it would be useful to know what experience the witness has had with the particular equipment involved. In automobile cases, it is useful to know whether the witness is a licensed driver and whether the witness has been directly involved in any motor vehicle accidents.

An investigator should determine whether the witness has been interviewed by anyone else and has given a statement to anyone else. If so, the witness may have a copy of the prior statement and may be willing to give a copy to the investigator. Indeed, some witnesses who have given one statement feel that should be enough and expect the parties to share that statement. If the witness does not have a copy of the statement, she or he may have a right to a copy and should be told about that right. In addition, the statement may be discoverable when the matter is put into suit, as provided by the Federal Rules of Civil Procedure.

How do lawyers and paralegals deal with witnesses who are mistaken about the facts because of a defect in either memory or perception? It is proper to tell or suggest to a witness that he or she may be mistaken about the fact in question and to explain the apparent reason for the mistake. It is proper to tell a witness that his or her version of the fact is inconsistent with physical possibility or with the observations of other witnesses who had an equivalent or better view. It is proper to ask a witness to conduct a detailed review or study of the fact in light of other circumstances or other evidence. The witness may or may not appreciate such help. A witness's response usually depends, in part, on how he or she is approached about the problem. If a witness feels that the investigator is applying pressure to improperly influence him or her, the witness will be, and should be, resistant, upset, and uncooperative. On the other hand, if the witness believes that he or she is being treated fairly and that the help may prevent him or her from making a mistake, the witness will be receptive and cooperative.

Usually, a paralegal's best approach is to inform the witness that "a bit of a problem" exists. Then the paralegal may explain the nature of the problem. A paralegal should not indicate to the witness that the witness is the problem, or that the paralegal knows the solution and is going to dictate to the witness. A paralegal should manifest a desire to help the witness to resolve the problem or solicit the witness's help to resolve the problem. A paralegal should be prepared to raise questions and offer suggestions that lead the witness to the truth. A paralegal can lead the witness through a reasoning process that takes into consideration all the critical issues that necessarily help the witness to recognize the truth. Hopefully, when the witness understands the big picture and understands how her or his evidence fits into it, the witness will see that her or his evidence is mistaken and why. Hopefully, the witness will be willing to abandon false beliefs in favor of the truth.

If the witness's error in perception or memory is understandable and readily justifiable, the witness, who needs to feel justified, may be more willing to accept having erred. The less justifiable the mistake, the more the witness will cling to it. That is human nature.

These considerations and approaches have no application where the witness is simply lying. Nevertheless, they may force the witness to add to the lie, and that will make cross-examination of the witness easier.

Suppose the witness mistakenly recalls that the accident occurred during daylight. A paralegal could explain to the witness that the police report shows the time of the accident as 9:00 P.M., and the dispatcher's records corroborate the time. The United States Weather Bureau records show that the sun set at 6:30 P.M. By 9:30 P.M., the accident scene would have been dark, except for artificial lighting. The witness may feel as though he has a very good recollection of the accident, and, consequently, believes that he had a good view of it. In this instance, the witness may have mistakenly remembered the accident as occurring during daylight. Or the witness's perspective may have left him with a faulty recollection of the natural lighting conditions. Artificial lighting may have made the scene seem as bright as daylight. Consequently, that is how the witness remembers the scene—as being in daylight. Witnesses do not want to make mistakes. Indeed, they are afraid of making mistakes. They usually do not resent being assisted. They should shun efforts perceived as misleading and improper.

Good planning helps investigators to keep their questions focused so that witnesses do not become impatient and annoyed. A plan helps an investigator to build naturally on the evidence as it becomes available. If an investigator obtains all the pertinent information on the first contact with a witness, the investigator will not have to return to ask more questions. That is important because witnesses are commonly less accommodating on second and third contacts. Indeed, repeat visits may lead to hostility.

■ WITNESS STATEMENTS

As a general rule, lawyers and investigators want **recorded statements** from witnesses, whether the statements are helpful to the client's case or adverse. An adverse witness is going to hurt the client's case no matter what. If the investigator has the witness's version of the matter in a recorded statement, the investigator can be pretty sure he or she knows what the witness will or will not testify to in court.

In a few situations, it may be better not to obtain a witness statement. For example, in states where a party must disclose witness statements to adverse parties, it may be better not to have a statement from a person who is adverse and whose version of the facts is not truthful. In such cases, it may be better to prepare a **memorandum of interview** concerning the witness's knowledge. A memorandum of interview does not have to be disclosed to the opposing side because it is part of the party's work product (Rule 26(b)(3)). It is merely the interviewer's notes. However, a witness who gives a recorded statement may require the lawyer to provide a copy of the statement to the witness, and then the witness may share the statement with the other party (Rule 26(b)(3)). An investigator must decide whether to obtain a recorded statement and if so, what type of statement to obtain and what to include in it.

A recorded statement provides a source of reference that is useful during the remainder of the investigation and at trial. Having the witness's version in writing provides the client with an increased comfort level because it removes some of the uncertainty about civil litigation. Nevertheless, recorded witness statements are hearsay and generally cannot be used as evidence to prove the facts contained in the statements. The witnesses will have to appear in court and give their testimony subject to cross-examination. This general rule has a few exceptions. A party's recorded statement may be put into evidence as substantive evidence *against* that party as an admission. A recorded statement may be used at trial to **impeach** a witness whose testimony contradicts it. (To impeach is to challenge a witness's testimony by showing the witness said or did something inconsistent with his or her present testimony.) In addition, a recorded statement may be used to prove facts contained in the statement when the witness is "unavailable" and the court is satisfied that the statement is trustworthy. Rule 804(b)(5) covers these exceptions as well as the following:

> A statement not specifically covered by any of the foregoing exceptions but having equivalent circumstantial guarantees of trustworthiness, [may be admitted] if the court determines that (A) the statement is offered as evidence of a material fact; (B) the statement is more probative on the point for which it is offered than any other evidence which the proponent can procure through reasonable efforts; and (C) the general purposes of these rules and the interests of justice will best be served by admission of the statement into evidence. However, a statement may not be admitted under this exception unless the proponent of it makes known to the adverse party sufficiently in advance of the trial or hearing to provide the adverse party with a fair opportunity to prepare to meet it, the proponent's intention to offer the statement and the particulars of it, including the name and address of the declarant.

Types of Witness Statements

The most common type of witness statement is a written statement that is signed by the witness. The signed written statement may be used at trial to impeach the witness if the witness testifies to something different from what was recorded in the statement. The witness's signature provides the foundation for using the statement for impeachment. If the witness denies that the signature is his or hers, the investigator must testify that the witness did read and sign the statement at the time and place shown on the statement. A second type of witness statement is an electronically recorded statement, such as an audiotape or a videotape. Ordinarily, a typed transcript is made of the recording, because a transcript is more convenient and easier to use. If the witness reads and signs the transcript, it may be used in the same manner as a written statement that is signed by the witness. A third type of witness statement is a stenographically recorded statement. A stenographer must attend the witness interview and record the witness's statements using shorthand notes or a stenographic machine. The notes are not self-authenticating and are not evidence of the interview. The notes may be used by the stenographer to testify to what she or he heard the witness say during the interview. Again, if the witness reads and signs the transcript made from the shorthand notes, it may be used in the same manner as a written statement that is signed by the witness. A fourth type of recorded statement is made from recording a telephone interview.

Each method of recording a witness statement has its own advantages and disadvantages. Therefore, an investigator must carefully consider which type of statement to obtain from each witness. These investigation statements do not have to be under oath. If a written statement *is* made under oath, it is usually described as an affidavit.

The manner in which an investigator should approach a witness depends, in part, on whether a statement is going to be obtained and how that statement is going to be recorded. For example, if there is reason to believe that a particular witness is not going to be cooperative, it may be

■ **EXHIBIT 9.1**

Form Statement

```
                                              FILE NO. _____
                    WITNESS REPORT OF ACCIDENT
                                        ___AM
DATE OF ACCIDENT_____19___TIME_____PM  PLACE_____

CITY_____ COUNTY_____ STATE_____

CAR A _____
             Make              Color         Direction Moving        Driver's Name

CAR B _____
             Make              Color         Direction Moving        Driver's Name

CAR C _____
             Make              Color         Direction Moving        Driver's Name

WHERE WERE YOU WHEN THE ACCIDENT HAPPENED?_____

IF YOU WERE IN ONE OF THE CARS INVOLVED, WHICH ONE?_____SEATED WHERE? _____

DID YOU SEE THE ACCIDENT HAPPEN?_____ SEE THE CARS AFTERWARDS?_____
```

COMPLETE DIAGRAM

Illustrate position of cars at time of collision:

```
STATE BRIEFLY HOW ACCIDENT HAPPENED_____
_____
_____
_____
_____
_____
_____

WERE THERE ANY STOP SIGNS OR TRAFFIC LIGHTS FACING CAR A?_____ CAR B? _____ CAR C? _____

WERE ANY STOP-AND-GO LIGHTS VIOLATED BY CAR A?_____ CAR B?_____ CAR C? _____

WERE ANY STOP SIGNS VIOLATED BY CAR A?_____ CAR B?_____ CAR C? _____

WHAT IF ANY TRAFFIC VIOLATIONS DID YOU SEE BY CAR A? _____

    CAR B?_____ CAR C? _____
```

PLEASE ANSWER ALL QUESTIONS ON BOTH SIDES

desirable to employ a stenographer to observe and record the interview, because the witness is not likely to sign a written statement and may avoid a tape recorder. An experienced stenographer is capable of being unobtrusive during the interview. Also, a stenographer may be a helpful witness for the investigator if the interviewee challenges the statement or complains about the conduct of the investigator.

Signed Written Statements. The procedure for obtaining a written, signed statement is very simple. The investigator may prepare the statement during the interview, or after the interview based upon the information obtained during the interview. The investigator has quite a bit of control over

WERE ALL LIGHTS BURNING ON CAR A?_____CAR B?_____CAR C?_____

WHAT, IF ANY, SIGNALS WERE GIVEN BY CAR A?_____CAR B?_____CAR C?_____

WHAT WAS THE SPEED OF CAR A?_____CAR B?_____CAR C?_____

WHAT WAS THE SPEED LIMIT?_____

WAS VISIBILITY RESTRICTED FOR DRIVER OF CAR A?_____CAR B?_____CAR C?_____
     (Indicate whether rain, snow, fog, dust, trees, shrubs, buildings, parked cars)

CONDITION OF ROAD OR STREET: DRY_____ICE_____SNOW_____WET_____MUDDY_____

WHERE WAS POINT OF IMPACT ON CAR A?_____

     CAR B?_____CAR C?_____

WHAT DEFECTS DID YOU SEE IN THE CONDITION OF CAR A?_____

     CAR B?_____CAR C?_____

WHAT MARKS OR DEBRIS DID YOU SEE ON THE ROAD?_____

WHERE WERE THEY WITH REFERENCE TO THE CENTER OF THE STREET AND WITH REFERENCE TO THE CARS INVOLVED?

_____

_____

LENGTH OF SKID MARKS, IF ANY, FROM CAR A?_____CAR B?_____CAR C?_____

WHAT WAS THERE ABOUT THE POSITION OF THE CARS, OR THE MARKS ON THE ROAD, OR OTHER FACTS THAT YOU

OBSERVED, TO INDICATE WHO WAS TO BLAME FOR THE ACCIDENT?_____

_____

WAS EITHER CAR ON THE WRONG SIDE OF THE ROAD?_____

WHAT DID YOU HEAR THE DRIVERS SAY AFTER THE ACCIDENT?_____

_____

WERE YOU INJURED?_____DID ANYONE ELSE APPEAR TO BE INJURED?_____IF SO, IN WHAT CAR?_____

WHO ELSE WAS A WITNESS TO THIS ACCIDENT?

     NAME _____ADDRESS_____

     NAME _____ADDRESS_____

          YOUR NAME HERE:_____AGE:_____

          ADDRESS:_____

          TELEPHONE: RESIDENCE_____BUSINESS:_____

          DATE:_____

what goes into a written statement and what is not included. Although the contents must be approved by the witness, he or she is almost never asked to prepare a written statement. One example of a statement that a witness does prepare is the form statement that insurance companies sometimes mail to witnesses (see exhibit 9.1). The witnesses are asked to fill in the blanks and make diagrams that show what they observed. The witnesses are asked to sign, date, and return the statement in an envelope that the insurer provides. Some law firms have used a similar approach where many witnesses are involved, such as with a hotel fire or airplane crash. Such statements are usually looked upon as preliminary contacts and are used to identify witnesses who have significant information and are cooperative.

The investigator almost always prepares the written statement for the witness to sign because most witnesses simply would not make the effort to prepare their own statement. The investigator may tell the witness that she or he is preparing a statement that the witness will be asked to sign. Or the interviewer may simply start asking the witness a series of questions and write down the answers in a statement format, which, at the end of the interview, the witness is asked to read and sign. The investigator's notes become the witness's statement.

The witness's own words should be used insofar as possible. The statement ought to be single spaced to reduce the possibility of interpolation. When the interview is finished, the statement is done. If the witness agrees that the statement is accurate, the witness should be encouraged to sign all pages. A lawyer cannot rely upon an unsigned statement. A witness cannot be impeached with a statement unless the witness has signed it. Consequently, a witness cannot be cross-examined from an unsigned statement. The witness statement ought to conclude with an acknowledgment showing that the witness has read it and received a copy. It is easy to make a copy for the witness to keep.

If the witness is reluctant to sign the statement, the interviewer should make it clear that he or she will give the witness a copy of the statement. The copy will be a valuable reference for the witness when other lawyers and investigators contact him or her. The witness's signature is the witness's assurance that this is the statement he or she gave and it is accurate. It is fair to point out that in one or two years, the witness's memory may not be as clear as it is currently, so signing the statement is assurance that it was true and correct when made. In other words, signing the statement is for the witness's own benefit and protection. If the witness's signed statement is totally beneficial to the investigator's client, the investigator may suggest to the witness that by signing it and retaining a copy, the witness can use the same statement if other investigators happen to contact the witness. The laws of some states require investigators to give witnesses copies of all signed statements. Rule 26(b)(3) requires a party to give a witness a copy of his or her statement if and when requested by the witness. Some courts require parties to provide copies of witness statements to the opposing parties when requested. Those states do not recognize the preparation of witness statements to be part of a party's work product or attorney's work product. According to Rule 26(b):

> Upon request, a person not a party may obtain without the required showing a statement concerning the action or its subject matter previously made by that person. If the request is refused, the person may move for a court order.

Electronically Recorded Statements.   Electronically recorded statements are increasing in popularity as recording devices become smaller and more reliable. Tape-recorded interviews relieve the investigator of the chore of writing the statement. Tape recordings are inexpensive to make. Tape recorders can be used so as not to be obtrusive. They permit the investigator and witness to enter into a natural dialogue. A tape-recorded interview may take less time than preparing a written, signed statement. Investigators must have in mind that some witnesses develop "stage fright" when they see a tape recorder. It is not that they intend to make any false statements; they are afraid that if they make a mistake, the recording will "trap" them. Some witnesses decline to be interviewed when they are told the procedure will be recorded. The investigator has very little control over exactly what goes into the recorded statement, whereas a written statement can be "edited" as it is made.

Generally, it is good to preview the subject with the witness before recording the interview. The preview gives the investigator an opportunity to determine exactly what the witness knows and is willing to say. The investigator can do a better job of framing questions and avoiding matters that are sensitive or counterproductive. When the investigator has obtained a good overview of the witness's knowledge, the interviewer may simply state that she or he would like to cover this same material in a recorded statement, and ask, "Would that be all right?" The recorder should be ready to be turned on. The interviewer should state his or her name, the name of the witness, the date, and the time of the interview. Then the witness should be asked to state his or her name and spell it. The witness should also be asked to give his or her address. Generally speaking, it is perfectly all right for the interviewer to ask **leading questions.** A leading question suggests the answer the interviewer wants. Witnesses do not mind, and leading questions do not impair the usual uses of recorded witness statements. On the other hand, answers given to leading questions are never as persuasive as the statements articulated by the witness in his or her own words.

Stenographically Recorded Statements.   Some statements are stenographically recorded. In other words, the investigator hires a stenographer to make a verbatim transcript of the interview. The stenographer may make notes in shorthand or by using a stenographic machine. Lawyers typically refer to stenographers as court reporters even though they do not necessarily work in a courtroom or for a court. The investigator must interview the witness in the presence of the stenographer, who records the questions and answers. Ordinarily, these statements are not made under oath, but they may be. After the interview, the stenographer uses her or his notes to prepare a transcript of the interview. The transcript usually resembles an oral deposition transcript.

A stenographic transcript provides a record of what the witness said. It preserves the information and may be used to refresh the witness's recollection when preparing for trial, but not when the witness is on the stand and testifying at trial. (When testifying, a witness may refresh his or her recollection only from a document that the witness has prepared himself or herself.) If the witness is willing to read the transcript and adopt its contents by signing the transcript, it may be used to impeach the witness if the witness tries to testify to something that is different than what is in the statement. If the witness declines to sign the transcript, the court reporter may testify from his or her notes concerning the witness's prior statements. The stenographer testifies to what he or she heard during the interview and may use the stenographic notes to "refresh" and confirm his or her memory. Technically, a stenographer's transcript cannot, by itself, impeach the witness; it is the stenographer who impeaches the witness. But a written statement that the witness has signed is, itself, evidence that can impeach the witness. Stenographically recorded statements are particularly useful when dealing with a witness who is uncooperative. A stenographer is an independent witness to the interview, and that may provide some protection if the witness should later claim that the investigator applied undue pressure to obtain the statement.

Telephone Interview Statements.   Some witness interviews are conducted by telephone. A telephone interview can be recorded, and a transcript can be made from the recording. The witness must be told that the conversation is being recorded. Telephone interviews are easy to make, quick, and inexpensive. Very little time and effort are needed to set up and conduct a telephone interview. A telephone interview causes the witness the least amount of inconvenience. On the other hand, telephone interviews are difficult for investigators to do well. The witness can easily terminate the interview. The investigator cannot see the witness, so cannot fully evaluate the witness. Too often, portions of telephone recordings are garbled. The audiotapes of telephone conversations are difficult to present and use at trial if the transcript of the recording is challenged.

Memorandum of Interview

In states where parties are required to exchange witness statements on demand, lawyers are reluctant to obtain statements except for very specific and compelling reasons, because they do not want to share their efforts with the opposition. In those states, a practice has evolved of making a memorandum of interview, which contains the witness information but is not directly adopted by the witness by signing it. A lawyer may supply a copy of the memorandum of interview to the witness so that the witness can refer to it. But the memorandum is not considered to be a recorded statement because it is not a verbatim recording and has not been signed by the witness. Rule 26(b) defines witness statements:

> For purposes of this paragraph, a statement previously made is (A) a written statement signed or otherwise adopted or approved by the person making it, or (B) a stenographic, mechanical, electrical, or other recording, or a transcription thereof, which is a substantially verbatim recital of an oral statement by the person making it and contemporaneously recorded.

Uses for Witness Statements

There are a number of reasons for obtaining a witness's recorded statement. A statement preserves the information the witness has. A statement may be used to refresh the witness's recollection when preparing for trial. It may be used to impeach the witness if the witness changes his or her version. A statement becomes part of the investigation file, so the investigator may compare it with other information and evidence. A statement may be shown to other witnesses to help them understand facts that are recorded in it. A statement may be shown to the opposing party as part of a settlement negotiation effort. A lawyer is much more comfortable preparing for trial knowing that the important witnesses have committed themselves to certain facts in recorded statements, because if a witness changes his or her testimony, the recorded statement shows the lawyer's good faith, and the statement may be used to impeach the witness.

Content of Witness Statements

An investigator must use common sense in determining what should go into a recorded statement and what, if anything, should be omitted. It might be nice to keep certain things out of the statement and out of evidence, especially things that the investigator knows are wrong and will cause the witness problems later on. If a statement is used at trial for any purpose, the whole statement might be received into evidence. No law or rule provides that a statement must be complete in every detail. But a witness has the right to object to giving or signing a statement that omits facts the witness considers to be important. The witness's sense of propriety must be respected. A statement must accurately reflect the witness's version of the facts insofar as the facts are recorded.

Accurate details help to make a witness's recorded statement authoritative and credible. Details help a lawyer to develop and present a sharp, clear picture of the transaction or occurrence at trial. This is true even though lawyers try to avoid going into unnecessary details at trial because such details only serve to confuse the issues and the jury. If a lawyer has a good understanding of the details, she or he can effectively cross-examine witnesses.

A good recorded statement, regardless of the type, should commit the witness to his or her version of the occurrence or transaction. It should clearly set forth the information, evidence, and facts that the witness knows and identify the sources of the witness's knowledge. For example, it is not enough to state that the witness saw a vehicle traveling at a certain speed. The statement must also show that the witness had an opportunity to accurately observe the vehicle's speed. The statement should note where the witness was when he saw the vehicle, where the vehicle was, how long he observed it, and the direction of travel. The statement should establish that the witness has good eyesight and has sufficient experience to make a reasonably accurate judgment concerning the speed of the vehicle in question.

A good statement should also record the witness's lack of knowledge about important facts. For example, it could properly note that the witness did not look for skid marks, does not know of any other witnesses, did not talk to any of the parties, is not acquainted with any of the parties, did not hear a horn sounded before the collision, did not see the traffic light, and so forth. Some signed statements are purely **negative statements.** A negative statement provides that the witness does *not* have the particular information or know the fact(s). Negative statements provide some insurance against having witnesses come forward at a later date with evidence that is harmful to the client's case. A good negative statement neutralizes the witness. If a witness indicates that he or she does not have certain information but will not give a statement to that effect, the witness's reluctance is a red flag that the witness may be hiding information or is aligned with the other side.

■ PREPARING WITNESS STATEMENTS

An investigator should not rush into writing out a statement for the witness. It is better to simply talk with the witness for a while to find out what the witness knows and what the witness's attitude is about the occurrence or transaction. After developing the basic facts known by the witness, the investigator should start writing out a statement for the witness to sign. The witness may or may not be told at the beginning of the interview that she or he will be asked to sign the statement. The written statement often begins with the date and place at the top, as shown in exhibit 9.2.

Having the witness's signature on each page makes the statement more reliable, authoritative, and easier to use. It assures the witness that it is his or her statement. It helps to protect not only the witness, but the investigator and the party who is relying upon the statement. If the witness is reluctant to give a signed statement, the investigator may point out that, like it or not, the witness is already involved in the matter. It will be easier for everyone if the witness cooperates by "doing the right thing." The witness should have a record of his or her observations, and the proposed statement can be that record. The statement will be a convenient reference for the witness if and when the case comes up for trial.

Investigators commonly make minor errors in a written statement. When errors are made, the investigator should identify them to the witness and ask the witness to initial the corrections. The witness's initials in the body of a written statement are evidence that the witness has read and corrected the statement; therefore, the inference is that the final product is true and correct and specifically approved by the witness. Indeed, some investigators make it a point to make at least one mistake so that the witness has the opportunity to make at least one correction in the body of the statement.

Witnesses will be more cooperative and responsive if they feel the investigator is being candid, fair, and sensitive to their concerns. As a last-resort kind of argument, an investigator may tell a reluctant witness that if he or she will not give a signed statement, the lawyers will have to arrange to take the witness's deposition. The witness will have to appear for the deposition at some time and place selected by the lawyers. The witness will have to give the information, probably in greater detail, and under oath.

■ **EXHIBIT 9.2**

Written Witness Statement

[date]
[place]

Statement of Jasmine E. Carter

I live at _____ . I am _____ years of age and employed at _____ . My parents are _____ , and they live at _____ . They usually know where I am if I have to travel out of state. On [date], I was a witness to an accident at

***

I have read the above statement consisting of three pages. Yes
The statement is true and correct. Yes
I have received a copy of this statement. Yes

_____ [witness signature] _____

The choice is the witness's. An uncooperative witness may be subpoenaed for a deposition. Usually, depositions cannot be taken until after the matter has been put into suit. (Rule 30(a)). However, if good cause is shown, a deposition can be taken before suit. (Rule 27(a)). Unlike the taking of depositions, the procurement of statements does not expose the witness to the opposing side.

■ PRESERVING EVIDENCE

Once an investigator has identified an item of evidence, steps should be taken for **preserving the evidence** and maintaining its authority. Physical evidence comes in many forms. It may be an entire automobile or a machine or a mechanical part or a piece of glass or an instrument or a document, etc. If the custodian of the physical evidence is not a party, and therefore is not subject to the court's jurisdictions and rules, the investigator should inform the custodian about the importance of the evidence and the necessity of preserving it for use in the litigation. If the custodian will not part with it, the investigator should offer assistance to make sure it is properly stored. If some expense will be involved, suitable arrangements must be made to cover those expenses. The custodian should be informed that the case might not be resolved for many, many months and that the evidence must be retained until it is no longer needed. It may be possible to subpoena the evidence and place it under the court's jurisdiction.

Seldom is an investigator fortunate enough to be on the scene of an accident soon enough to preserve all the relevant evidence; however, it is surprising how long the effects of an event do remain, whether the event is an airplane crash, a shooting, a slip-and-fall accident, or another kind of occurrence. Even if the skid marks and debris from an automobile collision are already gone, good photographs of the accident location may be used to illustrate the conditions as they did exist. For example, photographs taken within hours of the accident may show the condition of the street, its construction, and its general appearance. A witness may be able to use such photographs to illustrate the location of skid marks as they were at the accident scene. If photographs or plats or similar items are used during the investigation or to prepare witnesses to testify at trial, any marks you have made on them might disqualify them from being used at trial. For example, if witness A has drawn skid marks on a photograph and witness B attempts to use the photograph at trial, A's markings could be considered as "leading" witness B. It is safest to have more than one set of photographs or other graphics, and make marks only on expendable copies.

Photographs

Photographs may be used to preserve evidence, such as the "accident scene," so that jurors can see it. Photographs may be used to help jurors visualize objects that cannot be brought to the courtroom for their inspection. Photographs may be used for illustrative purposes, that is, to help a witness describe the things she or he observed. An investigator may use photographs during the investigation as an aid to interviewing witnesses. Usually a witness can be more specific about the facts if she or he has one or more photographs to look at while describing them. In addition, photographs often help witnesses to recall facts. If an investigator has a good set of photographs available when interviewing a witness, the photographs may help the investigator to avoid being misled by the witness whose perspective is wrong or whose memory is bad or who is biased.

An investigator should collect as many photographs as possible from the witnesses and make as many additional photographs as reasonably possible. An investigator should err on the side of taking too many pictures, rather than not enough. The same guidelines for gathering, preserving, and using still photographs apply to motion pictures and video pictures.

A photograph that depicts a fact material to the case, such as a skid mark, defective stairway step, or body wound, may be evidence of that fact. To be evidence of the fact, the photograph must show the subject matter in the same condition as it was at the time of the occurrence. The jury sees the fact by looking at the photograph. The witness must lay a foundation for use of the photograph by identifying when the photograph was taken and explaining that it shows the subject matter as it was at the time in question. With that foundation, the jury may rely upon the photograph as a tool for determining the truth. For example, a photograph of an accident scene that shows conditions as they were at the time of the accident is evidence of those conditions. If the photograph happens to show a car parked near the situs of the accident, the jury may conclude that the parked car was there, even though the witnesses do not remember the parked car. On the other hand, photographs that do not show exactly the same conditions and circumstances that existed at the time of the occurrence are not, in themselves, evidence of facts. At most, they have some illustrative value.

Illustrative photographs are useful because they show similar objects or similar scenes or similar circumstances. Illustrative photographs may be used at trial to help a witness describe what the witness observed and knows, but they are *not* evidence. The evidence is the witness's testimony. The judge may not allow a jury to take illustrative exhibits to the jury room to examine and consider as part of their deliberations. The jurors must rely upon the testimony, not the illustrative exhibits. There is too much danger that the jury may forget that the illustrative exhibit is not proof of anything. Consequently, jurors see the illustrative exhibits only while they are being used by the witness in the courtroom.

Court rules provide that each party may ask every other party to disclose whatever evidence another party has or knows about. Consequently, photographs that are evidence must be disclosed and made available to other parties if and when requested. The underlying philosophy of the courts is that all parties must have equal access to the evidence. Furthermore, such photographs must be protected from loss or destruction. A party who causes the loss of material evidence is in real trouble. The party or lawyer is subject to all of the sanctions provided by Rule 37(a)(4) (see chapter 8). On the other hand, photographs that an investigator has made that are merely illustrative are not sacrosanct. If a party loses an illustrative photograph, it is only that party's loss. An illustrative photograph need not be disclosed to other parties. However, as a general rule, courts require parties to disclose in advance of the trial all witnesses and exhibits the parties intend to use at trial. Therefore, an illustrative photograph that a party intends to use at trial will have to be disclosed.

Suppose that a month after the plaintiff's slip-and-fall accident on the defendant's stairway, the defendant's investigator took photographs of the stairway. After the photographs were developed, the investigator discovered that they show some debris on the steps. What should the investigator do about the pictures? They are bad pictures. They are not evidence. They should be destroyed, and new photographs should be taken that do not show debris on the steps. However, if the photographs had been made immediately after the accident and showed the condition of the stairway as it was at the time of accident, they would have to be preserved and disclosed. They would be evidence and irreplaceable.

To take photographs for use in civil litigation, a good 35mm camera is usually best. A 50mm lens is usually best because it is neither a wide-angle or a telephoto. A 50mm lens tends to show the subject in the most natural configuration. Wide-angle photographs taken with a 28mm lens may be kept out of evidence because they distort the scene too much. The photographer should consider the purpose for the photographs before taking them, and how they might be used. Will the photographs be illustrative, or evidence? Just because they are taken long after an accident does not mean that they will not be evidence. For example, a photograph taken of a dented fender six months after the accident may still be evidence of the dent. Once the fender is repaired, that photograph will the best evidence of the dent.

The subject should be nicely framed, but the photographer must also be aware of what and who are in the background. If the photographs are going to be used to help the jury to visualize the subject, it is important to provide a perspective that makes the jurors feel truly acquainted with the subject. When they look at the photographs, they should feel that they are seeing the entire scene, not just what the photographer wants them to see.

Photographs should be taken in a sequence, beginning well away from the subject so that the subject is placed in context. Looked at one after another, in sequence, the photographs should bring the viewer closer and closer to the subject and then show the various facets of the subject. For example, suppose the case centers upon the condition of an interior step of a stairway in an apartment house. The photographer should begin the sequence by taking a couple of photographs that show the entire front of the apartment house and the buildings on each side. Then she should take photographs of the back and sides. She should take a series of photographs in front that bring the viewer closer and closer to the front door. She should take photographs with the front door open and entering the foyer. Then she should show the hallway with the stairway, moving closer and closer to the stairway. Some photographs should show the entire stairway from the bottom, side, and top. Then a series of photographs should move the viewer to the step in question. The step should be photographed from each possible angle. The set of photographs taken in this manner makes the jurors feel as though they have visited the scene. The photographer must make a record of the date and time the photographs were taken, the direction of each view, relevant measurements, relevant colors, and who was present.

Lawyers face some potential problems when deciding which photographs of a set to use. In the preceding example, although the photographs of the back of the apartment house may be "interesting" and may help the jurors to feel as though they are familiar with the accident site, are they relevant? What if they show a lot of debris and disrepair? The defendant will want to keep those photographs out of evidence because they would tend to prejudice the court and jury against the defendant. For that very reason, the plaintiff would want the court to receive the photographs into evidence. If the defendant's investigator took the photographs, they would not have to be disclosed to the plaintiff because they are not material evidence.

An investigator cannot always know the value and purpose for which a photograph will be used. By way of illustration, an investigator might take a photograph of the street where an accident occurred, to show the location of the stop sign. That photograph might later become important because it shows there were no skid marks on the street at the time the photograph was made. Sometimes the absence of something may be as important as the presence of something. But how does the investigator know what is missing and that the missing thing is important? He or she does not know. Nevertheless, good photographs taken in the proper manner will generally meet a client's needs and be fully usable in litigation.

Records

Almost any transaction or occurrence that ends in civil litigation has some relevant records. The records may have been generated as a result of the occurrence, as where the police or the transportation board prepares a report on an automobile accident. The records may be part of the transaction or occurrence, as in a medical malpractice case where records concerning the patient's care and treatment are routinely prepared by the physician and hospital, or in a business transaction case where the parties may have kept many records to reflect their contentions about the transactions. The records may be related to the dispute but not to the transaction or occurrence, as in a personal injury claim where the plaintiff's past employment and tax records are relevant to his claim for loss of income.

Records that are under the client's control are readily available. Copies should be made to use in the investigation. Many records are public and are available for the asking. Official records and reports that were generated by the transaction or occurrence often provide the names and addresses of additional witnesses and should be obtained as soon as possible.

Some records cannot be obtained without signed authorizations, such as tax returns, hospital records, medical records, police reports, employment records, school records, and official death records. Each law office has its own forms for obtaining such records. The custodian of such records may have a preferred form, and the custodian's preference must generally be honored. If the custodian's requirements become too unreasonable, the records may be obtained by taking the custodian's deposition and having the records subpoenaed for inspection and copying at the deposition (see Rule 45(a)).

The client should sign the necessary authorizations for such records at the first meeting. It is usually a good idea to leave the authorization undated until they are used. That way, if there is some delay before the authorizations are used, they will be current. One hospital association arbitrarily decided not to honor authorizations that are more than six months old—a rule that is easily circumvented by not dating the authorizations until they are to be used.

If the authorization is to be signed by someone other than the client, it should be dated when signed, even though it is not always convenient or desirable to use the authorization right away. For example, it may be preferable to wait until an injured plaintiff returns to work before obtaining the plaintiff's employment records and personnel file. In this case, the decision when to obtain the records will be influenced by whether or not the defendant's lawyer is going to be able to obtain another authorization at a later date.

Using Experts

A party should not overlook the possibility of employing experts who know about the subject matter to assist with the investigation. For example, if a plaintiff is considering bringing a medical malpractice action against a physician or hospital, it is useful to have another physician or nurse review all the patient's records to determine whether proper procedures were followed in a timely manner. A party may hire an accident reconstructionist to assist with the investigation of an accident. Reconstructionists are available to help with all kinds of accidents, including automobile, airplane, and industrial accidents and explosions. In a malpractice action against an accountant, the plaintiff should retain another accountant to review the records and advise whether they were properly prepared. An expert may be able to locate important publications concerning the subject matter. The publications may be authorities that can be used as evidence, as provided in Rule 803(18), or they may merely provide information about the subject that is useful in dealing with the evidence and preparing the case for trial.

A paralegal may conduct the search for a competent expert who is willing to provide timely assistance. There are several national organizations that act as clearing houses for obtaining expert witnesses for litigants. A paralegal may prepare a letter to an expert outlining the nature of the problem, summarizing the information that is available, describing the areas of concern, and stating the scope and terms of the expert's engagement. A paralegal may collect data for the expert to review, and may be the expert's contact for additional inquiries. A paralegal may work directly with a retained expert, and may report the expert's opinions and recommendations to the client.

■ ETHICAL CONSIDERATIONS

Suppose that immediately before trial, the client confesses that the information she supplied in a written, signed statement is false. The lawyer and paralegal have been relying upon the information in preparing the case for trial, but the statement has not been disclosed to anyone else. What course of action should be taken? The client cannot be allowed to use fraud or deceit against the adverse party. As officers of the court, lawyers have a duty to prevent clients and witnesses from testifying falsely. Since the false information has not yet been communicated to the other parties or to their lawyers or to the court, the lawyer does not need to disclose that the client has lied. If false information had been supplied to the opposing side, through answers to interrogatories or in some other manner, the opposing party would have to be told of the error, but not necessarily how the error occurred. If the client is unwilling to allow corrections to be made, the lawyer is faced with a dilemma. The lawyer must not disclose privileged communications. However, the lawyer must not permit his client to perpetrate a fraud upon the court. The dilemma is resolved in favor of disclosing the privileged information to the court. The lawyer would also have to withdraw from the case if the client persists with the lie.

SUMMARY

I. Purpose of investigation

    A. Find evidence and information relevant to the disputed facts.

    B. Collect evidence with which to prove or disprove alleged facts.

    C. Preserve evidence.

    D. Prepare and organize evidence for use at trial.

II. Guidelines

    A. Establish an investigation plan.

        1. Identify the purposes for the investigation.

        2. Establish priorities.

        3. Keep the plan flexible to change as warranted.

    B. Begin the investigation as soon as possible

    C. Begin by obtaining the client's version of the transaction or occurrence.

        1. Pay attention to the details.

        2. Test claims and assumptions against physical fact.

    D. Build on the evidence as it is acquired.

    E. Preserve the evidence.

        1. Witness information

            a) Depositions before suit

            b) Statements

                (1) Signed

                (2) Recorded

            c) Memorandum of interview

            d) Letter to witness regarding the gist of the witness's information.

        2. Scene: measurements, diagrams, photographs, models

        3. Documents (always record sources)

        4. Considerations

            a) Making or keeping evidence to be admissible in court

            b) Keeping evidence authoritative and therefore persuasive

    F. Evaluate evidence for the following:

        1. Completeness—Check on records and other documents volunteered by the opposing party; there should be no need to verify records supplied pursuant to discovery rules by a lawyer.

2. Accuracy—Even determinations made in official investigations may need to be verified.

3. Availability, now and in the future

4. Authenticity—For example, watch for unsigned copies of affidavits, statements, and documents.

G. Keep the "big picture" in mind while collecting and evaluating evidence.

H. Be concerned about negative evidence and the absence of evidence. For example:

1. Absence of skid marks

2. Absence of physical complaints, symptoms, findings

3. Absence of property damage

I. Do not let appearances mislead you or cause you to make false assumptions.

J. Do not be too quick to discard available evidence. Evidence that at first may not seem relevant may become critical as the investigation continues.

K. Collect the evidence now and sort it out later. Evidence that at first seems detrimental may turn out to be very helpful.

III. Procedure

A. Obtain the client's version.

B. Visit the scene of the occurrence.

C. Collect all the documents relevant to the transaction.

D. Locate and interview eyewitnesses.

E. Interview friendly witnesses.

F. Interview neutral witnesses.

G. Interview the potential adverse party if she or he is not represented by a lawyer.

H. Obtain official records and documents concerning the transaction or occurrence.

I. Locate photographs and make photographs.

1. Photographs that show facts are evidence.

2. Photographs that are illustrative may help witnesses testify to the facts.

IV. Interviewing The Client

A. Record the client's version of the transaction or occurrence as soon as possible.

B. Record details even if their importance is not obvious; details make a pattern and provide a basis for recalling other facts.

C. Probe to make sure you have obtained all the available information. Clients often have more information than they realize.

D. Avoid stopping and correcting the client until you are confident you know what happened and how it happened. Wait to point out mistakes, inconsistencies and "holes" in the client's version of the matter.

E. View the accident scene or accident location with the client as soon as possible, and have the client demonstrate what happened, insofar as that is possible.

F. When the client does not know what happened, find out what the client believes probably happened. This gives you a better understanding of the client's assumptions and expectations about the case.

G. Form a mental picture of the critical events of the occurrence. The mental picture should be constructed out of the evidence that you have obtained. Voids in the mental picture point to a need for more evidence.

H. Have the client make a diagram, if appropriate. This diagram does not have to be to scale, but the mere act of preparing a diagram helps people to orient their thinking, and reinforces the memory about conditions at an accident scene, for example.

V. Witnesses

A. Determine the best circumstances for conducting the interview: scene, work, office, home, telephone, restaurant.

B. Decide whether the client should participate in the interview to help the witness and to promote relations with the witness.

C. Determine whether a statement should be obtained from a witness.

D. Determine the purpose for which a statement will be used if one is to be obtained: preservation of information, impeachment, negation of a witness's role, justification of an intended settlement, or other disposition.

E. Determine how much of what the witness has to say should be included in the statement.

F. Determine whether the witness will be available and accessible in the future.

VI. Witness statements—What information should be included in a witness statement?

A. General rule: The client's statement should be complete and as detailed as possible. Preserve the client's privilege by protecting against disclosure of the statement.

B. Independent witness statements should be accurate, but need not include everything.

C. An adverse party's statements should be accurate and all-inclusive; do not omit anything, whether good or bad.

D. Statements should be as factual as possible, but opinions should be used when they are the only way to express information.

E. When making a recorded statement an interviewer should use leading questions to develop the client's version of the facts.

    F. If the client says she was traveling only twenty-five miles per hour at the time of the accident, and you believe her, then say to the witness, "Wouldn't you agree that Ms. Fredericks was driving at not more than twenty-five miles per hour?" Do not ask, "Was Ms. Fredericks traveling more than twenty-five miles per hour or in excess of the speed limit?"

    G. If a recorded telephone statement can be taken on the second contact, you can be better prepared to ask the right questions and avoid the wrong questions.

    H. Determine whether the witness should be given a copy of the statement.

VII. Preparing witness statements

    A. Extend yourself to establish rapport.

    B. Cultivate cooperation.

        1. Make the witness feel appreciated.

        2. Stress civic duty.

        3. Show the witness why his or her information is important.

        4. Establish a line of communication with the witness.

        5. Determine whether the witness will be available when needed.

    C. Determine how to find the witness if he or she were to move.

    D. Make the witness appreciate that you are being fair with him or her.

VIII. Preserving Evidence

    A. Take photographs.

        1. Cameras with a 50mm lens do not distort.

        2. Objects should be photographed from several angles to obtain several perspectives.

        3. Photographs should be taken in sequence, from a distance leading up to the particular subject, so that the viewer can see the scene and objects in context.

        4. Do not "touch up" the accident scene before taking pictures.

        5. Clean up the accident location. (Pictures of location do not purport to show conditions as they were at the time of the accident. However, no one should ever tamper with the appearance of the accident scene.) Distorted or prejudicial photographs should not be received into evidence.

        6. The witness must lay a foundation for the use of photographs at trial.

            a) Photographer: date, time, camera, lens, direction, distances, subject matter

            b) Reasonably accurate portrayal of subject matter

            c) Picture as evidence, such as the accident scene

      d) Picture as illustrative evidence, to help the witness explain what the witness saw

    7. It is better to take too many pictures than not enough. Take pictures of the entire scene or location even though the relevance may not yet be evident.

  B. Evidence from witnesses should always be weighed against physical fact.

  C. The evidence should make a pattern or a picture. If part of the "picture" is missing, something is wrong with the evidence.

  D. Use experts to help conduct the investigation.

    1. Experts are very useful for identifying problems, and for preserving information and evidence.

    2. Experts are often able to suggest additional areas of inquiry and use of scientific literature.

    3. Engineers are particularly useful in dealing with claims involving machines, structures, real estate, and products.

KEY TERMS

accident scene	negative statement
recorded statement	leading question
memorandum of interview	preserving the evidence
impeach	

REVIEW QUESTIONS

1. Why should you prepare an investigation plan?
2. List five considerations for preparing an investigation plan.
3. Of what use are photographs during the investigation?
4. Under what circumstances is it preferable to obtain a memorandum of interview rather than a witness statement?
5. Under what circumstances is it all right for a paralegal to try to have a witness change her or his version of an occurrence?
6. Why is it important to obtain background information about an independent witness?
7. What advantage does a tape-recorded witness statement have over a handwritten, signed witness statement?
8. What advantages does a handwritten, signed statement have over a tape-recorded statement?
9. Why is it significant that a witness statement is considered to be hearsay?
10. Is a paralegal required to give the witness a copy of the witness's signed statement?
11. How does a typical signed witness statement differ from an affidavit?
12. What should you do about a substantive error you make in a written witness statement?

10

INTERROGATORIES

Written interrogatories are the most basic and economical discovery procedure used in civil litigation. A written interrogatory is merely a written question propounded by one party to another party. The author of an interrogatory is the **proponent,** and the party who must answer the interrogatory is the **deponent.** Each question must be singular and clearly stated. It may have subparts stated separately, but each subpart counts as a separate interrogatory. Though interrogatories are inherently questions, they may be stated as either questions or imperatives. For example, an interrogatory may be phrased "What is the date of your birth?" or "State the date of your birth." Interrogatories may be used to discover relevant facts, evidence and information. An interrogatory is relevant if it is reasonably calculated to lead to discovery of admissible evidence. Interrogatories may be used to obtain copies of relevant documents or information contained in documents that are under the control of the deponent. Interrogatories are used to identify tangible evidence and its custodian or location.

■ PROCEDURE

Rule 33 of the Federal Rules of Civil Procedure authorizes a party to serve written interrogatories upon any other party, but interrogatories may not be served upon a person who is not a party. The parties do not have to be adverse to each other to be able to serve interrogatories upon each other. Thus, codefendants who have not cross-claimed against each other may serve interrogatories upon each other. Rule 26(f) precludes parties from serving interrogatories if they have participated in a discovery planning meeting, as provided by Rules 26(d) and (f). In most state courts, the plaintiff may serve interrogatories with the complaint or anytime after commencement of the action. If the plaintiff serves interrogatories before the defendant has appeared in the action by serving an answer or motion, the interrogatories must be served in the manner provided by Rule 4. The defendant may serve interrogatories upon the plaintiff even before the answer is due. The defendant commonly serves interrogatories with the answer. The Rules contain no provision for serving interrogatories before commencement of the action. If discovery is needed before a suit can be brought, the proponent must resort to an oral deposition as provided by Rules 27 and 30.

The deponent must serve answers to interrogatories within thirty days of the date that interrogatories were served upon the deponent. If the proponent served the interrogatories by mail, the deponent has thirty-three days in which to serve the answers (Rule 6(e)). In state courts, if the plaintiff serves interrogatories upon the defendant along with the complaint or shortly after serving the complaint, the defendant has forty-five days after service of the complaint in which to serve the answers. In other words, the defendant has another twenty-five days after serving the answer to the complaint. Rule 6(b) provides that a party may move the court ex parte for an order enlarging the time for answering, if the party makes the motion *before* the time prescribed by the Rules has expired.

■ USES

Parties use interrogatories to obtain information from each other about the facts, evidence, and even legal theories. An interrogatory is not objectionable merely because the deponent's answer necessarily involves an opinion about the case or about the facts, or concerns the deponent's contentions. Interrogatories may be used to find out what evidence the deponent does *not* have. An interrogatory imposes an affirmative duty upon a deponent to obtain information that the deponent may not have at the time but that is under the deponent's control and is therefore available to the deponent. Interrogatories may ask about any matter that is within the scope of Rule 26(b). The principal limitations on the scope of interrogatories, as on other discovery procedures, is that the subject matter must not be privileged, must not be work product and must be relevant to the case. For purposes of discovery, an inquiry is relevant if it is calculated to lead to discovery of evidence that will be admissible at trial.

Interrogatories are particularly useful for obtaining basic background information about the opposing party, such as the party's address, date of birth, marital status, employment history, accident history, medical history, litigation history, criminal convictions, educational background, use of other names, and social security number. A party may use interrogatories to force the deponent to reveal sources of information such as the identity of a witness; the existence of witness statements, photographs, records, particular documents; the identity of tangible things; and even the subject matter of conversations. The information obtained through the deponent's answers often provides the basis for conducting additional investigation and pursuing more detailed discovery. The main limitation on interrogatories is that they do not give the proponent any opportunity to cross-examine the deponent. On the other hand, the answers to interrogatories may be used at trial to cross-examine the deponent. Also, the answers lack spontaneity in that they are edited by the deponent's lawyer. Despite these minor limitations, interrogatories play a very important role in civil litigation.

One function of the initial interrogatories is to discover the identity of witnesses known to other parties. A proponent is entitled to discover the identity of all witnesses that the other parties know about. A deponent may be required to disclose witnesses by stating their names and addresses, and whether the deponent has obtained statements from them. A proponent may not use interrogatories to require the deponent to say what the witnesses know about the transaction or occurrence. Nor may interrogatories be used to find out what witnesses the deponent intends to call upon to testify at trial.[1] Most courts allow interrogatories that require the deponent to identify witnesses by categories, such as all persons who witnessed the accident, all witnesses who arrived after the accident, or witnesses who have information concerning damages. The deponent is not required to summarize the information that she or he believes each witness has; interrogatories asking for such information are objectionable and should not be answered. Once the identity of a witness is disclosed, it is up to each party to obtain the information that the witness has, by interviewing, obtaining a statement, or taking the witness's deposition—whatever the situation requires.

Initial interrogatories commonly ask for the deponent's version of the transaction or occurrence. For example, in a case involving an automobile accident, the defendant proponent could properly serve this interrogatory to the plaintiff: "Describe fully how you claim the accident occurred." The interrogatory contemplates that the deponent will state the facts upon which the plaintiff bases the claim of negligence. A proper response by the plaintiff deponent could be, "The defendant entered the intersection in violation of the traffic signal (red light) and struck the right side of the automobile in which the plaintiff was riding as a passenger; the defendant was negligent for violating the traffic light, failing to keep a proper lookout, failing to keep his automobile under control, and traveling at an excessive rate of speed." This answer gives the defendant a good picture of the plaintiff's version of the accident. The interrogatory answer helps to focus the rest of the defendant's investigation and discovery. The interrogatory does not expect the deponent to describe the entire claim or to describe all the details of the accident.

The answers to interrogatories may be used to establish that the opponent does not have certain evidence or does not have evidence concerning a particular fact. For example, when the defendant serves interrogatories requiring the plaintiff to disclose the identity of witnesses to the accident, the plaintiff may answer that she does not know of any witnesses. This disclosure may allow the defendant to stop spending effort and money to locate witnesses who do not exist. The interrogatory has eliminated a potential problem.

If the deponent should try to produce a surprise witness at trial, after claiming that he or she has no witnesses, the court, on motion, should preclude the witness from testifying, or the court may order a postponement of the trial, allowing the defendant additional time in which to

1. Nevertheless, when a case nears trial, it is common for courts to order the parties to disclose the witnesses they intend to have testify. The information is for the court, so that the court can manage its own schedule.

prepare. The court may order the deponent to produce the witness for an oral deposition so that the opposing party can find out everything about the witness and the witness's expected testimony. The court may require the delinquent party to pay all the costs of the oral deposition. This procedure gives the "surprised party" an opportunity to find out whether he or she really needs more time to prepare for trial and if so, how much. A deponent's disclosure that he or she is not aware of any relevant documents, photographs, or other tangible evidence gives the proponent grounds for excluding from evidence any nondisclosed items or obtaining a postponement of the trial.

■ FORMAT

Parties usually serve interrogatories in sets. In other words, it is rare for a party to serve only one interrogatory at a time. A party's set of interrogatories is a group of questions the party currently wants answered. Later, the party may have more questions to ask and will submit another set of interrogatories.

Parties never group interrogatories into sets on the basis of subject matter or some other classification. For example, when the defendant serves initial interrogatories upon the plaintiff, the defendant does not serve one set concerning liability and another set concerning damages.

Each interrogatory in a set must be numbered for convenient reference. Each new set should begin with the next number after the last number of the previous set. Thus, if the first set ends with interrogatory 20, the second set should begin with interrogatory 21.

It is a common practice to divide an interrogatory into subdivisions, and there is no reason to avoid that form if it fits the needs. For example:

1. For each witness statement obtained by the defendant, state the following:
   a. the name and address of the person who interviewed the witness
   b. the date on which the statement was obtained
   c. the means by which the statement was recorded
   d. the name and address of each person who was present when the statement was obtained
   e. whether the witness has been given a copy of his or her statement

■ NUMBER AND CONTENT

Interrogatories should not be unreasonably burdensome in their number or in their demand for information. The relevancy and importance of the questions should be weighed against the burden and inconvenience to the deponent.

Rule 33 limits to twenty-five the number of interrogatories that a party may serve upon another party. However, the parties may stipulate to a larger number. Some state courts and the local rules of some federal district courts limit to fifty the number of interrogatories that may be served upon another party. Each subdivision counts as a separate interrogatory in courts that limit the number of interrogatories. If the case involves two defendants, the plaintiff may serve up to the prescribed limit on each defendant. Suppose a husband and wife bring an action to recover money damages for the wife's injuries sustained in an automobile accident. The defendant wants to serve more than twenty-five interrogatories to obtain information about the wife's background, accident, injuries, exhibits, and so forth. The defendant could serve twenty-five interrogatories on the wife and another twenty-five on the husband. None of the interrogatories served upon the wife should be duplicated in the set served upon the husband; duplication wastes time and effort. It is proper to ask the husband questions that would normally be put to the wife if there were no limit on the number of interrogatories.

Even if the court does not limit the number of interrogatories that may be asked, the proponent should not propound an interrogatory without having a specific purpose and a reasonable need for the information. It is all too easy for the proponent to serve a myriad of questions that require the opponent to spend days collecting useless information. If interrogatories are served just to make the file look substantial or to satisfy the client's curiosity or to harass the deponent, the proponent has abused the process. The deponent has a right to object to improper interrogatories or the misuse of interrogatories (Rule 37). However, litigants should rarely have to ask the court for protection from harassment through improper interrogatories. Paralegals and lawyers must act responsibly, with restraint, and use interrogatories properly.

Each interrogatory should be limited to a single question and a single subject. Each interrogatory should be short, specific, and to the point. Some lawyers try to ensure specificity and clarity by using a list of definitions at the beginning of each set of interrogatories. The set of definitions should help to keep the interrogatories more concise.

Each interrogatory should be drafted so that it is easy to answer. For example, if it is possible to obtain the needed information by having the deponent answer yes or no, the interrogatory should be phrased for a yes or no answer. Then the deponent will be less likely to put off answering, and the answer cannot be misinterpreted.

Preprepared interrogatories, or form interrogatories, are acceptable and frequently used, but they must be directly applicable to the case. It is a bad practice to serve interrogatories of a type that were drafted for another case and do not really fit the issues in the present case. If the proponent's office has sets of form interrogatories, she or he should carefully select from the sets only interrogatories that are actually relevant.

Carefully drawn interrogatories promote appropriate, responsive answers with significant information. The deponent cannot easily avoid the gist of a carefully drawn interrogatory. On the other hand, poorly drafted interrogatories frustrate and irritate the deponent and the deponent's attorney. If an interrogatory is poorly phrased, the deponent has good grounds for objecting and not answering the interrogatory, or the deponent may avoid the question by using a nonresponsive answer, because the proponent will be reluctant to ask the court for an order compelling the deponent to provide a better answer. If the proponent does try to compel a different answer, the court may simply direct the proponent to redraft the interrogatory.

One fault commonly found in poorly drafted interrogatories is that two interrogatories are used where one will do. For example: (1) "Do you know of any witnesses to the accident?" (2) "If your answer to the preceding interrogatory is yes, state the name and address of each witness." The two interrogatories would have been stated more simply and better as one imperative: "State the name and address of all witnesses to the accident."

■ SCOPE

An interrogatory may be used to obtain mere information. For example, it may ask whether the deponent knows of any witnesses to the accident. The answer will not be useful evidence, but may lead to evidence. An interrogatory may be used to obtain evidence. For example, it may ask the opposing party to describe that party's conversations with the police about how the accident happened. The deponent's answer may be used by the respondent at trial as evidence. An interrogatory may be used to obtain a more definitive statement of the deponent's allegations in the complaint or answer. For example, the defendant's answer may allege that the plaintiff assumed the risk of her injuries. The plaintiff may serve an interrogatory demanding to know, specifically, the facts upon which the defendant bases the assumption-of-risk defense. Or suppose the complaint alleges that the defendant breached an express warranty. The defendant may ask the plaintiff to state fully the terms of the alleged express warranty. An interrogatory may be used to obtain the deponent's explanation about the law's application to specified facts. For example, if the defendant contends that the plaintiff's claim is barred by the statute of limitations, the plaintiff could ask, in a series of interrogatories, when and on the basis of what facts the defendant claims that the cause of action accrued.

An interrogatory must be "calculated" to obtain evidence or information that will lead to the discovery of evidence that is admissible at trial. The proponent must have some intent and expectation of obtaining usable evidence. Otherwise, an inquiry is nothing more than the proverbial "fishing expedition." Mere "fishing" is impermissible; it is an abuse of the discovery process.

The plaintiff's initial set of interrogatories usually asks the defendant to disclose the identity of all witnesses; the defendant's version of the transaction or occurrence; and the existence of evidence such as documents, photographs, reports, and so forth. In personal injury actions, the plaintiff commonly asks whether the defendant knows of any other accidents or claims in which the plaintiff has been involved. This information helps the plaintiff's attorney to determine whether the defendant may have some impeaching evidence against the plaintiff.

The defendant's initial set of interrogatories usually asks similar questions about the plaintiff's version of the transaction or occurrence and about the evidence the plaintiff has. In addition, the defendant ordinarily needs to inquire about the circumstances affecting the plaintiff's claim for damages. The defendant must determine what the plaintiff claims about the nature and extent of the alleged loss. The defendant usually asks questions concerning the manner in which the plaintiff has calculated the damages. It is often useful for the defendant to ask what amount of money the plaintiff claims for each item of loss. Each circumstance affecting the amount of damages is a proper subject for an interrogatory. Suppose the plaintiff is claiming twenty thousand dollars in damages for his damaged automobile. The defendant needs to know the original cost of the automobile; when it was purchased; from whom it was purchased; whether the automobile can be repaired or has to be replaced; the depreciated value of the automobile immediately before the accident; whether the automobile had been in any prior accidents; the age of the automobile in terms of years and miles; the estimated or actual cost of repairing the automobile; whether the plaintiff obtained more than one estimate for repair or replacement; the plaintiff's basis for depreciation; the availability of supporting documentation such as repair bills, invoices, and receipts. Interrogatories may be used to obtain information about witnesses who have information about the alleged damages.

The defendant is also entitled to know whether the plaintiff's loss was covered by the plaintiff's own direct-loss insurance. A person buys direct-loss insurance to protect herself or himself against damage to the person's own property, such as a fire insurance policy to protect the insured's own home, whereas a person buys liability insurance to protect herself or himself from legal responsibility for causing injury to another person or damage to another person's property. The insurance information is relevant because the defendant is entitled to know who else has any interest in the subject matter and outcome of the case. The direct-loss insurer may have a subrogation right and may be another source of evidence that would be admissible at trial. For example, the insurer may have photographs relevant to the damages, repair estimates, repair bills, and statements.

Technically, the availability of liability insurance is not relevant to accident cases because insurance does not affect issues of liability or damages. Discovery of insurance is allowed, however, because it may significantly affect the parties' willingness or ability to settle their dispute. The most efficient means of obtaining insurance information is through written interrogatories. A proponent may ask whether the deponent has any liability insurance that will pay any of a judgment against the deponent. The proponent is entitled to discover the name of the insurer, the identity of the particular insurance policy, the amount of the available coverage, and whether there is any dispute over the coverage (Rule 26(b)(2)). If there is a dispute over coverage, the proponent should consider making a demand for the policy in question, pursuant to Rule 34.

Interrogatories may be used to find out how the opponent contends the law applies to facts in the case. According to Rule 33(c),

> An interrogatory otherwise proper is not necessarily objectionable merely because the answer to the interrogatory involves an opinion or contention that relates to fact or the application of law to fact, but the court may order that such an interrogatory need not be answered until after designated discovery has been completed or until a pre-trial conference or other later time.

For example, in an automobile accident case, the defendant may require the plaintiff to specify all acts and omissions that the plaintiff attributes to the defendant and claims were negligent. The plaintiff and her lawyer must answer the interrogatory with specific allegations such as unlawful speed (specifying miles per hour), failure to yield right-of-way, driving on the wrong side of the highway, failure to signal a turn, failure to keep a proper lookout, and so forth. In a products liability case, the plaintiff would have to disclose circumstances that the plaintiff contends made the product defective in its design, fabrication, warnings, or instructions. The plaintiff's answers to such interrogatories enable the defendant to focus the rest of the investigation and discovery procedures on the particular acts or omissions related by the plaintiff. The Federal Rules of Civil Procedure had to give interrogatories this role of clarifying and supplementing the parties' pleadings because the Rules permit most pleadings to state the facts in a general, broad statement. Rule 9 still requires certain matters to be pleaded with particularity, including fraud, mistake, time, place, and special damages, but in general, parties are expected to obtain the details through interrogatories.

If, at trial, the plaintiff attempts to prove that the defendant was negligent in some respect not identified in the plaintiff's answer to interrogatories, the defendant may be able to exclude the plaintiff's evidence bearing on that issue, or obtain a postponement of the trial so that he or she can prepare on the "new" issue. For example, if the plaintiff's answer to interrogatory only specifies the defendant's excessive speed as a cause of the automobile accident, and, at trial, the plaintiff attempts to prove that the defendant's brakes were negligently maintained, the defendant may be able to exclude any evidence about the condition of the brakes, or obtain a continuance of the trial so that the defendant can adequately prepare on the issue. The plaintiff may pose the same type of interrogatory to the defendant concerning affirmative defenses asserted in the answer. In this way, interrogatories enable the parties to concentrate on specific issues and fully prepare on the issues.

Interrogatories may be used to obtain information about any claim or defense, whether in a contract, tort, or statutory case. This role is not in conflict with the rule against disclosure of the attorney's work product. Interrogatories requesting such information do not require disclosure of what the deponent or deponent's lawyer has done to develop or substantiate the legal theories or legal conclusions. Remember, the plaintiff's complaint and defendant's answer are sufficient to state a cause of action or an affirmative defense by merely alleging it in general terms.

Interrogatories are frequently used to obtain information about the existence of business records and their contents. Rule 33(c) gives the deponent the option to extrapolate the requested information or to produce the records for inspection and copying by the proponent. The primary considerations in deciding how to proceed are the time, expense, and inconvenience involved. If the parties cannot agree upon which procedure to use, the court will decide for them.

Interrogatories are useful to obtain information about conversations between parties and between a party and another person or persons. Interrogatories cannot be directed to nonparties, so the proponent can obtain only the deponent's version of a conversation with other persons. Interrogatories concerning the deponent's version of a conversation should request disclosure of the exact words, or disclosure of the substance of what was said if the deponent avers that she or he cannot recall the exact words. It is also important to discover who else was present and may have heard the conversation. Was a record or memorandum of the conversation prepared? Who made the record or memorandum? Who has custody of it? The deponent's answers to interrogatories usually provide a basis for substantive inquiry when the deponent's deposition is taken.

As a general proposition, the scope of inquiry through interrogatories is the same as in other discovery procedures. But one very important exception exists. In most states, interrogatories are the only means for obtaining information about expert witnesses whom an opposing party expects to have testify at trial. A proponent may serve interrogatories to obtain information about the identity of the deponent's experts, the subject matter to which an expert will testify, and the grounds for the expert's opinions. If the proponent can show exceptional circumstances to the effect that the proponent cannot obtain facts or opinions on the same subject, then, upon motion and court order, the proponent may be allowed to take the deposition of the deponent's expert. Most states do not require disclosure of the identity of experts who were consulted but whom the deponent or deponent's lawyer does not intend to have testify. Consultation with an expert who is not selected to testify is considered part of the attorney's work product and not discoverable.

For example, if the deponent's expert conducted tests on something that is no longer available to be tested, the party seeking discovery has a right to know about the details of the test. The only fair way to obtain all the necessary information is to cross-examine the deponent's expert in a deposition. The deponent cannot keep the expert from being discovered and deposed by claiming that the deponent does not expect to call upon the expert to testify at trial.

Interrogatories are very useful for obtaining information and sources of information and for identifying evidence. But interrogatories are not useful for cross-examining the deponent. The deponent has the opportunity to ponder the questions and consider the answers, so the answers are never spontaneous. In fact, the answers are usually prepared by the deponent's lawyers and paralegals, so the answers are stated in their words. Each discovery tool has its special uses and limitations, and each discovery task should employ the best discovery method.

■ AMENDMENTS TO FEDERAL RULES

State court and federal rules had been very similar until December 1, 1993, when the federal courts established a requirement that parties meet and prepare a discovery plan that they can submit to the court for approval. The parties may not initiate discovery until they have their discovery plan as provided in Rule 26(b)(2):

> Except when authorized under these rules or by local rule, order, or agreement of the parties, a party may not seek discovery from any source before the parties have met and conferred as required by subdivision (f)(Rule 26(d)).

Rule 33 provides that the parties may serve not more than twenty-five interrogatories, including subparts, upon each other party, unless the parties agree in the discovery plan to a greater number or unless a court order allows more.

Rule 33(b) requires the party and her or his lawyer to sign the answers to interrogatories. If a party objects to any interrogatory, the objection must be supported by "reasons." If the deponent fails to object to an improper interrogatory by the time the answers are due, the deponent waives the objection (Rule 33(b)(4)).

Rule 33(c) discusses interrogatories that ask for opinion or information related to facts:

> An interrogatory otherwise proper is not necessarily objectionable merely because an answer to the interrogatory involves an *opinion or contention that relates to fact or the application of law to fact,* but the court may order that such an interrogatory need not be answered until after designated discovery has been completed or until a pretrial conference or other later time [emphasis added].

The problem with such interrogatories is that the deponent cannot adequately deal with them until he or she has all the evidence available to consider. For example, if the defendant is asked to state all the facts upon which he claims that Avery Cantrell is not his employee, he should have an opportunity to make sure he has all the facts that can be obtained.

Rule 33(d) gives the deponent the option to produce business records rather than the information demanded in an interrogatory, where the source of the information is the records. Then the burden shifts to the proponent to study the records and secure the information wanted. The rule clarifies that the deponent must provide the records in the same condition and same order in which they are ordinarily kept.

The deponent's answers to interrogatories are subject to the mandates of Rule 26(g):

> (1) Every disclosure made pursuant to subdivision (a)(1) or subdivision (a)(3) shall be signed by at least one attorney of record in the attorney's individual name, whose address shall be stated. An unrepresented party shall sign the disclosure and state the party's address. The signature of the attorney or party constitutes a certification that to the best of the signer's knowledge, information, and belief, formed after a reasonable inquiry, the disclosure is complete and correct as of the time it is made. The court must strike any response or objection that is not duly signed.

■ ANSWER FORMAT AND CONTENT

As interrogatories are usually served in sets, the answers are similarly prepared and submitted in sets. The deponent must answer each interrogatory separately. In other words, the deponent may not prepare a lengthy narrative that seems to cover all the questions, and leave it to the proponent to separate the information and apply it to the interrogatories. Each answer must be complete, in writing, and under oath (Rule 33(a)). Although the Federal Rules of Civil Procedure do not require a reiteration of the interrogatory, the best practice is to restate each interrogatory and then state the answer after or below it. This practice makes the answers convenient to use. The rules of many state courts require this procedure.

Answers should respond by using the same wording and form as the interrogatories when it is reasonable to do so. For example, if an interrogatory has used subdivisions, the answer should respond to those same subdivisions. Short, declarative sentences are best. Sometimes a single word may suffice, such as *yes* or *none* or a date. If the interrogatory is not relevant to the particular facts, the answer may be "not applicable." The deponent is not required to answer in full sentences. Answers may be made upon information and belief as well as upon knowledge. If an answer is not made upon actual knowledge, the notary clause should state that it is "made upon information and belief." For example, when the president of a corporation signs answers on behalf of the corporation and the answers are based upon information gathered by various employees, the answers should reflect that circumstance. Rule 33(a) does not require the deponent to identify the sources of the corporation's information, but if sources are not disclosed, the proponent may ask for them in another set of interrogatories.

The deponent must sign her or his answers to interrogatories. The signature is made under oath. The deponent's lawyer must sign any objections to interrogatories. A corporate officer or authorized agent may sign for a corporation. If specifically authorized by the corporate party, the lawyer handling the case may sign on behalf of the corporation.

■ OBJECTIONS

If an interrogatory is improper for any reason, the respondent may state an objection in lieu of an answer. Or the respondent may answer the interrogatory **subject to objection.** For example, if an interrogatory asked whether the deponent had ever been convicted of a crime, the deponent may answer that he has not had any convictions for the past ten years and object to the question insofar as it applies to convictions before that (see Rule 609(b)). When a deponent objects to an interrogatory, the proponent has the right to move the court for an order compelling the deponent to answer. There is no time period within which the objection must be noticed for hearing. On the other hand, if a discovery plan is in effect, that plan may provide such time periods. If no effort is made to compel discovery until the case reaches trial, a judge is not likely to be sympathetic to the motion. In the absence of a motion to compel an answer, the law presumes that the proponent of the interrogatory concurs in the respondent's objection.

Interrogatories are not subject to objection on the grounds that they call for the deponent to state an opinion or contention relevant to her or his own claims or defenses. An interrogatory may properly ask for another party's explanation concerning the application of law to certain facts. If such a question were put to the deponent in the course of an oral deposition, the question would be objectionable because the answer requires a legal analysis. But since a lawyer prepares the deponent's answers to interrogatories, such interrogatories are permissible (Rule 33(b)).

■ ANSWER PROCEDURE

Ordinarily, the answers to interrogatories are drafted by a lawyer or paralegal for the client's signature. The answers must be based upon the collective information available to the party, the party's lawyer, the party's employees, and the party's agents. They must be accurate and complete in light of all the information *available* to the deponent, not just according to what the deponent happens to know. In other words, the deponent has a duty to make reasonable inquiry to obtain the information called for by the interrogatories. However, if the information is unknown to the deponent and is *equally* available to the proponent, the deponent is under no duty to do the proponent's work. An interrogatory requesting such information is subject to objection.

The deponent must sign and serve answers to interrogatories within thirty days after the interrogatories were served. Objections to interrogatories must be served within the same time period. Usually objections are served with the answers. For example, if the defendant serves interrogatories upon the plaintiff by placing them in a United States mailbox on June 1, the thirty-day period begins to run on June 2. Another three days is added because service was by mail (Rule 6(e)). Therefore, the answers to interrogatories must be served on July 5. The time period actually ends on July 4, but that is Independence Day, a legal holiday, so another day must be added. If the legal holiday were not the last day of the time period, it would not extend the time for answering (Rule 6(a)).

Parties frequently accommodate each other by voluntarily granting reasonable extensions of time. Parties may stipulate to modify the discovery rules in almost any manner that is convenient for them. One exception is that the time limitations prescribed by Rule 33 may be extended only by court order (Rule 29); Rule 29 prevents the parties from upsetting the court's discovery plan and schedule. The customary procedure for obtaining a court-ordered extension of time is for the parties to enter a stipulation in writing that sets forth a reasonable extension and the reasons the extension is necessary. The stipulation is then made the basis for a motion in which the court is asked to issue an order that comports with the stipulation. Courts generally encourage the parties to accommodate each other on discovery matters, and grant extensions freely.

A proponent may serve an interrogatory that asks the deponent about the contents of various business records. The amount of time and effort required to examine the records to obtain the information could be substantial, even unreasonably burdensome. Rule 33(c) authorizes the deponent to respond to the interrogatory by simply offering to produce the records for the proponent to examine. The rule says that "the specification [answer] shall be in sufficient detail to permit the interrogating party to locate and identify . . . the records from which the answer [information] may be ascertained." The deponent must allow the proponent to have reasonable access to the records and must permit copying. If the proponent cannot understand the records or it would be unreasonably expensive for the proponent to examine the records, a court could require the deponent to answer the interrogatory by preparing a compilation, abstract, or summary and could charge the proponent for the reasonable cost of doing so.

■ ANSWER USES

A party's answers to interrogatories may be used at trial "to the extent permitted by the rules of evidence" (Rule 33(b)). However, a party cannot introduce into evidence his or her own answers to interrogatories even if the party had personal knowledge of the facts and the facts are relevant and so forth. The deponent cannot use his or her own answers to interrogatories because they are self-serving hearsay. A possible exception is that answers to interrogatories might be admissible at trial on behalf of the deponent if the deponent dies before trial (see Rule 804(b)(5).

The most common basis for receiving into evidence a party's answers to interrogatories is that the answers constitute the party's admissions. For example, if a defendant in an automobile case admits in his answers to interrogatories that he did not stop for the stop sign, the plaintiff may offer the answer into evidence to prove the stop sign violation. Answers to interrogatories may be used for impeachment purposes, that is, to contradict the deponent's testimony at trial. For example, if the deponent's answers to interrogatories state that the deponent was traveling forty miles per hour as she entered the intersection, but, at trial, the deponent testifies to a speed of only thirty miles per hour, the inconsistency may be shown for its impeachment effect. Also, the answer of forty miles per hour constitutes substantive evidence as an admission of a party.[2]

Would the proponent always try to impeach the deponent with inconsistent answers to interrogatories? Not necessarily. Suppose the deponent states in her answers to interrogatories that her speed was twenty miles per hour as she entered the intersection, but, at trial, she admits to a speed of forty miles per hour. Should the proponent show the jury that the deponent's prior answer is inconsistent and impeaching? Perhaps. Like so many things about trial strategy, it depends upon how the evidence fits into the big picture and the overall strategy. The proponent's lawyer is going to have to make a judgment call, and he may not have much time to consider all the ramifications. What may be lost by not showing the inconsistency? Perhaps the deponent will recall that the speed was only twenty miles per hour after all, and the jury may believe the deponent.

Suppose the defendant served interrogatories that asked the plaintiff to fully describe all personal injuries she sustained in the accident, and the plaintiff described only head and neck injuries in her answers. Then, at trial, the plaintiff testifies that she has had a lot of lower-back pain since the accident. Her failure to refer to this pain in her answers to interrogatories may be used to impeach her claim of a lower-back injury, and her credibility. It may be substantive evidence tending to show that she did not have any back injury. However, the deponent's answers to interrogatories are not judicial admissions, which means that they do not conclusively establish the facts indicated in the answers against the deponent. This is one important difference between Rule 33 answers to interrogatories and Rule 36 responses to requests for admissions. In the preceding example, the plaintiff's answers to interrogatories merely affect the weight the jury may or should give to the deponent's testimony.

■ ABUSES AND SANCTIONS

If the deponent wrongfully withholds or conceals information by giving incomplete or misleading answers, the deponent is subject to sanctions (Rule 37).

---

2. Substantive evidence is any evidence that supports a verdict. Not all impeachment evidence is substantive evidence. Some impeachment evidence is heard by the jury only for the purpose of discrediting a witness but cannot be considered by the jury as proof of any facts in dispute between the parties.

If the deponent believes that the proponent's interrogatories are excessively burdensome or constitute harassment, he or she may move the court for a protective order limiting the interrogatories in number or in scope (Rule 26(c)). The new Federal Rules and the rules of practice in some state courts limit the number of interrogatories, including subdivisions. If a set of interrogatories exceeds the specified number, the deponent may refuse to answer any of the interrogatories or may choose the twenty-five interrogatories that he or she prefers and answer only them. Courts that limit the number of interrogatories also provide a means for obtaining a court order authorizing more interrogatories when more are necessary. The limitation helps to reduce the use of nuisance interrogatories.

SUMMARY

Written interrogatories are the most basic and economical discovery procedure used in civil litigation. They are useful for obtaining basic information from the opposing party. Therefore, the plaintiff commonly serves interrogatories with the complaint, and the defendant commonly serves interrogatories with the answer. The respondent's answers will be used as a basis for conducting the investigation and conducting more discovery.

Interrogatories should not be used to obtain information a party already knows. A party should not harass another party by serving interrogatories concerning issues in which the proponent has no real interest.

Each interrogatory must be numbered separately. If two or more sets of interrogatories are used, the new set should begin with the next number following the last set. If the court's rules limit the number of interrogatories that may be served, the rule applies to subparts as well. Otherwise, lawyers and paralegals could circumvent the limitation by creatively using subpart questions.

Paralegals must be able to prepare interrogatories and answers to interrogatories. They should give careful consideration to the drafting of each interrogatory to make sure it is clear, is not overly burdensome, and is within the permissible scope of discovery, and that they have not used two interrogatories where one will do. Form interrogatories may be used only when they are relevant. If the proponent's office has a set of form interrogatories, she or he should select from the set only the interrogatories that are truly relevant.

The scope of inquiry through interrogatories is determined by Rule 26. Interrogatories may be served to obtain information, evidence, clarification of the pleadings, and a party's explanation of how the law applies to specified facts. A proponent may serve an interrogatory that asks the deponent about the contents of various business records. If the proponent cannot understand the records or it would be unreasonably expensive for the proponent to examine the records, a court could require the deponent to prepare a compilation, abstract, or summary and could charge the proponent for the reasonable cost of doing so. In the past, written interrogatories were the primary means for finding out about the opponent's experts and expert opinions, and in some states, that still may be true. Under the new Federal Rules, the parties must provide reports from their expert witnesses. An interrogatory answer is the product of the party and the party's lawyer or paralegal. Interrogatories do not afford any opportunity to cross-examine the deponent about the answer. However, the answer provides a basis for cross-examination at trial.

A deponent's answers must be complete in light of the information that is available to the deponent, not just what the deponent happens to know. In other words, the deponent has a duty to make reasonable inquiry to obtain the information called for by the interrogatories. Interrogatory answers cannot be used in lieu of live testimony at trial because they are not subject to cross-examination when made. However, answers to interrogatories may be used to cross-examine the deponent. It does not matter that the wording of the answers was that of the deponent's lawyer or paralegal; the deponent is stuck with the answers. An adverse party may offer an interrogatory answer into evidence as an admission by the deponent. However, the deponent may explain or even contradict an answer to an interrogatory. The answer may be impeaching or even considered by the jury as substantive evidence, but the answer is not conclusive in the way that a Rule 36 admission is.

If the deponent believes that the proponent's interrogatories are excessively burdensome or constitute harassment, he or she may move the court for a protective order limiting the interrogatories in number or in scope. The deponent must sign and serve the answers to interrogatories within thirty days after they were served. If an interrogatory is improper for any reason, the respondent may state an objection in lieu of an answer, or the respondent may answer the interrogatory subject to an objection. Objections to interrogatories must be served within the same time period as the answers.

The new Federal Rules provide that a party may serve not more than twenty-five interrogatories, including subparts, upon another party, unless the parties agree in the discovery plan to a greater number or unless a court order allows more. The new rules require the party and lawyer to sign the answers. If a party objects to any interrogatory, the objection must be supported by "reasons." If the deponent fails to object to an improper interrogatory by the time the answers are due, the deponent waives the objection.

KEY TERMS

proponent
deponent
subject to objection

REVIEW QUESTIONS

1. When may interrogatories be served upon a nonparty?
2. When may the plaintiff first serve interrogatories upon a defendant?
3. Under what circumstances may the deponent offer her or his interrogatory answers into evidence?

4. How may the deponent try to obtain additional time in which to answer a set of interrogatories?

5. Interrogatories are particularly valuable for obtaining what kind of information?

6. When is the deponent's lawyer required to sign the answers to interrogatories?

7. How many *sets* of interrogatories may one party serve upon another?

8. When is a party able to discover the expert opinions of an expert with whom the opponent has consulted but whom the opponent does not expect to have testify at trial?

9. If the deponent does not have the information with which to answer an interrogatory, what must the deponent do to comply with the spirit of the discovery rules?

10. How does an admission in an interrogatory differ from an admission made in the party's pleading or a Rule 36 admission?

11

EXPERT WITNESSES

Civil litigation is becoming more complex and increasingly dependent upon experts. Experts can provide assistance in a variety of ways in addition to testifying at trial. An expert may be retained to review the client's claim or defense in order to determine how to go about gathering evidence to develop and support the client's position. Experts are familiar with sources of information, such as the identity of other experts who can provide advice and testimony. They are familiar with relevant literature and how to obtain it. Experts can help start the investigation on the right path by postulating how and why the problem arose. As facts and evidence are obtained, experts can assess the strengths and weaknesses of the client's case and the opponent's case. Even though the ordinary juror has a good education, jurors often need experts to help them understand the significance of certain evidence and to explain how the evidence applies to the facts. Lawyers are constantly finding new ways of using information from expert witnesses to develop parties' claims and defenses.

Civil litigation is conducted on the premise that the jury should decide the case on the basis of the facts, and not on the basis of witnesses' opinions, conclusions, or suppositions. The reasons for the premise are valid. A verdict based upon the facts is a fair verdict. The prejudicial effect of witnesses' opinions and conclusions ordinarily outweighs their probative value. The limitations on opinion evidence promote objectivity and fairness. Nevertheless, the rule against opinion evidence has quite a few exceptions, and the use of expert witness testimony is an important one.

■ OPINIONS AND CONCLUSIONS

Experts are allowed to use their education, training, and experience to form **expert opinions,** which they may express to the jury to help the jury

259

understand disputed facts or the application of the evidence to disputed facts. Rule 702 of the Federal Rules of Evidence outlines this permission:

> If scientific, technical, or other specialized knowledge will assist the trier of fact to understand the evidence or to determine a fact in issue, a witness qualified as an expert by knowledge, skill, experience, training or education may testify thereto in the form of an opinion or otherwise.

Although expert witness opinions are admissible in evidence, conclusions by witnesses, whether or not experts, are not.

The Federal Rules of Civil Procedure and the Federal Rules of Evidence do not define *opinions* or *conclusions*, probably because the subject is too esoteric and any definitions that could be devised would be riddled with exceptions.

Opinions

An opinion may be described as an informed judgment derived from facts and developed in light of the witness's education, training, and experience with such facts. An opinion is more than mere deductive reasoning that leads to a conclusion. The facts upon which an opinion is based may have been observed by the witness or merely communicated to the witness. A witness's belief about a particular matter or subject is not an opinion if it is nothing more than an assumption, speculation or a guess. An opinion must be based upon **reasonable certainty.** Reasonable certainty means that the fact is more than probable; it is the degree of certainty upon which an expert would rely to make important decisions.

Take this example of an expert opinion that would be admissible in evidence: A patient seeks treatment for a rather sudden onset of nausea with abdominal pain, indications that the pain is beginning to localize in the right lower quadrant of the abdomen, and a low-grade fever. The physician will probably make a differential diagnosis that includes the possibility of appendicitis. The physician will probably elect to check the patient's abdominal reflexes, order a white blood count, and observe the patient for a while. If the patient's condition worsens and the white blood count is greatly elevated, the physician may form an opinion that the patient probably has appendicitis. Until the physician is able to form this opinion, she will elect not to operate. In other words, the opinion must have a degree of certainty about it before the physician will act upon it. The diagnosis or opinion cannot be confirmed until the operation is performed and the physician can actually see the inflamed appendix. Until then, the opinion has the possibility of being mistaken even though it is very reasonable and well supported. The patient would not want the physician to wait until she knows for sure that the appendix is inflamed before operating, because then it may be too late. On the other hand, the patient does not want the physician to operate on the basis of a mere guess that the appendix is inflamed and might need to be removed.

In the foregoing example, a medical doctor brings his or her education, training, and experience to the problem to form an expert opinion about the patient's malady. A person who does not have medical training could only guess about the nature of the problem.

An opinion differs from a conclusion in that a conclusion is merely a process of reasoning from the established or presented facts without any element of expertise added to form a judgment about the matter. In the preceding example, the physician had a number of facts to consider: nausea, presence of pain, location of pain, type of pain, elevated temperature, elevated white blood count, change in abdominal reflexes, and so forth. The physician could actually observe some of these facts, such as the elevated temperature. Some of the facts were merely reported to the physician, such as the pain. Some of the facts were observed by others, such as the elevated white blood count, which was determined by a laboratory technician. These facts might cause a layperson to suspect that the patient has appendicitis, but without the expertise of a physician, the layperson's suspicions would be nothing more than conjecture. The physician had to call upon her education, training, and experience to convert the history, symptoms, and findings into a diagnosis. The diagnosis is an opinion, at least until after the surgery. After surgery the condition would be a known fact.

The law uses experts' opinions almost the same way as the physician used the diagnosis in this example. The expert may take into consideration the facts that are ordinarily important to professionals in forming opinions. But not until the opinion has a reasonable degree of certainty to it will the law permit the jury to rely and act upon it. In the example, the physician's education and experience are essential to the formation of her expert opinion. A jury would not have the necessary experience to know the significance of the history, symptoms, and findings that were necessary to the preoperative diagnosis. Therefore, if the question of fact before a jury were whether the patient has appendicitis, the physician's opinion would help the jury make that determination.

Bear in mind that another expert might have made a different diagnosis based upon reasonable certainty. Because physicians do not always agree and there is room for honest disagreement, patients often choose to obtain second opinions before submitting to treatment. The law recognizes that the jury is entitled to hear experts who disagree and to choose from among their opinions. The jury usually makes its choice on the basis of the relative competence of the experts and the reasons those experts give for their opinions.

Conclusions

A layperson with an average education and ordinary intelligence can make conclusions by reasoning from the facts, usually just as well as an expert. A jury should conduct its own analysis of the facts to arrive at its own conclusions about the facts. The lawyers will suggest conclusions in their final arguments. There is no good reason to have experts also argue for conclusions. Therefore, mere conclusions are not received into evidence, but expert opinions are.

The following example should be helpful to differentiate between expert opinions and a layperson's conclusion. Suppose two salesmen have rented an automobile for a business trip. One is driving, and the other is a passenger. The driver misses a turn in the road, causing the automobile to go into the ditch and roll over, and both salesmen are thrown out. Both salesmen die instantly. A question arises as to which salesman was driving the automobile and, presumably, responsible for the accident. A thorough, careful investigation of the accident scene shows the position of the bodies and of the men's belongings, the path of the automobile, the types of injuries sustained, and the salesmen's fingerprints within the automobile. Salesman A had a fractured skull, and the windshield in front of the passenger's seat was shattered by the occupant's head having struck it. Salesman B's fingerprints are all over the steering wheel, whereas only one indistinct print on the wheel might be salesman A's. An accident reconstruction expert could take all these facts and conclude that salesman B was driving. But a jury using its own experience and common sense could reasonably arrive at the same conclusion without input from the reconstructionist. The reconstructionist's education, training, and experience with similar cases would add very little to the analysis or determination of the facts. Therefore, the reconstructionist's conclusion should not be deemed as useful to help the jury to understand the evidence or to determine a fact in issue (Rule 702). The jury should make the conclusion from the facts. The witnesses should only testify to what they observed.

■ EXPERT WITNESS QUALIFICATIONS

A witness must qualify as an expert before the court will allow the witness to express any expert opinions. The foundation is laid through preliminary testimony in which the witness shows that she or he has special education, training, or experience in the subject matter. Lawyers place great importance on the witness's credentials: the extent of the witness's education, training, and experience. The better the expert's qualifications are, the more persuasive her or his testimony is likely to be. Some courts allow the expert to supply a written **curriculum vitae** as evidence of the witness's qualifications. A curriculum vitae is a written description of the witness's education, work experience, publications, membership in professional associations, and professional awards or recognition. If a party elects to offer a curriculum vitae into evidence to establish the expert's qualifications, the expert should not be allowed to reiterate the contents when testifying, because the evidence is cumulative, that is, redundant. There are some advantages to having the expert testify to his or her qualifications and some benefits from using a curriculum vitae instead. The trial lawyer must decide which is best for the case. Usually, witnesses testify to their own qualifications. Just how much education or experience an expert is required to have is a matter left to the **sound discretion** of the trial judge. This means that the trial judge has a great deal of latitude in such matters. The witness qualifies if the judge concludes that the witness's opinions would probably help the jury to understand other evidence in the case (Rule 702). The tendency seems to be for trial judges to resolve any doubt on the side of allowing the testimony, rather than excluding it.

Again, a person may qualify to be an expert witness by showing that he or she has had special education, training, or experience in a subject that is relevant to the case. A highly trained surgeon qualifies to be an expert about medical procedures. A mechanic with less than a high school education may qualify concerning matters with which the mechanic is familiar through on-the-job training and experience. A machine operator may qualify solely by reason of experience. A truck driver may qualify on the basis of experience concerning the proper methods of loading and operating a particular type of truck. Billy Martin, former manager of the Yankees baseball team, once testified as an expert witness to explain how and why a batter may lose control of the bat and let it fly even while gripping it properly.

■ USE OF EXPERT OPINION EVIDENCE

Certain types of litigation, such as professional malpractice cases, usually require expert testimony to establish a prima facie case of liability. For example, suppose a bridge collapses and a malpractice action is brought against the structural engineer who designed the bridge. The collapse itself does not establish that the engineer failed to use due care in preparing the bridge's design or specifications. To prove malpractice, the plaintiff must prove that the engineer failed to comply with the standards, practices, or procedures applicable to structural engineers. The plaintiff must also prove that the engineer's deviation from applicable standards was a direct cause of the bridge's failure. A jury could not be expected to know or determine, from the jurors' collective experience, what the professional standards are, so it could not determine whether the engineer violated the standards. Someone who is familiar with the standards of the profession, usually a member of the profession, must describe the applicable standards for the jury.

If a juror happened to be an expert, the juror could not substitute his or her expertise for that of the witness, because the juror is not sworn, not subject to cross-examination, and the verdict would be based upon matters outside the record. If a lawyer believes that his or her client's evidence would be better understood and appreciated by an expert, the lawyer may want to keep the expert as a juror. On the other hand, a lawyer who is hoping to win on the basis of some technicality or sympathy may want to strike the potential juror from the panel.

Most medical malpractice cases require expert testimony to establish the standards applicable to the defendant physician. Without such testimony, the evidence is insufficient to prove a case of negligence (malpractice) against the physician. Similarly, just because a lawyer loses a case, that does not mean the lawyer has been negligent in preparing for the trial or in presenting the case. An action for malpractice against the lawyer requires evidence that the lawyer neglected professional standards relevant to the preparation or presentation of the case.

The defendants in malpractice actions usually qualify as expert witnesses and may express their opinions concerning the correctness of their own conduct. Experts may make almost any field or subject more understandable, and lawyers are using the input of experts with increased frequency. A person does not have to have a strong academic background to be an expert where the subject in question is not based upon higher learning. An automobile mechanic who did not finish high school may qualify as an expert concerning automobile repair work. A party who *is* an expert may testify as an expert.

Some cases do not require expert witness testimony, but expert testimony is allowed because it will help the jury to better understand the evidence and its application to the disputed facts. For example, if two automobiles have a head-on collision on a two-way highway and no one survives or witnesses the event, expert witnesses may be able to reconstruct how the accident occurred by studying the skid marks, location of debris, points of impact on the vehicles, point of impact on the roadway, consequential damage, gyrations of the cars after impact, and so forth. The jurors could use their own knowledge and experience and probably do a pretty good job of determining, from the same evidence, what happened. Nevertheless, the experts' observations and opinions may help the jurors; therefore, courts tend to allow experts to reconstruct an accident where there are no witnesses. Some courts would hold that if eyewitnesses can testify to what happened, no experts should be allowed to reconstruct the accident for the jury. The apparent need for expert testimony is diminished if an eyewitness observed the occurrence.

The use of expert testimony does not always make the jury's job easier, because, more often than not, each party is able to find an expert who will contradict the opinions of the opposing expert. The jury then has to choose between two or more experts and their opinions. The net effect may be that the jury hears the experts "argue" the case from the witness stand, in addition to hearing the lawyers' final arguments. Many jurors have some difficulty with the idea that honest experts can differ in their opinions. This is also a concern for some scholars who are interested in improving the system. Most trial lawyers appreciate that this is a problem, so they focus not on the expert's opinion, but on the *reasons* for the opinion.

The tendency to use the opinions of expert witnesses in order to prove matters that really do not require expert testimony seems to be increasing. Reliance on accident reconstruction experts is leading this trend. These experts examine the accident scene, talk to witnesses, read the parties' depositions, examine the vehicles involved in the accident, review their scientific data and tables, and then undertake to explain *how* and *why* the accident occurred. At first blush, this seems to be a very logical approach, but equally qualified experts commonly come to diametrically opposed conclusions. In automobile accident cases, reconstruction experts may get by expressing conclusions concerning the point of impact, angle of collision, speeds of the vehicles at impact, speeds of the vehicles when the brakes were applied, and so forth. Many of these professional expert witnesses engage in a good deal of sophistry. The trend toward relying on experts when their testimony is not needed is not healthy for the legal system. Jurors should decide cases on the facts.

Although courts allow experts to testify concerning a broad range of subjects, some limits have been imposed. Expert witnesses may not testify concerning what the law is or how the law applies to the facts of a case. As a general rule, an expert may not testify as to whether the defendant had a legal duty to the plaintiff. An expert may not interpret contracts or statutes for the jury. An expert may not give opinion testimony about how the law applies to a certain set of facts. These are all functions of the judge. For instance, an expert in insurance law would not be allowed to testify, as an expert, concerning the meaning and application of an insurance contract. The court (judge) must interpret the contract and tell the jury how it applies. In any case, a judge must interpret applicable statutes and tell the jury how the statutes apply to the facts.

As a rule, experts are not supposed to tell the jury how they believe the jury should decide the case. The rule as commonly phrased says that the expert must not invade the province of the jury. However, this rule has some gray areas and is "bent" from time to time. For example, in medical malpractice cases, the parties' experts are usually allowed to testify to the standards of the profession and that the defendant did or did not comply with the standards. The problem is addressed by Rule 704 of the Federal Rules of Evidence. It provides, in part, that "testimony in the form of an opinion or inference otherwise admissible is not objectionable because it embraces an ultimate issue to be decided by the trier of fact." Therefore, where opinion testimony is essential to help the jury, it is admissible even though the opinion may, in effect, tell the jury how the expert thinks the jury should decide the case. Otherwise, the court should not allow experts to influence the jury by testifying how the jury should answer special verdict questions or otherwise decide the case. For example, an expert witness should not be allowed to testify that the plaintiff or defendant was "negligent."

■ DISCOVERY OF EXPERTS' OPINIONS

Good trial preparation requires each side to find out as quickly as possible about the other side's expert witnesses, their opinions, and the grounds for their opinions. It usually takes quite a bit of time to fully analyze an expert's reasoning processes, check the expert's data, and check on the expert's background. In addition, it usually takes time to locate opposing expert witnesses who are knowledgeable, authoritative, and persuasive. The rules balance the need for such information against the principle that each party must obtain his or her own evidence.

If courts were to allow unbridled access to the adverse party's hired experts, the very heart of the adversary system would be threatened. If experts could be interviewed or deposed like ordinary witnesses, opposing parties could discover much of each other's work product through the expert witnesses. This is true because experts obtain most of their information, at least initially, from the lawyer. They discuss most of the facts and even the legal theories. In other words, hired experts are often given the entire plan for trying the case. This is the information that would be sought when interviewing or deposing them.

Sometime after the lawyer and expert have consulted, the expert may decide, for one reason or another, that she or he cannot or does not want to help. Or the lawyer might decide against using the testimony of that particular expert even if she or he is willing to help. If their communications were subject to discovery, the disclosures could be devastating. The theories advanced and rejected in the course of their frank discussions might be used against a party. Statements of facts and assumptions about facts made only tentatively might be used against the party in an effort to suggest a lack of certainty or apparent inconsistency.

The Federal Rules of Civil Procedure have, with some difficulty, steered a course calculated to preserve the adversary nature of civil litigation and yet make available to each party essential information about the opposing party's experts and their opinions. To begin with, the Rules distinguish between experts with whom a party or a party's lawyer has merely consulted and experts who have been selected to testify at trial. A party does not have to disclose the opinions of experts who have provided advice or information for the case but will not be called upon to testify at the trial.

Absent very unusual circumstances, those experts are of no consequence to the case.

The opinions of the experts who will testify at trial are subject to disclosure. A party may require any other party to disclose experts who have been selected to testify at trial. In addition, those experts' opinions and the grounds for their opinions are subject to discovery through written interrogatories directed to the party who has retained the experts.

The court may prohibit a party from using any expert witness whom the party failed to disclose in a timely manner. Lawyers need time to prepare a deal with an adverse party's experts, and court procedures make time allowances accordingly. A party will not be allowed to secure an advantage by failing to comply with discovery requirements, even if the nondisclosure is inadvertent.

■ INTERROGATORIES

In many state courts, information about experts who have been selected to testify at trial may be obtained only through written interrogatories unless, for good cause shown, a court orders that some other means of discovery, such as an oral deposition, be used. The new Federal Rules of Civil Procedure require parties to produce reports from experts they have retained and expect to testify at trial. State court rules are patterned after the old Federal Rule 26(b)(4). Volumes have been written concerning the rule's application. The practice in most states is to allow a party to serve interrogatories to obtain the retained expert's identity, a description of the subject matter about which the witness will testify, a statement of the facts relied upon by the expert for the opinion, and the **grounds,** or bases, for the expert's opinion.

Exhibit 11.1 is a typical set of interrogatories used to obtain information about another party's expert witnesses. An expert's report that is prepared and produced pursuant to Rule 26(b)(4)(A) should provide the same type of information in a narrative form.

The first two interrogatories in exhibit 11.1 should be easy to understand. The answer to the second interrogatory should describe fully each

■ EXHIBIT 11.1

Set of Interrogatories for Expert Witnesses

For each expert witness you intend to call upon to testify at the trial, do the following:

1. State the name, age, address, and employment of each such expert.
2. Describe in detail the qualifications of each expert with particular reference to the subject matter on which each expert may testify at trial.
3. State fully the opinions to which each expert is expected to testify.
4. Describe in detail the facts upon which each expert relies for each opinion, respectively.
5. State a summary of the grounds for each opinion to which each expert is expected to testify.
6. Identify by author, title, publication date, and publisher all writings that your experts may use at trial as learned treatises.
7. Identify separately any document that you intend to call to the attention of any expert witness upon cross-examination.

expert's education, training, and experience. Interrogatory 3 asks for each expert's opinion. In the example of the patient who presents symptoms of appendicitis, the physician would testify that in her opinion the patient has appendicitis and is in need of surgery to treat the problem.

Interrogatory 4 asks about the facts relied upon by the witnesses as a basis for each opinion. In the preceding example, the facts are the patient's history of nausea, localized abdominal pain, low-grade fever, elevated white blood count, and worsening symptoms during observation. Interrogatory 5 asks for the grounds for each expert's opinion. In the example, these are that the syndrome of symptoms and findings presented by the patient is most commonly associated with appendicitis; these symptoms are all consistent with appendicitis; the syndrome tends to rule out most other maladies, such as food poisoning, which could cause some of the symptoms; the onset of symptoms and the progression of the symptoms are consistent with appendicitis; and the witness has treated other patients with similar symptoms, and they had appendicitis.

Interrogatories 6 and 7 require disclosure of publications upon which the plaintiff's experts rely as authorities to support their opinions. Experts commonly justify their opinions by looking to textbooks and professional journals for authorities who seem to agree with them. Since the Rules of Evidence allow experts to use learned treatises to "bootstrap" their opinions, it is a good idea to find out, in advance, what publications the experts may use (Rule 803(8)). Apparent support from one or more publications may be additional grounds for an expert's opinions.

How should interrogatories be used in the typical case? Suppose the plaintiff suffered an injury when a five-year-old metal extension ladder collapsed while he was on it; he was carrying a heavy object and was near the top when the ladder's tread and side rail bent and gave way; and the ladder and the plaintiff fell to the ground. The plaintiff claims that the ladder was defective and that the manufacturer is strictly liable in tort because of the alleged defects. The complaint may or may not specify the type of defects claimed. Countless types are possible, including defective materials, a defect in the metal creating a localized weakness, a defect in design such as the treads being too narrow or too thin or inadequate fasteners being used, or failure to warn the user about foreseeable dangers such as the need to position the ladder at only certain angles or about the danger of overextending or overloading the ladder. The plaintiff discloses that he has an expert who will testify that the ladder is defective. What information can the defendant obtain through written interrogatories directed to the plaintiff?

The defendant can secure the expert's identity, including name, address, curriculum vitae, relationship to plaintiff, and description of area of expertise. Next, the defendant may inquire about the subject matter to which the expert may testify. The answers to the defendant's interrogatories should specify the defect or defects claimed. For example, they may state that the ladder was defective because the metal in the side rail had fissures in it making the ladder too weak to support ordinary loads. The defendant is entitled to obtain a summary of the grounds for the expert's opinion. The grounds are the expert's reasons, calculations, and the application of standards of the industry. The interrogatories should demand disclosure of all tests conducted by the expert, such as analysis of cross sections of the side rail at the point where it collapsed, any microscopic examinations, and X-ray studies conducted to show the presence of fissures. The expert presumably determined the load strength by testing and making calculations. The expert will have to disclose his tests of the ladder's load strength and the methods by which the determination was obtained.

A lot of information can be obtained through interrogatories that are carefully drawn and properly answered. Nevertheless, the effectiveness of discovery of expert opinions through interrogatories does have significant limitations. The answers to interrogatories do not give an adverse party the opportunity to evaluate the expert's personal appearance. In the previous example involving a metal extension ladder, can the expert express himself orally? Does the expert appear authoritative? Does the expert recognize that other formulas or other methods of calculating the strength of the metal used in the ladder are accepted in the industry and give different results? Can he rule out the possibility that the alleged fissures developed at some time after the ladder was sold to the plaintiff? Have comparisons been made with other ladders? Can he rule out consumer misuse? If so, how? What weaknesses in his theory is he aware of? What tests did the expert conduct that do *not* support the opinions expressed in the answers to interrogatories? With whom has the expert consulted for advice and guidance in forming the expressed opinions? Who has already expressed disagreement with the stated opinions?

The involvement of an expert witness adds another dimension to the case. If one party hires an expert to testify, it almost becomes mandatory for the other parties to obtain experts to counteract the testimony of the first expert. In all probability, if a party looks hard enough, she or he can find a professional expert to conjure up a theory helpful to the case. Any use of information from experts substantially adds to the cost of preparing and trying cases.

■ EXPERTS' REPORTS

It is customary to obtain written reports from experts. Written reports are desirable because they reduce the opportunity for misunderstanding. A lawyer needs to know exactly what his or her experts are saying and what their testimony will be. Most state courts preclude discovery of experts' reports, except in rare circumstances. A lawyer's consultation with experts for advice and guidance is treated as the lawyers' work product. The experts' reports are similarly treated as the attorney's work product. The protection afforded to experts' reports permits and encourages open, candid discussions between lawyers and their experts. The state court rules recognize that, in almost every field, experts may have bona fide disagreements and hold different opinions. It is perfectly reasonable and proper for a lawyer to consult with a number of experts before choosing one to testify. There is no reason why a party should be limited to the opinions of the first expert the party happens to consult. The consultation with experts not selected to testify is considered the attorney's work product and is not discoverable by other parties. For this reason, as a general rule, discovery concerning experts who have been consulted but not retained to testify is very limited.

Notwithstanding the limitations on discovery of the opinions and reports of experts, parties commonly give their opponent a copy of an expert's report. They do so for several reasons. The report may be very persuasive and offered in the hope of settling the case. The parties may agree to exchange reports for, in effect, an even trade. Or, by producing an expert's report, a lawyer may seek to avoid the inconvenience of answering interrogatories concerning the expert's opinion.

A party should not take too much comfort in obtaining the opposing party's experts' reports. The reports may not contain or provide as much information as would proper answers to interrogatories. The reports may not contain all the information available through the experts. The reports may be selective and especially prepared for the opposition. One must always be on guard for diversionary tactics, although it would be unethical to supply a false report. Use of a false report should subject the lawyer to disbarment or worse.

On rare occasion, a party may be entitled to discover the opinions of another party's expert who is not going to be called to testify at a trial. This requires a showing to the court that "exceptional circumstances" make it impracticable to obtain facts or opinions on the same subject matter by other means. Suppose a woman buys a bottle of soda pop, consumes about half of it, and becomes ill about an hour later. She assumes that the soft drink caused her illness. Her husband has the remaining soda pop analyzed by a local chemist. The chemist finds nothing unusual in the sample. Two months later, the husband takes the remainder of the soda pop to another chemist, who purports to find a toxin in it. The foreign substance is not ordinarily found at the bottling plant but is common to households. When an action is commenced months later, none of the soda pop is left for the defendant vendor to have analyzed. For obvious reasons, the plaintiffs may elect not to ask the first chemist to testify. Would it be fair to deny the defendant vendor the right to have the information that is available through the first chemist? No.

Suppose some of the soft drink were still available for an independent analysis by a chemist to be chosen by the defendant. Should the defendant, nevertheless, be entitled to the first expert's opinion, analysis, factual date, and records? Probably yes. The soft drink may have been contaminated after the first chemist completed her analysis. Therefore, the *same* subject matter is not necessarily available for analysis.

If an expert is uncooperative after the court has authorized a deposition to be taken, the court may compel the expert to appear for a deposition and to testify, by serving a subpoena upon the expert. An expert may be compelled by subpoena to produce records for inspection at the deposition. Violation of a subpoena subjects the expert to a contempt-of-court order. A party is presumed to be able to control a hired expert, so ordinarily subpoenas are not used. If a party cannot control an expert witness and obtain reasonable cooperation, she or he should notify the other side so that the witness can be placed under subpoena.

When a party seeks to use or benefit from the efforts of an expert originally hired by another party, he or she may be required to pay a "fair portion" of the expert's fee and expenses already incurred by the other party. Ordinarily, the parties or the court determines how the expense should be assessed, before the discovery is conducted (Rule 26(b)(4)(C)).

In an ordinary case, answers to interrogatories provide sufficient information about the opponent's experts to make additional means of discovery unnecessary. Frequently, lawyers agree to exchange experts' reports, as they exchange medical reports pursuant to Rule 35, as an alternative to answering interrogatories. Parties should use the most expeditious methods of discovery available in order to keep down the cost of litigation. The determinant must be whether the procedure is adequate to obtain the information that is or should be available.

■ AMENDMENTS TO RULE 26

The federal courts have adopted a different approach to dealing with expert witnesses. Parties must disclose their expert witnesses and written reports as part of the discovery plan. Rule 26(a)(2) provides the following:

> (A) . . . [A] party shall disclose to other parties the identity of any person who may be used at trial to present evidence under Rules 702, 703 or 705 of the Federal Rules of Evidence.
>
> (B) Except as otherwise stipulated or directed by the court, this disclosure shall, with respect to a witness who is retained or specially employed to provide expert testimony in the case or whose duties as an employee of the party regularly involve giving expert testimony, be accompanied by a written report prepared and signed by the witness. The report shall contain a complete statement of all opinions to be expressed and the basis and reasons therefore; the data or other information considered by the witness in forming the opinion; any exhibits to be used as a summary of or support for the opinions; the qualifications of the witness, including a list of all publications authored by the witness within the preceding ten years; the compensation to be paid for the study and testimony and a listing of any other cases in which the witness has testified as an expert at trial or by deposition within the preceding four years.
>
> (C) . . . In the absence of other directions from the court or stipulation by the parties, the disclosures shall be made at least 90 days before the trial date or the date the case is to be ready for trial or, if the evidence is intended solely to contradict or rebut evidence on the same subject matter identified by another party under paragraph (2)(B), within 30 days after the disclosure made by the other party. The parties shall supplement these disclosures when required under subdivision (e)(1).

The amended rule requires a full disclosure, going well beyond what courts have required in the past. Indeed, most courts did not require the production of a report. The parties merely had to provide a summary of the expert's opinions, the facts upon which the expert's opinions were based, and the grounds (reasons) for the opinions.

Rule 26(b)(4)(B) limits discovery with regard to experts who will not testify at trial:

> A party may, through interrogatories or by deposition, discover facts known or opinions held by an expert who has been retained or specially employed by another party in anticipation of litigation or preparation for trial *and who is not expected to be called as a witness at trial only* as provided in Rule 35(b) or upon a showing of exceptional circumstances under which it is impracticable for the party seeking discovery [the proponent] to obtain facts or opinions on the same subject by other means [emphasis added].

The question arises, How does a party know about an opposing party's expert who has not been named as a witness? It appears that the opposing party need not voluntarily disclose the existence of such experts. However, if a party serves an interrogatory asking for disclosure of experts who have been consulted but who are not expected to testify, the interrogatory must be answered. According to Rule 26(b)(5),

> When a party withholds information otherwise discoverable under these rules by claiming that it is privileged or subject to protection as trial preparation material, the party shall make the claim expressly and shall describe the nature of the documents, communications, or things not produced or disclosed in [a] manner that, without revealing information itself privileged or protected, will enable other parties to assess the applicability of the privilege or protection.

Therefore, a party may be required to disclose the existence of an expert who has been consulted but who is not expected to testify. A party may serve interrogatories to obtain the date of the consultation, the subject matter of the consultation, the nature of the expert's expertise, whether the expert prepared a report, and the date of the report. Apparently, a proponent may not ask the deponent why the deponent has elected not to have the expert testify or what the expert's opinions are.

■ PARTY AS AN EXPERT

The collapse of a roof on a large, new building is almost certain to engender litigation. Even if no one is injured, a very large property damage claim is still likely. The owner will look to someone to compensate her for the loss. If the owner's loss is covered by insurance, the insurer will probably have subrogation rights against whomever is liable for the collapse by reason of negligence, strict liability, breach of warranty, or even breach of contract. It is not at all unusual for the building's owner or insurer to bring a negligence action against the architect, general contractor, and selected subcontractors in these kinds of cases. The defendants usually serve cross-claims making everyone adverse parties. Each party usually has his or her in-house experts on the business payroll. More often than not, however, the parties hire independent experts (outside experts) to assist and advise concerning the litigation. Rule 26(b)(4) does not protect a party who happens to be an expert from having his or her deposition taken and opinions discovered. The rules do not protect expert employees from having their depositions taken concerning their expert opinions relevant to a claim. The adverse party may inquire into the expert's background, education, training, experience, relationship to the matter at issue, and opinions about the claim. The work product limitation applies only to experts who are hired for the purpose of assisting with the particular litigation.

What if the plaintiff's lawyer serves a **notice for taking depositions** on the defendant's employees who are experts but who had nothing to do with the particular matter of concern? May the plaintiff's lawyer ask them, for instance, questions about the structure that collapsed and for opinions about the adequacy of design, materials, fabrication methods, and so forth? Rule 26 does not seem to cover this situation. Probably a court would quash the notice for taking their depositions if the defendant showed by affidavit that they had no connection with the project. If they were deposed, they could probably elect to have no opinions concerning the subject matter. The party taking their depositions should compensate them for their time.

Otherwise, courts would be encouraging "fishing" for expert opinions, trying to secure such opinions through "admissions."

If a patient sues a physician for medical malpractice, the defendant physician will probably hire another physician to review the medical case to determine whether the defendant has committed malpractice. The same hired physician may conduct a Rule 35 independent medical examination of the plaintiff. Thus, the one expert may have two distinct roles. Each role must be handled separately. If the plaintiff asks for a report on the independent medical examination, Rule 35 requires that the physician who conducted the examination must provide a complete report. This report is available through the party who requested the examination—not directly from the independent medical examiner. The Rule 35 report should discuss the patient's medical history, the findings, the diagnosis, and so forth. However, that report should *not* discuss the malpractice issues. The expert witness should prepare a separate report concerning the malpractice allegations. The examining physician should also make a separate report concerning her or his evaluation of the alleged malpractice. That phase of the case and evidence falls under Rule 26(b)(4) and is protected as part of the defendant attorney's work product.

■ CROSS-EXAMINATION OF EXPERT WITNESSES

The most fruitful areas for cross-examining experts are their background, the sources of their information, the assumptions they have made as a basis for their opinions, and the reasons (given or not given) for their opinions. The lawyer who has the most experienced expert may try to compare the experts' backgrounds. The concessions and admissions of an expert witness are not necessarily admissions of the party who retained the expert.

■ COSTS

Expert witnesses are expensive. They require payment for the time analyzing the problem, rendering their opinions, and participating in legal proceedings. The Rules provide guidelines for determining who shall pay an expert for time spent in discovery proceedings. When an expert's opinion is sought through interrogatories, the party who hired the expert must pay the expert's fees for the time spent helping to answer the interrogatories. If an oral deposition is ordered, the party who takes the deposition must pay a reasonable fee for the time the expert spends testifying. The party who takes the deposition should not have to pay for time the expert spends preparing for the deposition. The party who retained the expert should pay for any preparation time. The preparation time is not at the request of the party who requested the deposition, nor is it for that party's benefit.

An expert cannot extort an excessive fee from the opposing side. If the parties and the expert cannot agree on what amount is reasonable, the issue may be submitted to the judge for determination. If the judge awards a smaller fee than is acceptable to the expert, the expert's remedy is to obtain the balance from the party who retained him or her.

■ SANCTIONS

If a party fails to disclose an expert as a potential witness, the expert may not be allowed to testify at trial. Another common sanction is to allow the complaining party to take the expert's deposition and require the delinquent party to pay all of the complaining party's expenses. It is preferable to err on the side of disclosure.

SUMMARY

When scientific, technical, or other specialized knowledge will help the trier of fact to understand the evidence or to determine a fact in issue, a witness qualified as an expert by knowledge, skill, experience, training, or education may testify thereto in the form of an opinion or otherwise. Trial court judges have broad discretion in deciding whether the "expert" is qualified and whether the "opinions" may be helpful to the jury. A person may qualify to be an expert solely through experience in the field.

An expert's opinions are admissible in evidence because they go beyond mere deduction and reasoning. An expert takes the evidence, as the jury has heard it, and provides a perspective that the jurors could not have because of their limited training and experience. The expert provides the benefit of additional knowledge.

An expert's opinion must be based upon a reasonable probability of accuracy. That means the expert, being intellectually honest, must believe that the opinion is more likely true than not true. When an expert expresses an opinion about the future, the opinion must be stated in terms of reasonable certainty. For example, a physician may testify as an expert that the plaintiff's injury was caused by the accident in question. This opinion must be based upon reasonable probability. The same physician may testify that the plaintiff's injury will require medical treatment for the rest of the patient's life. This opinion must be based upon reasonable medical certainty. Certainty is a higher standard of belief than probability. An opinion that is reasonably certain is not subject to any serious doubt.

An opinion differs from a conclusion in that a conclusion is merely a process of reasoning from the established or presented facts without any element of expertise added to form a judgment about the matter. Any ordinarily intelligent person may do the reasoning to arrive at a conclusion. A witness's conclusions drawn from the evidence that is available to the jury are not admissible into evidence. A witness's conclusions about the facts are not admissible as evidence.

A witness must qualify as an expert before the court will allow the witness to express any expert opinions. An expert qualifies by testifying to his or her own education, training, and experience in the field. Some courts allow the expert to supply a written curriculum vitae as evidence of his or her qualifications. In malpractice actions, the defendant usually qualifies as an expert witness and may express an opinion concerning the correctness of his or her own conduct. A person does not have to have a strong academic background to be an expert where the subject in question is not based upon higher learning. An automobile mechanic who did not finish high school may qualify as an expert concerning automobile repair work. Experts may make almost any field or subject more understandable, and lawyers are using the efforts of experts with increased frequency.

Certain types of litigation, such as a professional malpractice case, usually require expert opinions to establish a prima facie case of liability. The plaintiff must have an expert in the particular field identify the profession's standards, practices, and procedures so that the jury can determine whether the defendant violated the professional standards. The expert witness may be allowed to conclude that the defendant's conduct did or did not violate the applicable professional standards. It takes testimony from someone who is familiar with the standards of the profession to describe the standards. In the absence of expert testimony, a jury would in all likelihood only be guessing if it tried to decide whether the defendant acted according to the standards of the profession. Most trial lawyers try to make their expert witness's opinions more persuasive by having the expert explain the reasons for those opinions.

A party does not have to disclose the identity of experts who have provided advice or information for the case but will not be called upon to testify at the trial. The experts who will testify at trial are subject to disclosure. A party must disclose, through answers to interrogatories, the opinions of the experts who will testify for that party at trial. Interrogatories are written questions directed to another party used to obtain information and evidence from the other party. Interrogatories may be used to obtain the expert's identity, a description of the subject matter about which the witness will testify, a statement of the facts relied upon by the expert for the opinion, and the grounds (reasons) for the expert's opinion. If a party fails to make a timely disclosure of an expert witness, the court may prohibit the expert from testifying, or may order the delinquent party to produce the expert for a deposition at the delinquent party's expense. Lawyers need time to prepare to deal with an adverse party's experts.

There are significant limitations to discovery of expert opinions through interrogatories. The answers do not give an adverse party the opportunity to evaluate the expert's personal appearance or ability to express himself or herself orally. Nor is there an opportunity to cross-examine the expert.

Notwithstanding the limitations on discovery of the opinions and reports of experts, parties commonly give their opponent a copy of an expert's report. The new Federal Rules require each party to provide to the other a report signed by the expert or experts who will testify. The report must contain all the essential information to which the expert will testify at trial. If the expert's testimony deviates from the report, the report could be used to impeach the expert. The party who hired the expert must pay for the report.

KEY TERMS

expert opinions	curriculum vitae
reasonable certainty	grounds
sound discretion	notice for taking depositions

REVIEW QUESTIONS

1. What factors determine whether a court will allow the parties to present expert witness testimony?

2. What factors determine whether a person qualifies to testify as an expert witness?

3. When is an expert's opinion discoverble in federal court?

4. When is a party required to disclose the expert opinion of a consultant whom the party does not intend to call upon to testify at trial?

5. What elements determine whether a person has sufficient competence to testify as an expert witness?

6. Is expert testimony limited to matters involving science and engineering?

7. Is an expert required to disclose the fact that he or she has testified in other cases?

8. May the parties define the scope of discovery for expert opinions as part of their discovery plan?

9. Is a detrimental statement by a party's expert witness an admission of the party?

10. What is meant by the grounds for an expert's opinion?

11. If a party elects to take the deposition of another party's expert witness, who must pay the expert's fee?

12. If a retained expert refuses to issue a written report, what remedy does the opposing party have?

12

ORAL DEPOSITIONS

Oral depositions are the mainspring of civil litigation discovery. Rule 30 of the Federal Rules of Civil Procedure authorizes any party to take the oral deposition of any other party and of any witness, concerning any fact relevant to the case. The procedures for scheduling and taking oral depositions are simple and practical. Whenever an oral deposition is taken, a record or transcript is made of the deponent's testimony. The transcript is used for trial preparation and during the trial. Taking an oral deposition is moderately expensive but usually well worth the cost. No other method provides as much detailed information from an adverse party or witness.

■ DEFINITIONS

An oral deposition is a legal procedure in which the lawyer for a party to a civil suit may question any other party and witnesses about matters relevant to the litigation. The term **deposition** is synonymous with *testimony*. It is also used to indicate the *procedure* for taking a person's testimony and the *transcript* of a person's testimony. Lawyers commonly describe the interrogation process as "taking a deposition." A *deponent* is a person who testifies under oath. The word **depose** means "to make an oral or written statement under oath"; it is synonymous with *testify*. Sometimes the word *depose* is used to describe the act of taking a person's deposition. To illustrate, "I will depose the witness next week" means "I will take the witness's deposition next week." It is often necessary to look to the context in which these words are used to determine their meaning.

An affidavit is a written statement made under oath. A deposition, whether written or oral, differs from an affidavit in that a deponent is subject to cross-examination by all interested parties, whereas an affiant (person who makes an affidavit) is not.

A party schedules the deposition of another party or witness by serving on all other parties a **notice of deposition** or **notice of taking deposition.** Lawyers commonly refer to the service as merely noticing the deposition— for example, "The plaintiff noticed the defendant's deposition for March 15."

■ PURPOSES

Lawyers use oral depositions to find out what the deponent (party or witness) knows or does not know about the case. This type of deposition is commonly called a **discovery deposition.** When a lawyer takes a deposition, the lawyer engages in a dialogue with the deponent. This gives the lawyer an opportunity to ask follow-up questions that force the deponent to fully respond. The lawyer not only hears the deponent's testimony, but has the opportunity to observe the deponent's demeanor while testifying. The lawyer has the opportunity to gauge how well the deponent knows what he or she is talking about. The lawyer has the opportunity to question the witness about documents and other tangible evidence while the evidence is in front of them. A deposition cross-examination usually reveals the strengths and weaknesses of the deponent's testimony. Usually, the lawyer can evaluate the deponent's authority and credibility.

A deponent's oral deposition testimony must be recorded by stenographic means or electronically in the form of a video or audio recording. When an audio or video recording is made, a written transcript is not necessary. Nevertheless, any party may choose to have a written transcript made from an audio recording, because written transcripts are easier to use for some purposes. When a party or witness is not available to testify at trial, a deposition transcript (record) may be presented to the jury in place of the deponent's live testimony. Some depositions are used at trial as substantive evidence; some are used only for impeachment purposes.

■ ROLE OF PARALEGALS

Since taking a person's oral deposition is tantamount to eliciting testimony in court, and transcripts may be used at trial as evidence, only lawyers may take a deposition for use in civil litigation. Only lawyers may interrogate the deponent and make objections. Although paralegals are not authorized to conduct the actual interrogation, they may make arrangements for depositions, including noticing the deposition. Paralegals may collect and organize the exhibits to be used in a deposition. They may prepare outlines of the critical facts and opinions to be covered. Paralegals often attend depositions to observe deponents, to make notes about the testimony and reports. Paralegals may review a deposition transcript with the client to help the client make corrections and additions as authorized by Rule 30(e).

Paralegals often review, correct, and index deposition transcripts to make them more usable at trial. A lawyer may ask a paralegal to sit in on a deposition when the lawyer intends to ask no questions of the deponent but wants a report on what the deponent says and on the kind of appearance the deponent makes. A paralegal may help to prepare a client or nonparty witness to testify in a deposition.

Arbitration is becoming increasingly popular. More and more claims are being submitted to arbitration tribunals for resolution. Most arbitration procedures are patterned after court procedures but are somewhat more streamlined. A person does not have to be a lawyer to be able to fully participate in the arbitration of a matter. If the parties to an arbitration engage in discovery, paralegals may conduct the discovery, including taking depositions. Indeed, a paralegal may make the presentation before the arbitration tribunal, including interrogating the witnesses and making the arguments.

■ SCHEDULING AND NOTICING DEPOSITIONS

The plaintiff is not generally permitted to take the defendant's deposition during the first thirty days following service of the summons and complaint. The Rules recognize that the defendant and his or her lawyer would have difficulty preparing for it that quickly. Furthermore, the legal and fact issues are not framed until the defendant serves an answer to the complaint. However, if a compelling reason exists, the plaintiff may move the court for an order allowing her or him to take the deposition of the defendant or of a witness during those first thirty days. The plaintiff must show good cause, that is, special need, for the accelerated date. Rule 30(b)(2) specifies three situations (exceptions) that automatically give the plaintiff the right to take an early deposition: (1) the deponent is about to leave the judicial district and will be at least a hundred miles from the place where the trial is to be held; or (2) the deponent is about to leave the United States; or (3) the deponent is about to leave on a voyage to sea. No court order is necessary if any of these reasons are stated in the notice, with a brief explanation. Progressive illness, impending death, and a call to military service are additional situations in which a court would probably order an accelerated date for a deposition.

Rule 30(a) says that "leave [of the court] is not required . . . if a defendant has served a notice of taking deposition or otherwise sought discovery." Therefore, once the defendant initiates any discovery procedure, the plaintiff is at liberty to schedule the defendant's deposition—even during the first thirty days after service of the summons and complaint. This means that as soon as the defendant serves initial interrogatories upon the plaintiff, the plaintiff may schedule the defendant's deposition to be taken at a reasonable time.

The party who notices a deposition may select the time and place. A deposition should be taken at a place convenient for the deponent and a majority of the parties' lawyers. Most depositions are taken in the office of the lawyer who scheduled them, but depositions may be held almost anywhere, such as at a courthouse, hospital, hotel, airport meeting room, or private home.

A lawyer schedules a deposition by preparing, serving, and filing a notice of taking deposition, which must state the deponent's name and the time and place of the deposition. Sometimes the party who requires a deposition does not know the name of the person to be deposed but can describe her or him; for example, the notice could describe the deponent as "president of the defendant corporation." The notice of deposition may require a party to bring documents or other tangible items to the deposition for inspection, copying, and photographing.

A copy of the notice must be served upon each party, and the original filed with the court. A notice must give everyone a *reasonable time* in which to prepare for the deposition. The Rules purposely avoid specifying a certain number of days for the notice, because need and circumstances vary. If the designated time and place are inconvenient for a party, that party may make a motion to quash the notice of deposition (Rule 30(b)(3)). Fortunately, lawyers try very hard to accommodate each other and each other's clients. In many communities, the party who wants to schedule a deposition contacts the other parties' lawyers before noticing the deposition and tries to obtain a consensus for a mutually convenient time. Again, professionalism is an important key to the success of the civil justice system.

A notice for taking a deposition states that the deposition will be taken at a specified time and place before an officer who is authorized to administer oaths (Rule 28). The officer is usually the stenographer who records the testimony. Every law office has its preferred form for the notice. The notice must state the deponent's name and address, if known. Otherwise, the deponent may be identified by description. Exhibit 12.1 is a sample of a notice for taking the deposition of a party. The notice must bear the title of the action and be signed by a lawyer. Deposition notices are usually served by mail.

An extra copy of the notice of deposition should be made for the court reporter to keep. The notice provides the reporter with most of the information she or he needs, including the title of the action, court file number, correct spelling of the deponent's name, names of the lawyers who are appearing, and identity of the lawyers' respective clients.

■ AMENDMENTS TO RULES 30 AND 32

The December 1, 1993, amendments to Federal Rules of Civil Procedure 30 and 32 significantly changed oral deposition procedures but not their purpose or use. Rule 30 provides that an oral deposition may not be noticed or taken before the parties have the discovery plan. A party cannot take more than ten depositions, unless the other parties agree or the court authorizes more. The rule still provides that the notice for taking a deposition

---

■ **EXHIBIT 12.1**

Notice of Deposition

PLEASE TAKE NOTICE that the oral deposition of Roberta Jones will be taken on the seventh day of May, 1995, at 10:00 A.M. at 2205 Parkway South, Chicago, Illinois, before [name of officer or court reporter], and Roberta Jones shall present herself at said time and place for the purpose of her oral deposition.

[date]   /s/_____

must give the parties and deponent a "reasonable" time in which to prepare for the deposition (Rule 30(b)(1)). Rule 32(a)(3) adds the following:

> [N]or shall a deposition be used against a party who, having received less than 11 days notice of a deposition, has promptly upon receiving such notice filed a motion for a protective order under Rule 26(c)(2) requesting that the deposition not be held or be held at a different time or place and such motion is pending at the time the deposition is held.

The notice must state the method by which the deposition will be taken. It must specify how the testimony will be recorded, that is, by stenography, sound, or sound and visual. The party who noticed the deposition may pay the cost of recording the testimony. In addition, "[a]ny party may arrange for a transcription to be made from the recording of a deposition taken by nonstenographic means" (Rule 30(b)(2)). The party who wants the transcription must pay for it. Rule 30(b)(7) authorizes parties to take oral depositions by telephone or other remote electronic means.

Rule 30(b)(4) provides that the deposition must be taken before an officer who is duly authorized to administer oaths. The officer shall begin the deposition by stating her or his name and business address; the date, time, and place of the deposition; the name of the deponent; and that the oath was duly administered to the deponent. The officer is required to list or note the names of all persons in attendance and parties represented. The rule states that if the deposition is electronically recorded, the record must not distort the appearance of the deponent or lawyers.

The procedure for examining witnesses is supposed to be the same as if the examination were being conducted in court. Rule 30(c) covers this point:

> Examination and cross-examination of witnesses may proceed as permitted at the trial under the provisions of the Federal Rules of Evidence, except Rules 103 [having to do with the court's rulings on objections] and 615 [having to do with the exclusion of witnesses so that one witness cannot hear another's testimony]. . . . All objections made at the time of the examination to the qualifications of the officer taking the deposition, to the manner of taking it, to the evidence presented, to the conduct of any party, or to any other aspect of the proceedings shall be noted by the officer upon the record of the deposition; but the examination shall proceed, with the testimony being taken subject to the objections.

Rule 30(d) explains and qualifies this mandate:

> (1) Any objection to evidence during a deposition shall be stated concisely and in a non-argumentative and non-suggestive manner. A party may instruct a deponent not to answer only when necessary to preserve a privilege, to enforce a limitation on evidence directed by the court, or to present a motion under paragraph (3).

The proscription against "suggestive" objections is to prevent lawyers from using an objection to suggest to the witness how to answer a question. The rule fails to allow objections to the form of the question, as where the questions may be argumentative, repetitious, or abusive. Formerly, lawyers were expected to state their objections and the reasons for their objections, so that the court could look at the transcript and see if they made a sincere effort to resolve their differences. To some extent the protection is maintained in Rule 30(d)(3):

At any time during a deposition, on motion of a party or of the deponent and upon a showing that the examination is being conducted in bad faith or in such manner as unreasonably to annoy, embarrass, or oppress the deponent or party, the court in which the action is pending or the court in the district where the deposition is being taken may order the officer conducting the examination to cease forthwith from taking the deposition, or may limit the scope and manner of the taking of the deposition as provided in Rule 26(c). . . . Upon demand of the objecting party or deponent, the taking of the deposition shall be suspended for the time necessary to make a motion for an order. The provisions of Rule 37(a)(4) apply to the award of expenses incurred in relation to the motion.

Rule 30(d) describes some additional limitations that may be imposed on oral depositions:

(2) By order or local rule, the court may limit the time permitted for the conduct of a deposition, but shall allow additional time consistent with Rule 26(b)(2) if needed for a fair examination of the deponent or if the deponent or another party impedes or delays the examination. If the court finds such an impediment, delay or other conduct that has frustrated the fair examination of the deponent, it may impose upon the persons responsible an appropriate sanction, including the reasonable costs and attorney's fees incurred by any parties as a result thereof.

The deponent still has the right to read the transcript or listen to the recording and make changes "in form or substance" (Rule 30(e)). The deponent does not have to sign the transcript unless the changes are made, but the deponent must give a reason for each change. The officer appends the changes to the transcript. The changes must be made within thirty days after the transcript is made available to the deponent. Otherwise, the deponent waives the right to make them.

Rule 30(f) provides that the officer shall file the transcript and exhibits with the clerk of court. However, most courts do not want the transcripts on file. They provide by local rule that the party who noticed the deposition shall take custody of the transcript and safeguard it. The party who "owns" the exhibits used by the deponent may retain them, or the exhibits may be kept with the deposition transcript. According to Rule 30(f),

Documents and things produced for inspection during the examination of the witness, shall, upon the request of a party, be marked for identification and annexed to the deposition and may be inspected and copied by any party, except that if the person producing the materials desires to retain them, the person may (A) offer copies to be marked for identification and annexed to the deposition and to serve thereafter as originals if the person affords to all parties fair opportunity to verify the copies by comparison with the originals, or (B) offer the originals to be marked for identification, after giving to each party an opportunity to inspect and copy them, in which event the materials may then be used in the same manner as if annexed to the deposition.

The amended rule follows procedures that evolved under the former Rules.

Amended Rule 32(a) allows the parties to use a deposition for any purpose at trial if the deponent is not available. A deponent is not available if the deponent is dead, is more than one hundred miles from the place of trial, is ill, for some reason cannot be subpoenaed, or is in prison. A lawyer usually makes an affidavit to show that the deponent is unavailable. If a paralegal has made the investigation and tried to subpoena the witness, the paralegal's affidavit is used. A party must not procure the witness's un-availability so that the deposition can be used.

Amended Rule 32(c) provides that the deposition transcript may be used to impeach the witness at trial. But if the deposition is used at trial when the deponent is not available, the testimony must be presented orally. In other words, someone must read the testimony to the jury. If the testimony was electronically recorded, the recording may be played to the jury. The court cannot allow the jury to take the deposition testimony into its deliberations, because that would place an undue emphasis on the recorded testimony.

■ OBTAINING A LAWYER

If a person's deposition is taken within thirty days after service of the summons and complaint, owing to circumstances specified in Rule 30(b)(2), but a party was unable to obtain a lawyer to represent her or him at the deposition, the deposition may not be used against the party (Rule 30(b0(2)). The Rules require due diligence on the part of each party to obtain a lawyer, and the burden of persuading the court is on the party. Suppose the plaintiff sued three defendants, and the summons and complaint were served upon each defendant at two-week intervals, so that the last defendant was served four weeks after the first defendant was served. Within five days after the last complaint was served, the plaintiff notices the deposition of a nonparty witness to be taken in the plaintiff's lawyer's office in just seven days, because the deponent intends to move out of state permanently. The reason for taking the deposition early is, as required, stated in the notice (Rule 30(b)(2)). The first defendant served has appeared in the case by serving an answer. The notice for deposition may be served upon her by mail, but personal service upon the lawyer is preferable because of the shortness of time (Rule 5(b)).

The second defendant has retained a lawyer, but the lawyer has not yet interposed an answer. If the plaintiff's lawyer can nevertheless find out who the lawyer is, service of the notice of deposition should be made upon that lawyer (Rule 5(b)). Otherwise, service of the notice must be made upon the defendant by delivering it to her personally or by mail (Rule 5(b)). Again, personal service is preferable because of the shortness of time. The third defendant has had the summons and complaint for only five days. He promptly delivered them and the notice of deposition to his liability insurance agent, who, in turn, delivered them to the liability insurance company's claim department in another town for processing. The third defendant probably will not have a lawyer by the time the deposition is taken, notwithstanding due diligence on his part. Under those circumstances, the deposition could not be used against him at trial. But suppose, through some "miracle," the liability insurer is able to provide a lawyer in time. Then the lawyer's appearance at the deposition would result in a waiver of any defect in the notice and service of the notice (Rule 32(a)).

■ ATTENDANCE

A party who notices a deposition must serve the notice upon *all* other parties (Rules 5(a) and 30(b)(1)). The procedure for scheduling an oral deposition is intended to make sure all parties have the opportunity to appear and participate. If a party does not receive due notice of a deposition, the deposition transcript cannot be used against that party for any purpose.

The lawyer who noticed the deposition must attend, and so must the deponent. Other parties are not required to attend (Rules 30(g)(1)) and 37(d)). However, if a party has received due notice and elects not to attend a scheduled deposition, the deposition may be used against that party just as though the party had attended and participated. For example, the deposition testimony could be used to support a motion, or it could be used as substantive evidence at trial if the deponent were unavailable to testify. A party who elects not to attend a deposition may, nevertheless, use the deposition transcript or recording at trial for any proper purpose (Rule 32).

If a party is *not* served with notice of taking the deposition, but the party or lawyer attends the deposition anyway, the deposition may be used against that party the same as if notice had been duly served. A party's or lawyer's appearance at the deposition constitutes a waiver of any defect in the notice or in the service of the notice. A party who does not receive due notice of a deposition may take the deponent's deposition at another time. A party who does not receive notice of the deposition is, nevertheless, entitled to buy and use a copy of the deposition transcript.

When a nonparty witness is willing to appear for a deposition without being subpoenaed, the noticing party may avoid the expense and inconvenience of obtaining and serving a subpoena. However, if the nonparty witness fails to appear at the scheduled time and place, the party may be required to reimburse the other parties for their time and expense, including attorney's fees, incurred by reason of the aborted deposition. If the nonparty witness has been served with a subpoena, the noticing party cannot be blamed for nonappearance and costs cannot be assessed against the party or her or his attorney (Rule 30(g)(2)). In addition, the nonparty witness is subject to being held in contempt of court.

When the party who serves the notice fails to appear to take the deposition, he or she may be required to pay the costs incurred by all parties who did appear (Rule 30(g)(1)). Consequently, if a party decides to cancel or postpone a deposition, he or she must make sure that everyone is duly notified about the change.

A party's lawyer may elect to appear at an oral deposition by submitting written questions through the party or lawyer who scheduled the deposition. The written questions and the deponent's answers are incorporated into the reporter's stenographic notes and the deposition transcript. This procedure is seldom used but can be very valuable. Suppose a third-party plaintiff schedules the deposition of a witness to be taken halfway across the country, but the testimony is going to be relevant only to the third-party claim against the third-party defendant. The plaintiff's lawyer may avoid the expense of traveling to the deposition by submitting a few questions in writing. The written questions must be served upon the lawyer who noticed the deposition and who will be taking it. The written questions must be placed in a sealed envelope, which is not opened until the deposition begins. The lawyer gives the written questions to the deposition officer (court reporter), who then presents the questions to the witness. This procedure lacks flexibility and allows no opportunity for follow-up questions for clarification or to develop a point that suddenly appears to be more important than was previously believed.

All parties have a constitutional right to attend any deposition, whether of a party or of a nonparty, and cannot be excluded by a court order. A corporate entity has the right to have a designated person attend on its behalf, in addition to the corporation's lawyer. The parties may agree to allow observers (Rule 29). For example, a representative from the defendant's liability insurance company might want to observe the deposition of the plaintiff to evaluate the claim.

The Rules do not state who may not attend depositions. Nevertheless, there is a general consensus that a deposition in a civil action is not a public meeting. News reporters do not have a right to attend, and the parties may agree to exclude certain persons, such as witnesses. If a party objects to a nonparty witness's attending the deposition, that party may move the court for an order **sequestering** (keeping out) witnesses pursuant to Rules 26(c)(5) and 615; a party cannot be sequestered. The most common reason for a party to exclude witnesses from a deposition is to keep them from hearing what other witnesses have to say. The testimony of one witness may cause another witness to change her or his testimony in some way. Suppose two bartenders were witnesses to a fight in the bar. Inconsistencies in their versions of the fight are more likely to develop if neither hears the testimony of the other. However, if witnesses are trying to be honest and helpful to the court, it is probably better for everyone if they all have the opportunity to hear each other. Consequently, sequestration of witnesses is the exception.

■ SUBPOENAING A NONPARTY DEPONENT

A notice for taking deposition is a mandate to appear for the deposition at the time and place scheduled. No subpoena is necessary. Nevertheless, it may be desirable, if not necessary, to subpoena a nonparty deponent. A court obtains jurisdiction over the person of a nonparty when a subpoena is served upon that person. The procedure is simple. A paralegal may prepare the notice for taking the nonparty's deposition. The notice must be signed by a lawyer. The paralegal may prepare the notice for taking the nonparty's deposition. The notice must be signed by a lawyer. The paralegal serves the notice upon the other parties. The paralegal must take the original copy of the notice and proof of service to the clerk of court for filing. The clerk of court will give the paralegal a subpoena form to complete. The subpoena contains the same information that is in the notice for taking the deposition. If the nonparty lives in another district (state), the paralegal must file the notice of deposition with the clerk of court in that district. The court in the district in which the deposition is to be taken must issue the subpoena. Rule 45(a)(3) provides as follows:

> An attorney as officer of the court may also issue and sign a subpoena on behalf of (A) a court in which the attorney is authorized to practice; or (B) a court for a district in which a deposition or production is compelled by the subpoena, if the deposition or production pertains to an action pending in a court in which the attorney is authorized to practice.

A subpoena may be served upon the deponent anywhere within the district (state) of the court that issued the subpoena. A federal district court's subpoena may be served "at any place without [outside] the district that is within 100 miles of the place of the deposition, hearing, trial, production, or inspection specified in the subpoena (Rule 45(b)(2)).

A **subpoena duces tecum** tells the recipient that he or she must appear at the time and place stated to give testimony and produce for inspection and copying designated records, documents, or "tangible things." A subpoena may be used to compel a nonparty to permit an inspection of real property that the nonparty owns or occupies (Rules 45(b) and (d)). If the deponent finds the demand for inspection, documents, or things too burdensome, the deponent may serve and file an objection to inspection stating the grounds for the objection. The objecting party must deliver the objection before the deposition is to be taken. If more than ten days' notice was given for taking the deposition, the objection must be served within ten days. When an objection is made, the party serving the subpoena has the right to move the court for an order compelling production (Rule 45(d)). Otherwise, by electing to proceed with the deposition, the party who noticed the deposition must assume that the documents will not be available for the deposition. A subpoena must clearly identify all the items the deponent is to produce at the deposition. A copy of the subpoena duces tecum must be attached to the notice of deposition served upon the other parties.

When it is necessary to bring a motion to compel a nonparty deponent to produce documents or things for inspection, a copy of the notice and motion must be served upon the deponent. She or he has a right to appear in opposition to the motion (Rule 45(d)). The motion must be served on the person personally, as provided by Rule 4(d)(1), not by mail, because the nonparty has not appeared in the case.

A subpoena may be served by the United States marshal or by anyone who is at least eighteen years of age and not a party to the suit. It must be delivered to the deponent along with a witness fee for one day's attendance and a mileage fee as set by statute (Rule 45(c)). On occasion, disputes arise concerning the time of service or whether a subpoena was served in a proper manner. In that event, the original copy of the subpoena and proof of service must be filed with the court. The proof of service must state specifically the date of service and describe the manner of service, including the name of the person who made the service.

When a nonparty corporation is subpoenaed, the subpoena must clearly inform the corporation of its duty to respond by designating someone to appear at the deposition on its behalf. The person who does appear must be able to speak for the organization concerning the subject matter. The subpoena may cite and quote the rule.

A nonparty deponent cannot be required to travel outside the county in which he or she lives or is regularly employed, to give a deposition. However, Rule 45(d) provides that a deponent may be subpoenaed to appear for a deposition in the county in which he or she transacts business in person. By implication, he or she must regularly transact business in that county. If the deponent is not a resident of the district (state) in which the deposition is to be taken, the subpoena may require the deponent to appear in the county in which the subpoena was served or within a one-hundred-mile radius of the place of service. If those two alternatives are not satisfactory, the party noticing the deposition has to obtain a court order setting another reasonably convenient place (Rule 45(d)(2)).

Almost no one wants to be subpoenaed for a deposition or a trial. Subpoenas tend to scare most people. A subpoena may make a person feel as though the whole weight of the court is upon her or his shoulders. Consequently, a lawyer runs a significant risk of alienating a witness by dropping a subpoena on her or him. It is a good idea to personally explain to the witness before the subpoena is served why the subpoena is being used. If a better reason cannot be found, the witness can be told that the Federal Rules of Civil Procedure require it. A witness may be more comfortable if told that in case of an emergency, she or he can be released from the subpoena. To obtain a release, she or he should contact the lawyer who caused the subpoena to be served. The lawyer's name and address are on the subpoena. If the witness has cogent reason for being unable to appear, she or he may be released and other arrangements may be made.

A witness must not be allowed to think that if the witness avoids testifying at the scheduled time, he or she will never have to testify. A witness may have a hundred reasons why he or she cannot be available. The witness should be counseled against putting off the inevitable. Some witnesses hide themselves when they have advance warning that they may be served. Therefore, legal professionals should be careful about telling others about plans to subpoena someone. When a person disobeys a subpoena, he or she may be held in contempt of court. A person who is found to be in contempt of court may be punished by imprisonment—although contempt is not a crime (Rule 45(f)). Note that the rules for subpoenaing a deponent for an oral deposition are not necessarily the same as those for subpoenaing a witness to testify at trial.

■ DEPOSITION PROCEDURE

A court reporter records the lawyer's appearances and the identity of every other person who attends the deposition. The reporter records the date and time when the deposition begins. The court reporter makes a verbatim record of the entire proceeding. On occasion, one of the lawyers may have a preliminary statement to make for the record. If the parties have entered into any stipulations concerning the deposition, they may be stated for the record. The officer (court reporter) administers an oath to the deponent.

The lawyer who noticed the deposition begins the interrogation. The first questions usually concern the witness's identity and background: name, address, age, marital status, birth date, birthplace, employment, social security number, and criminal record. The other areas of questioning concern the transaction, occurrence, liability, and damages. Each question is supposed to be singular and clearly stated. Lawyers give careful attention to the context and meaning of their words and the words used by the deponent. For example, consider the question "Did you make a left-hand turn?" and the answer "Right." Does "Right" mean "A right turn" or "Correct"? A lawyer must make sure that each question is clearly stated and the deponent's answers are meaningful, clear, and responsive. A lawyer may ask leading questions and otherwise cross-examine the deponent if he or she is an adverse party or a **hostile witness** (Rule 611(b)(c)). (A hostile witness is one who is aligned with an another party or who is recalcitrant while testifying.) There is no set limit on the number of questions that a lawyer may ask. Nor is there any time limit. The questions must not become repetitious or irrelevant. A deponent does not have the right to "go off the record."

When the first lawyer finishes asking questions, the other lawyers ask their questions, in turn. The lawyers seldom argue or raise concerns about the order in which they may ask questions. When more than one interrogator is present, it is common to have a second round of questioning, because the additional questions and answers seem to prompt more questions. The deponent is entitled to have her or his own lawyer present to give advice, even if the deponent is not a party to the suit. When all the interrogators are through asking questions, the deponent's own lawyer *may* ask questions. The deponent's lawyer would not ask questions in a discovery deposition, except for clarification of testimony. Only if the lawyers agree to an intermission may the court reporter stop recording the dialogue.

■ SUFFICIENT FOUNDATION

The largest worry a lawyer has when taking an expert's deposition for use at trial is that the lawyer may fail to show that the expert's testimony is competent. The expert's opinion testimony is inadmissible unless the expert is shown to be an expert and good grounds (foundation) support the expert's opinion. The court will not rule on the admissibility of the evidence until the trial. The deponent's testimony must be competent in order to be admissible in evidence at trial. In this regard, an expert witness's opinion evidence is not competent if it lacks sufficient foundation. The foundation is laid by presenting evidence that shows that the expert has special training and experience in the field and sufficient knowledge and information to have an opinion that will help the jury to understand the case. If the necessary foundation is not laid during the deposition, the expert's opinions cannot be used.

Nonexpert witnesses are seldom permitted to give opinion testimony. But when they are, the deposition must show that they had an opportunity to observe, understand, and recall the events about which they are to testify. Failure to make the necessary showing subjects the evidence to objection on the grounds of lack of foundation. Again, presenting such testimony by deposition is worrisome and risky because sufficient foundation may not be laid in the deposition. The lawyer taking the deposition does not have a final ruling on the admissibility of the evidence until trial, and a deficiency in foundation cannot be supplied then. Suppose a nonexpert witness is asked for her opinion about the speed of a vehicle she observed. She saw the automobile for two seconds (or five seconds or fifteen seconds). Was the length of time sufficient to make a valid observation? The value judgment falls within the discretion of the trial judge. Fair-minded judges may differ on the ruling—hence, the lawyer's concern about the adequacy of foundation. In all probability, two seconds is not enough time to form a valid opinion about a vehicle's speed. Five seconds may or may not be a sufficient period of time, depending upon the witness's age and experience. Ten seconds certainly is ample time for a qualified witness. But suppose the deponent is only ten years old; would the deponent qualify to form an opinion of speed? Or suppose the deponent is fourteen years old; is that old enough? The decision will ultimately be made by the trial judge, who has a great deal of latitude in such matters.

■ SCOPE OF INQUIRY

The scope of permissible inquiry in discovery depositions is much broader than in court. A lawyer may examine the deponent about any matter that is relevant to the issues as framed by the pleadings. Evidence is relevant if it has a tendency to prove or disprove a fact in issue. But since a major purpose for taking depositions is to *discover* facts and evidence, the examination of the deponent is considered to be not too broad if the questions are reasonably calculated to lead to discovery of evidence admissible at trial. Therefore, the standard adopted by courts and applied by lawyers is to permit examination as long as it is not excessively burdensome or abusive. For example, in a case where the plaintiff is seeking money damages for personal injuries caused by an accident, the plaintiff's lawyer is likely to ask questions about the defendant's background, including such things as the defendant's past employment, education, past residences, military service, and criminal convictions. A court should not preclude such inquiry even though it has very little to do with the facts of the accident. On the other hand, a court would not condone a line of questioning that is calculated to harass or embarrass the deponent. It would be unfair, and thus not permissible, to question the deponent about the *details* of a divorce or other personal matter. As part of the discovery procedures, it is proper to ask whether the deponent has given a deposition in any other case and if so, in what cases. Sometimes it is difficult to determine where relevant discovery ends and witness abuse begins.

■ HYPOTHETICAL QUESTIONS

Hypothetical questions are not common in depositions. Many lawyers contend that they are not calculated to discover admissible evidence. They are not useful as a means of discovering facts. However, they may be used to obtain an adverse party's expert opinions, especially in malpractice actions.

Hypothetical questions are primarily used as a means of obtaining opinion evidence from a witness who does not have sufficient personal knowledge of the facts to give an opinion. If the facts can be proved through other witnesses, an expert is permitted to assume the truth of those facts and, relying upon them, give an opinion concerning their effect. But when hypothetical questions are used in depositions, the most common purpose is to try to get the witness to establish a legal duty owed by one party to another. This is especially true in tort actions involving professional malpractice, in construction accident cases, and in products liability cases.

Suppose a question exists as to whether a general contractor is responsible for erecting restraints around the floors of a multilevel building. An ironworker fell from the second structural level while the steel beams, columns, and flooring were being installed. He was an employee of the steel erection company that had a subcontract for the work. No other subcontractors were on the job. Only ironworkers were allowed on the steel framework while it was being erected. A lawyer might ask the general contractor's superintendent whether he would take action to prevent an ironworker from engaging in an unsafe act. If so, what action would he take? What is his authority to act? More specifically, if the superintendent saw an ironworker on the second floor who was repeatedly throwing down objects in a pedestrian area, would the superintendent speak directly with the ironworker to stop him? Could he cause the ironworker to be taken off the job? Does his authority to act come through the contract, subcontractor union contract, or customs and practice? The probable answers are that the superintendent has no authority or power to stop the ironworker's misconduct. But if the superintendent were to answer that he could stop the ironworker's misconduct, that answer in the deposition might be used to establish a legal duty to protect the ironworkers from themselves. The deposition would be used at trial to try to establish that the general contractor has a legal duty to put up perimeter restraints for the ironworkers.

The vice of conducting discovery through the use of hypothetical questions is, for instance, that if the superintendent denies any responsibility for supervising the ironworkers, the opposing lawyer will contend that the superintendent's opinions lack foundation. But if the superintendent recognizes some authority or responsibility, the superintendent's statement will be used against the general contractor as an admission at trial. So the hypothetical question is frequently a "heads I win, tails you lose" effort to get admissions from another party. Rarely is a hypothetical question used to actually discover facts or evidence.

The deponent's lawyer may try to avoid the problem by preparing the deponent to cope with hypothetical questions by explaining the interrogator's objectives and going through some examples. The deponent's lawyer may try to object to the use of hypothetical questions unless and until the examiner establishes that the witness has authority to give opinions and accepts the witness's authority. Only then do the witness's opinions have relevancy. The interrogator may then create a problem for himself or herself. A paralegal should discuss this subject thoroughly with a supervising lawyer to determine how to handle such matters. A paralegal may be assigned the task of preparing some hypothetical questions to be used in a deposition or at trial. This is not an easy assignment. Many lawyers have considerable difficulty preparing intelligible, useful, and relevant hypothetical questions.

■ OBJECTIONS

Objections concerning the form of the questions must be made during the deposition; otherwise, they are waived. The rationale is that if an objection is made during the deposition, the effect can be corrected. As part of the adversarial nature of civil litigation, the objecting party is obligated to flag evidence problems by making appropriate, timely objections. Leading and argumentative questions are prime examples of the kind that are objectionable owing to form rather than substance. On the other hand, questions and answers that are fundamentally inadmissible in evidence may not be used at trial merely because objections were not made during the deposition. According to Rule 32(d)(3)(A),

> Objections to the competency of a witness or to the competency, relevancy or materiality of testimony are not waived by failure to make them before or during the taking of the deposition, unless the ground of the objection is one which might have been obviated or removed if presented at that time.

At trial, the parties may try to persuade the judge that the grounds for an objection made for the first time at trial could have been obviated had the objection had been made during the deposition while the witness was available to provide the missing information.

When an objection is made, the lawyer who asked the question may rephrase the question or abandon the question or insist upon an answer. If the interrogator insists that he or she is entitled to an answer, the deponent's lawyer has to decide whether or not to let the deponent answer subject to the objection. By making the objection, the lawyer has protected the record in the sense that if the deposition is used at trial, a judge will have to rule on the objection before the question and the deponent's answer can be read to the jury. However, if the deponent answers subject to the objection, the objectionable question gets answered and the interrogator obtains information to which the interrogator may not be entitled. The alternative is to adjourn the deposition and ask the court to rule on the objection.

In an oral deposition, when an objection is made to a question or an answer or an exhibit, the customary practice is to receive (hear) the evidence subject to the objection (Rule 30(c)). If the evidence were precluded by the objection, and later the court determined that the objection was not valid, the witness's deposition would have to be taken again concerning the omitted matters. By being received, subject to the objection, the evidence is available. If the evidence is not admissible at trial, the court may order it stricken from the deposition transcript when it is offered at trial. The jury will never hear it. Also, the lawyer who made the objection may find that the answer is actually helpful to his or her theory and may decide to withdraw the objection. Or the lawyer may decide that the answer is innocuous and not worth fighting about. Rule 32(d)(3)(A) gives parties the right to object to deposition questions, answers, and other evidence for the first time at trial when the objections concern the competency of the witness (Rule 601), competency of the testimony (Rules 602, 701, 702, and 703), and relevancy of the testimony (Rules 401–411).

On occasion, a question may be so prejudicial (damaging) to the deponent, if answered, that her or his lawyer decides the deponent should not answer, even subject to objection. Questions concerning privileged communications and records, and questions concerning an attorney's work product often fall into those categories. Two alternatives are available to the deponent: the deponent's lawyer may elect to stop the deposition at that point, or the lawyers may agree to proceed with other questions and finish the deposition. Then the party seeking discovery may make a motion to compel answers to the questions to which objections were made. If the court sustains the objections, the deposition need not be resumed. If the objections are overruled, the deponent may be allowed to respond to the specific questions by answering written interrogatories. That would be more convenient and more economical than resuming the deposition. The court is authorized to award costs and attorneys' fees in favor of the party whose position was correct (Rules 30(d) and 37(a)(4)). This is discretionary with the court.

If problems arise during a deposition being conducted away from the home district, the parties may apply to the federal district court in which the deposition is being taken for a resolution. For example, if it appears to one or more of the parties that the deposition is being taken so as to embarrass or oppress the deponent, either he or she or another party may stop the deposition and move the court in that district for an order terminating the deposition or limiting the scope of the deposition or directing the manner of the taking of the deposition (Rule 26(c)). It would be inconvenient for everyone to have to return to the home district court, obtain a ruling, and then journey once again to the place where the deposition is being taken. Rule 30(c) appears to reserve to the home district court the obligation of ruling on the admissibility of the evidence at trial. If the deposition is terminated by order of a court other than the home district, the deposition cannot be resumed until ordered by the home district court, that is, the court in which the action is pending. The deponent or party has an absolute right to demand that the deposition be suspended until the court rules on his or her objection. The party or lawyer at fault may be required to pay the expenses of the motion and deposition (Rules 30(d) and 37(a)(4)).

■ MOTION TO SUPPRESS

A party may move the court for an order suppressing the use of a deposition, or any part of it, if some irregularity occurred. The burden rests upon the moving party to persuade the court that the deposition is invalid or that its use would cause prejudice outweighing its value to the court and jury. The motion to suppress must be made promptly after the error or irregularity in the proceedings has been discovered (Rule 32(d)(4)).

■ DEPOSITION RECORD

The deposition testimony is often recorded by stenographic means (shorthand or stenotype) unless the parties stipulate to another means or the court orders that another method be used (Rules 29 and 30(b)(4)). The transcript contains each question, answer, statement, and stipulation made during the oral deposition.

The deposition may be recorded electronically to make an audio or a video recording. If the deposition is to be used at trial, an electronic record will have to be played for the jury. That is fine when the parties want the entire deposition presented, but it is a nuisance to play excerpts from an electronic recording.

Video has the advantage of showing the witness to the jury. One disadvantage is that a video recording is expensive. In addition to the cost of the typed transcript, there is the cost of the videotape, video operator, and equipment. The room used for the deposition must be large enough to accommodate the lights, camera, and other paraphernalia. A video recording is cumbersome to make and to show at trial. It is also difficult to edit. For example, if the court upholds ten of the objections made during the taking of the deposition, the sound will have to be turned off when those questions and answers are reached. It is not impossible, just awkward and inconvenient. Also, a video recording seems to magnify the problems witnesses have speaking or articulating their answers. Some witnesses are even more nervous on camera than when testifying in court in person. The pauses between questions seem to be eternal. Discussions between the lawyers may seem more argumentative. On the other hand, a witness who is authoritative and who makes a good physical appearance usually makes a good presentation in a video deposition. Some lawyers prefer to present a doctor's medical testimony by video because of the difficulty of scheduling doctors to appear in court. Sometimes it is less expensive to present expert medical testimony at trial by video than to have the doctor appear in person.

Making a good videotaped deposition requires experience and careful planning. If a law firm has its own video equipment, the firm may want its paralegals to develop expertise in operating the equipment.

Any party has a right to have a stenographic record and transcription made of a deposition even if some other means has been agreed upon or ordered by the court. However, the party who wants the stenographic record must pay for it (Rule 30(b)(4)). A typed transcript is the most convenient form of record with which to work when preparing for trial and at trial.

The party who noticed the deposition does not have to order a transcript for the court, or for himself or herself, or for anyone else. If any party does order a transcript, the court reporter is required to file the original copy with the clerk of court. He or she must place it in a sealed envelope displaying the title of the action, the name of the deponent, and the date of the deposition. If the reporter cannot deliver the transcript to the clerk, he or she must send it by registered mail (Rule 30(f)).

When the court reporter files the original copy of the deposition transcript with the clerk of court, she or he must inform the lawyer who took the deposition, specifying the date of filing. In turn, the lawyer who noticed and took the deposition must notify all other parties that the original transcript has been filed (Rule 31(c)). This is done by serving a notice of filing of deposition. If this procedure is not followed, the original transcript may not be on file when the case is reached for trial. Nevertheless, a custom has developed among lawyers in many jurisdictions to stipulate on the record that they "waive notice of filing." If notice of filing is waived, the lawyer who took the deposition should still make sure that the original transcript is duly filed. Lawyers frequently waive notice of filing simply to lessen the amount of paperwork.

The court reporter may sell copies of the transcript to anyone who wants them—whether or not a party to the action. Lawyers commonly search for and obtain copies of depositions given by an adverse party in other cases. They may be able to find out about a party's other litigation by examining the litigation indexes kept by the clerk of court. The court files are available for public inspection. The clerk also keeps a list of all documents filed in connection with each case, so it is relatively easy to determine whether a person's deposition was taken in a case.

The easiest way for a nonparty to obtain access to a deposition transcript is to contact one of the lawyers who was involved in the case and review her or his copy. The transcript is not a privileged document. It is easy to make a photocopy of a transcript. If for some reason it is not desirable to contact one of the lawyers, the court reporter who took the deposition can make a copy from her or his stenographic notes. Usually reporters do not retain copies of transcripts. It is cheaper and more convenient to try to find an existing copy.

■ DEPONENT'S VERIFICATION OF DEPOSITION TRANSCRIPT

The deponent has a right to read the deposition transcript in order to make corrections or changes before it is filed with the court and before it is used for any purpose. The court reporter is required to submit the transcript to the deponent as soon as it has been prepared. The deponent must review the transcript and make corrections within thirty days from the date it is received. The deponent may correct any errors in her or his testimony whether the errors are of *substance* or of *form*. The deponent must make a written statement giving reasons or an explanation for each change made.

The usual procedure for making changes is for the deponent and her or his lawyer to review the transcript—not necessarily at the same time. Each notes the apparent errors and proposed corrections she or he thinks are necessary. They discuss the matter. The lawyer then prepares an addendum or errata sheet, which the deponent must sign under oath. The addendum is then sent to the court reporter, who must append the correction sheet to the end of the transcript. The deponent must sign a certification and verify that she or he has read the deposition and that, as changed, it is correct. A paralegal should be able to help the client make the corrections.

A deponent may waive the right to make changes and corrections in the transcript if the parties agree (Rule 39(e)). The deponent does so by stating at the conclusion of the deposition that he or she waives the right to read and sign the transcript. The court reporter notes the oral waiver in the transcript. If the deponent waives the right to review the transcript, he or she necessarily relies upon the accuracy of the stenographer (court reporter). In many cases, lawyers advise their client to waive the right to read and sign because usually substantive changes are not needed. The changes concerning form (such as spellings) are obvious and do not really affect anyone's legal rights. It is easier to simply rely upon the accuracy of the reporter. Most court reporters are very capable, conscientious, and reliable.

A deponent automatically waives the right to review and correct the transcript if she or he fails to make the corrections within thirty days after the transcript is submitted by the reporter. Day 1 of the thirty-day period begins on the day after the deponent or deponent's lawyer receives the transcript (Rule 6(a)). If the deponent does not sign the transcript, the court reporter is supposed to make a statement in the transcript explaining why the deponent was unable or unwilling to sign it. The transcript may then be used as though it has been signed by the deponent.

■ DEPOSITION SUMMARIES

Paralegals may be asked to prepare summaries of discovery deposition transcripts. Lawyers need deposition summaries to abstract essential information for convenient reference. They use summaries when preparing for trial. Sometimes clients or a client's insurer needs a deposition summary to evaluate the case. Lawyers in private practice who represent corporations are often required to provide detailed reports to management or the head of the legal department, including summaries of important depositions.

No one format is used for a deposition summary. Indeed, the format of choice depends upon the purpose for which the summary will be used. A deposition may be summarized in a letter as a narrative. The letter may or may not refer to pages of the transcript where the information is located. This kind of summary is usually made by a person who attends the deposition and reports on the testimony before the transcript is available. It is useful for insurance companies and as a general reference. Narrative summaries are often used by lawyers who oversee the handling of a case but are not directly involved in the discovery process.

If a deposition summary is going to be used for trial preparation, citations to the transcript are indispensable. The trial preparation summary may paraphrase testimony or quote critical testimony. When this format is used, it is preferable to leave a wide margin for editorializing. The summary may be chronological so as to parallel the transcript, or categorized by subject matter.

Paralegals must understand the legal issues, fact issues, and parties' legal theories to know what to include in a deposition summary and what may be safely left out. They will become more efficient as they gain experience.

Narrative Summaries

A malpractice action has been brought against a doctor of chiropractic who allegedly failed to diagnose a sixteen-year-old girl's slipped capital femoral epiphysis. The epiphysis is a growth plate at the end of the femur in the hip socket. When it has slipped, it has detached from the femur. The condition is quite painful. It can be corrected by surgery. The plaintiff's condition was eventually diagnosed by a medical doctor and surgically repaired. The plaintiff claimed that if the diagnosis had been made earlier, while she was treating with the chiropractor, she would have made a full recovery. Instead, she was left with a disability and the prospect of having to have a hip replacement in the future. The chiropractor contended that he treated her for a different problem caused by a fall while playing. She recovered from that problem, and she terminated her treatment. She returned a year later with symptoms that were similar but due to a new injury. After three weeks of treatment, he realized that she was not improving and referred her to a medical doctor. In the meantime, she had been seen by a medical doctor who did not observe any hip problem.

The plaintiff's lawyer took the treating doctor's deposition to use at trial. The summary in exhibit 12.2 was prepared to report to the chiropractor's insurance company, which was managing the defense of the case. This summary is primarily for the client's information. It has not been prepared as a synopsis for use at trial. The information gleaned from the deposition transcript has been put into subject matter paragraphs regardless of where the information is contained in the transcript. No page references are given because the client does no need to refer to the transcript. The legal assistant has minimized use of the expression "The witness testified that. . . ." The entire report is about Dr. Ellen Wales's testimony, so that need not be said in the report. The summary attempts to relate the testimony to the parties' theories of the case. These asides are quite apparent and do not require disclaimers that the author is providing commentary. The summary is authoritative. If the client wanted the responsible lawyer to evaluate the case, the lawyer could use this summary when making the analysis and evaluation.

Trial Preparation Summaries

The deposition summary in exhibit 12.3 was prepared for the trial lawyer's use. It provides the page of the transcript where the information may be

■ **EXHIBIT 12.2**
Narrative Summary

DR. ELLEN WALES'S DEPOSITION SUMMARY

Dear Mr. Insurance Supervisor:

Dr. Ellen B. Wales's videotaped deposition was taken on July 30, 1994. The following is a summary of Dr. Wales's testimony.

Dr. Wales is a medical doctor who specializes in orthopedic surgery. Orthopedic surgery deals with the skeletal system of the body and all supporting structures including muscles and ligaments. She has practiced orthopedic surgery since 1973. Before that, she practiced general medicine from 1962 to 1968 approximately. She became board certified in orthopedic surgery in 1973. Dr. Wales is an assistant professor of orthopedic surgery at the University of Minnesota. She has also supervised the Knee Clinic at the local veterans hospital since 1976. Dr. Wales is affiliated with Superior Orthopedics located in St. Paul. Superior Orthopedics has nine orthopedic surgeons. The medical group services St. Joseph's, St. John's, Midway, and Divine Redeemer Hospitals. All members of this group are on the staff of the University of Minnesota Hospital and of the local veterans hospital. Dr. Wales also travels to Forest Lake and Hastings, and Grantsburg, Wisconsin, to provide consulting services to the smaller communities. She first met the plaintiff while providing consulting services in Hastings.

Dr. Wales has had a great deal of experience diagnosing and treating slipped capital femoral epiphyses. A slipped capital femoral epiphysis is most common in children who have not yet reached their full growth. Children who are eleven to fifteen years old and obese are particularly vulnerable to injury. The slip (break) may occur owing to a traumatic incident, or there may be no history of any apparent trauma. The condition usually goes through four discrete stages. The symptoms and patient presentation vary depending upon the stage. In the first stage the patient has some knee and hip pain. In stage 2 the patient has increased hip pain, thigh pain, groin pain, and a distinct limp. In the third stage the patient has more pain, and the affected leg may turn out or rotate outward. In the fourth stage the patient has an emergency condition. In each stage the slippage has advanced. In the fourth stage the epiphysis has completely separated from the head of the femur.

Dr. Wales first saw Susan Smith on May 3, 1991, at the Orthopedic Clinic located in Hastings. She happened to see Smith walk to the front door and into the office. Her mother helped her sit down because she was limping. She could have made the diagnosis from just seeing how she walked. She noted that she was somewhat obese. On examination she found that Smith had groin and thigh pain and pain that went into her knee. She walked with a "short-leg" gain. Her left leg was shortened several centimeters and externally rotated outward. She could not flex her hip up or bring it out straight. She could bring it out laterally, but the movement caused a great deal of pain. She had little or no rotation of her left hip. The diagnosis of slipped capital femoral epiphysis was clear even without X-rays. Nevertheless, Dr. Wales took "frog-leg" views of the plaintiff's pelvis and hip point to confirm the diagnosis. The X-rays showed a grade 3 slipped capital femoral epiphysis.

Dr. Wales testified that there are grades of slippage. A preslippage condition could last as long as one year. It may or may not be symptomatic. The patient's condition would be expected to progress to a grade 1. Dr. Wales testified that it did not take long for Smith to go from a preslip to a grade 3. She was not blaming Dr. Marcus Santos [the chiropractor] for Smith's slipped capital femoral epiphysis.

Dr. Wales put pins in Smith's hip at United Hospital. She drilled the pins across to hold the joint from falling off anymore. She tried to have the growth center closed

—*Continued*

—Continued

so that it would not be vulnerable to any more slippage or injury. because of the surgery, Smith's growth center has prematurely closed and completely fused. The plaintiff's ball and socket are not matched.

Dr. Wales opines that a direct relationship exists between the symptoms Smith presented to Dr. Santos in February 1990 and Dr. Wales's diagnosis of a grade 3 slipped capital femoral epiphysis in May 1991. She believes the slip began in February 1990. She bases her opinion on the fact that children with slipped capital femoral epiphysis who have come in early, before the actual slip, experience groin and thigh pain. They may or may not have a normal gait. They sometimes complain of knee pain. This is called the preslip stage, and if the condition is caught at this stage, surgery usually restores full function. The epiphysis is surgically nailed in place, and normal growth continues. Dr. Wales believes the diagnosis of slipped capital femoral epiphysis could have been made in February 1990 by exam and X-rays. If X-rays were taken in February 1990, yielding the diagnosis of early slippage, it would have been a grade 1 slippage. Appropriate orthopedic care would have included a surgical pinning of the hip.

Dr. Wales's opinion takes into consideration the fact that Smith did not have pain in her hip from February 1990 [when Dr. Santos discharged her from his care] until March 1991. She testified that sometimes children who have initial slippage can settle down and will not slip any further for a significant period of time. Children who have slippage that continues have a synovitis, or an inflammation of the hip joint. They produce excess fluid and have pain from the distension of the sack around the hip joint. If Smith had a quiescent period during which no slippage occurred, then the fluid could have been reabsorbed, and she would not have had as much pain as she had in the past. Dr. Wales testified that Susan's development of a significant limp in March 1991 indicates that the epiphysis slipped again, to change her condition to a grade 3.

The delay of almost a year in diagnosis caused a repairable problem to turn into a permanent problem. Dr. Wales could not obtain a good alignment because of the delay and increased slippage. Smith will experience untoward wear and tear on her hip joint during her early adult years, and this will lead to the need for at least one hip replacement. During her lifetime, she may need two or three hip replacements. Her leg is externally rotated and is somewhat shorter. This will lead to degenerative arthritis and increased pain. A new hip joint will cost approximately twenty-five thousand dollars. A hip joint replacement is considered to be a temporary procedure. If the procedure is performed on a patient in his or her forties, one can pretty well guarantee that a second total hip replacement will be needed eight to twelve years later. Smith can no longer partake in any sporting activities or running. She has difficulty riding a bike.

If the slipped capital femoral epiphysis had been diagnosed in February 1990 when she was under the defendant's care, Smith would now have a normal hip. She would not have any restrictions. In Dr. Wales's opinion, Dr. Santos's chiropractic adjustments did not provide any "medical" benefit for her limp. Dr. Wales knows that chiropractors are not licensed or qualified to treat slipped capital femoral epiphysis. She believes that Dr. Santos's treatment harmed Smith's hip condition by keeping her from seeing a qualified medical doctor.

Dr. Wales knew Smith fell while playing in gym class, and hurt her knee. That is the problem for which she originally consulted Dr. Santos in February 1990. Although

—Continued

—Continued

the chiropractor's records show that she progressively recovered to the point that she was symptom free, Dr. Wales feels that she was not in fact symptom free. In other words, she disagrees with the records. She has no explanation for why the plaintiff did not return to Dr. Santos or see another doctor if she was continuing to have symptoms during the year. It appears that neither she nor the plaintiff's attorney are aware of the record that the plaintiff did see another medical doctor during the year, and that doctor did not observe symptoms of a slipped epiphysis. Dr. Wales talked to Smith's mother at great length. The mother told Dr. Wales that Smith had been having a great deal of difficulty over the past three months and was having trouble in gym class. Dr. Wales concluded that Dr. Santos's confidential history indicated that Smith was limping on the left leg and had fallen during her gym class. He believes that Smith had a grade 1 slip at that time. She had a sheer force to her hip when she fell on her knee in gym. The limp indicated that she had an effusion and pain in her hip.

We will continue to keep you advised of any further developments.

Very truly yours,

Carol Munson
Legal Assistant

obtained or verified. The subject matter is identified by a generic topic. The information is reviewed in the same order as in the deposition transcript. The legal assistant has been careful to provide all the pertinent names and dates. She has not provided any commentary on the merits of the testimony or related the testimony to the parties' legal theories.

The plaintiff was involved in two motor vehicle accidents and one work-related injury, and asserted a claim that a treating chiropractor caused a herniated disk in his cervical spine. He brought suit to recover money damages for his personal injuries. He claimed that the December 1990 automobile accident caused a minor neck strain but permanently injured his right shoulder and right elbow. He claimed that the January 1991 accident did not cause any injury; however, the other driver did make a claim against him for injuries. He received a traffic ticket for that accident. He injured his lower back at work in March 1991. He started treating with the defendant chiropractors for that injury. He alleged that on April 9, 1991, Dr. Sarah Jackson adjusted his neck in such a manner that she caused the intervertebral disk at C6–7 to herniate and press on the nerve root at that level. The pressure on the nerve caused pain in his neck and weakness and numbness in his left hand. In July 1993, his treating neurologist referred him to a neurosurgeon, who arranged for a magnetic resonance imaging (MRI) scan of his cervical spine. The scan showed that he did not have a herniated disk at all, but had a large bone spur that predated even the first automobile accident.

■ **USE OF DEPOSITIONS IN TRIAL PREPARATION**

A person who is going to testify at trial must study his or her deposition transcript. The deponent can be sure that the lawyer on the other side of

■ **EXHIBIT 12.3** Trial Preparation Summary

DEPOSITION SUMMARY OF
Michael Strike
Taken on April 26, 1993

File No.

PAGE	TOPIC	DESCRIPTION
8	Personal	Deponent is presently single. He was married from 1971 to July 1990. He was divorced in Spencer. His former wife's name is now Paula Jean Lund. She resides at 801 Ninth Avenue SE. They have a daughter, Jennifer, who is twenty, and a son, Jonathon, who is seventeen. His son lives with him at 2285 Ahrens Hill Road North. His daughter is a junior at Moorhead State.
9	Occupation	He is a recreational therapist for the state of Iowa. He has had that job for eight years. Before that he was a recreation program assistant for the state. He worked at Spencer Regional Treatment Center for one or two years. Before being a program assistant he was a human services technician for the state at Spencer Regional Treatment Center. Before that, when he was eighteen, he worked for Viking Coca-Cola Company.
10	Recreational Therapist	Recreational therapists program recreational activities for developmentally disabled persons. They write programs, implement programs, do one-on-one training, provide leisure counseling, and so forth.
11	Recreational Therapist	Recreational therapists have professional responsibilities for the implementation of a program. They direct the line staff to implement the programs they write. They counsel, observe, do quality assurance tasks, and so forth.
11	Physical Requirements of a Recreational Therapist	Recreational therapists model the activities they are teaching their clients. In other words, they demonstrate and participate in the activities. They may include any kind of aerobic activity, lift weights, play baseball, anything that involves socialization and physical activity.
12	Education	The deponent has a bachelor of science degree in physical education and a bachelor of science in art education, K through 12. He obtained the degrees from St. Cloud University in 1978 through 1982. He graduated from Spencer High School in 1971.
12	Weight	He has weighed approximately two hundred pounds since June 1991. He did take off some extra weight the year he was getting divorced, in 1989, by bicycling, lifting weights, and running.
13	Self-Defense Courses	Occasionally he conducts seminars for women in self-defense through the school system. The last time he conducted a seminar was March 1993. In that month he made approximately $220 from the self-defense classes. He was unable to conduct one seminar owing to his arm and shoulder injuries. He would have made approximately $300.

—Continued

■ **EXHIBIT 12.3** Trial Preparation Summary, *Continued*

—Continued

15	Certification in Therapeutic Intervention	Instructors are certified in therapeutic intervention every year through the state of Iowa. Therapeutic intervention is the method the state has authorized for control of residents who become assaultive and aggressive. The deponent is an instructor. He was picked by his supervisor and then trained by state certified instructors through a one-week workshop.
16	Decoy Business	He believes he started his decoy work in the mid-1970s. He started it as a hobby and turned it into a business. A friend of the family, John Bale, thought a market existed and asked him if he was willing to do it for money, and he responded, "Sure." He is no longer in the decoy business. He got out of the business about the same time he was involved with the neck injury. His wife helped him for a period of time. He is now able to do the basic rough shapes, but he is unable to do detailing, as it requires a steady hand. His tax returns show he made $122 in 1989 in the decoy business. He made only that much because he did not have his wife's assistance in the business. In 1990 he did not sell any decoys. Since his automobile accident of 1990, he has only been able to partially complete one decoy. In some years he made $5,000 in this business. The decoys sold for $350 to $450 each. They were sold to the Harris Gallery in Storm Lake.
21	Loss of Feeling in Fingers/Decoy Business	He does not have any feeling in his index finger, the finger next to it on the left hand, and his thumb. If you do not have feeling when you are wood burning, you dig too deep. You have to have dexterity to do symmetrical lines. At this point in time, he does not have plans to continue with the decoy business unless something turns around as far as the numbness in his hand.
23	Treatment since January	At the beginning of the year, he went through a bout of bronchitis and started having trouble with his neck because of the heavy coughing. He saw Dr. Peter Fowler, who referred him back to that Physical Therapist Greg Phillips. Phillips gave him a grip test, which revealed that he had 120 pounds of grip strength in his right hand and 50 pounds in his left. He is left-handed. The physical therapist was happy that he showed up because his condition was deteriorating. Phillips put him in traction and massage and had him do exercises to strengthen his left hand. Now his grip strength is back up. He has an appointment to see Dr. Fowler this week.
24	Appointment with Dr. Fowler for Right Shoulder	He scheduled an appointment to see Dr. Fowler, as his shoulder has been giving him a lot of trouble. He is losing mobility and strength in it. It is painful to lift heavier objects. Since this is a problem that was dealt with before, he is going to ask that he be referred back to Phillips for physical therapy for his right shoulder.
24	Podiatrist	He saw a podiatrist for a bone spur on his right heel that aggravated the Achilles tendon.

—Continued

■ **EXHIBIT 12.3** Trial Preparation Summary, *Continued*

—Continued

24	Right Shoulder	His right shoulder feels as if it is stretching away from the socket. Dr. Fowler managed to resolve some of the problems the last time the doctor worked on it. He has trouble lifting heavy objects, twisting, turning, swinging anything, sleeping and so forth. It is very painful.
25	Physical Activities	He walks and sometimes jogs. However, he cannot jog too much because it shakes things around the he stiffens up quickly. He is not able to do any other body strengthening things that he was able to do before. Any strenuous midsection exercises seem to affect his neck.
26	Lifting Weights	He is not now on a weight training program. Occasionally, he would go in and lift weights with the clients. He would occasionally demonstrate the use of weights at his job, but he has a recreational assistant who generally will take over those duties.
26	Recreational Assistant Moser	His recreational assistant is Randy Moser, who lives in Spencer.
26	Strength Training	Before the accident, he did have a strength training program. He would lift weights three times a week at the Spencer Regional Treatment Center. There was a universal gym. He was not worked with the universal gym since the accident in 1990. He has done limited amounts of strength training. his shoulder has been bothering him the last two months, so he has not lifted.
28	Current Complaints	He is concerned about the numbness in his hand getting worse. He is worried that when he was able to do repetitive activities, like shoveling snow, he had a lot of pain in his left elbow. Also, his right shoulder has gotten weaker. He wonders what the longevity of the treatment is going to be. He has lost flexibility in his neck. One of the problems he has as an instructor of therapeutic intervention is that a lot of times he is not able to demonstrate some of the techniques and has to defer to the other instructor, Karen Stuneck, who lives in Spencer.
29	Neck	He used to be able to move his neck a lot more. Now when he moves his neck beyond a certain point it is very painful. He is not currently receiving treatment for his neck problem. He was treated for it in February.
29	Medications	He is not taking any medications.
30	Neck	He has not been prescribed any home exercises for his neck problem. In the last year, his neck has stayed about the same.
30	Left Hand Complaint	He has loss of sensation in his thumb and first two fingers since April 1991. He has lost dexterity.
30	Left Arm Complaint	If he does anything repetitive, he has a burning, painful sensation across his elbow, which is like lateral epicondylitis. He was given cortisone by Dr. Fowler after the accident in the joint. Anything repetitive causes problems. That is why he does not lift weights anymore.
32	Prior Neck Problem	He denies any neck problem before 1990. Medical records indicate he fell off a ladder in 1987, hurting his neck. When

—Continued

■ **EXHIBIT 12.3** Trial Preparation Summary, *Continued*

—Continued

		questioned, he remembered falling off the ladder and testified that he might have had a stiff neck. He probably saw a doctor one time, but he does not recall any continuing symptoms from that fall.
33	Prior Right Shoulder Problems	He initially did not recall having any right shoulder problems before 1990. When questioned, he remembered that he did separate his shoulder while skiing at Ski Gull. He was going down a hill too fast and leaned into the hill and separated his shoulder. At the time of the 1990 automobile accident, his shoulder was not bothering him from the separation. He was lifting weights and was in pretty good shape before the car accident.
34	Reason for First Seeing a Chiropractor	In March 1990 he stopped a resident from dropping weights on the resident's chest. He hurt his lower back, which led him to see the defendant chiropractors. He does not recall treating with chiropractors before that.
35	First Visit to Dr. Frazee's Office/Neck Problems	His lower-back pain was acute and he was unable to see his orthopedic surgeon. He had heard from Janet Wagner at work that she had had good luck with Moira Frazee's office. Any neck symptoms he had as a result of the accident had resolved themselves before he went to the chiropractor. He did not have any big problems with his neck. He was very satisfied with the treatment he received at St. Joseph's Medical Center.
36	Neck Problem	Right after the automobile accident of 1990, he did have a stiff neck, for which he saw Dr. Fowler.
36	Prior Elbow Problems	Before the automobile accident of 1990, he does not recall having any left elbow problems.
37	Golfing	He did not golf last year or the year before. It was one of the things he enjoyed doing. he will not be able to play golf in the foreseeable future. He attempted to play twice with some friends but gave it up, as it was too frustrating. He is a certified golf coach. That is part of his teaching certificate. He was a pretty decent golfer, and it was frustrating to play badly. He does not have the rotation to golf. Golfers need grip strength and dexterity in their fingertips. When he tried to golf, he experienced shoulder and elbow pain. He used to play golf four times a month.
39	Waterskiing	He has had to give up waterskiing. He tried it once last year and could not get out of the water because he did not have the arm or shoulder strength to hold himself up.
39	Running and Walking	He walks and runs approximately two and a half to three miles three times a week. Physical problems depend on the road surface, how he slept, or how he feels during warm-up stretching. Stretching is a necessity. His hip will hurt, and his shoulder will hurt from holding his arms. When that happens, he starts walking. He runs less now than he did before.
40	Subject Accident	On December 21, 1990, he had been visiting his girlfriend Wagner, for a week at Christmas in Bayfield, Wisconsin. He was on Interstate 35 heading south at 2:45 in the afternoon when

—Continued

■ **EXHIBIT 12.3** Trial Preparation Summary, *Continued*

—Continued

		the accident occurred. He had just crossed the bridge across Lake Superior and was approaching an incline. The visibility was bad, and all the traffic had slowed and eventually stopped because of a snowplow ahead. The roadway was slippery. As soon as he stopped, he looked in his rearview mirror because some of the traffic had been moving at a higher rate of speed than he would have deemed safe. He saw Alfred Walker's car approaching from the rear. Walker had his lights on, and the deponent stated, "I think we're going to be hit." He grabbed onto the steering wheel and reached across Wagner. Walker's car hit him with enough impact to break his seat back and total out the back of the car. The back end of the car was pushed to the windshield.
42	Walker's Vehicle	Walker's vehicle was a 1978 Thunderbird. Walker could not open the doors and had to crawl out the window.
42	Highway 35	Interstate 35 is a four-lane highway. Two lanes are northbound, two are southbound. Both southbound lanes were stopped before the accident.
42	Subject Accident	The deponent did have his lights on. He was stopped for maybe two minutes before he was hit. He was wearing his seat and shoulder belts. On impact he was pitched forward and felt a burning sensation in his left arm from hanging on to the steering wheel. He then pitched back, and the seat back broke. He was concerned about his passenger. Wagner banged her head against the window. She had not been ready for the impact, and by the time he told her they were going to be hit, she was not braced. His left hand had been holding on to the steering wheel, his right hand he had put out in front of his passenger. He does not know if his left elbow hit anything inside the car. He just knew they were going to be hit and hit hard.
44	Theory of Stopped Traffic/Plow	His theory in regard to why the traffic was stopped was that a blue light was flashing from a road plow up ahead that was not moving. He believes it was a wing plow, which stopped traffic in both lanes.
44	Vehicle Trajectory	His car was pushed forward into the guardrail in the left-hand lane.
44	Conversation at the Scene	After the impact, the deponent got out and looked at the damage. He and Walker agreed that it was better that they both get off the road so that someone else would not get hit. Because their cars both ran, they decided they would go up the road a quarter mile and take an off-ramp to a grocery store, where they exchanged numbers and called the highway patrol. Walker appeared to be shaken up and said it was hard to see. The traffic started to move right after the accident.
45	Treatment after the Accident	The deponent received treatment from a doctor at the Spencer Medical Center after the accident.
45	Second Accident	He was involved in another accident on January 18, 1991, near Spencer. He had stopped at a stop sign at a pile of snow. He

—Continued

■ **EXHIBIT 12.3** Trial Preparation Summary, *Continued*

—Continued

		could not see traffic coming from the north because of the snow. Most of the traffic comes from the south, so he looked that way. He was hit from the north. His back quarter panel was hit. The police came and investigated the accident. He does not have a claim against the other driver, Harlan Olson. His left rib cage was bruised. He believes he bruised his ribs on the armrest. The deponent had been driving a 1988 Honda Accord.
49	Claim against Him	Olson is suing him for the second accident. Notification his attorney received said that Olson was hurt. However, Olson did not seem hurt at the scene.
49	Damage to Deponent's Vehicle	His vehicle sustained substantial damage to the rear quarter panel and was repaired. He was surprised that they would fix it. The damage was probably in excess of three thousand dollars. Horace Mann Insurance Company would know the cost of repair.
50	Incident Resulting in Chiropractic Treatment	On March 13, 1991, he was spotting for a resident on an incline bench press. The resident pushed the bar up and dropped it. The deponent grabbed it before it came down too hard. He was concerned that the weight might hit the patient, and the bar might break if it was dropped from any distance. He was not in a good position to stop the downward motion of the weight. He was somewhat bent over. The deponent immediately felt a pinch in his lower back. He reported the incident to his employer. The next day he went to get chiropractic treatment.
53	Conversation with Chiropractor	He told the chiropractor he injured his back in a weight lifting incident at the state hospital. He did not tell the chiropractor about the automobile accident, as he felt that he had recovered from that accident.
53	Time Lost from Work	His answers to interrogatories state he missed 137 hours of work. This was covered by workers' compensation. He knows he received a check from somebody in February 1991. He does not recall who it came from.
55	Medical Bills	He believes he submitted his medical and chiropractic bills to Mann.
56	Other Injuries	Other than the two automobile accidents and the incident where he hurt his lower back, he has not been involved in any other automobile accidents or hurt himself in any other way.
57	Income from Decoys	The most money he has ever made in one year from making decoys was five or six thousand dollars. He sold the decoys for $350 to $400 in Storm Lake.
57	Education	He has a degree in fine arts and art education.
58	Girlfriend	His girlfriend is Janet Wagner. She resides at 6047 Fourth Street North, Nisswa. She is thirty-nine years old.
58	Income from Decoys	He earned five or six thousand dollars in 1987 and 1988.
59	Fall from Ladder	He believes it was 1987 when he fell off the ladder and developed a stiff neck. He does not recall what treatment he might have had as a result of the fall. He saw whoever was on call at the Spencer Medical Center.

—Continued

■ **EXHIBIT 12.3** Trial Preparation Summary, *Continued*

—Continued

60	Loss of Feeling in Left Thumb	He has a loss of feeling in his left thumb. It began in April 1991 after manipulation. It occurred at the same time he lost feeling in his left hand. The deterioration of his condition took place over a period of time. He does not specifically recall when he noticed it.
61	Medical Bills	He has submitted his medical bills to Mann. He does not believe he has any medical bills outstanding.
61	Olson's Claim	Olson has made a claim against him. Olson is being represented by the Van Drake Law Firm in Spencer.
62	Wagner's Injuries/ Conversation	After the accident, the deponent asked Wagner how she was. She said she got a bump on the side of her head from hitting the door window. She might have complained of a headache. He does not recall. Wagner asked the deponent how he was. The deponent said he was shaken up but seemed to feel OK. He cannot recall if he said he had a headache.
63	Neck Discomfort	He did have neck discomfort following the accident, but he did not tell that to Dr. Anne Jackson [the chiropractor he saw at Dr. Frazee's office on March 14, 1991].
63	Numbness	He had numbness in the front of his left hand in addition to his index finger and middle finger. Basically the numbness was along the perimeter of the hand.
64	Recommended to Dr. Frazee	He went to Dr. Frazee's office on March 14, 1991. He had hurt his lower back the previous day. The individual who recommended Dr. Frazee's office had problems between her shoulder blades. She is currently a patient of Dr. Frazee's. She has never complained about Dr. Frazee. She likes him.
65	First Visit to Dr. Frazee	He does not recall any adjustment on his first office visit on march 14. He received massage and heat. X-rays were taken. He saw Dr. Jackson. He does not recall Dr. Jackson's diagnosis.
65	Second Visit	His second visit to Dr. Frazee's office was on March 19. He saw Dr. Jackson. His neck was not adjusted.
66	Third Visit	At his third visit on March 21, he saw Dr. Jackson. On that day he told Dr. Jackson he was having some headaches. Dr. Jackson asked if he had ever had adjustments on his neck for headaches. He had not. Dr. Jackson suggested that he try an adjustment to see if it would help his headache. A cervical adjustment was administered. He does not recall any problem following the adjustment. He was shocked how loud it was. He did not experience an increase of discomfort in his neck following the adjustment.
67	Fourth Visit	The next chiropractic treatment took place on March 26. He was still having headaches. Dr. Jackson suggested that he try a cervical adjustment. When the doctor finished the adjustment, he felt no worse. He felt that he was being taken care of professionally and his condition was being treated appropriately.
69	Fifth Visit	His next treatment at the Frazee Clinic was April 2. He again had treatment to his lower back. He does not recall if he had treatment to his neck.

—Continued

■ **EXHIBIT 12.3** Trial Preparation Summary, *Continued*

—Continued

69	Sixth Visit	His sixth visit to the chiropractor was on April 9. His back seemed to be getting better. He was not doing anything for his back aside from getting chiropractic adjustments. He had been able to continue working notwithstanding his back discomfort. He was feeling better than he had when he first came in on March 14. He believes he had a cervical adjustment. Other than his lower-back pain, he still had recurring headaches. He believes Dr. Jackson indicated that she was going to try cervical adjustments at different levels to see if she could find a trigger point for the headaches. When he left, he felt the treatment was a little more vigorous than the prior treatments. He made no complaints to the doctor. He scheduled another treatment.
72	Seventh Visit	His seventh visit was on April 11.
72	Subsequent to the April 9 Adjustment	After the April 9 adjustment, which occurred on his lunch break, he went back to work. He felt funny, so he basically did paperwork. He worked until 8:30 in the evening. He went home after work. He was with his son. He took ibuprofen.
73	Injuries from December 21, 1990, Accident	He is not aware that he struck his left elbow against anything. He was braced against the steering wheel. He might have had some slight swelling of the left elbow. He went to see a doctor for his left elbow.
74	Asleep on Couch	On the night of April 9, 1991, he watched television while lying on the couch with two pillows. The next day, April 10, his neck was very sore.
74	Neck Pain	On April 10, after he got out of bed, his neck was very sore. His head was cocked toward his shoulder. He could not move in any direction comfortably. The pain was very severe. He had used two pillows to support his shoulders and neck while lying on the couch.
76	Contact with Dr. Frazee's Office	On April 10, in the morning, he contacted Dr. Frazee's office to see if he could get into see Dr. Jackson. He was told that Dr. Jackson was not in but Dr. Frazee was in her Storm Lake office. He made arrangements to be seen by Dr. Frazee at the Storm Lake office. He did go to work on the tenth.
78	Others Who had Knowledge of Neck Problems/Medication	His recreational assistants and his secretary showed concern. He probably took some Advil.
78	April 11 Visit	He saw Dr. Frazee in Storm Lake on April 11. He drove himself to the doctor's office, which was approximately twenty-two miles away.
79	Conversations with Dr. Frazee	He told Dr. Frazee that he last had an adjustment from Dr. Jackson on April 9. He also told the doctor that he had slept on the couch for a while with two pillows and later had severe neck pain. Dr. Frazee examined his neck. Dr. Frazee probably explained to him that a chiropractic adjustment could not be given to him because of the pain. The deponent thought maybe Dr. Jackson had messed up and Dr. Frazee could straighten out his problem. It was his original intention to see Dr. Frazee because that is who he was referred to.

—Continued

■ **EXHIBIT 12.3**   Trial Preparation Summary, *Continued*

—*Continued*

81	Treatment with Dr. Frazee	He continued treatment with Dr. Frazee for several office visits. He does not recall if Dr. Frazee gave him any type of adjustments.
81	MRI	He and Dr. Frazee discussed an MRI. Dr. Frazee felt it would be a good idea. The deponent made arrangements to have an MRI on April 29, 1991.
82	Physical Therapy/ Traction	After the MRI he received physical therapy prescribed by a medical doctor. Along with physical therapy treatments, he had traction to his neck. The traction seemed to make it feel better when he was having it. He also had a home traction unit. Along with the traction, he received massage and heat. It was the same treatment he was receiving for his lower back at the chiropractor's office. He does not recall having any discomfort during his physical therapy. Traction felt good.
83	Medical Attention after December 21, 1990, Accident	The first treatment he received following the automobile accident on December 21, 1990, took place at the Spencer Medical Center on December 26. He gave a history of having stiffness in his neck immediately following the automobile accident. He complained of having recurring headaches. He experienced a slight discomfort when the therapist worked on his elbow. He let the doctor know. He told the doctor of the changes and sensations he was experiencing in his left arm, fingers, hand, and shoulder. Dr. Kenneth Galbraith released him to return to work without any restrictions as of July 11, 1991. The doctor told him he was very happy with the progress being made in physical therapy. The doctor told him that if he did not straighten out his problems, he would probably be a candidate for surgery. However, he progressed.
85	First MD Seen after Development of Wryneck Condition	The first medical doctor he saw after having the development of the wryneck condition was Dr. Phyllis Thomas. He explained to Dr. Thomas that the pain began in his neck the day after the chiropractic treatment.
86	April 15, 1991, Visit to Dr. Thomas	In addition, he was having pain in his left shoulder and down to his elbow.
86	April 25 Visit	On April 25 he saw Dr. Thomas and reported having shoulder and neck pain that radiated into his elbow.
87	May 8 Visit	On May 8 he reported to Dr. Thomas, for the first time, having problems with a tingling down into his hand and fingers. The day of his MRI was the day he went on vacation. He was suffering a few symptoms of this during his vacation.
87	Vacation	He and Wagner went on vacation to New York City to see some shows and visit the Statute of Liberty. He was suffering symptoms at this time. The second day there, he was not sure if he should hop a flight back to Spencer and check himself into the hospital. Since the automobile accident of December 21, 1990, he had also gone to Michigan skiing in February. In addition, he had just returned form Arizona. He did a lot of walking there.

—*Continued*

■ **EXHIBIT 12.3** Trial Preparation Summary, *Continued*

—Continued		
89	Additional Visits to Dr. Jackson	Before discontinuing his chiropractic care, he saw Dr. Jackson for his back and neck. He did not complain to Dr. Jackson that she had done something unusual to his neck. He usually does not complain.
90	Traction to Neck	The therapist usually does manual traction where she places her hands basically underneath the deponent's whole back. At that time she would ask the deponent how he felt. When using the mechanical device, the doctor gave him the stirrup to hang on to. The deponent would be in control and would not go beyond what was comfortable for him. He was reclining on the treatment table when the traction was administered to his neck.
90	Current Problems	Currently, his left elbow is better. He can use it normally although he has to avoid repetitive motions. Shoveling snow is very hard on it, as is lifting repetitively. He experiences problems with his elbow first and then his shoulder.
92	Causation of Problems	He does not know what the causation of his problems is. All he knows are the results. He is not a neurologist or orthopedic surgeon. He does not have any judgment as to what incident or incidents have caused his problems.
92	Dr. DeKoster	He has not personally been examined by Dr. David DeKoster. Dr. DeKoster only reviewed his records.
93	Complaint Regarding Headaches	Before the chiropractors did the first adjustments to his neck, he does not recall complaining to them about headaches. He had a cold, and they discussed the possibility of his having a sinus infection.

the case will have studied it. If the deponent's testimony at trial is inconsistent with (differs from) her or his deposition testimony, the inconsistency may be brought to the attention of the jury. The inconsistency is called **impeachment.** The jury may consider evidence of impeachment when determining whether to believe the witness.

A person who is going to testify at trial may study the deposition testimony of other witnesses to see what they say about the same subjects. Lawyers study deposition transcripts to prepare their examination of the deponents and to prepare to examine other witnesses who will be testifying on the same subject matter. A transcript helps the lawyer to know what questions to ask at trial. When a lawyer takes the deposition of an opposing party, the lawyer's questions reflect the theory that the lawyer is pursuing. That is another feature that lawyers consider when reviewing their clients' discovery deposition transcripts. Deposition transcripts are regularly used to refresh the deponent's memory in preparation for trial. A transcript may be used to educate a witness about points of contention.

■ USE OF DEPOSITIONS AT TRIAL

A deposition transcript may be used at trial to present testimony regardless of the purpose for which the deposition was originally taken. Therefore, if a lawyer elects not to ask a witness any questions in a deposition taken for purposes of discovery, he or she is gambling on the witness's availability for the trial. Usually, it is a risk worth taking because most lawyers do not want to prove or disclose the case in a discovery deposition.

A transcript may be used at trial in lieu of the deponent's live testimony if the deponent is unavailable for trial. A deponent is considered unavailable for trial if he or she is deceased, is more than one hundred miles from the place of trial, is ill, is in prison, or has not responded to a subpoena. Other reasons may be accepted by the court as establishing the witness's unavailability (Rule 32(a)(3)). Under certain circumstances, a deposition taken in one case may be used in another case (Rule 804(b)(1)).

Presentation to Jury

Deposition testimony may be presented to the jury in various ways. The manner chosen depends upon the amount of testimony to be presented, the lawyer's personal preference, and economics. The simplest and most economical method is for the lawyer to read the pertinent parts of the deposition to the jury. Depending upon the rules of the particular court, the lawyer may stand in front of the jury or sit in the witness box and read the transcript. The lawyer or court makes an introductory statement telling the jury what the lawyer is going to do and why the deposition is being read in lieu of the witness's personal appearance. The introductory statement should explain that the witness testified under oath, subject to cross-examination; when and where the deposition was taken; and who was present. Then the lawyer may state for the court record which pages and lines will be read. While the lawyer reads the questions and answers, the other lawyers watch their copy of the transcript to make sure it is read accurately. When the lawyer finishes reading the portions he or she feels are important to the case, the other lawyers may read any other portions they feel are relevant. The deposition testimony is admissible only if it otherwise comports with the rules of evidence.

This method of presenting deposition testimony is satisfactory if the reading is short; it is not very satisfactory if all or a substantial portion of the deposition is to be read. It is too monotonous for the jury to listen to one person read more than just a few pages. Also, it is difficult for the jury to follow questions and answers when one person reads both.

Another method of presenting deposition testimony is for someone, such as a paralegal, to sit in the witness stand, in place of the deponent, and read the deponent's testimony while a lawyer reads the questions. Each lawyer reads his or her own part. This method helps to establish a dialogue that is much easier for the jury to follow and to appreciate. The procedure is less boring. An effective reader can make himself or herself appear to be the deponent. Sometimes a reader makes a better appearance than the deponent.

Here are some guidelines for reading a deposition to a jury: The reader must read very slowly, with pauses between sentences. Otherwise, the jury has difficulty assimilating the evidence. Jurors are supposed to look for conflicts in the evidence. They must have a moment to reflect on what they are hearing. Natural pauses occur when a witness testifies in person, which too often are omitted in reading the testimony. The reader must make a conscious effort to inject appropriate pauses. The reader should look at the jury as much as she or he can. If the deponent used exhibits while testifying, the reader should use the exhibits in the same way. The reader should not just say, "Here, the deponent pointed to the photograph." The reader must put herself or himself into the role of the witness. Some playacting is involved. The reader must be prepared to pronounce all the words correctly, especially medical terms. The reader must be well-groomed and must also dress for the role to be played.

The deposition may be presented to a jury in a videotape, which allows the jury to see and hear the witness. A video presentation has obvious advantages over the other methods where the witness makes a particularly good appearance and effectively uses exhibits to explain the facts. However, the replay equipment has to be set up in the courtroom for the presentation of the evidence and arranged so that the judge, jury, and lawyers are able to see the video picture. If an objection is made, the whole production must be stopped until the court can rule on it. Usually a video picture shows only the deponent and the exhibits. After a while, a video picture of one person tends to become tedious. The witness may become quite uncomfortable being on camera for a long time. It is like having someone constantly staring at you. Notwithstanding these problems, the trend is toward more and more use of video deposition testimony.

Impeachment

A deposition may be used to impeach a witness, whether or not the witness is a party (Rule 32(a)(1)). A witness is impeached by showing that on some previous occasion, the witness made statements that are inconsistent with her or his testimony at trial. The inconsistency is shown merely by reading the portion of the deposition that appears to be inconsistent with what the witness says in court. The jury is instructed, at the end of the trial, to consider any impeachment when evaluating a witness's credibility.

Impeachment merely affects the weight or credibility of the testimony, not its admissibility. However, impeaching statements made by a party may be used as substantive evidence against the party. Substantive evidence is any evidence that supports a verdict. Out-of-control statements by a nonparty are not substantive evidence because they are not always under oath or subject to cross-examination, and the jury was not able to hear and observe the person when they were made. The jury's verdict should be based on the sworn testimony the jurors hear in court when they can observe the witness.

Impeachment does not cause the witness to be disqualified from testifying or even subject the witness to penalties. On the other hand, if a witness is guilty of perjury, that would be a basis for finding the witness in contempt of court, and criminal charges could be brought against the witness.

Any portion of a party's deposition may be presented by the adverse party as a party admission (Rule 32(a)(2)). A party's admissions in a deposition constitute substantive evidence as well as impeachment evidence when used against the party.

It is relatively easy for lawyers to use depositions, which are on file with the court, to show inconsistencies between the deposition testimony and testimony at trial. For example, suppose that in a personal injury action, the plaintiff testified at trial that her various aches and pains began immediately after the accident. This testimony appears to be at variance with her deposition testimony, in which she admitted that her lower-back discomfort did not begin until two months after the accident in question. A delay of two months in the onset of pain suggests that the accident did not cause the problem. The impeachment could be accomplished in the following manner on cross-examination:

Q: You will recall, Ms. Johnson, that on May 10, 1994, you appeared, with your attorney, at my office for your deposition?

A: Yes.

Q: At that time, you testified concerning your accident and the injuries you sustained?

A: Yes.

Q: Before testifying, you took an oath to tell the truth, the whole truth, just as you did before testifying here in court?

A: Yes.

Q: Ms. Johnson, you will recall that during your deposition I asked you the following questions, and you gave the following answers.

A: Well, I don't know!

Q: Please listen. Beginning at page 24, line 10, you testified as follows:

> Q: Right after the collision occurred and the cars came to rest, how did you feel?
>
> A: Shook up; kind of sick.
>
> Q: Well, did you have any specific aches or pain?
>
> A: Yes. My neck began hurting, and I had a headache.
>
> Q: Where was your headache located?
>
> A: In the back of my head.
>
> Q: When did the headache begin?
>
> A: Right away.
>
> Q: Did you have any other pains while at the accident scene?
>
> A: No.
>
> Q: Are you claiming any other injuries to your person besides your head and neck?
>
> A: Yes.
>
> Q: What?
>
> A: My back hurts.
>
> Q: Where does your back hurt?
>
> A: In the lower part, here [indicating].
>
> Q: When did that begin to bother you?
>
> A: It came on kind of gradual.
>
> Q: Well, when did you first become aware of the problem? What were you doing?
>
> A: I'm not too sure.

Q: So you can't say whether it was two months, six months or any particular time after the accident?

A: I know it wasn't six months—maybe two months.

Q: That's your best recollection?

A: Yes.

Q: Do you remember what you were doing when you first noticed that your lower back was uncomfortable?

A: No.

Q: Now, just where in the lower back do you have this pain?

A: Here [indicating].

Q: Let the record show that the witness has pointed to an area just below the waistline, directly over the spine. Have I accurately described the location to which you were pointing?

A: Yes.

[*End of deposition*]

Q: Now, that was your testimony when your deposition was taken, wasn't it?

A: Yes.

Q: And that was the truth—your testimony under oath?

A: Yes, but after the deposition I talked with my husband about it, and he said I complained about my back hurting the same day of the accident.

Attorney: Your honor, I move that the witness's last answer be stricken as not responsive and on the grounds that it is hearsay.

Court: The last answer is stricken, and the jury is instructed to disregard it.

Q: Certainly your memory about the accident and related events would have been better when your deposition was taken than now.

A: I don't know.

Q: You do not have any current recollection as to when your back started hurting, do you? That is, of your own memory.

A: Well, we talked about it, and I'm just trying to remember—it's been so long, and I've seen so many doctors.

Attorney: I move that the last answer be stricken as not responsive.

Court: The last answer is stricken, and the jury is instructed to disregard it.

[*End of trial testimony*]

It may be hard to believe that the witness lied, that is, committed perjury in either her deposition or her court testimony. Nevertheless, she was inconsistent; both answers could not be correct. She was quite satisfied to yield her recollection to that of her husband. But she cannot testify as to his recollection, because that would be hearsay testimony. Perhaps her husband will be allowed to testify concerning his observations of her condition, and such testimony would help to rehabilitate the witness. The jury will be instructed that it may and should consider impeachment of the witness or of the witness's testimony when weighing the believability of the testimony. The deposition testimony concerning the onset of the plaintiff's back pain is substantive evidence, because it is the prior statement of a party. Based upon the deposition testimony, the jury could decide that the plaintiff's back pain did not begin until two months after the accident.

A witness may also be impeached in other ways. Any time a witness's testimony at trial is shown to be inconsistent, in some material respect, with prior statements or conduct, the inconsistency constitutes impeachment. If, for example, a witness testifies that he saw that he traffic light was green for the plaintiff, another witness would be allowed to testify that she heard the first witness state that she was not looking at the traffic light at the time of the collision. The impeaching witness must come to court and testify under oath. A witness can also be impeached by simply reading pertinent portions from his or her deposition transcript. The safeguards against abuse are in the court reporter's certification that the transcript is accurate and in the witness's right to read and verify the transcript before it is used. As part of trial preparation, a lawyer or paralegal should make sure that all depositions that will be used at trial have been properly filed.

A witness may be impeached by her or his recorded statement if the contents of the statement differ from the witness's testimony in court. The necessary foundation for using a recorded statement to impeach a witness is more difficult than that for using a deposition transcript (see Rule 613). If the statement is in writing and is signed by the witness, the cross-examination may be conducted as follows:

Q: Do you recall that on [date] you were interviewed by a Ms. Chin [a paralegal] about this accident?

A: No. Well, maybe. I'm not sure. I've talked to so many people, and it has been a long time.

[*Counsel has statement marked as defendant's exhibit 1 for identification.*]

Q: I am now showing you a document marked as defendant's exhibit 1. Can you identify it?

A: No.

Q: I am showing you the bottom of the second page. Is that your signature?

A: It appears to be.

Q: Do you now recall that on the date shown here, [date], you were interviewed at your home concerning this accident?

A: Could be.

Q: At that time you were asked about your version of the accident as you saw it.

A: Perhaps.

Q: Please take the exhibit now and read it to yourself.

A: Yes, I seem to recall it.

Q: This is your signature?

A: Yes.

Counsel: I offer defendant's exhibit 1 into evidence.

Court: For what purpose, Counsel? I don't see the connection yet.

Counsel: The exhibit is being offered for impeachment purposes.

[*At this point the plaintiff's counsel would probably demand to see the statement, as provided in Rule 613.*]

Court to witness: Is that your signature and your statement?

A: Yes.

Court to plaintiff's counsel: Is there any objection?

Counsel: Yes. No foundation has been laid for the exhibit, and it is not impeaching.

Court: Objections overruled. Exhibit received.

[*Note that the contents of the document cannot be referred to until after the exhibit is received into evidence.*]

Q: You stated, at the time you gave this statement, that you did not see the traffic light before the collision.

A: I don't specifically remember saying that.

Q: Please read with me. Now referring to defendant's exhibit 1: "I was standing at the southwest corner waiting for a bus which would be coming from the west. I was looking westerly when I heard the collision behind me. I turned around right away. The southbound car (white convertible) was stopped in the middle of the intersection. The eastbound car (Ford) slid sideways and came to rest at the northwest corner of the intersection. It was turned almost 180 degrees around. I could see the driver of the Ford was slouched over. As soon as I was sure that no other cars were coming, I ran over to the Ford."

Q: Now, that is what your signed statement said, isn't it?

A: That's what it says.

Q: And when you gave that statement, you were trying to be truthful—to give a truthful account of what you observed?

A: Yes.

Q: And you did not intend to claim that you saw things that you didn't see?

A: But the statement doesn't say everything I saw . . .

Q: When you signed it you considered it to be accurate, didn't you?

A: Yes.

Q: If an important point had been left out of the statement, you would have brought that to the attention of Ms. Chin when she took the statement, wouldn't you?

A: Well, I didn't know what she thought was important.

Q: We're talking about what you think is important.

A: [No response]

Q: No further questions.

Redirect Examination

Q: Is this written statement, defendant's exhibit 1, in your handwriting?

A: No.

Q: But the signature is yours?

A: Yes.

Q: Did you choose the wording used in this statement?

A: No.

Q: Did you choose the things to be said or included in the statement?

A: No.

Q: Were you told when this statement was being written down that you would be asked to sign it?

A: No.

Q: Were you given a copy of the statement?

A: No.

Q: Did you read it before signing it?

A: Well, I just sort of glanced over it, and it looked OK, so I signed it. I think she told me I had to.

Q: Did you, in fact, look at the traffic light?

A: Yes, I did.

Q: What color was it?

Counsel: Objection. The question is objected to for lack of foundation—there is no showing of just when the observation was made, and the witness has disqualified himself.

Court: Perhaps a little more foundation should be laid.

Counsel: Yes, I was just about to do that, Your Honor.

Q: You say you did take notice of the traffic signal light?

A: Yes, sir.

Q: Just when did you make this observation of the light?

A: Soon as I heard the crash and turned around—when I looked to see if any other cars were coming; that's when I saw that the light was green for east-west–bound traffic.

Q: No further questions. Thank you.

Recross Examination

Q: Let's see now. On direct examination this morning, you said that you saw the light before the crash, but now you say you saw it after the crash. Is that right?

A: I guess the statement refreshed my memory.

Q: Are you familiar with the intersection? Do you catch a bus there every day?

A: No. I go that way to see my sister sometimes.

Q: Where is the traffic light located—the one you observed after the collision?

A: There is only one. It sort of hangs on a wire over the center. I saw the light that faces west, and it was definitely green.

Q: But you said that you saw the Ford sliding sideways and turning around and coming to rest at the northwest corner.

A: Yes.

Q: You saw all that, and then you saw the driver of the Ford slumped over?

A: Yes.

Q: And you felt that you should get over to help him?

A: Yes.

Q: You realized that there might be an emergency right there in front of you?

A: I don't know if I. . . . Well, yeah, sort of.

Q: As soon as you could see that no cars were coming, you dashed right over to the Ford?

A: Yes.

Q: Isn't it true that you could not see the color of the light by looking from the place where you were standing, the bus stop?

A: I don't know. I saw the light, and it was green.

Q: But after hearing the crash, seeing the Ford slide to a stop, and looking for other traffic in the area—about five or six seconds lapsed before you could have looked at the light?

A: I didn't time it. You don't have a stopwatch.

Q: It would have been at least five seconds, wouldn't it?

A: Four, maybe five, I suppose. Something like that.

Q: You didn't tell Ms. Chin when she interviewed you on [date], when this statement was given, that you saw the light, now did you?

A: No.

Q: Why not?

A: She didn't ask.

Q: And you didn't think she was interested or needed that information from you?

A: If she'd asked, I would have told her. I talked to a lot of people. And I was getting kind of tired of it all.

Q: You didn't tell the investigating police, either, that you saw the light, did you?

Counsel: Objection. That's irrelevant and calls for hearsay.

Court: Overruled.

Q: You may answer. Did you tell the police that you saw the light?

A: They were too busy. I gave them my name.

Q: I have no further questions of this witness.

Recross Examination

Q: There is no doubt in your mind about it, is there? You did see the light?

Counsel: The question is objected to on the ground that it is repetitious, leading, and suggestive.

Court: Sustained.

Q: Thank you, Mr. [Witness]. That will be all for now. You are excused.

The signed statement has almost the same value and effect for impeachment purposes as a deposition. But the statement is more cumbersome to use because it must be identified and the witness must acknowledge that it is his or her statement. If, in the preceding example, the witness had continued to deny that the signature was his, the person who took the statement would have to be called as a witness to identify the statement and relate the circumstances under which the statement was given. Then it becomes the paralegal's word against that of the witness. If the statement had been secured by the attorney who was examining the witness, a further problem would be introduced because an attorney is forbidden by ethics to testify in a case he or she is trying. It would be very difficult for the attorney to put the statement into evidence if the witness remained adamant that he did not sign it.

SUMMARY

An oral deposition is a procedure by which a party's lawyer may question another party and witnesses about matters relevant to the litigation. The word *depose* means "to give testimony." Testimony is a statement, oral or written, made under oath, that is offered as evidence of a fact. A *deponent* is a person who testifies under oath. The term *deposition* is synonymous with *testimony*. It also may be used to indicate the *procedure* for taking a person's testimony, to describe the *transcript* made from a person's testimony. The interrogation of a witness is often characterized as the "taking of a deposition." Sometimes the word *depose* is used to describe the lawyer's act of taking a person's deposition. It is often necessary to look at the context in which these words are used to determine their meanings.

An affidavit is a written statement made under oath. A deposition, whether written or oral, differs from an affidavit in that a deponent is subject to cross-examination by all interested parties. A party schedules the deposition of another party or witness by serving a *notice of deposition* or *notice of taking deposition* on all the other parties. Lawyers commonly refer to the service as merely noticing the deposition.

Lawyers take oral depositions to find out what the deponent (party or witness) knows or does not know about the case. This type of deposition is commonly called a discovery deposition. A deposition may be taken to preserve the deponent's testimony for use at trial. All the parties have a right to cross-examine the deponent. When a lawyer takes the deposition of a party or witness, the lawyer has the opportunity to evaluate the deponent's demeanor, authority, and sincerity.

Paralegals may collect and organize the exhibits to be used and prepare outlines concerning the critical facts and opinions to be covered. Paralegals often attend depositions to observe deponents, to make notes about the testimony and reports. Paralegals may review a deposition transcript with the client to help the client make corrections and additions as authorized by Rule 30(e). Paralegals often review, correct, and index deposition transcripts to make them more usable at trial. A lawyer may ask a paralegal to sit in on depositions when the lawyer intends to ask no questions of the deponent but wants a report on what the deponent said and on the kind of appearance the deponent makes. A paralegal may help to prepare a client or nonparty witness to testify in a deposition. If the parties elect to arbitrate their dispute, paralegals may conduct the discovery, including taking depositions. Indeed, a paralegal may make the presentation before the arbitration tribunal, including interrogating witnesses and making the arguments.

A nonparty deponent cannot be required to travel outside the state in which she or he lives or is regularly employed in order to give a deposition. However, Rule 45(b)(2) provides that a federal district court may subpoena the witness to travel anywhere within the district and up to 100 miles outside the district to appear for a deposition. The deponent is entitled to have a lawyer present to give advice, even if the deponent is not a party to the suit.

It may be necessary to subpoena a nonparty deponent. The party wishing to subpoena the nonparty must take the original copy of the notice for taking deposition and proof of service to the clerk of court for filing. The clerk of court will give the party a subpoena form to complete. If the nonparty lives in another district (state) the party must file the notice of deposition with the clerk of court in that district. The court in the district in which the deposition is to be taken must issue the subpoena.

A subpoena may be served upon the deponent anywhere within the district (state) of the court that issued the subpoena. A federal district court's subpoena may be served "at any place without [outside] the district that is within 100 miles of the place of the deposition, hearing, trial, production, or inspection specified in the subpoena" (Rule 45(b)(2)).

A subpoena duces tecum may be used to compel a nonparty to produce for inspection documents or other tangible things, or to permit an inspection of real property that the nonparty owns or occupies. If the deponent finds the demand for documents, things, or inspection too burdensome, the deponent may serve and file an objection to inspection stating the grounds for the objection.

A non-party deponent cannot be required to travel outside the county in which he or she lives or is regularly employed, to give a deposition. However, Rule 45(d) provides that a deponent may be subpoenaed to appear for a deposition in the county in which he or she regularly transacts business in person. If the deponent is not a resident of the district (state) in which the deposition is to be taken, the subpoena may require the deponent to appear in the county in which the subpoena was served or within a one-hundred-mile radius of the place of service. If those two alternatives are not satisfactory, the party noticing the deposition has to obtain a court order setting another reasonably convenient place (Rule 45(d)(2)).

A notice for taking a deposition states that the deposition will be taken at a specified time and place before an officer who is authorized to administer oaths. The deposition transcript may be used at trial or to support a motion against any party who received notice of the deposition, regardless of whether the party was represented at the deposition. A party's appearance at a deposition constitutes a waiver of any defect in the notice or defect in the service of the notice. A party who does not receive notice may take the deponent's deposition at another time. A party who did not receive notice is entitled to buy and use a copy of the deposition transcript even though he or she was not represented at the deposition.

All parties have a right to attend any deposition, whether of a party or of a nonparty. A corporate entity has the right to have a designated person attend on its behalf in addition to the corporation's lawyer. The parties may agree to exclude certain persons, such as witnesses, from observing the deponent testify. The news media has no right to attend. The parties may agree to allow observers. When the party who serves the notice fails to appear to take the deposition, he or she may be required to pay the costs incurred by all parties who did appear.

Each question in a deposition is supposed to be singular and clearly stated. Lawyers give careful attention to the context and meaning of their words and the words used by the deponent.

An expert's opinion testimony is inadmissible unless the witness qualifies as an expert on the basis of his or her education, training, and experience. The witness qualifies if the judge determines that the witness is significantly more knowledgeable about the subject than a jury of laypersons. It must appear to the judge that the expert has good and sufficient evidence (foundation) upon which to base an opinion. The foundation is laid by disclosing to the court and jury the evidence which the expert knows about, has considered, and has relied upon to form the opinions that she or he has reached. If the necessary foundation is not laid during the deposition, the expert's opinions cannot be presented to the jury by reading the expert's deposition transcript.

Non-expert witnesses may give opinion testimony only when the evidence must come in that form, and there is a showing that the witness had an opportunity to observe, understand, and recall the events upon which the opinion is based. For example, a witness may need to describe lighting conditions, or the condition of a floor or highway, by expressing an opinion. Failure to make the necessary showing makes the evidence subject to objection on the grounds that it lacks foundation. If the lawyer who takes the deposition does not lay the necessary foundation, the deposition testimony will not be received into evidence at trial. The judge has a great deal of latitude in determining what constitutes sufficient foundation.

The scope of permissible inquiry in discovery depositions is much broader than in court. A lawyer may examine the deponent about any matter that is relevant to the issues as framed by the pleadings.

Hypothetical questions are used to obtain opinion evidence from a witness who does not have sufficient personal knowledge of the facts to give an opinion. When the facts can be proved through other witnesses, an expert may assume the truth of those facts and rely upon them to give an expert opinion concerning their effect. However, when hypothetical questions are asked during a cross-examination in a deposition, the likely purpose is to get the witness to admit to a legal duty owed by one party to another. This is especially true in tort actions involving professional malpractice, construction accident cases, and product liability cases. The hypothetical question is frequently a "no win" situation for the witness. Hypothetical questions are rarely used in a cross-examination to discover facts or evidence. The deponent may avoid the problems raised by hypothetical questions by refusing to answer a question on the grounds that it is entirely speculative, or the deponent may qualify her or his answers to the point that the answers are meaningless.

Objections concerning the form of the questions must be made during the deposition; otherwise, they are waived. When an objection is made, the lawyer who asked the question may rephrase the question or abandon the question or insist upon an answer. If the interrogator insists that he or she is entitled to an answer, the deponent's lawyer has to decide whether to let the deponent answer subject to the objection. By making the objection, the lawyer has protected the record in the sense that if the deposition is used at trial, a judge will have to rule on the objection before the question and the deponent's answer can be read to the jury.

Questions concerning privileged communications and records and questions concerning an attorney's work product are improper. When the deponent objects on those grounds and the interrogator insists upon an answer, the deponent's lawyer may stop the deposition (walk out) at that point, or the lawyers may agree to proceed with other questions and finish the deposition. They can obtain a ruling on the objection at a later time.

A party may move the court for an order suppressing the use of a deposition, or any part of it, if there is some irregularity in the proceedings. The burden rests upon the moving party to persuade the court that the deposition is invalid or that its use would cause prejudice outweighing its value to the court and jury. The motion to suppress must be made promptly after the error or irregularity in the proceedings has been discovered.

An oral deposition may be taken stenographically or in a video or audio recording. The recording must be a verbatim record of the entire proceeding. The party who noticed the deposition does not have to order a transcript for the court, or for himself or herself, or for anyone else, but if any party orders a transcript, the court reporter must file the original copy of the deposition transcript with the clerk of court.

The deponent has a right to read the deposition transcript in order to make corrections or changes before it is filed with the court and before it is used for any purpose. The court reporter is required to submit the transcript to the deponent as soon as it has been prepared. The deponent must review the transcript and make corrections within thirty days from the date it is received. The deponent may correct any errors in her or his testimony whether the errors are of substance or of form. The deponent must make a written statement giving reasons or an explanation for each change made to the transcript. A deponent automatically waives the right to review and correct the transcript if she or he fails to make the corrections within thirty days after it is submitted by the reporter. Day 1 of the thirty-day period begins on the day after the deponent or deponent's lawyer receives the transcript.

Lawyers use deposition summaries to collect essential evidence for easy reference. Summaries may be used in preparation for trial, to report to the client on the status of the case, or for the information of a client's insurance company.

A lawyer may present deposition testimony to the jury by reading from the transcript or by having someone, such as a paralegal, sit in the witness stand, in place of the deponent, and read the deponent's testimony while a lawyer reads the questions. The deposition may be presented to a jury through a videotape, which allows the jury to see and hear the witness. A video presentation has obvious advantages over other methods where the witness makes a particularly good appearance and effectively uses exhibits to explain the facts.

A lawyer may read part of the adverse party's deposition to the jury to impeach the party or as a party's admissions. The admissions are substantive evidence upon which a jury may base its verdict. However, deposition testimony may not be used the same as Rule 36 admissions.

The new Federal Rules provide that an oral deposition may not be noticed or taken before the parties have prepared a discovery plan. A party cannot take more than ten depositions, unless the other parties agree or the court authorizes more. The Rules provide that the notice for taking a deposition must give the parties and deponent a "reasonable" time in which to prepare for the deposition.

KEY TERMS

depose

deposition

notice of deposition

notice of taking deposition

discovery deposition

sequestering

subpoena duces tecum

impeachment

REVIEW QUESTIONS

1. List four reasons for taking a person's oral deposition rather than using interrogatories.

2. How many oral depositions do the Federal Rules of Civil Procedure allow?

3. Under what circumstances may a paralegal take a deposition?

4. Why would a deponent waive the right to read and correct a deposition transcript before it is filed with the court?

5. What kinds of changes may a deponent make in a deposition transcript?

6. How does the deponent makes changes in a deposition transcript?

7. Can the deponent's original answers have any role in the trial even though they were duly changed as authorized by the court's rules?

8. For what reasons might a party take another person's oral deposition by video rather than have a court reporter make a stenographic record?

9. What advantages does a deposition transcript have over a video recorded deposition?

10. May a paralegal handle the mechanics of making a videotaped deposition?

11. How much notice must a party give for taking a witness's deposition?

12. On what grounds may a party object to questions asked of him or her in an oral deposition?

CHAPTER

13

PREPARATION OF CLIENT FOR AN ORAL DEPOSITION

OUTLINE

Preparing to Meet the Client

Scheduling Meetings to Prepare for the Deposition

Meeting with the Client

Deposition Procedures

The Client's Testimony

Discovery Deposition Guidelines

Cross-Examining the Client

Following Up After the Deposition

SUMMARY

KEY TERMS

REVIEW QUESTIONS

The primary method of determining what an adverse party knows or does not know about the case is to take the party's deposition. Oral depositions are the mainspring of discovery because no other method of discovery provides so much information about the deponent. When a lawyer takes the deposition of an opposing party, the lawyer obtains more than just evidence and information about the case. The lawyer has the opportunity to evaluate the deponent's appearance and authority. In other words, the lawyer can determine whether the deponent will be a strong witness or a weak witness; whether the deponent is able to give testimony in an authoritative, persuasive manner; whether the deponent understands the interrelation of the evidence and the theory of the case; whether the deponent has some concerns; whether the deponent is willing to go to trial; and whether the deponent is prepared. The lawyer will evaluate the deponent's testimony not only by what is said but by how it is said. The lawyer can even evaluate the preparedness of the other lawyer by the way the deponent answers questions or the inability of the deponent to answer questions. If the deponent makes mistakes while testifying, the mistakes can severely damage the deponent's ability to prove a claim or defense at trial. Also, the mistakes can significantly diminish the value of the claim or defense for purposes of settlement. As always, good preparation is the key to successful handling.

Paralegals are playing an ever increasing role in preparing clients for their deposition. To be able to prepare a deponent, paralegals must thoroughly understand the purpose of depositions, the uses of depositions, and the procedures for taking depositions, as well as the case at issue and the role of the deponent in the case. They cannot reasonably expect to assume this kind of responsibility until they have had an opportunity to observe the deposition process in operation and have received on-the-job training by a supervising lawyer. Every lawyer tends to have a little different approach and a different emphasis in preparing for depositions, and paralegals must honor the lawyer's preferences.

There is no one method or formula for preparing a client for a deposition. The order of the various steps in the preparation may be changed, and some steps may be omitted entirely, depending upon the particular case. Even so, certain witness guidelines are always applicable, regardless of whether the client is a plaintiff or a defendant and regardless of the type of case involved. The best preparation for a deposition is to actually take the client through a question-and-answer session—a mock cross-examination. The deponent should be asked the same questions the opposing lawyer is expected to ask and in the same manner.

Though a paralegal must impress the client about the importance of the deposition, he or she must avoid making the client nervous about it. Therefore, the paralegal should try to appear relaxed and confident about the question. The paralegal and the deponent should look upon the discovery deposition as a positive and useful experience. The deposition gives the client experience testifying, and that is beneficial. As a result of the paralegal's thorough preparation, the client realizes that he or she can handle it. After going through an oral deposition, the client should feel more confident about the case and about testifying at the trial. The client may use the deposition transcript to help prepare for the trial. The opposing lawyer's questions tend to disclose information the other side has and does not have. The paralegal may be able to gauge how well the other side understands the case and how well prepared the interrogator is. The interrogator's questions also tend to reflect the facts the other side considers important. So the paralegal can learn about the other side even as the client's deposition is being taken. The Rules do not limit the number of times a party's deposition may be taken. However, the practice is to require a party to appear only once, unless subsequent developments create a need to supplement the prior deposition. For example, if the plaintiff is involved in a subsequent accident, that would give good reason for another deposition.

■ PREPARING TO MEET THE CLIENT

The first step is to prepare to meet with the client. In other words, the paralegal needs to prepare for the preparation. The paralegal begins by making sure she or he understands all parties' legal theories and the paralegal's own side's theory of the facts. The parties stated their legal theories in their pleadings. Those legal theories frame the legal issues that remain to be resolved. Remember, the legal issues determine what facts are material to the case; the material facts (also thought of as essential or controlling facts) determine what evidence is relevant; and relevant evidence tends to prove or disprove any disputed fact. If evidence is relevant, it is usually admissible at trial. From a review of the file, the paralegal should be able to determine what happened, why it happened, and how it happened.

The client's testimony must be truthful. The paralegal must not lead the client into error. The client's deposition testimony must be consistent with the client's testimony at trial. If the testimony at trial conflicts with the testimony in the deposition, the discrepancies will be brought out by the opposition to impeach or discredit the testimony at trial. Furthermore, any misstatements made during the deposition are subject to being used against the client as admissions. The consequences of impeachment and admissions can be disastrous. Clients appreciate competent guidance by persons who are sincerely interested in their welfare.

As part of the preparation to meet with the client, the paralegal should try to anticipate the problems in the case. He or she should start with the basic disagreement or disagreements on the facts and determine the reasons for them. Then the paralegal can determine how best to deal with the problems. He or she should develop a plan for dealing with each anticipated problem. The overall objective is to make sure the client's testimony is consistent with the legal team's theory of the case. If the client's version of the facts does not agree with the team's strategy, the strategy must be revised *before* the client's deposition is taken. Again, the truth is sacred. Lawyers and paralegals have a duty to the courts to prevent clients from testifying falsely. An effort to establish consistency in the theory of the case, the testimony, and other evidence must be part of a larger effort to find and prove the truth.

The paralegal should review the pleadings and the correspondence, especially opinion letters, to identify particular problems and proposed solutions. He or she should make notes about the important points of agreement and disagreement. The paralegal should examine all parties' answers to interrogatories to find areas of agreement, areas of disagreement, and inconsistencies. He or she should study the investigation materials to obtain details about the transaction or occurrence in issue. While studying the investigation materials, the paralegal should do the following:

1. Determine what facts are indisputable and what facts apparently are not disputed, and whether inconsistencies appear in the investigation file to date. The case should be built around these facts.

2. Decide which disputed facts are really important to the parties' theories of the case.

3. Consider whether the client's version of the facts is consistent with physical facts.

4. Consider whether the client's version of the facts is consistent with probability, common experience, and common sense.

5. Consider whether the client's version is believable.

6. Determine whether the client's version of the facts requires testing or correction.

7. Decide whether any of the photographs and documents in the file will be used as exhibits.

8. Consider whether the client should be allowed to make any drawings or sketches during the deposition. Such drawings may be useful for the case. Even though a drawing made during a deposition is not to scale, it may be used at trial to cross-examine the deponent.

It may be a good idea not to let anyone mark on exhibits that may be used at trial. If an exhibit bears marks on it before it is presented to the witness, and the witness merely adopts the position suggested by those marks, the exhibit may be subject to objection as "leading" the witness. Leading questions are objectionable. Furthermore, answers to leading questions lack persuasiveness.

9. Examine original transaction documents.

If the case involves an accident, the paralegal should do the following:

1. View the situs of the accident when necessary to obtain an understanding of how the accident occurred. (The situs is the place where the accident occurred; *situs* and *location* are to be distinguished from *accident scene,* which implies that the conditions are exactly the way they were at the time the accident happened.) Consider meeting the client at the situs.

2. Establish and verify all relevant measurements, and relate the measurements to corresponding time factors.

3. Make sure that all speed, distance, and time factors correlate with the party's theory of what happened and how it happened.

4. Choose a theory of claim or defense that fully accommodates the applicable law and known facts. The theory concerns what happened, how it happened, and why it happened. Again, the theory may have to change as new information and evidence is obtained.

5. Find out what the trial lawyer's expected theme is. The trial lawyer should have a theme for the trial. A theme is not the same as a theory. A theme is an attitude or approach that permeates the entire trial, culminating the final argument. The theme may be that the opposing party is lying, or that the other party's case mistakenly relies upon a certain expert's opinion, or that the opponent's expert is relying upon incorrect facts. Typically, a personal injury claim is tried in light of the theme that the plaintiff has suffered a great deal of pain, and the suffering will continue in the future unless the jury provides the claimant with the verdict the plaintiff is requesting. Typically, the defendant's lawyer's theme is that the jury must follow and apply the law without sympathy. The paralegal should have the trial lawyer's theme in mind and incorporate it into the client's preparation.

6. Consider how the material facts will likely be proved at trial. Consider what evidence will be produced to prove those facts and how that evidence will be presented. The paralegal must remember that the evidence must be admissible to be usable.

7. Determine what the client's role will be in developing the material facts. If the case will turn on a critical fact, and the client is the only source of evidence for that fact, everything that is even remotely relevant to that fact must be carefully examined and coordinated in the client's preparation. For example, assume the client is the defendant, who survived a collision at an intersection controlled by a traffic light. The other driver did not survive. There are no eyewitnesses other than the client. What must the client know to defend himself? He must know where his car was when he first saw the green light, and when he last noticed the color of the light. He must know where

the traffic light was located at the intersection. He must know that the red light is at the top and the green light is at the bottom of the signal. If the intersection has more than one light, he must know which one he watched. He should know how long the light was green for him; the time sequence for the light, to keep him from becoming confused by time factors; the location of the other car when he first noticed it; at what point he applied his brakes; the point of collision on the cars; the point of collision on the roadway. What does he know? What did he tell the police?

On the other hand, if the client's testimony about a particular fact is not critical, the client may be better off to defer to more authoritative witnesses or evidence. Suppose both drivers survived, and immediately after the accident the adverse party told the client the accident was the adverse party's fault. If no one else heard the admission, the client must be prepared on this point with great care. But if several witnesses heard the adverse party, it will be enough to prepare the client to relate the statement and context generally. Of course, the paralegal cannot tell the client what to say. When the paralegal makes suggestions to a client about how to say something, she or he must make sure the client is comfortable with the suggestions and understands that they are only suggestions. In the final analysis, the testimony must be that of the deponent.

8. Consider whether the client needs to be prepared to make a diagram to illustrate how the accident occurred or some other relevant fact. If so, the paralegal must allow time to prepare a diagram as part of the preparation for the deposition.

9. Decide whether the client's spouse should or should not attend. Ordinarily, most lawyers prefer to exclude the client's spouse from the preparation and testimony. However, if the client *needs* a spouse to be present, that is all right. If both spouses are going to testify, they should be prepared together. However, a client and an independent witness should *not* be prepared together, because communication with the independent witness is not privileged. The independent witness could be compelled to testify to anything and everything he or she heard said to the client.

The paralegal can prepare the client for the deposition by instructing the client how to handle the questions that will be posed by the opposing lawyer. If the client becomes comfortable with the deposition procedure and has a good deposition, the paralegal may win the undying gratitude of a pleased client. The key to success is adequate preparation, which usually includes a mock cross-examination. There is no reason why an experienced paralegal should not be involved in the examination.

■ SCHEDULING MEETINGS TO PREPARE FOR THE DEPOSITION

Plenty of time should be left for meeting the client and preparing her or him for the deposition. Although lawyers commonly spend only an hour preparing a client immediately before a deposition, that is not sufficient. Ideally, the preparation should be done in two sessions. The first meeting should cover all the issues considered in preparing to meet with the client, with an emphasis on locating and solving problems. During the hiatus between meetings, the legal professional and the client will have time in which to locate documents, pin down additional facts, and resolve problems that have been identified. The second meeting should focus on the client's anticipated testimony. The client will be more comfortable and relaxed during the first meeting if she or he does not have to testify that day.

The meetings may be scheduled through a letter like the one in exhibit 13.1.

■ MEETING WITH THE CLIENT

The paralegal's discussions with the client are privileged; therefore, neither the paralegal nor the client can be required to disclose to anyone else what the two said during discussions. This privilege must be explained to the client. The client must be told that no one is entitled to know what was

■ **EXHIBIT 13.1**

Letter for Scheduling
Meetings with a Client

Dear Alice Rose:

Today we received a notice from the defendant's lawyer demanding that you appear for a discovery deposition in his office on [date] at [time]. You may recall that when we first undertook to prosecute this case on your behalf, we discussed the likelihood that the lawyer would exercise his right to take your deposition.

The defense lawyer has a right to ask you questions about the accident. You will have to answer his questions under oath. The lawyer will try to find out what you know about the accident and what you do not know. A verbatim transcript will be made of his questions and your answers.

The deposition procedure is fairly informal. Only the defendant's lawyer, [the client's trial lawyer], a court reporter, and I will be present for the deposition. The defendant has a right to attend, but it is not likely he will choose to do so.

I want to help you prepare for the deposition. It would be best if we could plan on two meetings in which to conduct our preparation. The first meeting should be as soon as your convenience will permit. I have blocked out the morning of [date] on my calendar, hoping that time may fit into your schedule. We shall need at least two hours so that I can bring you up to date on your case, explain the issues, explain the deposition procedure, and discuss your testimony. Please let me know whether the date I have chosen is good for you.

Our second meeting must be on the day before the deposition. At that time we shall actually go through a mock examination, much like the procedure we expect the defense lawyer to use. I am sure that by the time we complete our preparation you will feel completely confident about testifying and about your case. This deposition gives us an opportunity to show the defense that our case has merit. I fully expect that after the defense lawyer has heard your testimony, the defense will be interested in discussing settlement with us.

I look forward to hearing from you shortly.

Sincerely yours,

Shawna Montgomery
Paralegal

said during preparation for a deposition. Even the court cannot properly inquire about these discussions. Sometimes a client needs to be assured that it is proper to prepare for the deposition. When the client testifies, he or she may acknowledge meeting with a lawyer or paralegal to prepare for the deposition, but the client will not be required to relate the matters discussed. Maybe even more important, the client should be cautioned against mentioning that certain subjects were discussed. This exemption does not mean that the subjects themselves are privileged; it means only that the adverse party cannot discover what the legal professional and the client said about the subjects during their meetings.

When preparing a witness who is not a client for a deposition, the opposing lawyer may ask about the discussions the witness had with his or her lawyers or paralegals. The witness should be assured that it was proper to meet and that he or she will have to acknowledge the meetings if asked. The witness should be prepared to give innocuous answers to questions like "What did the paralegal tell you to say?" For example, the witness should be prepared to answer, "I was told to tell the truth" or "I told him the same things I'm telling you" or "She just said that you would ask questions about the accident and that I should listen carefully to the questions and answer the questions. We talked about the basketball game and so forth." A savvy witness will try to steer to another subject.

The paralegal who is preparing a client must know how she or he wants the meeting to proceed and must direct its course. The paralegal must not let the meeting get sidetracked. The client and the client's testimony are usually the most important aspects of the trial, so it is worth spending whatever time it takes to prepare them. The paralegal should strive to obtain the client's trust and confidence. The first step is to help relieve the client's natural apprehensions about the lawsuit and about testifying. The more apprehensive or nervous the client is, the more likely she or he is to make mistakes. An overly apprehensive deponent is doomed to failure. For most of us, the unknown is the principal cause of fear and nervousness. The paralegal's job is to make the client feel comfortable about the case and about her or his role in it. Nevertheless, the client must appreciate that it is her or his lawsuit and that the paralegal is there to help. The paralegal must show a concern for the client's needs, comfort, and convenience, and manifest an interest in the client and the client's problems. This interest is reflected in what is said and how it is said. The paralegal must conduct herself or himself in a professional manner; try to be authoritative in a pleasant, caring way; and not be casual or try to be funny. The paralegal is in charge. She or he is responsible for the success or failure of the client's deposition. The paralegal should speak authoritatively about the facts and show the client she or he knows the details.

Visiting the Situs

The first meeting may require a visit to the situs of the accident. The paralegal and the client should visit the situs together. They should take a camera and a measuring tape. Hopefully, most of the essential information is already in the file, because the legal team has conducted a good investigation and documented all the findings. Nevertheless, it is a good idea to be prepared to verify and document what is found at the accident location.

For one thing, the scene may have changed significantly, and any changes should be documented. Then if the opponent testifies on the basis of the way the scene looks now, as opposed to how it looked at the time of the accident, the client's side is well on its way to a win.

Giving an Overview and Discussing Deposition Procedures

Many lawyers prefer to begin the client's preparation by explaining the mechanics of the deposition procedure. Others prefer to begin by giving the client an overview of the case and then discuss the deposition procedures. Either way, the paralegal should let the client know that he or she understands the facts and has a plan or strategy for dealing with the adverse party's claim or defense. As part of the overview, the paralegal may explain the fact issues so that the client can understand how his or her testimony fits into the case as a whole. The paralegal should explain the legal issues in terms that a layperson can understand. When the client asks questions, that helps the paralegal to know that the client understands what is being said. However, if the client starts asking questions about the case that are irrelevant to what is being said, the client may be told that he or she is getting ahead of the process. The client's questions should not be allowed to disrupt an organized approach to the preparation.

Identifying the Facts and the Legal Theories

The next step is to identify the facts that are disputed and the facts that are not contested. Then the paralegal can explain the opponent's theory about the facts, that is, how the opponent is going to attempt to prove her or his version of the disputed facts. The explanation will help the client to better understand the context of the interrogator's questions and their relevancy. As a result, the client will have a better understanding of the consequences of her or his answers. If the client understands the big picture, the client will have a frame of reference that should help her or him to give clear, authoritative answers with confidence.

Exploring the Client's Version of the Facts

Next, the paralegal should explore the client's version of the facts. Even though the client's version is highly questionable, the paralegal must listen to the client's explanation before making any suggestions about possible errors. He or she must try to understand the client's explanations, because the client may be right, and the paralegal may be wrong in his or her analysis. The paralegal must not lead the client into perjury, errors, or discomfort. If the client's case is lost, it should be lost for the right reasons. Nevertheless, if the client's belief about certain facts is clearly wrong, the paralegal must help the client to understand the truth. He or she should determine the client's foundation for the false beliefs, then put the fact issues into context. The paralegal should discuss with the client what is physically possible and what probably happened. He or she should explain to the client what the other evidence in the case is and what it shows. The paralegal should try working through the evidence in a logical manner by asking simple questions that cause the client to discover the truth for himself or herself. Suppose the paralegal is helping the plaintiff with a personal injury claim that arose from an automobile accident. Both cars entered an uncontrolled intersection at the same time. The client was on the right and had the right-of-way. The client claims the defendant was going fifty miles per hour and made no effort to stop. Photographs show only minimal damage to both cars. The defendant admitted to the police that she was going ten miles per hour at contact, and the paralegal thinks maybe the defendant was going between ten and fifteen miles per hour. The combined speeds of the two cars could have caused the injury the client sustained. The paralegal should consider the following approach:

Q: I have talked with your doctor. He says your injury could have resulted from the combined speeds of your car and the defendant's car, even if the defendant was going only ten miles per hour. Why do you think the defendant might have been going faster?

A: The collision was such a shock. There was a tremendous noise. She must have been way down the block, because I looked and there was no car near the intersection as I approached. Suddenly, there she was.

Q: The police report and these photographs show two vans parked along the curb. They could have momentarily obstructed your view of the defendant's car. Her car could have been behind them. She admitted to going ten miles per hour. Don't you think it is possible, just possible, her car was blocked from your view when you looked to your left and then back to your right?

A: The way she was going, she must have been farther back.

Q: Neither car had much damage. If she were moving fifty miles per hour, wouldn't you expect more damage?

A: I suppose.

Q: Her car didn't move after the point of collision, did it?

A: No, not that I remember.

Q: How far does a car move in one second if it is going fifty miles per hour?

A: I don't know; I never figured it.

Q: Well, the charts show it moves 77 feet per second. You were traveling ten miles per hour as you entered the intersection. At ten miles per hour, you traveled 15 feet per second. She must have been about the same distance back. In three seconds you traveled 45 feet to the point of impact. If she was going fifty miles per hour, she would have traveled 225 feet in three seconds. It hardly seems possible that she could have been that far back when you were only 45 feet from the point of collision.

A: What about it?

Q: Well, if she was going ten to fifteen miles per hour, we can see how your view was blocked, but if she was 150 feet back, the parked trucks would not have blocked your view.

A: But if she was going faster, doesn't that mean the accident was her fault?

Q: No. Speed isn't our concern. You had the right-of-way. Our concern is whether the defendant's lawyer can contend that you didn't keep a proper lookout. He will argue that you didn't see that which was in plain sight. You told the police that you didn't see the defendant's car until it was about to enter the intersection.

A: Do you think that my estimate of her speed is off?

Q: Yes. I think the shock of the collision made you feel that the defendant was traveling faster than she really was.

A: Could be. I never thought about it that way. Maybe she could have been going ten or fifteen miles per hour.

The paralegal should try to keep the client from becoming emotionally committed to a mistaken view of the facts. She or he should try to make it easy for the client to let go of false beliefs about the facts. A client will become resentful if the client thinks the paralegal is trying to lead her or him into error. But the client's first version may be right. The paralegal must not cause the client to make a mistake. The paralegal's job is to help the client avoid making mistakes.

Discussing the Client's Testimony

In a discovery deposition, the deponent's best answer is the shortest answer. But each answer must be sufficiently complete to be truthful. It is entirely natural for the client to want to justify himself or herself by fully explaining what he or she did and why. That is exactly what the opposing lawyer wants. The opposing lawyer wants to find out everything about what the client knows and does not know. The client should be instructed not to volunteer information. The client should not explain an answer unless the question specifically requires an explanation. The client may understand the importance of not volunteering information if the paralegal explains that the more the opposing lawyer finds out about the client and the client's version of the facts, the better the lawyer can prepare for trial. There is no reason to help the opponent any more than the law and professionalism require. As a general rule, the client's best answer in a discovery deposition is the client's shortest answer.

There are exceptions to the general rule that the client should not volunteer information. The paralegal's overall strategy may require the client to provide certain testimony (information) in the deposition. Consequently, the paralegal may want the client to volunteer that information. Or the deponent's lawyer may decide to ask questions that the other lawyer fails to ask. When a lawyer elects to ask the client questions in a discovery deposition, those questions and their answers should be discussed or rehearsed in advance. For example, the plaintiff in a personal injury action may want to settle before trial, but the defendant will not know the full monetary value of the injuries unless the defendant's lawyer finds out all about the injuries. The plaintiff's deposition strategy may be to provide a full picture of the injuries. The plaintiff may have to volunteer information to present that full picture. Consequently, plaintiff deponents often volunteer information about their pains and disabilities. Another example is where the deponent's lawyer has in mind making a motion for summary judgment, and the client's testimony on a certain point is essential to the motion. The client should be prepared to volunteer the information.

On occasion the deponent's lawyer needs to ask clarifying questions to protect the deponent. A witness may think she or he said one thing, but it came out quite differently. The deponent's lawyer must decide whether to explain and correct the mistake before the deposition is concluded. The alternative is to correct the mistake when the transcript is submitted for review. If the correction is made during the deposition, the deponent's lawyer may elect to use leading questions in an effort to avoid augmenting the mistake. If the lawyer is not quite sure how the client will respond to the attempt to correct the mistake, the better practice is to correct the mistake as provided by Rule 30(e). Either way, the mistake may have opened the client to impeachment. A third alternative is to do nothing about the apparent mistake and deal with it at the time of trial with an appropriate explanation.

The paralegal should assure the client that, through the paralegal's help, he or she is going to be fully prepared to deal with all the questions the opposing lawyer will ask. The client should be given confidence that he or she is going to be an excellent witness. The client should be encouraged to look upon the deposition as a positive experience because it will help the client to be fully prepared to testify at the trial. The introductory meeting with the client should help the client to understand where his or her testimony fits, why certain questions will be asked, and the probable effect of his or her answers on the outcome of the case. The paralegal should strive to develop a dialogue with the client, rather than lecture the client. The client will understand and retain much more if he or she actively participates in the preparation.

■ DEPOSITION PROCEDURES

The paralegal will help make the client more comfortable by explaining the procedures and physical arrangements for the deposition. The deposition will probably be taken at the office of the lawyer who noticed (requested) it. However, it could be taken almost anywhere—a courtroom, an airport, the deponent's home, or a hospital. The primary consideration is availability of the deponent and convenience of a majority of the people involved.

Members of the public and news media do not have a right to attend discovery depositions. Each party has a right to be present and to hear any witness testify. More often than not, the parties elect not to attend discovery depositions. Nevertheless, it can be very useful to have a client attend another party's discovery deposition. The experience may help the client to prepare for her or his own deposition. The client may obtain a better appreciation for the problems in the case. The client may be able to suggest additional questions to put to the deponent. Another potential benefit is that a party's presence seems to keep the deponent from exaggerating and minimizing. Psychologists might say that it is easier to lie about a person than it is to lie to the person. A person's presence can make a difference, psychologically, for the deponent.

At the client's deposition, everything the client says is recorded, verbatim, by a stenographer, who is usually referred to as a court reporter. Since the client's testimony is under oath, the client is subject to the penalties of perjury. The court reporter may not stop recording unless the attorneys agree that he or she may. The client does not have a right to make statements "off the record"; however, if it is necessary to interrupt the deposition, the lawyers usually can agree upon suitable arrangements.

The length of the deposition depends upon the type of case and the extent of the deponent's involvement. In a typical accident case, the plaintiff's deposition lasts between one and two hours. If more than one lawyer interrogates the deponent, the deposition is going to be longer. The defendant's deposition typically lasts about one hour. But a deposition may last as long as several days. No time limit is prescribed unless the Rule 26 "discovery plan" or a court order imposes a limit.

The lawyer who is assisting the client will be present throughout the deposition to protect the client from improper questions and other types of abuse. The client should be told that lawyers have a right to ask questions about almost anything, but when an improper question is asked, her or his lawyer will object. The lawyer may instruct the client not to answer the question. In that event, the interrogator has a right to adjourn the deposition and seek a court order compelling the client to answer the question. In the alternative, the interrogator may complete the deposition and later seek a court order that requires the witness to answer the question. If the client's lawyer objects to a question, that may be a signal to the client that the question presents some problem. Indeed, the lawyer may state the grounds for the objection, and those grounds may help the client to understand why the question is a problem.

One approach to preparing the client is to explain that if an objection is interposed, the client should remain silent until he or she receives instruction about what to do. The lawyer who asked the question may rephase the question or go on to another question. If the interrogator insists on an answer, the lawyer will have to decide whether to let the deponent answer subject to the objection. An answer is made subject to objection when the client's lawyer objects to the question and states the grounds for the objection but allows the deponent to answer.[1] If the lawyer allows the client to answer the question subject to the objection, the client should have the court reporter read back the question so that the client can make sure he or she understands it. The lawyer's objection may provide a clue to the problem, so the client should listen carefully to the objections and grounds. The client should listen carefully to any discussion the lawyers have about the question and objection, because the discussion might help the client to understand the dangers in the question. Sometimes a lawyer makes objections simply to educate the deponent. For example, the following questions were put to a landlord in an action brought by tenant:

Q: How long had the stairway light been burned out before the plaintiff fell on the stairway?

Objection: The question is objected to on the grounds that it assumes facts not in evidence and is argumentative in form. The defendant does not know that the plaintiff fell on the stairway.

Q: You don't deny that the plaintiff fell on the stairway, do you?

A: I don't know that he fell.

Q: Well, how long was the light out?

A: I don't know that it was burned out. I heard from the plaintiff's wife that she changed the bulb in the stairway after the plaintiff went to the hospital. I understood that she put in a brighter lightbulb.

---

1. A lawyer preserves the objection by making an answer subject to objection. At some later time the parties can ask a judge to rule on the objection. The lawyer does not protect against disclosure of the information required by the question, but may prevent subsequent use of the information. Also, the lawyer avoids the expense and inconvenience of stopping the deposition and obtaining a court ruling on the objection.

This witness was adequately prepared on the points in issue. The objection helped the witness to focus on the problem.

■ THE CLIENT'S TESTIMONY

The client must understand the reasons why the opposing party wants the client's discovery deposition. The paralegal should explain, in a general way, the purpose and uses of a deposition. Uses that the client should know about include the opposing lawyer's interest in getting acquainted with the client and observing her or him testify. The lawyer wants to evaluate the client's appearance, authority, and believability. The lawyer wants to find out what the deponent knows and does not know about the occurrence or transaction in issue. In addition, the lawyer wants to force the deponent to commit to a particular version of the facts, so that the lawyer will know what she or he will face at trial. The lawyer will look for inconsistencies in the deponents testimony. The lawyer will seek to obtain additional sources of information. Through all of this, the opposing lawyer will evaluate the client's preparedness and, consequently, the preparedness of the client's legal team. The client's presentation reflects directly upon the lawyer and paralegal who prepared the client for the deposition. Finally, the opposing lawyer may try to intimidate the client to make the client fearful about testifying at trial. The paralegal must allay the client's fears.

The client must understand the big picture: the claim, the defenses, the legal issues, the fact issues, and the posture of the case. The paralegal must explain the theory of the claim and defenses. He or she must explain what facts are controverted and what facts are not disputed. This is the trial lawyer's theory of the facts; it is a theory that the paralegal must believe is true and salable. All of this will go a long way toward making the client an effective witness.

In most cases, the parties' legal rights and obligations are determined by a few key points. The paralegal must identify the key points for the client. Then she or he must tell the client how the opponent will try to develop a version of those key issues. The paralegal must explain to the client how the opponent's lawyer will try to develop that version in the client's deposition.

The paralegal should explain to the client the use of exhibits, including the procedure for identifying exhibits, marking exhibits, laying foundation for exhibits, and offering exhibits. Remember, the purpose of a foundation is simply to show that the exhibit is what it purports to be. The client may be asked to make sketches relevant to the occurrence or things in issue. If that is likely, it would be well to practice before the deposition. Some lawyers take the position that a deponent does not have to *create* evidence in a deposition, so they do not permit a client to make drawings or sketches. Other lawyers make sketches in advance of the deposition. They produce the prepared sketches if and when the client is asked to make one.

The client will be asked what she or he has reviewed to prepare for the deposition. The examiner will want to look at and copy any document or thing the client has used. In addition, the examiner will ask if the client has relied upon the document (such as a statement) to refresh her or his memory and whether it did refresh her or his memory. Therefore, the paralegal should not allow the client to review any document that the legal team does not want to share with the opponent. The client should not even examine her or his own statement unless the opponent has already obtained a copy. The client can be fully prepared without looking at statements or other confidential documents. If the client reviews a document or statement in preparation for the deposition, it will be claimed that the client is testifying from a refreshed recollection. Some courts have held that the examiner has a right to look at any document a witness has used to refresh her or his recollection in preparation for a deposition or trial.

The client should be told to be polite but reticent. Regardless of whether the interrogator is aggressive, or abusive, or personable and pleasant, the client should remain polite and reticent.

The paralegal should explain that the burden is on the interrogator to make each question clear. If the deponent does not understand a question, it is not the deponent's fault. The deponent has the right to have the questions made clear. Each question should be singular. The client should be on guard for multiple questions.

The paralegal should explain that the client's lawyer will protect the client from improper questions by making timely objections. The deponent should create a definite pause following each question. The pause gives the deponent's lawyer an opportunity to object and to protect the deponent. Furthermore, it gives the deponent the opportunity to think through the answer before it becomes a matter of record. When the deponent's lawyer objects to a question, the deponent should not answer unless and until the lawyer authorizes an answer. The paralegal should help the client choose the words that best describe the facts that relate to critical issues. The paralegal may ask the client to repeat significant words. She or he may even ask the client to write the words to reinforce memory of them. Some important words in an accident case are *impact, contact, bump, tap, moment, second, split second, instantaneous.* The client should avoid the word *guess*, and instead use the word *estimate* or *approximately.* In a personal injury case, the plaintiff should be helped to explain the nature, location, and type of pain she or he has been experiencing. For example, pain may be described as sharp, dull, an ache, shooting, burning, and so forth.

Some questions may center upon **negative evidence.** This happens when one of the parties is trying to prove that something did not happen. For example, a party may testify, "I didn't see any turn signal" or "I didn't hear any horn" or "I didn't hear anyone shout a warning" or "I didn't hear any gun" or "I didn't see any light in the hallway." The deponent must be prepared to explain that he or she would have heard or seen the event if it had happened. Furthermore, there is a better way of describing the absence of a fact or event. The deponent will be more authoritative if he or she states, for instance, "I could see that the other car did not have any turn signal flashing." This is a positive statement about the absence of a turn signal.

The client should be instructed to be careful of questions that contains the word *duty* or *responsibility*, because the interrogator may be trying to obtain an admission to some *legal duty* that the client does not really have. A client must be prepared to "deny" facts, assertions, and allegations that are not true. Sometimes interrogators ask questions in a manner that indicates they have evidence that the deponent said or did something the deponent did not actually say or do. For example, the interrogator may ask the client whether the client denies making a certain statement to an investigating police officer. The way in which the question is phrased may cause the client to worry that somebody claims she did make the statement. Consequently, the client may be reluctant to deny having made the statement. A failure to make the denial will mitigate against the client's authority. Similarly, the client must be prepared to deny facts that may seem reasonable but are devastating in their effect, such as when the interrogator says, "You may have been going thirty-one miles per hour in this thirty-mile-per-hour zone."

One objective of the opposing lawyer in taking the client's deposition is to discover what the client does not know about the case. The opposing lawyer may ask a lot of questions for which the client has no answers. The client should not be afraid to admit not knowing the answers. A deposition is not like a test in school where the student is expected to know the answers because the subject matter has been covered in the book or in class. A deponent can testify only to the things that he or she observed and now remembers. A deponent should never *guess* about anything when giving sworn testimony. On the other hand, a client should be cautioned against saying he or she does not know the answer merely because that is an easy way to avoid controversy.

Sometimes a witness does not realize that she or he does know the facts. The witness believes that certain facts are true because she or he has read about them or heard about them from someone. The client should not affirm a statement about a fact if the client does not have personal knowledge about the fact. The deponent should say that she or he does not know the answer when she or he really does not know. But once the deponent states that she or he does not know or remember the particular fact, the deponent is at the mercy of the other parties and witnesses. Again, the client must be urged not to say "I don't know" or "I don't recall" merely because that is an easy out.

Suppose the client testifies that she cannot recall whether she discussed the accident in issue with the other party. The other party may contend that the two did talk and that the client admitted that the accident was her fault. The client will have difficulty refuting the other party's claim because the client is on record that she does not remember whether they talked about the accident. Similarly, if a client says he does not recall how fast he was going, the other side may come up with some very damaging figures from unreliable witnesses. But the client cannot dispute the figures because he has admitted he does not recall the speed. Sometimes a deponent believes that a question about speed or distance requires an exact answer, so the client initially says, "I don't know." The deponent may expect the lawyer to ask another question to have the deponent estimate the speed or distance, which the deponent could do with reasonable reliability. However, the interrogator has the answer he or she wants and may not ask any follow-up questions. The client must be prepared to cope with such questions. When necessary, a client should be prepared to say, "I cannot recall right now, but I can obtain that information for you." When asked where the deponent will search for the information, the deponent need not pin himself or herself down: "I'm not too sure just where I need to look, but I will look!"

The paralegal must explain to the client the application of any pertinent legal privileges, such as the physician-patient privilege, the privilege against disclosing communications with the client's spouse, and the privilege against self-incrimination. In addition, the lawyer should explain any applicable statutory privileges.

The paralegal must anticipate that the examiner will ask questions from records prepared by the client and colleagues. He or she must determine whether any of the client's reports are privileged or otherwise protected from discovery. The paralegal should caution the client not to voluntarily refer to documents that should not be discoverable. The new Federal Rules require parties to disclose the existence of privileged documents, but not the contents.

■ DISCOVERY DEPOSITION GUIDELINES

The following guidelines will help clients testify in a deposition. These guidelines cannot be found in any statute, rule of procedure, or other book. The guidelines are mostly common sense, but also take into consideration some of the peculiarities of the Rules of Evidence and court procedures. Though the guidelines are useful for a deponent in a discovery deposition, they do not necessarily apply to testifying in trial before a jury. This is because the objectives and purposes are different in the two situations. Specifically, in trial a party must testify to educate and persuade the jury; in a discovery deposition the deponent's objective is to disclose only what needs to be disclosed. The witness should comply with these guidelines throughout the time the opposing lawyer is in the area. The client cannot drop his or her guard just because the lawyer has said, "No more questions."

Tell the Truth. Testimony is given under oath. A witness who testifies falsely is subject to the criminal penalties of perjury—a felony. Jurors are instructed that if they conclude that a witness has testified falsely, they may disregard everything the witness said. There is no surer way to lose a case than for a party to be caught in a lie. Telling the truth means testifying accurately—without exaggerating or minimizing. A witness must not fabricate or twist the facts. Her or his opinions must comport with what the witness actually believes.

Lawyers are obligated to prevent clients from perpetrating frauds upon the courts. They must not allow clients to testify falsely. Lawyers must not present evidence they have reason to believe is false. As officers of the court, lawyers are subject to severe penalties for allowing clients to abuse the procedures or rules. The adversary system is effective at finding the truth. If a party tries to win a case on the basis of false testimony, that party is fighting against heavy odds and faces severe penalties.

A witness who takes the stand intending to lie looks anxious and uneasy and tends to overcompensate in various ways. The witness may have actually believed that he or she could deceive everyone, but when the witness takes the stand and faces the jury, he or she is not so sure. If the witness took the stand in good faith but suddenly has lied, there is a sudden change in the witness's demeanor. It is human nature. This is one reason the adversary system for examining witnesses is effective for getting at the truth.

The nature of the adversary system assumes that each party will give herself or himself the benefit of any actual, honest doubt concerning a disputed matter. For example, if a motorist honestly believes she was not exceeding a thirty-mile-per-hour speed limit, but did not look at the speedometer to determine her actual speed, she should testify to what she believes her speed was. She should be prepared to deny driving any faster than she believes she was. She must candidly admit that her opinion of speed is based upon experience and is merely an estimate; she was not looking at the speedometer. But she should refuse to speculate that she may have been going faster than she truly believes she was.

A client may indicate that she or he wants to be told what to say. The client must be firmly told that she or he is to tell the truth and only the truth.

Be Sincere. Sincerity is one hallmark of a persuasive witness. Second to sincerity is authority. A witness appears sincere when the witness appears to believe what she or he says. A witness appears authoritative when the witness is able to remember and describe details about the facts to which she or he testifies. The client should be polite with everyone, including the opposing lawyer, before, during, and after the deposition. Other qualities that add to the client's appearance are confidence, directness, and thoughtfulness.

A lawsuit is a serious matter for all concerned. Seldom is there occasion for wisecracks or jokes. If the witness has an opportunity to poke fun at another person, the temptation should be resisted—even if the witness sees it as a means of "putting a lawyer in his place." As often as not, someone will be offended. A joke may well boomerang. If a duel of sharp-tongued wit develops, the forum favors the lawyer because only the lawyer is authorized to initiate questions.

Listen Carefully to Each Question. A witness should feel certain that he or she understands the question before answering. The burden is on the lawyer to make each question clear and understandable. If the witness does not understand a question, it is not the witness's fault or problem. The lawyer must repeat or rephrase the question if asked to do so. A witness has the right to ask the lawyer for clarification of a question. When the witness realizes that the onus is on the lawyer to make the witness understand, the witness feels much more comfortable and confident. The witness is less reluctant to admit that she or he did not hear or understand a question.

The witness should be encouraged to reflect on each question for a moment and silently phrase the answer before responding aloud. This procedure helps the witness to avoid interrupting the lawyer's questions. Unless cautioned, deponents are inclined to answer before a question is completed. When a deponent answers too quickly, the deponent is likely to make mistakes. In addition, the deponent complicates the court reporter's task because it is nearly impossible to record the statements of two people talking at the same time. The usual consequence is that the court reporter has to stop everyone, and the questions have to be repeated.

When a witness takes a moment to reflect upon the question and to think through the answer, the witness's lawyer has an opportunity to interpose objections if the question is improper. When a witness answers too quickly, she or he loses that protection. A witness should even be cautioned against permitting the opposing lawyer to hurry her or him by showing impatience or irritation. Lawyers know that a thoughtful witness is less likely to be tripped up, and may try to pressure the witness to answer more quickly.

A witness can hardly be too thoughtful or deliberate when testifying in a deposition. Testimony at trial presents a little different situation. There, excessive hesitancy or delay may be interpreted, rightly or wrongly, as uncertainty or a lack of authority or even a lack of candor. Pauses and little delays do not show up in a deposition transcript unless a video system is used, and it is quite unusual to videotape a discovery deposition.

Answer Just the Question.   The purpose of a discovery deposition is to find out what the deponent knows and does not know. The more information the interrogator obtains, the better the interrogator can prepare for trial. The client should not help the interrogator by volunteering information or by providing explanations that are not specifically called for by the questions. A witness should strive to make answers responsive, direct, and specific. The deponent's best answer is the shortest answer, provided that answer is truthful. Short answers help to make the witness appear polite, authoritative, and nonargumentative. They usually keep the testimony brief and provide the least help to the opponent. A deponent may be inclined to volunteer information when the deponent does not understand the question, or wants to explain how he or she happens to know the answer, or simply wants to emphasize his or her importance. A talkative deponent tends to gravitate to the problems in the case that are most bothersome to him or her. A verbose deponent opens new subjects and areas for questioning. The more the deponent talks, the greater the opportunity for inconsistencies.

The client should feel as though she or he is a well of information and the interrogator has to dip into the well with each question. If the client feels as though the information is being pulled out, then the client is handling a discovery deposition correctly. The client should not feel like a fountain that gushes forth information. This does not mean that the client should be uncommunicative, stubborn, or difficult.

Each question is supposed to be singular, not multiple. A deponent should only have to think about one question at a time. A deponent can help to keep his or her answers short by declining to answer multiple questions. Although it is the deponent's lawyer's responsibility to watch for and object to multiple questions the deponent can also watch for vague and multiple questions. Whenever such a question is asked, the client may ask to have it made more specific even if his or her lawyer does not object.

Keep in mind that these guidelines should help a client prepare for a discovery deposition. They may not apply to a client's testimony at trial. Short answers may appear to be evasive. They keep the client from presenting her or his version of the facts. Indeed, full, narrative answers are the rule at trial, because the purpose of testifying is too fully inform and persuade the jury. Short answers do not do that. In addition, most lawyers who handle plaintiffs' personal injury cases feel that the plaintiffs' deposition testimony should give full, descriptive answers to all questions relative to the plaintiffs' injuries and losses.

Do Not Guess. A witness should candidly admit to not knowing the answer to a question rather than guess at the answer. Generally speaking, a wrong guess can do more harm than a lucky guess can help. It is usually evident when a witness is merely guessing. If jurors determine that a witness is prone to guessing, they are inclined to discount the witness's testimony as a whole. A witness's authority is severely diminished by guessing. What is worse, a wrong guess may be interpreted as false testimony.

The rule against guessing does not mean that a witness should refrain from giving estimates or judgments or opinions or best recollections. By way of example, a witness may not know the exact width of the roadway in question, but may be able to make a reasonably accurate estimate. A reasonably reliable estimate is not a mere guess. The law usually does not require exactitude. Nor does the law require perfect recall. The law *does* require the witness to *believe* that his or her memory and judgment are reasonably accurate.

To express some degree of uncertainty without guessing, witnesses often use expressions such as "to the best of my memory," "as best as I recall," "I believe," or "I'm not certain, but. ..." Whenever a witness is constrained to qualify an answer in this manner, he or she loses some authority and persuasiveness. These expressions should be avoided in depositions and at trial. The client should be told that everyone assumes the client is testifying to only what the client believes is true. Therefore, the client need not qualify answers by saying she or he does not know the answer for sure but believes the answer to be true. For example, when the client is asked for a time, distance, or location, the client may respond with the answer that she or he believes is true by just stating it. The client need not volunteer that the answer is only an estimate. If asked whether the testimony is merely an estimate, the answer is yes. If the interrogator asks whether the time was clocked or the distance measured, the answer is a simply no. Again, the best answer is the shortest answer. Otherwise, a witness is inclined to say something like "I don't know what it is, but I'd guess that it's about fifteen feet." Such an answer may disqualify the witness from having and giving a reasonable estimate of the distance in question simply because the witness used the word *guess*. But if the witness has never made an estimate of the time or distance or whatever, the only proper answer is, "I don't know."

If a party testifies that he or she does not know the answer to a particular question, that gives the other side an opening to have evidence on the subject that may go unchallenged. For example, if the plaintiff testifies in his deposition that he cannot recall whether he talked with the defendant at the scene of the accident, he is in a difficult position at trial to refute the defendant's testimony that the plaintiff admitted at the scene that the accident was his fault.

The client should be made aware that if she or he cannot remember a certain fact at the time of the deposition, but believes the fact or information can be obtained, the client should so indicate. Perhaps the information is available in records or a diary or is subject to recall later. A statement to that effect keeps the door open to supply the information after the deposition is completed. The subsequent production of the evidence will not be looked upon with suspicion. By agreeing to try to obtain the requested information, the client keeps from being discredited by producing the information at a later date.

Do Not Be Suspicious or Defensive.   A deponent should show respect for the lawyers and the process. A deponent should be polite but reticent. A deponent should exhibit a positive attitude about testifying, whether in a deposition or at trial. A positive attitude reflects confidence. A deponent should not assume an attitude of hostility. A deponent should not presume that the adverse lawyers will be abusive or will ask tricky questions. Any apparent hostility tends to mitigate against the deponent's appearance of objectivity and, therefore, against her or his effectiveness as a witness. If the opposing lawyers appear to be overbearing and abusive, the deponent should make a conscious effort to remain polite but reserved. A deponent should never try to be clever or humorous.

Answer Out Loud.   We frequently communicate by signs and gestures, such as a nod of the head or a shrug of the shoulders. But the court reporter may not see gestures and is not required to record them. So each answer must be stated orally and loud enough for everyone in the room to hear. Deponents should use the word *correct* rather than the word *right*. They should use *yes* or *no* rather than *uh-huh* or *uh-uh*.

Do Not Show Anger or Impatience.   A witness must consciously strive to avoid losing his or her temper. A display of temper usually reflects adversely on the witness though the anger may be perfectly justified. A deponent may even feel like the star of the show because of his or her justified indignation. But a display of temper creates a risk of being offensive and adds to the possibility of becoming confused. The risk of damage is too great. A witness who loses his or her temper tends to lose perspective, forgetting the big picture. He or she is much more subject to making avoidable errors. A show of anger is likely to cause the deponent to forget the other guidelines for testifying. Once a feeling of anger takes over, it is likely to grow and fester. It seldom goes away spontaneously. When in trial, a lawyer usually tries to obtain a court recess when the opposing lawyer has the client angry and not thinking clearly. But it is not easy to obtain a recess for the benefit of a party who is undergoing a cross-examination. A witness should try to respond to each lawyer the same way, in a polite, courteous, reserved manner.

Give Reasonable Opinion Evidence.   As a general rule, lay witnesses are not permitted to give opinions about facts—just the facts. Many conditions, situations, and "facts" in ordinary human experience can only be described in the form of opinions. Courts recognize this. For example, witnesses seldom determine the speed of a motor vehicle in an accident by seeing the speedometer or obtaining a radar reading or clocking the vehicle. A witness who is reasonably familiar with motor vehicles and who observed a vehicle long enough to form an opinion is allowed to state an opinion or estimate of the automobile's speed in miles per hour. The witness gives an opinion concerning facts. A witness is not permitted to state an opinion that the automobile was going "fast" or "slow." Also, a witness is allowed to give an opinion of a distance in some unit of measurement: feet, yards, miles, and so forth. Again, she or he may not state an opinion that the subject was "close" or "far."

When a witness describes a street as "slippery" or a room as "fairly dark" or rainfall as "heavy" or a streetlight as "dim" or an embankment as "steep" or elevator doors as "fast," he or she is giving an opinion. But how else can an ordinary person describe such conditions? There is no other practical way.

If opinion evidence is admissible, the witness should be sure that it is reasonable in light of the witness's own experience and in the experience of most people. The witness's opinion should be tested against physical facts. The most common area of opinion evidence involves time and distance estimates. Remember, a witness must not guess. A witness may have the opportunity to revisit the accident scene to make comparison observations to help make an accurate estimate about a speed or distance. If a moving object is involved, the correlation between time and distance should be considered, as in the following:

Estimating Speed

Miles per hour	Equals	feet per second
5		7
10		15
20		29
30		44
40		59
50		73
60		88

When a witness is questioned about a speed, distance, or time, the witness should first determine whether or not he or she has a valid estimate or judgment. If so, then he or she must decide whether to express an opinion in terms of a range or a precise measurement. For example, a witness could estimate skid marks to be forty to fifty feet long, or forty-five feet long. Either approach is legitimate and reasonable. However, tactics or strategy may determine that one approach is preferable in a particular case.

A witness must be prepared to stay with an estimate if challenged. The challenger usually begins by forcing the witness to "admit" that the figure given is only an estimate, not a measured quantity. Next, the lawyer may ask the witness to admit that, for instance, the estimate could be off (slower or faster) by one, two, or three miles per hour, and later the lawyer may suggest it could be off by even five miles per hour. Again, the cross-examiner will resort to the phrase "Isn't it possible?" If the estimate could vary by five miles per hour more or less, that creates a spread of ten miles per hour. Pretty soon, it appears that the estimate is of no value at all. Not only is the estimate likely to be rejected as unreliable, but the witness's authority—if not credibility—has been impaired. The solution is for the witness to refuse to speculate about the possibility that the estimate could be slightly off. When asked if she could have been traveling one mile per hour slower or faster than estimated, the witness should respond that her best estimate is as previously stated, and she will not speculate about mere possibilities. Even if the questioner persists, the witness should continue in her refusal to go beyond the original estimate. She thereby avoids weakening her testimony. The same principle applies to almost any type of estimate involving measurements.

Ensure That Memory and Observations Comport With Physical Laws. Estimates and memory should be tested against natural laws and physical or scientific fact. For example, if a witness has the impression that a motor vehicle collision occurred at thirty miles per hour, but the property damage is slight, the witness's observation or memory is in error. When preparing the witness to testify, the lawyer and paralegal must gently show the witness that his present recollection or estimate is not possible. Then they must try to determine what the facts are. If the witness's recollection cannot be refreshed, and if in fact he has no valid estimate or recollection, he must not try to fabricate evidence.

Do Not Overemphasize Honesty. A witness should avoid using expressions such as "to be honest with you," "to tell you the truth," "if I remember right," "to the best of my recollection," or "it seems to me." These expressions weaken the witness's authority and credibility. Testimony should be given without equivocation and without qualification unless absolutely necessary.

Avoid Hypothetical Questions. Hypothetical questions relate to fact situations that are merely assumed to be true for the purpose of having the witness render an opinion or otherwise comment on the assumed facts. The facts used in hypothetical questions must be supplied by other testimony or exhibits. Hypothetical questions have a legitimate and important role in trials. However, it is questionable whether they may properly be used in discovery depositions. Clients must answer questions about the facts of a case. They must tell what was done and what was not done. They must tell what they know. A witness must admit a lack of knowledge when she or he really does not know. But a client should not speculate about what she or he would do or not do in hypothetical situations. The basic reason for this is that it is nearly impossible to prepare adequately for all conceivable hypothetical situations. A secondary reason is that many hypothetical questions that are used to test a witness's knowledge, judgment, or expertise are irrelevant to the case at hand. Suppose a witness is asked, "How many feet would it take for you to stop your automobile when traveling at ten miles per hour? twenty miles per hour? fifty miles per hour?" Most people would be guessing at the answers. On occasion, a question is phrased as a hypothetical question but is actually based upon the facts of the present case. In that event, the witness must be prepared to answer.

Follow Instructions. If an objection is made, the witness should remain silent until the interrogator asks a new question or rephrases the question or until the witness's lawyer says the question may be answered notwithstanding the objection. Whenever the lawyers disagree about the propriety of a question, they must decide what to do. The witness has no responsibility to do anything until his or her lawyer provides specific directions.

The deponent's lawyer might object to a question but immediately follow up with a direction to the witness that the question may be answered "if you understand it." The usual purpose of such an objection and instruction is to warn the witness that the question is dangerous and possibly confusing. The witness should be particularly careful of this question.

A deponent may elect to read the deposition transcript to make corrections in form and in substance. Often deponents are advised that they may waive the right to review and sign the transcript. However, if either the deponent or the lawyer thinks the transcript should be reviewed, the right to review and make changes should not be waived. The witness should be told during the preparation about the right to read the transcript before it is certified and filed. If the lawyer decides at the end of the deposition that it is all right to waive the right to read and sign, the lawyer will ask the deponent whether he or she wishes to waive the right. That is a signal to the witness that the lawyer believes a waiver is acceptable. The witness may still indicate that he or she prefers to review it. If the lawyer wants the witness to review the transcript, he or she will simply tell the reporter to make the transcript available for review.

The client must be prepared to deal with estimates of time and distance. The client should be educated concerning the physical facts so that the client can give estimates, judgments, and approximations that are accurate and authoritative. The paralegal and client may need to visit the scene to do this. Good estimates can be very important in accident cases. The paralegal must decide whether the estimate should be a single figure or a range. For example, depending upon the legal team's theory and strategy, the client may estimate speed as a range of forty to fifty miles per hour or as a single figure of forty-five miles per hour. The estimate must comport with other physical facts and what is reasonable. It must not be a mere guess. Once selected, the range or figure should be firm even though the client must acknowledge that it is only an estimate. For example, if the client estimates a speed as being thirty miles per hour, the client should not admit that it could have been thirty-two or thirty-five miles per hour. Instead, the client should respond that thirty miles per hour is the client's best estimate, and he or she is not going to discuss or argue about possibilities.

Sometimes a client has difficulty remembering some of the details and needs help to determine how to deal with the questions that are expected. Again, the client must not be led into error and must not testify falsely. With that caveat in mind, here are some suggestions: The client may give herself or himself the benefit of any honest doubt. The paralegal should determine what is consistent with physical fact and with other established facts. The paralegal should consider what probably happened. Once the client has reconstructed the situation and is confident that she or he is correct, the client should testify confidently from that belief. Again, the client should avoid using qualifying expressions, such as "to tell you the truth" or "to be honest" or "as best as I can recall."

■ CROSS-EXAMINING THE CLIENT

After the client has been instructed in the guidelines for testifying, the next step is to test the client by interrogating the client just as though his or her deposition were being taken. This gives the client an opportunity to use the guidelines and to practice phrasing answers. As questions and problems arise, the paralegal should stop the mock interrogation to discuss them.

The mock cross-examination should not be conducted in a hostile manner. Instead, unless the paralegal knows to the contrary, the paralegal should assume that the opposing lawyer will be very personable and will try to induce the client to volunteer information. The mock examination should be well focused, searching, and calculated to raise the problems anticipated. It should begin with background questions. The paralegal should ask about the client's past employments, previous addresses, prior accidents, education in detail. She or he should ask about members of the client's family. These background questions will help the client to develop a feel for listening and answering. The paralegal should establish a cadence that includes a significant pause following each question.

Then the paralegal should move to some more difficult subjects, such as past criminal convictions, conversations with the opposing party, speeds, distances, and so forth. The paralegal should try jumping from one subject to another to see if the client is able to cope with the changes. He or she should determine whether the client can recall critical dates, times, distances, words. If the client has trouble with them, he or she should write them down. The act of writing is an aid to recall. The paralegal should use repetition until the client overcomes whatever problems develop. The paralegal should not assume that by just talking about the problem and explaining it he or she can ensure that the client will handle the problem correctly in the deposition. The client must rehearse until the problem is no more.

The client must be helped to deal with questions that call for narrative answers, such as "Then what happened?" or "Tell me about everything you saw" or "How did the accident occur?" The client should not give narrative answers, only short answers. To prevent a narrative answer to the last question, the client could state, "Your client struck my car." The examiner should be forced to pursue the interrogation by using specific questions.

The client must be prepared for standard questions—for example, "Have you given any statements to anyone?" or "What material have you reviewed to prepare for this deposition?" or "Why couldn't you stop?" or "What did you tell [the policeman] about the accident?" In the last case, the answer might be, "The same thing I have told you" or "I told him that your client struck my car."

The paralegal should ask some questions that are improper in form so that the client develops a sense for them, and explain how the client will be protected from such questions during the deposition. Again, questions are improper in form if they are multiple, are argumentative, are abusive, or wrongly assume facts that are not true. The paralegal should try objecting to some of his or her own questions, as though the paralegal were the client's lawyer, so that the client can see the objection procedure in operation. If it were to appear that the cross-examination was being conducted in bad faith, the deponent may elect to leave the deposition. The deponent may make a motion to the court to officially terminate the deposition, or the interrogator may make a motion to compel the deponent to proceed with the deposition.

■ FOLLOWING UP AFTER THE DEPOSITION

After the client's deposition has been completed, the paralegal should spend some time with the client. Clients usually need assurance that they did all right. The paralegal should find out whether the client believes she or he had any problem. Sometimes clients worry about something that really is not a problem, and the paralegal can put the client's mind at ease.

If there is a problem, it should be addressed as soon as possible. The client is entitled to the paralegal's help to gain peace of mind. Hopefully, when the client's deposition is finished, the paralegal and the client will have an increased confidence about the case.

This is also a good time to discuss possible additions and corrections to the transcript and to confirm arrangements for reading and signing the deposition transcript. A deponent has the right to read the deposition transcript to make sure that it accurately states her or his testimony. The court reporter must submit the transcript to the deponent, or the deponent's lawyer, as soon as it has been transcribed. The deponent has thirty days in which to review the transcript and make corrections. The corrections may be changes or additions. They may relate to form, such as spelling, or to substance, such as where the deponent testified in the deposition that he saw that the traffic light was red, and changes the transcript to state that the light was green (see Rule 30(e)). Changes may be necessary because the court reporter made a mistake in reporting the testimony or the deponent made a mistake. The deponent must give a reason for each change, whether the change relates to a mistake by the court reporter or the deponent. The explanation may be as simple as "misspelled," or it may be very detailed and self-serving. For example, the reason might be something like: "My estimate of the width of the road was wrong. After the deposition, I measured the width, and found it was 42 feet wide. Therefore, I have changed my answer on the basis of the new information." As a general rule, the deponent will have the opportunity to state or read the reason to the jury in trial if the opposition informs the jury about the original answer or otherwise uses the original answer. The corrections and reasons must be made in writing and are added to the end of the transcript.

A deponent does not have to read and sign the deposition transcript; he or she may waive this right. If the deposition was short and nothing of consequence was covered and the court reporter is totally reliable, the choice to waive may be reasonable. The only reason to waive the right to read and sign the transcript is that the review may be inconvenient. Also, some lawyers believe that if the client is impeached by the deposition transcript because of an inconsistency, the effect of the impeachment is less devastating if the deponent did not read and sign it. The deponent may waive the right to read and sign by simply stating the waiver on the record at the end of the testimony.

If the deponent wants to review the transcript, the deponent's lawyer instructs the court reporter to provide a transcript for review, along with a correction page. There are some good reasons for having the client read the transcript and make changes. The client may have made a misstatement during the deposition, and that error can be easily corrected in the review. If the deponent agreed during the deposition to investigate the availability of additional information, the information may be supplied in the correction sheet. If either the deponent or the deponent's lawyer thinks the transcript should be reviewed, the right to review should not be waived. By making corrections in the manner provided by Rule 30(e), a lawyer may avoid subsequent problems, such as malpractice or client dissatisfaction.

Most courts allow the opposing party to present to the jury the deponent's original answer notwithstanding a proper correction. In effect, the court allows the deponent to be impeached by the inconsistent statement even though Rule 30(e) expressly reserves the right to make changes. The point is that the right to make corrections and changes is not a panacea for poor preparation. Still, a correction mitigates against the effects of impeachment, because the Rules specifically provide for making corrections in this manner.

SUMMARY

A lawyer who takes the deposition of an opposing party has the opportunity to evaluate the deponent's appearance and authority. The lawyer can determine whether the deponent will be a strong witness or a weak witness; whether the deponent is able to give testimony in an authoritative, persuasive manner; whether the deponent understands the interrelation of the evidence and theory of the case; whether the deponent has some concerns, whether the deponent is willing to go to trial; and whether the deponent is prepared. To be able to prepare a deponent for a deposition, a paralegal must thoroughly understand the purpose of the deposition, the potential uses for the deposition, and the procedures for taking depositions, as well as the case as a whole and the role of the deponent in the case. The paralegal must not tell the client what to say, other than to tell the truth, but he or she can advise a client *how* to testify.

The paralegal and the client have an obligation to correct any misstatement as soon as it is discovered. Even if the misstatement is corrected in the manner provided by the Rules, the opposing side may use it against the client as an admission or for impeachment. Therefore, careful preparation is essential.

While preparing to meet with the client, the paralegal should determine what facts are indisputable and what facts apparently are not disputed. The case should be built around those facts. The paralegal must determine which disputed facts are really important. He or she must consider whether the client's version of the facts is consistent with physical facts. The paralegal must consider whether the client's version of the facts is consistent with probability, common experience, and common sense, whether it is believable. The paralegal must decide whether to test or correct some aspect of the client's version and if so, how to do that. He or she must decide whether any of the photographs and other exhibits on file will be used as exhibits during the deposition and how they should be used. The paralegal must decide whether the client should be allowed to make any drawings or sketches during the deposition. Finally, the paralegal must examine original transaction documents.

Photographs of the accident scene are evidence, not merely illustrative exhibits. They must be protected against loss and alteration. They must be disclosed to the other parties. Photographs of the accident location that do not show conditions that prevailed at the time of the accident are merely illustrative and not, in themselves, evidence; therefore, such photographs need not be disclosed unless they are going to be used at trial.

The paralegal must choose a theory of claim or defense that fully accommodates the applicable law and known facts. The theory concerns what happened, how it happened, and why it happened. The paralegal must think about how the material facts will likely be proved at trial, what evidence will be produced to prove those facts, and how that evidence will be presented.

Ideally, the client will be prepared in two sessions. The first meeting should cover all the issues considered in preparing to meet with the client, with an emphasis on locating and solving problems. The paralegal must consider whether the client needs to be prepared to make a diagram to illustrate how the accident occurred or some other relevant fact. During the hiatus between meetings, the paralegal and the client will have time in which to locate documents, pin down additional facts, and resolve problems that have been identified. The second meeting should focus on the client's anticipated testimony.

When the paralegal meets with the client, he or she should try to relieve the client's natural apprehensions about the lawsuit and about testifying. An apprehensive witness is doomed to mistakes and failure. For most of us, the unknown is the principal cause of fear and nervousness. When the client understands the big picture, the client has a frame of reference that helps him or her to understand individual questions and to answer with confidence. Even though the client's version of the facts is highly questionable, the paralegal must listen to the client's explanation before making any suggestions about possible errors. She or he must try to understand the client's explanations, because the client may be right. The paralegal must not lead the client into perjury, errors, or discomfort.

The client's deposition testimony must be consistent with the client's testimony at trial. The client must not plan on having any "aside" conferences during the deposition. Nevertheless, if necessary, a lawyer can interrupt the deposition to have a conference with his or her client. Prepare the client to answer basic discovery questions, such as:

What have you reviewed to prepare for the deposition?

What has your insurer told you to say?

Have you given a statement to anyone?

Have you ever said anything different?

Do you deny that. . . .?

What did you tell the police officer or investigator?

Where would you go to find out the answer to the last question?

The paralegal should explain to the client the use of exhibits, including the procedure for identifying exhibits, marking exhibits, laying foundation for exhibits, and offering exhibits. The witness may be asked to make sketches relevant to the occurrence or things in issue. It would be well to practice before the deposition if that is likely.

The examiner will want to look at and copy any document or thing the client has used to prepare for the deposition. In addition, the examiner will ask if the client has relied upon the document (such as a statement) to refresh his or her memory and whether it did refresh his or her memory. Therefore, the paralegal should not allow the client to review any document that you the legal team does not want to share with the opponent.

If the deponent's lawyer objects to a question, the deponent should remain silent until she or he receives instruction about what to do. The lawyer who asked the question may rephrase the question or go on to another question. If the interrogator insists on an answer, the deponent's lawyer will have to decide whether to let the deponent answer, notwithstanding the objection. If the lawyer allows the client to answer the question subject to the objection, the client should have the court reporter read back the question to make sure the client understands it.

The following guidelines are helpful to deponents in discovery depositions:

1. A deponent must tell the truth.

2. A deponent should strive to appear sincere, that is, to believe what he or she is saying.

3. A deponent should strive to appear authoritative by being direct and specific, and paying attention to details.

4. The deponent should listen to each question carefully and make sure he or she understands the question; the question must be meaningful to the deponent.

5. The deponent should avoid volunteering information and giving explanations that are not specifically required by the question.

6. The deponent should not guess about anything; estimates and opinions should comport with what is possible and probable.

7. The deponent should not be defensive during the interrogation.

8. The deponent must answer each question out loud.

9. The deponent should avoid being impatient and showing anger.

10. The deponent should avoid hurrying and give his or her lawyer an opportunity to object to improper questions.

These same guidelines do not necessarily apply to testifying at trial.

A deponent has the right to read the deposition transcript to make sure that it accurately states his or her testimony. The deponent has thirty days in which to review the transcript and make corrections. The corrections may be changes or additions. The corrections may relate to form, such as spelling errors, or to substance, such as where the deponent testified that something was "black" but changes the answer to "white."

KEY TERMS

negative evidence

REVIEW QUESTIONS

1. May a paralegal conduct a mock cross-examination of the client? Explain.

2. Why should the client be cautioned against giving narrative answers in a discovery deposition?

3. What can you do to help a client who is obviously confused about the facts about which she or he will be questioned by the opposing lawyer in a discovery deposition?

4. Is it better to correct the client's deposition testimony by asking clarifying questions at the end of the deposition or by making corrections in the errata sheet provided by the court reporter?

5. How many times may a party take the deposition of another party?

6. Why might a lawyer allow his or her client to answer an improper question subject to an objection?

7. What options does the deponent have where she or he believes that the interrogation is being conducted in bad faith?

8. Why should the deponent not review her or his privileged, written statement in preparing for a discovery deposition?

9. Why should you instruct a client not to guess when testifying?

10. Why do lawyers sometimes try to use hypothetical questions in discovery depositions?

MEDICAL EXAMINATIONS AND RECORDS

Many civil actions are concerned with a party's physical, mental, or blood condition. Such cases present a difficult problem for courts because the subject matter is under the exclusive control of one party. Also, a person's medical records, hospital records, and communications with physicians are privileged against disclosure. That means a court cannot order the physician or patient to disclose them, unless the patient waives the privilege.

Actions to obtain money damages for personal injuries are probably the most common type of lawsuit that focuses upon a party's physical and/or mental condition. Others include actions to determine whether an employee is able to do his or her work, a person is entitled to disability insurance benefits, a person is mentally competent, a person's disability was caused by his or her work, or a person is emotionally stable and fit enough to have custody of a child. In each instance, the fact question is basically a medical question.

A court could have significant problems trying to require a party to submit to a medical examination. A medical condition may be very personal. A medical examination may cause some embarrassment. Medical tests may be invasive, that is, they may pierce the skin or otherwise enter the patient's body. Some medical tests are painful and may subject the patient to a risk of harm. It is perfectly understandable that a person may be reluctant to undergo such tests. But how is the defendant to evaluate the plaintiff's claim and prepare to defend against it without an independent medical examination of the plaintiff? Or if the defendant's medical condition is in issue, what right does the plaintiff have to an independent medical examination of the defendant? How can the court provide to the parties equal access to the evidence without being able to require a party to undergo an independent medical examination? The Federal Rules of Civil Procedure deal with these problems in Rule 35, which seeks to protect both parties' interests.

■ RIGHT TO AN INDEPENDENT EXAMINATION

As part of the checks and balances in the civil justice system, Rule 35 provides that the court may order the plaintiff to appear for an independent medical examination if the defendant can show to the court **good cause** why the defendant needs more examinations of the plaintiff. The legal phrase "good cause" means there must be a substantial reason for the medical examination. The good cause requirement prevents defendants from making unjustified demands for medical examinations of plaintiffs.

Showing good cause is not a formidable task. Ordinarily, the defendant need merely show that the plaintiff has put her or his medical condition in issue, and the defendant needs an independent medical examination to be able to evaluate the nature, extent, and cause of the plaintiff's medical condition. Some states require the plaintiff to submit to an examination only if the plaintiff has put her or his medical condition in issue. In other words, the defendant cannot raise a question about the plaintiff's condition and, on that basis, require the plaintiff to submit to an independent medical examination. Suppose the plaintiff claims that the defendant transmitted a disease to her or him. The plaintiff does not have a right to obtain an independent medical examination of the defendant to determine whether the defendant has the disease, because the defendant did not put her or his condition in issue.

A court may require only a party to the lawsuit, or someone who is directly under the control of a party, to undergo a Rule 35 independent medical examination. If a corporation is a party, the adverse party cannot use Rule 35 to obtain an independent medical examination of the corporation's employees or agents. When a parent brings a lawsuit on behalf of a child, the child is considered a party and may be required to submit to an independent medical examination. The child is under the parent's legal control.

The rules of civil procedure in most states provide that when the plaintiff commences an action to recover money damages for personal injuries, the plaintiff thereby waives his or her medical privilege, at least to some extent. The extent of the waiver varies from state to state. The waiver may be total, or it may be limited to a relinquishment of privilege concerning the plaintiff's medical records and reports so that they become discoverable. The federal courts follow the laws of the state concerning medical privilege and its waiver. Therefore, the application of Rule 35 and its procedure is often subject to and qualified by state law. However, state law cannot be so narrow as to preclude a federal court from granting an independent medical examination when appropriate under the parameters established by Rule 35.

If a plaintiff refuses to submit to a medical examination, in spite of a court order finding that good cause has been shown, the court has two options: the court may dismiss the plaintiff's lawsuit, or the court may resolve the disputed medical facts against the plaintiff. If the defendant is the disobedient party, the court may strike (disallow) his or her answer and find the defendant in default. If a party is in default, judgment may be entered against him or her without having a trial. A court may *not* hold a party in contempt of court for refusing to submit to an independent medical examination. This means the plaintiff or defendant who refuses to be examined cannot be fined or incarcerated for violating the court order.

Suppose the parties were involved in an automobile collision at an intersection. The defendant wants to have the plaintiff's eyes examined because he contends that the plaintiff's vision is defective and that condition prevented the plaintiff from keeping a proper lookout and caused the accident. The eye condition is physical, and the best way of determining it is to have a medical examination. However, unless the plaintiff has placed the condition of her eyes in issue, the defendant does not have a right to an independent examination of the plaintiff and most courts would not allow him to obtain one. But if a defendant puts her or his physical condition into issue as a defense, the defendant may be required to submit to an examination. For example, a man had a sudden, unexpected heart attack while driving his car. He went off the road and killed some children. He claimed that the heart attack made the accident unavoidable. He was required to submit to an independent medical examination. Similarly, if the defendant were to claim insanity as a defense in a civil action, the plaintiff could insist on an independent psychiatric examination of the defendant.

The defendant may request a Rule 35 medical examination at any stage of the litigation, subject to the court's scheduling order. A party may not use a request for an examination to delay the trial. Nevertheless, the court has in some cases ordered the plaintiff to submit to a medical examination during the trial where the plaintiff has asserted a new claim since the independent examination.

Rule 35 does not limit the number of independent examinations the defendant may obtain. However, it must appear that an examination is reasonably necessary before a court will require the plaintiff to submit to one.

■ REASONS TO OBTAIN AN INDEPENDENT EXAMINATION

If the plaintiff gives the defendant access to the records and reports of the plaintiff's treating physician, the defendant's lawyer may elect to rely upon them to evaluate the case, especially if the treating physician has a reputation for being capable, objective, and candid. Also, many soft tissue personal injury cases are settled by liability insurance companies without an independent medical examination. (**Soft tissue** injuries are injuries involving muscle strains and sprains or bruises and contusions that generally heal without problems.) The need for an independent examination arises when the plaintiff does not have a treating physician and both parties want to make sure there is no hidden or latent injury before entering into a final settlement, or where the defendant's lawyer is not willing to rely upon the evaluation of the plaintiff's treating physician.

There are many reasons why the defendant's lawyer may feel that the treating physician's evaluation is inadequate or even in error:

- The defendant may believe that the treating physician's records and reports do not fully or accurately portray the plaintiff's condition.

- The treating physician may have obtained an inadequate or erroneous medical history. For example, the treating physician's report may describe the accident, the plaintiff's back injury, the treatment, and so forth, but fail to consider the plaintiff's prior back conditions.

- The treating physician may have an incomplete or erroneous accident history. For example, the plaintiff may have indicated to the physician that the defendant's automobile was traveling forty miles per hour when it struck the rear of the plaintiff's truck, whereas the evidence shows that the impact was minor and did not even move the plaintiff's vehicle.

- The findings recorded by the treating physician may be inconsistent with the plaintiff's subjective complaints. For example, the plaintiff may have testified in her deposition that she had severe lower-back pain immediately after the motor vehicle accident and was disabled because of it. On the other hand, the treating physician's records report some neck pain but no lower-back pain and no treatment for lower-back pain. The symptoms may vary from time to time, in an inexplicable way, to raise a doubt about their validity.

- The treating physician may not have sufficient expertise in a pertinent area. For example, in one case a general practitioner concluded that the plaintiff had a back strain following an automobile accident. But the defendant's independent examiner was an orthopedic surgeon who concluded that the symptoms and examination findings were not typical of a muscle strain. The specialist ordered X-rays that showed that the plaintiff had a kidney stone. The stone was removed, and the plaintiff had no more back pain. Since the plaintiff had associated his back pain with the accident, so had his family doctor.

Sometimes the defendant's lawyer has more detailed information about the accident history and the plaintiff's conduct following the accident than the treating physician appears to have. Occasionally, the defendant may suspect some collaboration between the patient and the treating doctor, and therefore feel a need for an *independent* evaluation. The suspected collaboration is rarely outright falsification. Rather, it is usually a matter of exaggeration and minimizing. In an extreme but true case, the plaintiff was a forty-eight-year-old homemaker who had stopped her automobile in response to a traffic light. The defendant's semitruck "bumped" the rear of her car. She told her treating physician that her car was struck forcefully and she was thrown about in the interior. She felt dazed, and soon her neck, left arm, and shoulder began to hurt. The physician's diagnosis was that she suffered a strain of the muscles and ligaments in her neck and shoulders. He undertook to treat her with medications and physical therapy for several years. At one point the treating physician called in a psychiatrist for consultation, who determined that the plaintiff was neurotic and a hypochondriac. These psychiatric problems were deep seated and had existed long before the automobile accident.

The defendant arranged for a Rule 35 independent medical examination by an orthopedic surgeon. The surgeon concluded that there was no objective evidence of injury or disability, but based upon the accident and medical history, as related by the plaintiff, and the continued symptom of pain in the neck and left shoulder, the plaintiff had a musculo-ligamentous strain without any apparent disability of the shoulder or neck. The surgeon had to assume the correctness of the plaintiff's subjective symptoms and medical history.

After the independent medical examiner testified in accordance with his report, the defendant's lawyer asked him to assume as true certain additional facts to which the defendant truck driver testified. Specifically, the truck driver said the truck was almost stopped at the moment of contact; the contact merely caused a scratch on the chrome strip on the right rear fender of the plaintiff's automobile, as shown by photographs; the plaintiff's automobile was not moved by the contact; the vehicles remained together after they came in contact; the plaintiff stepped out of her automobile immediately after the accident; and the plaintiff did not appear injured and did not complain of any injury while at the accident scene.

The independent examiner testified that if the additional accident history were true, he would have to conclude that the plaintiff was not physically injured in the accident, because there would have to be some movement of the plaintiff's automobile before she could have experienced any overstretching of her musculature. Her subjective complaints could not be attributed to a physical injury.

The psychiatrist's diagnosis then provided the logical explanation for the plaintiff's overreaction to the accident and for her continued symptoms. The independent examiner had the psychiatrist's records available and was able to use them when he testified. The jury determined that the plaintiff was not injured at all. The accident provided her with an opportunity to secure secondary gains, including help with her housework, sympathy, and the opportunity to visit the doctors regularly. The possible recovery of money damages was less important to her than these other considerations. The result of this case would have been quite different if the defendant had not been able to have an independent medical evaluation and opinion.

■ TREATING PHYSICIAN'S ROLE

Although a treating physician may be partial toward his or her patient, the physician is not expected to be an advocate. The Rules of Evidence presume that patients are candid with their physician when they seek medical treatment. The Rules assume that the plaintiff fully believes that the information she or he gives to the physician is for the purpose of obtaining the correct diagnosis and correct treatment. Therefore, the statements made by a patient to a treating physician are admissible into evidence as an exception to the rule against hearsay evidence.

When treating a patient, a physician is not expected to cross-examine the patient concerning the patient's accident history, medical history, and symptoms. The treating physician does not have any responsibility to prove or establish the patient's claim. The treating physician is expected to obtain the information needed to make an accurate diagnosis and to prescribe the proper treatment. Consequently, a patient who tries to fabricate a claim or embellish a claim may easily mislead a treating physician.

■ INDEPENDENT EXAMINER'S ROLE

The lawyer who orders an independent medical examination needs to have an objective, candid, accurate report. The examiner does not help the lawyer by providing a report that minimize the examinee's injury or presents the wrong analysis or reaches the wrong conclusions.

An independent examiner may be expected to be more skeptical about the plaintiff's accident history, prior medical history, subjective complaints, and symptoms than is a treating physician. The independent examiner is expected to look for inconsistencies between the symptoms, symptoms and history, and symptoms and findings. The examiner also looks for medical improbabilities, such as a claim of permanent injury where there are no objective findings. The examiner has a right to ask the plaintiff about almost anything relevant to the bodily condition in issue.

■ SELECTING AN INDEPENDENT EXAMINER

A party considers several issues when selecting an independent examiner. The trial lawyer must have complete confidence in the examiner's ability to do the necessary tests. The examiner must be competent to do the medical analysis. The lawyer relies upon the examiner (physician) to understand the medical problems and their relationship to the lawsuit. The physician must be willing to prepare a comprehensive report that the defendant can use to evaluate the case. In addition, the defendant must rely upon the physician to substantiate the report by testifying at trial when necessary. The physician must be able to explain the findings, diagnoses, and prognosis in the report and at trial.

The law recognizes that a lawyer may have some difficulty finding an examiner who can fulfill all these considerations. Consequently, most judges give lawyers broad latitude in selecting their independent examiners. The plaintiff may not like the examiner chosen by the defendant, but it takes a significant reason to disqualify that examiner. One reason that might suffice is that the examiner provided treatment to the plaintiff in the past. Another is that the plaintiff has sued the examiner in another lawsuit. The plaintiff could not disqualify the examiner on the grounds that the examiner happens to know the defendant or knows the defendant's lawyer or has a reputation for testifying in particular types of cases. The selected examiner cannot be disqualified on the grounds that the plaintiff's lawyer does not like the examiner and thinks the examiner may not be fair or honest. If the plaintiff wants to challenge the examiner's integrity, the challenge must be made by showing specific acts of dishonesty or prior wrongdoing. For example, a professional licensing board's findings of prior wrongdoing could be used for that purpose.

The defendant's lawyer must find a physician who is not only competent to conduct the examination, but willing to do it at a time and place that comport with the requirements of the litigation. Many physicians simply refuse to do medical examinations for litigants. Some physicians have decided they will do examinations and will provide detailed written reports, but will not testify in court. They will testify only by way of deposition, including videotaped deposition. If the defendant's lawyer insists upon having an examiner who will testify in court, the commitment to testify should be part of the initial arrangements between the defendant and the physician. Another consideration is the cost of the examination, report, and court appearance. Some physicians insist upon payment for their report even before the report is prepared.

The defendant must decide what kind of an independent examination should be obtained. Should the examination be conducted by a medical doctor (physician), osteopath, psychologist, chiropractor, or other practitioner? Since these practitioners are from different schools of the healing arts, they may have different theories about the problem, administer and prescribe different types of treatment, and apply different standards for evaluating the plaintiff's condition. If a medical doctor is selected to do the examination, should the examiner be a specialist? If so, which specialty is most directly related to the case? The type of treatment the plaintiff has selected often helps determine who should conduct an independent examination. For example, many states have no-fault insurance laws that require automobile insurers to pay their own insureds' medical expenses for treatment to the extent that the treatment is reasonably necessary. A question may arise as to whether the insured's continued treatment is necessary. If the patient is being treated by a doctor of chiropractic, the automobile insurer may want to have the opinion of another chiropractor. The same question may be presented in a workers' compensation case where the employer contends that the employee has received too much treatment.

The defendant has great leeway in selecting an independent examiner. The defendant may determine the type of examination because the examination is for the defendant's purposes. This is true in both discovery and trial preparation. Courts do not select examiners for the parties. However, a court may prohibit an examiner selected by the defendant from conducting the examination if some unusual problem exists, as where the examiner previously served as the plaintiff's treating physician.

Most law firms have contacts with individuals in the various professions who qualify to do independent examinations. Lawyers like to work with expert witnesses who, based upon past experience, they know will do a good job for the client. If none of these professionals can do the examination, they can probably recommend other qualified persons. Also, many organizations specialize in locating expert witnesses and examiners for litigants. The defendant's lawyer should make sure the examiner selected is duly qualified in his or her profession and will qualify to testify.

■ SCHEDULING AN INDEPENDENT EXAMINATION

The timing of an independent medical examination may significantly affect the examination's usefulness. If the plaintiff is claiming injuries due to an accident and the preliminary indications are that the injuries are quite minor, good strategy may dictate that the defendant obtain an independent medical examination right away. An early examination can establish an early date for the plaintiff's medical recovery. The examiner can probably give an opinion that the plaintiff is ready to return to work or can return to work within a week or two. An early examination is usually sought where an insurance company is attempting to cancel benefits to an insured or a claimant.

If the plaintiff has clearly sustained serious, long-term injuries, the defendant may want to wait awhile before obtaining an independent medical examination, because the purpose of the examination is to evaluate the plaintiff's recovery, not the nature or extent of the injuries. If the examination is performed soon after the injury, another examination may be required for evaluating the claim.

The defendant schedules the examination for a time and place that are convenient for the examiner and for the plaintiff. The date and time are usually selected through the physician's secretary. Although Rule 35 does not impose any geographic limitations or requirements, courts are inclined to require the defendant to arrange for examination in the county where the defendant resides or works. If the parties cannot agree, the court will determine the time and place.

The defendant must give the plaintiff sufficient notice to prepare for the examination. The plaintiff may have to arrange to take time away from work or arrange for baby-sitting or arrange for transportation. If the plaintiff does not have suitable transportation, the defendant may be required to provide it. Generally, however, the plaintiff must pay her or his own expense in traveling to and from the place of the examination.

Unless the court's order sets the time for the examination, the defendant's lawyer or paralegal sends a letter to the plaintiff's lawyer confirming the arrangements. It is a good idea to request the plaintiff's lawyer to contact the plaintiff immediately to ensure the plaintiff's availability. If the plaintiff fails to keep the appointment, he or she may be responsible for the physician's charge for reserved time. This is true whether the examination was scheduled by agreement or by court order.

Most independent medical examinations are arranged by mutual agreement between the parties without any specified conditions or limitations. Lawyers and professional examiners understand that the scope of an independent examination should be limited to what is reasonably necessary. Professional people who do independent examinations know that they must conduct those examinations in a way that comports with the standards of their profession, and that is what the courts require.

■ MOTION TO COMPEL AN INDEPENDENT EXAMINATION

Sometimes, problems arise concerning the defendant's right to have the plaintiff examined. If the plaintiff refuses to submit to an independent examination, the defendant must move the court for an order compelling the plaintiff to submit. A sample motion to compel an examination appears in exhibit 14.1.

If the plaintiff opposes the motion, she or he will have to serve and file an objection to examination, in which the plaintiff will state the grounds for the opposition. The grounds may concern the time, place, examiner, scope of the examination, or manner in which the examination is to be conducted. A judge then decides that the examination should go forward as scheduled or imposes necessary limitations.

The defendant hereby moves the court for an order requiring the plaintiff to submit to an independent medical examination for the purpose of diagnosis and evaluation of the plaintiff's alleged injuries.

This motion is made pursuant to Rule 35 of the Federal Rules of Civil Procedure.

The defendant has arranged for the plaintiff to be examined by Dr. Carol Ellingboe on March, 4, 1995, at 2:00 P.M. The examination is scheduled to be conducted at Dr. Ellingboe's office at 2050 Abbott Street, Suite 657, Boston, Massachusetts. Dr. Ellingboe is licensed by the state of Massachusetts to practice medicine, and specializes in neurology. The scope of the proposed examination is a complete physical and neurological examination to evaluate the plaintiff's claim of head, neck, and back injuries.

The grounds for this motion are that the plaintiff has put her bodily and mental condition into issue through the allegations set forth in her complaint, and the defendant needs an independent medical examination and opinion for the purpose of evaluating the plaintiff's claim and preparing his defenses.

This motion is based upon the plaintiff's complaint and the attached affidavit of counsel.

_____

Attorney for Defendant

Rule 35(b)(3) recognizes that the parties often stipulate to independent medical examinations. The rule provides that the parties' agreement shall be construed to comport with the basic requirements of Rule 35 unless it expressly and clearly provides otherwise. Parties do not seek court orders unless a dispute arises about the number of examinations, the length of an examination, the scope of an examination, or the manner in which an examination is to be done. For example, the plaintiff may want her spouse, attorney, or treating physician to attend the examination with her. As a rule, courts do not allow the plaintiff to have her attorney or treating doctor observe the examination. The plaintiff's lawyer does not have a right to interview the examiner. Rule 35 does not authorize the plaintiff to take the deposition of the independent examiner. Nevertheless, the plaintiff may take the examiner's deposition pursuant to another rule if good cause is shown. Only if unusual circumstances exist will a court permit someone to attend the examination of an adult. However, many courts have authorized either party to make an audiotape recording of the examination.

■ CONFIRMING AN INDEPENDENT MEDICAL EXAMINATION

The defendant should send the examiner a letter confirming the arrangements for the examination. The letter should fully inform the examiner about relevant details of the accident, the nature of all the plaintiff's complaints, the type of treatment received, the treating physician's diagnoses, and a prognosis. The defendant should include copies of the treating physician's reports and records along with instructions to use the enclosures for background information and to guide or focus the history taking and examination. Nevertheless, the examiner should base his or her report upon the history the plaintiff gives to the examiner and the examiner's own findings. The evaluation and conclusions must be the examiner's own.

The letter to an independent medical examiner in exhibit 14.2 illustrates the use of Rule 35. It also illustrates the value of an independent medical examination. Notice that the writer has carefully developed *relevant* details.

Paralegals are often asked to prepare this type of letter to the independent examiner. The letter gives the examiner a good deal of background, so that the examiner can put the examination in perspective and give special attention to any unique problems, such as inconsistencies in the medical records. The letter should indicate whether the defendant is interested in having additional examinations if reasonably necessary. Sometimes the plaintiff may have multiple medical problems, but only one or two problems are really debatable.

■ INDEPENDENT EXAMINATION PROCEDURE

A bodily injury claim usually involves many separate but related medical questions, such as Did the occurrence cause any injury? If so, what injury resulted? Is the plaintiff's past medical history contributory? Does the plaintiff have any physical impairment? If so, how much? What is the nature of the impairment? Has the physical impairment caused any disability, that is, inability to work or do daily living tasks? Was the past medical and chiropractic treatment reasonably necessary? Is the impairment temporary or permanent? Does the plaintiff require future medical care? If so, for how long, and how much will it cost? Did the bodily injury cause any pain? Is the pain subject to control by medication? Will the pain continue into the future? If so, for how long? Are the plaintiff's symptoms explainable on a basis other than the accident in question? Did the plaintiff obtain the proper medical treatment?

To answer these questions, the independent medical examiner needs to determine the nature, extent, and consequences of the plaintiff's abnormal physical or mental condition. To do this, the physician must consider the plaintiff's past medical history, current medical history, subjective complaints, and findings. The process requires the examiner to compare the plaintiff's various statements about her or his history, symptoms, and complaints to determine whether they have been consistent and whether the plaintiff has been consistent in their reporting. Do the complaints comport with the type of injury diagnosed? If the symptoms recur (come and go), what causes them to return? When do they recur? Is there a pattern? Is there evidence of normal progressive healing? The examiner must try to determine whether **subjective complaint and subjective symptoms** are corroborated by **objective medical findings,** which the examiner can observe by sight, touch, or sound. A complaint or symptom is subjective when it is merely the patient's voluntary response. A scar on the face is objective. An atrophied limb is objective. A headache is subjective. Muscle pain is subjective. A limited range of motion in the body may be objective or subjective. A lack of consistency suggests the plaintiff's complaints and symptoms may be exaggerated or even fabricated. If the diagnosis is based solely upon the patient's history and subjective complaints, there is no actual medical corroboration of the injury or disability.

■ **EXHIBIT 14.2**

Letter to Examiner, Confirming Independent Medical Examination Arrangements

January 7, 1995

Adam Goldes, MD
Medical Arts Building, 1000 Fifth Street
Dallas, Texas

Re: Diersen vs. Machacek
OUR FILE: 37610

Dear Dr. Goldes:

This letter will confirm the arrangements we have made for an independent neurological examination of Elizabeth Diersen to be conducted by you at your Medical Arts office at 9:00 A.M. on March 4, 1995. Mrs. Diersen is represented by Attorney Thomas Rice. His telephone number is 555-1555. The arrangements for this examination were made through his office.

Mrs. Diersen is claiming neck and back injuries, which she attributes to a rear-end-type automobile accident. She is also claiming a problem with headaches, dizziness, and pain in her right thigh.

Mrs. Diersen was born on January 21, 1967. She is now twenty-seven years of age. She is married to Paul Diersen, who is thirty-three years of age. They have one child. Mrs. Diersen completed high school. Her past gainful employments have been light assembly work. She worked with hand tools and circuit boards. She states that she has not been involved in any other motor vehicle accidents. She broke a couple of ribs many years ago when she fell in a school parking lot. Otherwise, she has enjoyed good health.

The automobile accident in question occurred Monday, March 6, 1994, about 7:00 A.M. on State Highway 5 in Eden, Texas. Mrs. Diersen stopped her Ford Mustang for a traffic light. She was in a line of traffic backed up from the light. Without any warning, she suddenly felt her car pushed ahead an undetermined distance. She did not strike the car in front of her. She did not hear any contact at the rear of her car. Her car seats had high backs. Her head struck the back of the seat. She did not strike anything else within the car. She did not sustain any cuts, bumps, swelling, or bruises.

Apparently my client, Mr. Robert Machacek, bumped the rear of an automobile driven by Ms. Rhea Bellman, and Ms. Bellman's car was pushed against the rear of Mrs. Diersen's automobile. Photographs show very minor damage to the back of the Diersen car. All three cars were drivable. Neither Ms. Bellman nor Mr. Machacek was injured. Mrs. Diersen did not feel injured at the accident scene. She continued to work, called her husband, found herself feeling very upset about the accident, and started crying. Her husband was off work that day. He came to the plant, examined the car, and drove it home. Mrs. Diersen left work early and drove their camper vehicle home. Upon her husband's suggestion, she saw Dr. F. P. Ekrem that same afternoon. He is a general practitioner at the Spencer Clinic. Mrs. Diersen's complaints then included a headache and slight thigh tenderness. On examination, Dr. Ekrem found that the reflexes in Ms. Diersen's upper and lower extremities were normal, and she had an excellent range of motion in her neck with minimal tenderness at extremes. She had slight occipital tenderness at the left, minimal vertebral tenderness in the neck, and no muscle spasm. No X-rays were taken. Tylenol and Valium were prescribed.

Mrs. Diersen returned on March 17 complaining of neck discomfort. Dr. Ekrem records the following:

—Continued

—Continued

While working she has her head in one position looking downward, causing some neck strain. She also has to cut wire, and there is associated bending. She has constant pain with bending down, then straightening up.

He found a good range of motion in her neck with tenderness at the extremes of motion. His diagnosis was neck and lower-back strain and sprain. He felt she could return to work, gave her a booklet on back care, and prescribed outpatient physical therapy.

Mrs. Diersen returned April 12, complaining of more back pain, especially while doing household activities and picking up her child. She was having pain in her thigh and calf on the left side. These symptoms worsened toward evening. Dr. Ekrem found a full range of motion of the neck with no muscle spasm. The straight-leg–raising test was negative. Her back pain was identified as being at the insertion of the paraspinal muscles at the iliac crest posteriorly. Dr. Ekrem notes that *Mrs. Diersen* felt she could not go back to work.

Dr. Ekrem last saw Mrs. Diersen on August 15, 1994, but in the meantime, she started seeing Chiropractor Jane Zimmerman. When Mrs. Diersen saw Dr. Ekrem in August, she was complaining of dizziness and continued pain, the location of which is not specified. He felt she might benefit from physiotherapy. He suspected that the dizziness was due to postural hypotension.

Chiropractor Zimmerman's first examination was April 28, 1994. She treated Mrs. Diersen's neck and lower back with chiropractic manipulation. Sometimes the adjustments were painful. Chiropractor Zimmerman explained to Mrs. Diersen that her spine was out of alignment, and that was causing her symptoms. She referred Mrs. Diersen to Chiropractor James Brandt for a consultation. She last saw Mrs. Diersen in July 1994. Her services were discontinued because Mrs. Diersen was unable to pay her bill and because the Diersens moved from Eden to Crystal, Texas.

On July 28, 1994, Mrs. Diersen started treatment with Chiropractor Donna Wahlen. Chiropractor Wahlen felt she had myocytis of the cervical, dorsal, and lumbar spine. She was treated with chiropractic adjustments, ultrasound, and so forth.

It appears that Chiropractor Wahlen referred Mrs. Diersen to D. L. Anderson and Dr. Anna Schut for a neurological evaluation. She was examined by one of them on September 6, 1994, when she was complaining of dizzy spells, neck pain, and lower-back pain. Dr. Anderson records that the lower-back pain did not begin until about a week after the accident. According to her history, the physical therapy she had received at Methodist Hospital as prescribed by Dr. Ekrem had not provided any help. The problem with dizziness began while she was under Chiropractor Zimmerman's care. The neurological examination was essentially normal. Specifically, testing of muscle strength and reflexes in the extremities was normal. Sensation was normal throughout the body. No Hoffman or Babinski signs were present. Gait and leg swinging were negative. The Romberg test was negative. However, she demonstrated some limitation in the range of motion of her neck. In this regard, Dr. Anderson states the following:

> However, the patient has a long, thin, angular neck probably capable of more range of motion than is elicited at this time. She has palpable muscle spasms in the cervical muscles bilaterally as well as the upper trapezius muscles, particularly on the left side.

He found the motion in the dorsal and lumbar spine to be within normal limits. However, again, he describes "palpable muscle spasms bilaterally over the lumbosacral

—Continued

■ **EXHIBIT 14.2**

Letter to Examiner,
Confirming Independent
Medical Examination
Arrangements, *Continued*

—Continued

spine." The straight-leg–raising test was negative at ninety degrees. The cause of her dizziness was not determined.

Dr. Anderson eventually had Mrs. Diersen admitted to the Eden Health Center for testing. She was also evaluated by Dr. Schut. An electromyogram dated September 20, 1994, was negative for both lower extremities. Ms. Sylvia Rush, psychologist, conducted an evaluation. A Minnesota Multiphasic Personality Inventory [psychological test] showed Mrs. Diersen to be significantly neurotic. In addition, Ms. Rush felt she sought secondary gain by obtaining financial benefits from her insurance coverage and other benefits that exceeded her wage loss. She also felt that Mrs. Diersen wanted to remain at home with her child rather than work. Though Mrs. Diersen states her home and family life is good and satisfying, the indications are to the contrary.

During the September 1994 hospitalization, a myelogram was performed and interpreted by radiologist L. O. Campbell. His conclusion is as follows:

> Congenital partial sacralization of L5. Bilateral small extradural defects at L4–5 suggesting central bulging disk at this level.

Dr. David Olson, who was called in for consultation by Dr. Anderson, concluded that surgery was not appropriate at the time, but he does not rule it out for the future.

More recently, Mrs. Diersen has come under the care of a psychologist named Stanley Baker at Clifton Court in Dallas. He is putting her through various physical stress activities that cause her to shake. The purpose is to release her tensions. He massages her neck. They talk. So far she has gone through seven such sessions at fifty dollars a session. She thinks Mr. Baker is helping her a lot. She intends to continue seeing him.

Mrs. Diersen's medical expenses now exceed eleven thousand dollars. She remains off work. She is apparently seeking social security disability benefits. She appears highly motivated to cling to her symptoms.

Please provide me with a narrative report on your examination and findings. Certainly psychiatric and psychological evaluations are necessary. Thank you for your very able assistance in this matter.

Very truly yours,

Constance McKenzie
Paralegal

■ MEDICAL TESTS COMMONLY USED TO DIAGNOSE INJURIES

Many medical tests are commonly used for diagnosing injuries, including the following:

- ■ ordinary X-rays, which show the condition of the bone
- ■ computerized tomography (CT) scans, which show some bone conditions and soft tissue conditions, and their interrelationship
- ■ magnetic resonance imaging (MRI) scans, which show soft tissue conditions, including some brain injuries
- ■ electromyograms (EMGs), which test the electrical function of nerves and muscles

- electroencephalograms (EEGs), which test brain wave function and may help to show whether the patient has a brain injury

- myelograms, which are a special type of X-ray of the spine that are useful in diagnosing injuries and abnormalities of the spinal nerve roots and spinal cord and intervertebral disk

- angiograms, which are a special type of X-ray that shows the condition of blood vessels

- psychometric tests, which evaluate a person's mental and emotional status and functioning

- diskograms, which are a special type of X-ray used to evaluate the condition of intervertebral disks in the spine; this type of test has come into disfavor and is being used with less frequency

- reflex tests, which help to show whether the peripheral nerves and/or the central nervous system has been injured or impaired

- range-of-motion tests, which test the movement of extremities (arms and legs) and all the joints in the body

- skin sensory tests, which indicate whether an apparent nerve injury corresponds with the expected nerve pattern

When the treating physician obtains such tests, the results ordinarily are available to the parties as part of the patient's medical-hospital records. The test results are quite objective and seldom need to be repeated. Even if physicians differ in their interpretation of the tests, the raw data is usually available to both sides for review and evaluation. The one significant exception is the interpretation of an electromyogram. Electromyography is a study of the electrical activity of nerves and muscle activity. The electrical activity is measured and evaluated by sound and by readings on an oscilloscope. No record is made of the measurements themselves during the testing. The examiner simply records his or her interpretation of the waves on an oscilloscope.

■ RISKY AND PAINFUL MEDICAL TESTS

If the plaintiff's own physician has not conducted or obtained appropriate, relevant tests, the independent examiner may want to do them. However, a problem occurs if the tests are painful or subject the patient to some risk of harm. A court will not order the plaintiff to submit to risky or painful tests. For example, courts do not require plaintiffs to undergo an angiogram. In an angiogram, a physician injects dye into the patient's bloodstream and then takes X-rays to determine whether there is some defect or obstruction in a blood vessel. The test carries with it a small risk of stroke and even death. The test may be perfectly justified when the patient is seeking diagnosis and treatment for a serious problem, but generally is not justified for purposes of litigation.

Courts do not require plaintiffs to submit to **invasive testing,** or testing that requires cutting into the body, such as a laparoscopy or arthroscopy. However, courts routinely require plaintiffs to submit to electromyograms, to test muscle and nerve function. Courts also order plaintiffs to undergo electroencephalography, to test electrical activity of the brain. Both tests require the insertion of small needles into the patient's skin. The tests are considered uncomfortable but not painful.

If the plaintiff will not voluntarily submit to a risky, painful, or invasive test, the test may not be done. Furthermore, courts do not allow the defendant to cross-examine the plaintiff about her or his refusal to submit to the tests. On the other hand, the defendant's lawyer is allowed to cross-examine the treating physicians about the availability of the tests to help make a definitive diagnosis. The physician can then explain why she or he has not recommended the tests. If the plaintiff's own treating physician recommended the tests for aiding in treatment, the jury can decide why the plaintiff declined. On occasion, the plaintiff voluntarily submits to the tests because they are indeed useful and the defendant has to pay their cost. For example, the plaintiff's physician may not have ordered a MRI because of its cost. But the defendant may be happy to pay the cost to try to prove that the plaintiff is not as badly hurt as the plaintiff is claiming. The plaintiff may agree to the test hoping to find out more about her condition at the defendant's expense.

■ SCOPE OF EXAMINATION

Courts are pragmatic about the scope of independent medical examinations. They are not inclined to impose specific limitations; instead, they generally defer to the examiners' professional judgment.

Rules 35 does not impose any limit on the amount of time an independent medical examination may take. The examiner may take as much time as the type and scope of the examination reasonably requires. The examiner should not waste the plaintiff's time by making the plaintiff wait either before or during the examination. Nevertheless, some inconveniences are common, and the client should be prepared to be tolerant and accepting of the independent examination procedure.

If the defendant wants more examinations than the plaintiff is willing to undergo, the defendant's remedy is to make a motion and show good cause why additional examinations are necessary. If the plaintiff sustained multiple injuries and has been treated by several specialists, a court is likely to allow the defendant to have two or more specialists covering different fields. The defendant can strengthen the motion by having the first examiner provide an affidavit in which he or she recommends a second examination by a specialist. If a long delay occurs between the independent medical examination and the trial, the defendant may be entitled to a repeat medical examination to prepare for trial, especially if the plaintiff has continued to receive treatment and is claiming a permanent injury.

An independent medical examination may exceed the scope of the plaintiff's claim of injury because the examination also establishes a baseline concerning the plaintiff's condition. A good independent medical report should establish the outside limits of the plaintiff's claim of injury so that if new complaints develop after the examination, those new complaints cannot be attributed to the defendant. Also, the plaintiff could be involved in another accident after the independent examination, in which case the first examination should be very useful in separating the injuries and quantifying any aggravation of the prior injury. For example, the plaintiff's claim against the defendant may be limited to the plaintiff's lower back. Nevertheless, the examination may properly include the plaintiff's legs, upper back, neck, and more. Sometimes the defendant's lawyer arranges for a battery of psychometric tests though the plaintiff is merely claiming a bodily injury. The reason is that many bodily complaints may be caused by a person's mental state, so the plaintiff's mental state must be evaluated. Probably the most common example is the person who has neck pain and occipital headaches that recur daily and do not improve with the passage of time. The symptoms could be due to a physical injury to the musculature of the neck, but tension and anxiety due to stress at work or home may cause the same symptoms.

If a dispute arises over what is reasonably necessary, a court may place limits on the scope of an examination and prescribe the manner in which the physician must conduct the examination. As a practical matter, the plaintiff must signal the need for particular limitations. For example, if the plaintiff is pregnant and should not be subjected to X-rays, she should raise the problem and suggest the limitation. A court may protect the plaintiff from medical tests or procedures that do not comport with the subject of the litigation. For example, if the plaintiff is claiming neck pain and headaches due to an automobile accident, there is probably no reason to require the plaintiff to submit to tests for venereal diseases. A court may impose conditions and limitations to protect the plaintiff's privacy and sensibilities.

The examiner may ask about the plaintiff's medical and accident history. The examiner may ask the same kinds of questions, even searching questions, that a treating physician might ask. However, an independent medical examiner should not prescribe any treatment, and should not make any comment to the patient about the patient's condition, the examiner's findings, or the plaintiff's current treatment regimen. On the other hand, if the examiner concludes that the treating physician has the wrong diagnosis or is providing the wrong treatment, the examiner may say that in the report.

It is perfectly proper for the lawyer and examiner to confer about the examination and case, just as it is proper for the plaintiff's lawyer to meet with the treating physicians to obtain information that the treatment records and consultation reports may not contain.

Court rules have provided for independent examinations for nearly fifty years, and during that time there has been very little evidence of abuse by the examiners. There are probably several reasons for this. The defendants' lawyers generally select highly qualified professionals to conduct independent examinations, because they have to rely upon the examiner to be persuasive. If an examiner were to do anything improper during the examination, that could severely damage the case and harm the examiner's professional reputation. In addition, lawyers and legal assistants prepare plaintiffs for independent examinations by carefully explaining the procedures, the limits on the examinations, and the plaintiffs' right to end an examination if the examiner exceeds the boundaries.

■ INDEPENDENT EXAMINER'S REPORT

Customarily, the independent medical examiner submits a written report to the defendant. The defendant uses the report to evaluate the plaintiff's claim of injury, disability, need for treatment, and so forth. Sometimes the defendant's lawyer confers with the examiner about the plaintiff's condition and matters covered in the report, because the report is ambiguous or raises new questions or did not answer all the questions posed to the examiner. Unfortunately, not all reports are complete in every respect.

Although it is not specified by Rule 35, a competent medical report always contains a recitation of the plaintiff's **past medical history** and a **current medical history** about the present physical or mental condition. A past medical history is a concise description of the patient's prior accidents, injuries, illnesses, and treatment. A current medical history describes the onset of the patient's current problem, including the accident, onset of symptoms, treatment, and improvement or lack of improvement. It has become popular for physicians to prepare their records using the **SOAP** format. *S* stands for *subjective*. Subjective information includes the patient's relevant history and relevant complaints or symptoms. *O* stands for *objective*. Objective information includes the physician's findings from the examination and tests. *A* stands for *assessment*. Assessment information is the physician's diagnosis. *P* stands for *plan*. The physician's plan is the prescription for treatment and observation.

Rule 35 provides that the examiner's report shall contain "the examiner's findings, including results of all tests made, diagnoses and conclusions." A physician's **findings** include whatever the physician noted about the patient's condition, whether normal or abnormal, that relates to the medical condition at issue. A **diagnosis** is the physician's determination about the plaintiff's medical condition. It may be a **working diagnosis** or a **definitive diagnosis.** A working diagnosis is merely the physician's best estimate concerning the patient's condition. It is tentative and subject to change as the physician obtains more information. Nevertheless, it usually gives the physician a basis for beginning treatment. A definitive diagnosis is reasonably certain and is usually the final diagnosis. Rule 35 expects a final diagnosis. A *conclusion,* as used in Rule 35, is the physician's determination about how the medical condition relates to the subject of the litigation. For example, the examining physician may make a definitive diagnosis that the patient has a herniated disk in his lower spine. Rule 35 requires the physician's report to take the next step and describe how the herniated disk affects the patient in terms of pain, physical impairment, and disability. The report should also state whether additional treatment is necessary, and if so, what kind of treatment and for how long.

Exhibits 14.3, 14.4 and 14.5 consist of a typical independent medical examination report and its attachments.

These reports illustrate the types of medical inquiries and considerations involved in independent medical examinations. They also show why parties can develop differences of opinion concerning the medical aspects of personal injury cases. Though the sample reports have been modified by changing names, dates, and places, they are based upon an actual case. The physician who prepared the examination report appreciated the importance of thoroughness and detail. Those qualities lend authority to the physician's opinions.

The independent medical examination report provides the lawyers with information for evaluating the case and preparing for trial. It also serves another valuable function: when the case reaches trial, the independent examiner may base her or his testimony upon the contents of the report.

EXHIBIT 14.3

Independent Medical Examiner's Report

Dear Ms. McKenzie:

On March 4, 1995, I examined this twenty-seven-year-old female whom you so kindly referred for a neurological and psychiatric evaluation.

Family History

The patient's mother is sixty and well. Her father is sixty-two years of age and well. She has two brothers and one sister. Her husband is thirty-four years of age and presently is unemployed. She has one boy, age three. The patient graduated from Eden High School in 1985.

Personal History

This patient denies any serious illnesses. She had a tonsillectomy at the age of five. Her appendix was removed in 1983. In December 1989 the patient had a pyelonephritis and some bladder polyps removed by Dr. Walonick at the Eden Hospital.

Present Illness

The patient was involved in an automobile accident on March 6, 1994. It occurred about 7:00 in the morning at Highway 5 and Mitchell Road. She was driving her car and was struck from the rear. At the time of the impact, she said that her head hit the back of the seat but that nothing happened to her. She was not knocked unconscious and actually did not feel very much. The police came, and information was exchanged. She went on to work. She said she rested in the ladies' room and after an hour went home.

At about 2:00 in the afternoon she saw her family physician, Dr. Ekrem. He examined her but did not take any X-rays. He gave her some Valium and told her to go home, rest, and take a couple of days off work. At that time she said her left leg was aching.

The patient rested at home, and, according to the patient, her neck started to bother her later in the day. Two days later she attempted to go back to work, and a few days after this she developed some soreness in her back. She went back to Dr. Ekrem, who sent her for some physiotherapy on an outpatient basis at the Methodist Hospital. She went there two or three times a week for about five weeks, and kept working off and on. Finally, on March 21, 1994, she was put on medical leave. According to the patient, the physiotherapy did not help.

The patient then went to Jane Zimmerman, a chiropractor in Eden, who took X-rays and adjusted her neck and back. Chiropractor Zimmerman also gave her a neck-and-back brace. Chiropractor Zimmerman sent her to a Dr. James Brandt, a chiropractor, for a consultation sometime in June 1994. Later the patient moved to Crystal, Texas, where she went to Dr. Donna Wahlen, a chiropractor. She took adjustments from Dr. Wahlen, starting out three times a week and now sees the doctor as necessary.

The patient was having some dizzy spells, so she went to a Dr. Malmoud, who apparently is a partner of Dr. Ekrem. He felt that she was possibly having hypotension, but when he examined her, her blood pressure was all right.

The patient was referred to Dr. Anna Schut and Dr. D. L. Anderson. They examined her and gave her physiotherapy in their office, and on two occasions she has been hospitalized. The first time was in April 1994, where she was given in-hospital physiotherapy for two weeks, and rehabilitation for her neck and back. This was at the Eden Hospital. In September 1994 Dr. Anderson put her back in the Eden Hospital, where a myelogram was done. Dr. David Olson, who looked at the myelogram, said she might have a low midline ruptured disk. She was put on an exercise program and given a better back brace, but this did not cure her.

—Continued

—Continued

The patient has also been seen by Dr. Hammond for an insurance examination. About a year ago she went to a doctor in Kellogg Square, who examined her, but she cannot remember his name. She had a social security examination at the university but does not know the doctor's name. In addition, she has been to Dr. Walonick for her kidney problems, at the request of Dr. Anderson. She is still seeing Dr. Anderson about once a month.

The patient was sent to a psychologist, Mr. Stanley Baker, at Clifton Court. He has his wife, Sandy Baker, help him. They talk with the patient, and, according to the patient, they talk about the lawsuit, the attorneys involved, letters that are coming to her. They try to get her to relax. They give her neck massage and put her in unusual positions. According to the patient, she will stand, bent over, for a long period of time, or they may have her stand against the wall or even on her head. She has seen Mr. Baker about ten or twelve times, and she thinks he might be helping her. According to the patient, the Bakers are giving her advice about what to do about the examinations.

The patient has been seen by people from rehabilitation. Two names are Betty Johnson and Maddy Boll. They have told her how to fill out the application blanks for rehabilitation benefits. They have told her she will continue to be paid as long as she earns less money than she earned in the job she had when she was injured. They got her a job at the Spa Petite in Eden, which she has been on for three days. She said she shows the members how to use the equipment, and she is on a running and exercise program with the members of the club. The patient volunteered to me that she will continue to be paid by rehabilitation as long as her compensation from Spa Petite is less than she had when she was working for EMT Electronics.

The patient presently takes only ampicillin for a strep throat, which was prescribed by Dr. Ekrem. If her headaches become too bad, she takes Excedrin or Tylenol 3.

Prior to her employment with EMT Electronics, she did electronic soldering for Ross Shadow. After this, she had a child and at one time worked for Kentucky Fried Chicken preparing food and waiting on tables. According to the patient, she had a cortisone shot in her left hip at one time for bursitis. When she was in the hospital, as well as having a myelogram, she had an electromyogram of her left leg. According to the patient, she does not think she is getting much better. She said all the therapy she has taken has really not helped very much as far as her neck, leg, and back are concerned. She said the doctors might think she is better, but she really is not.

Present Complaints

1. Daily headaches. These are bioccipital and bifrontal. They last a couple of hours and are relieved by Excedrin. The headaches are not associated with any nausea or vomiting and generally come on about noon.

2. Dizzy spells. She gets these approximately once a day. They consist of a light-headedness rather than a vertigo.

3. Some stiffness and discomfort in her neck and shoulders (primarily left). This is brought on by anything, and any type of paperwork or keeping her neck in one position bothers her.

4. Pain in the lower back. This is a stiffness and soreness and is always present. She wears a brace from time to time, particularly when driving or if she is going to sit for a long time.

5. Aching in her left leg, primarily in the thigh or hip region. This is worse in the evening. It is bothered by cold. Coughing and sneezing do not produce pain.

—Continued

—Continued

At this point, the patient has no blurred vision or double vision. She does not have any complaints as far as her chest and abdomen are concerned. She has had no syncope or convulsions. She is sleeping better on a water bed. The patient's appetite is good. She does a lot of exercises but does not play tennis, golf, or any sports. She does a fair amount of walking.

Physical Examination

The patient is five feet five inches tall and weighs 123 pounds. She is well developed and well nourished. Blood pressure is one hundred over seventy, pulse is sixty-six, respirations are eighteen. Teeth and gums are normal. Eardrums are normal. Throat is negative. The chest is clear to auscultation and percussion, and there are no cardiac irregularities or murmurs. The abdomen reveals no masses, or tenderness or scars, except for appendectomy.

Neurological Examination

Cranial Nerves

The patient can smell test odors. The visual acuity is 20/20-2 bilaterally without correction. The visual fields were normal. The ophthalmoscopic examination did not reveal any evidence of any increased intracranial pressure, hemorrhages, or exudates. No optic atrophy. Good pulsation of the veins. The third, fourth, and sixth cranial nerves were normal. The pupils were equal and reacted to light. No nystagmus. No facial asymmetry. No hypesthesia of the face or cornea. Hearing revealed to be normal.

Sensory Functions

The examination of the body to cotton, pinprick pain, and vibration and position sense was normal.

Motor Functions

The patient has a good grip bilaterally, and there is no atrophy, hypertrophy, twitching, or tremor of the musculature.

Body Measurements (in Inches)

Parts	Right	Left
Biceps	$9^{3}/_{4}$	$9^{1}/_{2}$
Forearm	$7^{1}/_{2}$	$7^{1}/_{4}$
Wrist	$5^{3}/_{4}$	$5^{3}/_{4}$
Hand	7	7
Thigh	$14^{1}/_{2}$	$14^{1}/_{2}$
Calf	$12^{1}/_{2}$	$12^{1}/_{2}$

Movements

The patient's neck goes through a full range of motion in all directions without any complaint of pain or evidence of spasm. The patient bends over to ninety degrees and comes about one inch from her toes. Straight-leg–raising tests go to ninety degrees. She is able to walk on her heels and toes and do a deep knee bend.

The patient has some tenderness over the left intertrochanteric bursa, indicating a bursitis in this area.

Coordination

The patient's gait is normal. The finger-to-finger, finger-to-nose, and heel-to-knee tests were done normally.

Reflexes

All the reflexes were present and equal. The toe signs were negative. She does not have any bowel or bladder dysfunction, and speech is normal.

—Continued

■ **EXHIBIT 14.3**

Independent Medical
Examiner's Report,
Continued

—Continued

X-Rays

Roentgenograms were made of the cervical spine in the anteroposterior, lateral, and both oblique directions.

Diagnosis

Negative for evidence of old or recent fracture or other bone or joint abnormality. A normal curvature is seen in flexion and extension.

Conclusion

Negative cervical spine study.

Roentgenograms were made of old or recent fracture. There are no productive or destructive changes and the disk spaces are maintained. The fifth lumbar vertebra is transitional. The sacroiliac joints and hips appear normal.

A few droplets of contrast material are seen in the spinal canal as the result of a previous myelogram.

An IUD is identified and appears to be normal in location.

Electroencephalogram

Basic alpha rhythm is ten per second. This is an awake record with some eye blink artifact, movement, and tension artifact. Some low-voltage and low-voltage fast activity. No evidence of any localized or diffuse spiking, slow waves, or delta activity. No amplitude asymmetry. No seizure discharges of any sort. Photic stimulation did not produce any driving response. Hyperventilation did not produce any buildup or slowing.

Impression

Within normal limits.

Electromyogram

An electromyogram was done by Jane E. Wilson, MD, on March 6, 1995. She found the entire left leg to be normal. A copy of her entire report is included with this letter.

Echoencephalogram

This echoencephalogram demonstrates a normal position for the midline echo complex.

Minnesota Multiphasic Personality Inventory

This was a valid test. There was a marked evaluation on hysteria or conversion reaction. Some mild depression and hypochondriasis were noted. This profile indicated the patient had tension within herself that was being converted to psychosomatic or psychophysiological symptoms. The symptoms undoubtedly have a secondary gain.

Psychological Examination

This patient was evaluated by Patrick Noble, PhD, Licensed Consulting Psychologist, on March 7, 1995. A copy of his entire report is included with this letter. His summary is as follows:

> The testing reveals an immature, dependent person who has a basic personality that is in keeping with an individual who could easily siphon off her psychological conflicts into physiological manifestations. This type of personality develops over the years and is closely related to the fact that she apparently lived in a situation where she felt she was being controlled by a rather overpowering mother figure. Thus, her only out is to develop symptomatology to blame her psychological difficulties onto some medical problem.

—Continued

—Continued

Conclusions

If one considers the mechanism of the accident, it is very difficult to imagine that really very much did occur to this patient. She had no symptoms at the time of the accident, and the back pain did not come on for several days. She could have had a very minimal strain of her neck, but one would expect that this would have disappeared with time. She has been overexamined and overtreated, and has had a tremendous number of chiropractic appointments. She has been going from doctor to doctor in an attempt to be cured, and this is not possible because 95 percent of her symptoms are psychological in nature. She has recently returned to work, as a demonstrator at the Spa Petite. The patient's complaints are of headaches, light-headedness, pain in the neck and both shoulders, lower-back pain, and aching in her left leg.

The physical examination is entirely normal for any abnormality as a result of this accident.

A complete neurological examination is negative. She does have bursitis in the left intertrochanteric bursa, and this is probably producing discomfort in the left leg. This is a degenerative affair and not related to the accident. She has had an injection of hydrocortisone in this area in the past.

X-rays of the cervical spine were normal. An X-ray of the lumbosacral spine was negative. A few droplets of contrast material were seen in the spinal canal, which was the result of a previous myelogram.

The electroencephalogram was normal.

The echoencephalogram was normal.

An electromyogram of the left leg was entirely normal.

The Minnesota Multiphasic Personality Inventory shows definite evidence of a conversion reaction with **secondary gain.** This secondary gain is obviously that the patient does not have to go to work, but can stay home and receive more compensation than she would get if she were working. In this respect a compensation neurosis is present.

The psychological testing showed

> an immature, dependent person who has a basic personality that is in keeping with an individual who could easily siphon off her psychological conflicts into physiological manifestations. This type of personality develops over the years and is closely related to the fact that she apparently lived in a situation where she felt she was being controlled by an overpowering mother figure. Thus, her only out is to develop symptomatology to blame her psychological difficulties onto some medical problem.

A great number of the patient's symptoms are very close to consciousness. She has been told that a lot of her symptoms are based on tension and that they are not organic in character. A lot of this is very close to being a conscious mechanism, particularly with her desire not to return to work and to enjoy life at home as long as she can obtain financial rewards. The financial reward is paramount in her mind. This mechanism is so close to consciousness that it is really not far from malingering. These mechanisms have been investigated by psychologists who have treated her, and have been disregarded by her physicians and chiropractors. I find no evidence, from a clinical standpoint, of a herniated lumbar intervertebral disk. There is no weakness, reflex disturbance, or atrophy, and movements are excellent. The pain, I believe, is a result of the bursitis, which is not attributable to the accident.

Sincerely yours,

Adam Goldes, MD

■ EXHIBIT 14.4

Attached
Electromyography
Report

ELECTROMYOGRAPHY REPORT

PATIENT: Mrs. Elizabeth Diersen

DATE: March 6, 1995

Nerve Conduction Studies

Nerve	Motor Conduction Velocity	Distal Motor Latency	Motor Response Amplitude
Left peroneal	46.5 meters/second	5.0 milliseconds	5.0 millivolts

Left Lower Extremity Needle Electrode Studies

Muscle	Insertional Activity	Motor Unit Activity
Iliopsoas	Normal	Normal
Rectus femoris	Normal	Normal
Vastus lateralis	Normal	Normal
Vastus medialis	Normal	Normal
Tibialis anterior	Normal	Normal
Extensor digitorum longus	Normal	Normal
Peroneus	Normal	Normal
Medial gastrocnemius	Normal	Normal for strength of contraction
Soleus	Normal	Normal
Gluteus maximus	Normal	Normal
Lumbar paraspinal	Normal	Normal

Summary

The motor conduction velocity, distal motor latency, and action potential are normal in the left peroneal nerve.

The needle electrode examinations reveal no significant variation from normal.

Impression

The above electromyographic studies are within normal limits.

Jane E. Wilson, MD

He or she may not even remember the plaintiff and the examination by that time. The physician commonly reads the report almost verbatim. A skilled defense lawyer can establish a dialogue with the physician although the physician is primarily reading from the report.

■ RIGHT TO AN INDEPENDENT EXAMINER'S REPORT

The plaintiff is entitled to a written report that specifies the independent medical examiner's findings, test results, diagnoses, and conclusions. The plaintiff must request the report through the defendant, not directly from the examiner. Indeed, the plaintiff should not have any contact with the examiner, except for the examination itself. The defendant must arrange with the examiner to obtain the report for the plaintiff. The lawyer who arranged for the examination may have some input to make sure that the

PSYCHOLOGICAL EVALUATION

RE: Elizabeth Diersen

TESTS ADMINISTERED: Hillside Short Form of the Weschler
Belleview Examination
Rorschach
Kahn Test of Symbol Arrangement
Sentence Completion

This lady indicates that she was in an accident 4-6-94. She states she was not unconscious and was not hospitalized, and her only symptom was headache. At the present time she states her symptoms are "headaches and dizziness, left leg aches, neck and lower-back aches." Currently she is on no medication except Tylenol 3 for headaches. In the past she apparently has had various medications. She states she does not smoke, drinks occasionally, and does not use drugs. She indicates she started a job last week, working at a health club. In terms of social activity, she states they don't do much because it is too expensive and they tend to sit around home and watch TV, although they do some camping.

The patient states she comes from a family of four children, where she is the oldest. Her father is a truck driver, and her mother is a waitress. She has been married four years. Her husband currently is unemployed and has worked for the Milwaukee Railroad in the past and has been laid off for about eight or nine weeks. There is one child of this marriage, a boy age three. The patient states she completed high school. She indicates she has had no serious illnesses except for appendicitis resulting in an appendectomy. She has no history of any other serious accidents.

The patient is a rather stoic-faced individual who has very little expression on her face. Speech is coherent, relevant, and under good control and shows no loose associations. Affective responses are felt to be somewhat flat at this time, and one gets the impression she may have some feelings of depression. There are no evidences of psychotic ideation. The patient is considered to be of average intelligence, is oriented in contact, and shows good comprehension, good attention span, and no loss of recent or remote memory.

This patient has been tested previously. The evaluation done in March 1989 indicated she was immature and had some self-esteem problems, with a diagnosis as an immature woman in stress with a self-esteem issue, unexpressed anger, and some sadness in relationship to her heterosexual life.

Testing at this time reveals a woman of average intelligence with a prorated IQ of 109. She continues to show the same type of immaturity and dependency that she apparently showed when she was tested previously. It would appear that she has been unsuccessful in separating from parental figures in the past and has more or less been living in a situation where the mother figure assumed a very domineering and controlling role. As a result of this, the patient has developed a very passive, dependent, and somewhat negativistic approach in dealing with her interpersonal life. She has problems also in attaining an adult heterosexual relationship and apparently will have some marital problems if this is not cleared up in the near future. The unresolved hostile feelings are still seen, although they may very well relate to her resentments over how she has been treated in the past. The testing also indicates that she more than likely tends to siphon off her emotional problems into this accident as a way of attempting to resolve her psychological problems. It may also very well be, even at the present time, that her financial conditions intensified her symptomatology, for she knows no other way of coping with the current changes except to maintain her symptomatology.

—Continued

■ **EXHIBIT 14.5**
Attached Psychological Evaluation

■ **EXHIBIT 14.5**

Attached Psychological
Evaluation, *Continued*

—Continued

In summary, the testing continues to reveal an immature, dependent person who has a basic personality that is in keeping with an individual who could easily siphon off her psychological conflicts into physiological manifestations. This type of personality develops over the years and is closely related to the fact that she apparently lived in a situation where she felt she was being controlled by a rather overpowering mother figure. Thus, her only out is to develop symptomatology to blame her psychological difficulties onto some medical problem.

> Patrick Noble, PhD
> Licensed Consulting Psychologist

report comports with the requirements of Rule 35 and otherwise meets the parties' needs. After all, physicians are not expected to know what is required by the Federal Rules of Civil Procedure. If a fee is charged for the report, the defendant must pay it.

Usually, the defendant simply sends to the plaintiff a copy of the report the examiner provided to the defendant. However, Rule 35 allows the defendant to order a separate report for the plaintiff. Rule 35 requires the examiner's report to be complete and entirely candid. It is best if the parties work from the same report. The independent examiner is subject to cross-examination from the report, and the cross-examination may cover matters that the examiner omitted from the report.

Generally, the defendant arranges with the physician, even before the examination, to provide a written report on the independent examination. Consequently, there is seldom any problem about obtaining a report for the plaintiff. If the independent examiner fails or refuses to submit a report, the defendant can do very little. If necessary, the defendant could subpoena her or his own expert witness for a deposition.

If the examiner refuses to produce a report to the plaintiff as provided by Rule 35, the plaintiff may subpoena the examiner to appear for a deposition. That is no problem for the plaintiff. A court would probably require the defendant to pay the costs the plaintiff incurred in taking the deposition. As an alternative, the plaintiff may simply move the court to exclude the examiner from testifying at the trial. That is probably the simpler solution and is usually the most effective for the plaintiff. After all, if the plaintiff takes the examiner's deposition, the court has no reason to prevent the defendant from having the benefit of whatever the expert may have to say.

Since an independent examiner is considered an expert witness, the party presenting him or her may be compelled under Rule 26 to reveal the substance of the expert's testimony. Rules 26 and 35 are not exclusive of each other. The parties may agree between themselves to use another method of discovery to obtain medical reports, hospital records, and medical opinions. Usually, the procedures outlined by the Rules work well, and litigants apply them without difficulty.

■ OBLIGATION TO PROVIDE TREATING PHYSICIANS' REPORTS

When the plaintiff demands a copy of the independent medical examination report, under federal rules, he or she becomes obligated to provide the defendant's lawyer with copies of all reports she or he has obtained from treating physicians. The plaintiff's failure to comply would preclude the treating physicians from testifying. In most jurisdictions, however, the plaintiff's medical records become available to the defendants when the plaintiff commences the action, because commencement of the action automatically waives the plaintiff's medical privilege.

The plaintiff's lawyer must obtain the plaintiff's records to give to the defendant if the lawyer does not already have them. If the treating physician charges the plaintiff for reproducing the records, that expense cannot be passed on to the defendant—just as the defendant cannot charge the plaintiff for obtaining a copy of the independent examination report. A plaintiff remains under a continuing obligation to produce new reports as she or he continues to receive treatment.

The court has authority to require either party to pay the bill for a treating physician's report. If the plaintiff does not want the treating physician's report and does not intend to call that physician as his or her own witness at trial, the court may require the defendant to pay the cost of having the report prepared. Another problem is presented if the physician refuses to render a report until the plaintiff pays the physician's bill for providing medical treatment. Occasionally, a plaintiff finds himself or herself unable to pay for medical expenses until the litigation concludes.

On occasion, a party may receive treatment from a physician who does not want to be bothered by preparing a report summarizing his or her findings and conclusion. This creates a problem for both sides. The physician is not a party to the action and cannot be punished by the court. Under the circumstances, either party could probably secure the physician's deposition. The party who wants the deposition may compel the physician to attend by serving a subpoena upon him or her. If a court orders the reluctant physician to appear and testify in a deposition because he or she refused to prepare a report, the physician may elect to prepare the errant report.

■ PREPARING A CLIENT FOR AN INDEPENDENT EXAMINATION

A paralegal can have a significant role in arranging for Rule 35 independent examinations, whether representing plaintiffs or defendants. When representing the defendant, the paralegal may arrange for the plaintiff's examination. She or he may select the examiner; establish the criteria for the examination; negotiate the terms and conditions under which the examiner will take the assignment; and negotiate with the plaintiff's lawyer for mutually satisfactory stipulations concerning the time, place, scope, and manner for conducting the examination. The paralegal may schedule the examination; collect and assemble the documents that the examiner needs in order to conduct the examination; and prepare the letter to the examiner that allows him or her to focus on the particular problems in the case. The paralegal may prepare a stipulation for the plaintiff's lawyer that confirms the terms, conditions, and scope of the examination, or sometimes a mere letter will suffice. When the paralegal receives the examiner's report, he or she may tell the client the results of the independent examination and its value to the case. If the plaintiff requests a report, the paralegal may handle those arrangements as well. When necessary, the paralegal should be able to prepare the motion and supporting documents necessary to compel an independent medical examination. The paralegal should also be able to prepare an objection to examination with supporting affidavits.

The paralegal serves the client and the legal system by fully describing for the client the purpose, scope, and manner of the independent examination so that the client is not unduly nervous about going through it. Presumably, when the law firm accepted the client's case, the client was told that the defendant would likely request an independent examination. That is the best time to give the client an overview of procedures, including those for depositions, interrogatories, and independent examinations. The paralegal should make sure the client understands what things she or he need not reveal to the examiner, such as the client's conversations with the paralegal, the lawyer, or the client's spouse. However, the independent examination is part of the discovery process, and it is not the paralegal's job to keep the examiner from discovering facts that are duly discoverable. The paralegal must reassure the client that the examination is routine for this type of case.

Letter of Confirmation to the Client

The paralegal should confirm the examination arrangements with a letter to the client that provides an overview. Most clients appreciate having information and instructions in a letter that they can keep for reference. The letter could be similar to the one in exhibit 14.6.

Meeting with the Client

When the paralegal meets with the client, he or she should again assure the client that the examiner will be professional and do nothing to hurt the client. The paralegal should describe and explain all the tests the examiner is likely to conduct. Some excellent books describe clinical examinations and the tests physicians commonly use to evaluate patients. Some continuing legal education programs explain orthopedic, neurological, and chiropractic examinations and demonstrate many of the tests used. Some law firms have videotapes that demonstrate the tests. Being forewarned, the client should have less anxiety about the examiner and the purpose for the examination.

The paralegal should tell the client to treat the examiner with respect and to cooperate throughout the examination. She or he should tell the client that the examination really begins from the moment the client enters the physician's office, because at the very outset, the physician may observe how the client walks, sits, and moves.

Some tests may be repeated during the examination to see whether the client's responses are consistent. If they are not consistent, there is reason to believe the client has tried to deceive the examiner. The paralegal should help the client to avoid inconsistent responses and statements by cautioning the client against exaggerating or minimizing symptoms and complaints.

The client should try hard not to let the examiner upset him or her. A client who exhibits a positive attitude while undergoing an independent examination makes a favorable impression on the examiner and on the defendant's lawyer. That can only benefit the client's case. If the examiner senses any lack of candor, that will probably be reflected in the examination

Dear [client]:

As we anticipated, the defendant's lawyer has made a demand for an independent medical examination. The law allows the defendant to choose a licensed [type of practitioner, such as medical doctor, chiropractor, psychologist] to examine you at a time and place that is reasonably convenient for you. Ordinarily the defendant is entitled to only one examination, but sometimes circumstances require an additional examination. At this point the defendant is only asking for the one examination. The examination is now scheduled for [date] at [time].

The defendant's purpose for requesting the examination is to determine the nature and extent of your injuries and the effect your injuries are having upon you. The examiner will provide the defendant with evidence that the defendant will use to evaluate your claim and will use at trial if the case cannot be settled.

The examiner is not permitted to conduct any tests that pose a risk to you. You are not required to submit to any tests that would be painful. The examiner is a licensed professional. She [or he] will treat you with respect and consideration.

We have to assume that the examiner selected by the defendant will look for weaknesses in our claim. We feel that it is important for you to understand how the examination will be conducted and what the examiner is likely to do during the examination. We want to explain to you your rights so that you can guard against any inadvertent intrusions into your privacy. Therefore, if you will telephone me, we can arrange to meet to prepare for the examination.

Please do not feel concerned about the defendant's request for the examination. It does not mean the defendant is aggressively contesting your injury claim. Indeed, it means the defendant is taking your claim seriously and wants to know more about it. We will be entitled to obtain a complete report of the examination. The person who conducts the examination must prepare the report. Usually the report helps both parties to evaluate the case and will help settlement negotiations.

I look forward to hearing from you soon.

Very truly yours,

[Paralegal]

■ **EXHIBIT 14.6**

Letter to Client, Confirming Independent Medical Examination Arrangements

report. The paralegal should urge the client to be on time and to be patient if the examiner is a little late or seems to be a little slow.

The paralegal should prepare the client to accurately relate her or his medical history and accident history. The paralegal should preview the important items in the client's history and symptomatology, that is, collection of symptoms.

The paralegal should explain that if the examiner goes beyond the scope of what is reasonably necessary, the client has the right to refuse the test. For example, in the typical bodily injury case, a pelvic examination is not necessary. If the examiner proposes to do a pelvic examination, the client should know that it is all right to say no.

On occasion, plaintiffs take diaries and notes to help answer the examiner's questions. No law prohibits doing so, but juries often react negatively to a plaintiff's apparent need for notes. Furthermore, the examiner will probably mention any diary in her or his report, and then the defense lawyer will want to look at the diary to see what else might be in it. Diaries and notes tend to complicate the case for the plaintiff, rather than help.

The paralegal should prepare the client to answer questions such as the following:

Pain

When did the pain start?

Can you relate the onset of the pain to an incident, activity, or time period?

Did the pain begin after some activity?

Have you experienced this same type of pain before?

Has the pain increased in severity?

Has the pain increased in frequency?

Has the pain increased in the affected area?

At what time of the day is the pain the worst?

What activity increases the pain?

What movements increase the pain?

Does any activity reduce the pain?

Is the pain continuous, or does it come and go?

Does the intensity of the pain fluctuate?

What causes the pain to increase? coughing? sneezing? bowel movements? walking? standing? sitting? deep breathing?

Where is the pain located?

Does the pain radiate to another part of your body? If so, what route does the pain take?

What medications help?

What medications do not help?

Is the pain improving with the passage of time?

Activities

How are your daily living activities affected?

How are your job activities affected?

Is there anything that you now cannot do at all?

What things can you do but suffer pain while doing them?

What things can you do but suffer pain afterward because you did them?

What activities had you given up but now resumed?

It may help the client to know that everyone has a different pain threshold. People seem to feel pain differently. Nevertheless, most physicians try to grade pain on a scale of 1 through 5. The scale may be as follows:

1. minimal

2. mild or uncomfortable

3. moderate or distressing

4. severe or horrible

5. excruciating

The paralegal should help the client to fully describe his or her condition. For instance, it may be a good idea to supply groups of adjectives that help to describe pain:

Flickering	Sharp	Hot	Tender	Punishing	Tight
Quivering	Cutting	Burning	Taut	Grueling	Numb
Pulsing	Lacerating	Scalding	Splitting	Cruel	Drawing
Throbbing		Searing		Vicious	Squeezing
Beating	Pinching		Tiring	Killing	Tearing
Pounding	Pressing	Tingling	Exhausting		
	Gnawing	Itching	Sickening	Annoying	Cool
Jumping	Cramping	Smarting	Suffocating	Troublesome	Cold
Flashing	Crushing	Stinging		Miserable	Freezing
Shooting			Fearful	Intense	
	Tugging	Dull	Frightful	Unbearable	Nagging
Pricking	Pulling	Sore	Terrifying		Nauseating
Boring	Wrenching	Hurting		Spreading	Agonizing
Drilling		Aching	Wretched	Radiating	Dreadful
Stabbing		Heavy	Blinding	Penetrating	Torturing
				Piercing	

A physician may choose a pain medication based upon his or her assessment of the grade and type of pain.

SUMMARY

A party may require another party to submit to an independent medical examination only if the party to be examined has put his or her physical, mental, or blood condition in issue and the moving party can show good cause for the examination.

Most of the time the parties agree to the time, place, and terms of an independent medical examination without having to obtain a court order. A court may require only a party to the lawsuit, or someone who is directly under the control of a party, to undergo a Rule 35 independent medical examination. An employer cannot be compelled to produce an employee for an independent medical examination.

In most states the plaintiff waives her or his medical privilege, at least to some extent, when the plaintiff commences an action to recover money damages for personal injuries. The extent of the waiver varies from state to state. At a minimum, the plaintiff's medical records and reports become available.

If a plaintiff refuses to submit to a medical examination in spite of a court order finding that good cause has been shown, the court has two options: the court may dismiss the plaintiff's lawsuit, or the court may resolve the disputed medical facts against the plaintiff. If the defendant is the disobedient party, the court may strike (disallow) his or her answer and find the defendant in default. If a party is in default, judgment may be entered against him or her without having a trial.

A party need not submit to medical tests that are painful or that subject the patient to some risk of harm. A court may not hold a party in contempt of court for refusing to submit to an independent medical examination.

A defendant's lawyer may elect to rely upon the plaintiff's medical records and reports to evaluate the plaintiff's case, especially if the treating physician has a reputation for being capable, objective, and candid. However, if the lawyer does not have confidence in the accuracy, completeness, or authority of the treating physician's records and reports, the lawyer should arrange for an independent medical examination. The treating physician may have obtained an inadequate or erroneous medical history or an incomplete or erroneous accident history. The findings recorded by the treating physician may be inconsistent with the plaintiff's subjective complaints. The treating physician may not have sufficient expertise in the area. Independent medical examinations are also appropriate when the plaintiff does not have a treating physician and both parties want to make sure there is no hidden or latent injury before entering into a final settlement. Occasionally, the defendant may suspect some collaboration between the patient and treating doctor, and thus desire an independent evaluation. Suspected "collaboration" is rarely outright falsification; usually it is a matter of exaggerating and minimizing. Sometimes the defendant's lawyer has more detailed information about the accident history and the plaintiff's conduct following the accident than the treating physician.

A treating physician is not expected to cross-examine the patient concerning the patient's accident history, medical history, or symptoms. A treating physician *is* expected to obtain the information he or she needs to make an accurate diagnosis and to prescribe the proper treatment. Consequently, a patient who tries to fabricate a claim or embellish a claim may easily mislead a treating physician. A treating physician does not have any responsibility to prove or establish a patient's claim. Although a physician may be partial toward her patient, a physician is not expected to be an advocate. There is a difference.

The lawyer who retains an independent medical examiner needs a report that he or she can rely upon to evaluate the case. A lawyer cannot properly evaluate the case if the independent examiner made the wrong analysis or reached wrong conclusions. A report that is conservative to the point that it distorts the patient's condition or prognosis may cause the defendant's lawyer to misevaluate the claim.

An independent examiner may be expected to be more skeptical about the plaintiff's accident history, prior medical history, subjective complaints, and symptoms than is a treating physician. The independent examiner is expected to look for inconsistencies between the symptoms, symptoms and history, and symptoms and findings. The examiner also looks for medical improbabilities, such as a claim of permanent injury where there are no objective findings.

The lawyer relies upon the independent examiner to understand the medical problems and their relationship to the lawsuit. The physician must be willing to prepare a comprehensive report that the defendant can use to evaluate the case. In addition, the defendant must rely upon the physician to substantiate the report by testifying at trial when necessary. The physician must be able to explain the findings, diagnoses, and prognosis in the report and at trial.

The defendant must schedule the examination for a time and place that are convenient for the examiner and for the plaintiff. The defendant must give the plaintiff sufficient notice to prepare for the examination.

Only if there are unusual circumstances will a court permit someone to attend the examination of an adult. However, many courts have authorized either party to make an audiotape recording of the examination.

A party who schedules an independent medical examination should send a letter to the examiner confirming the arrangements for the examination. Paralegals are often asked to prepare this type of letter to the independent examiner. The letter should fully inform the examiner about relevant details of the accident, the nature of all the plaintiff's complaints, type of treatment received, and the treating physician's diagnoses and prognosis. The letter should include copies of the treating physician's reports and records and any special instructions for obtaining important background information. The letter should provide a guide for taking the patient's history to make sure no critical facts are omitted. The letter gives the examiner information that he or she can use to focus the examination and give special attention to any unique problems, such as inconsistencies in the medical records. However, the examiner must base the report upon the history of the plaintiff gives to the examiner and the examiner's own findings, not the information supplied by the paralegal or lawyer. The report should indicate whether the examiner believes that additional examinations are necessary.

An independent medical examiner needs to determine the nature, extent, and consequences of the plaintiff's abnormal physical or mental condition. To do this, the physician must consider the plaintiff's past medical history, current medical history, subjective complaints, and findings. The process requires the examiner to compare the plaintiff's various statements about her or his history, symptoms and complaints to determine whether they have been consistent and whether the plaintiff has been consistent in their reporting. The examiner must try to determine whether the subjective conditions are corroborated by objective medical findings.

The results of the treating physician's tests ordinarily are available to all of the parties from the patient's medical-hospital records. Usually the tests and results are objective and need not be repeated. Even when physicians differ in the interpretation of tests, the raw data is usually available to both sides to review and evaluate. Some of the tests commonly used for diagnosing injuries include: ordinary X-rays; computerized tomography (CT scans); magnetic resonance imaging (MRI scans); electromyograms (EMG); electroencephalograms (EEG); myelograms; angiograms; psychometric tests; discograms; reflex tests; range of motion tests; and skin sensory tests.

Rule 35 does not impose any limit on the amount of time that an independent medical examination may take. The examiner may take as much time as the type and scope of the examination reasonably require. If the defendant wants more examinations than the plaintiff is willing to undergo, the defendant's remedy is to make a motion and show good cause why additional examinations are necessary.

A court will not order the plaintiff to submit to risky tests or tests that induce significant pain. Courts do not require plaintiffs to submit to invasive testing, such as laparoscopy or arthroscopy. However, courts routinely require plaintiffs to submit to electromyograms to test muscle and nerve function. Courts order plaintiffs to undergo electroencephalography to test electrical activity of the brain. Both tests require insertion of small needles into the patient's skin. Courts do not allow the defendant to cross-examine the plaintiff about his or her refusal to submit to risky or painful tests. On the other hand, the defendant's lawyer is allowed to cross-examine the treating physicians about the availability of the tests to help make a definitive diagnosis. If necessary, the treating physician can explain why he or she has not recommended certain tests. If the plaintiff's own treating physician recommended the tests for aiding in treatment, the jury can decide why the plaintiff declined. Courts are inclined to defer to the examiner's professional judgment whether tests are necessary and justifiable. A paralegal should prepare the client to be tolerant and accepting of the independent examination procedure.

An independent medical examination may exceed the scope of the plaintiff's claim of injury because the examination also establishes a baseline concerning the plaintiff's condition. A good independent medical report should establish the outside limits of the plaintiff's claim of injury so that if new complaints develop after the examination, those new complaints cannot be attributed to the defendant. Also, the plaintiff could be involved in another accident after the independent examination, in which case the first examination should be very useful in separating the injuries and quantifying any aggravation of the prior injury.

The plaintiff is entitled to a written report that specifies the examiner's findings, test results, diagnoses, and conclusions. The plaintiff must request a report through the defendant, not directly from the examiner. If the independent examiner fails or refuses to submit a report to the defendant who ordered the examination, the defendant can do very little. If necessary, the defendant could subpoena his or her own expert witness for a deposition. If the examiner refuses to produce a report to the plaintiff as provided by Rule 35, the plaintiff may subpoena the examiner to appear for a deposition. That is no problem for the plaintiff. A court would probably require the defendant to pay the costs the plaintiff incurred in taking the deposition. As an alternative, the plaintiff may simply move the court to exclude the examiner from testifying at the trial. That is probably the simpler solution and is usually the most effective for the plaintiff. After all, if the plaintiff takes the examiner's deposition, the court has no reason to prevent the defendant from having the benefit of whatever the expert may have to say.

By demanding a copy of the independent medical examination report, the plaintiff becomes obligated to provide the defendant's lawyer with copies of all the treating physicians' reports concerning the condition in issue. The plaintiff's failure to produce the reports precludes the plaintiff from having the treating physician(s) testify. In most state courts, however, the plaintiff's medical records become available to the defendants when the plaintiff commences the action. Usually, the federal district court will adopt procedures that are consistent with the state court procedures when not in direct conflict with federal law.

The plaintiff's lawyer must obtain the plaintiff's records to give to the defendant if the lawyer does not already have the records. If the treating physician charges the plaintiff, his or her patient, for reproducing the records, that expense cannot be passed on to the defendant, just as the defendant cannot charge the plaintiff for obtaining a copy of the independent examination report. The plaintiff remains under a continuing obligation to produce new reports as the plaintiff continues to receive treatment.

If a party receives treatment from a physician who does not want to be bothered by preparing a report that summarizes his or her findings and conclusion, the party who wants the information may take the reluctant physician's deposition. If an independent examiner refuses to submit a report to the defendant who ordered the examination, there is very little the defendant can do about it. If necessary, the defendant could subpoena his or her own expert witness for a deposition. If the defendant refuses to produce a report to the plaintiff as provided by Rule 35, the plaintiff may subpoena the independent examiner to appear for a deposition. As an alternative, the plaintiff may simply move the court to preclude the examiner from testifying at the trial. That is probably the simpler solution and, usually, the most effective for the plaintiff. After all, if the plaintiff takes the examiner's deposition, there would be no reason for the court to prevent the defendant from having the benefit of whatever the expert may have to say in the deposition. An independent examiner is considered an expert witness. A party who retains an expert may be compelled under Rule 26 to reveal the substance of the expert's testimony. Rules 26 and 35 are not entirely exclusive of each other. Parties may agree between themselves to other methods of discovery to obtain medical reports, hospital records, and medical opinions.

Paralegals have a significant role in arranging for Rule 35 independent examinations, whether representing plaintiffs or defendants. They may arrange for the plaintiff's examination; select the examiner; establish the criteria for the examination; negotiate the terms and conditions under which the examiner will accept the assignment; and negotiate with the other lawyer for a mutually satisfactory time, place, scope and manner for conducting the examination. A paralegal may schedule the examination, collect and assemble the documents that the examiner needs to conduct the examination, and prepare the letter to the examiner that allows him or her to focus on the particular problems in the case. A paralegal may prepare a letter or stipulation to confirm the terms, conditions and scope of the examination. A paralegal may summarize the examiner's report for the client. When a motion is necessary, a paralegal should be able to prepare the motion and supporting documents necessary to compel or resist an independent medical examination. Arrangements for a client's medical examination should be confirmed by letter. Most clients appreciate receiving their instructions in a letter they can keep for reference.

KEY TERMS

good cause	invasive testing
soft tissue injuries	past medical history
secondary gain	current medical history
motion to compel an examination	SOAP
objection to examination	findings
subjective complaint	diagnosis
subjective symptoms	working diagnosis
objective medical findings	definitive diagnosis

REVIEW QUESTIONS

1. Can the defendant move the court for an order requiring the plaintiff to submit to an independent examination to be conducted by a doctor of chiropractic?

2. How many independent medical examinations may a party request?

3. What information must the independent examiner include in her or his report?

4. Does a party have a right to take the deposition of the physician who conducted an independent medical examination on him or her?

5. Should you instruct your client to avoid volunteering information to the independent examiner? Why or why not?

6. Is it ethical to describe to the client what medical tests the independent examiner is likely to perform and the reasons for those tests?

7. What is the consequence of the plaintiff's request for a copy of the independent medical examiner's report?

8. Is the plaintiff required to pay for a copy of the independent medical examination report prepared by the defendant's examiner?

9. May the plaintiff's lawyer attend an independent medical examination conducted by the defendant's doctor?

10. May the plaintiff tape-record the independent medical examination that he or she is ordered to undergo?

11. What remedy does the defendant have if the plaintiff refuses to submit to an independent medical examination ordered by the court?

CHAPTER

15

INSPECTION OF PROPERTY, DOCUMENTS, AND THINGS

OUTLINE

Demand for Inspection

Written Response to Demand for Inspection

Limitations on Inspections

SUMMARY

KEY TERMS

REVIEW QUESTIONS

A premise of the Federal Rules of Civil Procedure is that the parties must have equal access to the evidence. Sometimes parties need access to property that another party owns or controls, because that property is evidence or contains evidence. The property in question may be **real property,** which includes land, structures on the land, and fixtures, or **personal property,** which is anything that is not real property, such as documents, business records, vehicles, instrumentalities, recordings, and witness statements. The Rules describe *documents* as including writings, drawings, graphs, charts, photographs, phonograph records, and other data compilations from which information can be obtained. The scope of the Rules is so broad that the term *things* is used to identify all the forms of property that are subject to inspection, testing, measuring, photographing, and copying.

Rule 34 provides a procedure by which a party may obtain access to any property that is in the custody or under control of another party. The property must be or contain evidence relevant to the litigation, or the inspection must be calculated to lead to the discovery of admissible evidence. Rule 26(b) determines the scope of relevancy for the inspection of property, the same as it does for other discovery procedures. A tangible item is relevant evidence if it is capable of proving a disputed fact or tends to prove the fact.

Rule 34 does not provide access to property owned or controlled by a person who is not a party. A court may order a party to produce property for inspection only if the party owns the property or has legal possession of it. In other words, the property must be subject to the party's control. Tenants and lessees do not own the property they possess, but they do have control of it. As a party to a lawsuit, a tenant or lessee could be required to produce the leased property for inspection.

An owner or possessor of property may have many reasons for being reluctant to allow another person to have access to the property. A possessor may have a legitimate fear that the other person might damage it or lose it or change it in some manner. Or the possessor may simply want to keep other parties from having equal access to the evidence.

Sometimes the parties' needs and concerns raise difficult problems for the courts to balance. A court must balance the parties' needs. Rule 34 attempts to provide that balance and keep the procedure fair and inexpensive. Rule 34 operates with very little court involvement. For example, unlike the party who wants to see another party's report on an independent medical examination, the party who wants to inspect another party's property does not have to make a motion and show good cause as a prerequisite.

A legal assistant may handle the arrangements on behalf of the party who demands the inspection (the proponent) or for the party who has custody of the property (the respondent).

■ DEMAND FOR INSPECTION

A written **demand for inspection** may be made upon a party as soon as that party appears in the case. Therefore, the defendant could serve a demand for inspection on the plaintiff immediately after receiving the complaint. The plaintiff could serve a demand for inspection on the defendant as soon as the defendant serves the answer. A paralegal may prepare and serve the demand for inspection, but a lawyer must sign it.

Elements

The demand must identify the property to be inspected with "reasonable particularity" (clearly). It should state the time and place of the proposed inspection, and describe the scope and proposed terms of the inspection.

Description of Property. Rule 34 does not require the demand for inspection to use legal descriptions, serial numbers, or precise names or locations to identify the property. The demand may describe the property generically or by category. However, it must not be so broad or vague as to be a mere "fishing expedition." For example, a demand for inspection is objectionable if it merely says, "Produce for inspection and copying all the documents upon which you base your claim." A demand for inspection could properly state, "Produce for inspection and copying all your payroll records for the year 1995." If a party has a question about the existence or identity of property he or she thinks ought to be inspected, the party should serve interrogatories or take depositions to identify the property, its location, its owner, and custodian.

Rule 34 places the burden upon the proponent to make the designation clear so that the respondent knows what property the proponent wants to inspect. If a dispute develops over whether the respondent has produced the property specified in the demand for inspection, the burden lies with the proponent to persuade the court that the request did specify or include the property in question.

Time and Place. The proponent should choose the time and place for the inspection on the basis of what is practical and most convenient for everyone. For instance, if the inspection involves only a few documents, it should be conducted at the office of the lawyer who represents the respondent or at the respondent's address. On the other hand, if the property is a large machine, the inspection should be conducted at the place where the machine is regularly used or stored. If the inspection requires testing that can only be done in a laboratory, the laboratory must be designated in the demand, and it would be appropriate to name the scientist or engineer retained to conduct the tests. The purpose of the inspection may affect the timing of the inspection. For example, if the purpose is to photograph the interior of a manufacturing facility, it may be preferable to schedule the inspection after regular business hours.

Manner of Inspection. A demand for inspection must describe the manner of inspection, which includes the purpose and scope of the inspection. The proponent must describe what he or she intends to do with the property during the inspection. An inspection may be as simple as just looking at the property or measuring it or photographing it. Most inspections are conducted to photocopy documents.

The generality of Rule 34 encourages parties to find the method and manner of inspection that is the most convenient for all persons concerned. Consequently, parties commonly request other parties to produce specified documents not by going through an inspection meeting, but simply by mailing copies of the documents to the requesting party. The proponent may receive more documents than he or she would have selected at a formal inspection, but the savings in time may be worth the cost of some extra copies. This approach is particularly helpful when the documents are all on microfilm, which is very tiring to review. Customarily, the proponent agrees to pay the reasonable cost of having copies made. Before making the copies, the parties should be sure they have a meeting of minds concerning the probable quantity and costs.

If the inspection involves a large quantity of business documents, it is customarily conducted at the place of business where the documents are used. The respondent must produce business records in the same form and condition as they are used in the respondent's business. Rule 34 has this provision to prevent parties from taking documents out of their context. When taken out of context, documents are more difficult to understand and may give the proponent a distorted picture of the facts.

Duplicate photographs can be made from negatives or from the photographs themselves; it is somewhat cheaper to work from negatives. Usually, the respondent who has custody of photographs arranges to obtain duplicates for the other parties so that the respondent does not have to give possession to another party. It is appropriate to impress upon the processor that the photographs are evidence to be used in court and the processor must protect them against loss or damage. The party who requests the copies must pay the cost of having them made. Sometimes photocopies of the photographs may suffice, especially for trial preparation. Photocopies are inexpensive and may provide an adequate reference. Usually the original photographs are available when needed for comparison.

The proponent of an inspection may need to do some **destructive testing.** For example, a party may demand the right to take a sample of the property to do tests on it. It may be necessary to obtain samples by taking soil borings, concrete borings, or samples of steel from metal structures. Unless these invasive procedures would cause some significant harm to the property, a court would order the respondent to allow the inspection and testing. Suppose the case involves the crash of an airplane, and there is reason to believe the crash was caused by metal fatigue. The proponent may need a piece of the metal to test in the laboratory, and the piece cannot be returned in its pretested condition. The proponent's demand for such testing may result in a disagreement over whether the test should be done and over the limitations on any such testing. Sometimes only a court can resolve such a disagreement.

You may ask, How can destructive testing ever be done and be fair to all the parties? Over the years, some creative solutions have been devised. For instance, a court may order the parties to choose one or more "experts" who can document the property's appearance and condition before the test. The court may order the parties to agree on an expert to do the destructive test, so that all parties are confident about the validity of the test. If the parties cannot agree on an expert, the court has the power to appoint an expert to conduct the test, and each party may have his or her own expert observe the test. In addition, the court may allow the parties to make video recordings of the test while it is being conducted, including commentary.

A more difficult problem is presented when the demand for inspection of property involves plans to totally destroy the property. For example, suppose the controversy centers upon the flammability of an article of clothing, and only a few small pieces of the clothing remain. The tests will destroy the remaining fragments. In all probability, all parties need the same tests. The usual and best solution is to have the parties' experts agree on a testing procedure in which everyone participates. A paralegal may videotape the procedure and test results. If the parties cannot agree on how the tests should be done, the court may appoint an expert to do the tests in the manner preferred by him or her. A judge should try to get the parties to agree upon the selection of the expert, but if the parties cannot agree, the court has the power to make the decision without their agreement (see Rule 706 of the Federal Rules of Evidence).

Procedure

Rule 34 states that the proponent must give the respondent a reasonable notice for the inspection. The rule does not state a minimum amount of time, but it does provide that the respondent shall have at least thirty days in which to prepare a response to the demand:

> The party upon whom the request is served [respondent] shall serve a written response within 30 days after the service of the request, except that a defendant may serve a response within 45 days after service of the summons and complaint upon that defendant.

If the demand for inspection is served by mail, add three days (Rule 6(e)). The rule makes no provision for serving a demand for inspection with the complaint. Nevertheless, demands for inspection, like interrogatories, may be served with the complaint, in which case the time period for answering is extended by fifteen days.

If the proponent needs to have the inspection earlier than Rule 34 permits, and the respondent is uncooperative, the proponent may move the court for an order setting a shorter period. This motion must be served on all the parties; unlike a motion to enlarge a time period, a motion to shorten the time cannot be made ex parte (see Rule 6(b)). The other parties must have the opportunity to object to a shorter period.

Rule 29 provides that the parties may not stipulate to enlarge the time for responding to a demand for inspection. Stipulations extending the time provided in Rules 33, 34, and 36 for responses to discovery may be made only with the approval of the court. The parties can do just about anything they want to do to accommodate each other concerning discovery. However, Rule 29 is clear: if the cooperation ends, neither party may look to the court to enforce a stipulation that enlarges the time. The reason for Rule 29's proscription is that courts must not lose control over scheduling.

Form

The demand for inspection must be served upon all parties although it applies to property under the control of only one party. The demand does not have to be in any particular form.

Formal Written Demand.   For convenience, Form 24 of the Rules Appendix for Forms is duplicated in exhibit 15.1.

Informal Written Demand.   Sometimes lawyers make the arrangements through correspondence rather than service of a formal demand. Although a lawyer must sign a formal demand for inspection, the paralegal may sign whatever letters are used to arrange or confirm Rule 34 inspections.

Suppose the paralegal has used an informal approach to obtaining some documents on behalf of the plaintiff, and when the case comes to trial it appears that the defendant has not produced the documents. What can the paralegal do? The paralegal's side is in a very good position to move

---

■ **EXHIBIT 15.1**

Demand
for Inspection

Plaintiff A. B. requests defendant C. D. to respond within [enter number of days; must be at least thirty but may be more] days to the following requests:

1. That defendant produce and permit plaintiff to inspect and to copy each of the following documents: [List the documents either individually or by category and describe each of them.]

   [State the time, place, and manner of making the inspection and performing any related acts.]

2. That defendant produce and permit plaintiff to inspect and to copy, test, or sample each of the following objects: [List the objects either individually or by category and describe each of them.]

   [State the time, place, and manner of making the inspection and performing any related acts.]

3. That defendant permit plaintiff to enter [describe property to be entered] and to inspect and to photograph, test or sample [describe the portion of the real property and the objects to be inspected].

   [State the time, place, and manner of making the inspection and performing any related acts.]

Signed: _____

the court for whatever relief is appropriate—from monetary sanctions to a mistrial. However, the burden is on the client (the paralegal) to show that the "request" was clear and specified the documents in question. Again, a letter is sufficient. It does not matter that the paralegal did not serve a formal Rule 34 demand for inspection. If the informal request was in writing and is clear, and the defendant did not object and "indicated" that she would comply with the request or purported to comply with the request, the court should protect the paralegal's client from the other party's noncompliance. Rule 37(a)(2) provides, in part, as follows:

> [I]f a party, in response to a request for inspection submitted under Rule 34, fails to respond that the inspection will be permitted as requested or fails to allow inspection as requested, the discovering party may move for an order compelling an answer, or a designation, or an order compelling inspection in accordance with the request.

In addition, the court may issue protective orders.

Parties should never rely upon an *oral* understanding. Rule 29 specifies that any modification of the discovery procedures must be by written stipulation. If a party makes an oral agreement concerning discovery matters, she or he must send a confirmation letter as soon as possible and make sure the letter purports to state the *entire* agreement between the parties.

Subpoena Duces Tecum. If the property is under the control of a nonparty, Rule 34 cannot be used to obtain access. A subpoena duces tecum must be used as provided by Rule 45. When dealing with property of a nonparty, a court cannot order destructive testing or order the nonparty to do something to the property, such as move it to another location for the convenience of the parties.

A subpoena duces tecum may be used to compel a party to produce personal property, including documents, for inspection. A subpoena duces tecum requires the same kind of information as a written demand for inspection. The subpoena must be served upon the person who has custody of the property to be inspected. It must describe the terms and scope of the proposed inspection. It must be used in connection with the custodian's deposition. Therefore, all other parties to the action have a right to attend the deposition and inspection. The subpoena must be issued by a court that has jurisdiction over the deponent custodian.

A party may be compelled to produce tangible items for inspection and copying pursuant to a subpoena duces tecum as an alternative to a written demand for inspection. On occasion a party may want to use a subpoena rather than make a Rule 34 demand. For example, the party may not have time in which to make a Rule 34 demand. Or the party's principal objective may be to take the other party's deposition, and the party wants to question the deponent about a few of her or his documents; a subpoena duces tecum may be used to require the party to bring those documents to the deposition.

A subpoena cannot be used to obtain access to real estate even when the property is under the control of a party. If a party needs to obtain access to land or a building that is under the control of a nonparty who is uncooperative, the party's only recourse is to obtain a court order against the occupant. Such orders are usually termed orders to show cause.

■ WRITTEN RESPONSE TO DEMAND FOR INSPECTION

A respondent's written response to the demand has two functions. It must tell the proponent to what extent the respondent will comply with the terms of the demand as stated. It must also state all objections the respondent has to the demand. It is not enough to simply object. The respondent must give specific reasons for each objection. The written response may suggest alternatives to the terms proposed by the demand.

Procedure

Although Rule 34 gives the respondent thirty days in which to serve a response, the respondent should confirm acceptance of the demand or object as soon as possible, because the parties usually have a lot of preparations to make and coordinating to do. The proponent may have other people to contact, such as experts who have been scheduled to do the actual testing, photographing, or the like. On the other hand, the proponent ought to have allowed sufficient time between the date on which the written response is due and the date of the proposed inspection to make alternative plans in case the respondent objects to the inspection as demanded. Suppose a party has proposed an inspection of a complicated machine and needs the help of an engineer to do the inspection. If the proponent receives the respondent's objection on the thirtieth day, he will need additional time to make other arrangements with the engineer. Proponents should try to anticipate these kinds of problems by planning ahead.

If the written response proposes some modifications, conditions, or limitations on the inspection, the proponent may accept the modifications as a counterproposal. When parties cannot agree upon a mutually convenient time and place for the inspection or cannot agree upon the manner in which the inspection should be conducted, the proponent may move the court for an order that specifies when, where, and how the proponent may conduct the inspection. The proponent has the onus of making the motion. If the court concludes that either party has acted unreasonably, the court may impose sanctions as provided by Rule 37.

When the opponent serves a demand for inspection that arbitrarily designates a time and place for the inspection, a party may reply that the designated time is not convenient and suggest other arrangements. The party could save time and inconvenience by telephoning the lawyer for the opponent and explaining her or his intention to permit an inspection and work out an inspection program that the opponent can subsequently confirm in a new demand for inspection or letter. Or the party's written response may set forth the new terms of the inspection. Once an agreement has been reached on the particulars, either party may confirm the agreement by letter, but the letter must clearly specify all the terms and conditions of the inspection. Lawyers recognize that other discovery efforts may be delayed until the inspection is completed. Therefore, parties usually try to hasten inspections, rather than delay them.

Objections to Inspection

When the respondent objects to a demand for inspection, the respondent must specify the reasons for each objection. If an objection concerns only part of a request for inspection, that should be clearly indicated. The respondent should use narrative explanations rather than technical legal objections. The respondent's objections to a demand for inspection must be served within the thirty days allowed by Rule 34. If the demand for inspection is served with the summons and complaint, the defendant has forty-five days in which to serve objections. A proponent cannot require an inspection before the written response is due.

The respondent should decide, as soon as possible, what position he or she is going to take concerning the demand for inspection, and advise the proponent so that the proponent does not waste time, effort, and money in preparing for an inspection that will not take place. For example, if the plaintiff has demanded an inspection to take place in forty days, the defendant may cause the plaintiff a great deal of inconvenience by waiting until the thirtieth day to serve objections. This is an area where the parties should extend themselves to provide cooperation. One thing courts always consider when they rule on parties' discovery motions is whether the parties have been diligent. Diligent parties who act in good faith are seldom penalized and seldom have to pay costs in connection with discovery motions.

Form

The initial response to a demand for inspection may be a written statement indicating that the respondent will comply, or the respondent may submit a list of requirements concerning the proposed inspection (Rule 34(b)). Exhibit 15.2 is a sample **written response to demand for inspection.**

■ **EXHIBIT 15.2**

Response to Demand for Inspection

Defendant hereby responds to plaintiff's demand for inspection pursuant to Rule 34 of the Federal Rules of Civil Procedure:

1. Plaintiff's lawyer and the experts designated in the demand for inspection may enter defendant's plant at Des Moines, Iowa, for the purpose of inspecting the conveyor system belt system on Thursday, January 5, 1995, between the hours of 2:00 P.M. and 5:00 P.M.
2. Plaintiff's representatives may take still pictures and motion pictures of the conveyor system in operation.
3. Plaintiff's experts may make measurements of the conveyor system and appurtenances.
4. Defendant objects to plaintiff's proposal to take sample swatches of the conveyor belt because that would seriously damage the integrity of the belt and conveyor system. Furthermore, B. F. Goodrich Company presumably has samples of the type of belt in question.
5. Defendant does not have any plans or specifications for the installation of the conveyor system. Therefore, defendant will not produce any plans or specifications at the scheduled inspection.
6. The only report of the accident in question was made for the defendant's liability insurer. The report was not made in the ordinary course of the defendant's business. It was made for the insurer in anticipation of litigation. The report is privileged and work product. It is not subject to discovery.

_____

Attorney for Defendant

■ LIMITATIONS ON INSPECTIONS

Rule 34 cannot be used to compel a party to prepare a document that does not already exist. For example, the plaintiff could not use the rule to compel the defendant to make a summary of the defendant's business records. On the other hand, the defendant may offer to make and provide a summary of the records, and the plaintiff may accept the summary instead of inspecting voluminous records.

Rule 34 cannot be used to obtain documents that are privileged or that are a party's work product as defined by Rule 26(b)(3). Suppose the plaintiff has brought an action to recover money damages for personal injuries, and the plaintiff's lawyer has obtained a copy of the plaintiff's hospital records. Could the defendant require the plaintiff to produce those copies for inspection and copying? Yes. The privilege has been waived by commencement of the action. The fact that the party (lawyer) only has copies of the records is immaterial. Those copies are under the plaintiff's control and subject to inspection. The hospital records are not the plaintiff's work product. If the plaintiff's lawyer takes a signed statement from an independent witness concerning the party's accident, the statement qualifies as attorney work product because it was prepared in anticipation of litigation. Nevertheless, the witness has a right to obtain a copy of her or his own statement. But another party does not have a right, under Rule 26 or 34, to obtain a copy of the statement from the lawyer who obtained it. If the witness obtains a copy, the witness could allow other people to see and copy the statement. Some states require parties to produce witness statements on demand.

Rule 34 provides the means to obtain copies of a party's income tax returns when the party's income is relevant to the litigation. Even if a party does not retain copies of his or her income tax returns, copies are available from the government, so the tax returns are under the party's "control." Income tax returns may be relevant to prove or disprove the plaintiff's claim for loss of income due to a personal injury or claim for breach of a contract. The defendant's income tax returns may be relevant to the plaintiff's claim against the defendant for punitive damages.

SUMMARY

Each party must have access to all the evidence before trial, including the tangible evidence that is in an opposing party's custody or control. Rule 34 gives every party the right to examine the property under the control of an adverse party, whether the property is real estate; personal property; documents; or things, such as machines and instruments. The right to inspection includes the right to measure, test, photograph, and make copies. Even destructive tests may be warranted. Property is subject to inspection whether it is potential evidence, or it contains evidence, or the inspection may lead to the discovery of evidence.

A party need only serve a demand for inspection. It need not move the court for an order for an inspection, unless the respondent refuses to cooperate. If the inspection must be made sooner than Rule 34 permits, the party who wants the inspection may move the court for an order accelerating the time period. The motion cannot be made ex parte. The sanctions provided by Rule 37 apply to inspection abuses. Rule 34 applies only to property that is under the control of another party. It cannot be used to obtain access to property that is under the control of a nonparty.

When a party receives a demand for inspection, that party must respond in writing within thirty days. The response must affirm that the inspection will be permitted, unless specific objections are made, and the objections must be supported with reasons. if an objection is made, the burden is upon the party who wants the inspection to move the court to compel the inspection.

Rule 34 cannot be used to obtain documents that are privileged. Rule 34 cannot be used to force the opposing party to make charts or summaries or compilations or photographs. The party whose property is inspected has a right to observe the inspection.

KEY TERMS

real property   destructive testing
personal property   written response to demand for
demand for inspection   inspection

REVIEW QUESTIONS

1. For what purpose can a party demand the right to inspect real estate that is under the control of another party?

2. What determines the place of the inspection?

3. What information must be contained in a demand for inspection?

4. Why must the demand for inspection be in writing?

5. When can you use a subpoena duces tecum to obtain access to real estate in order to photograph the property?

6. When might you choose to subpoena a party's records rather than use a written demand for inspection?

7. What is one good reason why a proposed inspection should not go forward at the time and place scheduled in the written inspection demand?

8. What right does the respondent have to copies of the product of the proponent's inspection of the respondent's property?

9. What action may a respondent take to a demand for inspection of documents that the respondent would have to create from other documents that do exist?

10. How should the respondent answer a written request for inspection if the respondent does not have the specified property but knows where the property is?

REQUESTS FOR ADMISSIONS

OUTLINE

Parties to a civil action need to identify areas of agreement as well as areas of disagreement. As soon as the parties recognize and confirm their areas of agreement, they can focus their remaining discovery and trial preparation on the disputed matters. Pleadings do a good job of identifying areas of disagreement, but little to identify areas of agreement. The allegations in pleadings are too general to deal with the myriad of facts that usually underly each cause of action. Furthermore, at the time the parties serve their pleadings, they may not have enough information to be able to admit facts that later become clear. With that in mind, the Federal Rules of Civil Procedure provide a means by which parties can narrow the areas of dispute. The procedure is simple. A party merely requests the other party to admit a specified fact. The party to whom the **request for admissions** is directed is under an obligation to respond in good faith and admit the fact if she or he knows it to be true.

When requests for admissions are properly used, all parties benefit. The party who has the burden of proving an admitted fact benefits most, so that party has good reason to request the admission. Each party benefits because the admissions narrow the areas of dispute, reduce the number or scope of issues to be tried, minimize trial preparation, and even shorten the trial. Everyone avoids unnecessary time and expense. Using requests for admissions is probably the most expeditious and inexpensive method for establishing particular facts.

Rule 36 does not use the word *admit* in a bad or negative sense. When a respondent duly admits that a specified fact is true, the fact is no longer subject to dispute. The fact is established, proved, uncontrovertible for all purposes of the case in which the admission is made. The proponent is relieved of the obligation of presenting evidence to prove the fact. Although

Rule 36 is part of the discovery rules (Rules 26 through 37), a request for admission is not truly a discovery device.

■ TYPES OF REQUESTS FOR ADMISSIONS

Requests for admissions may relate to facts, opinions, statements, and the genuineness of documents. They may even relate to the application of law to facts. Requests for admissions may relate only to facts and opinions that are relevant to the lawsuit.

Statements

The reference to statements in Rule 36 is not a reference to recorded or signed witness statements. Instead, it concerns utterances and remarks made by someone orally or in writing. A common example is the plaintiff's statement at the accident scene that he or she was not injured. In another example, the plaintiff in a personal injury action involving an automobile may have exclaimed right after the accident, "It's all my fault! I didn't see you coming!" The defendant may ask the plaintiff to admit that he made those statements at the accident scene. The request for admissions could be phrased in one of the following ways:

> Please admit you spoke to the defendant at the accident scene.
>
> Please admit you stated to the defendant that the accident was your fault.
>
> Please admit you made the statement, "It's all my fault."
>
> Please admit you stated to the defendant that you did not see the defendant coming.
>
> Please admit you stated to the defendant, "I didn't see you coming."
>
> Please admit you told the investigating police officer that your speed was forty miles per hour.

Note that in any of these forms, the request only requires the plaintiff to admit that he made the statement. The plaintiff may admit to having made the statement, but at trial deny that the statement was true. Consequently, there should be a follow-up request, such as, "Please admit that your statement was true."

Facts

When the proponent wants the respondent to admit several related facts, the proponent should state each fact separately. A separate statement makes each request more clear and more difficult for the respondent to avoid admitting. For example, if the proponent wants the respondent to admit that the respondent did not stop for the stop sign before entering the intersection and that the respondent was driving Joanne Barlow's car, the requests should be made separately. Suppose the plaintiff alleges that the defendant company's taxicab struck the plaintiff and left the scene, and a witness identified the taxicab by its number. The driver of the cab has left the state and cannot be found. The taxicab company denies that its cab was involved in the accident. The plaintiff could serve requests for admissions such as the following:

> Please admit that the defendant owns a taxicab that carries the number 222.

Please admit that the defendant's taxicab, number 222, is painted yellow with black trim.

Please admit that the defendant's taxicab, 222, was in service on [date].

Please admit that Joanne Barlow had possession of taxicab 222 from 4:00 P.M. until 12:00 midnight on [date].

Please admit that the intersection of Fourth Street and Third Avenue is located within Joanne Barlow's operating territory.

Please admit that on or about [date], the defendant had the right front fender of taxicab 222 replaced or repaired.

Please admit that the attached photograph fairly depicts taxicab 222 as it appeared immediately before the right front fender was repaired.

Please admit that Joanne Barlow no longer works for the defendant taxicab company.

Please admit that you do not know where Joanne Barlow lives or works.

Please admit that Joanne Barlow terminated her employment with the defendant on [date].

The facts in these admissions may have been discovered by taking the deposition of the company's employees, such as the dispatcher, payroll supervisor, and service supervisor. It would be easier to prove the facts by simply reading the defendant's admissions to the jury than it would be to bring the defendant's employees into court to testify. The requests will be useful in developing the case even if the admissions do not conclusively establish the plaintiff's case against the taxicab company. Each fact is material and important to showing that the defendant's taxicab probably was involved in the accident.

On occasion a party may testify in a deposition in one case to facts that are adverse to that party in a second case. That party deponent may be confronted with a request for admissions in the second case, asking him to admit that he made the statements and that the statements were true.

The following examples of requests for admissions relate to specific facts of various kinds:

1. Please admit that defendant entered the intersection in question without stopping for the stop sign.

   [*This request might be prompted by a notation in a police accident report that the defendant admitted to the investigating officer that she did not stop for the stop sign. The admission to the officer is evidence of the defendant's fault but is not conclusive on the fact. Obtaining the admission pursuant to a request makes the violation indisputable. Perhaps a follow-up request should be used, as in request 2.*]

2. Please admit that defendant stated to Officer Burt Jones that defendant did not stop for the stop sign in question.

   [*This request involves the same subject matter but a different fact, that is, the fact of a conversation. The defendant's admission that the conversation took place is not an admission that the stop sign violation occurred.*]

3. Please admit that defendant was acting in the course and scope of her employment for the ABC Corporation at the time and place of the accident described in plaintiff's complaint.

   [*The existence of an agency relationship is a common fact issue. An employer (principal) is legally responsible for an agent's torts committed in the course and scope of the agent's employment. The matter of agency may also be a mixed question of law and fact.*]

4. Please admit that defendant <u>delivered</u> <u>four tons</u> of <u>wheat</u> to <u>plaintiff</u> on <u>September 5,</u> 1995.

   [*Though the request is a single, simple sentence, it contains a request for admission of five separate facts. Each fact is underlined. If the controversy centers only around the* value *of the wheat delivered, the plaintiff may be able to admit all five of the facts without any difficulty. But if a dispute exists over how many tons were delivered, all the facts but the quantity should be admitted by the plaintiff. This same request could be directed by the plaintiff to the defendant to establish that the defendant delivered* less *wheat than he contracted to deliver.*]

5. Please admit that plaintiff was not wearing her eyeglasses at the time of the accident referred to in the complaint.

6. Please admit that the accident referred to in the complaint occurred at 6:04 P.M.

7. Please admit that the signature that appears on the attached promissory note (copy) was made by defendant.

8. Please admit that plaintiff was familiar with the stairway on which she fell.

9. Please admit that on [date] defendant received written notice of a defect in the pipe in question.

10. Please admit that the sidewalk on which plaintiff fell was

    a. four feet wide

    b. made of cement

    c. dry

    d. used by plaintiff at least three times a month for one year before plaintiff's alleged accident

11. Please admit that defendant negligently caused the accident described in the complaint.

    [*Although negligence and causation are issues of fact, they are also the ultimate questions of fact, which establish the defendant's legal liability. If the defendant is constrained to admit that he was negligent and that his negligence caused the accident or injury, he is one step away from admitting liability. Requests for admissions may relate to ultimate questions of fact.*]

12. Please admit that defendant breached the contract described in plaintiff's complaint.

    [*Breach of the parties' contract is another ultimate fact issue. If the defendant is constrained to admit breaching the contract, she still may not be liable to the plaintiff if she can prove some affirmative defense.*]

13. Please admit that defendant signed the attached promissory note as the drawer of the note.

14. Please admit that plaintiff used the stairway on ten or more occasions before the accident in question.

Genuineness of Documents

Requests for admissions may relate to the **genuineness** of document. The kinds of documents that are regularly made the subject of requests for admissions include the parties' contract, the parties' lease agreement, a party's bank check, a notice delivered to a party, a business letter, a record of account. Rule 36 does not define *genuine*, but there is not much disagreement about its meaning. A document is genuine if it is what it purports to be. If a document is genuine, it is not a forgery or an imitation. It is not bogus. Usually, it is obvious from the face of a document what it is.

By admitting that a document is genuine, the respondent acknowledges that the document exists and was duly prepared. The respondent admits that the dates, signatures, and statements in the document were entered as appears from the face of the document. The respondent admits that the signatures were made by the persons who purported to sign the document. On the other hand, the respondent does not admit that the content of the document is necessarily accurate. For example, if the proponent asks the respondent to admit that a witness statement is genuine, the respondent's admission establishes that the witness statement was made, dated, and signed, but the respondent is not committed to the truth of the contents of the statement. If the proponent wants the respondent to admit facts contained in the statement, the proponent will have to submit additional requests concerning those facts. Also, for example, if the proponent asks the respondent to admit that a business record is genuine, the respondent's admission merely establishes that the record was duly made and kept in the course of business. Again, the admission that the document is genuine does not establish that the business record is accurate. The proponent could ask the respondent to admit that the contents of the document are accurate.

A proponent may ask the respondent to admit the genuineness of documents possessed by either proponent or the respondent. If the proponent has possession, the proponent must "furnish" the document to the respondent by delivering it or at least making it available for inspection. A strict reading of Rule 36 places a burden on the proponent to provide the original to the respondent. In practice, however, the procedure is to attach to the request a good, clear photocopy of the document in question and ask the respondent to admit that the document represented by the photocopy is genuine. For example, if the proponent wants the respondent to admit that a certain bank check was prepared, signed, endorsed, and negotiated as those facts appear on the face of the check, the proponent may attach to the request for admissions a clear photocopy of the check and incorporate the photocopy by reference. Proponents commonly ask respondents to admit that the photocopy attached to the request is a true and correct copy of the original; however, that should not be necessary. If any question is raised about the accuracy of the photocopy, the proponent has the obligation to produce the original for inspection—unless the respondent has the original.

There should be no difficulty obtaining an admission that a document is genuine when the document is known to be valid. Then requests may be used to obtain admissions concerning the date of execution, identity of signatories, place of execution, and consideration paid for the document.

If a party admits that a certain document is genuine, he or she does not, thereby, admit that it is also admissible in evidence. For example, a defendant may admit that a certain photograph of the plaintiff's decedent at the accident scene is genuine—is that of the decedent and accurately shows his mutilated body. However, the photograph is still subject to the objection that it is inflammatory and therefore its prejudicial effect outweighs its probative value. Or a document that is admittedly genuine may nevertheless be excluded from evidence because it contains statements that are mere hearsay.

Requests for admissions may be used to help ensure that a certain document will be received into evidence, or at least to show that the necessary foundation for the document exists. For example, the following requests may be directed to the plaintiff in a tort action where the defendant is claiming that the plaintiff previously executed a release:

1. Please admit that the attached release of all claims is genuine.

2. Please admit that plaintiff signed the attached release on the date specified therein.

3. Please admit that plaintiff received the money described in the release as the consideration.

4. Please admit that the monies plaintiff received in exchange for the release have not been tendered or returned to defendant.

The plaintiff's admissions to these requests should greatly facilitate the defendant's trial preparation.

Opinions

Requests for admissions may relate to opinions of either laypersons or experts. The proponent probably will not be able to obtain an admission that the proponent's expert's opinions are correct, but this does happen. Each opinion must be clearly stated in a separate request so that the respondent knows exactly the scope and extent of each admission. Requests for admissions of opinions are useful when the proponent finds some admissions in the respondent's expert's reports that tend to favor the proponent. The proponent may *establish* those favorable opinions by asking the respondent to admit them. Again, there are two benefits: the proponent does not have to spend time and money proving those particular opinions, and the opinions become irrefutable. The opinions are taken out of the realm of controversy.

The following examples of requests for admissions relate to various kinds of opinions that could be relevant and admissible at trial:

1. Please admit that when you observed defendant at the scene of the accident in question, you observed that defendant was not intoxicated.

   [*Or the request could be phrased to establish the defendant was intoxicated. Either way, the matter of sobriety is an opinion.*]

2. Please admit that while you were at the accident scene you did not form an opinion of whether or not the plaintiff was intoxicated.

   [*Sometimes it is just as important to establish the absence of an opinion as the existence of an opinion.*]

3. Please admit that the sidewalk on which plaintiff fell was slippery owing to ice at the time she fell.

   [*"Slippery" is an opinion. The presence of ice is a simple fact.*]

4. Please admit that Dr. Sawra Karimi's charges in the amount of five hundred dollars for services to plaintiff were reasonable.

   [*This type of request is used frequently by plaintiffs in personal injury actions, especially if the lawyer does not intend to have the physician or hospital administrator appear at trial to testify. However, if the plaintiff refuses to permit the defendant's lawyer to talk with the physician, the defendant probably will not have available the necessary information to confirm the truth of the request. The value of the physician's services depends upon many issues including the physi-*

cian's experience, time spent, and skill. Such information usually is not available in the records. Therefore, unless the plaintiff will permit the defendant to interview the attending physician, the defendant properly denies the request on the basis that she or he lacks sufficient information upon which to make the admission.]

5. Please admit that the lumber delivered by defendant to plaintiff according to the contract in question complied with the specified grades and qualities.

    [*The grade or character of products is often a matter of opinion.*]

6. Please admit that the fair market value of plaintiff's automobile before the accident was four thousand dollars.

    [*The market value of personal property is usually a matter of opinion, unless the property is the kind that has a regular market, such as stock that is traded on a stock exchange.*]

7. Please admit that the ignition point for natural gas is 3,300 degrees.

    [*The ignition point of any material is a scientific fact, but the fact is ordinarily proved through expert opinion testimony. It is doubtful that a court would take judicial notice of such a scientific fact. A court would probably require the parties to present evidence to prove the fact, absent a stipulation or Rule 36 admission.*]

8. Please admit that rust caused the steel bar joists to fail.

    [*The cause of the joists' failure is a matter of fact. However, the fact would have to be proved by expert opinion testimony, unless the court were to determine that the jury could simply look at the steel joists and see, as any layperson could, that they were weakened by rust and gave way because of the weakened condition.*]

Application of Law to Facts

If an admission pertains to the application of law to certain facts, the court takes judicial notice of the admission. The admission becomes part of the **law of the case.** That means the parties have agreed it is the rule of law that determines their legal rights and obligations in this case. They have accepted it as the applicable rule, and perhaps a controlling law, even if they happen to be wrong. The same consequence flows when the parties try a case and an error occurs to which no one objects.

The following examples of requests for admissions involve the application of law to facts:

1. Please admit that at the time the contract was signed by Joseph Linder, he was acting within the course and scope of his agency for plaintiff.

    [*The existence of an agency and the scope of the agency depend upon the existence of a legal relationship that may be created in various ways.*]

2. Please admit that defendant was negligent in the operation of his airplane.

    [*The admission may be directed to the ultimate question of fact, which requires the application of law to a collage of facts. If the admission is made and negligence is thereby established, the issues of causation and damages still need to be established.*]

3. Please admit that on October 1, 1995, plaintiff was an employee of defendant who is entitled to benefits under the terms of defendant's contract with the teacher's union dated August 1, 1995.

4. Please admit that at the time plaintiff was discharged from her employment by defendant, she was a tenured teacher within the meaning of the contract referred to in the complaint.

    [*If certain conditions must be proved to establish tenure, the admission may save considerable time and effort proving those conditions.*]

5. Please admit that defendant's failure to stop for the stop sign was a proximate cause of the automobile accident in question.

[*Proximate cause is probably the most subjective legal conclusion in tort law. Appellate courts are reluctant to hold, as a matter of law, that any set of facts necessarily establishes that an alleged cause is a proximate cause of an accident.*]

■ PREPARING REQUESTS FOR ADMISSIONS

Paralegals may draft requests for admissions, but a lawyer must read and sign them. A request for admissions must be in writing and duly served upon the respondent. If the action involves other parties, a copy of the request must be served upon the other parties. A request for admissions must clearly state that it is made pursuant to Rule 36, to keep it from appearing to be some incidental inquiry about the case. The parameters of the rule are succinctly stated in the rule:

> A party may serve upon any other party a written request for the admission, for purposes of the pending action only, of the truth of any matters within the scope of Rule 26(b)(1) set forth in the request that relate to statements or opinions of fact or of the application of law to fact including the genuineness of any documents described in the request. Copies of documents shall be served with the request unless they have been or are otherwise furnished or made available for inspection and copying.

The proponent may serve a single request for admissions or a number of separate requests in one form. Either way the document containing the request or requests is entitled *request for admissions.* There is no limit on the number of requests that may be served, whether in one group or in several groups.

The burden is upon the proponent to specify the fact or opinion clearly. The respondent should not have to guess at the scope or purpose of the request. The respondent should be able to easily understand the request and should not have to worry that it may contain some hidden problem.

A request should be phrased so that the respondent is able to respond with a simple admission or a denial. Although Rule 36 provides for **qualified admissions** and **qualified denials,** the need for a qualification should be the exception to the rule. Whether a qualified response is called a qualified admission or denial, Rule 36(a) requires the respondent to identify that portion of the request that is true. If the request is essentially true but technically flawed, the respondent should state the fact or facts in a manner that meets the spirit of Rule 36(a). To illustrate, suppose the request asked the respondent to admit that his automobile is red. If the respondent's automobile is maroon, the response should state the automobile is maroon and not merely deny the request. If a request asked the respondent to admit that the accident occurred at 9:00 o'clock in the morning, the respondent could give a qualified response by admitting that the accident occurred at 9:10 o'clock in the morning. If a request asked the respondent to admit that snow was falling at the time of the accident, the respondent could properly make a qualified denial by stating that the wind was blowing surface snow across the roadway.

Each request must be singular. Each request must deal with only one subject. If a request uses a word that requires a specific definition, the definition must be stated separately. In the words of Rule 36, "Each matter of which an admission is requested shall be separately set forth." But even then, a response may admit only a portion of the request. For example, a request to a defendant that he admit he occupied certain real estate during the year 1981 may draw a response that he occupied the premises only during the month of January 1981. If he occupied the premises only in 1979, he could simply deny the request without qualifying the answer by "admitting" he occupied the premises in 1979. The qualifying information is outside the scope of the request.

The wording of each request for admission should make clear the scope of the request. Suppose the lawsuit centers around a counterfeit document and both parties know the document is counterfeit, but a dispute exists over who prepared the document and who signed it. The concept of genuineness would be difficult to use in this situation. Neither party would ask the other to admit that the document is what it purports to be. Nevertheless, a proponent may request the respondent to admit that *this* copy is a true copy of the counterfeit document; that the document in question is a counterfeit; that the opponent has possession of the original counterfeit; that the opponent knows (or does not know) who actually signed the counterfeit document.

The more specific and clear a request, the more difficulty the respondent will have avoiding it. Requests for admissions lose their value when they are overly broad or ambiguous. A misuse of requests for admissions increases the cost of litigation and creates friction between the parties.

It is customary to preface the request with Rule 36's statement that the request will be used "for purposes of the pending action only." Whether or not the request for admission notes the limitation, it is appropriate for the respondent to preface her or his admissions with that restriction.

The request must state the amount of time the proponent has allowed for the respondent to respond. The proponent cannot grant less than thirty days, but may grant more time. If the proponent subsequently grants more time than was specified in the request for admissions, the grant should be confirmed in writing. The Rule 36 time period is very important because if the respondent does not serve the response within the designated time, the requests are deemed admitted.

■ LIMITATIONS ON REQUESTS FOR ADMISSIONS

Requests for admissions may be served only upon parties to the civil action. A proponent should serve requests for admissions only when the proponent knows a fact is true or a document is genuine. Requests for admissions may not be used to "fish" for (seek discovery of) information or facts. Requests are not a substitute for interrogatories and depositions. The more clear it is that the fact or document is true, the more reason for establishing it by way of a Rule 36 admission. The test for determining whether to serve a request for admission is whether the proponent, not the respondent, knows or believes the fact is true or the document is genuine.

It is perfectly proper to serve a request for admissions even though the respondent strongly disagrees with the request. The request places an onus on the respondent to verify her or his position. If the respondent wrongly denies the request, the respondent may be required to pay the costs the proponent incurs to prove the respondent mistakenly refused to admit.

When the proponent believes the respondent should admit the particular facts but suspects the respondent may not do so, the proponent may follow each request for admissions with interrogatories that ask "discovery"-type questions. For example, a request for admissions could be framed, "Please admit that you are the owner of the vehicle bearing state license plate number XYZ-333." The interrogatory that complements the requests could be, "If you deny the foregoing request for admission, state the name and address of the person you claim is the owner of said vehicle." This is another example of using the discovery tools to complement each other.

The most common reason for obtaining an admission that a document is genuine is to avoid the necessity of preparing and presenting evidence to establish the validity of the document. Once a document is shown to be genuine, the document will probably speak for itself. In other words, the contents of the document will provide the relevant information and can be read to the jury or by the jury. A party should consider asking additional requests for admissions that provide the foundation for the document to be received into evidence. For example, suppose a party has a ten-page hospital record he wants to put into evidence, and he does not want to incur the expense of having a hospital administrator come to the trial to provide the foundation for the record. The party may prepare a request that asks the respondent to admit that the hospital record is genuine; that the ten pages attached to the request are true and correct copies of the originals; that if the proper person were called to testify, that person would testify that the record was prepared and kept in the ordinary course of the hospital's business; that the record was prepared and maintained for the purpose of providing medical care and treatment to the plaintiff. The party might even ask the respondent (the defendant in this instance) to admit that the amount of the hospital's charges for the proponent's treatment was fair and reasonable. The treating physician can testify that the hospital care was necessary and due to the accident in question.

■ CONSEQUENCES OF NOT RESPONDING

The plaintiff may serve requests for admissions with the summons and complaint or any time thereafter until the court establishes a cutoff date. Once the defendant has appeared in the case by serving an answer or motion, requests for admissions may be served by mail upon the defendant's lawyer. The defendant must serve a response to the request for admissions within thirty days after service of the request or within forty five days after service of the summons and complaint, whichever period is longer.

The defendant may serve requests for admissions any time after the action has been commenced. The request for admissions may be served by mail upon the plaintiff's lawyer. The plaintiff has thirty days in which to serve a response to the request. If service is by mail, three days may be added (Rule 6(e)).

If the respondent fails to serve a response within the allotted time, the request is deemed admitted. If the respondent inadvertently makes admissions by failing to respond, the respondent's only recourse is to move the court for leave to withdraw the admissions—even though no admissions have actually been made. As a rule, the court will not allow the delinquent respondent to avoid the admissions unless the respondent can show both that the failure was due to excusable neglect and that the admissions are wrong. Therefore, if the respondent needs more time in which to respond to a request for admissions, the respondent should obtain an extension of time in writing before the response is due. If the proponent will not voluntarily extend the time period for responding, the respondent must move the court for an order extending the time. Rule 6 permits the respondent to make an ex parte motion for an extension of time.[1] If the respondent obtains an extension of time on invalid grounds, the proponent may move the court to rescind the order.

Rule 36 does not require the proponent to do anything to show that the respondent did not respond to the request for admissions within the time allowed. The proponent's affidavit of service of the request should be sufficient to establish service of the request. Nevertheless, the proponent should prepare and serve upon the respondent an **affidavit of no response.** The affidavit should state the date on which the request was served; that no extension of time in which to answer was granted; that the respondent has not served a response as of the date of the affidavit; and that the request is deemed admitted for purposes of the pending action, as provided by Rule 36. When the respondent's lawyer receives the affidavit of no response, the lawyer will have to accept the fact that the admissions are made or take immediate steps to withdraw the admissions inadvertently made. The affidavit is useful because it prevents the defaulting party from claiming excusable neglect or inadvertence as a basis for withdrawing the admissions at trial.

■ TYPES OF RESPONSES TO REQUESTS FOR ADMISSIONS

When a respondent receives requests for admissions, the respondent has several alternatives: (1) deny the request, (2) admit the request, (3) assert an inability to admit or deny the request *and* explain in detail his or her reasons, (4) make a qualified denial, (5) object to the request. If the respondent elects to deny the request, the response may designate the request by repeating it and then state, "Denied." Rule 36 states the requirements for a denial or qualified denial:

> A denial shall fairly meet the substance of the requested admission, and when food faith requires that a party qualify his answer or deny only a part of the matter of which an admission is requested, he shall so specify so much of it as is true and qualify or deny the remainder.

If the respondent elects to admit the request, the respondent may intentionally let the time for responding expire, so that the request stands admitted; or serve a response that simply states the request is "admitted"; or repeat the request in a statement form. When the last approach is used, the response says; "[Name of party] admits that [request repeated word for word]."

The respondent may not evade responding to a request for admissions by simply stating he or she does not have the information with which to

---

1. An ex parte motion is made to the court without giving notice to the other parties in the case. Most motions are invalid unless duly served upon all parties as provided by Rule 5.

respond. The respondent is under an obligation to make "reasonable inquiry" to obtain the information. A respondent makes **reasonable inquiry** if he or she contacts people and reviews documents that are conveniently available to the respondent and asks for the information. The document or people who have the information need not be under the respondent's control. If the respondent makes the contact, and the people who have the information will not provide it, that explanation is a sufficient response. If the information is obtainable through another party, the respondent may be under an obligation to consult with the other party. On the other hand, the respondent does not have to travel or incur significant expense or conduct an investigation to determine where the information is or who has it.

Suppose the proponent requests the respondent to admit that Third Avenue is forty-eight feet wide from curb to curb at its intersection with Sixth Street. The intersection is in the same town as the respondent's residence. The respondent will have to drive to the intersection, measure it, and admit or deny the fact. However, suppose the accident in question occurred three years ago; the roadway has been reconstructed; and the request asks the respondent to admit that at the time of the accident, Third Avenue was forty-eight feet wide. If the respondent does not know, she does not have to conduct an investigation to determine who may know or what old records might provide the information. The proponent cannot shift to the respondent the obligation of investigating the facts. May the proponent ask the respondent to admit that the respondent does not know the width of Third Avenue as it was at the time of the accident? Yes. If the respondent does not have that information and cannot obtain it, the respondent should admit the fact that he or she does not know the width. More than likely, the respondent would provide an answer that contains an estimate or range on the width. The estimate would constitute a qualified denial.

If the respondent does not have the information with which to admit or deny and has made reasonable inquiry, the respondent may answer by stating that he or she "cannot admit or deny" the request, and then state the reasons why. The response is treated as a denial. Suppose the respondent did not have the information requested and contacted the people who did have the information, but those people would not voluntarily provide the information to the respondent. This is the kind of situation in which the respondent can justify neither admitting nor denying. The respondent does not have to take the deposition of the persons who have the information for the purpose of responding to another party's request. That would be an unreasonable burden on the respondent. The proponent of the request can conduct additional discovery if that is required.

An objection has the effect of a denial. When would the respondent have occasion to raise an objection? A request for admission is subject to the same relevancy requirement that applies to discovery procedures. The proponent cannot require the respondent to admit to a fact that is not relevant to the case. The proponent cannot require the respondent to admit a matter that is privileged. For example, the plaintiff in an automobile accident case could not request the defendant to admit that the defendant told his wife he went through the stop sign, because conversations between spouses are privileged.[2] One well-publicized privilege is the Fifth Amendment privilege against self-incrimination. If the proponent has served a request upon the respondent to admit that the respondent committed an act that was criminal, and the respondent and his lawyer know that he did commit the criminal act, the respondent cannot avoid the request for admissions by asserting the Fifth Amendment privilege. If he does refuse to admit or deny on that ground, the request stands admitted. On the other hand, the admission by silence could not be used against the respondent in a subsequent criminal action.

A party may object to a request on the grounds that it is too vague or unintelligible, but the safer course is to make a qualified admission by stating what is admitted, in the respondent's own words.

A request is objectionable if it is made for an improper purpose. For example, it is not proper to request the respondent to admit that she cannot or will not challenge a certain expert witness's qualifications to testify in the case. The expert's qualifications are not a matter of a fact and do not otherwise come within the purview of Rule 36. Such a request is directed at discovering the respondent's trial strategy, and that is not authorized.

■ PREPARING RESPONSES TO REQUESTS FOR ADMISSIONS

Paralegals may prepare a response to a request for admissions, but the respondent or the respondent's lawyer must sign it. The response does not have to be signed under oath; it is not testimony. Nevertheless, a party's response to a request for admissions may be used at trial in the place of evidence. Suppose the respondent admits she was the owner of the automobile at the time of the accident in question. Instead of questioning the party about that fact, the proponent of the request could stand before the jury and read the request and the response. When the judge instructs the jury at the end of the trial, the judge should tell the jurors they must accept the fact of ownership admitted in the response as true. They may not find otherwise.

■ CONSEQUENCES OF DENYING REQUESTS FOR ADMISSIONS

Rule 37(c) provides that the proponent who proves a fact or the genuineness of a document that the respondent denied may move the court for an order allowing the proponent to recover the costs the proponent incurred in proving the truth, including reasonable attorneys' fees. The rule provides that the court "shall" grant the proponent's motion for recovery of costs, unless the court finds that the request as drafted was objectionable, or that the request did not concern a matter that was really important to the case, or that the respondent had reasonable grounds to believe that the fact was not true or the document was not genuine. The respondent may assist himself or herself in this regard by carefully detailing the reasons why he or she cannot admit the request. Rule 37(c) leaves a nice catchall exception by

---

2. However, if a party says something to her or his spouse and the remark is overheard by another person, the remark is not privileged. A privileged communication retains its privileged status only as long as the owner of the privilege protects the privilege.

allowing the respondent to show "other good reason for the failure to admit." These criteria are very subjective and give the trial judge a great deal of latitude. The wording implies that the judge should lean toward disallowance of costs unless the respondent acted in bad faith. However, bad faith is *not* the test or standard.

If the proponent believes that a response is evasive, the proponent may move the court for an order "to determine the sufficiency of the answers [responses] or objections (Rule 36(a)). If the court determines that the respondent's response or objection is without merit, the court may order the respondent to answer the request. If the court determines that a response or objection is specious, the court may deem the request to be admitted. The court orders the request admitted. Another alternative is for the court to give the respondent a specified period of time in which to amend the response or face the consequences of an erroneous response.

Exhibit 16.1 is a sample of a negative response to requests for admissions. Requests for admissions should not be used as a substitute for a trial concerning fact issues over which there is a bona fide dispute.

■ EXAMPLE REQUEST AND RESPONSE

The set of requests for admissions in exhibit 16.2 contains an example of each type of request authorized by Rule 36. Notice that the requests are short, singular, and specific, except for number 4, which is poorly drafted. These requests are directed to a contested issue: ownership and legal responsibility for the operation of an automobile that allegedly caused the plaintiff's accident and injuries. The proponent wants to show that Raoul Esteban, who is a party to the case, was the owner of the automobile Theresa Pavoloni was driving when it struck the plaintiff's automobile. Esteban claims he was not the owner because he sold the automobile to Pavoloni shortly before the accident. Esteban is Pavoloni's father.

Defendant Esteban responds to the plaintiff's request for admissions as shown in exhibit 16.3. (*Note:* The response should repeat each request, but that step has been omitted from this example.)

■ EFFECT OF RULE 36 ADMISSIONS

A Rule 36 admission conclusively establishes the admitted fact for the purposes of the "pending action only." The purpose of Rule 36 admissions would be thwarted if a party could easily avoid an admission once it has been made. Consequently, Rule 36 prevents a respondent from withdrawing or changing an admission, unless the respondent can obtain the proponent's agreement or a court order allowing the change. The respondent must show the court good cause for allowing the withdrawal or change. As part of the good cause requirement, the respondent must show that the withdrawal or amendment will not **unfairly prejudice** the proponent of the request. A party is unfairly prejudiced if the party has relied upon the admission and the evidence is no longer available to prove or disprove the

■ **EXHIBIT 16.1**
Negative Response to
Requests for Admissions

RESPONSE TO REQUEST FOR ADMISSIONS

TO: Plaintiff and _____ , her attorney,

Come now defendants Dwight G. Hall and Willard Rosen and for their response to plaintiff's request for admissions state:

REQUEST No. 1. That the reasonable value of the medical expenses incurred by plaintiff as a result of the injuries received by plaintiff in the accident of September 20, 1994, are as follows:

Dr. Jerome Cowan	9-15-94 through 9-22-94	$ 92.00
Dr. Marilyn Berwin	9-22-94 through 2-5-95	308.00
Dr. Rebecca Copes	10-15-94 through 10-31-94	125.00
Midwest Medical Ctr.	9-21-94 through 9-27-94	1,082.60
Metro. Medical Assoc.	1-19-94 through 5-18-94	31.00
Drs. Peter, Elmer, and Hinkel	3-5-90	75.00
Prescriptions	10-3-94 through 7-15-95	21.00
TOTAL		$1,734.70

RESPONSE: DENIED

Defendants Hall and Rosen object to the request for admissions for failing to provide adequate documentation and information concerning these requests for admissions seeking to impose upon defendants the burden of securing copies of records at defendants' expense and reviewing those records at defendants' expense. Defendants have been unable to make reasonable inquiry of the various physicians due to plaintiff's failure and/or refusal to provide authorizations permitting defendants' counsel to interview them. Therefore, the information, known to defendants or information readily obtainable by defendants is insufficient to enable them to admit the request for admissions.

As of this time, plaintiff has not authorized defendants' counsel to interview the attending physician and hospital personnel. Therefore, defendants cannot verify the matters set forth in the various bills attached to plaintiff's request for admissions. Nor are defendants able to determine the qualifications, experience, or expertise of the various providers of health care to determine whether or not their charges for medical services are reasonable. If plaintiff would specify the amount of time spent by each provider of health care for each service rendered, defendants would be in a better position to evaluate the truth of the requests. Also, plaintiff should supply a copy of all hospital and medical records that are the bases for making the charges reflected in the bills attached to the request for admissions.

REQUEST No. 2. That if the proper parties were called to testify, they would testify that each of the aforementioned expenses for medical care and attention referred to in request for admission 1 was reasonable.

RESPONSE: DENIED. Please refer to response 1.

REQUEST No. 3. That in the event you deny either request for admission 1 or request for admission 2, supra, state the name, address, age, occupation, and employer of every person whom you will call to testify to dispute the reasonableness of such medical expenses.

RESPONSE DENIED. Please refer to response 1.

Dated: November 10, 1995   _____

                                                            Attorney for Defendants

Plaintiff Evan Schmidt requests defendant Raoul Esteban, within thirty days after service of this request, to make the following admissions:

1. You owned the automobile that Theresa Pavoloni was operating at the time of the motor vehicle accident described in the plaintiff's complaint.

   [*The plaintiff has requested admission of a fact. The fact is ownership of the automobile. In most cases, there is no dispute over the ownership of the vehicles, but in this case there is.*]

2. As owner of the automobile that Pavoloni was driving at the time of the parties' accident, you are vicariously liable for any legal liability that Pavoloni may have for said accident.

   [*The plaintiff has requested admission of the application of law to a given fact. Again, ownership is the fact. The plaintiff wants Esteban to admit that an owner is vicariously liable for the legal liability of the driver. That is the current law in all states. It is a simple legal proposition.*]

3. Pavoloni deposition exhibit 1 is a true and correct copy of the state certificate of title to the automobile that Pavoloni was operating at the time of the accident described in the plaintiff's complaint.

   [*The plaintiff has requested admission of the genuineness of a document. A document is genuine within the meaning of Rule 36 if it is what it purports to be.*]

4. While riding as a passenger in the automobile being driven by Pavoloni when the accident occurred, you observed the plaintiff's automobile before the collision and formed an opinion that the plaintiff's automobile was traveling at less then thirty miles per hour at the moment of the collision.

   [*The plaintiff has requested Esteban to admit to an opinion. Rule 36 allows the proponent to request the respondent to admit lay opinions and expert opinions when relevant. In this case, Esteban had already expressed the opinion in his deposition. The request will keep Esteban from subsequently changing the opinion. Note that this request is too lengthy and too involved to be a good one.*]

fact that was admitted. A proponent cannot be unfairly prejudiced if the respondent can show to a certainty. As part of the good cause showing, the respondent should show that the admission is not only wrong, but was made inadvertently. In this regard, a respondent is in a much better position to obtain relief from the court if the admission was duly made in writing rather than the result of letting the time period for responding expire without admitting or denying. Where a party can show that an admission is clearly a mistake, the court should allow the respondent to correct the error, but a respondent has a heavy burden when he or she tries to avoid a Rule 36 admission.

A fact may be admitted in answers to interrogatories or in a deposition. However, the deponent may subsequently deny or qualify the admission when testifying at trial. The only adverse consequence to the deponent is that the change may be impeaching. The jury may consider the change in the deponent's testimony in evaluating the deponent's credibility. On the other hand, a Rule 36 admission of a fact is conclusive and absolute, albeit not totally irrevocable. It cannot be explained away, assuming the request and the admission were clearly drafted. Courts characterize a Rule 36 admission as a judicial admission.

A Rule 36 admission is binding upon the proponent and the responding party. Though the Rules do not specifically say so, an admission is not binding upon a party who did not propound the request or was not required to respond to the request. Therefore, if a request for admissions is served by the plaintiff on one defendant and admitted by that defendant, the admission does not affect any other defendant.

The use of requests for admissions should facilitate trial preparation and the trial by establishing the truth. Is there a duty to correct a response that was true when given but subsequently became incorrect? Yes. What if the respondent denied a fact is true but subsequently discovered the fact is true? Does the respondent have a duty to correct the response? Yes. What if a party erroneously makes an admission? Does it make any difference whether the error was technical or inadvertent or now clearly demonstrable or always subject to some doubt? Yes.

■ **EXHIBIT 16.3**

Response to Request for Admissions

1. Denied. Although defendant Raoul Esteban was the registered owner of the automobile Theresa Pavoloni was operating at the time of the accident, the automobile in question had been sold to Pavoloni one week before the accident, as explained more fully in Esteban's deposition.

   [*Ownership is a fact. The fact will turn upon the validity of the purported sale.[1] The proponent has not succeeded in eliminating ownership as a fact issue.*]

2. Denied. Defendant Esteban objects to the request as hypothetical and not a request for application of a law to an admitted fact. The defendant denies that he is vicariously liable for punitive damages claimed by the plaintiff even if it is determined that Esteban is vicariously liable for the automobile accident in question.

   [*Request 2 is dependent upon how the respondent answered request 1. If request 1 had been admitted, presumably request 2 would have been admitted, except for the punitive damages issue that the respondent raised. The respondent found the request to be too broad and challenged the request even while denying it. It is proper and desirable for the respondent to point out defects in a request. The respondent called the requested fact hypothetical because he denies that it is true, but it still might be true.*]

3. Subject to response 2, admitted, that deposition exhibit 1 is genuine.

   [*The respondent has not admitted ownership by admitting that the document is genuine. The admission means that the proponent will not have to have a witness come to trial and testify in order to lay foundation for the use of the document.*]

4. Admitted.

   [*Suppose the request had been framed, "Please admit that in your deposition you testified the plaintiff's automobile was traveling less than thirty miles per hour at the time of the collision." What would be the effect or value of such a request? If the respondent admitted the request, would that prevent the respondent from giving a different opinion of speed at trial? If the respondent tried to change his testimony at trial to opine that the plaintiff's speed was forty-five miles per hour, would the change be in violation of Rule 36, or mere impeachment? A good argument could be made that the admission, as phrased, simply affirms what was stated in the deposition but does not commit the respondent to the less-than-thirty-miles-per-hour speed.*]

---

1. The law of most states places the burden of proof on the registered owner to show that he or she no longer owns the vehicle. Other states provide that registration is conclusive on the issue of financial responsibility for an accident.

■ RESCINDING A RULE 36 ADMISSION

An admission duly made is not irrevocable. The party who mistakenly made the admission should first request the opponent for permission to withdraw or correct the admission. If the parties can resolve the problem by agreement, usually reduced to a formal stipulation, that is the quickest and easiest method of handling it. Otherwise, admission may be withdrawn or modified only by permission of the court pursuant to a timely motion.

A motion to rescind a Rule 36 admission must (1) specifically request permission to withdraw or amend the admission, (2) state precisely how the proposed amended admission would read, (3) explain the reason for the amendment or withdrawal, (4) explain why the other parties will not be prejudiced by the correction. The motion should be supported by affidavits to establish facts relevant to the motion. Withdrawal of an admission may adversely affect another party's claim or defense in a significant manner. That does not mean the party has been prejudiced; the truth does not prejudice a party. However, if a party's ability to prove the truth has been prevented or hindered, as where a witness had died or other evidence has been lost, that party has been prejudiced. Also, a party is prejudiced if he or she is deprived of time in which to investigate or conduct discovery to gather evidence that was available. A motion to withdraw or amend an admission ought to anticipate these time and availability-of-evidence problems.

SUMMARY

Lawyers should strive to identify the areas of agreement as well as the areas of disagreement concerning the facts and the application of law to the facts. At some point before trial the parties may appreciate that some of the material facts are not disputed or should not be disputed. After identifying the areas of agreement, the parties may take steps to establish that there is no controversy concerning the particular facts. If a fact is clearly true, the party may avoid spending time, effort, and money to prove the fact by obtaining an admission that the fact is true. Admissions eliminate adverse surprises at trial and save the court's time.

Requests for admissions may relate to facts, opinions, statements, and the genuineness of documents. They may even relate to the application of law to facts. Requests for admissions may relate only to fact and opinions that are relevant to the lawsuit. A lack of relevancy is grounds for objecting to a request for admissions. However, a respondent does not admit relevancy by admitting the requested fact or opinion.

The proponent should state each request for admissions clearly. The proponent should prepare the requests so as to make it easy and comfortable for the respondent to admit each request.

An admission to a request for an admission takes the fact or opinion out of controversy. The fact or opinion is established for all purposes of the case in which the admission is made. The admission cannot be used against the respondent in another civil action. An admission may be withdrawn only with the proponent's consent or by a court order.

The respondent must serve a response in the form of an admission, denial, or objection within thirty days or within the time provided in the request if more than thirty days. If the respondent fails to respond, the request stands admitted. A proponent may serve and file an affidavit of no response to establish that the fact or opinion is now duly admitted by default. Rule 36 does not require an affidavit of default, and the decision whether or not to use such an affidavit is a strategic decision.

A respondent has a general duty to make reasonable inquiry to ascertain or corroborate requested facts or opinions. A respondent may not deny a request merely because it contains a minor, technical defect. A denial must "fairly meet the substance of the requested admission." A respondent may qualify an admission by identifying problems in the request or providing certain parameters that limit the scope and application of a response.

A request may be used to establish the nonexistence of a fact or document. Requests may be used in conjunction with interrogatories. Requests may relate to conclusions of law that are relevant to the case. An admission duly made may be read to the jury. The written response (admission) may not be submitted to the jury as an exhibit.

KEY TERMS

request for admissions
qualified admissions
qualified denials
genuineness

law of the case
unfair prejudice
reasonable inquiry
affidavit of no response

REVIEW QUESTIONS

1. Describe the consequences of a respondent's erroneous admission that she does not have a recorded witness statement from a particular witness.

2. How many requests for admissions may be served upon any one party?

3. State two reasons for serving requests for admissions concerning a fact that the proponent already knows is true.

4. What is the criteria for determining whether a party may properly serve a request for admissions?

5. What is the consequence of mistakenly denying a request for admission that was correct?

6. What is the consequence of failing to respond to a request for admissions within the time allowed for the response?

7. If a party realizes before trial that he mistakenly admitted a request for admission, what course of action should the party take to avoid the effect of the admission?

8. May requests for admissions be used in conjunction with interrogatories?

9. When may a respondent refuse to respond to a request for admissions on the grounds that the admission may violate her right not to incriminate herself?

10. How is a request for admission and its response presented to a jury during the trial of a civil action?

11. To what extent is a respondent required to seek out information he or she needs in order to admit or deny a requested fact?

A **fact brief** is a written analysis that identifies each material (controlling) fact concerning each claim and each defense, and the evidence to prove or disprove them. The analysis identifies the sources of the evidence, addresses the admissibility of the evidence, and anticipates how the evidence may be countered or opposed. The analysis must be conducted on an objective basis to be of value.

Lawyers do not routinely compile fact briefs when they prepare for trial, but they should always go through the kind of analysis that they would make in preparing a fact brief. Some law schools require students to prepare fact briefs as part of their trial advocacy courses. A fact brief may be used in a continuing education course to teach lawyers how to handle a new type of case. Our purpose here is to study legal analysis.

When a lawyer or paralegal prepares a fact brief, he or she necessarily conducts a methodical review of the fact issues and the evidence. The analysis will show whether the case is ready for trial and identify any deficiencies in the evidence that has been gathered. The analysis must be objective, by taking into consideration the opponent's evidence as well as the party's own. The preparation of a fact brief forces the legal team to anticipate how the opponent will use the evidence. More than anything else, a fact brief tells the paralegal and trial lawyer what more needs to be done to make the case ready for trial.

An airplane pilot uses a checklist to make sure he or she takes care of each preflight item. A fact brief is a custom-made checklist that helps the legal team determine whether it has all the evidence needed to prove every material fact and that helps the team determine the best way to present and use the evidence. Its primary value is in the preparation, where the analysis is done. A lawyer would never share her or his fact brief with the opposition. It is the ultimate work product document.

A fact brief may deal with the entire case in great detail, like the sample in exhibit 17.1, or it may deal with only one aspect of the case. The purpose remains the same: to ensure that the client is ready to go to trial and that the legal team has the basis for a winning strategy. A fact brief considers

■ **EXHIBIT 17.1**
Fact Brief

Abstract of Pleadings

Complaint	Answer	Reply, or None Required
On June 7, 1984, plaintiffs and decedent entered into an agreement whereby plaintiffs agreed to give up their home and to move into decedent's house, and to take care of decedent and his house until his death.	Denied—that plaintiffs agreed to care for the decedent.	Responsive pleading
In consideration of the agreement, decedent promised to convey his house and lot at Seventy-Four Golf Terrace, Edison, Minnesota, to plaintiffs.	Denied	
Plaintiffs gave up their home, moved in with William Brown, and fully performed their part of said agreement.	Denied—that plaintiffs performed their part of the agreement.	
Decedent devised his house to Edward Bordon in his will dated July 20, 1994, instead of devising his real property to plaintiffs as required by the agreement.	Denied—the existence of the agreement to devise decedent's property to plaintiffs.	
Plaintiffs performed personal services valued at thirty thousand dollars.	Denied—the performance of the services. No cause of action exists. Agreement is unenforceable because it is within the statute of frauds. Plaintiffs have been fully compensated by the salary of one hundred dollars a month, free rent and utilities, and the two-thousand-dollar bequest in the decedent's will.	

Issues

1. No agreement existed between the decedent and the plaintiffs whereby the decedent agreed to devise his real property at Seventy-Four Golf Terrace, Edison, Minnesota, to the plaintiffs in return for their services.

—Continued

—Continued

2. The services were not satisfactorily performed by the plaintiffs, and therefore they breached the contract, if there was one.

Defendant's Case-in-Chief

1. No agreement was made between the plaintiffs and the decedent whereby the decedent promised to convey his real property at Seventy-Four Golf Terrace, Edison, Minnesota, in return for the performance of services by the plaintiffs, for the facts are as follows:

   a. The complaint states that only one arrangement was made between the plaintiffs and the decedent.

   b. This arrangement was initiated and consummated on June 7, 1984, during a dinner party at the decedent's home, given in honor of Dr. Olson.

   c. Negotiations and statements concerning the arrangement were made during a card game in the presence of Dr. Carl Olson, William Mitchell, John Hughes, and William Brown, the decedent.

   d. The terms of the alleged arrangements were substantially these: The Hugheses agreed to move into the upstairs apartment of the decedent's home, and to take care of the yard and walks and perform other external maintenance on the house; in return the decedent agreed to pay the Hugheses one hundred dollars a month and to provide the apartment and utilities at no cost.

   e. At no time during the negotiations or the ensuing arrangement was any reference or mention made concerning the decedent's house, or any agreement to devise said house to the plaintiffs at the decedent's death.

   f. This proposal was made by the decedent to John Hughes, and after a short discussion with Mrs. Hughes, the plaintiffs accepted these terms.

   g. No mention was made by either party that the plaintiffs would be personally caring for the decedent.

   The law is as follows:

   Whether a contract was made is primarily a question of fact to be determined by the trial court. The burden is upon the plaintiff to prove the fact of the contract and its terms. The terms of the contract must be definite and certain, and the contract must be established by clear and convincing evidence. The oral contract is within the statute of frauds and may be enforced only through an action in equity.

2. The plaintiffs failed to satisfactorily care for the decedent's house and yard as provided by the contract.

   a. The plaintiffs failed to rake the leaves, as a result of which the yard usually appeared unkept in the fall and spring and aroused ill will among several of the neighbors.

   b. The plaintiffs failed to mow the grass at reasonable intervals, causing large portions of the lawn to become infested with crabgrass and other noxious weeds.

   c. The plaintiffs were normally several months late in changing the storm windows and screens and failed entirely to change the storm windows in 1993.

   d. The plaintiffs never shoveled the snow from the sidewalks.

   e. The plaintiffs failed to remove an accumulation of ice from the front sidewalk, the accumulation having occurred from the runoff of an eaves spout.

—Continued

—Continued

As a result, a passing neighbor fell and broke his ankle, and under threat of an action at law, the decedent paid $750 to the claimant as a settlement.

f. The reason for the lack of care given to the maintenance of the yard and house, besides irresponsibility, may be that the plaintiff was gainfully employed as a paintbrush salesman and, in carrying on his business, had little time to devote to the property.

g. The decedent did some of the outside work himself, when it became apparent that it would not otherwise be done.

h. The plaintiffs sporadically helped the decedent clean the lower floor of the house, and the decedent normally did his cleaning himself.

i. The decedent did his own cooking, laundry, and other personal duties.

j. The plaintiffs, although friendly with the decedent, remained apart from the decedent in both their everyday life and social activities. Mrs. Hughes was often out with her friends and entertained often in the apartment.

k. Robert Burger, the decedent's attorney, acted as the decedent's financial adviser and kept all his accounts.

l. As compensation for the arrangement, the plaintiffs received one hundred dollars a month, free rent, and utilities. They also received a bequest of two thousand dollars in the decedent's will.

m. The decedent was at all times in good physical condition and capable of caring for himself.

The law is as follows:

When an oral agreement is made unenforceably by the statute of frauds and does not merit specific performance, the plaintiff may recover only damages for services rendered under the agreement under the theory of quasi contract, and the measure of such recovery will be the value of the services rendered less the benefits the plaintiffs received under the contract. Nor can the plaintiff recover damages for breach of the oral contract. The value of the property to be devised is not a measure of recovery.

To recover specific performance, the terms of the contract must be definite and certain. The services must be performed under the terms of the contract. To merit specific performance, the services must be of a peculiar and personal nature. If the part performance of the contract is as beneficial to the plaintiff as to the decreased, specific performance will not be allowed.

Anticipated Case of Plaintiff

1. An oral contract existed in which the decedent promised to devise his house and lot to the plaintiffs: "If you come live with me and care for me and my house until I die, I will devise you my house." Mr. Hughes: "I accept."

Meet this by disputing the terms of the alleged contract and by contending that these terms do not specify that the plaintiffs were to assume a peculiar domestic relationship with the decedent.

2. The plaintiffs are entitled to recover thirty thousand dollars for the value of the services they performed.

Meet this by showing the services were not fully and adequately performed. Show what the proper measure of recovery is, and show that the plaintiffs have been fully compensated. Show the plaintiffs' failure to present their claim in probate court. Also show the actual value of the services the plaintiffs allegedly performed.

—Continued

■ **EXHIBIT 17.1**

Fact Brief, *Continued*

—Continued

3. The decedent made statements to neighbors to the effect that the plaintiffs were to receive the property when the decedent died.

   Meet this by showing that the witness is a friend of the plaintiffs and is biased. Show that the plaintiffs never objected to the will. Also show that the plaintiffs made statements adverse to their pecuniary interest.

4. The plaintiffs will testify as to their close relationship with the decedent.

   Meet this by showing that the decedent addressed the plaintiffs by their last names and did not appear well acquainted with them at the party on June 7, 1984. Show that the decedent was interested in activities with his own friends, that he was independent and capable, and that the relation was merely friendly. Show that Mr. Hughes worked a large number of hours each week, and that Mrs. Hughes was absorbed with her friends and community interests.

5. The plaintiffs will testify that they gave up a lease at a loss of one hundred dollars, a five-thousand-dollar-a-year job, and friends in moving from Anoka.

   Meet this by showing that the plaintiffs moved into a nice apartment and had many new friends, and that the plaintiff appeared to be fully employed.

Memo of Testimony-in-Chief for Defendant

1. William Mitchell, witness

   a. As to relationship with the decedent—
   Was longtime friend.
   Did work for same railroad. Is now retired.
   Lives at Seventy-Two Golf Terrace.
   Was hunting and fishing companion of decedent.
   Had conversation with decedent about getting someone to help him.
   Suggested calling minister.
   Decedent told him of the minister's suggestion.

   b. As to the oral agreement—
   Was invited to the dinner party of the decedent on June 7, 1984.
   Knew purpose of the party.
   Was with decedent when Olson asked if he could bring plaintiff.
   Was member of the card game and heard negotiations.
   Heard the terms: one hundred dollars a month, apartment, and utilities for services.
   Was with decedent at all times during evening and helped straighten up.

   c. As to the will—
   Was present when drawn up.
   Will was made on July 20, 1985, in evening.
   Will was drawn in presence of the plaintiffs.

   d. As to the quality of the work performed—
   Always had seasonal work done much before plaintiffs.
   William Brown did some of the yard work.
   Plaintiffs painted porch, but it had to be repainted.
   Noted specific items of disrepair and unperformed or misperformed services.
   Decedent did own cooking, and enjoyed it.
   Decedent did his own housecleaning, and laundry professionally.

   e. As to the decedent's health—
   Decedent's health was excellent for his age.

—Continued

—Continued

Accompanied decedent on hunting and fishing trips.

Decedent's illness of 1985 was a mild heart attack.

Decedent recovered in one and one-half months—two-week confinement to house.

Subsequent to illness, decedent was as sound as before—fishing, officer in church.

   f. As to the plaintiff's living quarters—

Complete apartment in second floor of decedent's house.

Originally furnished for Paul Smith and wife while going to university.

Outside entrance.

2. Robert Burger, witness

   a. As to the will of decedent—

Was called to hospital on July 20, 1985, to draw up will.

Reads the will to the court after identifying signature.

Plaintiffs were present when will was made.

All persons were in position to hear provisions—read provisions to decedent.

Plaintiffs did not object to provisions and have not to date.

Decedent was specific and clear on provisions he desired.

   b. As to the decedent's financial matters—

Decedent was a client for ten years.

Took care of all monthly expenses, as decedent did not wish to be bothered.

Paid taxes, utilities, and other monthly bills.

Paid the plaintiffs $100 a month by check.

Canceled checks were sent to decedent—does not know their whereabouts.

Paid threatened claim in amount of $750 as a settlement.

Thought claim valid because unnatural condition.

Took over decedent's investments in 1982.

Told by decedent that plaintiff was incompetent to invest and lost money.

Finally back into stable securities.

   c. As to the upstairs apartment in decedent's house—

Knew of the previous occupancy by Smith and wife.

Had advised what kitchen equipment to buy.

Has gone through it—five rooms and bath, all necessary facilities.

Is an expert in real estate—sells, buys, has made many leases.

Is familiar with decedent's neighborhood and price of apartments.

Rental value is one hundred dollars plus utilities.

   d. As to the decedent's health—

Saw him every month or two during the six years.

He was as alert and active after the illness as before.

3. Allen Anderson, witness

   a. As to the quality of work done by the plaintiffs—

Went by decedent's house every day on way to the bus.

Grass was never cut on time—crabgrass and noxious weeds set in.

Storms and screens were never changed on time.

Storms were never removed in 1993.

Sidewalks were never shoveled, except for a few times when decedent did it.

Leaves were never raked unless decedent did it—heard neighbor complain.

Saw plaintiff painting porch, later saw another painter doing it.

Fell on sidewalk and fractured left ankle.

Was off work for three weeks.

—Continued

■ **EXHIBIT 17.1**

Fact Brief, *Continued*

—Continued

      Told attorney to start action, but settled with decedent for $750.

      Fall occurred from hump of ice that had accumulated from eaves spout.

  b. As to the plaintiff's hours away from home—

      Many times saw plaintiff leaving house at 8:00 A.M.

      Often noticed him driving into the yard at about 5:00 P.M.

      Was given a ride to work by plaintiff several times.

      Plaintiff told him business was good and he was working long hours.

      Business was rushing during spring, summer, and fall, according to plaintiff.

  c. As to the plaintiff's statements adverse to his interest—

      During one ride, plaintiff said he hated to leave house when old man died.

      During another ride, said too bad the old man had relatives.

      State that witness had nothing against plaintiff; thought him OK.

Memo of Anticipated Testimony for Plaintiff

1. Raymond Quin, friend of the decedent's, will probably be called to testify to the terms of the oral agreement.

  a. See that he testifies only to facts within his own knowledge.

  b. Determine his relation with the plaintiffs. Impeach by use of friendly witness by showing intimacy with the plaintiffs.

  c. Test his certainty of the agreement.

  d. Have him corroborate the purpose of the party.

2. John Hughes, plaintiff, will probably be called to testify to the extent of his services and also to the oral agreement.

  a. See that he testifies only to facts within his own knowledge.

  b. See that he does not testify to any part of the oral agreement.

  c. Bring out the fact that he is an interested party.

  d. Impeach on investments and personal services by friendly witnesses.

3. George Robb, friend of the decedent's, will probably be called to testify to the quality of services performed by the plaintiffs, and subsequent statements of the decedent indicating his obligation to the plaintiffs.

  a. See that he testifies only to facts within his own knowledge.

  b. Determine how he observed the performance of the services.

  c. Counter subsequent admissions by the plaintiffs' statements to Anderson.

not only the adequacy of the client's evidence, but also how to maximize persuasiveness.

If a fact brief is more detailed than the one in exhibit 17.1, it is a **trial notebook.** A trial notebook is like a manuscript for a play. Some lawyers use it as a guide for presenting their case—particularly a complex case. A trial notebook may contain the questions and expected answers for each witness.

A fact brief is different from a **trial brief.** Lawyers prepare trial briefs to inform the judge about the law applicable to the case. A trial brief discusses the facts only insofar as necessary to provide a basis for the discussion of the law. A trial brief does not discuss how the party intends to prove the facts.

When a paralegal has the opportunity to help a trial lawyer prepare a case for trial, the paralegal will be more effective if he or she takes the time to prepare a fact brief. But if the paralegal does not have the time to draft a fact brief, he or she should at least conduct the analysis that goes into one. A fact brief helps the preparer to understand what facts are material to the case. A lawyer begins the preparation by reviewing the pleading. The pleadings should provide much of the basic information about the occurrence or transaction that gave rise to the litigation. The paralegal's review should follow these steps:

1. Set the complaint and the answer side by side and compare the allegations, admissions, and details.

2. Ascertain the elements in the plaintiff's cause of action and in the defendant's affirmative defenses. Consider what facts must be proved to satisfy those elements.

3. Identify and list the facts that each side must prove.

4. Determine what facts have been *conclusively established* by admissions in the pleadings, by Rule 36 admissions, by stipulations between the parties, and by the court's pretrial order. The remainder of the analysis will be conducted around those established facts.

5. Identify and describe the disputed facts. When the paralegal expresses the fact issue, the paralegal helps ensure that she or he understands the problem. By articulating the fact issue, even to herself or himself, the paralegal sharpens her or his thinking and recognizes important considerations. Checklists are important because they force a person to actually do what she or he is supposed to do.

6. Examine the evidence that has been gathered through investigation and discovery procedures.

7. Consider whether the legal team has all the evidence needed to establish each material fact to the client's cause of action or affirmative defense. If the client is defending against a claim or counterclaim, the paralegal must determine whether the opponent has all the evidence he or she needs to prove the claim. The paralegal must be objective.

8. Decide what evidence will be used to prove each material fact and how that evidence will be offered at trial. Specifically, through which witness or exhibit can or should the evidence be presented? Should the evidence be presented through more than one source?

9. Anticipate the evidence the opponent has on each material fact.

10. Decide how to counter the opponent's evidence on each material fact. Can the evidence be kept from the jury by making a motion in limine?[1] Can the evidence be excluded by making a legal objection to its admissibility? Can the source of the evidence be discredited as unreliable? If the source is a witness, is the witness subject

1. A motion in limine is used to exclude evidence that the moving party expects another party to offer during the trial. "In limine" literally means "at the threshold." The motion is made at the threshold of the trial out of the jury's hearing. The purpose is to prevent the jury from knowing anything about the objectionable evidence by keeping the opposing party from making any reference to the evidence. As a general rule, courts prefer not to rule on the admissibility of evidence until the evidence is actually offered, so the judge can assess the importance of the evidence in the context of the other evidence.

to impeachment on a collateral issue? Is there other evidence with which to contradict the opponent's evidence? Should that evidence be saved for rebuttal? Is there other evidence with which to explain or qualify the opponent's evidence? All these questions must be considered for each item of evidence, concerning each material fact.

The same kind of analysis must be made from the opponent's perspective. In other words, a trial lawyer must think about how the opponent will try to keep her or his evidence from being heard by the jury. The lawyer must anticipate the opponent's objections and prepare to meet them with argument and legal authorities. The lawyer must consider how to protect favorable witnesses just as much as how to attack adverse witnesses. The paralegal can help the trial lawyer by making sure the evidence is available and organized and its integrity is maintained.

The sample fact brief in exhibit 17.1 is concerned with an action to enforce a decedent's oral contract to make a will. The plaintiffs claim they had a contract with the decedent in which he promised to bequeath his house to them if they would take care of him for the rest of his life. Unfortunately for the plaintiffs, the decedent's will left the house to the defendant. This fact brief is one prepared by the defendant's lawyer to guide his trial preparation. The defendant wanted to sustain the will and keep the house for himself.

The defendant's lawyer has decided to challenge the plaintiff's claim that the decedent had made a contract to devise the property to the plaintiffs. This means he must find ways to avoid and discredit the plaintiffs' evidence. In addition, he is going to claim that even if the plaintiffs did have a contract with the decedent, they cannot enforce the contract because they breached it by not providing the services they claim they provided to him.

Some cases are so simple or routine that an experienced lawyer would not make even a cursory fact brief. However, even in the most simple case, a trial lawyer goes through the mental process of coordinating the evidence and fact issues. A paralegal may be asked to prepare an analysis of the facts and evidence considering the legal issues as outlined by the client's lawyer. The paralegal should try using the fact brief approach. The analysis must deal with the facts and evidence from the client's perspective *and* from the opponent's perspective. To be useful, the review or preview and the analysis must be objective.

The real value of a fact brief is its preparation. A fact brief is a lawyer's ultimate work product. Its structure forces a lawyer or paralegal to specifically examine each important factor that goes into the trial. For example, if the preparation of a brief leads a paralegal to discover that the client's answer to an interrogatory is wrong, she or he must act to correct the mistake by making a disclosure of the mistake and the true facts (Rule 26(e)(2)).

SUMMARY

The preparation of a fact brief begins with a comparison of the pleadings and determination of what facts remain contested. The fact brief identifies each material fact, the evidence that will be offered by each side to prove the fact, the source of the evidence, and how best to present or counter the evidence. A fact brief is an analytical tool that may be used by paralegals and lawyers to determine whether the case is ready for trial and to help prepare a trial strategy. When a paralegal or lawyer prepares a fact brief, he or she is forced to fully examine the case to determine whether the client has the ability to prove a prima facie case and whether the client has a persuasive case. If the paralegal or lawyer approaches the preparation properly, he or she will be very objective about the evidence and will give due consideration to the sources of evidence and all conflicts in the evidence.

Although the value of a fact brief is in the preparation, a fact brief could be turned into a trial notebook, which some lawyers use to guide their presentations, especially in complex litigation. A trial brief serves an entirely different purpose. The parties prepare trial briefs to help the trial judge to determine and apply the applicable law to the facts of the case. A trial brief is an assist to the court, whereas a party never shares a fact brief with the court or with the opposing party.

KEY TERMS

fact brief   trial brief
trial notebook

REVIEW QUESTIONS

1. For whom does a paralegal or lawyer prepare a fact brief?

2. What is the principal purpose for preparing a fact brief?

3. Do the Federal Rules of Civil Procedure require the parties to prepare preliminary fact briefs as part of their discovery plan?

4. At what point in the development of a case is a fact brief most valuable to the preparer?

5. May a fact brief that is prepared for one case be used in another case?

6. To what extent does a fact brief contain citations of legal authority?

7. Would a lawyer commit malpractice if he or she did not compile a fact brief when preparing for a trial?

8. Does a fact brief have to encompass the entire case in order to be useful?

9. What action must a lawyer and paralegal take, if during the preparation of a fact brief, they discover that their client's answer to the opponent's interrogatory is incomplete because it fails to disclose information that they have and that was duly requested in the interrogatory?

FINAL TRIAL PREPARATION

As soon as the parties realize they have a dispute, everything the parties do to gather evidence and develop their claims and defenses is trial preparation. In the final preparation, which the parties do shortly before the case commences trial, the paralegal and trial lawyer must organize the evidence and prepare it for presentation in court. At this point, all the witnesses have been identified and interviewed. Each witness has been committed to a version of the facts, usually in a deposition or a signed statement. Admissions have been made pursuant to Rule 36. The parties have resolved some disputes through written stipulations filed with the court. Nevertheless, the parties have been unable to settle the case. Now the parties must prepare for trial. A paralegal and trial lawyer may have a month in which to prepare, or they may have only a few days. The final trial preparation should never be left to the last minute.

The evidence must be prepared so that the trial lawyer can present it in its most effective form and manner. The lawyer or paralegal must prepare the witnesses to testify. The legal professional cannot tell them *what* to say, but the team can explain to them *how* to say what they need to say. All these activities and concerns come under the general heading of trial preparation. Trial preparation has the additional value of helping the parties to further evaluate the case for purposes of settlement.

■ TRIAL STRATEGY

A party's trial strategy is dictated by a combination of the client's version of the facts, the legal theories, and the available evidence. Legal theories must be considered in light of the impact that one legal theory may have on another. For example, assume the facts of the case are such that the plaintiff may be entitled to recover punitive damages from the defendant, in addition to compensatory damages. At first blush, it seems logical to pursue both claims. However, there are some ramifications that must be considered. Suppose the defendant has no assets with which to pay the punitive damages, and her liability insurance policy does not cover punitive damages. In that event, the plaintiff would likely never collect the punitive damages award. That fact must be considered in light of the common belief that juries may award less compensatory damages when they award substantial punitive damages in the same case. By pursuing a punitive damages claim, the net effect might be to reduce the client's net recovery of damages. Therefore, the better strategy may be to give up a potential claim for punitive damages.

Suppose the plaintiff was riding with the defendant when the defendant drove off the road into a tree, causing the plaintiff to be injured. The evidence shows that the defendant had consumed several beers shortly before the accident and may have been intoxicated. That could explain why the defendant lost control of the car and would establish that the defendant was negligent. However, suppose the defense is that the defendant was intoxicated, the defendant's condition was obvious, the risk of riding with the defendant was apparent, and the plaintiff assumed the risk of riding with him. Instead of presenting evidence of the defendant's intoxication, the plaintiffs lawyer needs to concentrate on showing why the plaintiff did not know the defendant was in no condition to drive. The legal professional must look at the case as a whole—the big picture. When he or she has evidence that proves one fact, it may disprove another fact. The lawyer and paralegal must have an overall strategy in order to appreciate what needs to be done and the best way of doing it.

The legal team needs to have a plan for presenting the client's case-in-chief and a plan for meeting the opponent's case-in-chief. In some respects, a trial is like a game of chess. The lawyer and paralegal must have an overall plan—a grand strategy. But they must have flexibility to deal with changing circumstances. They must make their moves, but also anticipate the countermoves. For example, if the opponent has a very strong witness concerning a crucial fact, the strategy must cope with it. The lawyer and paralegal must find a way of neutralizing the witness or the witness's evidence. Is there an objection the trial lawyer can make to keep the witness from testifying? Is there an objection the lawyer can make to keep the jury from hearing the crucial testimony? Are there similarly capable witnesses who can counter the opponent's witness? Can the witness be impeached by a prior statement? Is there circumstantial evidence that contradicts the witness? Can the client's side obtain some favorable testimony from the witness to leave the jury in a quandary about the overall significance of the testimony? Trial strategy must consider all the possible alternatives, and there usually are several. Lawyers may strongly disagree over the best strategy. There is no one best strategy. Furthermore, a strategy that works for one lawyer may not work for another.

■ SCHEDULING A TRIAL

When a case is filed in federal court, it automatically moves toward trial along with other cases. Some cases are accelerated on the calendar, and some are delayed because of special circumstances. In most instances, each case moves up according to the court's schedule and the presiding judge's wishes. The parties are expected to be ready for trial when called. Most state courts also have procedures that keep cases moving toward trial. However, in some courts a case may not be placed on the active trial calendar until a party has certified that the case is ready for trial. Paralegals should know which procedure the courts in her or his jurisdiction follow.

Historically, federal and state courts have scheduled cases for trial by conducting periodic **calendar calls.** The presiding judge selects twenty to fifty of the oldest cases on the docket and orders the trial lawyers handling those cases to appear for a calendar call. At the calendar call the judge asks each lawyer if his or her case is ready for trial. When a lawyer claims the case is not ready for trial, the lawyer has to explain the reasons. If the judge considers the reasons to be valid, the case is stricken from the trial calendar, usually on condition that it will be ready at the next calendar call. Occasionally, lawyers who are not ready for trial are forced to start trial anyway. Sometimes judges insist upon knowing whether the lawyers have discussed settlement and whether settlement is possible. Some judges require the lawyers to reveal how far apart the demand and the offer are. Some judges even want to know the amount of the plaintiff's demand and the amount of the defendant's offer. On the other hand, many judges do not want to know anything about the amount of the settlement offers and demands, because they are concerned that such information might influence them in their handling of the case.

The judge schedules the cases that are ready for trial in the order in which they were filed with the court. Sometimes the court modifies the chronological order to accommodate cases that have special problems and have to be tried at a particular time. If a party needs to have the case start trial on a certain day, the party can move the court for a **day certain** setting. If the moving party shows good cause for a day certain, the court can schedule the case to begin on a particular day. Day certain settings are reserved for cases that involve many parties and many witnesses, particularly when they have to travel long distances.

After the calendar call, the court issues an order listing the order in which the cases are to be tried. The list of cases alerted for trial is called the ready calendar or given some similar name. Lawyers who have cases on the ready calendar communicate with the lawyers who have cases ahead of theirs to find out how those cases are progressing, so that they can find out when their own cases might be reached for trial.

Usually the parties have at least one week between the calendar call and the commencement of the trial. Once the series of trials begins, a party may have no more than a half day's notice. When the clerk of court calls during the morning hours to tell the lawyer that her or his case will begin at 1:30 P.M., the paralegal can provide invaluable aid to get everything ready.

When a court is unable to dispose of all the cases that have been set for trial during the term, the remaining cases are usually given a priority setting at the next calendar call to ensure that they will not be passed over again. A court's inability to try the cases as scheduled may cause the parties considerable expense and frustration. However, no one has been able to devise a system that completely solves the problem of keeping the courtrooms busy and the cases tried when they are ready. If a court avoids scheduling too many cases, so that all scheduled cases are reached for trial, some cases will probably settle and the court will run out of work before the end of the term.

Today, most courts have **scheduling conferences** and **pretrial conferences** that take the place of calendar calls. The presiding judge conducts a scheduling conference soon after the case is filed with the court. A scheduling conference concerns only one case. The judge and lawyers try to establish a schedule for conducting discovery, for hearing dispositive motions, for a pretrial conference and a trial date. They try to select dates and times that are reasonable and convenient for everyone. However, the primary consideration is to ensure that the case is duly prosecuted by the parties and brought on for trial to end the dispute. The court tries to schedule the pretrial conference to be held after discovery has been completed but before the parties' final trial preparation will begin.

Courts are giving cases more individual attention by allowing the parties to participate in the preparation of scheduling orders. Rule 16(b) of the Federal Rules of Civil Procedures provides that a court has discretion to make a **scheduling order** at any time and to set a trial date. A scheduling order that sets a trial date pursuant to Rule 16 is usually part of a comprehensive schedule that deals with all aspects of the case leading to the trial, such as discovery, motions, settlement conferences, and so forth. If one or more of the parties determine that the schedule is not realistic, the parties have to move the court to modify the schedule. Otherwise, the case goes to trial as scheduled. A pretrial conference order may also deal with various trial management problems.

If a case has been placed on the calendar for trial but the parties agree that it really is not ready, the court will usually accept the parties' stipulation to have the case stricken. If a case is struck under such circumstances, it may be reinstated by a stipulation that leads to the appropriate court order, or it may be reinstated by a motion made by one or both parties. However, if a party is not ready to go to trial because he or she has been dilatory, the court has authority to order the case to trial despite the disastrous consequences that an immediate trial may have for the dilatory party. A party's neglect or dilatory conduct should not work to the prejudice or disadvantage of any other party. Otherwise, a dilatory party could obstruct justice. Justice should not be delayed. A good case, whether for the plaintiff or the defendant, deteriorates with the passage of time. Consequently, a poor case may improve with the passage of time.

■ ALERTING THE CLIENT AND WITNESSES

Regardless of the manner in which the case is set for trial, as soon the paralegal and the trial lawyer receive a trial date, one of them must notify the client about the trial schedule. The paralegal should be able to tell the client when the trial will start and how long it will last, so that the client can arrange to be available for the entire trial. A surprising number of clients wonder why they have to attend the entire trial. The client should be there for every minute of the trial. The client should be there to help with problems as they occur and to see how the case develops.

Furthermore, the legal team does not want the jury to infer that the client is not really interested in the case. An officer should personify a company.

The lawyer and paralegal must alert all the witnesses that the case has been scheduled for trial and tell each witness when he or she will be needed to testify. If a witness is cooperative, the paralegal may simply telephone the witness to alert him or her. When there is time, a paralegal should follow up with a letter confirming the arrangements. If a witness is uncooperative, the paralegal should subpoena the witness as provided by Rule 45. The word *subpoena* means "under penalty of law." A person who has been duly served with a subpoena must appear in court at the designated time and bring along the items specified in the subpoena.

Lawyers must have their witnesses in court at the time they are needed. When a subpoena is served upon a witness or party, the onus shifts from the lawyer to the person subpoenaed to be at court at the designated time. If the witness fails to appear as scheduled, the lawyer is in a good position to obtain a delay of the trial or even to obtain an order for a **mistrial,** because of the unavailability of the evidence. (An order declaring a mistrial voids the trial. The trial must start again from the very beginning, including selection of a new jury.) A party who has taken the precaution of subpoenaing a reluctant or forgetful witness cannot be blamed or penalized for the witness's failure to appear. The court may order the sheriff or marshal to find the witness and bring the witness to court for an explanation and possible punishment. A person who fails to comply with a subpoena may be held in contempt of court. On the other hand, a trial lawyer has no recourse against a witness who fails to show up but has not been subpoenaed.

Subpoenas are also served because a witness may need one to show to his or her employer to justify getting off work. Some public officials and some hospital personnel have rules that prevent them from going to court without a subpoena. Sometimes such people only need the subpoena for their office records, so they do not insist upon actually being served. The subpoena may be sent to them by mail. However, if the subpoena is not duly served, it is unenforceable. If the witness does not appear as requested, the lawyer has no recourse through the subpoena. The lawyer cannot tell the judge the witness was subpoenaed if the witness was not duly served. If a witness must appear at a particular time and if there is any doubt about whether the witness will come to court when needed, it is better to serve the subpoena as provided by Rules 45 and 4.

Service of a subpoena is the only means that a party has to compel a reluctant or unreliable witness to come to court. A subpoena gives a court jurisdiction over the person who has been duly served, just as service of summons and complaint gives the court jurisdiction over a party. However, a courts authority over a witness is limited to requiring the witness to appear and testify.

If the lawyer and paralegal want to be sure the opposing party will attend the trial at a particular time so that she or he can be called for cross-examination, they can compel the party to appear by serving a subpoena. An alternative is to ask the court to state in the pretrial order that the opposing party must make herself or himself available for cross-examination. The parties are already under the court's jurisdiction, but no rule says a party has to attend the trial, unless the party is specifically ordered or subpoenaed.

That could be a real problem if the opposing party has evidence that is critical to the client's claim or defense.

Subpoenas may be obtained from the clerk of court, sometimes called the court administrator. Sometimes it is difficult to know exactly when the witness will be needed. Consequently, the legal team may not know what time to designate in the subpoena. They can accommodate the witness and protect themselves by designating the earliest time the witness might be needed, but tell the witness he or she may remain at home or at work until the court is ready, if he or she will stay near a telephone so that the lawyer and paralegal can call the witness on short notice. If the witness fails to show up, they have all the protection of the subpoena. Only the court or the lawyer who caused the subpoena to be served may release the witness from the subpoena. The release may be given as a simple oral statement.

■ PRETRIAL CONFERENCES

Rule 16(c) authorizes district courts to conduct pretrial conferences to facilitate trial preparation and management. The judge may initiate the pretrial conference, or one of the lawyers may ask the court to schedule the conference. A pretrial conference is a meeting between the presiding judge and the lawyers. Sometimes the parties are allowed to attend. The meeting may be held in the courtroom or in the judge's chambers. The rule even authorizes the judge to conduct the meeting by a telephone conference. Sometimes the judge has a court reporter make a verbatim record of the meeting. The purpose of having a record is to preserve the parties' stipulations and commitments. Furthermore, the court may make orders during the conference that need to be preserved.

Purpose

Rule 16 includes several purposes for pretrial conferences.

Simplify the Fact Issues and the Legal Issues. The court simplifies the issues by obtaining the parties' agreement to eliminate claims, defenses, facts, and even evidence that has no merit or relevancy. For example, if at the time the defendant interposed the answer she believed that the plaintiff's claim would be barred by the statute of limitations but new information shows that the statute of limitations is not applicable, the defense should be withdrawn. The judge may ask a party's lawyer how he or she intends to prove the defense, what evidence he or she has, and what precedent supports application of the rule of law claimed by the lawyer. The judge's questions may persuade the lawyer or party to voluntarily dismiss a claim or defense.

The judge's pretrial order may order **frivolous** claims and defenses stricken. A claim or defense is frivolous if there are no facts to support it or the legal theory is contrary to established law. Any party who prosecutes a frivolous defense or claim is subject to sanctions and possibly to disciplinary action. The sanctions may include the assessment of costs, an order striking the party's pleadings, or even an award of judgment in favor of the opposing party. A lawyer and/or the party could even be held in contempt of court (see Rule 11).

Determine the Necessity of Amending the Pleadings and Establish Time Limitations for Doing So. The pretrial conference is a time to correct or amend pleadings as needed. The need for amendments may arise from new information a party obtained after the initial pleadings were served. Rule 15 provides the means for amending pleadings by motion. But the pretrial conference presents the ideal opportunity to take care of such "housekeeping" matters, and perhaps the last opportunity to do so. The plenary power of the court enables the court to order amendments at the pretrial conference though no party served a notice of motion to amend.

Explore the Possibility of Obtaining Parties' Admissions to Uncontroverted Facts. The pretrial conference gives the judge and the lawyers the opportunity to discuss the facts and how the parties intend to prove the facts. To the extent the parties can agree on some facts, the court's **pretrial order** states the parties' agreement. The effect is similar to that of a signed stipulation or Rule 36 admission. The agreement saves time and expense and reduces some of the uncertainties of litigation. The parties may not agree on the application or effect of certain evidence and exhibits, but that does not prevent them from stipulating to the evidence. They may stipulate to the foundation for exhibits. For example, the parties commonly agree (stipulate) to foundation for hospital records so that the medical record librarian does not have to come to court to identify the records. The parties also commonly stipulate that copies of records may be used at trial in place of the originals. Parties may agree on the reasonableness of charges for medical care without agreeing that the medical care was necessary or even caused (necessitated) by the accident. When parties stipulate to the foundation for an exhibit they agree that the exhibit is what it purports to be, or what they say it is.

Deal with Legal Issues. The court may conclude that the case raises particularly difficult legal issues concerning jurisdiction, evidence, jury instructions, constitutionality, or other legal problems. The court may request (order) the lawyers to file memorandum of law concerning the issues. The memorandums may be due at the time of trial or before. Or the court may schedule another pretrial conference for dealing with difficult issues.

Consider Limiting the Number of Expert Witnesses. Lawyers are tending to increase their use of expert witnesses to prove their claims and defenses, even when experts are not needed and even though expert testimony is expensive and time-consuming. So far the courts have not seriously tried to limit the number of experts who may testify to an issue. Nevertheless, courts have retained the right to limit the number of experts that a party may call. Suppose the plaintiff brings a medical malpractice action against his physician, a hospital, and a medical products manufacturer, alleging that each was negligent and caused his injury. The plaintiff will need an expert witness to testify to the medical problem, another to testify that the defendant violated the standard of care of medical doctors, and another to testify to the alleged product defect. Clearly, the plaintiff will be entitled to have three expert witnesses. But suppose the plaintiff wants to have three expert witnesses testify that the physician did not comport with medical standards and four expert witnesses testify about the alleged product defect. The plaintiff might want to use so many experts simply because the number might influence the jury. The judge would seriously question whether so many experts would be helpful to the jury. Certainly, that many experts are not necessary. The opposing party usually feels compelled to hire an equal number of experts. A court must be pragmatic about the number of experts a party may call, and keep the presentation fair to both sides.

Consider Referring the Matter to Arbitration or Mediation or a Referee. Courts and lawyers are showing increased interest in **alternative dispute resolution,** sometimes called **ADR.** It is useful when both parties want to conclude the dispute as quickly and economically as possible. The special rules of some courts now require the parties to go through nonbinding ADR before the case may be tried. The parties may accept the ADR award, or the parties may convert the ADR award to a judgment and dismiss the case, or a party who disagrees with the award may insist upon going ahead with a jury trial. In the last event, if the party who insisted upon a trial does not obtain a ''better result'' in the trial, that party may be required to pay the opposing party's trial expenses. The jury would not be told about the parties' use of ADR or the ADR award.

Explore Other Matters That May Help the Court Facilitate a Disposition of the Case, Including Encouraging the Parties to Discuss Settlement. Approximately 90 percent of all cases settle before or during trial. Since so many cases do settle, the civil justice system is trying to devise ways to help the parties settle earlier; sooner is better. Therefore, Rule 16(c)(9) expressly authorizes the presiding judge to use her or his office to encourage settlement negotiations or ADR.

Attendance

Rule 16 requires that the lawyer who attends the pretrial conference must have authority to make stipulations and to make admissions of the type authorized by the rule. A lawyer cannot refuse to admit a fact or dismiss a claim or defense on the grounds that he or she does not have authority to make the commitment. Nevertheless, the lawyer or other representative does not have to make unreasonable agreements or admissions that are not well justified. If the lawyer does not have the client's authority, the client must attend the conference in person.

If an insurance company is interested in the case, although not a named party, the insurance company's representative is often invited to attend the conference, especially if the insurance company has retained the authority to make stipulations and admissions. An insurance company may be interested in the outcome of the case because it provides liability insurance to the defendant or because it has a subrogation right to some of the litigation proceeds. When a liability insurer controls settlement negotiations, it is particularly important for the representative to attend the conference.

■ ORGANIZING THE EVIDENCE

The process of organizing and evaluating the evidence usually begins with a review of the investigation materials, interrogatory answers, experts' reports, and oral deposition transcripts. Some evidence that seemed very important in the early stages of the case may be less significant at this stage because of stipulations or admissions made pursuant to Rule 36. On the other hand, some evidence that at first seemed minor may have become critical because it bears on an apparent conflict in the anticipated testimony. Some lawyers like to begin organizing the evidence after composing their final arguments. They decide what they want to be able to tell the jury. Then they try to make sure the evidence will support the proposed argument. There is no established formula to guide trial preparation. Each lawyer must decide when to begin each phase of the preparation and determine how to coordinate the preparation. Nevertheless, some fundamental considerations are applicable to most cases.

The lawyer and paralegal must be objective when evaluating the evidence, whether the evidence is the client's or the opponent's. Just because they have a witness who will testify favorably on an important point does not mean the jury will believe the witness or the witness will not cause the client problems in some other regard. Since almost all evidence is introduced through witnesses, it is logical to organize the evidence around the individual witnesses—the client's and the opponent's. The legal team should begin by identifying the remaining fact issues, and then determine what role each witness can have concerning each fact issue. Not all witnesses will have a connection with all the fact issues. Some of the opposing party's witnesses will have some evidence that is helpful to the client's case. Next, the lawyer and legal assistant should determine what evidence can be presented through each witness, whether the evidence is testimony or exhibits. They may have to introduce some evidence through witnesses aligned with the opponent. They should consider whether each witness can confirm or give support to evidence introduced through another witness.

For each disputed fact the lawyer and paralegal will have a witness listed who can help to prove the client's version of the fact. For each witness they will have a list of the evidence that can be presented through that witness. They must note the source of each item of evidence. If the evidence is testimony, the source is the witness. If the evidence is in an exhibit, the exhibit must be identified. The legal team must identify sources for impeaching evidence such as the answers to interrogatories, deposition transcripts, witness statements, photographs. If either side is going to present expert testimony, the important points should be gleaned through the experts' reports depositions, and answers to interrogatories. The important information must be extracted.

The facts established by admissions in the pleadings and in response to Rule 36 requests do not require evidence to be proved at trial. They are conclusively established. The jury will be told that those facts are established and that the jury is to accept those facts as incontrovertible. Therefore, as part of the overall trial strategy, no evidence should be presented that conflicts with those established facts. Indeed, the lawyer and paralegal should find ways of using the admissions to support the client's theory of the case and the client's evidence. Similarly, they should avoid using evidence that conflicts with the physical facts. Indeed, they should make sure that all the client's evidence comports with the physical facts. If a theory or evidence does not comport with physical fact, it is not possible and not believable. For example, if a party's version of an intersection collision is that "suddenly the other car appeared before me," the only reasonable inference is that the party was not keeping a proper lookout. Cars do not "suddenly appear" in intersections. Or if the client is the defendant, and she says she just "bumped" the plaintiff's car, but photographs show five thousand dollars' worth of damage, the client's description of the accident is not consistent with physical fact. The client's evidence of a "bump" will be rejected. The really negative consequence of improbable evidence is that a jury is inclined to be suspicious of any other testimony or other evidence offered by the witness giving that evidence.

For another example, if the defendant's answer admits that her automobile struck the plaintiff's automobile, because that is what the defendant believes, it is self-defeating to offer testimony that is contrary to the admission—even if the defense has found a witness who believes the defendant did not strike the plaintiff's automobile. If the admission in the answer is in error, it should be corrected, if possible, by stipulation or court order. Similarly, if the defendant has good photographs showing that her automobile left skid marks twenty feet long leading to the point of collision, it would be counterproductive for the plaintiff to offer "eyewitness" testimony that the defendant made no effort to stop before the collision. Or suppose the plaintiff wants to testify that the defendant's car was traveling thirty miles per hour, or more, when it struck the plaintiff's car. However, photographs show that the contact caused only a slight dent in a fender and the repair bill is consistent with only minor damage. If the plaintiff were to *mistakenly* testify to a thirty-mile-per-hour collision, the testimony would adversely reflect upon the plaintiff's own credibility. The plaintiff's testimony conflicts with common experience and the physical facts. The trial lawyer's strategy and preparation must deal with this kind of problem.

The lawyer and paralegal must make sure the evidence is admissible, then decide how the evidence should be presented to be most persuasive. For example, foundation for the admissibility of hospital records could be established by the hospital administrator, or by stipulation, or maybe through a treating physician who made entries in the records and is otherwise familiar with how the records are made and kept. Each method has its own advantages and disadvantages. Testimony from the hospital administrator or a medical records librarian may be more impressive to the jury, but more expensive for the client and more time-consuming for the trial. Is it worth the cost? Suppose the opposition is willing to stipulate that the client's expert witness is qualified to give the expert opinions stated in the expert's report, but by so stipulating the opposition wants to exclude the expert's résumé and background evidence. Although the stipulation would make certain the expert will qualify and would shorten the expert's testimony, it might take away from the authority of the client's case.

The lawyer and paralegal should decide whether their tangible evidence is in the best form for use. For example, should enlargements be made of some of the documents and photographs? Should some illustrative exhibits be made, to help the witnesses explain the facts to which they will testify? It may be apparent that the client is going to have great difficulty explaining how the automobile collision occurred. If the client had a scale drawing of the intersection to use, maybe she could do a much better job of educating the jury about what happened and how it happened. In that event, a scale drawing should be prepared, and model cars to go with it.

Each item of evidence a party presents should complement the other evidence. For example, in medical malpractice cases the defendant physician can present medical and hospital records that were made contemporaneously with the patient's treatment. Entries would have been made by the physician and by hospital personnel. The physician's testimony should find support in the records, so that the records and the testimony complement each other. If a significant inconsistency exists, even a suspicious omission, the physician's case loses some credibility.

When there are conflicts in the client's evidence, the lawyer and paralegal must try to resolve them. They should first try to determine whether the conflicts are actual or merely apparent, in the sense that they *seem* to exist but do not really exist. Apparent conflicts often arise from a misunderstanding of the evidence or false assumptions about the evidence or false assumptions about the facts. One way of dealing with misconceptions and false assumptions is to reinspect the occurrence situs. An inspection may show why one witness could make an observation that another witness at another location could not make or would make differently. The phenomenon is known as a parallax. If the case involves a transaction, such as the breach of contract to construct a building, it may be necessary to examine the building—not just the written contract. When the legal professional sees the alleged problems with the structure, he or she may have a better feel for the evidence. Personal observations will help the lawyer and paralegal to communicate with the client and with the witnesses. Experienced trial lawyers know they have to have personal knowledge about the subject to be able to conduct an effective cross-examination.

Finally, the lawyer and paralegal should always try to keep the evidence interesting to the jury and judge. The evidence should build as it tells the client's story.

The legal professional must pay attention to the details. Careful development and use of details gives authority, credibility, and persuasiveness to the client's case. When the details are carefully developed, and kept interesting and consistent, the rest of the case almost takes care of itself.

■ PREPARING THE CLIENT TO TESTIFY

Preparing the client to testify at trial requires at least two meetings, and sometimes more. The value of the preparation fades quickly with the passage of time; therefore, it must be done shortly before the trial. A paralegal may take a major role in preparing a client for trial, including preparing the client to testify. The paralegal needs to explain to the client the status of the case. Hopefully, the status is good. All the evidence that is reasonably available has been obtained. The paralegal needs to explain what will happen at the trial, that is, the trial procedures. This helps the client to be less anxious about the trial. She or he should preview the trial lawyer's strategy and explain what the client may do to help during the trial. For example, the client should carefully listen to the witnesses testify and be prepared to discuss their testimony with the trial lawyer during recesses. The paralegal should be candid with the client about any problems in the case about the uncertainties of litigation. She or he should explain how the client should conduct herself or himself while at the courthouse and during the trial. The client should be pleasant and on her or his best behavior. The client should try to develop a positive attitude about the jury by presuming that the jurors like her or him.

If the client's discovery deposition was taken, the paralegal should make sure the client has a copy of the transcript to study. The client must review the transcript before the trial. This is one of the reasons for having two meetings. At the first meeting, the paralegal and client can review the transcript, emphasizing important parts. The client should study the transcript. In the next meeting, the client's testimony must be prepared. The client should be put through a direct and cross-examination. In the first meeting, the paralegal may highlight significant points in the transcript for the client to emphasize, but the paralegal should not use highlighting excessively, because it loses its significance. Furthermore, the client must study the entire transcript, not just the highlighted parts.

The client should be encouraged to write down questions as they occur to him or her during this preparation phase. The paralegal can answer the questions when the two next meet. If the client does not write down questions and suggestions, the client will likely forget some of them before the next meeting. When that happens, the client worries that there was something important to ask and become anxious about not being able to remember what it was. This is a time for making lists of things to do in order to make sure nothing is forgotten or overlooked. Making and using lists are part of thorough preparation.

The client needs to establish rapport with the jury. Unless the client is a professional actor or has been schooled in public relations, she or he is going to need much help. A client must look and feel comfortable, not only while testifying, but throughout the trial. The hallmarks of a good witness are *sincerity* and *authority*. The appearance of sincerity comes from the presentation, the manner in which the witness testifies and from the witness's demeanor. A witness appears sincere when the witness appears to believe what he or she is saying. The appearance of authority comes from an ability to remember and relate the facts, an ability to cope with factual details, and a confident attitude without arrogance or a tendency to be overbearing.

The paralegal may explain to the client the legal theory of the claims, the legal theory for the defenses, the evidence that is available to both sides, and the steps that are being taken to prepare for the trial. This information will help the client to feel more comfortable about the upcoming trial and confident that he or she is well represented. The paralegal also needs to explain the trial procedures so that the client understands what is expected of him or her. The client may have already had the experience of testifying in a deposition. However, the guidelines for testifying in a discovery deposition do not necessarily apply to testifying in trial. Remember, the objectives in the discovery deposition were different. In the deposition, the lawyer was not trying to prove a claim or defense; at trial, he or she is. Testimony at trial is focused and offered for a purpose, not to obtain information.

When preparing for the discovery deposition, the client was told to just answer each question briefly—to not explain the answer, not volunteer information. That was good advice for handling the discovery deposition. However, it is not good advice for testifying at trial to a judge or jury. When the client testifies at trial, the lawyer wants the client to educate and persuade the judge and jury. A witness who merely answers each question with a short statement does not educate or persuade listeners. Short answers at trial make the witness look evasive and defensive. Instead, the client should be instructed to tell her or his version openly, in full sentences and paragraphs. The client should use every question as an opportunity to tell the jury what the jury needs to know about the case.

It takes much preparation to be able to make that kind of presentation without appearing overbearing. The first step is to get the client to testify using full sentences, not just words and phrases. The client should think in terms of the points in controversy. The client's answers should be designed to explain those points fully. This is true whether the question comes from the client's lawyer or from the opponent's lawyer. Ideally, a witness should respond to all questions in the same manner, no matter who asked them. In other words, it is counterproductive for a witness to appear open and friendly toward his or her own lawyer but hostile and defensive when questioned by the opposing lawyer.

The best preparation is an actual direct examination and cross-examination. A mock examination will identify the problems and weaknesses in the client's testimony. The client should be asked some "trick" questions that assume facts favorable to the opposition. The client should be helped to deal with such questions to the point that the client's lawyer will have very little need to object to improper questions, because the client has "all the answers." The client should write down the important facts and figures to reinforce his or her recall. But the client must understand that he or she cannot take any notes to the witness stand. The client may take a copy of the deposition transcript and will have access to the exhibits, but nothing else may be used as an aid while testifying.

If an exhibit is going to be offered into evidence through a particular witness, the procedure should be explained to the witness. If the witness shows any uncertainty, the procedure should be rehearsed.

The client should not appear to know her or his "story" so well that it appears to be fabricated. That could happen if the client memorizes prepared testimony. The client should know the facts to which she or he will testify, but not memorize a presentation. The facts should be committed to memory. But that is quite different from memorizing a "script." The client's credibility will be enhanced if she or he reflects briefly on each question before answering. She or he should answer questions directly, in a deliberate manner. The client should look at the jury while testifying and at the lawyer while the lawyer is asking a question.

The following recommendations for testifying in court before a judge and jury should be helpful:

1. Have a positive attitude about the trial and about the jury. Look upon the trial as an opportunity to obtain deserved justice.

2. Be polite in and out of the courtroom. Do not overreact to the evidence or anything else that happens during the trial. Never lose your temper. Do not make jokes. Regardless of what happens during the trial, remain calm and deliberate. Try to be relaxed. While testifying, if you become irritated, tired, confused, or physically uncomfortable, ask for a short recess or just a drink of water.

3. Try to keep the big picture in mind. It provides a frame of reference. Become acquainted with what the other witnesses will probably say

when they testify. If the testimony of other witnesses conflicts with yours in some significant respect, be sure you know why the conflict exists and know how you are going to deal with the facts underlying the conflict when on the witness stand.

4. Avoid discussing confidential matters in the presence of strangers, other witnesses, or jurors. The privilege status of attorney-client communications is lost if either permits another person to hear or see the communication.

5. Make written notes about important developments during the trial so that they can be discussed later, during recess.

6. Act interested and sincere on the stand and anywhere you might be observed by members of the jury, opposing party or lawyer.

7. When a lawyer asks a question, whether on direct examination or cross-examination, look at the lawyer. When answering questions, look at the jury at least two-thirds of the time and the lawyer who asked the question about one-third of the time. Avoid looking at the ceiling, out the window, or at the floor. Do not steal furtive glances at your lawyer, as if to say, "I really made a good point!" or "Please help me!"

8. Explain your answer when it seems appropriate. A witness has the right to answer fully. This right cannot be abridged. The opposing lawyer may object on the grounds that your answer is not responsive. Do not be concerned if the judge sustains the objection and instructs you to "just answer the question." The jurors will not be unhappy with you, provided you are trying to tell them something about the case at hand. If the lawyer objects that the answer is not responsive or went beyond the question, you should not feel as though you did anything wrong, as long as you feel your answer is relevant to the question.

9. If you realize that you have given an incorrect answer, correct the mistake as soon as you realize it. You can simply tell the judge that you want to correct something you said earlier, and the judge will tell you that you may speak now or that it can be taken care of when your lawyer has the opportunity to ask questions. Your request will be a signal to your lawyer that you have something more to say about a matter already covered.

10. Avoid expressions such as "to tell you the truth" or "to be honest with you" or "to the best of my knowledge." If you believe the testimony is true, there is no need or reason to qualify it. These phrases weaken the testimony and take away from your authority. If you are dealing with an *estimate* or *judgment*, use those words. Remember, a mere *guess* cannot be received into evidence.

11. Avoid exaggerating and minimizing.

12. Visit the accident location and study it. Compare the site with photographs of the scene and diagrams that may be used as exhibits.

13. Do not argue, fence, or joke with the lawyers while you are on the witness stand. Statements suggesting disagreement should not be made in a disagreeable manner.

14. If a lawyer tries to put you on the defensive by starting a question with "Do you admit that . . ." it may be appropriate to tell the lawyer you do not know what he or she means by "admit," but you do *agree* with the statement.

15. Do not deny that you prepared yourself to take the stand by reading your deposition transcript, viewing the accident scene, examining the exhibits, and conferring with your lawyer. But do not let the opposing lawyer suggest that you do not have an independent recollection of the facts to which you have testified. You cannot testify to something that someone else has written or that is based upon what you heard from someone else. You must base your testimony upon what you observed and know of your own knowledge. You may testify from something that you wrote when the information was fresh in your mind. But then the writing becomes the best evidence, and the entire writing may come into evidence whether you want it to or not.

16. Do not refer to insurance unless specifically advised by your lawyer, before taking the witness stand, that insurance is a proper subject in the case. The judge, lawyers, and other witnesses will carefully avoid mentioning insurance, because there is the belief that jurors might be too generous if they think they are awarding insurance benefits or money. An improper reference to insurance could cause a mistrial.

The client should be told about the trial procedures so that the client understands what is happening as it happens. The client will be more comfortable knowing that the case is going as it should. In this regard, the client needs to know that the lawyers will meet with the judge in chambers for a few minutes to discuss questions of law, scheduling of witnesses, preliminary motions, and possibly settlement. Lawyers select a jury by conducting a voir dire examination, which is a cross-examination limited to a person's qualifications to be a juror. When the trial lawyer has completed the voir dire examination of a prospective juror or the panel, the paralegal should ask the client for her or his impressions of the potential juror and supply that information to the lawyer. Therefore, the client should pay close attention to the selection process. Nevertheless, the lawyer will decide which jurors to strike. The client should listen carefully to the opening statements, as these will provide a good preview of the case. The client should be encouraged to tell the paralegal or the trial lawyer if either lawyer makes a misstatement in the opening statement. This suggestion will cause the client to listen more carefully and more thoughtfully. If a lawyer is told that he or she made a misstatement in the opening statement, that gives the lawyer a chance to correct the problem later in the trial. The client should listen carefully to the opposing lawyer's opening statement because the lawyer will probably explain exactly how he or she is going to prove the case. The lawyer's opening statement gives the opposition a good idea what evidence the laywer has to offer.

The client should be forewarned that, as a party, he or she may be called for cross-examination by the opponent during the opponent's case-in-chief. The client cannot be compelled to take the stand unless the client is in court. For this reason, the opposing party may serve a subpoena upon the client to make sure the client is in court and subject to cross-examination (Rule 43(b)).

The more familiar the client is with the procedures, the more comfortable the client will be. The client will make a better presentation if he or she is comfortable. A client will be more comfortable knowing what to expect.

■ PREPARING WITNESSES

The case file should contain all the witnesses' home addresses, business addresses, and telephone numbers, and the names and telephone numbers of persons who know how to contact the witnesses, such as relatives, employers, coworkers, and so forth. When the court gives a trial date, the witnesses must be notified so that they can arrange to be available. They should be asked to confirm their availability. A party should not take a chance on a witness's availability. The sooner a witness's scheduling problem is addressed, the easier it is to solve the problem, or at least to obtain consideration from the court.

Witnesses do not have any legal duty to cooperate with the parties and their lawyers outside court. Parties can require witnesses to come to court by serving subpoenas on them, and once in court witnesses can be required to answer questions under oath. But witnesses do not have to come to a lawyer's office to discuss the case. So if they talk to a lawyer and legal assistant, they are doing a favor. In the end, they are also helping themselves. By cooperating in the trial preparation, witnesses have the opportunity to find out what kinds of questions will be asked at trial and to obtain help with how to answer questions. In addition, they have the opportunity to see the exhibits that will be used—diagrams, photographs, business records, summaries, and the like.

Some witnesses require more preparation than others. For example, an experienced police officer who testifies in court regularly may not be interested in having help with her testimony. Nevertheless, the lawyer or paralegal should make the effort to meet and discuss the officer's expected testimony. The better the officer's understanding of the areas of dispute, the better she can explain to the jury what the jury needs to know. The officer probably has a wealth of information that she could present, but much of what she could say may be unimportant because it may not be relevant to contested facts. Every case is unique, so even experienced witnesses benefit from a little preparation. In turn, by preparing the witness, the legal team benefits its own preparation. It is a two-way process.

Lawyers must not tamper with evidence or produce false testimony. And they must not let their clients or paralegals do it either. As officers of the court, lawyers are subject to strict supervision. They cannot tell a witness *what* to say, but they can tell a witness *how* to say it. If the witness is friendly and aligned with the client, a lawyer and paralegal can prepare the witness in much the same way as they would prepare a client. The one important difference is that no privilege exists, so anything they say to each other is subject to disclosure.

Handling Uncooperative Witnesses

An independent witness who is not entirely cooperative may not appreciate efforts to educate him or her and cultivate his or her cooperation. The witness's response to those efforts will depend, in part, on how he or she approached and the nature of the problems. Common sense dictates that a witness should be approached in a friendly, open, respectful manner. An attempt should be made to develop the witness's interest in the case and its outcome. The witness should be made to feel important, because the witness *is* important. An independent witness may misinterpret such contact as an illegal effort to tamper with the evidence. The witness must be assured that it is appropriate, even necessary, for the lawyer and paralegal to contact him or her to discuss the case. Suppose the witness has a different view of the evidence than they have. They must find out the reasons for the apparent mistake or inconsistency in the evidence. The witness must be asked to review the transaction or occurrence with the lawyer and paralegal to help them understand the witness's version. The lawyer and paralegal should be prepared to ask questions as the witness explains what he or she observed. They should identify the apparent inconsistency in a way that does not challenge the witness's veracity or competency. They do not want the witness to become defensive. They should not give the witness occasion to reiterate the erroneous version until the inconsistency has been resolved, because the more a witness repeats the erroneous version, the more he or she becomes committed to it. That is just human nature.

It is common for witnesses to an accident to immediately take sides. They feel that they know who was right and who was wrong. And they might be correct. Consequently, a witness may not want to even talk with a representative of the party she or he considers to be at fault. But if the witness is told what the real problem is, the witness will likely cooperate. For example, a witness to an automobile collision at an intersection may "know" that the accident was the defendant's fault. Consequently, he does not want to talk with the defendant's lawyer or investigator. However, once the witness is told that the defendant acknowledges that the accident was his fault and the only reason he is defending is that the plaintiff's claim for damages is excessive, the witness might be more cooperative with the defendant's representatives. The lawyer and paralegal should try to convey to independent witnesses the idea that they and their client are taking a reasonable position in the matter.

When the lawyer and legal assistant have to cope with an uncooperative witness, they should consider using exhibits, especially photographs, as bait to catch the witness's interest. Even hostile witnesses are usually interested in seeing exhibits pertinent to what they have to say at trial. The lawyer and paralegal should consider beginning the discussion with points where there is no real disagreement. They should show the witness that there are areas or points of agreement; then, step by step, show the witness how her or his testimony fits into the big picture. Hopefully, once the witness senses that the interviewer is a sincere and pleasant person who appreciates the witness's cooperation, the witness will become more cooperative and receptive. Occasionally, a witness who harbors an erroneous belief will abandon it when the case is put in perspective. Even if the witness will not abandon the erroneous idea, she or he may be less adamant about it at the trial.

Interviewing Two or More Witnesses Together

Sometimes it is desirable to have a meeting with two or more witnesses together so that they can help each other to recall pertinent details and avoid unnecessary inconsistencies. Again, the witnesses should be given an overview of the case so that they can appreciate how their testimony corresponds to the other evidence. They should be told to freely acknowledge this meeting and discussion at trial. They should also be prepared to explain that they were only told to tell the truth.

Compensating Witnesses

If a party has offered to compensate an independent witness for testifying at trial because the witness will lose time from work or have some expenses, the party should assure the witness that this reimbursement is proper. The witness should be told to freely acknowledge the agreement or payment when asked about it. Sometimes the exact amount of the witness's expenses cannot be determined until the trial is completed. In that event, the best answer to any cross-examination questions about the amount is to explain that the amount has not been determined but the witness expects to be reimbursed for expenses. A party cannot offer to pay for testimony, only for time and expense.

A different situation is presented when dealing with expert witnesses who do charge for their services, including testifying. The size of the fee is subject to disclosure. Indeed, the expert witness may be asked about the amount charged for testifying in other cases. If the fee is exorbitant, the jury has a right to infer that the witness is selling testimony—that the witness would say whatever the party asked if the price were right. When a jury learns that an expert witness charges a contingent fee, so that the expert gets paid only if the party who retained her or him wins the case, the expert's credibility will be destroyed. Again, a jury may properly conclude that the witness is merely a "hired gun" who will say anything for a fee. Even if the expert is reluctant to discuss her or his fees, that will reflect adversely against the witness and the party who presented the witness. Part of preparing the witness is making sure that the matter of fees and charges is appropriately handled.

Dealing with an Erroneous Version

If the case involves an accident, the lawyer or paralegal should try to take the witness to the location of the accident so that the two can visualize what happened and how it happened. If the witness persists with an erroneous version, he or she must be told how that version is contrary to other undisputed facts, or contrary to physical facts, or inconsistent with the observations made by other witnesses who had as good a view or a better view. It is counterproductive to do this in an argumentative way. It must be handled as though the witness is doing a favor to even speak with the trial team. The lawyer or paralegal has to educate the witness by asking questions, rather than dictating answers. If the witness's version conflicts with photographs of the accident scene, the witness should be shown the photographs. When the witness's version conflicts with another witness's deposition testimony, the witness may be shown the deposition transcript. The witness may insist that the photographs or other witnesses are wrong.

But once witnesses have had an opportunity to see what the other witnesses say, what the other evidence is, and how their testimony fits into the big picture, most are willing to correct an honest mistake. Witnesses usually appreciate help to avoid embarrassment and unnecessary complications with the legal system. It might even be helpful to let the witness know that the trial team can appreciate how she or he could have misinterpreted or incorrectly remembered the particular fact. Lawyers and legal assistants must use great care not to lead any witness into error. The penalty for doing so could be severe.

Suppose the police accident report shows that the accident in issue occurred at 9:30 P.M. The United States Weather Bureau's records show that the sun set at 8:45 P.M. and the weather was overcast. Nevertheless, a witness who has essential and reliable testimony to offer about the collision has the mistaken idea that the accident happened in daylight. By taking the witness to the accident location under similar conditions, it may be possible to show the witness that the artificial lighting from the streetlights and stores made the area seem "bright as day." There should be no concern that this extra effort will hurt the client's case in any way. No undue influence is applied. These efforts with the witness merely show the jury, if they come out at trial, that the party has a sincere interest in establishing the truth. Once the reason for the witness's error in perception or recollection is discovered, the witness's mistake can be explained and justified. Of course, this approach is not helpful where the witness is simply lying.

Subpoenaing Witnesses

A subpoena should be served as soon as possible on witnesses who are not cooperative but who are essential to the client's case. A person who fails to comply with a subpoena may be held in contempt of court. The penalty could be incarceration or fine or merely a stern lecture. Even more important to the lawyer, the client can obtain a recess or delay in the proceedings until the United States marshal brings the witness to court. The onus is on the lawyer to have his or her witnesses in court and ready to testify when needed. However, that onus switches to the witness if the lawyer has served a subpoena on the witness. Consequently, it may be prudent to subpoena even cooperative witnesses, because if a witness were to become unavailable, the subpoena would justify a recess or even a continuance of the trial.

A party may look into the availability of the opponent's witnesses as well as her or his own. Contacting witnesses aligned with the opposition is ethical provided no privilege is violated. For example, it would be ethical for the defendant's lawyer to telephone the office of the plaintiff's treating doctor to find out whether the doctor will be in town during the week the case has been set for trial. If the doctor will be out of town for a convention, such information could be significant in evaluating the case. Furthermore, it is always useful to know whether the opposition is doing its homework and preparing for trial.

There are times when an independent witness prefers to be subpoenaed to come to court so that his or her appearance is viewed as not voluntary. A subpoena protects the witness from appearing to be aligned with one side against the other. Public officials and police officers often ask to be subpoenaed for that reason. Another example is where the testimony of the plaintiff's treating physician favors the defendant, but the physician does not want to appear to be voluntarily testifying against his or her patient. The physician may be more comfortable about testifying if placed under a subpoena.

A subpoena must designate the time and place the witness is to appear to testify. But the lawyer who subpoenas the witness may not know precisely when the witness will be needed. This problem can be handled by designating in the subpoena the earliest probable time that the witness will be needed and asking the witness to cooperate by staying near a telephone so that she or he can be reached on very short notice. This way, the witness may wait at home or work until contacted. The alternative is for the witness to sit in the courtroom and wait for her or his turn. The wait could be hours or even days. A party takes a bit of risk by accommodating a witness in this manner. But a lawyer incurs a larger risk by not subpoenaing a witness whose reliability is questionable.

United States marshals usually serve federal court subpoenas. However, any person eighteen years of age or older, who is not a party to the suit, may serve subpoenas in civil cases (Rule 45(c)). The process server must pay to the witness the established witness fee. Also, the witness must be paid a fee based upon the mileage from his or her home to the courthouse. If there is any doubt about the mileage, the process server should be sure to tender enough. Failure to tender an adequate payment could make the service defective. The process server's affidavit of service must state the time, place, manner of service, and amount of fees paid. The affidavit of service may be filed with the court if needed. The affidavit will be needed if the witness fails to appear. The affidavit is a party's proof that the witness was duly served.

◼ PREPARING EXHIBITS

The court's pretrial order may require the parties to have all their exhibits "marked for identification" before a magistrate before the trial begins. The parties are supposed to stipulate to the foundation for all marked exhibits, unless an actual dispute exists concerning the foundation. If a party has failed to disclose and mark an exhibit as ordered, the exhibit may not be received into evidence. The Federal Rules do not establish any particular system for identifying exhibits. However, local court rules may mandate a method to maintain uniformity. The trend is to use numbers, rather than letters, to identify all exhibits.

Exhibits must be carefully examined to make sure they do not contain any inappropriate markings or notations. Once in a while a photograph gets marked up by a witness, or a sticker used for organizing the exhibits is left on an exhibit. Underlining of passages in documents, notations in the margins, and Xs used in photographs to pinpoint locations might cause the exhibits to be inadmissible or reduce their authority. For example, while preparing a witness for her deposition, someone might have penciled on a photograph the point of impact. A new photograph should be obtained from the negative so that an "undamaged" photograph can be used at trial. Markings made on an exhibit before the witness uses the exhibit in court are considered hearsay evidence (out-of-court unsworn statements) or leading questions (questions that suggest the answer the lawyer wants). If the markings cannot be explained, they may preclude the necessary foundation for the exhibit and make the exhibit inadmissible.

Photocopies may need to be made of documents that will be used as exhibits at trial, because once a document has been received into evidence, the clerk of court takes custody of the exhibit and the parties may not have access to it after court hours. Photocopies are useful for preparing witnesses to testify and for preparing the final argument and for preparing for post-trial motions. Even photographs may be photocopied, and photocopies may be adequate for this collateral use.

■ PROPOSED VERDICT

Three types of verdicts are rendered: general, special, and general with interrogatories (see Rule 49). When judges use special verdicts, they commonly ask the parties to submit a proposed verdict form. Most law firms have a collection of special verdict forms that can be tailored to a new case. A paralegal may handle the initial selection and preparation of the preferred form. (See chapter 19 concerning the various types of verdicts and their applications.)

■ JURY INSTRUCTIONS

Most courts require the parties to submit proposed jury instructions before the trial begins. Again, most law firms have a collection of jury instructions that can be tailored to fit a new case. A paralegal may help the trial lawyer by selecting and organizing the preferred instructions. If a party duly submits proper "requested instructions" and the court fails to give one of those instructions, the court's omission may give the client grounds for an appeal. Most judges have their own boilerplate instructions with which they are comfortable and which they ordinarily use despite a lawyer's requests. Nevertheless, it is always a good practice to submit requested jury instructions.

SUMMARY

In the final phase of trial preparation, the paralegal and trial lawyer must focus on trial strategy. They must identify the fact issues and make sure all the evidence gathered is available. They must alert the client and witnesses of the trial date. They must check on the availability of the opponent's witnesses. They must make sure they have evidence to address each fact issue. The paralegal must not forget that the trial lawyer can offer evidence through the opponent's as well as the client's witnesses.

Courts hold pretrial conferences to help the court and the parties prepare for trial. The two primary objectives of pretrial conferences are to settle the case or to simplify the case for presentation. Each judge seems to have a different philosophy and approach for inducing the parties to conduct serious settlement talks. A court may simplify the fact issues by securing agreement and concessions from the parties. A court may simplify the legal issues by securing the parties' agreement to eliminate certain claims or defenses. In addition, a court may order certain claims or defenses stricken for lack of merit. A party may raise a legal issue by making a motion, or the court may raise a legal issue sua sponte. A court may make rulings that exclude certain evidence. A judge may require or allow amendments of the pleadings. A judge may ask the parties to make a formal admission concerning certain material facts. The judge may order the parties to submit legal memorandums dealing with particularly difficult issues. The court may ask the parties to submit all or part of the action to arbitration or mediation. The court may limit the number of expert witnesses each side may use.

A party's evidence must not conflict with the laws of nature or the physical facts or with facts established by stipulation or admission. It should be organized around the witnesses so that the trial lawyer can effectively cover everything that needs to be covered with each witness. The lawyer and paralegal must be objective about the client's evidence and the opponent's evidence. Each facet of the client's evidence should be consistent with every other aspect of the evidence.

The client and witnesses should be prepared shortly before the trial is to begin. The lawyer and paralegal should explain the trial procedures, the big picture, and where each witness's testimony fits into the case as a whole. The client and witnesses must appear sincere and authoritative. The trial team cannot tell a witness what to say, but they can tell the witness how to say what he or she needs to say.

The courts may require the parties to mark all their exhibits for identification before a magistrate before the trial begins. The parties must be prepared to stipulate to the foundation for exhibits, unless there is an actual dispute concerning the foundation. If a party has failed to disclose and mark an exhibit as ordered, the court may refuse to receive the exhibit into evidence. Local court rules usually mandate a method for marking exhibits to maintain uniformity. The exhibits must not contain any inappropriate markings or notations on them. Occasionally a photograph gets marked up by a witness, or a sticker used for organizing the exhibits is left on an exhibit. Highlighting passages in documents, making notations in the margins of the documents, or inserting Xs in photographs to pinpoint locations may cause exhibits to be inadmissible or reduce their authority. If a marking cannot be explained, the exhibit may be inadmissible into evidence. Consider making photocopies of documents that will be exhibits at trial, because once documents have been received into evidence, the parties may not have access to them. Extra photocopies are useful for preparing witnesses to testify and for preparing the final argument and post trial motions.

There are three types of verdicts: general verdicts, special verdicts and general verdicts with interrogatories. Lawyers like to submit proposed verdict forms, and paralegals may assist with their preparation. Courts usually require parties to submit proposed jury instructions before the trial begins. Paralegals may help the trial lawyer by selecting and organizing the proposed instructions. If a party duly submits proper requested instructions and the court fails to give one of the requested instructions, the court's omission may give the client grounds for an appeal.

The trial team must not be beguiled by the evidence it has organized. The lawyer and paralegal must remain objective about the evidence and the case. If they do not see any problem in the case, they need to look again and look harder. When all the evidence seems to favor the client and no problems are apparent, something has been overlooked. Good trial preparation is tedious, complex, and sometimes frustrating, but necessary and worth all the effort. It becomes easier with experience. There are logic and reason to what must be done. As a paralegal gains experience, she or he can assume greater responsibility for initiating and conducting trial preparation.

KEY TERMS

calendar calls	mistrial
day certain	frivolous
scheduling conference	pretrial order
pretrial conferences	alternative dispute resolution
scheduling order	(ADR)
pretrial conference order	

REVIEW QUESTIONS

1. Why is it important to develop the details when preparing for trial?

2. What must you do if you have two witnesses, each with a somewhat different version of a fact?

3. What is the first thing you should do in response to a trial alert?

4. What are the principal differences in how a party testifies in a discovery deposition and at trial?

5. How does trial strategy differ from a party's legal theory of the case?

6. Why might a party subpoena an opponent to come to the trial?

7. What kinds of matters may be covered at a pretrial conference?

8. Why does Rule 16 require the lawyer to have authority to make admissions and stipulations on behalf of the client at pretrial conferences?

9. May a party's liability insurer send a representative to attend the pretrial conference?

10. What are the hallmarks of a good witness at trial?

11. When is a claim or defense considered frivolous?

19

JURIES AND VERDICTS

Most litigants prefer to have their case decided by a jury rather than by a judge. Litigants tend to be suspicious of decisions made by one person regardless of that person's qualifications and apparent conscientiousness. Litigants seem more concerned about being treated impartially than wisely. Many lawyers feel that judges may tend to be influenced by the numerous, similar cases they have handled in the past. By contrast, the inexperience of jurors allows jurors to approach a case with a fresh perspective, and they will probably have considerable interest in the proceedings. Also, most trial lawyers prefer decisions by consensus of a group rather than a decision by one person. Some people say the jury system is for losers, because a loser usually finds a jury verdict more palatable than a judge's adverse decision. A prevailing party has less concern with who made the decision.

■ THE RIGHT TO TRIAL BY JURY

The federal Constitution and all state constitutions guarantee the right to trial by jury whenever the claim is for money damages. The United States Constitution, Seventh Amendment, states this guarantee:

> In Suits at common law, where the value in controversy shall exceed twenty dollars, the right of trial by jury shall be preserved, and no fact tried by a jury shall be otherwise re-examined in any Court of the United States than according to the rules of the common law.

The constitutional mandate means that whenever a claim is for money damages, the parties have a right to request and obtain a trial by jury. The constitution does not give the parties a right to trial by jury when the parties seek equitable relief, such as specific performance of a contract or injunctive relief. A **petit jury** is the jury that tries cases, whether criminal or civil. A petit jury is distinguished from a grand jury which is an investigatory body that determines whether a crime has been committed and whether a person should be indicted for the crime. A petit jury is drawn from a jury panel of veniremen. The panel of veniremen is drawn from the community as a whole.

■ THE JURY'S ROLE

The jury's only function is to resolve fact issues; a jury does not determine issues or questions of law. The jury must find the facts from the evidence. The jurors are supposed to use their common knowledge and experience to evaluate the evidence to determine the facts. Once the jury determines the facts, the law must be applied to those facts. The jury states its findings in its verdict. The jury must use the evidence to determine what happened, how it happened, and who did what and when.

After determining the basic facts concerning the transaction or occurrence, the jury must determine the ultimate questions of fact. In a negligence action, the ultimate facts are determined by asking questions like these: Were the parties negligent? Was a party's negligence the proximate cause of the loss? If both parties were causally negligent, what are their percentages of causal negligence? What sum of money would provide full compensation? In a contract case, the ultimate facts are whether the parties had a valid contract; whether the defendant breached the contract; whether the plaintiff breached the contract; and what sum of money would fairly compensate the plaintiff for loss of the benefits of the contract. The ultimate fact issues are conclusions of fact that are drawn from the basic facts. Furthermore, an ultimate fact cannot be determined without applying rules of law to the conclusions drawn from the basic facts.

The Constitution makes the jury's determination of facts final. The jury's determination, as reflected in its verdict, cannot be set aside merely because the trial judge or the appellate court judges believe it is the wrong conclusion. The determination is final, provided competent evidence supports it and it is consistent with applicable law. The trial judge or reviewing judges may be required to determine whether sufficient evidence supports the jury's determination concerning one or more material facts. More than a scintilla (trace) of evidence must exist to prove a fact before a court can sustain a jury's verdict finding in favor of the fact. Furthermore, if there is no dispute concerning the material facts, there may be no fact issue for the jury to decide. A verdict cannot be based upon evidence that leaves a disputed fact subject to mere speculation. Suppose the plaintiff's decedent is found dead in a railroad switching yard and was probably struck by a train, but no one knows when or just how the accident happened. If those facts were presented to a jury, the jury could not find that the railroad was negligent or otherwise liable for the accident, because the verdict would be based upon mere speculation that the railroad did something wrong. By the same token, a judge's determination that certain evidence is inadmissible may have the effect of keeping an essential fact from being proved. The parties have a right to have the jury decide the facts when some credible evidence supports the fact determination. Otherwise, the court must resolve the facts against the party who has the burden of proof.

A judge may take months to decide a case and issue the order, whereas a jury usually decides the critical fact issues within a matter of hours or within a day or two. Juries help to expedite litigation and the court's business by relieving judges of a very taxing function.

■ MAKING A DEMAND FOR JURY

Rule 38 of the Federal Rules of Civil Procedure prescribes the procedure a party must follow to obtain a jury trial. A plaintiff may serve and file a **demand for jury** by noting the demand on the complaint. The jury demand is usually made at the bottom of the complaint and labeled as such. The defendant may make a demand for jury on the answer in the same way. Or either party may serve a demand for jury in writing as a separate document. The written jury demand must be served and filed within ten days after service of the last pleading, whether the pleading is an answer to the complaint or an answer to a cross-claim or an answer to a third-party complaint.

The party who serves and files a demand for jury may specify particular fact issues to be tried to the jury, leaving all nonspecified fact issues to be determined by the trial judge as the fact finder. An unqualified demand for jury leaves all disputed facts subject to determination by the jury. If a party receives a demand for jury that is limited to a specific issue, she or he has ten days in which to serve a **counterdemand for jury** that specifies additional fact issues or in which to serve an unqualified demand for jury. Usually a party makes a general demand because he or she can always waive the right to a jury at any time—assuming the other parties do not object (Rule 38(d)). In other words, the defendant's jury demand protects the plaintiff's right to a trial by jury, and vice versa. The defendant could not withdraw his or her demand so as to preclude the plaintiff from relying upon the initial demand for jury.

If a party fails to follow the requirements of Rule 38 to demand a jury, the party automatically waives the right to a jury. In that event, a judge acts as the fact finder as well as the determiner of the law.

■ ABSENCE OF A DEMAND FOR JURY

If neither party makes a demand for a jury in the manner prescribed by Rule 38, the judge may nevertheless order a jury trial if she or he believes that is preferable. The judge may order a trial by jury on the basis of a party's motion or make the order sua sponte, that is, on the judge's own initiative.

Why would a judge encourage a jury trial? When a case is tried without a jury, the judge must consider and evaluate the evidence to resolve the disputed issues of fact. The role of a fact finder is often difficult, stressful and time-consuming, whether the fact finder is a jury or judge. When a judge acts as a fact finder, the judge must prepare a document called **Findings of Fact, Conclusions of Law** and **Order for Judgment.** It is a single document that has three separate parts. The judge must specify the material facts that he or she found from the parties' evidence. The judge must articulate his or her conclusions of law that apply to determine the parties' legal rights and obligations. The judge must order the clerk of court to enter a judgment as specified in the order. Judges commonly attach memorandums of law to their orders to explain the rationale for the findings and decision. This is a time-consuming process.

A judge may elect to use an advisory jury even in cases where the parties have not requested a jury or the parties do not have a constitutional right to a jury trial. For example, parties do not have a right to a jury trial in actions to reform a written contract, to obtain an injunction, or to obtain a divorce. A judge need not accept the determinations made by an advisory jury. The judge remains ultimately responsible as the fact finder in such cases.

A judge cannot choose to have a jury hear cases in which the United States government is the defendant if the action against the government is pursuant to a statute that expressly provides that trial shall be without a jury. A party who sues the government cannot be denied due process of law by not receiving a jury trial because, historically, the federal government is immune from suit. Where a statute waives governmental immunity permitting an action against it without a jury trial, the plaintiff can hardly complain about the waiver of immunity being only partial.

■ SELECTION OF JURORS

Jurors are selected for service at random from voter registration lists in the district or division in which the court sits. Some courts use a combination of voter lists and driver's license lists in an effort to obtain a broad cross section. Each potential juror must fill out a juror qualification form. To be a juror, a person must meet certain minimum requirements. A juror must be a citizen of the United States, at least eighteen years of age, able to read and write, able to understand the English language, physically capable of participating, and mentally competent to serve. A person may be disqualified from service if he or she has been convicted of a crime punishable by imprisonment for one year or more or has criminal charges pending against him or her for such a crime. A juror's term of service may not exceed thirty days, unless more time is needed to finish a trial that commenced within the thirty-day period. Federal courts may not call persons for jury duty more than once during any two-year period.

When a jury panel is needed, the clerk of court issues subpoenas to persons who are on the jury list. The court may serve the subpoenas by registered mail or have the United States marshal serve them. The subpoena tells each person served that failure to appear as directed subjects her or him to a fine of one hundred dollars or three days' imprisonment or both. A person may be excused from jury service only if she or he can show an "undue hardship" or "extreme inconvenience." The showing only postpones the term of service. Jurors may be called upon to hear and decide either criminal cases or civil cases during a single term of service.

The prospective jurors go through an indoctrination session that usually includes a lecture and a motion picture. They are also given a booklet that explains their role and duties. Paralegals should make an effort to find out what their local indoctrination program includes. The clerk of court will be able to provide a copy of the jurors' booklet. Lawyers sometimes use information in the jurors' booklet in their final arguments.

NUMBER OF JURORS

The United States Constitution does not specify how many individuals are to be on a jury. Historically, the number has been twelve. That number has been maintained in criminal cases to the present time. Rule 48 provides that federal district courts shall seat not fewer than six and not more than twelve persons for the jury. There is no provision for a party to ask for a particular number of jurors between six and twelve. The Rules Advisory Committee believes there is an implied constitutional right to have at least six persons on a jury. The committee has observed that courts should avoid allowing verdicts by fewer than six jurors because smaller juries tend to be erratic. Most lawyers and judges who remember working with twelve-person juries believe that twelve-person verdicts were less likely to go to extremes. Therefore, verdicts rendered by twelve-person juries were somewhat more predictable. Nevertheless, the trend is to use smaller juries. The preference for smaller juries is simply for economy. With smaller juries, the government has fewer people to pay, and the trials may be somewhat shorter.

Most civil actions are now tried to six jury members plus one or two additional members. Judges commonly impanel more than six jurors because jurors cannot be added once the trial has begun, and if one or more jurors become ill or otherwise unavailable to return a verdict, the judge might have to declare a mistrial. The judge must declare a mistrial whenever an irreparable problem arises that prevents the parties from having a fair trial. If the number of jury members became less than six, that would be an irreparable problem. For example, if the court seats eight jurors but subsequently releases two from service because of illness, the remaining six jurors can decide the case. On the other hand, if the court seats only seven jurors and two become ill so that they cannot complete the trial, the judge will have to declare a mistrial. Having one or two or more additional jurors provides a measure of protection against having a mistrial.

ALTERNATE JURORS

In state courts, when the parties anticipate that the case may last more than a week, it is common to add one or two **alternate jurors** to the panel. Alternate jurors are selected to serve only if a regular juror becomes sick or otherwise unavailable during the trial. The alternate jurors are usually the last members of the jury panel called to the jury box. The alternate jurors participate in the trial in the same way as other jurors during the trial. In fact, they might not even know they are alternates. Some judges are concerned that if jurors are told they are alternates, they might assume they will not have to decide the case and might not pay close attention to the evidence.

The alternate jurors participate until the very end of the trial. They hear the final arguments. They listen to the judge's instructions on the law. Ninety percent of the time they are excused from further service when the other jurors are sent to the jury room to deliberate. Consequently, if a juror becomes ill during the deliberations, there is no alternate juror to take over that juror's responsibilities.

If both parties agree on the record, the alternate jurors may participate in the deliberations the same as the regular jurors. In that event, the case is decided by the seven or eight persons on the jury. The verdict must be unanimous, unless the parties stipulate on the record that a fraction of the jurors may return the verdict. The lawyer who has the burden of proof may be reluctant to have alternate jurors participate in the deliberations, because the lawyer may feel that he or she would then have more minds to persuade. For the same reason, the defendant usually wants larger juries. The principal reason the plaintiff's lawyer may agree to have an alternate deliberate is that the lawyer may feel the alternate is the "best" juror and will favorably influence the others.

In federal court there are no alternate jurors. If seven or more jurors are impaneled, to make sure that the required number of six is met, all of them deliberate and participate in the verdict. All jurors who are impaneled and who are still sitting when the case is submitted participate in the jury's deliberations and verdict.

■ IMPANELING THE JURY

The parties are entitled to have their case heard and decided by an impartial jury composed of individuals who are competent to understand the evidence, who will listen to the evidence and try to determine the truth, and who will follow the law without favor or bias. Courts ensure the parties' right to an unbiased, competent jury by conducting a voir dire examination of the veniremen members. The **veniremen** are all those on the panel from which a jury is drawn. A **voir dire examination** is a cross-examination under oath concerning the veniremen's qualifications to be jurors. The court instructs the veniremen that they must answer the questions truthfully.

Rule 47 provides that the voir dire examination may be conducted by the lawyers or the judge or both:

> The court may permit the parties or their attorneys to conduct the examination of prospective jurors or may itself conduct the examination. In the latter event, the court shall permit the parties or their attorneys to supplement the examination by such further inquiry as it deems proper or shall itself submit to the prospective jurors such additional questions of the parties or their attorneys as it deems proper.

The judge has broad discretion in deciding what questions may be asked. If the court decides to ask all voir dire questions, the lawyers have a right to submit written questions to the judge. Some judges require the lawyers to submit proposed voir dire questions before the trial begins. The judge then selects the questions she or he believes are relevant and reads those questions to the jury.

The judge directs the clerk to bring twenty or more veniremen to the courtroom. They are seated in the spectators' section of the courtroom. The clerk then reads the names and addresses of twelve or more jurors, depending upon how many veniremen the judge wants in the jury panel. As each venireman's name is read, that person is instructed to take a seat in or near the jury box. The lawyers watch how each venireman walks to his or her seat, to see whether the potential juror has any physical impairments. The lawyers watch to see whether the venireman is carrying anything such as a book, a newspaper, knitting, or the like. They try to observe whether the veniremen manifest any confusion or uncertainty or reluctance. They note how each venireman is dressed and groomed. They watch to see whether the veniremen indicate any familiarity with other persons in the courtroom.

The process continues until the desired number of veniremen have been seated in or near the jury box. The size of the panel depends upon the number of jurors that will be needed to try the case and the number of veniremen that the parties will strike during the voir dire examination. Assume the judge wants to impanel eight jurors. The case involves one plaintiff and two defendants who are adverse to each other. Each of the three parties is entitled to three peremptory challenges (objections not accompanied by a reason), for a total of nine. The judge may assume that not more than two veniremen will be stricken for cause. Based upon these assumptions, the judge will need to seat at least nineteen veniremen (eight jury members plus nine possible peremptory challenges plus two possible challenges for cause) for the voir dire examination. Those nineteen veniremen make up the jury panel.

The clerk or judge administers an oath to the members of the jury panel, requiring them to truthfully answer questions about their background and qualifications.

■ CHALLENGES FOR CAUSE

A member of the jury panel may be **challenged for cause** when the voir dire examination shows that the venireman is biased or appears to be biased. **Actual bias** exists when a venireman acknowledges that she or he cannot be totally fair or has a close relationship with one of the parties. This bias may be against a party or for a party. Or a venireman may be biased because of some experience with the type of case. If a venireman is related to one of the parties or to one of the lawyers, or works for a party, or has some other connection with the case, there is **implied bias,** and the member will be excused by the court even if the person claims she or he can be fair.

A judge may determine sua sponte that a panel member should be stricken for cause. When a lawyer seeks to have juror stricken for cause, the lawyer must make a motion to strike the panel member. The motion is usually made at the judge's bench, out of the panel's hearing, because it may be denied and the lawyer's remarks might cause that juror to be prejudiced toward the lawyer or client. Furthermore, the discussion at the bench could unduly influence other members of the panel if they heard it.

A venireman who has actual or implied bias will be stricken for cause before the next panel member is examined. Each party has an unlimited number of challenges for cause. Whenever a panel member is stricken from the panel for cause, the court adds another member to the panel. A judge must try to keep veniremen from feigning bias for the purpose of evading jury service.

■ PEREMPTORY CHALLENGES

A **peremptory challenge** is an objection to a venireman being a juror that a party may make without having or giving any reason for the objection. A party uses peremptory challenges to eliminate panel members he or she cannot strike for cause.

In federal district court, each party is entitled to three peremptory challenges:

> In civil cases, each party shall be entitled to three peremptory challenges. Several defendants or several plaintiffs may be considered as a single party for the purposes of making challenges, or the court may allow additional peremptory challenges and permit them to be exercised separately or jointly. All challenges for cause or favor, whether to the array or panel or to individual jurors, shall be determined by the court. (28 U.S.C.A. § 1870).

Some state courts limit the number of peremptory challenges to two. Each party *must* exercise those challenges. Consequently, the lawyers may be constrained to strike panel members they would like to have serve as jurors.

Note that when two or more parties are aligned in the prosecution of a claim or defense, those parties may be required to share the allotted number of peremptory challenges. For example, when the plaintiff sues the owner and the driver of an automobile to obtain money damages for injuries, the owner and the driver may have to share their peremptory challenges. If a husband and wife have brought an action to recover money damages for the wife's injuries, they are aligned and must share their peremptory challenges. On the other hand, parties who are adverse to each other do not have to share peremptory challenges. Parties are adverse to each other if the pleadings raise issues between them. For example, cross-claims make codefendants adverse. The same circumstances determine whether or not plaintiffs must share peremptory challenges.

Once in a while a lawyer announces to the jury panel that she or he finds all the panel members to be acceptable and waives the right to strike. Lawyers who engage in that kind of bravado are asking for trouble. They are evading their responsibility to the court and merely trying to ingratiate themselves with the jury.

The parties exercise their peremptory challenges by noting on the clerk's jury list which veniremen are to be stricken. The defendant's lawyer must exercise the first peremptory strike. Then the plaintiff strikes one venireman from the panel. The process is repeated until all strikes have been used.

Most states still provide for alternate jurors. Lawyers know who the alternate jurors will be. They avoid "wasting" their peremptory strikes on alternates because usually alternates do not participate in jury deliberations.

■ VOIR DIRE EXAMINATION

The purpose of the voir dire examination is to enable the parties to obtain fair, impartial jurors who will conduct themselves responsibly and according to the law. But trial lawyers look for more. They try to determine whether anything in a juror's background would adversely affect the juror's willingness to be fair to *their* client. It is only natural that lawyers also try to determine whether any of the potential jurors might have attitudes or experiences or relationships that make them favor the client or disfavor the opposing party. In other words, lawyers look for jurors who will be sympathetic to their client and who will be indifferent or adverse to the opposing party.

Lawyers are not supposed to use the voir dire examination to indoctrinate the jury or ingratiate themselves with the jury. Nevertheless, a fine line separates being friendly and "selling." Of course, a lawyer must have his or her trial strategy well in mind while conducting the voir dire examination. Unfortunately, lawyers overstep the bounds of proper voir dire examination on occasion. That is one reason federal courts impose strict limitations on the questions that may be asked and the manner in which they may be asked.

The Judge's Introductory Remarks

The judge begins the voir dire examination by telling the jury panel members why they have been assembled and the purpose of the examination, which is to determine each venireman's qualifications. The judge briefly explains the nature of the case, identifies the parties, and introduces the lawyers, and may define some of the issues. The judge identifies the probable witnesses from lists the parties must submit as provided by the court's pretrial order. The purpose is to determine whether the jurors are acquainted with any persons who may testify. If it turns out that a venireman does know a party, lawyer, or witness, the nature of the relationship must be explored to determine whether the venireman could and would be fair to all the parties.

The judge's introductory remarks may be similar to the following:

> Members of the jury panel: You have been summoned to this courtroom so that of your number six may be selected to hear, try, and determine this case. You might be an excellent juror in ninety-nine out of one hundred cases; however, because you may be acquainted with one or more of the parties, lawyers, or witnesses, or because you have a present leaning one way or another about this case or this type of case, you may be considered to be biased or prejudiced concerning this case. What we need are six persons from varying walks of life who will diligently seek the truth; who will fairly and impartially and without fear or favor try the issues of fact; and who will decide this case upon the evidence adduced here in the courtroom and upon the law that will be given to you by me.
>
> In order that we may ascertain if you are a proper or qualified person to sit as a juror in this case, first I, then counsel, will ask you questions about your qualifications. In so doing, it is not the lawyers' intention to pry into your private life, but it is their duty to select a jury of the quality and character indicated. Please be open, frank, and responsive to the questions put to you so that justice may be done between the parties.
>
> So that you may intelligently respond to questions put to you testing your qualifications, I shall briefly state the identity of the parties, the nature of the case as reflected by the pleadings, the identity of the lawyers, the names of possible witnesses, and certain fundamental rules of law applicable to this case and all cases of like character.

At that point, the court introduces the parties and lawyers.

Methods of Questioning

Two methods are used to conduct the voir dire examination. In one method, the panel members are questioned one at a time and accepted or stricken before the next juror is questioned. This is the procedure that is most commonly used in criminal cases. It is somewhat cumbersome and does not give the lawyers an opportunity to compare all the veniremen before exercising their precious peremptory challenges. The procedure may cause a little more embarrassment for the veniremen and lawyers because a peremptory challenge has to be exercised before going on to the next juror. The other method for conducting the voir dire examination is for the court and attorneys to question the panel as a whole before the parties exercise their peremptory challenges. In this method the jurors know that six of their number must be stricken even though all of them may be perfectly acceptable, whereas in the first method each juror is accepted or rejected personally by the parties before the lawyers have the opportunity to question the remaining jurors. Both methods require the parties to move to strike a juror for cause while that particular juror is being questioned. The parties cannot wait until the end of the voir dire to make challenges for cause.

Types of Voir Dire Questions

The judge and lawyers may ask questions of the veniremen concerning the following: age; occupation; family; education; past and present occupations; prior jury experience; experience with similar occurrences or transactions; experience with litigation as a party or witness; attitude toward the judicial system or type of lawsuit in question; attitude toward the parties or witnesses; willingness to follow and apply the law; and willingness to set aside natural feelings of sympathy. This list is by no means all-inclusive.

In most federal district courts the judges ask all the questions put to the veniremen. A lawyer must submit her or his questions to the judge in writing before the trial begins, but has no opportunity to actually talk with the veniremen. In most state courts, the lawyers are allowed to conduct the voir dire examination, or at least participate significantly. The voir dire examination provides the only opportunity the lawyers have during the trial to talk with the jurors. Although some critics complain that lawyers spend too much time trying to sell their case during the voir dire, most trial lawyers believe that *their* voir dire examination is essential to obtaining a fair-minded, qualified jury.

When lawyers engage in the voir dire examination, they may provide a little background information about the parties, the transaction or occurrence, and the parties' claims so that the veniremen appreciate the significance of the voir dire questions and make responsive answers. Again, a fine line separates describing these matters and making an argument about them.

The techniques lawyers use differ greatly, but always the primary objective is to weed out undesirable jurors from the panel without causing annoyance or embarrassment to anyone. Lawyers may object to improper questions, as where a question is calculated to engender sympathy for one of the parties or exacts a promise from a venireman or argues the case. Lawyers must not ask questions for the purpose of prejudicing the jury against the opposing party. The objection is made on the grounds that the question is "improper voir dire." The objection does not have to be any more specific. The case is not supposed to be tried in the voir dire examination.

Most experienced trial lawyers try to engage veniremen in a conversation. They do this by using a venireman's answer as the basis for the next questions. Soon they have a dialogue going. Lawyers try to make each venireman feel that they are very nice, sincere people.

Lawyers may not ask veniremen to put themselves in the client's position. For example, it would be impermissible to ask a juror, "How would you feel about this injury if it had happened to you?'' They may not ask questions that suggest the defendant has liability insurance or that imply the defendant has a limited amount of liability insurance. However, a judge may ask veniremen whether they are employed by an insurance company that has an interest in the outcome of the case. The judge does not identify the interest or who is insured, but merely asks about any connection the veniremen might have with the insurance company. Usually the context of the question makes it clear that the defendant has some liability insurance.

Paralegal's Role

While the voir dire examination is being conducted, the paralegal should listen to what the veniremen say, but also to *how* they respond to the questions. The paralegal should consider whether each venireman is equally pleasant and open with each of the lawyers. Does a venireman hesitate to answer some kinds of questions? Do any of the veniremen have difficulty hearing or understanding the questions? If they do, they will probably have the same difficulty during the trial. The paralegal should note his or her observations and impressions for the trial lawyer to consider when it comes time to decide which jurors to strike from the panel. He or she should encourage the client to evaluate the veniremen and compare feelings about them. Does a juror show a dominant or submissive personality? Is the juror really interested and willing to be conscientious about deciding the case? Does the juror's position in the community indicate that the juror would follow the law even if he or she disagreed with the law or dislikes the consequences of applying the law? Does the client want strict jurors or free spirited jurors?

Procedure

In most courts the defendant's lawyer begins the voir dire examination. The rationale is that this balances the trial because the plaintiff's lawyer has the right to make the first opening statement. When the defendant's lawyer completes her or his portion of the voir dire examination, the plaintiff's lawyer repeats the process from the plaintiff's perspective. When both sides have concluded their voir dire examination, they are required to exercise their peremptory challenges to reduce the jury panel from twelve or more to no less than six jurors. In most state courts each adverse party has at least two peremptory strikes.

In personal injury cases, the defense lawyer usually concludes the voir dire examination by asking the jurors to set aside their natural feelings of sympathy, to keep an open mind about what the evidence proves until they have heard all the evidence, and to follow the court's instructions on the law even if they feel that the law should be different. The plaintiff's lawyer usually concludes his or her examination by asking the jurors to listen carefully to the evidence and to give to the case the same thoughtful consideration they would want for their own important matters.

The judge or lawyers who conduct the voir dire examination may question the veniremen in the order in which they were seated or question the panel as a whole. In the latter event, the usual procedure is for the examiner to ask a question to the panel, and each juror is supposed to raise a hand when the question applies to her or him. Then the examiner pursues the matter with each juror who raised a hand. This is the faster method and tends to avoid unnecessary repetition. Nevertheless, lawyers consider it to be the least satisfactory method because it does not allow a dialogue between the veniremen and the lawyer. Lawyers want to have a conversation with each venireman because often the manner in which a venireman expresses herself or himself is almost as important as what she or he says. The whole process is very subjective. Consequently, the more interaction a lawyer generates, the better feel the lawyer has for each venireman's competency and attitudes.

Most lawyers believe that the jury selection in criminal cases is extremely important to the outcome of the trial. They see the jury selection as being as important as the trial itself. Consequently, the voir dire examination in a criminal case may take several days and be as long as the actual trial. Lawyers tend to place somewhat less importance upon the voir dire examination in civil cases.

■ PRELIMINARY INSTRUCTIONS

When the six to twelve jurors have been selected, they must take an oath to follow the court's orders and the law. The following is typical of oaths administered to jurors:

> You each do swear that you will impartially try the issues in this case and a true verdict give according to the law and the evidence given you in court; your own counsel and that of your fellows you will duly keep, you will say nothing concerning the case, nor suffer anyone to speak to you about it, and you will keep your verdict secret until you deliver it in court. So help you God.

The court may remind jurors that they must act upon reason and good judgment, not on the basis of feelings, emotion, or speculation. The judge may give some preliminary instructions, such as the following:

> As to the law of this case, it will be given to you by me at the appropriate time. However, you are instructed that you must take the law exactly and precisely as I shall give it to you, that you must apply such law to the facts as you find them to be from the evidence, and that you must render your verdict accordingly, regardless of where the "chips may fall." The court (trial judge) does not make the law, but merely declares it in a given case. The law comes from federal and state constitutions, from federal and state statutes, and from declarations contained in judicial decisions stating the public standards of rights and duties in matters not covered by the constitutions and statutes. In this connection, you are instructed that if judges and juries were not bound by these tangible statements of the law, If in each lawsuit the judge or the jury could set up private and personal standards of rights and duties as a basis for deciding the case, one would never know in advance of a decision how he or she should have acted in a particular situation and no one would be safe. Cases arising from similar relationships or circumstances must be decided on settled principles of law and not on the notions of the trial judge or of a jury. Accordingly, it must be readily apparent to you that even though you may have an opinion as to what the law is or should be, you must set that aside; you must accept and apply the law exactly and precisely as I shall give it to you. I cannot at this time instruct you as to all rules of law applicable to this case because I have not as yet heard the evidence.
>
> I have some general instructions that I think will be of assistance. Our hours are generally 9:30 A.M. to 12:00 P.M., 1:30 P.M. to 5:00 P.M. Those hours

may be modified or extended depending upon circumstances. For example, should a witness's testimony be near completion at the customary recess time, we would tend to continue so that the witness would not need to come back for the next session.

Promptness, of course, is extremely important, and I am sure I need say no more about that.

During the morning session, about midway, and the afternoon session, about midway, we will take a fifteen-minute recess. On those occasions, as well as during the noon hour and after hours, you will be among the public. Do not discuss this case or the subject matter of the case with anyone. Once the case is over and you have rendered your verdict and you have been discharged from the case, then you may speak as fully and freely as you wish. On the other hand, if anyone should inquire, it is up to you. You may say, "I've done my best; I'd rather not discuss it."

You know where the accident occurred. Please do not go out and view the premises. You are not investigators. You are to determine the facts from the evidence submitted here in the courtroom, so keep that in mind.

You must try to keep an open mind until all the evidence has been presented and until you have been instructed, by me, concerning the applicable rules of law. The plaintiff will proceed with his case first, followed by the case-in-chief of each defendant. If new material is submitted, the plaintiff will have the right of rebuttal. If new material is submitted on rebuttal, then each defendant will have a right of rebuttal. In that way, all of the evidence that is proper and competent will be submitted to you without repetition.

After all the evidence has been presented and the parties have rested their case, you will have the opportunity to hear the attorneys' summations. The attorneys will review the evidence and draw conclusions from it. They will also discuss the rules of law as they apply to the evidence. Prior to those summations, I will have discussed with counsel the law that I have determined applies to the case and that I will give to you. The summations may be—and usually are—of assistance to you, but the responsibility of decision is yours, not that of the attorneys.

When you enter the jury room, you will have all the tools with which to determine the facts of the case and to apply the law in an appropriate manner. In the meantime, do not jump to conclusions as each witness takes the stand. You must keep an open and objective mind while the case is being presented. You should maintain that same objectivity when you commence your deliberations.

You may take notes if you wish. However, those notes are your own personal notes for refreshing your own memory. If your memory has then been refreshed so that you can say, "Now, of my own knowledge, I know this was said," or whatever the case may be, then you may say that to your fellow jurors. But your fellow jurors should not use your notes to refresh their memory. Such notes are no more authoritative than another juror's memory. There is a danger that when writing notes, you will not hear other important evidence.

There may be, from time to time, conferences here at the bench. Those conferences with counsel are intended to be out of your hearing. They involve questions of law or procedure, not questions of fact. Do not attempt to overhear our conversation. Under no circumstances should you guess the subject of our conversations and permit that to bear upon your determination of facts or the ultimate issues of the case. If you were to do so, your decision or determination would be based not on solid facts and the law, but on speculation and conjecture—which is repugnant to good judicial administration.

If at any time during the trial something of a personal nature bothers you, come to me about it. I am sure I can handle it so that it will not be detrimental to any party. But do not ask me what the evidence is, because that is solely within your province. That is your responsibility. As I indicated before, you should not consider or even know what I think of the evidence.

Sometimes, after the jury commences deliberations, a disagreement arises as to what a witness may have said—and it seems simple to call the court and say, "May we come back and have the court reporter read a witness's testimony?" I do not permit that except under unusual circumstances. In all probability, I will have started another trial. Counsel have perhaps gone their respective ways and may be trying another lawsuit—even in another county. In order to have you come back in and have portions of the testimony read to you, I would have to contact counsel, get them back, and recess my current case. And then, after I have permitted the reading of that one witness's testimony, the attorneys may be constrained to point out that, in fairness, the testimony of other witnesses who touched upon that subject ought to be read; otherwise, one facet of the case may be overemphasized. By the time I complied, we would be trying the case all over again.

When you fail to hear a question of an attorney or an answer of a witness, speak up, raise your hand. I will make sure that it is read back at that time, in its proper context and without any fear of possible overemphasis. Do not wait until the end of the testimony or end of the trial. It will be too late then to go back.

The judge should caution jurors against discussing the case with anyone. They may not even discuss the case among themselves until they receive their instructions on the law and begin their deliberations. There is a danger that some jurors would become advocates for a particular position before hearing all the evidence and receiving their instructions on the law. For the same reason, jurors are often urged to avoid making strong, unretractable statements at the beginning of their deliberations.

Some courts allow jurors to take notes. However, the judge cautions that an individual juror must not use her or his notes to influence other jurors. Notes are not necessarily more reliable or authoritative than another juror's memory. One reason for this is that a juror may be so busy writing that the juror may not be listening. The juror's notebooks are collected and kept by the clerk during evening recesses to prevent anyone from tampering with them and to keep them from being lost.

There is a trend in the courts for judges to give the jury some preliminary instructions concerning the probable applicable law even before any evidence is received. These preliminary instructions are usually repeated at the end of the trial. They may cover guidelines for evaluating evidence and some of the **substantive law** such as definitions of negligence and proximate cause. (Substantive law is the law that establishes the parties' legal rights and duties. It is distinguished from procedural law.) These preliminary instructions should help the jury to follow the evidence and appreciate the significance of the evidence.

Most courts give the jurors preliminary instructions to help them evaluate the evidence as the evidence is presented. The instructions on evaluating evidence may or may not be repeated at the end of the case when the court instructs the jury concerning the substantive law. The instructions on evaluating the evidence may be similar to the following:

DIRECT AND CIRCUMSTANTIAL EVIDENCE

A fact may be proved by either direct or circumstantial evidence, or by both. The law does not prefer one form of evidence over the other.

A fact is proved by direct evidence when, for example, it is proved by witnesses who testify to what they saw, heard, or experienced, or by physical evidence of the fact itself. A fact is proved by circumstantial evidence when its existence can be reasonably inferred from other facts proved in the case.

EVALUATION OF TESTIMONY—CREDIBILITY OF WITNESSES

You are the sole judges of whether a witness is to be believed and of the weight to be given to the testimony of each. There are no hard and fast rules to guide you in this respect. In determining believability and weight, you should take into consideration, as to each witness, the following:

the witness's interest or lack of interest in the outcome of the case

the witness's relationship to the parties

the witness's ability and opportunity to know, remember, and relate the facts

the witness's manner and appearance

the witness's age and experience

the witness's frankness and sincerity, or lack thereof

the reasonableness or unreasonableness of the witness's testimony in the light of all the other evidence in the case

any impeachment of the witness's testimony

any other circumstances that bear on believability and weight

You should rely upon your own experience, good judgment, and common sense.

EXPERT TESTIMONY

A witness who has special training, education, or experience in a particular science, profession, or calling is allowed to express an opinion. In determining the believability and weight to be given such opinion evidence, you may consider, among other things, the following:

the education, training, experience, knowledge, and ability of the witness

the reasons given for the witness's opinion

the sources of the witness's information

considerations already given you for evaluating the testimony of a witness

Opinion evidence is entitled to neither more nor less consideration by you than the other fact evidence.

EVALUATION OF DEPOSITION EVIDENCE

Testimony may be presented to you by way of videotaped deposition. The testimony of a witness who for some reason cannot be present to testify in person may be presented in this form. Such testimony is under oath and is entitled to neither more nor less consideration by you because it was so presented. You are to judge its believability and weight in the same manner as you would have had the witness been present in court.

IMPEACHMENT

In deciding the believability and weight to be given the testimony of a witness, you may consider three types of evidence:

Evidence that the witness has been convicted of a crime. In doing so, you may consider whether the kind of crime committed indicates the likelihood of the witness telling or not telling the truth.

Evidence of the witness's reputation for truthfulness.

Evidence of a statement by or conduct of the witness on some prior occasion, that is inconsistent with the witness's present testimony. This evidence may be considered by you only for the purpose of testing the believability and weight of the witness's testimony and for no other purpose. However, if the statement was given under oath or the witness is a party or an agent of a party in the case, the evidence of the prior inconsistent statement or conduct may be considered as substantive evidence bearing on the issues in this case as well as for testing the believability and weight of the witness's testimony.

■ JURY DELIBERATIONS

When a case is submitted to the jury for its determination, it usually takes several hours for the jurors to review the evidence and reach a verdict. Five to six hours is an average length of time for deliberations in a typical civil case that arises from an accident.

While the jury is considering the case, the trial judge may begin trying another case or may conduct other essential business of the court. When the trial judge acts as the fact finder, he or she must conduct a careful review of the evidence, just as the jury does, and then prepare a written findings of fact, conclusions of law, and order for judgment. Most lawyers believe that the time required for a judge to go through this procedure well justifies the expense of the jury system. Just as important, it often takes the trial judge a long time to make his or her decision—sometimes months. During that period of time, it is said that the judge has the case "under advisement." The delay may cause the parties a great deal of anxiety and inconvenience. Yet lawyers are very reluctant to pressure a judge for an earlier decision.

■ TYPES OF VERDICTS

The trial judge selects the type of verdict the jury must use and designates the form in which the verdict is to be submitted. Three types of verdicts may be used in civil actions: general, special, and general with interrogatories. The type of verdict a judge chooses to use is not determined by the kind of case. Rather, the choice is based upon the complexity of issues and the need to identify facts and issues for purposes of appeal.

The type of verdict most commonly used in the past was the **general verdict.** A general verdict is very succinct. The jury simply states that it "finds for the plaintiff" in a stated amount of money, or the jury "finds for the defendant," which means the plaintiff recovers no money damages. If the defendant prevails on his or her counterclaim, the amount is stated for the defendant.

Currently, the most common type of verdict is the **special verdict,** which consists of specific questions concerning the disputed facts and/or ultimate questions of fact to which the court applies the law. The jury must answer each question, thereby resolving the basic issues of fact. The court then applies the law to the facts as determined by the jury and issues an order for judgment accordingly. The jury's answer to each question may be short; usually yes or no. For example:

1. Did defendant sign the promissory note (plaintiff's exhibit A)? _____ (yes or no)

2. Was the defendant negligent? _____ (yes or no)

3. If your answer to question 2 is yes, was the defendant's negligence a direct cause of the accident? _____ (yes or no)

4. If your answer to question 3 is yes, what amount of money would fairly compensate the plaintiff? _____

One very pragmatic reason for having a special verdict is that if some error occurs in the course of the trial but it can be determined from the special verdict that the error did not affect the outcome of the case, the error is not prejudicial and cannot be made grounds for an appeal. Rule 49(a) anticipates the possibility that when a court uses a special verdict one or more important fact issues may be left out of the verdict. The omission may be inadvertent or intended. The rule prevents the omission from becoming prejudicial error by providing that the parties waive the right to a trial by jury concerning any issue of fact that is omitted unless, before the jury begins its deliberations, the party who wants a jury's determination of the fact duly asks the court to submit the questions to the jury. The party should make the request in writing, and the request must clearly appear on the record. Otherwise, the fact issue, if material to the judgment, must be determined by the judge as the fact finder.

For the **general verdict with interrogatories,** the court requires the jury to find for the plaintiff or the defendant and also to answer certain specific fact questions. The fact questions must be phrased so that the jury can answer them with short, specific answers, such as yes or no. Rule 49(b) recognizes that one or more of the jury's interrogatory answers may result in an inconsistency with the general verdict or that the interrogatory answers may themselves be inconsistent. The rule instructs the court how to deal with inconsistencies. The court may tell the jury that the answers are inconsistent and ask the jurors to deliberate further to make the answers consistent. Or the court may declare a mistrial and try the case again with a new jury.

■ QUOTIENT VERDICTS

Some courts instruct jurors that they must not render a **quotient verdict,** in which each juror decides for herself or himself how much money the plaintiff should recover. Each juror's amount is added to the others, and the total is divided by the number of jurors. The resulting number is accepted by the jurors as the proper award. For example:

Juror	Award
1	$1,000
2	2,000
3	2,000
4	0
5	500
6	6,000
Total	$11,500

$11,500 ÷ 6 = $1,916.67, which is the verdict.

Such verdicts are improper because the amount awarded is not necessarily what the individual jurors have determined is the correct amount based upon the law and the evidence. A quotient verdict is a method of compromise that has no basis in the law or the evidence. In the preceding example, jurors 4 and 6 greatly influenced the result. What would have happened if juror 6 had selected twenty thousand dollars as the proper amount, believing that the other jurors would be too low?

■ ADDITIONAL INSTRUCTIONS

Occasionally, jurors determine that they need clarification on some point of law or procedure, so they notify the judge, through the bailiff, that they need additional instructions. The judge then summons the lawyers to the courtroom so that they can hear the jury's question and help the judge resolve it. The judge has the ultimate responsibility to handle the problem. Ideally, the lawyers will agree on the solution. Their agreement precludes the problem from being a basis for a subsequent appeal. Usually the problem can be solved by rereading the instructions already given to the jury.

Sometimes, before signing a special verdict, the jury wants to know what effect the answers will have. The judge's customary answer is that they are not supposed to concern themselves with the consequences of the verdict—just the truth. They should "let the chips fall where they may." However, some states have laws or rules that permit the judge and lawyers to tell the jury about the effect of their answers to a special verdict.

■ UNANIMOUS VERDICT

Rule 48 says a verdict must be unanimous unless the parties stipulate that some designated lesser number may agree on a verdict:

> Unless the parties otherwise stipulate, (1) the verdict shall be unanimous and (2) no verdict shall be taken from a jury reduced in size to fewer than six members.

Suppose that after five days of trial, the case is submitted to a jury that has eight members. After a full day of deliberation, the jury forewoman tells the judge the jury is deadlocked. Seven jurors are able to agree on a verdict, but one is holding out. The parties could stipulate that they will be bound by a verdict rendered by the seven who do agree. The Rules Advisory Committee clarifies this issue:

> In exceptional circumstances, as where a jury suffers depletions during trial and deliberation that are greater than can reasonably be expected, the parties may agree to be bound by a verdict rendered by fewer than six jurors. The court should not, however, rely upon the availability of such an agreement, for the use of juries smaller than six is problematic for reasons fully discussed in *Ballew v. Georgia,* 435 U.S. 223 (1978).

A stipulation to a verdict by less than six is not inconsistent with the rule that requires that at least six jurors consider the case. If the parties do not stipulate, they have a right to a unanimous verdict.

The laws of the some states provide that a jury's verdict must be unanimous if it is returned within six hours after the case is submitted to the jury. However, after six hours of deliberation, a jury may return a five-sixths verdict. One dissenting juror cannot prevent a verdict from being final. In other words, after at least six hours of deliberation, the verdict does not have to be unanimous. If the jury has seven or eight members, one holdout cannot prevent a verdict. If the court impanels twelve jurors, ten of the twelve may return a five-sixths verdict. When a jury returns a five-sixths verdict, all five or all ten of the concurring jurors must concur with all parts of the verdict. They must agree to all the answers in a special verdict. All the concurring jurors must sign the verdict. The dissenting juror does not sign the verdict. Otherwise, when a verdict is unanimous, only the foreperson signs the verdict. The five-sixths rule results in fewer **hung juries** and fewer new trials. (A jury is hung when the necessary number cannot agree on a verdict as a whole.)

◼ RENDERING THE VERDICT

The judge receives the jury's verdict in open court. The lawyers and parties have a right to be present. The lawyers may ask to have the jury **polled** for the purpose of confirming that each juror concurs in the verdict. The jury is polled by the judge who merely asks each juror whether she or he concurs in the signed verdict. The juror must answer aloud and the court reporter records each juror's answer. Once in a great while a juror who had some reservation about the verdict decides to repudiate the verdict when polled. Usually, the lawyers waive the right to poll the jury.

Many courts do not require the parties and lawyers to wait at the court for the verdict. The lawyers may elect not to be present when the verdict is delivered. The judge or clerk notifies them of the verdict by telephone within minutes after the verdict is received. The clerk enters judgment on the judgment roll in accordance with the terms of the order for judgment.

◼ POSTVERDICT JURY CONTRACTS

Jurors do not have to talk to anyone about their verdict, their deliberations, or any other aspect of the trial after the case is concluded. On the other hand, no law prohibits a juror from talking to the parties, lawyers, media reporters, or anyone else about the case. If it should appear that the jury or any of its members was guilty of misconduct in the course of the trial, that could be a basis for setting aside the verdict. If either party learns about or even suspects that there has been misconduct by the jury, the party must tell the trial judge. The court, not the parties, must conduct an investigation of the alleged misconduct. Interviewing jurors after the verdict may not be used as a subterfuge to find error for obtaining a new trial. Any contact the parties or lawyers or paralegals have with jurors after the trial may result in a waiver of the right to complain about jury misconduct.

Jurors who participate in the trial of a civil action and return a verdict are usually enriched by the experience. They provide an important service to their government and community. They derive a better understanding of the judicial system and have a better appreciation for its value. They help to maintain a system that has been instrumental in preserving domestic peace and tranquility for over two hundred years. Within a few days after their service ends, jurors usually can set aside the worries and anxieties they may have had about their responsibilities, but their new respect for the civil justice system continues. It is the responsibility of judges, lawyers, and paralegals to help make their jury service a rewarding experience.

SUMMARY

Parties have a right to a jury trial in most civil actions. A jury resolves the controverted fact issues. A jury finds the facts on the basis of the evidence presented by the parties. Jurors may use their experience to evaluate the evidence but cannot substitute their knowledge or experience for the evidence. A jury must apply the law to the facts to resolve ultimate questions of fact. The court instructs the jury concerning the relevant rules of law and their application. The jury's determination of the facts is reflected in the jury's verdict.

A party requests a trial by jury by making a demand for jury on the party's pleading or serving and filing a written demand for jury within ten days after the last pleading has been filed. A party may request a jury trial on specified fact issues, leaving the remaining fact issues to be determined by the judge as the fact finder. A party waives the right to a jury trial by failing to make a demand for jury on the party's pleading or within ten days of service of the last pleading.

Parties do not have a right to a trial by jury when the plaintiff seeks equitable relief. When a case is tried without a jury, the judge determines the facts. The judge does not render a verdict. Instead, the judge prepares the court's findings of fact. Then the judge applies the substantive law to those facts by preparing the court's conclusions of law and its order for judgment, which tells the clerk of court how to prepare the judgment. The judgment declares the parties' ultimate legal rights and obligations in the matter. After the trial and judgment are entered, the case may end, or the prevailing party may have to take steps to enforce the judgment, or the losing party may appeal from the judgment. A petit jury is drawn from a jury panel of veniremen. The panel of veniremen is drawn from the community as a whole.

To qualify to be a juror, a person must be able to hear, be able to speak and understand the English language, and not have a felony conviction.

A jury may be composed of any number of jurors between six and twelve. The jury must have at least six members when the case is decided. Often more than six jurors are selected to serve to make sure that when the trial is finished six or more jurors are available to decide the case.

Federal courts do not use alternate jurors. Most state courts do use alternates.

The trial lawyers and judge conduct a voir dire examination of the jury panel members to determine the members' qualifications to be jurors. Since the party who has the burden of proof makes the first opening statement, the rules allow the other party's lawyer to begin the voir dire examination. The lawyers may not use the voir dire examination to argue the case, to persuade the jury about the case, to engender sympathy for a party, or to foster antagonism against another party. The jurors must answer the voir dire questions under oath.

Courts ensure the parties' right to an unbiased, competent jury by subjecting the veniremen to a voir dire examination. The examination is usually conducted by the judge and the lawyers. The questions must relate to the veniremen's qualifications. The veniremen must answer the questions under oath. If the judge decides to ask all voir dire questions, the lawyers have a right to submit written questions to the judge for the judge to ask. A venireman may be stricken for cause or because of actual or implied bias. Actual bias exists when a venireman acknowledges that he or she cannot be fair. If a venireman is related to one of the parties or one of the lawyers, or works for a party, there is implied bias, and he or she will be excused by the court even if the person claims he or she can be fair. A venireman may have a bias because of the nature of the case. A lawyer must make a motion to strike the venireman to remove him or her because of bias. Each party has an unlimited number of challenges for cause. Whenever a panel member is stricken from the panel for cause, the court adds another member to the panel.

Jurors may be excused for cause if they have some connection with the case. Each party has three peremptory challenges, which the party must use. A party does not have to justify a peremptory challenge.

Once selected, the jurors are not supposed to talk about the case with anyone, not even with their fellow jurors until they commence their deliberations. At that point they will have heard all the evidence and will have the court's instructions concerning the applicable law. Jurors may take notes, but they may not use those notes for any purpose other than to refresh their own recollection.

There are three types of verdicts. The judge decides which type to use. In a general verdict, the jury simply finds for the defendant or for the plaintiff and awards an amount of money damages. In a special verdict, the jury answers fact questions that the judge submits to them. The judge applies the law to the facts the jury determines, to draw conclusions of law. The judge orders entry of judgment based upon the conclusions of law. Courts use special verdicts most often. In a general verdict with interrogatories, the jury finds for the plaintiff or the defendant, but in addition answers specific fact questions relevant to the parties' dispute. The jury's answers to the interrogatories may help to resolve some collateral problem or merely assure the judge that the jury understood the problems in the case.

A jury must not resort to a quotient verdict. In a quotient verdict each juror decides for himself or herself how much money the plaintiff should recover, if any. The jurors' numbers are added together for a total amount which is then divided by the number of jurors. The quotient becomes the amount of the award. A quotient verdict is not a product of a reasoned consensus, and is easily affected by extreme positions taken by one or two jurors. A quotient verdict is a method of compromise that has no basis in the law or the evidence.

When jurors need clarification on some point of law or procedure they notify the bailiff who notifies the judge about the question or problem. The judge may contact the lawyers by telephone or summon them to the courtroom, so they can hear the jury's question and assist the judge to resolve it. The judge is ultimately responsible for resolving the problem. Often the problem can be solved by re-reading the instructions already given to the jury. A judge will usually refuse to tell the jury the legal consequences of proposed answers to special verdict questions. For example, if the jury wants to know whether the plaintiff will receive some compensation even if they find the defendant was not negligent, the judge would tell them to make true findings and not concern themselves with the consequences.

In a federal court a jury's verdict must be unanimous. However, the parties may stipulate that the verdict need not be unanimous. The stipulation must be on the record, and the parties must agree on what lesser number may concur to render a verdict. If the parties stipulate to a lesser number, the stipulated number of jurors, usually five of six, must agree to all parts of the verdict.

The judge receives the jury's verdict in open court. The lawyers and parties have a right to be present when the jury returns the verdict. The verdict is read in open court. The parties have a right to poll the jury to determine whether each juror truly concurs in the verdict as read. Rarely does a juror disavow the verdict. In civil actions, lawyers usually waive the right to poll the jury. Many courts allow the parties and lawyers to leave the court while the jury deliberates, and they do not have to be present when the verdict is returned. In that event, the judge or clerk telephones the lawyers to report the verdict to them.

Jurors do not have to discuss their verdict or deliberations with anyone. However, there is no rule of law that prohibits a juror from talking to the parties, lawyers, media reporters, or anyone else about the case. Lawyers often contact jurors after the trial for the purpose of finding out what the jury thought about certain aspects of the case. Lawyers may not contact jurors for the purpose of uncovering misconduct on the part of the jury in order to obtain a new trial. If contact with a juror should uncover some jury misconduct, the lawyer must not investigate further. Instead, the lawyer must report the matter to the court and let the court conduct the investigation. Any contact the parties, lawyers, or paralegals have with jurors after the trial may result in a waiver of the right to complain about jury misconduct.

KEY TERMS

petit jury
demand for jury
counterdemand for jury
findings of fact
conclusions of law
order for judgment
alternate jurors
venireman
voir dire examination
challenged for cause

actual bias
implied bias
peremptory challenge
substantive law
quotient verdict
general verdict
special verdict
general verdict with interrogatories
polling the jury
hung juries

REVIEW QUESTIONS

1. What is the maximum number of jurors that may be seated in a civil action in federal court?

2. How many alternate jurors may a federal court seat in a civil action?

3. How does the role of an alternate juror differ from that of a regular juror?

4. Why are jurors forbidden to discuss the evidence with each other before they begin their deliberations?

5. Who signs a general verdict?

6. If the jury members find that they have a disagreement about what the law is or how the law applies, what may they do?

7. Describe two problems that may arise because a juror takes notes about the evidence during the trial?

8. What are two bases on which a lawyer may object to another lawyer's question to a veniremember during the voir dire examination?

9. May you contact a juror after the trial is over to discuss with the juror his or her perceptions about the case?

10. If a party hears from a person employed at the courthouse that a particular juror may have conducted an independent investigation of the facts during the trial, contrary to the judge's instructions, may you interview the juror to determine whether she or he may have engaged in some misconduct that would give grounds for a new trial?

STRUCTURE OF A CIVIL TRIAL

A courtroom is like a laboratory where the parties conduct research, tests, and analyses of alleged facts to determine the truth about a transaction or occurrence. Like a carefully controlled scientific study, a trial follows strict protocols. Consequently, when parties resort to a trial, they give up the right to use their own standards, values, and procedures for resolving their dispute. A trial is governed by rules of procedure, rules of evidence, and rules of law. The structure and rules are designed to promote fairness and impartiality. The parties are treated equally. The outcome should not depend upon who the parties are or who the judge is or what lawyers try the case. Each party has the opportunity to present the evidence upon which he or she relies and to make an argument for the result he or she seeks. Once the facts are established, the court must apply the law to the facts so that the dispute can be resolved according to the law. The outcome should be predictable within a reasonable range of possibilities. If the outcome is extraordinary, some error likely occurred in the procedure or in the application of the law.

The judge presides over all aspects of the trial. The judge determines what rules apply and how they apply and what substantive laws apply. Lawyers are officers of the court. They are expected to help the judge manage the trial. Lawyers are expected to control their clients and witnesses by instructing them about the law, the procedures, and their responsibilities to the court. For example, lawyers are expected to keep their clients and witnesses from testifying falsely. Lawyers are expected to present their clients' evidence in a proper manner. Lawyers assist the court by making objections and motions when they believe the opponent or court has made a mistake. Lawyers must actively help to protect the court from fraud, deceit, and perjury. A paralegal is expected to assist the trial lawyer with all these important functions.

■ PRELIMINARY CONFERENCE

When the parties and lawyers report to the courthouse to begin trial, the judge usually has a preliminary conference with the lawyers. This conference may take less than ten minutes, or it may last all day. The conference may cover any of a number of subjects. Usually the judge wants to know whether the parties might settle. Some judges want to know the amount of money the plaintiff has demanded and the amount of money the defendant has offered. Other judges do not want to be told about the actual amounts, only whether the parties might settle and whether they want additional time to discuss settlement. Most judges give the parties a few minutes to pursue settlement negotiations if there is any reason to believe that negotiations might be fruitful. On the other hand, some judges have the attitude that the parties must negotiate on their own time, not on the court's time.

The preliminary conference gives the judge an opportunity to ask the lawyers questions about the case and to ask the lawyers how they intend to handle the case. Presumably the judge has reviewed the pleadings and other documents filed with the clerk. The judge will use the parties' pretrial disclosures to help her or him conduct the voir dire examination of the veniremen. Some courts have special rules that require each party to serve and file a **statement of case** that provides a current summary of each party's version of the facts, witnesses list, and exhibit list. The lawyers are expected to explain their legal theories and any problems they expect to arise during the trial. The judge and lawyers try to establish a schedule for the presentation of evidence. They will almost always run into a problem scheduling witnesses, but the problem can be minimized if the parties cooperate to establish a schedule. Some judges require the lawyers to submit their proposed jury instructions before the trial begins.

The lawyers may schedule **motion in limine** to be heard during the preliminary conference. The phrase *in limine* means "at the threshold of the trial." The principal purpose for motions in limine is to prevent foreseen problems from complicating or disrupting the progress of the trial. Motions in limine are not supposed to deal with substantive legal issues. These motions usually deal with problems concerning the admissibility of evidence and procedural issues. Motions in limine may be made orally on the record without notice. Nevertheless, they should be made in writing and filed with the court before the parties report for the trial. A written motion is usually supported by a memorandum of law.

Suppose the defendant has evidence that the plaintiff was intoxicated at the time of the accident in question. However, since the plaintiff was a passenger in the defendant's vehicle at the time of the accident, his intoxication has nothing to do with the cause of the accident or injuries. The plaintiff may make a motion in limine to prevent the defendant from offering evidence of the plaintiff's intoxication. The grounds for suppressing or excluding this evidence is that the prejudicial effect of the evidence outweighs its probative value. Motions in limine are also commonly used where the plaintiff has some very vivid photographs showing her or his injuries in their acute stage. The prejudicial effect of these photographs may outweigh their probative value. The judge has discretion to exclude all such photographs or to limit the number that the plaintiff may put into evidence. Similarly, a court may limit the number of photographs dealing with a particular subject in order to avoid repetition and the cumulative effect of such evidence. Repetition wastes time and tends to give undue emphasis to the matters repeated.

■ JURY SELECTION

The paralegal and the trial lawyer should carefully watch the veniremen as they walk from the back of the courtroom to take their seats in the jury box. They should observe whether any of the jurors have any physical impairments. Do they look at the paralegal and lawyer or the parties? How are they dressed, and how do they carry themselves? Do they appear confident and respond appropriately to questions, or do they seem confused? What have they brought with them to pass the time? If they have brought reading materials, are the materials books or newspapers or office work in a briefcase or . . .? These outward indicators may suggest questions that should be put to jurors. For example, in a personal injury case, the defense lawyer ought to be very concerned about a venireman who limps as she walks to the jury box. A venireman who has brought a supply of comic books to read may not be much interested in the parties' business transaction. An obviously shy person may not contribute to the jury's deliberations regardless of how strongly she may feel about the evidence and the facts of the case. Perhaps the trial lawyer wants a shy person for the particular case or prefers shyness to the other choices available.

The more the paralegal can observe about the veniremen, the more helpful he or she can be in the selection process. The paralegal should listen to what the veniremen say and to *how* they say it. He or she should be sure to obtain the client's input. The client may have some undescribable, subjective feeling about a venireman that causes the client to be uncomfortable. The trial lawyer must take the client's feeling into consideration. The paralegal may be able to discuss the acceptability of the veniremen with the client while the trial lawyer is conducting the voir dire examination (see chapter 19).

■ OPENING STATEMENTS

A lawyer has a right to make an **opening statement.** The purpose of this statement is to tell the jury what each party claims and what evidence each party will present to support or refute the claims. An opening statement helps the jury to understand how items of evidence fit together. It is like a road map to show the jury where the case is going and how the evidence will get them there. It gives the jury an overview of the case and a frame of reference in which to consider the evidence as it is received. The plaintiff's lawyer may state the amount of money damages the plaintiff claims. The defense lawyer may describe the defendant's affirmative defenses. The lawyers may state what they believe happened or did not happen.

A lawyer may use the opening statement to explain concepts, relationships, potential problems, technical subjects, terms, and procedures. For instance, if the trial involves a medical procedure, the lawyers may prepare the jurors to hear about the procedure by giving them a preliminary description. In a case involving electricity, it might be useful for a lawyer to define some of the terms and explain some of the principles to which the experts will testify. Depending upon local rules, the lawyers may be allowed to show illustrative exhibits during the opening statements.

A lawyer must not make any statement about the evidence that she or he knows is unsupportable. An opening statement is not supposed to be an argument. Although the lawyers may describe the evidence they intend to offer, they may not argue why the jury should believe that evidence or what the evidence proves. It is improper to characterize a party's conduct, or to argue the effect or consequences of the conduct, or to justify or condemn the conduct of the other party. Lawyers may not discuss the law or its application to the facts of the case during their opening statement.

Courts give lawyers quite a bit of latitude to "discuss" the claims, facts, and evidence in their opening statement. Some lawyers regularly preface their statement with "The evidence will show that . . ." This preface helps them to focus their statement on the evidence to be offered rather than argue the case. The phrase also tends to make an argument sound as though the lawyer is discussing the evidence. Watch for this tactic. For example, the statement "The evidence will show that the defendant was driving much too fast for conditions" is a thinly veiled argument and is objectionable. On the other hand, the statement "The evidence will show that the defendant was driving forty miles per hour in a thirty-mile-per-hour zone" could properly be made in an opening statement. The lawyer could not properly state that the defendant was negligent for driving forty miles per hour in a thirty-mile-per-hour zone, because that statement would involve the application of the law to the expected evidence.

The party who has the burden of proof makes the first opening statement because that party must present his or her evidence first. In most cases the plaintiff has the burden of proof. Therefore, in most cases the plaintiff's lawyer makes the first opening statement. The defendant's lawyer may make an opening statement immediately after the plaintiff's lawyer concludes his or her statement, or after the plaintiff **rests.** The plaintiff rests when the plaintiff has finished presenting his or her case-in-chief. Usually, a defendant's lawyer prefers to make his or her opening statement at the beginning of the trial, immediately after the plaintiff's opening statement. Most defendant's lawyers want the jury to appreciate, at the outset, that the case has two sides. A defendant wants the jury to know about the problems in the plaintiff's case and to follow the defendant's cross-examination of the plaintiff's witnesses. By making an opening statement directly after the plaintiff's opening statement, a defendant's lawyer is more likely to persuade the jurors to keep an open mind until they have heard all the evidence. The defense lawyer who waits until the plaintiff has rested to make an opening statement may have some surprise evidence or impeaching evidence that he or she does not want to discuss until the plaintiff is fully committed to a position.

The most common format for an opening statement is a chronological development of the facts with a description of the supporting evidence. A chronological approach is helpful because lawyers often have to present their evidence in bits and pieces in a disconnected fashion, so the chronological overview helps the jury to follow and understand the evidence.

An opening statement may be no longer than five minutes or as long as forty minutes. The Federal Rules of Civil Procedure do not impose a time limit, but some judges do. Most lawyers keep their opening statement to about twenty minutes. An hour is too long. If a lawyer spends that much time, it suggests he or she has not prepared and is not focused on the fact issues. A lawyer's opening statement should anticipate and complement the final argument he or she intends to make. Experienced trial lawyers believe that an opening statement should be no longer than necessary to give the jury a clear understanding about the client's case. There is real danger in saying too much.

The opening statement educates the opposing party as well as the jury. Consequently, no one listens more carefully to a lawyer's opening statement than the opposing lawyer. The trial lawyer may ask the paralegal to take notes on the opening statements. If the paralegal hears the trial lawyer make a misstatement, she or he must let the lawyer know because the lawyer may be able to correct the mistake during the trial. For example, if the lawyer misstates an important date and the paralegal catches the mistake, the lawyer can emphasize the correct date while questioning the witnesses. The same is true if the trial lawyer leaves out some important point. While listening to the opponent's opening statement, the paralegal should think about whether the statement reflects the strategy the paralegal and lawyer anticipated when preparing for the trial. If either lawyer makes assertions in the opening statement that are not borne out by the evidence, the failure can be devastating. At the end of the trial the trial lawyer should ask the paralegal to compare the evidence with both opening statements and identify deficiencies. Any deficiencies in the evidence will be used against the lawyer who overstated his or her case in the opening statement.

The paralegal should ask the client to listen carefully to the opening statements. The opponent's statements tells the client exactly what the opponent thinks is important and what the opponent is likely to ask during cross-examination. The client's lawyer's statement provides a nice reminder of what is important. Also, the client should listen for inadvertent misstatements and omissions in order to help his or her lawyer correct the mistake.

■ BURDEN OF PROOF

A court will not provide a remedy unless the party who has the burden of proving his or her claim establishes the claim through evidence. In the final analysis, the jury must believe that the claim is more likely true than not true. If the party who has the **burden of proof** leaves the jury in doubt about the claim, the claim has not been proved and the verdict must leave the parties in the status quo. Although the burden of proof in civil cases is not as great as in criminal cases, where guilt must be proved beyond a reasonable doubt, it is significant. On the other hand, most defense lawyers believe that it is important to show the jury what did happen (to have a theory of the case), and not merely raise doubts in the mind of the jurors about the plaintiff's claim.

The burden-of-proof jury instruction the judge gives at the end of the trial defines the burden:

> Whenever I say a claim must be proved, I mean that all the evidence by whomever produced must lead you to believe it is more likely that the claim is true than not true. If the evidence does not lead you to believe it is more likely that the claim is true than not true, then the claim has not been proved. Proof of a claim does not necessarily mean the greater number of witnesses or the greater volume of testimony. Any believable evidence may be a sufficient basis to prove a claim.

The jury must evaluate and weigh the evidence. The jury may decide that one witness is more believable than three other witnesses on a particular point. A trial lawyer takes all these factors into consideration when preparing a witness to testify, when cross-examining an adverse witness, when making an opening statement, and when making a final argument. Many cases have been lost or won because the jury simply was not convinced that the claim was more likely true than not true.

The party who has the burden of proof has the right and duty to present her or his evidence first. Since the plaintiff almost always has the burden of proof on the principal issue, the plaintiff almost always presents her or his evidence first. However, if the defendant were to have the burden of proof, the defendant would have the right to go forward with the evidence first. As an example, if the plaintiff entrusted her fur coat to the defendant to store during the summer season, and the coat was lost or damaged while in the defendant's possession, the defendant's storage company would have the burden of proving that it was not negligent. Therefore, the defendant would have the right and duty to present evidence first. In the absence of any evidence as to how the loss occurred, the legal presumption of negligence on the part of the storage company (bailee for hire) would control.

Another common example where the defendant has the burden of proof on the principal issue is where an insurance company has denied coverage solely on the basis of an exclusion in its insurance policy, and the plaintiff insured brings a lawsuit to recover benefits under the policy. The defendant's insurer has the burden of proving facts that bring the claim within the exclusion. Therefore, the defendant insurer has the first opening statement and must present its evidence first. However, if the insurance company denied coverage on the basis that the policy was not in force at the time of the insured's loss, the plaintiff insured would have the burden of proving that the policy was in force and that the loss is of the type covered by the policy. Then the plaintiff insured would have the first opening statement and would be the first to present evidence.

■ PLAINTIFF'S CASE-IN-CHIEF

The parties present their evidence in stages. The plaintiff must present all his or her evidence first. The defendant may object to the plaintiff's evidence and test the evidence through cross-examination, but the defendant may not offer any evidence until the plaintiff is through. The plaintiff's initial presentation is the plaintiff's **case-in-chief.** The plaintiff's evidence may anticipate the defendant's affirmative defenses, but that is not required. The plaintiff's lawyer indicates that he or she has finished presenting the plaintiff's case-in-chief by stating on the record that "the plaintiff rests." At that point the court and parties must determine whether the plaintiff's evidence has established a **prima facie case.** A party has presented a prima facie case when the party has presented enough evidence to meet the minimum requirements to prove a claim upon which the court can grant relief. The believability of the evidence is not a factor in determining whether the evidence the court received is sufficient to prove the claim. If the plaintiff fails to prove a prima facie case, the plaintiff's claim is subject to dismissal on a **motion for judgment as a matter of law** (Rule 50(a)(1)).

The plaintiff's evidence must do more than tell a story. It must do more than show that the defendant is a bad person or did something bad and that the plaintiff has a grievance. The plaintiff's evidence must prove a prima facie case by presenting evidence that, if believed, establishes all the elements necessary to the plaintiff's causes of action. The plaintiff's evidence establishes a prima facie case if it shows that the defendant breached a legal duty owed to the plaintiff. In addition, the plaintiff must show that the defendant's wrongful conduct (act or omission) was the direct cause of some injury, property damage, or other harm recognized by the law as compensable. For example, in a breach-of-contract action, the plaintiff must prove that a contract existed. The contract establishes the legal duty. The plaintiff must prove that the defendant breached the contract and that the plaintiff sustained a compensable loss because of the breach. In a negligence action, the plaintiff must prove that the defendant breached a legal duty by engaging in negligent conduct (act or omission); that the plaintiff sustained an injury or property damage; and that the defendant's negligence caused the plaintiff's injury or property damage.

■ DEFENDANT'S CASE-IN-CHIEF

When the plaintiff rests, the defendant's lawyer takes charge of presenting the evidence. The defendant's case-in-chief is much like the plaintiff's case-in-chief. The defendant's lawyer has three objectives in mind: the defendant must counter the plaintiff's evidence on the disputed facts; offer evidence to prove the facts that support the defendant's theory of the transaction or occurrence; and prove the defendant's affirmative defenses. Experienced lawyers know that it is not enough for the defendant to poke holes in the plaintiff's evidence. The defendant must have a theory about the case and develop that theory.

The plaintiff may not offer evidence during the defendant's case-in-chief. The plaintiff may only object to the defendant's evidence and challenge the evidence through cross-examination. The defendant must present evidence that, if believed, is sufficient to prove the elements of the alleged affirmative defenses. When the defendant's lawyer is done presenting the defendant's evidence, he or she must state on the record that "the defendant rests." If the defendant's evidence does not cover all the elements of the alleged affirmative defenses, the plaintiff may move for judgment as a matter of law dismissing the affirmative defenses (Rule 50(a)(1)).

■ PLAINTIFF'S REBUTTAL

The plaintiff has the opportunity to present **rebuttal evidence** after the defendant's case-in-chief. This evidence is limited to issues and facts that are covered by the defendant's evidence. The plaintiff cannot offer rebuttal evidence on matters not raised or covered in the defendant's case-in-chief. The plaintiff may not withhold evidence for use in rebuttal unless its purpose is truly for rebuttal. A party may not use the rebuttal as a means to ambush the opponent. When the plaintiff's lawyer is finished, she or he must again state that "the plaintiff rests."

■ DEFENDANT'S REBUTTAL

The defendant's rebuttal evidence is limited to the matters covered by the plaintiff's rebuttal evidence. The defendant's lawyer must repeat that "the defendant rests" when all the rebuttal evidence has been offered.

■ MOTIONS FOR JUDGMENT AS A MATTER OF LAW

After all the evidence has been presented and both parties have rested finally, each party has the right to make or renew its motions for judgment as a matter of law. Rule 50(a)(1) provides guidelines for granting such motions:

> If during a trial by jury a party has been fully heard on an issue and there is no legally sufficient evidentiary basis for a reasonable jury to find for that party on that issue, the court may determine the issue against the party and may grant a motion for judgment as a matter of law against that party with respect to a claim or defense that cannot under the controlling law be maintained or defeated without a favorable finding on that issue.

The motion for judgment as a matter of law is often called a **motion for directed verdict** in many state courts. Again, a party may make a motion for judgment as a matter of law as soon as the opposing party rests, and the motions may be renewed when both parties have rested finally.

■ PRESENTING EVIDENCE

Unless the court has ordered the witnesses sequestered, they usually sit in the spectators' section of the courtroom until called.[1] (Witnesses are usually not present until the day they are expected to be called.) After the voir dire examination and opening statements have been made, the plaintiff's lawyer calls the first witness to the stand. The clerk or judge administers the oath or affirmation to the witness. The witness identifies himself or herself to the court and jury. The lawyer who called the witness to the stand begins the examination. The lawyer should ask questions that allow the witness

1. Rule 615 provides that a party may move the court for an order excluding a witness from the courtroom so that the witness cannot hear the testimony of any other witness. The purpose is to keep a witness from being influenced by what some other witness says. However, a party cannot be excluded. A government or business organization has the right to have a representative present and that representative may not be excluded, pursuant to Rule 615.

to relate the information the jury needs to determine the facts. There is an art to asking questions that make the testimony flow and that keep the testimony interesting for the jury. The questions should produce testimony that builds the case. Each new question should reasonably follow from the witness's prior answers. Each question must be clear to the witness and to the jury. Each question should be singular, should not cover too much information. Each question must seek evidence that is relevant to the material facts.

The questioning may be a direct examination or cross-examination. A lawyer must conduct a **direct examination** of any witness who is aligned with her or his client and any independent witness the lawyer calls to testify. A direct examination question should not suggest the answer the examiner wants to hear. In other words, the information should come from the witness, not the lawyer.

Conversely, a lawyer may **cross-examine** any witness aligned with the opposing side, any witness who is overtly hostile, and any independent witness the opposing party calls to testify. On cross-examination the lawyer may lead the witness by asking questions that suggest the "correct" answer. The questions may be framed so as to keep their answer very specific—to keep the witness from volunteering beyond a question. When the witness goes beyond the narrow question, the lawyer may move to strike the answer as nonresponsive. Unless the lawyer is interrogating an adverse party or a witness aligned with the adverse party, the cross-examination should be limited to the matters covered in the witness's direct examination. For example, if the plaintiff's lawyer called the witness to testify about the plaintiff's injuries, the defendant's lawyer could cross-examine the witness about the injuries. But if the defendant's lawyer asks questions about the accident (a different subject), the plaintiff's lawyer could object that the cross-examination is outside the scope of the direct examination. The defendant could then ask the court for leave to call the witness as his or hers and cover the new material in a direct examination.

The plaintiff may require the defendant to testify as part of the plaintiff's case-in-chief. Indeed, it is very common for the plaintiff's lawyer to call the defendant as the first witness in the plaintiff's case-in-chief. The plaintiff might do this for a number of reasons. The plaintiff's lawyer can pin down the defendant's version of the facts and then attack that version. The plaintiff's lawyer may cross-examine the defendant about one or two matters where the defendant's credibility is particularly weak. This approach is often good strategy because it may make the plaintiff's case appear strong at the beginning. At that point, the defendant has not heard the testimony of any witnesses, so the defendant may be a little less prepared than she or he would be later in the trial. It is usually advantageous for a party to testify after hearing other witnesses, because the testimony of other witnesses may help to refresh and sharpen the party's memory.

When the plaintiff's lawyer concludes the cross-examination, the defendant's lawyer may conduct a direct examination of the defendant, or the lawyer may choose to reserve the direct examination until the defendant's case-in-chief. Most judges permit the defendant's lawyer to ask the defendant a few questions to clarify one or two points developed during the plaintiff's cross-examination that might be confusing or misleading if not promptly explained, and nevertheless reserve the right to conduct a full direct examination of the defendant during the defendant's case-in-chief.

A fact may be proved by direct evidence or circumstantial evidence or both. The law does not prefer one form of evidence over the other. A fact is proved by direct evidence when it is proved by a witness who testifies to what he or she saw, heard, or experienced, or by physical evidence of the fact itself. A fact is proved by circumstantial evidence when its existence can be reasonably inferred form other facts proved in the case. If a witness testifies that he saw the defendant's car skid to the point of impact, the witness has presented direct evidence of the fact. On the other hand, if the witness did not see the accident but did see skid marks on the road, proof of the skid marks is circumstantial evidence that the car skidded to the point of impact. For another example, a witness who testifies to the length of skid marks provides direct evidence concerning those skid marks. From that direct evidence a jury may also infer that the driver was near the point where the skid marks began when the driver saw the danger, the driver sensed the need to stop, the driver applied the brakes, and the driver was or was not keeping a proper lookout.

Although circumstantial evidence is indirect proof, it is not considered any less trustworthy or less credible than direct evidence. Therefore, the law does not prefer direct evidence over circumstantial evidence. When a jury is confronted with conflicting direct evidence and circumstantial evidence, it may elect to accept either. Circumstantial evidence requires some analysis and reasoning. Therefore, it is only as good as the jury's ability to analyze and reason. Matters of intent, motive, and knowledge often have to be proved through circumstantial evidence.

■ QUESTIONING WITNESSES

Lawyers prefer to call their witnesses in the order that permits them to effectively tell the client's story to the jury. Usually a chronological development is the most understandable and persuasive order for the evidence. Unfortunately, sometimes the importance of a chronological development of the evidence must take second place to the witnesses' schedules and availability. If a lawyer disregards a witness's convenience and subpoenas her or him for an inconvenient time, the witness may be vindictive and less helpful than if the witness had been accommodated. In personal injury cases, the lawyers on both sides find that it is very important to accommodate the doctors' schedules. To avoid scheduling problems, some lawyers resort to the use of videotaped depositions to present witnesses' testimony at trial.

A witness should be cautioned that anything taken to the witness stand is subject to being examined by the opposing lawyer. Consequently, most witnesses take nothing to the stand except their deposition transcripts. Medical doctors and expert witnesses take their "business" files with them. These witnesses will have to refer to their files, and the files may be received into evidence as exhibits. Expert witnesses expect to have their files examined by the opposing lawyer.

A lawyer who puts a witness on the stand should know all about the witness, including such things as the witness's criminal background. If a party presents a witness as "important" to the case and, the cross-examination shows the witness to be a bad person, the client may suffer from guilt by association. A lawyer who must present testimony from an unsavory witness may choose to mention the problem as part of his or her opening statement. In this way the lawyer prepares the jury with an explanation about the witness and disassociates the client from the witness even before the testimony begins. The witness will not be present to hear the opening statement and lawyer's disclaimer of the witness.

It is perfectly proper for a lawyer or legal assistant to talk with the opposing party's witnesses even during the trial, unless a witness is represented by a lawyer. Nevertheless, there is no basis for forcing a hostile or unfriendly witness to discuss the case, except by taking the witness's deposition. If a witness who appears to be aligned with the opposing side does decline to speak about the case, the witness's refusal may be brought out on cross-examination to emphasize the bias of the witness. A manifest bias works against the witness's credibility.

The lawyers have primary responsibility to examine the witnesses. However, a federal judge may ask questions too. Judges occasionally ask witnesses questions for clarification for the judge's own benefit and for the benefit of the jury. A judge has some control over the interrogation to keep it from being repetitious, to keep the questions from being unduly embarrassing, and to keep the lawyers from harassing witnesses (see Rule 611).

■ PRESENTING EXPERT TESTIMONY

A witness who has special training, education, or experience in a particular science, profession, or calling is allowed to express an expert opinion. An expert witness does not have to be a college graduate or otherwise have a strong academic background. Welders, mechanics, plumbers, and even lawyers may be expert witnesses concerning the matters in which they have special training and experience. The court must be satisfied that the expert witness's background does in fact qualify her or him to be an expert. The weight and credibility to be given to an expert's testimony is a matter for the jury to decide. Usually, an expert's persuasiveness depends upon the reasons the expert gives for her or his opinions, the soundness of the information upon which the expert has relied, and the expert's credentials and experience. The mere fact that the evidence comes from an "expert" does not mean the jury can or should give more weight or consideration to the evidence. Indeed, jurors could reject an expert's opinion on the basis that they find some circumstantial evidence to be more persuasive than that opinion. The Rules of Evidence permit expert witnesses to state their opinions when their opinions help the jury to understand evidence material to the case and when their opinions provide information that is not ordinarily available in any other form:

> If scientific, technical, or other specialized knowledge will assist the trier of fact to understand the evidence or to determine a fact in issue, a witness qualified as an expert by knowledge, skill, experience, training, or education, may testify thereto in the form of an opinion or otherwise. (Rule 702)

Expert witnesses may be retained to testify about almost any subject. There is a growing tendency for litigants to hire expert witnesses to prove how an accident happened. The experts are called reconstructionists. They analyze all the evidence and then present an explanation, in the form of an opinion, of how and why the accident occurred. Reconstructionists are asked to testify in many different types of accident cases, including construction site, automobile, airplane, even slip-and-fall accidents.

Courts should not let an expert witness act as an advocate and argue the facts of a case. Experts are not allowed to testify to what the law is or how the law applies to the facts of the case. Experts should not be allowed to do the jurors' reasoning for them by making deductions from the evidence, or to advocate certain conclusions. They should be allowed to explain technical evidence and facts the jury could not understand without their input.

A party runs a very real risk of losing credibility by calling too many expert witnesses. Two experts may be one too many. Experts do not always agree with each other even if they are testifying for the same party. They might arrive at the same basic conclusion, but their assumptions, analyses, and reasons may differ. These differences may weaken their overall authority. A skilled cross-examination may indicate that the expert witness would have given whatever opinion he or she was asked to provide.

The use of expert witness testimony adds considerably to the cost of preparing for trial and presenting the evidence. Scholars of jurisprudence have expressed a good deal of concern that courts should become sensitive to the overuse of expert testimony and should place additional restraints on its use. Some courts are beginning to discourage the hiring of experts when their testimony is not really needed to establish material facts.

■ MAKING OBJECTIONS

The trier of fact (jury) may consider and rely upon any evidence the court allows it to consider. Generally, courts allow juries to consider any evidence a party offers, unless a proper objection is made to the evidence in a timely manner. For example, hearsay evidence may be sufficient to prove a claim or defense if it is received without objection from the opposing party. If a party offers evidence that is contrary to the Rules of Evidence or contrary to law, the evidence is subject to objection. If the objection is timely and sustained, the evidence will not be received. If the evidence is not received, it may not be used by the court or jury to decide the case.

A lawyer is supposed to interpose an objection without interrupting the question but before the answer is given. If the witness answers anyway, the lawyer may ask the court to instruct the jury to disregard the answer.

A technical objection exists for every situation, and the lawyer should use it. The technical objection indicates the grounds for the objection without arguing the objection—for example, "Defendant objects to the question on the grounds that it calls for hearsay" or "Plaintiff objects on the grounds of lack of foundation." A lawyer must not argue the point by saying, "Defendant objects on the grounds of hearsay, because this witness would only be repeating what the witness heard from another person." The lawyer must state the proper grounds for the objection, because that helps the judge to focus on the problem. If a lawyer states the wrong grounds for an objection and the objection is **overruled,** the lawyer cannot complain that the evidence should have been included. (An objection is overruled when the court denies it and decides that the proffered evidence should be received.)

When an objection is **sustained.** the interrogator must rephrase the question or move to another subject. (An objection is sustained when the court agrees with it and refuses to allow the evidence.) If the interrogator believes the court has erred, she or he may request permission to approach the bench to discuss the issue out of the hearing of the jury. If the judge allows the request, both lawyers meet with the judge at the bench or in the judge's chambers to discuss the issue. The court reporter should record their discussion. Upon further consideration, the judge may reverse her or his previous ruling.

Trial lawyers are constantly deciding whether to object to evidence. In making this decision, a lawyer must first consider whether he or she has grounds for the objection. If grounds exist, then the lawyer must consider the value of making the objection by determining how the expected evidence fits into the theory and strategy of the case. Lawyers are reluctant to object too often and appear as though they are trying to keep vital information from the jury. An objection may not be sustained even when properly made. The judge may be wrong in overruling an objection, but the jury will not be aware that the judge is wrong. If the objection is overruled, it may only serve to highlight the evidence in the eyes of the jury. Furthermore, why object to evidence that could be received if presented by another witness or in another form, especially if it would be stronger evidence if properly presented?

An objection duly made and erroneously overruled establishes error in the record, which may entitle the objecting party to a new trial. However, an error justifies a new trial only if it is prejudicial. Some errors that cannot be considered prejudicial occur in most trials. If the answer to an improper question is sure to be innocuous, it may be better not to object. If the opposing lawyer can introduce the evidence in another way—for instance, by asking a different question or by rephrasing the question—it may be better not to object. Also, an improper question may open opportunities for cross-examination that otherwise might not be available. Making an objection should never be a mere reflex reaction.

When an objection is sustained so as to preclude a lawyer from presenting certain evidence, the lawyer has a right to make an **offer of proof,** out of the hearing of the jury, to show what the evidence is and what it would prove. The judge cannot prevent a party from making an offer of proof. The offer of proof helps the appellate court to appreciate the significance of the excluded evidence. It also gives the trial judge an opportunity to reconsider the ruling.

■ USING DEPOSITIONS

Deposition transcripts may be used at trial in various ways, whether the depositions were taken for discovery or to preserve testimony. The most common use is to impeach a witness whose testimony at trial differs from what the witness previously said in the deposition. If the inconsistency is significant, it may reflect adversely upon the witness's credibility. The jury must decide whether the deposition testimony is true or the court testimony is true.

If a deposition is used to impeach a witness who is not a party, the impeachment testimony may be considered by the jury only to test the witness's credibility. Out-of-court statements made by a nonparty are not evidence and cannot support a verdict. Such statements are hearsay;

furthermore, the witness has, in effect, retracted the prior out-of-court statement with testimony that is inconsistent with the prior statement. Technically, the out-of-court statement by a nonparty is not competent to establish any fact in the case. If a nonparty's court testimony is believed, that testimony will support a verdict even though the witness was impeached.

If a party made a statement in a deposition that is contrary to her or his testimony at trial, the opponent may offer the prior deposition testimony into evidence as the party's admission. The party's admission, even though it was made out of court, is substantive evidence that will support a verdict. Suppose the plaintiff stated in her deposition that she never saw the defendant's car before the collision, but testified at trial that she did see the defendant's car when it was still one hundred feet away. The defendant could offer into evidence the plaintiff's deposition testimony that she did not see the defendant's automobile, and the jury could base its verdict upon that testimony. A party's prior statement that is inconsistent with the party's testimony in court may also be used to discredit the party by impeachment of the party's testimony.

Suppose a nonparty witness testifies in his deposition that he saw the defendant driving fifty miles per hour in a thirty-mile-per-hour zone, and testifies at trial that the defendant's speed was twenty-five miles per hour. The witness's testimony is competent only to prove a speed of twenty-five miles per hour. The deposition testimony of a higher speed casts doubt on the witness's credibility, but the jury cannot use the out-of-court testimony as a basis for determining, as a fact, that the defendant traveled fifty miles per hour. On the other hand, if the defendant (a party) testified in his deposition that he was driving fifty miles per hour at the time of the accident and testifies at trial to a speed of twenty-five miles per hour, the jury can accept the "admission" in his deposition as substantive evidence and find that his speed was fifty miles per hour.

At the end of the trial, the jury is instructed to consider impeachment when evaluating the witnesses' testimony. Impeachment (a showing of inconsistency) does not necessarily mean the witness has lied. The witness is not necessarily guilty of perjury. Nor is the witness disqualified from testifying. Impeachment merely goes to the weight and believability of testimony.

A deposition may be used as the "best evidence" when a witness is not available to testify in court. This is true even though the deposition was taken only for discovery and not to present the witness's testimony, as provided by Rule 32(a):

> At the trial or upon the hearing of a motion . . ., any part or all of a deposition, so far as admissible under the rules of evidence applied as though the witness were then present and testifying, may be used against any party who was present or represented at the taking of the deposition or who had reasonable notice thereof, in accordance with any of the following provisions:
>> (1) Any deposition may be used by any party for the purpose of contradicting or impeaching the testimony of deponent as a witness, or for any other purpose permitted by the Federal Rules of Evidence.
>> (2) The deposition of a party or of anyone who at the time of taking the deposition was an officer, director, or managing agent . . . of a public or

private corporation . . . which is a party may be used by an adverse party for any purpose.[2]

(3) The deposition of a witness, whether or not a party, may be used by any party for any purpose if the court finds:

(A) that the witness is dead; or

(B) that the witness is at a greater distance than 100 miles from the place of trial or hearing, or is out of the United States, unless it appears that the absence of the witness was procured by the party offering the deposition; or

(C) that the witness is unable to attend or testify because of age, illness, infirmity, or imprisonment; or

(D) that the party offering the deposition has been unable to procure the attendance of the witness by subpoena;

(E) upon application and notice, that such exceptional circumstances exist as to make it desirable, in the interest of justice and with due regard to the importance of presenting the testimony of witnesses orally in open court, to allow the deposition to be used.

A witness may be "unavailable" due to death, illness, absence from the jurisdiction, or other circumstances. In the previous example, if the non-party witness is unavailable to testify at trial, his deposition testimony that the defendant was traveling fifty miles per hour is substantive evidence because he has not retracted his sworn testimony.

A party may offer into evidence any portion of an adverse party's deposition. The testimony may be read to the jury. The deponent may subsequently read to the jury other portions of the deposition to explain or clarify the testimony or to put the testimony into proper context. The transcript is not given to the jury, but it is made part of the court's record.

■ FINAL ARGUMENTS

A trial is structured to allow the lawyers to present **final arguments** to the jury after the jury has heard all the evidence but before the judge instructs the jury on the applicable law. Some courts have experimented with having the final arguments after the judge instructs the jury, but the procedure needs a neutralizing "buffer" between the arguments and the jury's deliberations.

The lawyers' arguments serve several important functions. They summarize the important evidence, reminding the jurors what they saw and heard during the trial. However, the court cautions jurors that they must rely on their own memories of the evidence and not on the lawyers' recollections. The lawyers can tell the jurors why they should believe (accept) certain evidence and disbelieve (reject) other evidence. They may explain to the jurors their theories on the facts. They may preview the law for the jury and suggest how the law applies to the facts.

Two common formats are used for the final argument. In some courts the plaintiff's lawyer must argue first. Then the defendant's lawyer may argue. Then the plaintiff's lawyer may make a short rebuttal argument. The rebuttal may be limited to as little as five minutes. More important, the rebuttal may not cover matters already argued by the plaintiff's attorney

---

2. This provision makes clear that the deposition of an officer of a corporation may be used *against* the party as substantive evidence or for purposes of impeachment or both.

and is limited to matters raised in the defendant's argument. The other format for final arguments has the defendant's lawyer argue first. The plaintiff's lawyer argues last because the plaintiff ordinarily has the burden of proof. When the defendant has the burden of proof, the defendant's lawyer should be last to argue. The lawyer who makes the first final argument does not have a right to rebuttal. Consequently, the lawyer who argues first must anticipate the opponent's argument. That is a difficult assignment.

The final argument gives the lawyers the opportunity to summarize the evidence and argue how the jury should apply the evidence to determine the facts of the case. The lawyers have a right to contend that certain evidence is believable or not worthy of belief. They may argue how the evidence proves or fails to prove a fact. They may comment on how the law applies to the facts. However, the judge's instructions will point out that the jury is to follow the law as the judge gives it. If the lawyers say anything about the law that is different from the judge's instructions, the jury is to disregard the lawyers' remarks. Each lawyer's objective is to persuade the jury that the client's claim or defense is correct.

The lawyers have a great deal of latitude in making their final argument. Only a few proscriptions have been put on final arguments: Lawyers must not misstate the facts or law. Lawyers may not try to invoke religious beliefs for or against a party. Lawyers may not ask the jurors to put themselves in the place of a party. Where a special verdict is used, lawyers may not tell the jury what legal consequences flow from the answers. For example, the plaintiff's lawyer may argue that the defendant was negligent and the jury should find that she was negligent. But the plaintiff's lawyer may not argue that unless the jury finds the defendant negligent, the plaintiff will not obtain any money damages. Lawyers cannot engage the jurors in conversation. The jurors may not ask questions. A lawyer may object to any improper statement the opponent makes in the final argument. If the objection is sustained, the judge tells the jury to disregard the statement. If a lawyer's argument is misleading, the opponent may be entitled to a corrective jury instruction. In that event, the judge not only tells the jury to disregard the lawyer's improper statement, but also tells the jury why the statement was wrong and what the evidence is or in what respect the law was misstated.

Lawyers have a right to know, before they make their final argument, exactly what the judge intends to tell the jury about the law. Lawyers often use charts in their final argument to illustrate points, compute money damages, list items of damages, list critical items of evidence, and so forth. Each lawyer has a right to know about charts the opposing counsel intends to use in its argument, unless the charts have been received in evidence as exhibits. Lawyers may refer to or use any of the exhibits that were received in evidence. They may read from documents, such as hospital records, received in evidence, but not from documents not received in evidence. Lawyers try to keep their argument to less than an hour in length. However, the length and complexity of the case determine the length and scope of the argument.

■ JURY DELIBERATIONS

After the final arguments, the judge instructs the jury on the law and the procedures the jurors must follow while deliberating. The instructions are always read by the judge to minimize the opportunity for error. They give the jury guidelines for evaluating the witnesses and evidence. The judge tells the jurors what they need to know about the substantive law in order to complete the verdict form. The judge reads the verdict form to the jurors and explains how they are to use it. It is becoming increasingly common for the judge to give the jurors a copy of the written instructions to take with them into their deliberations.

The jurors may ask the judge for additional instructions or have the instructions reread if they have difficulty understanding or remembering what they were told. Their questions must be made in writing. When the jury asks for additional instructions, the judge contacts the lawyers. The judge explains to the lawyers the jury's question and how the judge intends to answer or otherwise deal with it. The judge may ask the lawyers for suggestions or for them to agree (stipulate) to an answer. Regardless of the course of action taken, a record is made concerning the jury's question and its resolution. If the judge does give additional instructions, the lawyers have a right to be present and to make whatever objections they deem appropriate. If the judge merely rereads the instructions previously given, the lawyers may choose not to return to the courtroom to participate.

The jurors are encouraged to fully participate and fully discuss the case. They cannot communicate with anyone except the marshal or the bailiff who sequesters them. In civil actions jurors are allowed to go to their own home during the evening hours. They are forbidden to discuss the case with anyone, not even with other jurors, while in recess. On the other hand, if they want to continue with their deliberations, as is often the case, they are allowed to work into the night.

In federal court the verdict must be unanimous, unless the parties stipulate to a lesser number. In most state courts all six jurors must agree if they return a verdict during the first six hours of their deliberations. After six hours, five of the six may return a verdict, but all five must agree to all parts of the verdict. In other words, the same five must agree on all liability questions and all damages questions.

When the jury returns its verdict, the parties have a right to poll the jury ensure that all jurors really do concur. More often than not, the parties waive the right to poll the injury. The verdict is then filed with the clerk of court. If the court used a special verdict, which determines only questions of fact, the judge must use the verdict to prepare his or her own findings of fact, conclusions of law, and order for judgment. If the jury returns a general verdict, it simply finds for the plaintiff for a specified sum of money, or for the defendant. The clerk enters judgment on a general verdict.

■ TAXATION OF COSTS

The prevailing party is entitled to recover certain costs and disbursements incurred in the prosecution of the case. The recoverable costs are specified by statute or rule of the court (Rule 54(d)). The prevailing party must prepare a bill of costs and disbursements that itemizes the various costs claimed. The losing party is given an opportunity to object to the items listed and the amounts claimed. If objections are made, a hearing must be held on the objections. Otherwise, the clerk of court automatically enters the claimed costs as part of the judgment. If the defendant is the prevailing party, the defendant obtains a money judgment against the plaintiff for taxable costs. Before any judgment may be filed, the prevailing party must file an **affidavit of identification,** which fully describes the judgment debtor. Each court has a form or recommended form for this.

SUMMARY

The preliminary conference gives the judge an opportunity to ask the lawyers questions about the case and how they intend to handle the case. Some courts have special rules that require each party to serve and file a statement of case that provides a current summary of each party's version of the facts, witnesses list, and exhibit list. The lawyers are expected to explain their legal theories and any problems they expect to arise during the trial. The judge and lawyers try to establish a schedule for the presentation of evidence.

The lawyers may schedule motions in limine to be heard during the preliminary conference. The phrase *in limine* means "at the threshold of the trial." The principal purpose for motions in limine is to prevent foreseen problems from complicating or disrupting the progress of the trial. Motions in limine are not supposed to deal with substantive legal issues.

The paralegal and the trial lawyer should carefully watch the veniremen as they walk from the back of the courtroom to take their seats in the jury box. They should consider whether any of the jurors have any physical impairments. Do they look at the paralegal and lawyer or the parties? How are they dressed, and how do they carry themselves?

The purpose of an opening statement is to tell the jury what each party claims and what evidence each party will present to support or refute the claims. An opening statement helps the jury to understand how items of evidence fit together. The lawyers may state what they believe happened or did not happen. Lawyers may not argue why the jury should believe their clients' evidence or what the evidence proves. Lawyers are not supposed to discuss the law or its application to the facts of the case in their opening statement.

An opening statement sets the stage and gives the jury its first impression of the case. It must comport with a party's overall strategy. A lawyer's opening statement is sure to be tested by the evidence. The opponent will try to capitalize on any misstatements or inadequacies in the statement. The lawyer must not overstate the case, but she or he must tell the jury enough to make the jury appreciate that the client has a strong and just position. Like a good witness, the lawyer should strive to appear sincere and authoritative.

The party who has the burden of proof must present her or his evidence first. That party must present a prima facie; otherwise, the alleged claim will be dismissed as a matter of law. In determining whether a prima facie case has been proved, the court looks to see if the party has presented evidence to establish each element of the cause of action. The court does not consider the believability of the evidence or whether the evidence has been refuted by other credible evidence. When the jury decides whether a fact has been proved, it must determine whether the evidence shows that the fact is more likely true than not true. If the jury cannot reach that state of conviction from the evidence, the fact has not been proved by a fair preponderance of the evidence, and the jury must find against the claim.

The plaintiff's initial presentation of evidence is the plaintiff's case-in-chief. The defendant may object to the plaintiff's evidence and test the evidence through cross-examination, but the defendant may not offer any evidence until the plaintiff is done. The plaintiff's lawyer indicates that he or she has finished presenting the plaintiff's case-in-chief by stating on the record that "the plaintiff rests."

The defendant's case-in-chief counters the plaintiff's evidence on the disputed facts. The defendant must prove all the elements of her or his affirmative defenses. Good strategy requires the defendant to have a theory about the case and develop that theory during her or his case-in chief. When the defendant's lawyer is finished presenting evidence, she or he must state on the record that "the defendant rests." Then the rebuttal begins.

Rule 50(a)(1) provides guidelines for granting motions for judgment as a matter of law.

A lawyer must conduct a direct examination of witnesses aligned with his or her client and any independent witness the lawyer calls to testify. A direct examination question should not suggest the answer the examiner wants to hear. A lawyer may cross-examine any witness aligned with the opposing side, any witness who is overtly hostile, and any independent witness the opposing party called to testify. On cross-examination the lawyer may lead the witness by asking questions that suggest the desired answers. The questions may be framed so as to keep their answers very specific—to keep the witness from volunteering testimony beyond the question. When the witness goes beyond the narrow question, the lawyer may move to strike the answer as nonresponsive. A cross-examination should be limited to the matters covered in the witness's direct examination. The plaintiff may require the defendant to testify as part of the plaintiff's case-in-chief.

A fact is proved by direct evidence when it is proved by a witness who testifies to what she or he saw, heard, or experienced, or by physical evidence of the fact itself. A fact is proved by circumstantial evidence when its existence can be reasonably inferred from other facts proved in the case. Circumstantial evidence is not considered any less trustworthy or less credible than direct evidence. Therefore, the law does not prefer direct evidence over circumstantial evidence. Circumstantial evidence requires some analysis and reasoning. Therefore, it is only as good as the jury's ability to analyze and reason. Matters of intent, motive, and knowledge often have to be proved through circumstantial evidence.

It is perfectly proper for a lawyer or legal assistant to talk with the opposing party's witnesses even during the trial, unless a witness is represented by a lawyer. Judges occasionally ask witnesses questions for clarification for the judge's own benefit and for the benefit of the jury. A federal judge has unlimited authority to ask questions of witnesses.

The rules of evidence permit expert witnesses to state their opinions when their opinions help the jury to understand evidence material to the case and when their opinions provide information that is not ordinarily available in any other form. An expert witness does not have to have a strong academic background. The court must be satisfied that an expert witness's background does in fact qualify him or her to be an expert. The weight and credibility to be given to an expert's testimony is a matter for the jury to decide. Usually, an expert's persuasiveness depends upon the reasons the expert gives for his or her opinions, the soundness of the information upon which the expert has relied, and the expert's credentials and experience. The mere fact that the evidence comes from an "expert" does not mean the jury can or should give more weight or consideration to the evidence. Experts are never allowed to testify to what the law is or how the law applies to the facts of the case.

If a party fails to make a timely objection to the opponent's evidence, the jury may consider the evidence even though it would have been excluded if the objection had been made. A lawyer is supposed to interpose an objection without interrupting the question but before the answer is given. A technical objection exists for every situation. The technical objection indicates the grounds for the objection without arguing the objection. If a lawyer states the wrong grounds for an objection and the objection is overruled, the lawyer cannot complain that the evidence should have been excluded. When an objection is sustained, the interrogator must rephrase the question or move to another subject. An objection duly made and erroneously overruled establishes error in the record, which may entitle the objecting party to a new trial. However, an error justifies a new trial only if it is prejudicial. Making an objection should never be a mere reflex reaction. When an objection is sustained, a lawyer has a right to make an offer of proof to show what the evidence is and what it would prove. The judge cannot prevent a party from making an offer of proof. The offer of proof helps the appellate court to appreciate the significance of the excluded evidence. It also gives the trial judge an opportunity to reconsider the ruling.

A deposition of a party may be used to cross-examine the party and impeach the party. Statements in a deposition may be used against the party deponent as party admissions. The admissions are substantive evidence. The deposition testimony of a deponent may be used at trial in lieu of the deponent's live testimony if that deponent is unavailable to testify in person. Such testimony is received for all purposes, just as though the deponent were present in court.

The final arguments provide a summary of the important evidence, reminding the jurors what they saw and heard during the trial. The lawyers may tell the jurors why they should believe certain evidence and disbelieve other evidence. They may explain to jurors their theories about the facts. They may preview the law for the jury and argue how the law applies to the facts. A lawyer may not ask the jurors to put themselves in the place of a party. If a lawyer's argument is misleading, the opponent may be entitled to a corrective jury instruction. Lawyers have a right to know, before they make their final argument, exactly what the judge intends to tell the jury about the law. Lawyers may refer to or use any of the exhibits that were received in evidence.

After the final arguments, the judge instructs the jury on the law and the procedures that the jurors must follow while deliberating. The judge tells the jurors what they need to know about the substantive law in order to complete the verdict form. The jurors may not communicate with anyone during their deliberations, except the marshal or the bailiff who sequesters them. In civil actions, jurors are allowed to go to their home during the evening hours. They are under strict instructions not to discuss the case with anyone, not even another juror, until they reconvene. A violation of that mandate would result in a mistrial. In federal court the verdict must be unanimous unless the parties stipulate to a lesser number.

The prevailing party is entitled to recover certain costs and disbursements incurred in the prosecution of the case. The recoverable costs are specified by statute or rule of the court (Rule 54(d)). The prevailing party must prepare a bill of costs and disbursements that itemizes the various costs claimed. The losing party is given an opportunity to object to the items listed and the amounts claimed. Each court has a form or recommended form for this.

KEY TERMS

statement of case	rebuttal evidence
motion in limine	motion for directed verdict
opening statement	direct examination
rests	cross examination
burden of proof	overruled
case-in-chief	sustained
prima facie case	offer of proof
motion for judgment as a matter of	final argument
law	affidavit of identification

REVIEW QUESTIONS

1. What subjects are usually covered in the conference that the judge has with the lawyers immediately before trial?
2. When does the court hear motions in limine?
3. What is the general purpose of any motion in limine?
4. How may a paralegal help the trial lawyer with the jury selection?
5. What are the primary purposes of an opening statement?
6. What are the limitations on a lawyer's opening statement?
7. Which party may make the first opening statement?
8. Why is the formality of "resting" important?
9. What is a prima facie case?
10. What is meant by a fair preponderance of the evidence?
11. What are the limitations on rebuttal evidence?
12. Why do courts require lawyers to use formal, technical objections when they want to exclude improper evidence?

POSTTRIAL MOTIONS

A party who is dissatisfied with the results of the trial and who was prevented from having a fair trial may obtain relief from the verdict and judgment through one or more posttrial motions. Occasionally, both parties consider the verdict and judgment to be unsatisfactory and both may make posttrial motions.

Several types of posttrial motions may be made. The motions may be combined with one another and may be made in the alternative. The most common posttrial motions include those for the following:

a new trial

a new trial on the issue of liability only

a new trial on the issue of damages only

a new trial concerning a particular party's liability

additur to money damage award

remittitur from money damage award

judgment as a matter of law

In addition, if the case was tried to a judge without a jury, so the judge made findings of fact, conclusions of law, and an order for judgment, the moving party may move the court for amended findings of fact or amended conclusions of law or both. Recall that when a jury returns a special verdict, the judge must make findings of fact and conclusions of law based upon the answers to the special verdict questions.

A paralegal may be asked to prepare the posttrial notice of motion and to assemble the supporting documentation. The trial lawyer must decide which motions to make and the grounds for the motions. The lawyer must sign the motion papers.

There are countless possibilities for error in the trial of a case. Errors may arise from the trial procedures, rulings on the evidence, misapplication of the substantive law in the jury instructions, or other rulings. Regardless of the type of error, the moving party is entitled to posttrial relief if the error was "duly preserved" by a timely objection and was prejudicial. A party's timely objection to an error gives the judge an opportunity to consider the problem, deal with it, and correct it. If a party fails to bring an error to the attention of the court in a timely manner, the error is waived. A party may not wait until the trial is over and then complain about the error. Otherwise, parties would be tempted to covet error for the purpose of obtaining relief from any unsatisfactory trial result, instead of preventing and correcting error as it occurs.

The system requires lawyers to prevent error and to work to keep any errors from becoming prejudicial. When a lawyer objects to improper evidence or other error, the lawyer must be prepared to suggest solutions for correcting the error. For example, when a lawyer objects to improper evidence but the jury has already heard the witness's answer, the lawyer must ask the court to instruct the jury to disregard the answer. Or if the lawyer believes that a mere instruction is inadequate, the lawyer may move the court for a mistrial. If the motion for a mistrial is granted, the parties must start the trial from the beginning. They will even have to select a new jury.

The purpose of posttrial motions is to give the trial judge an opportunity to reconsider or further consider errors already brought to the judge's attention. In addition, a few errors, called **plain errors** or **fundamental errors,** may be noted for the first time in a posttrial motion. An appellate court will consider plain error in an appeal even though no objection was made during the trial. Plain error is very basic error that goes to the heart of the case. By characterizing an error in this manner, an appellate court acquires some discretion in deciding whether or not to deal with the problem. If the court concludes that a serious miscarriage of justice occurred, it may call the apparent error plain error and use that characterization as a basis for review and setting aside the lower court's judgment even though the error was overlooked during the trial stage. The system provides many checks and balances in an effort to ensure a fair trial and proper result according to law.

■ PREJUDICIAL ERROR

A party's mere disappointment in a jury's verdict is not grounds for obtaining a new trial or for appealing the case to a higher court. If the trial was conducted without any **prejudicial error,** there is no basis for changing the result. Error is considered prejudicial only if it appears that the error adversely affected the outcome of the case. Rule 61 provides guidelines for identifying prejudicial error:

> No error in either the admission or the exclusion of evidence and no error of defect in any ruling or order or in anything done or omitted by the court or by any of the parties is ground for granting a new trial or for setting aside a verdict or for vacating, modifying or otherwise disturbing a judgment or order, unless refusal to take such action appears to the court inconsistent with substantial justice. The court at every stage of the proceeding must disregard any error or defect in the proceeding which does not affect the substantial rights of the parties.

A large body of appellate law focuses on what constitutes a substantial right and when error is considered to be prejudicial. The important point to appreciate is that the court's error must be significant to warrant posttrial relief.

Assume that the plaintiff and the defendant were involved in a motor vehicle accident. The plaintiff was injured and brought an action in negligence to obtain money damages. The judge mistakenly allowed the plaintiff to present evidence that suggested the defendant was intoxicated at the time of the parties' accident, and the defendant duly objected to the evidence. The jury returned a verdict in favor of the plaintiff, awarding damages in a large amount but not so large as to be shocking. The defendant makes a posttrial motion for a new trial on all issues, claiming that the evidence of his intoxication was improperly allowed, and it prejudiced him. The judge must decide whether the jury might have found the defendant negligent because of the defendant's possible intoxication and whether a finding of intoxication affected the amount of the damages awarded; otherwise, the evidence was not prejudicial. The judge should consider the following issues: Intoxication is not, by itself, a basis for imposing civil liability. In this case, the plaintiff must prove that the defendant was negligent, such as by failing to keep a proper lookout or failing to yield the right-of-way or driving at an excessive speed. Without proof of some such act or omission, the plaintiff fails to prove a prima facie case of negligence whether or not the defendant was intoxicated.

The plaintiff's evidence that the defendant was intoxicated does not prove negligence. At most, it explains why the defendant failed to keep a proper lookout or failed to keep his motor vehicle under control. If the jury followed the jury instructions, and there is a presumption that it did, it must have found that the defendant committed some negligent act that caused the plaintiff's injury. If that is true, how could the evidence of intoxication be prejudicial? The judge must look at the other evidence concerning liability and decide whether it made liability a close issue. If there was evidence from which a jury could have found that the defendant was not negligent, the jury may have rejected that evidence if it concluded that he was drunk at the time of the accident.

Did the evidence prejudice the amount of the verdict? If the verdict was within an acceptable range, but high, the evidence may have affected the jury's evaluation. Jurors tend to award higher damages, almost as a penalty, against drunk drivers. On the other hand, if the award was low, the judge has to decide whether the jury might have made a compromise between awarding some damages and awarding none. If the judge concludes that the amount of the verdict was a compromise, the judge should award a new trial on damages as well as liability.

■ MOTION FOR NEW TRIAL

Where the alleged error may have affected the outcome of the case, but the court cannot ascertain how the case would have been decided if the error had not occurred, the remedy is to order a new trial in which the error will not be repeated. Any error in procedure, concerning the evidence or substantive law, that could have affected the jury's verdict is grounds for a motion for new trial. When prejudicial error is shown, the court should order a new trial. The new trial may be on all issues or only on the issues that could have been affected by the error. The moving party does not have to prove that the error did in fact affect the outcome, merely that the error could have affected the outcome. A new trial on all issues is often called a **trial de novo.**

A motion for a new trial must be served upon all parties within ten days after the entry of judgment (Rule 59). To illustrate, if judgment was entered on Monday, the ten-day period begins to run on Tuesday and the motion must be filed on or before the following Thursday.

A motion for a new trial must state the precise grounds for the motion. Proof of the error may be shown to the trial court by having a partial transcript of the proceedings prepared by the court reporter. The motion may be supported by affidavits of persons who have knowledge of the claimed errors. In addition, the motion is almost always based on the facts as recorded in the **judge's minutes,** or official notes, made during the trial.

The Rules provide that a trial judge may order a new trial within ten days after the entry of judgment even though neither party has made a motion for a new trial. The same power permits the trial judge to order a new trial on grounds that were not raised by the moving party's motion for a new trial. The order for a new trial must state the reasons or grounds for granting a new trial. An order denying the motion for a new trial needs no explanation.

A motion for a new trial is considered the first step to an appeal. In some state courts a motion for a new trial is a prerequisite to an appeal. It gives the trial judge an opportunity to consider and correct the alleged errors. It also gives the judge an opportunity to explain his or her reasons for denying the motion. In federal court a losing party may simply appeal from the judgment. In some appellate courts the scope of review is broader if the appeal is from an order denying a new trial rather than from the judgment.

■ COMMON GROUNDS FOR A NEW TRIAL

Misconduct on the Part of One or More Jurors.   If a juror were to conduct an investigation of the case outside of the courtroom, that would constitute misconduct that could require a new trial. A juror's contact with one of the parties or witnesses before or during the trial could give the appearance of favoritism or worse. A juror's false statement in the voir dire examination could be the basis for a new trial. A jury engages in misconduct by returning a quotient verdict.

Misconduct on the Part of the Prevailing Party.   If the prevailing party concealed evidence, concealed witnesses, suborned perjury, presented false testimony, made an improper, prejudicial remark during the final argument, or engaged in some other form of misconduct, the trial court should order a new trial in favor of the moving party. The misconduct must be substantial, prejudicial, and not corrected during the trial.

Discovery of New Evidence.   If the moving party can show the existence of new, additional evidence that could change the outcome of the case *and* that evidence could not have been discovered or obtained by the exercise of due diligence before the trial was completed, the judge may order a new trial. Parties must be diligent in gathering evidence for the trial. If a party finds that more time is needed to secure important evidence, the party may move the court for an order postponing trial. However, the moving party must be able to show the court that he or she has not been dilatory and that the delay of the trial will not cause substantial prejudice to other parties.

It would be unfair for a party to neglect to gather or present evidence and then use the omission to obtain a new trial. The moving party must show the court that the newly discovered evidence did not exist or was unavailable or could not have been found through the exercise of diligence. This rule probably illustrates the adversarial nature of civil litigation as well as any. It manifests the duty each party has to be self-reliant in obtaining and presenting evidence. The verdict is final, even if wrong, where the parties have had a full, fair opportunity to present their claims and defenses.

Inappropriate Award of Damages.   The amount of compensation to be awarded is peculiarly a question of fact for the jury. Nevertheless, courts have developed a sense of proportion about the adequacy or inadequacy of money damages for most types of cases. If the award does not shock the judge's conscience as being either too high or too low, it must stand. But an award that is manifestly unfair should be set aside and a new trial should then be ordered.

A new trial is appropriate whether the award is too much or too little. The new trial may be limited to the issue of damages only. A party who moves the court for a new trial on the issue of damages usually combines the motion with a request for an **additur** to the verdict if the award is too little or a **remittitur** to the verdict if the award is too much. An order for an additur increases the award to a specified amount. An order for a remittitur reduces the award to a specified amount. The trial judge may determine that a certain amount of money added to or taken away from the verdict will do substantial justice, and by ordering a change in the award, the expense of a new trial may be avoided. The judge may order that a new trial will not be held if the plaintiff will accept a smaller amount, or if the award is unconscionably small, if the defendant will agree to pay a specified additional amount. An order for an additur or remittitur does not have to be tied to an order for a new trial, but it usually is.

Suppose the jury returns a verdict for $100,000, and the judge concludes that amount is excessive. If the judge decides that an award of $75,000 would be fully adequate, the judge may order a remittitur of $25,000, reducing the verdict to $75,000. If the plaintiff accepts the reduction, the defendant's motion for a new trial on damages is denied; if the plaintiff refuses to accept the reduction, the defendant's motion for a new trial is granted. Similarly, a judge may order an additur for the plaintiff on the condition that the defendant agrees to pay the designated increased amount. If the defendant refuses to pay the additur, the plaintiff receives a new trial, and the defendant runs the risk of having to pay even more. In this example, the judge's knowledge about the pretrial settlement negotiations may influence her decision about what is a fair range for a verdict. If liability is not in dispute and the judge knows that the plaintiff was asking for only $20,000 for a settlement, the judge may worry that the jury's $100,000 award is excessive.

Occasionally, an injured plaintiff claims to have spent many thousands of dollars for medical treatment for injuries allegedly sustained in an accident, but the defendant is able to present persuasive evidence establishing that the medical expenses were not due to the accident in question or were not necessary. A very small verdict may result. Weighing the evidence and equities of such a situation can be a very difficult responsibility for the trial judge and appellate court. The courts are reluctant to substitute their own evaluation for that of a jury.

Unrectified Errors of Law at Trial.   If evidence was erroneously received or excluded at trial, the moving party must show that an objection was duly made and that the evidence could have affected the jury's verdict. When a case is tried to a judge without a jury, the judge may decide whether or not the disputed evidence actually affected her or his findings of fact or conclusions of law. A judge commonly has to make many rulings on evidence during a trial, and no judge will be correct all the time. Federal Rule of Evidence 103 discusses such rulings:

> Rulings on Evidence
>> (a) Effect of erroneous ruling. Error may not be predicated upon a ruling which admits or excludes evidence unless a substantial right of the party is affected, and
>>> (1) Objection. In case the ruling is one admitting evidence, a timely objection or motion to strike appears of record, stating the specific ground of the objection, if the specific ground was not apparent from the context; or
>>> (2) Offer of proof. In case the ruling is one excluding evidence, the substance of the evidence was made known to the court by offer or was apparent from the context within which questions were asked . . .
>> (d) Plain error. Nothing in this rule precludes taking notice of plain errors affecting substantial rights although they were not brought to the attention of the court.

If any of the rulings are erroneous and the error was duly brought to the judge's attention, the losing party is entitled to a new trial if he or she can show that the error probably adversely affected the outcome of the case. Technical errors of little substance are never the basis for securing a new trial.

A lawyer's objection to evidence is sufficient notice to the judge that admission of the evidence is error. The lawyer does not need to argue each evidentiary ruling or to make a specific exception to the judge's rulings. There may be a problem, however, where a lawyer objects to certain improper evidence but inadvertently states the wrong grounds for the objection.

If a lawyer believes that the court has misstated the law in the jury instructions, she or he is required to bring that error to the judge's attention before the jury commences its deliberations. Ordinarily, as soon as the judge finishes giving the instructions, she or he asks the lawyers whether there were any errors or omissions in the instructions. The lawyers must speak then or waive the right to complain. It is unnecessary to repeat objections about errors in the instructions that were fully discussed on the record, in chambers, before the judge undertook to instruct the jury. Also, a lawyer protects her or his record by filing written requested instructions that correctly cover the rule in question.

Verdict Not Supported by the Evidence.   If a party feels that he or she was entitled to a directed verdict on an issue because no evidence supported the particular claim or defense, and the motion for judgment as a matter of law was denied, he or she may make a motion for a new trial on that ground. Usually, it is very difficult to obtain a new trial on this ground, because almost any believable evidence on the issue is enough to carry the issue to the jury. The trial court, in effect, has a duty to sustain the verdict if that is reasonably possible. The court must resolve every reasonable doubt in favor of the verdict. This motion is always accompanied by a motion for judgment notwithstanding the verdict.

■ MOTION FOR JUDGMENT NOTWITHSTANDING THE VERDICT

The grounds for making a motion for judgment as a matter of law—a **motion for judgment notwithstanding the verdict**—are that the determinative issue must be decided as a matter of law, or the evidence is insufficient to establish the opponent's cause of action or affirmative defense, even though the jury has found in favor of the opponent. The standard for challenging the sufficiency of the evidence has been variously stated. The verdict should be set aside (1) if the verdict is contrary to the entire evidence or (2) if reasonable minds could not differ as to the correct outcome or (3) if no competent evidence reasonably tends to support the verdict. The grounds for granting judgment as a matter of law are the same as those for granting a Rule 56 summary judgment.

This posttrial motion may become necessary where the trial judge believed that the jury would not find as it did and the judge wanted the parties to have their case decided by the jury. Since the jury did the unexpected thing, the judge must now correct the error. Another situation that may give rise to a successful posttrial motion is where the judge does not have time to fully consider the requirements of the applicable law and, rather than make the jury wait for the court and lawyers to fully consider the law, decides to submit the case in line with the prevailing party's theory. After further consideration, the judge may conclude that the legal theory was wrong or unsupported by the evidence. To correct the problem, the judge may grant judgment to the losing party as a matter of law. This motion is usually combined with a motion for new trial (see Rule 50).

■ FORM OF A POSTTRIAL MOTION

Each motion should have four parts. The motion should state what relief the moving party wants the court to provide; the procedural rule, if any, by which the motion is made; each of the grounds, or reasons, for the motion; and the identity of the documents that the party claims supports the motion.

The motion in exhibit 21.1 is similar to one made by a defendant landlord who was held liable in negligence for the rape of a tenant committed by an assailant who entered the apartment through a ground-floor window. The landlord contended that the tenant had left the window open. The plaintiff tenant contended that the window lock was defective, consequently she was unable to lock the window. The landlord argued that if the tenant knew the lock was defective, which he denied, she had a duty

■ EXHIBIT 21.1

Posttrial Motions

Jane Ackerman,		File No. PI 95-002356

Jane Ackerman,

      Plaintiff,

vs.   NOTICE OF MOTIONS

               AND MOTIONS

Percy Smith,

      Defendant,

     File No. PI 95-002356

TO: Plaintiff and David O. Blake, her attorney, 386 North Magnolia Street, Suite 1500, Grand Building, St. Louis, Missouri 44551:

NOTICE OF MOTIONS

PLEASE TAKE NOTICE that the defendant will move the court for judgment notwithstanding the verdict, or in the alternative, for a new trial. Said motions will be heard before the Honorable Ann Balton in room C751 of the County Government Center, St. Louis, Missouri, on December 20, 1995, at 9:00 A.M., or as soon thereafter as counsel can be heard.

MOTION FOR JUDGMENT NOTWITHSTANDING VERDICT

The defendant hereby moves the court for an order granting judgment of dismissal to the defendant notwithstanding the special verdict.

This motion is made pursuant to Rules 50.02 and 59 of the Missouri Rules of Civil Procedure.

The grounds for the defendant's motion are that the defendant was entitled to a directed verdict at the conclusion of the plaintiff's case-in-chief and at the close of all the evidence. Specifically, the plaintiff's claim and testimony that she knew the shell lock on the window in question could not be engaged so as to keep the window from being opened from the outside, precluded the defendant landlord from having any legal duty to warn the plaintiff about the lock or to repair the lock in question. The plaintiff's second theory of negligence contradicted her first theory and was unsupported by the evidence. Specifically, the plaintiff testified that the window lock could not be engaged, and the plaintiff's counsel was allowed to argue that the assailant was able to force the window open from the outside because the shell lock used washers as spacers and that the defendant was negligent for having spacers in the lock.

The great weight of the evidence showed that the window lock in question was operable and the plaintiff failed to use the lock.

The jury's determination that the plaintiff sustained a loss of earning capacity in the amount of $250,000 is contrary to the great weight of the evidence and was the result of passion and prejudice. The award is excessive as a matter of law.

The grounds for these motions are stated more fully in the defendant's memorandum of law, which is served herewith.

This motion is made upon the court's minutes, files, exhibits, and records, including deposition transcripts used at trial, a partial transcript of the plaintiff's testimony, and the defendant's memorandum of law.

MOTION FOR AMENDED FINDINGS OF FACT, CONCLUSIONS OF LAW, AND ORDER FOR JUDGMENT

The defendant hereby moves the court for an order amending the court's findings of facts, conclusions of law, and order for judgment so as to determine that the defendant was not negligent and his alleged negligence was not a proximate cause of the plaintiff's injury.

—Continued

—Continued

This motion is made pursuant to Rule 52.02 of the Missouri Rules of Civil Procedure.

The grounds for this motion are that the findings of fact are contrary to the evidence and contrary to the great weight of the evidence and contrary to law.

This motion is made upon the files, exhibits, deposition transcripts used at trial, trial transcripts, and minutes of the court.

MOTION FOR NEW TRIAL

The defendant hereby moves the court for an order granting to the defendant a new trial on all issues.

This motion is made pursuant to Rule 59 of the Missouri Rules of Civil Procedure.

The grounds for the defendant's motion are as follows:

1. There were irregularities in the proceedings of the court that deprived the defendant of a fair trial, including the following:
   a. The plaintiff was permitted to argue that an event is foreseeable if it is a mere possibility.
   b. The plaintiff was permitted to argue two theories of liability that were in direct conflict with each other and that were contrary to the great weight of the evidence.
   c. The plaintiff did not offer evidence to rebut the legal presumption that an intentional criminal act is not foreseeable by the parties and is to be treated as a superseding cause of the plaintiff's harm.
2. There were irregularities in the proceedings by the prevailing party that prevented the defendant from having a fair trial.
3. Plain errors of law concerning admissibility of evidence occurred at trial, to which objections were made at the time.
4. The special verdict answers 1, 2, 3, 8, and 10 are not justified by the evidence.
5. The court's decision and order for judgment based upon the special verdict answers are not justified by the evidence.
6. The special verdict answers 1, 2, and 3 are contrary to law.
7. The court's decision and order for judgment are contrary to law.
8. The awarded damages for loss of earning capacity, future pain, and emotional distress are excessive in amount and appear to have been rendered under the influence of passion and prejudice.

These motions are made upon the court's minutes, files, exhibits, and records, including deposition transcripts used at trial and partial transcripts of testimony at trial.

JOHNSON AND JOHNSON

DATED: December 12, 1995   By _____

B. L. Bogat
Mary M. Cleary
Attorneys for Defendant
4200 Trenton Tower
333 South Sixth Street
St. Louis, Missouri 55402
(555) 555-5555

to take some other action to secure the window. Furthermore, the lease provided that the landlord was not responsible for repairing or maintaining the premises. If the tenant knew about the alleged defect, then the landlord had no further duty to warn or repair. There was also a question whether the landlord could be held liable for the criminal acts of the intruder. The jury returned a verdict for the plaintiff tenant, and the landlord duly moved for a new trial.

SUMMARY

There are several types of posttrial motions. The motions may be combined with one another and may be made in the alternative. The most common posttrial motions include those for the following:

    a new trial

    a new trial on the issue of liability only

    a new trial on the issue of damages only

    a new trial concerning a particular party's liability

    additur

    remittitur

    judgment as a matter of law

A party may move the court for amended findings of fact or amended conclusions of law or both in a posttrial motion. A paralegal may be asked to prepare a posttrial notice of motion and motion and to assemble the supporting documentation. It is the responsibility of the trial lawyer to determine which motions to make and the grounds for each motion. The lawyer must sign the motion papers.

The purpose of posttrial motions is to give the trial judge an opportunity to reconsider or further consider errors already brought to the judge's attention. However, plain error or fundamental error may be noted for the first time in a posttrial motion. Plain error is very basic error that goes to the heart of the case. A party does not have to show that he or she preserved an objection to plain error. Even plain error must be prejudicial to be grounds for a new trial.

Error must be prejudicial to be grounds for obtaining posttrial relief. Error is considered prejudicial only if it appears that the error adversely affected the outcome of the case. Rule 61 provides guidelines for identifying prejudicial error.

A motion for a new trial must be served upon all parties within ten days after the entry of judgment. The motion must specify the alleged error and provide verification of the error. The verification may be shown by a partial transcript, affidavits, exhibits, or the judge's minutes. The new trial may be on all issues or only on the issues that could have been affected by the error. The moving party does not have to prove that the error did in fact affect the outcome, merely that the error could have affected the outcome. A trial judge may order a new trial within ten days after the entry of judgment even though neither party has made a motion for a new trial.

The same power permits the trial judge to order a new trial on grounds that were not raised by the moving party's motion for a new trial.

The most common grounds for posttrial motions include misconduct on the part of one or more jurors, misconduct on the part of the prevailing party, discovery of new evidence, inappropriate award of damages whether excessive or inadequate, unrectified errors of law at trial, and a verdict not supported by the evidence. A lawyer protects his or her record by filing written requested instructions that correctly cover the rules of law in question. When a party moves for a directed verdict on the grounds that no evidence supported the particular claim or defense, the trial court has a duty to sustain the verdict if that is reasonably possible.

The grounds for moving for judgment as a matter of law are that the determinative issue must be decided as a matter of law, or the evidence is insufficient to establish the opponent's cause of action or insufficient to establish the opponent's affirmative defense, even though the jury has found in favor of the opponent. The standard for challenging the sufficiency of the evidence is that the verdict is contrary to all the evidence in the case or reasonable minds could not differ as to the correct outcome.

Every motion should state the relief the moving party wants, the rule that authorizes the motion, the grounds for the motion, and identification of the documentation that supports the motion.

KEY TERMS

plain error	additur
fundamental error	remittitur
prejudicial error	motion for judgment
trial de novo	notwithstanding the verdict
judge's minutes	

REVIEW QUESTIONS

1. How soon must a posttrial motion be made?
2. What is the criteria for deciding whether the court should order an additur?
3. Under what circumstances may an order for a remittitur be combined with an order for a new trial?
4. What role may a paralegal have in handling a posttrial motion?
5. What is meant by plain error, and how does it differ from other error?
6. In the absence of plain error, what two circumstances must be established to justify an order for a new trial?
7. What four parts should every motion contain?
8. What is the criteria for granting a motion for judgment as a matter of law?
9. When does a party move for amended findings rather than a new trial?
10. Who decides whether an error was prejudicial to the moving party?

22

JUDGMENTS

The civil courts can promise that a controversy will be permanently concluded. For better or for worse, the controversy is put to an end, and the government will act to protect the rights established through the litigation process and enforce the obligations. The dispute must be brought to a conclusion permanently so as to discourage the parties from resorting to violence and revenge. As long as the controversy lasts, it tends to fester.

A judgment is a court's final declaration of the parties' legal rights and obligations between them. The words *judgment* and *decree* may be used interchangeably. Historically, a decree was the ultimate determination by a court in equity that required a party to do something or not do something, and a judgment was an award or denial of money damages. Today, the distinction is not considered important.

If a court concludes that the defendant did not owe the plaintiff a legal duty or did not breach a legal duty or did not cause a loss or injury to the plaintiff, the court's judgment provides that the plaintiff's claim is dismissed or disallowed. On the other hand, if the court concludes that the defendant breached a legal duty owed to the plaintiff and caused a loss or injury to the plaintiff, the court's judgment is for an award of **money damages** for the plaintiff. The judgment declares that the defendant owes to the plaintiff a specified sum of money. The party who obtains an award of money damages is called a **judgment creditor.** The party who owes the money is called a **judgment debtor.**

Where the litigation concerned ownership of property, the judgment may declare which party is the owner of the property in question. The judgment may order a party to execute a deed or bill of sale to evidence the ownership. The judgment may declare that a party must do a certain act, such as vacate certain real property. The judgment may declare that a party must abstain from certain conduct that is deemed injurious to the other party's person or property. Thus, the judgment states the parties' legal rights and the relief or remedy the court has decided to provide to the parties.

A court may enter judgment upon a party's default, as where the party fails to appear in the case by filing a pleading or the pleading is stricken by court order as provided by Rule 37.

A party may offer to have a judgment entered against herself or himself for an amount of money that the party believes the opposing party is entitled to recover (Rule 68). An **offer of judgment** must be made at least ten days before trial is to begin, and it must remain open for at least ten days after it is made. It must include all accrued costs. It must be made in writing and may be served by mail or delivered to the opposing lawyer. The offer need not be filed with the court unless accepted by the opposing party. If the opposing party does accept the offer, the clerk of court shall enter judgment according to the terms of the offer. If the opposing party rejects the offer and fails to obtain a judgment for more than the offer, the offeror is entitled to recover costs and disbursements on the basis that the offeror is the prevailing party. A party may offer to let a judgment be entered because she or he recognizes the legal obligation but simply cannot pay it. There is no sense in resisting a valid claim.

When a case is tried to a jury and the jury returns a general verdict, the clerk of court enters the judgment on the basis of the jury's verdict (Rule 58). If the jury returns a special verdict or a general verdict with answers to interrogatories, the judge must prepare findings of fact, conclusions of law, and an order for judgment. The order tells the clerk of court how to state the terms of the judgment. The judge must approve the form of the judgment before it is officially filed. Approval is indicated by the judge's signature.

When a case is tried to a judge, the judge must prepare his or her own findings of fact, conclusions of law, and order for judgment. Whenever the decision of the court provides a remedy other than dismissal of the claim or an award of a specified amount of money, the judge must tell the clerk of court how to word the judgment (Rule 58).

A court's order for judgment may be similar to the one in exhibit 22.1.

Under the laws of most states, a judgment creditor is entitled to interest on the amount of the judgment. Interest begins to accumulate on the date the judgment is entered. In many jurisdictions, interest accrues on the jury's verdict from the day the verdict is rendered. Where interest is allowed on the verdict, that amount must be incorporated into the amount of the judgment.

The clerk of court notes the date on which the judgment was entered in the court's permanent records in a **judgment book** or file, sometimes

---

■ EXHIBIT 22.1

Court Order for Judgment

The above-entitled action came on for trial before the court and a jury, the Honorable Russell A. Smith, United States District Judge, presiding, and the issues have been duly tried, and the jury has duly rendered its verdict.

It is ordered and adjudged that the plaintiff, Robert I. Miller, recover from the defendant, Thomas Jones, the sum of twenty-five thousand dollars and his taxable costs.

Dated at Chicago, Illinois, this _____ day of October, 1995.

/s/ Raymond A. Johnson

Clerk of Court

called the judgment roll, but more often called the judgment book. The clerk of court is required to send to the parties a notice of entry of the judgment "immediately" after entering the judgment in the judgment book. In most states a judgment remains in force for ten years. Unless renewed *before* expiration, it automatically expires and becomes a nullity. A judgment is a public record. Any credit search includes a review of the judgment roll to determine whether the person who is the subject of the search has a judgment against him or her. A judgment may be a lien against the debtor's property.

The judgment may provide that the plaintiff is entitled to recover specific property or that she or he is the owner of certain property. Various forms of relief may be ordered by a court. Whatever its form, the relief is stated in the judgment. Rule 70 provides guidelines for enforcing the judgment:

> If a judgment directs a party to execute a conveyance of land or to deliver deeds or other documents or to perform any other specific act and the party fails to comply within the time specified, the court may direct the act to be done at the cost of the disobedient party by some other person appointed by the court and the act when so done has like effect as if done by the party. . . . If real or personal property is within the district, the court in lieu of directing a conveyance thereof may enter a judgment divesting the title of any party and vesting it in others and such judgment has the effect of a conveyance executed in due form of law. . . .

Courts are reluctant to allow the prevailing party to enforce a judgment before the losing party exhausts or waives his or her posttrial remedies. Rule 62 prevents the successful judgment creditor from enforcing his or her judgment for ten days following entry of the judgment. This gives the losing party an opportunity to make posttrial motions or decide whether to appeal. When the losing party appeals, he or she may be required to provide a bond that guarantees the judgment debtor's ability to pay the obligation. A party's inabiliy or failure to file a bond may preclude the appeal.

■ EXECUTION AND ATTACHMENT

A judgment is a valuable property right. When it is filed, it becomes a lien against the judgment debtor's property, insofar as the property is not exempt from seizure as provided by state law. A judgment for money may be assigned or transferred to another person. Such transfers should be in writing and filed with the clerk of court. State law determines the length of time a judgment remains enforceable. The federal courts follow and apply state law.

If the judgment is for a sum of money and the debtor cannot or will not pay it, the court may issue a **writ of execution,** which directs the executive branch of the government, usually a sheriff, to locate the defendant's property, seize it, and sell it in the manner prescribed by law. The usual procedure is to sell the property at a public auction with due notice given to the public and to persons who have special interests in the property. Usually, the property is held for a designated period of time during which the judgment debtor has an opportunity to **redeem** the property by meeting his or her obligation. Rule 69(a) provides for these actions:

Process to enforce a judgment for the payment of money shall be a writ of execution, unless the court directs otherwise. The procedure on execution, in proceedings supplementary to and in aid of a judgment, and in proceedings on and in aid of execution shall be in accordance with the practice and procedure of the state in which the district court is held, existing at the time the remedy is sought, except that any statute of the United States governs to the extent that it is applicable. . . .

A judgment creditor may be required to post a bond protecting the judgment debtor against any errors or improprieties that might occur when the property is seized and sold. The sheriff probably does not know the exact location of the judgment debtor's property. Therefore, it behooves the judgment creditor to provide the sheriff with whatever information she or he can about the identity and location of nonexempt property to be seized. The sheriff charges the creditor for her or his time and expenses, but these expenses ultimately become the responsibility of the judgment debtor.

Rule 62(a) precludes the judgment creditor from enforcing the judgment during the first ten days after entry in the judgment book. The ten-day period gives the judgment debtor an opportunity to decide whether to pay the judgment, make a posttrial motion, appeal, or take some other action to protect his or her interests. Rule 62(b) authorizes a court to stay enforcement of a judgment during the pendency of a motion for new trial or a motion for judgment as a matter of law. A party may seek an order staying enforcement of the judgment by making a separate motion or as part of the posttrial motion. However, the party who seeks a stay against enforcement of the judgment should not wait for the posttrial motion to be heard before securing the order staying enforcement of the judgment, or it may be too late.

Rule 64 provides that the parties to a federal civil action are subject to the posttrial remedies provided by the laws of the state in which the federal district court functions:

[A]ll remedies providing for seizure of person or property for the purpose of securing satisfaction of the judgment ultimately to be entered in the action are available under circumstances and in the manner provided by the law of the state in which the district court is held. . . . These remedies thus available include arrest, **attachment**,[1] garnishment, replevin, sequestration, and other corresponding or equivalent remedies, however designated and regardless of whether by state procedure the remedy is ancillary to the action or must be obtained by an independent action [emphasis added].

If a judgment has the effect of determining that property owned by the judgment debtor should be transferred to the judgment creditor, the court may order the judgment debtor to execute (sign) a quitclaim deed running in favor of the judgment creditor. If the judgment debtor refuses to do this, the court may appoint a trustee to do it for the judgment debtor. In some jurisdictions, the court is empowered to declare, "That which the judgment debtor should have done, is done." In other words, the court order, which declares that the judgment creditor is entitled to have the property

1. Attachment is a proceeding in which a judgment debtor's property is actually seized by the sheriff or U.S. marshal and held for the benefit of the claimant. A writ of attachment may be issued only after a hearing that provides due process protection, and will be granted only where there is good reason to believe that the opposing party will dispose of the property to avoid paying his or her legal obligation.

transferred to the creditor, has the effect of an actual deed. A judgment creditor ordinarily prefers to have an actual deed, rather than a court order; therefore, a creditor resorts to a court for transferring title only when the judgment debtor refuses to comply with the court's order to execute a deed. The judgment becomes a public record transfer of title and is accepted for filing by the local registrar of deeds.

■ SUPPLEMENTARY PROCEEDINGS

Sometimes neither the judgment creditor nor the sheriff can find any of the debtor's properties or monies, but the creditor believes the debtor does have assets. In that event, the judgment creditor is allowed to conduct **supplementary proceedings** to try to locate the debtor's monies and properties. Upon motion, a court that has jurisdiction over the judgment debtor will order the debtor to appear at a specified time and place for a deposition in which the debtor may be interrogated about earnings, properties, past transfers of property, and any expectancy of future acquisitions. The debtor may be asked about current and recent employments, salary, mode of payment, checking accounts, savings accounts, accounts receivable, and so forth. The debtor's testimony is under oath, so she or he is subject to the penalties of perjury. Rule 69(a) provides for these proceedings:

> In aid of the judgment or execution, the judgment creditor or a successor in interest when that interest appears of record, may obtain discovery from any person, including the judgment debtor, in the manner provided in these rules or in the manner provided by the practice of the state in which the district court is held.

If the debtor refuses to answer questions about the nature and extent of his or her properties and financial condition, he or she may be held in contempt of court. If found in contempt of court, the debtor may be incarcerated until he or she agrees to cooperate with the civil justice system.

Armed with the new information obtained through the supplementary proceedings, the judgment creditor can obtain a new writ of execution directed to the sheriff. The sheriff will again try to locate, seize, and sell the debtor's properties. If the sheriff is able to find cash, the money itself may be turned over to the judgment creditor. Again, the sheriff deducts her or his fees and expenses before the judgment creditor is paid. However, the judgment creditor's total recovery is not necessarily reduced by the amount of the sheriff's fees. If enough money or property is found, the judgment debtor ends up paying those costs.

A judgment debtor should not be subject to harassment by supplementary proceedings. Therefore, judgment creditors are allowed to have only a certain number of depositions during a year. A court order is required for each deposition. The proceedings are governed by state law. A judgment debtor may move the court for a protective order when the judgment creditor has become overly aggressive in trying to enforce the judgment.

■ GARNISHMENT

If a third person is indebted to the judgment debtor or holds monies or properties of the debtor, the judgment creditor may claim and recover such monies or properties through a **garnishment** action. The judgment creditor does this by serving a garnishment summons on the third person, who is designated as a garnishee. The summons informs the garnishee about the judgment debtor's indebtedness and the amount of it. It directs the garnishee to disclose to the judgment creditor the amount of money, if any, the garnishee is holding, such as in wages, a bank account, bonds, and so forth. The garnishee makes the disclosure by serving and filing a **garnishment disclosure.** Garnishment procedures are frequently used to tie up bank accounts and wages earned. In most states, if not all, wages have a partially exempt status, so only a fraction of the debtor's take-home pay may be seized.

If the garnishee's disclosure states that the garnishee does not hold any money or property that belongs to the judgment debtor, the judgment creditor may challenge the disclosure by moving the court for leave to serve a supplemental complaint upon the garnishee. The judgment creditor must show the court that there is probable cause to believe that the garnishee does have property or money that belongs to the judgment debtor and that should be available to pay the debt. If probable cause is shown, the court allows the judgment creditor to start a garnishment action against the garnishnee. The garnishee cannot relitigate the judgment debtor's liability, except to challenge the court's jurisdiction to render the judgment. Ordinarily, the only issue is whether the garnishee has any property or money that belongs to the judgment debtor. When the plaintiff obtains a judgment against the defendant in a personal injury action and the defendant contends that he has liability insurance that covers the loss but the insurer has wrongly denied coverage, as a judgment creditor, the plaintiff can serve a garnishment summons on the insurance company to force the insurance company to litigate the coverage issue.

■ TRANSFER OF A JUDGMENT

A judgment in one court may be transferred to another court in another jurisdiction for enforcement. The procedure is relatively simple. An authenticated, sometimes called exemplified, copy of the original judgment must be filed with the second court. The transferred judgment establishes the nature and extent of the debtor's obligation. As provided in the Untied States Constitution, the states are required to give full faith and credit to each other's judgments. The judgment debtor may contest the transferred judgment on the grounds that the original court lacked jurisdiction or that he or she has paid the judgment. Either of these defenses requires a trial to establish the truth. However, the judgment debtor cannot relitigate the merits of the case in which the judgment was obtained. A trial court may have lacked jurisdiction because it failed to obtain jurisdiction over the person of the defendant or over the subject matter, or because it went beyond its power in granting a particular remedy or it acted beyond its geographic limitations. The judgment is presumed to be valid. The judgment debtor has the burden of proving facts in avoidance of the judgment.

When a judgment creditor transfers the judgment to another jurisdiction and brings an action on that judgment to enforce it against the debtor, the judgment debtor cannot attempt to relitigate any of the issues that were decided or should have been determined in the first trial. For example, the judgment debtor cannot challenge the sufficiency of the evidence or the court's rulings on objections.

■ RELIEF FROM JUDGMENT

In a perfect judicial system, the courts would never need to open a judgment to correct a mistake. Although our system is good, it is not perfect. Occasionally, a judgment has been entered that ought to be modified or even set aside. Rule 60(a) provides that a court may correct clerical errors in a judgment at any time. The court may act on its own initiative or on motion by a party. A clerical error is any statement in the written judgment that does not comport with the court's actual intent. It may concern a number, name, omitted fact, or other such item.

A judgment may be set aside or modified on the grounds that it was obtained by the prevailing party through a fraud upon the court or upon the losing party, or on the grounds that there is newly discovered evidence that was not available to the losing party before the trial was completed (Rule 60(b)). In addition, Rule 60(b) contains a catchall provision that allows a court to set aside or modify a judgment on the grounds of "mistake, inadvertence, surprise, or excusable neglect." If a party seeks to vacate a judgment for any of the reasons stated in this paragraph, the motion must be made within one year after the judgment was entered in the judgment book.

Rule 60 does not limit the time in which a judgment may be challenged on the grounds that the court lacked jurisdiction in the case; therefore, the judgment is void if it is at any time successfully challenged on those grounds. Also, a judgment may be set aside because of subsequent events, as where the judgment debtor can show the court that she or he duly satisfied the judgment, but the judgment creditor failed to have the judgment satisfied.

■ TAXATION OF COSTS

After the judgment is entered, a party may apply to the clerk of court to compute and add **taxable costs** to the amount of the judgment. The clerk determines what costs the court will allow, as provided by statute, and adds those costs to the judgment. The taxable costs may include the party's filing fee, deposition costs, subpoena fees, and expert witness fees within prescribed limits. If a party is entitled to a recovery of his or her attorney's fees, the party must, within fourteen days after entry of the judgment, make a motion to obtain a court order allowing the attorneys' fees and determining the amount (Rule 54(d)). A paralegal may be asked to prepare the client's bill of costs and disbursements for taxing costs against the opposing party.

SUMMARY

A judgment is the court's ultimate expression of the parties' legal rights and obligations between them. The judgment is a valuable property right.

It is a lien against the judgment debtor's property. It may be used as the basis for seizing the debtor's property to satisfy the legal debt. Interest accumulates on the debt. The judgment remains in effect as a lien against the debtor's property until it expires. Most states provide that a judgment is good for a period of ten years. The judgment may be renewed and kept in effect longer by paying a nominal fee.

Once a judgment has been entered, the judgment creditor may institute supplementary proceedings in an effort to find the debtor's money and property with which to pay the judgment. The debtor may be required by subpoena to appear for a deposition and disclose her or his financial condition, including assets, employment, ownership of property, and claims against other persons. State statutes limit the number of times the judgment creditor can force the debtor to undergo examination.

A judgment may be used to garnishee a third person who is holding property that belongs to the judgment debtor. The judgment creditor serves a garnishment summons on the third person, who is designated a garnishee. The summons informs the garnishee that the judgment debtor owes the creditor a certain amount of money and directs the garnishee to disclose to the creditor the amount of money, if any, the garnishee is holding, such as in wages, a bank account, bonds, and so forth. The garnishee makes the disclosure by serving and filing a garnishment disclosure. Garnishment procedures are frequently used to encumber bank accounts and wages earned. In most states, if not all, wages are partially exempt from garnishment, so an employer need pay the creditor only a portion of the debtor's wages.

If the garnishee's disclosure states that the garnishee does not hold any money or property that belongs to the judgment debtor, the judgment creditor may challenge the disclosure by moving the court for leave to serve a supplemental complaint upon the garnishee. The judgment creditor must show the court that there is probable cause to believe that the garnishee does have property or money that belongs to the judgment debtor and that should be available to pay the debt. If probable cause is shown, the court allows the judgment creditor to start a garnishment action against the garnishee. The garnishee cannot relitigate the judgment debtor's liability, except to challenge the prior court's jurisdiction to render the judgment. Ordinarily, the only issue in a garnishment action is whether the garnishee has any property or money that belongs to the judgment debtor.

A judgment may be transferred to another jurisdiction and enforced in the same manner as a local judgment. The only basis for challenging a transferred judgment is that the court that rendered the judgment lacked jurisdiction over the judgment debtor or the subject matter of the litigation.

KEY TERMS

money damages	redeem
judgment creditor	attachment
judgment debtor	supplementary proceedings
offer of judgment	garnishment
judgment book	garnishment disclosure
writ of execution	taxable costs

REVIEW QUESTIONS

1. What purpose does a judgment serve?

2. Of what value is a judgment for money damages if the judgment debtor will not voluntarily pay the obligation?

3. What procedure may the judgment creditor use to force a judgment debtor to disclose the existence of the debtor's assets?

4. What protection does a garnishee have against harassing-type claims?

5. What protection does a judgment debtor have against a judgment creditor who is overly aggressive in trying to discover the debtor's assets?

6. Of what value is an offer of judgment to the offeror?

7. On what basis may a party obtain a default judgment against another party?

8. What is the difference between a judgment book, judgment roll, and a judgment docket?

9. What are two grounds for setting aside a judgment?

10. What is the time limitation for vacating a judgment on the grounds of fraud?

11. What is the time limitation for setting aside a judgment on the grounds that the court that granted the judgment lacked jurisdiction over the subject matter?

23

SUMMARY JUDGMENTS

OUTLINE

Material Fact Issues

Motion for Summary Judgment

Summary Judgment versus
Declaratory Judgment

Uses and Limitations of Summary
Judgments

Partial Summary Judgments

Procedure

SUMMARY

KEY TERMS

REVIEW QUESTIONS

When parties to a civil action agree about the material facts that gave rise to their lawsuit and disagree only about what the law is or how the law applies to those facts, the parties may obtain a judicial determination of their dispute without having a trial. The judicial procedure is called a **summary judgment.** Also, a party is entitled to a summary judgment if the opposing party is unable to produce evidence to establish necessary facts to prove that party's claim or defense. Rule 56 governs summary judgments. A party invokes the summary judgment procedure by making a motion for summary judgment. Motions for summary judgment have three principal uses or applications. They may be used to determine what the law is concerning a particular matter; or to have a court interpret a legal document, such as a contract; or to determine how the law applies to a given set of facts. Though motions for summary judgment are usually thought of as a defense tactic, they may be used effectively by plaintiffs to eliminate nonmeritorious affirmative defenses (Rule 56(a)). A summary judgment may resolve the entire case or only a part of the case.

■ MATERIAL FACT ISSUES

Rule 56 provides that a court shall order summary judgment "if the pleadings, depositions, answers to interrogatories, and admissions on file, together with the affidavits, if any, show that there is no *genuine* issue as to any *material fact* and that the moving party is entitled to judgment as *a matter of law.*" A summary judgment resolves only issues of law. Ideally, summary judgments are used when the parties agree to all the facts, but that seldom happens. Nevertheless, a dispute over some facts does not preclude a summary judgment if the disputed facts are not material to the legal issue.

511

Only material fact issues prevent a court from ordering a summary judgment. A fact is material if it controls application of the law to the case. Suppose the parties' dispute arose from a transaction in which the defendant made an oral offer to sell certain real estate at a specified price and the plaintiff accepted the offer, and subsequently the defendant refused to convey the property as promised. The plaintiff buyer sued to enforce the oral contract, and the parties disagree about the terms of the oral agreement. Notwithstanding this dispute, the defendant seller could move the court for summary judgment to dismiss the claim on the grounds that an oral contract for the sale of real estate is unenforceable. A contract to sell real estate must be in writing to be enforceable. The material (controlling) fact is that the purported contract was not in writing. In this scenario, the parties agree or admit that the alleged contract was not reduced to a writing. Although other facts are disputed, those other facts become immaterial to the application of a dispositive rule of law. (A rule of law is dispositive if it controls to resolve the entire case.) The judge can apply the law to the two undisputed material facts: that the contract was for the sale of land and was not in writing. On those facts, the defendant is entitled to summary judgment of dismissal. The clerk of court is authorized to enter a judgment in the judgment book based upon the court's order for summary judgment.

■ MOTION FOR SUMMARY JUDGMENT

A party may resort to a summary judgment motion only when the party can present all the material facts to the court in documentary form, including deposition transcripts, affidavits, exhibits, written stipulations, and Rule 36 admissions. A party could not use statements from his or her own pleadings to establish facts, but could use admissions in an opponent's pleading to show that a fact is not disputed. Rule 56(e) explains what is required:

> Supporting and opposing affidavits shall be made on personal knowledge, shall set forth such facts as would be admissible in evidence, and shall show affirmatively that the affiant is competent to testify to the matters stated therein. Sworn or certified copies of all papers or parts thereof referred to in an affidavit shall be attached thereto or served therewith. The court may permit affidavits to be supplemented or opposed by [transcripts of] depositions, answers to interrogatories, or further affidavits.

A party may not offer live testimony to support or oppose a motion for summary judgment. Sometimes an attorney's affidavit will be offered to support or oppose a summary judgment motion. Such affidavits are seldom appropriate, because they are usually submitted in the form of an argument or recite facts about which the attorney has no personal knowledge. However, if lawyers and paralegals develop certain facts in the course of their investigation, they can establish those facts, for purposes of a summary judgment motion, by reciting them, along with the evidence, in an attorney's affidavit.

The most common basis or ground for opposing a summary judgment motion is that the parties disagree about a material fact, and a trial must determine the facts. The party who moves for a summary judgment has the burden of showing that no material fact is in dispute. The moving party must show that the opponent's claim of a disputed fact is false or that the alleged disputed fact is not material to the grounds for the motion for summary judgment.

Occasionally, the parties agree that no fact issue exists, and they work together to submit the case to the court on a motion for summary judgment. In that event, the parties will probably make **cross-motions for summary judgment.** (Cross-motions means that each party has moved the court for the same order in his or her favor.) If the court determines there is a legitimate dispute concerning a material fact, the court must deny the motion for summary judgment. This is true even if both parties have moved the court for summary judgment.

When both parties agree on the facts and both parties want the court to decide the case on a summary judgment motion, the parties may prepare a *stipulation of facts* for the court to consider. District courts accept stipulations of facts even though Rule 56 does not expressly authorize their use in summary judgment motions. A written stipulation of facts is conclusive for and against the parties, so the parties must make certain the stipulation is accurate.

When a party serves a motion for summary judgment that is duly supported by documentary evidence, and the opposing party claims that there is a disputed material fact, the opposing party cannot merely deny that the moving party's evidence is correct and complete. Rule 56(e) states that the opposing party must come forward with documentary evidence of the type admissible in court, to show that a dispute exists on material facts:

> When a motion for summary judgment is made and supported as provided in this rule, an adverse party may not rest upon the mere allegations or denials of the adverse party's pleading, but the adversary's response, by affidavits or as otherwise provided in this rule, must set forth specific facts showing that there is a genuine issue [of fact] for trial. If the adverse party does not so respond, summary judgment, if appropriate, shall be entered against the adverse party.

This provision cannot be applied literally to all cases.

Suppose the plaintiff is a business invitee upon the defendant's premises and claims that she fell because of a small accumulation of water in the hallway of the defendant's building. If the defendant had no knowledge of the water or of the plaintiff's alleged accident, how can the defendant present "specific facts showing that there is a genuine issue for trial"? The defendant's affidavits will have to show that no one else reported any slippery condition or accumulation of water on the premises at the time of the plaintiff's accident and the plaintiff did not give the defendant notice of the alleged accident until days later. These are merely general denials, not specific facts that mitigate against the plaintiff's accident. Nevertheless, the allegations should be sufficient to preclude a summary judgment in the plaintiff's favor. A jury will have to decide whether there was a puddle of water; whether it existed for such a period of time that the defendant should have discovered it and removed it; whether the plaintiff actually fell on the premises; and whether the puddle caused the plaintiff to fall.

Affidavits made in support of motions for summary judgment and made in opposition to motions for summary judgment must be made upon personal knowledge. The facts stated must be admissible into evidence. The affidavits must show that the affiant is competent to testify concerning the facts set forth in the affidavits. Where the court is confronted with conflicting affidavits and believes that they have been made in good faith, the court must deny the summary judgment motion and let the case proceed to trial. There is no occasion for the judge to weigh the credibility of the affidavits or the quantity of evidence offered by the respective parties. The conflict concerning a material fact necessarily precludes summary judgment. Even though the court denies a summary judgment motion, the court may determine, and provide in its order, that certain facts are conceded and therefore, for purposes of the trial, established (Rule 56(d)). The effect is like that of a Rule 36 admission.

Rule 56(f) allows the opposing party to submit an affidavit to the court showing that she or he cannot obtain the necessary documentary evidence in time to oppose a summary judgment motion, but that the party believes the evidence can be obtained and will try to obtain it promptly. The affidavit must state what evidence the opposing party expects to obtain, from whom, and when, and in what form it will be presented to the court. It may be presented in the form of an affidavit, deposition transcript, Rule 36 admission, or a certified exhibit.

Rule 56(g) authorizes the court to award attorneys' fees and costs against any party who files an affidavit for the purpose of merely delaying the motion without having grounds for obtaining a delay. Furthermore, an affiant who gives a false affidavit is subject to criminal prosecution for perjury. Suppose the plaintiff moves the court for an order granting summary judgment, which the defendant wrongfully opposes using affidavits that are misleading and interposed in bad faith. The plaintiff spends five thousand dollars for attorneys' fees and other costs preparing for trial. The plaintiff is entitled to recover those costs because of the improper affidavits. The costs could be added to the plaintiff's judgment or made the subject of a separate order.

■ SUMMARY JUDGMENT VERSUS DECLARATORY JUDGMENT

A summary judgment is different from an action for declaratory judgment. Sometimes people confuse the two procedures. Whereas a summary judgment is the result of a motion, a declaratory judgment is a form of a legal action. A party uses a declaratory judgment to have a court construe a written document, such as a contract, or a statute before a cause of action has actually accrued, that is, before any damage or harm has occurred. A declaratory judgment seeks a declaration by the court that tells the parties what their respective rights and obligations are, and may be used to determine the parties' relationship or status.

A party may make a motion for summary judgment in a declaratory judgment action. For example, the plaintiff may bring a declaratory judgment action to have the court construe and apply the plaintiff's contract with the defendant. If the parties do not dispute the validity of the contract, they may move the court for summary judgment, asking the court to construe the contract and to tell them what it means and how it applies to their transaction.

■ USES AND LIMITATIONS OF SUMMARY JUDGMENTS

A court may decide, on a summary judgment, an action for breach of a written contract where the parties' dispute centers upon *how* the contract applies to their situation and not upon the parties' performance of the contract. The moving party must document the material facts and provide the court with the written contact and ask the court to construe the contract. After the court has determined what the contract means and what it requires, the court can apply the contract to the undisputed facts. Then the court can enter a judgment that determines the parties' rights and obligations under the contract. Specifically, the court can decide whether the defendant breached the contract and whether the plaintiff is entitled to recover money damages. The court could determine that the defendant did breach the contract, but leave for trial the issue of how much money damages the plaintiff is entitled to recover.

Cases in which a fact finder (jury) must make an ultimate fact determination are not well suited for a motion for summary judgment. For example, in most negligence actions a jury must decide whether the plaintiff or the defendant or both were negligent, and whether the negligence of either was a proximate cause of the plaintiff's injury. Since a jury decides negligence as a *fact issue,* a court could not decide the negligence issues and causation issues without a trial.[1] Rarely may a court find, as a matter of law, that a party was negligent or was not negligent. The criterion for determining whether a person was negligent is an objective standard based upon what a reasonable person would do or would not do under the same circumstances. Because a jury must decide whether a "reasonable person" would have been more careful, the jury determines, as a fact, whether the party was negligent. If the jury decides that the party did what a reasonable person would have done, then the jury finds that the party was not negligent. Similarly, the determination of the proximate (legal) cause of an injury or other harm is an ultimate fact issue. Rarely will a court decide the issue of causation as a matter of law. Consequently, in most negligence cases, even if the parties agree upon what happened and how it happened, a jury has to decide whether the act or omission was negligent.

Nevertheless, even some negligence actions may be decided on points of law. One example is where a dispute exists about whether the defendant owed a legal duty to protect the plaintiff from the risk that caused the plaintiff's injury or loss. The determination of whether a legal duty exists is a question of law for the court. Suppose the plaintiff was a customer in a service station and slipped on a small puddle of oil and fell. A jury would have to decide whether the station attendant was negligent for failing to discover the puddle of oil before the plaintiff fell and for not cleaning the floor to prevent the accident. The question of whether the attendant was negligent is a question of fact. But suppose the plaintiff was injured by a robber as the plaintiff was leaving the service station, and alleges that the service station was negligent for failing to protect him from the robber. A court could examine the undisputed facts and determine, as a matter of

---

1. Occasionally, a court determines that reasonable minds could not differ on how the ultimate question of fact should be decided. In that event, a judge may direct a verdict for the party who is entitled to prevail.

law, that the plaintiff and the attendant did not have a special relationship that required the latter to protect the plaintiff from the robber. The question or issue of whether the service station had a legal duty to protect the plaintiff is a question of law. If the defendant did not have a legal duty to protect the plaintiff, the defendant is entitled to a judgment of dismissal as a matter of law. The case could be resolved on a motion for summary judgment. If the court concluded that the service station did have a legal duty to provide some protection, a jury would decide whether the service station provided adequate protection.

If one party can show the court that the material facts are not in dispute, so that the case can be decided as a matter of law, a motion for summary judgment is appropriate. For example, in the typical automobile accident case, the cause of action accrues, and the statute of limitations begins to run, when the accident occurs. Suppose the applicable statute of limitations is two years. The date on which the action was commenced is easily determined from the clerk of court's records. If indisputable evidence shows that the action was commenced more than two years after the accident occurred, the plaintiff's claim is subject to dismissal as a matter of law. It does not matter that there is a dispute concerning liability and damages, because the statute-of-limitations defense is controlling and dispositive of the entire case. Therefore, for purposes of the summary judgment motion, the material facts are the facts relevant to the statute-of-limitations defense—that is, the date of the accident and the date on which the action was commenced. The plaintiff's complaint must state the date and place of the accident (Rule 9(f)). Consequently, the material facts are easily established in this example. The defendant is entitled to an order granting summary judgment of dismissal of the action.

Now suppose the plaintiff brought a negligence action against her physician for medical malpractice, and the defendant physician alleges the claim is barred by a two-year statute of limitations. The general rule in medical malpractice actions is that the statute of limitations does *not* necessarily begin to run when the malpractice occurs; it begins to run when the defendant physician ceases to treat the patient for the medical condition.[2] So the question arises, When did the defendant physician stop treating the plaintiff for the particular condition in question? In this case the physician's office records show the dates of the patient's office visits, all hospital visits made by the physician, and all significant telephone calls. According to these records, two years have elapsed since the physician had any contact with the plaintiff. The physician could move the court for summary judgment of dismissal on the grounds that the statute of limitations ran against the cause of action. The motion could be supported by the physician's office records, the physician's affidavit, and affidavits by personnel in the physician's office. If the physician's deposition has been taken, relevant testimony from the deposition could be used in support of the motion. It will be a simple matter for the court to apply the law to the facts if the facts are not controverted. But if the plaintiff submits an affidavit

2. In some states the statute of limitations does not begin to run until the patient acquires information that would cause a reasonable person to know that the physician committed malpractice. The rationale for the rule is that the patient's reliance upon the physician makes it tantamount to a fraud for the physician not to tell the patient "what went wrong" and the consequences.

claiming that she had a telephone conference with the physician about her condition during that two-year period, the affidavit would suffice to raise a fact issue concerning the date of the last treatment. The patient's affidavit, if credible, would preclude the court from granting summary judgment. It does not matter that the great weight of the evidence favors the motion for summary judgment.

Summary judgments are also useful in cases that concern the application of a municipal ordinance or state statute. Suppose an ordinance is adopted that provides that all property-line fences must have a two-foot setback. The plaintiff's fence is on the property line shared with a neighbor and was in existence long before the ordinance was adopted. The plaintiff could use the summary judgment procedure to obtain a court declaration that the ordinance does not apply to her fence. The facts are not in dispute; the issue concerns how the law is to apply to uncontested facts.

Suppose the plaintiff brought suit on a written contract in which the plaintiff claims that the defendant agreed to sell a certain parcel of land to the plaintiff. A dispute exists concerning one of the terms of the contract. If the parties agree that the contract is binding on them and that the only issue concerns the proper interpretation of the contract, the matter can be determined by summary judgment. However, if the court determines that the contract is ambiguous and that evidence outside the written document is necessary for a proper construction of the contract, there is an issue of fact that precludes the court from granting summary judgment.

■ PARTIAL SUMMARY JUDGMENT

A summary judgment may be granted to resolve only part of a case: it may dismiss a claim, a cause of action, an affirmative defense, or a party. A summary judgment may determine that a defendant is liable to the plaintiff, but leave for trial the question of whether the plaintiff is entitled to recover damages and how much. A summary judgment may be awarded to the plaintiff on the question of liability and damages against one defendant, but leave for trial the plaintiff's claims against another defendant in the same case. A summary judgment may dismiss one cause of action, but leave intact other causes of action against the defendant. For an example of the last instance, suppose the plaintiff brought an action against the defendant for injuries caused by a product the defendant sold, and the plaintiff's action is based upon breach of warranty and negligence. The breach-of-warranty claim is subject to a four-year statute of limitations, and the negligence claim is subject to a six-year statute of limitations. If the plaintiff commenced the action five years after the causes of action accrued, the defendant is entitled to a partial summary judgment dismissing the warranty claim.

For an example of a summary judgment used to defeat a defendant's affirmative defenses, suppose a property owner brought an action in trespass against the defendant for entering upon the plaintiff's property and removing trees. The defendant alleges in his answer that he had the plaintiff's consent to cut down and remove the trees. The plaintiff could move for dismissal on the basis of his affidavit that states he did not consent to the defendant's entry upon the land and did not consent to the defendant's removal of any trees. If the defendant were unable to refute the plaintiff's affidavit in good faith, the plaintiff would be entitled to a summary judgment that eliminates the affirmative defense of consent. That may lead to the court's determination as a matter of law that the defendant is liable for the plaintiff's damages, leaving the amount of damages as the only issue to be litigated (Rule 56(c)). The defendant cannot avoid a summary judgment by relying upon a general denial in his answer to the complaint. A general denial does not meet the thrust of a summary judgment motion. A party who defends against a motion for summary judgment must present specific facts and must do so in good faith (Rule 56(e)).

■ PROCEDURE

A defendant may serve and file a motion for summary judgment any time after the action was commenced. A plaintiff may not serve a motion for summary judgment until twenty days after commencement of the action. However, if the defendant serves a motion for summary judgment sooner, the plaintiff may immediately serve a motion for summary judgment. (An action is commenced when the complaint is filed with the clerk of court, even though the summons and complaint may not be served until days or weeks later.) A defendant may not serve a motion for summary judgment on a counterclaim until twenty days after the counterclaim was served. Furthermore, a defendant may not serve a motion for summary judgment on a cross-claim until twenty days after the cross-claim was served. Motions for summary judgment are seldom made until after the parties have completed their discovery procedures. Rule 6(d) provides that an ordinary motion must be served at least five days before the hearing, but Rule 56(c) provides that a summary judgment motion must be served at least ten days before the hearing. When any motion is served by mail, three days are added to the allotted time. A summary judgment is a **dispositive motion;** therefore, a party may need more than 10 days to prepare to resist the motion. (A dispositive motion is one that seeks to conclude the case, or at least conclude an issue in the case. Rule 56(f) provides that a party who opposes a motion for summary judgment has a right to a postponement of the hearing when that party needs more time to prepare. For example, a party may need to take a witness's deposition, so the deposition can be used to show facts that preclude the summary judgment. Suppose the defendant asserted a release as an affirmative defense and grounds for a motion for summary judgment. The plaintiff should be allowed time to take depositions of witnesses to prove the release was obtained by fraud.)

The moving party must serve all supporting affidavits and documents with the motion. The adverse party must serve and file any opposing affidavits at least one day before the hearing (Rule 56(c)). Though it does not clearly say so, Rule 56(c) contemplates that the moving party will receive the opposing affidavits at least one day before the hearing. Most courts have "special" or "local" rules that expand these time requirements.

A paralegal may prepare a motion for summary judgment for the approval and signature of the trial lawyer. Exhibit 23.1 is a sample of a summary judgment motion.

A party incurs some risk in making a motion for summary judgment. The risk is that the court will agree that no fact issue exists, but award summary judgment in favor of the nonmoving party, that is, the respon-

---

MOTION

Pursuant to Rule 56 of the Federal Rules of Civil Procedure, plaintiff hereby moves the court for an order determining that defendant is liable to plaintiff for money damages, in an amount to be determined by trial, for defendant's wrongful trespass upon plaintiff's property and destruction of plaintiff's trees.

This motion for partial summary judgment is made upon the grounds that defendant's answer admits that defendant entered plaintiff's property by mistake and mistakenly cut down plaintiff's trees and denies only the amount of plaintiff's loss.

There is no dispute concerning any material fact that would prevent the court from holding defendant liable in trespass as a matter of law.

This motion is made upon plaintiff's complaint, defendant's answer, and plaintiff's affidavit, which identifies the trees, their location upon plaintiff's property, and plaintiff's ownership. Further, plaintiff's affidavit shows that defendant did not have plaintiff's consent to enter upon plaintiff's land.

[Date]   _____

                                  Attorney for Plaintiff

---

dent. The court has authority to do so, and courts have done so. Consequently, the moving party ought to be sure about the law and be sure that he or she wants to take the position that the material facts are not in dispute. Also, a motion for summary judgment may force both parties to disclose some of their strategies.

SUMMARY

A party invokes the summary judgment procedure by serving and filing a motion for summary judgment. A party may avoid the expense and inconvenience of a trial if the party can obtain a resolution of the dispute through a summary judgment proceeding. Motions for summary judgment may be used to resolve issues of law to determine how the law is to be applied to a given set of facts. Defendants may use motions for summary judgment to obtain dismissal of a plaintiff's cause of action. Plaintiffs may use summary judgment motions to eliminate nonmeritorious affirmative defenses. A summary judgment may dispose of the entire case, or only a part of the case. Summary judgments allow courts to decide disputed questions of law and to decide how the law is to apply to a particular set of facts.

A dispute over some facts does not preclude a summary judgment if the disputed facts are not material to the dispositive legal issue. Only material fact issues prevent a court from ordering a summary judgment. A fact is material if it controls application of the law to the case.

A party may resort to a summary judgment motion only when the party can present all the material facts to the court in documentary form, including deposition transcripts, affidavits, exhibits, written stipulations, and Rule 36 admissions. A party could not use statements from his or her own pleadings to establish facts, but could use admissions in an opponent's pleading to show that a fact is not disputed. Supporting and opposing affidavits must be made on personal knowledge. The affidavits must set forth the facts that would be admissible in evidence. The affiant must show that he or she is competent to testify to the matters covered in the affidavit. All documents referred to in an affidavit must be attached to the affidavit or served with it. The court may permit affidavits to be supplemented or opposed by depositions, answers to interrogatories, or further affidavits. A party may not offer live testimony to support or oppose a motion for summary judgment. An attorney's affidavit is seldom appropriate, because the attorney usually has no personal knowledge about the material facts. However, lawyers and paralegals may develop certain facts, in the course of their investigation, that can be used to support a motion for summary judgment.

When the parties agree that no fact issue exists, they may work together to submit the case to the court on cross-motions for summary judgment. The party who moves for a summary judgment has the burden of showing that no material fact is in dispute. The moving party must show that the opponent's claim of a disputed fact is false or that the alleged disputed fact is not material to the grounds for the motion for summary judgment. If the court determines there is a legitimate dispute concerning a material fact, the court must deny the motion for summary judgment. This is true even if both parties have moved the court for summary judgment.

When both parties agree on the facts and both parties want the court to decide the case on a summary judgment motion, the parties may prepare a stipulation of facts for the court to consider. District courts accept stipulations of facts even though Rule 56 does not expressly authorize their use in summary judgment motions. A written stipulation of facts is conclusive for and against the parties, so the parties must make certain the stipulation is accurate.

An opposing party cannot defend against a summary judgment motion by merely denying that the moving party's evidence is correct or complete. The opposing party must come forward with documentary evidence of the type admissible in court, to show that a dispute exists on material facts. Rule 56(f) allows a party to submit an affidavit to the court, showing that the party cannot obtain the necessary documentary evidence in time to oppose the summary judgment motion, but that the evidence can be obtained and will be obtained promptly. The affidavit must state what evidence the opposing party expects to obtain, from whom, and when, and in what form it will be presented to the court. A person who gives a false affidavit is subject to criminal prosecution for perjury, and a party who relies upon a false affidavit may have to pay the opposing party's costs and attorneys' fees.

A summary judgment is different from an action for a declaratory judgment. Sometimes some people confuse the two legal procedures. A party brings a declaratory judgment action to have a written document, such as a contract, or a statute construed before a cause of action has actually accrued. A party brings the action to obtain a judicial determination of the parties' rights before any harm or loss has occurred. A party may make a motion for summary judgment in a declaratory judgment action and in other types of civil actions.

Cases in which a jury must determine an ultimate fact are not well suited for summary judgment motions. The ultimate fact is central to the dispute and is certainly material. Consequently, most negligence cases cannot be resolved through a summary judgment motion. However, where there is a controlling legal issue, a negligence action may be subject to resolution through a motion for summary judgment, as where there is a question about whether the defendant owed the plaintiff a legal duty or where the statute of limitations clearly applies.

A defendant may serve and file a motion for summary judgment any time after the action was commenced. A plaintiff may not serve a motion for summary judgment until twenty days after commencement of the action. However, if the defendant serves a motion for summary judgment sooner, the plaintiff may immediately serve a motion for summary judgment. A defendant may not serve a motion for summary judgment on a counterclaim until twenty days after the counterclaim was served. Furthermore, a defendant may not serve a motion for summary judgment on a cross-claim until twenty days after the cross-claim was served. Motions for summary judgment are seldom made until after the parties have completed their discovery procedures. A summary judgment motion must be served at least ten days before the hearing. When any motion is served by mail, three days are added to the allotted time. A summary judgment is a dispositive motion; therefore, a party may need additional days or weeks to prepare to resist the motion.

KEY TERMS

summary judgment
cross-motions for summary
   judgment

dispositive motion
stipulation of facts

REVIEW QUESTIONS

1. What are the potential benefits to a party who makes a motion for summary judgment?

2. In what form must the evidence be presented to support a motion for summary judgment?

3. At what point in a civil action may a defendant make a motion for summary judgment?

4. When is a disputed fact considered material so as to preclude a summary judgment?

5. How could a moving party use an opposing party's signed, but unsworn statement to establish a fact to support a motion for summary judgment?

6. May a party move the court to order a partial summary judgment?

7. May a party use admissions in pleadings to support a motion for summary judgment?

8. May a party use her or his own answers to interrogatories to oppose a motion for summary judgment?

9. May a party use the opponent's responses to requests for admissions to support a motion for summary judgment?

10. May a court grant summary judgment *against* the moving party?

APPEALS

Appellate courts exist to correct errors. They do not retry cases. They do not decide who was right and who was wrong. They do not make judgments about the fairness of the outcome or the reasonableness of the verdict. Appellate courts correct errors by vacating (voiding) the lower court's judgment and ordering a new trial or by ordering entry of a different judgment as a matter of law. They decide issues of law.

A party has the right to have an appellate court review her or his case to determine whether the trial court committed any error that adversely affected the outcome of the case. The appellant must specify the errors. The errors may arise from the trial court's procedures or the trial court's misstatement of the law or the trial court's misapplication of the law. An appellate court examines the trial court's record in light of the alleged errors and determines whether some error occurred and whether the error may have prejudiced the outcome of the trial. The system does not allow a party to appeal merely because he or she is disappointed or strongly disagrees with the result. An appellate court will not reverse on the grounds that the appellate court would have come to a different conclusion from the evidence or would have preferred a different outcome.

The party who prosecutes an appeal is referred to as the **appellant.** The party against whom an appeal is prosecuted may be called the **appellee,** although many state courts identify that party as the **respondent.**

Some error occurs in almost every trial. The civil justice system does not require judges and lawyers to be perfect, because perfection in litigation is unattainable. At most, the system can hope to provide a fair trial that is unaffected by significant errors. Therefore, an appellate court will not reverse a trial court's judgment or order a new trial unless the appellant can show there was a significant error that could have affected the outcome. In other words, the error must be *prejudicial* to be appealable. Appealable errors may arise from the misapplication of substantive law or in trial procedures. In either event, the party who appeals has the burden of persuading the appellate court that the alleged error was prejudicial. The appellant must show that if the law had been correctly applied, there is good reason to believe that the trial court's verdict or decision would have been different.

Although appellate work is highly technical and tends to be focused upon legal issues, a paralegal can be helpful in this area, especially if the paralegal was involved in preparing the trial. A paralegal may be asked to outline portions of the trial transcript in much the same way that depositions are outlined and summarized. Paralegals may help to prepare the exhibits, assemble a brief's appendix, proofread drafts of a brief, check citations, and shepardize[1] cases. If a paralegal is familiar with the facts of the case and has good writing skills, there is no reason why he or she could not help to write the statement-of-facts section of a brief.

■ APPELLATE SYSTEM

A party has the right to appeal from a federal district court judgment to the circuit court of appeals for the circuit in which the district court is located. Each state is a separate judicial district. The federal judicial system has eleven circuit courts of appeals and the Court of Appeals for the District of Columbia (a map showing the circuits follows the glossary). Appeals to circuit courts of appeals are governed by the Rules of Appellate Procedure.

The United States Supreme Court is the highest federal appellate court. In most cases, an appellant appeals from a district court's judgment to a circuit court of appeals. Subject to a few exceptions, parties do not have a right to appeal to the United States Supreme Court.

A relatively small proportion of cases are appealed. The system tends to favor the party who prevailed at trial. Several circumstances mitigate against appealing a district court's judgment: Appeals are expensive. The amount in controversy may not justify the cost and effort that go into an appeal. An appeal may be significantly more expensive than the trial. The appeal process may take more than a year. If a money judgment has been made against the appellant, the appellant must file an appeal bond that protects the judgment creditor, and appeal bonds cost money; furthermore, interest accrues against the judgment. The system tends to favor the party who prevailed at trial; a large majority of the cases that are appealed are affirmed. The appellate process is very exacting.

■ NOTICE OF APPEAL

An appellant initiates an appeal by serving and filing a **notice of appeal.** The notice of appeal must be filed with the clerk of the federal district court

---

1. **Shepardize** is a colloquial legal expression. To shepardize a case is to use the *Shepard's* citation system to find out whether other courts have considered the case and what the courts have said about the case. By using *Shepard's Citations,* one can determine whether the case has been overruled, questioned, followed, distinguished, approved, or ignored. Courses on legal research cover methods of using resources like *Shepard's Citations.*

within thirty days of the date on which the judgment was entered. The notice of appeal may be similar to the one in exhibit 24.1.

The appellant must pay a filing fee of one hundred dollars to the clerk. The district court may require the appellant to file a **cost bond** or give other security to guarantee that the appellee's costs will be covered. If a judgment has been made for a sum of money against the appellant, some state courts require the appellant to file a **supersedeas bond** that protects the prevailing party for the amount of the judgment. The bond guarantees that the judgment creditor can collect the amount of the judgment docketed in the trial court, as well as taxable costs. The parties commonly stipulate to a waiver of these appeal bonds. This way, the appellant avoids the initial cost of the bonds. The appellee benefits because if the appellee loses the appeal, the appellant could tax the cost of the bond against her or him.

■ RECORD ON APPEAL

The appellant must order a transcript of the trial from the official court reporter within ten days after filing the notice of appeal. The appellant must make arrangements with the court reporter to pay the reporter's fees for transcribing the testimony. The trial transcript, exhibits, and district court file—which make up the record on appeal—must be sent to the clerk of the court of appeals. The transcript usually includes all the testimony, motions at trial, and jury instructions. However, the lawyers may stipulate that certain parts of the record may be omitted. Frequently, the opening statements and closing arguments are omitted. If the appeal is concerned only with a liability issue, the testimony concerning damages may be omitted, and vice versa. The original transcript must be filed with the clerk of court by the reporter. The appellant must supply at least one copy of the transcript to each party.

■ APPELLANT'S BRIEF

The appellant must prepare a brief on the law and an appendix to the brief. The appendix consists of the pleadings and other documents filed with the district court in connection with the case. It also contains pertinent portions

■ EXHIBIT 24.1

Notice of Appeal

NOTICE OF APPEAL

[Title of Cause]

To: Plaintiff Claire Romano and Angela Von, her attorney:

    Notice is hereby given that [name], defendant above named, hereby appeals to the United States of Appeals for the _____ Circuit from the final judgment entered in this action on the _____ day of _____ , 1995, in the above entitled action on [date of judgment].

                              _____

                                  Attorney for Defendant
                                    Address

of the transcript relating to the issues to be submitted to the court of appeals. The appellant is required to tell the respondent which portions of the transcript he or she intends to include in the appendix. The appellee may ask the appellant to include additional portions, and if the appellant refuses to do so, the respondent may arrange to supplement them by preparing a respondent's appendix.

The appellant has only forty days in which to prepare the appellant's brief and appendix, after the original record is transmitted to the clerk of the appellate court. The Rules allow the appellee only thirty days in which to reply to the appellant's brief. If more time is needed for preparing the brief and appendix, the appellant must make a request for it before the forty-day period expires. The request is made to the district court—not to the appellate court.

The Rules limit the appellant's brief to fifty pages. An appellant's brief has several sections. It must contain (1) a statement outlining the nature of the case; (2) a chronological review of the case, listing the date on which the action was commenced and each important procedural date thereafter; and (3) a concise, nonargumentative statement of the facts that were established through the pleadings and the evidence at trial. Most lawyers consider preparation of the statement of facts to be the most difficult part of good brief writing. The statement must be truthful, must not be argumentative, and must fully support the client's version of the case. Each important fact must be supported by a reference to the transcript or exhibit where it may be found in the record. The appellant must state the legal issues to be decided by the appellate court. If the appellee disagrees with the appellant's phrasing of the issues, the appellee may submit a statement of the issues in her or his brief. Too often the parties cannot even agree on the issues to be examined and argued.

The body of the brief is an argument on the law as the law applies to the evidence or facts of the case. The appellant attempts to persuade the court of appeals that the trial court committed one or more errors and the errors prejudiced the outcome of the case. The argument may be concerned with how the appellant was prevented from proving the facts or how the trial court misapplied the law. Although a verdict may be set aside where it is manifestly contrary to the weight of the evidence, the appellant is not permitted to argue that the verdict is wrong. The appellate court assumes that the verdict is consistent with the evidence that favored the appellee. Any evidence favoring the appellant, which is inconsistent with the verdict, is presumed to have been rejected by the jury. The jury cannot reject admissions and stipulations. That is another good reason for using Rule 36 requests for admission as much as possible.

If more witnesses and exhibits supported the appellant's theory of the evidence, that is of no importance on appeal. Suppose the plaintiff claims to have sustained a brain injury in an accident; the evidence showed he was attended by six physicians; one of the six physicians said the accident caused the plaintiff's alleged brain injury; one of the physicians had no opinion on the issue; four of the physicians were emphatic that the accident could not have caused any brain injury; and one independent medical examiner, chosen by the defendant, testified that, to a reasonable medical certainty, the accident did not cause any brain injury. If the appellate court determined that the one physician who supported the plaintiff's claim of brain injury was competent to render such an opinion and that adequate foundation supported the physician's opinion, the verdict would stand even though the greater number of witnesses testified to the contrary.

The appellate court is not supposed to act as a superjury. Its function is to make sure that the law was correctly stated and applied, and that the trial procedures were properly followed. However, suppose that in the preceding example the only witness to support the plaintiff's claim of a brain injury was a psychologist, and all the medical doctors concluded there was no brain injury. An appellate court would be constrained to set aside a verdict for the plaintiff, because the psychologist's testimony would not be competent to establish a medical fact. The trial court's error, in that event, goes not to the mere weight of the evidence, but to the admissibility and competency of the evidence.

Most appeals are the result of a dispute about the law, as distinguished from a dispute over facts or trial procedures. A disagreement about the law may be based upon a dispute over what the law is. For instance, the parties may disagree about the meaning of a statute. Suppose a statute of limitations provides a two-year limitation on actions against physicians and hospitals. Does the statute apply to claims against osteopaths and chiropractors? A court must decide. The dispute may be over which law applies to the parties' transaction or occurrence. For example, one party may argue that a federal law applies, and the other party contends that a state law controls. A disagreement about the law may be based upon a dispute over how the law applies to the parties' transaction or occurrence. For example, the law is clear that an insurance policy provides coverage only for accidental occurrences. But is an employer's wrongful discharge of an employee an accident where the employee unexpectedly becomes ill because of emotional upset due to the wrongful discharge? In other words, is the terminated employee's illness an accidental occurrence that invokes insurance coverage for the employee's claim against the employer? A court must decide. The rules of law are clear, but a court must determine how those rules apply to the particular facts.

The parties' arguments on the law usually rely heavily upon statutes and the precedent of other cases that have dealt with the same or similar problems. Prior cases decided by the court in which the appeal is pending are considered most persuasive. If a decision is directly in point, it should be determinative. A court should follow the precedent of its own decisions until the court expressly overrules the prior decisions. Parties look to the decisions of other jurisdictions as instructive and persuasive, but not controlling. Of course, the more similar a prior case is to the pending case, the more persuasive the prior decision is. An appellant may show that many other appellate courts have decided the issue differently than the court in which the appeal is pending, and urge the court to overrule its prior decision. The opinions rendered by other appellate courts are particularly helpful when they contain a clear, forceful rationale. Furthermore, courts strive for uniformity in the law and are reluctant to reach a decision that is inconsistent with what other courts are doing. By way of example, many states have rules of civil procedure that use the same language as the Federal Rules of Civil Procedure. State courts are inclined to follow federal decisions that interpret and apply the federal rules. However, state courts are not bound by the federal court interpretations and federal precedent merely because their rules contain the same language.

The last section of an appellant's brief is the conclusion. Customarily, the conclusion states the legal issue or issues in a positive way, indicating how the party wants the court to rule or hold. For example, if the issue is whether a chiropractor is a physician within the meaning of the statute of limitations, the conclusion might state, "Therefore, the statute of limitations applies to a doctor of chiropractic, the same as any other health care provider; otherwise, the statute unconstitutionally discriminates between persons in the same class." The conclusion should also specify the relief requested by the appellant—that is, a new trial or a judgment as a matter of law. A good conclusion is concise—not a rehash of the argument.

■ APPELLEE'S BRIEF

The appellee has thirty days from the date the appellant's brief is received, in which to prepare and file a responsive brief. However, an appellee can well anticipate what the issues and arguments will be, especially if the appellant made posttrial motions, so the appellee ought to start working on the brief as soon as the notice of appeal is served. The appellee argues in support of the trial court's rulings and contends that the errors that did occur were not prejudicial. The format of the appellee's brief is the same as that of the appellant's brief.

■ APPELLANT'S REPLY BRIEF

The appellant may file a twenty-five-page reply brief. This brief may address only the arguments made in the appellee's brief. An appellant's reply brief may not be used to advance new issues or new arguments.

■ AMICUS CURIAE

Once in a while, an appellate matter raises an issue of law that may have a substantial effect on persons or companies that are not parties to the suit, and they may want to participate in the appeal. They may apply to the court for leave to file an **amicus curiae** brief—a brief by a "friend of the court." No one has an absolute right to file an amicus brief. The court considers the nature of the applicant's interest in determining whether or not to permit the appearance. The parties have an interest in who will participate and to what extent, but they have no veto power over a motion for leave to file an amicus brief. An amicus party is never given the right to make an oral argument to the court.

■ ORAL ARGUMENT

The clerk for the circuit court of appeals schedules the appeals for an oral argument before three or more of the court's judges. Each circuit court of appeals has eight or more judges. If a case has unique importance, all the judges in the circuit may hear the oral argument and participate in the decision making. When all the judges participate, it is called an **en banc hearing.**

The parties usually have at least thirty days' notice of the hearing date. An appellate court ordinarily hears three or four arguments during a morning's session. Each case is allotted one hour or less. Therefore, each lawyer has only thirty minutes or less in which to present an oral argument. The appellant may be allowed to save some of the allotted time for replying to the appellee's argument. During the arguments, the judges ask such questions as they deem useful. The appellate judges almost never state what their decision will be. However, a lawyer is often able to make an educated guess about the probable outcome by the nature of the judges' questions and by their apparent attitude toward the issues.

The judges who hear the oral argument confer immediately after the argument and determine how the case should be decided. One of the judges writes the opinion for the court. The judge then circulates the draft opinion to the other judges for additions or corrections. As soon as they reach a consensus on a final draft, the judge who authored the opinion signs the opinion. The opinion is then filed with the clerk of court, who sends a copy of the opinion to each party.

If one or more of the judges disagrees with the **majority opinion,** they may write a **dissent,** which is published along with the majority opinion. On occasion, a judge may agree with the result reached by the majority, but disagree with the reasons given for the majority decision. The judge may then file a **concurring opinion,** in which he or she explains why and how the rationale of the majority opinion should be qualified. A unanimous decision is usually considered to be more forceful authority for use as a precedent. If a court is closely divided in reaching a decision, the decision might be overruled the next time it comes before the court. On occasion, the appellate court judges are evenly divided on how the case should be decided. The consequence is that the trial court's decision breaks the tie: the trial court's judgment is affirmed.

An appellate court's decision is usually rendered within six months after the oral argument. The length of time depends upon many circumstances. In some cases the appeal has taken more than a year.

■ MOTION FOR REHEARING

Upon receiving the appellate court decision, the losing party may determine that some controlling fact or legal issue has been overlooked by the appellate court. The remedy is to file a motion for rehearing, in which the moving party sets forth the reasons why a rehearing is necessary. If the written motion convinces the court that a rehearing is justified, a rehearing is ordered. More often than not, motions for rehearing are denied without explanation. If the court does grant a rehearing, that does not mean the court will hear another oral argument. A second oral argument is extremely rare. Whatever is to be done will normally be done in writing.

■ APPEALS TO THE UNITED STATES SUPREME COURT

Only a small percentage of the cases that go to the circuit courts of appeal are carried to the United States Supreme Court. Furthermore, in only a very few types of cases do the parties have an absolute right to appeal to the Supreme Court.

A party appeals to the Supreme Court by petitioning the Court for a writ of certiorari. The writ is an order for the lower court to transmit its record to the Supreme Court so that the Supreme Court can inspect the proceedings and determine whether any irregularities took place.

Every year many petitions for writs of certiorari are filed, but the Court grants only a small percentage of them. At least four of the nine Supreme Court justices must vote in favor of granting the petition. A petitioner must try to persuade the Supreme Court that the case is unusually important— that it has ramifications beyond its effect on the parties. For example, the Supreme Court is likely to grant review if two circuit courts have reached opposite conclusions on the law, and a decision by the Supreme Court is needed to harmonize the law; when federal courts differ in how they handle a particular issue or type of case, litigants start shopping for the more favorable forum. If an appeal raises significant constitutional questions or questions of general importance to the nation, the appeal may be accepted. The amount of money or property in question is not a major determinant of whether the Supreme Court will elect to hear the case.

◼ STARE DECISIS

Appellate courts have inherent power to overrule their prior decisions and to propound new rules of law. However, an appellate court cannot disregard a statute, unless the court finds the statute is unconstitutional. To a large extent, the stability of our legal system depends upon the reluctance of appellate courts to change rules of law once decided. The principle is referred to as stare decisis.

Most changes in the law should come through the legislative process. Appellate courts cannot change laws enacted by the legislature; however, courts can change their interpretation of statutes, and that can have almost the same effect. An appellate court may determine that a statute is invalid because the statute violates the Constitution or was enacted by a procedure that was defective in some way. A statute may be too vague to be enforceable, thus violating due process. At times, an appellate court recognizes that it erred in propounding a rule of law and overrules its prior decision by declaring a new rule of law.

◼ ORDER FOR NEW TRIAL OR REVERSAL

When an appellate court determines that a trial court committed prejudicial error, the appellate court may **vacate** the trial court's judgment and order entry of judgment in favor of the appellant. When a judgment is vacated it is nullified as though it never had existed. In that event, the litigation is put to an end: the trial court's judgment is **reversed.** Or the appellate court may determine that an error was committed but the appellant is not entitled to judgment on the present state of the record. The appellate court may then **remand** the case to the trial court for a new trial. A new trial may be ordered on all issues or on certain specified issues. For example, a court may determine that the error in question did not affect the jury's determination of liability in favor of the plaintiff against the defendant, but did affect the jury's determination of the amount of damages awarded to the plaintiff. Under those circumstances, the court could direct the trial court to have a new trial on the issue of damages only. In that event, the first trial was of some value to the parties. In light of the appellate court's decision, the parties may be able to settle their dispute without actually going through another trial.

■ TAXABLE COSTS

The appellate courts have broad discretion in determining what costs should be awarded to the parties in connection with the appeal. The appellate court's decision specifies what costs, if any, are allowed and to whom the costs are awarded. Costs are not always awarded to the prevailing party.

■ EXTRAORDINARY APPEALS

On rare occasions, a party may ask an appellate court for a **writ of mandamus,** which is an order that requires the trial judge to do a particular act, or a party may seek a **writ of prohibition,** which is an appellate order that prohibits the trial judge from doing a particular act. These appellate writs are obtained during prosecution of the case, usually before the trial. For example, the parties might disagree over the scope of discovery in one party's deposition. The deponent may contend that the questions require disclosure of privileged information and that any disclosure of the information would cause irreparable harm. If the trial judge ordered the deponent to answer the questions anyway, the deponent could seek a writ of prohibition from an appellate court, to prevent the trial judge from enforcing the order.

SUMMARY

An appellate court does not sit in judgment of the fairness of the outcome. It corrects errors by vacating the lower court's judgment and ordering a new trial or by ordering entry of judgment as a matter of law. It examines the record of the trial court, pursuant to the notice of appeal, to determine whether the trial court followed proper procedures and correctly applied the substantive law. An appellate court will not reverse on the grounds that it would have preferred a different outcome. An appellate court will not reverse a trial court's judgment or order a new trial unless there was an error that may have affected the outcome. In other words, the error must be prejudicial to be appealable.

A paralegal may help with various aspects of an appeal. A paralegal may outline portions of the trial transcript in much the same way that depositions are outlined and summarized. Paralegals may help to prepare the exhibits, assemble a brief's appendix, proofread drafts of the brief, and check citations. A paralegal who has a good understanding of the facts of the case and who has developed good writing skills could help to write the statement of facts in a brief.

An appellant initiates an appeal by serving and filing a notice of appeal. The notice of appeal must be filed with the clerk of the federal district court within thirty days of the date on which the judgment was entered.

The appellant must order a transcript of the trial from the official court reporter within ten days after filing the notice of appeal. The appellant must make arrangements with the court reporter to pay the reporter's fees for transcribing the testimony. The trial transcript, exhibits, and district court file make up the record on appeal. The transcript usually includes all the testimony, motions at trial, and jury instructions. The parties may stipulate that certain parts of the record may be omitted. The appellant must supply at least one copy of the transcript to each party.

The appellant's brief is limited to fifty pages. It must contain (1) a statement outlining the nature of the case; (2) a chronological review of the case, listing the date on which the action was commenced and each important procedural date thereafter; and (3) a concise, nonargumentative statement of the facts. The brief must state the legal issues that are to be considered—the reasons for the appeal. It must contain an argument concerning the applicable law. Most lawyers consider preparation of the statement of facts to be the most difficult part of good brief writing. The statement must be truthful, must not be argumentative, and must fully support the client's version of the case. Each important fact must be supported by a reference to the transcript or exhibit where it may be found in the record. The appellant must state the legal issues to be decided by the appellate court. If the appellee disagrees with the appellant's statement of the issues, the appellee may submit a different statement of the issues.

The argument is the main part of an appellant's brief. The appellant attempts to persuade the appellate court that the trial court committed one or more errors of law and the errors prejudiced the outcome of the case. The appellate court assumes that the verdict is consistent with the evidence that favored the appellee. Any evidence favoring the appellant, which is inconsistent with the verdict, is presumed to have been rejected by the jury. If more witnesses and exhibits supported the appellant's theory of the evidence, that is of no importance on appeal.

The parties' arguments rely upon statutes and the precedent of other cases that have dealt with the same or similar problems. A prior decision that was made by the same appellate court and is directly in point should be controlling and dispositive. An appellate court should follow the precedent of its own decisions until it expressly overrules the prior decisions. Parties look to the decisions of other jurisdictions as instructive and persuasive, but not controlling. Opinions rendered by other appellate courts are particularly persuasive when they provide a clear, forceful rationale for the decision.

The brief's conclusion should state how the party wants the court to rule or hold and the specific relief the appellant wants—that is, a new trial or a judgment as a matter of law. A conclusion should not rehash the argument.

The appellee has thirty days from the date the appellant's brief is received, in which to prepare and file a responsive brief. The appellee ordinarily argues in support of the trial court's rulings and that any errors that did occur were not prejudicial. The format of the appellee's brief is the same as that of the appellant's brief.

An appellant's reply brief is limited to twenty-five pages and may address only the arguments made in the appellee's brief. A reply brief may not be used to advance new issues or new arguments.

A person who has a major interest in the outcome of an appeal because the appeal will have precedential value may petition the appellate court for leave to file an amicus curiae brief. The court considers the nature of the petitioner's interest and the significance of the case in deciding whether to permit the person to appear in the case. The parties have no veto power to keep a non-party from appearing as a friend of the court. The amicus brief is not supposed to take sides in the case. An amicus party is to address only the legal issue that directly affects his or her interests.

The circuit court of appeals clerk schedules the appeals for oral argument before three or more of the court's judges. An appellate court ordinarily hears three or four arguments during the course of a morning's session. Each lawyer has only thirty minutes or less in which to present his or her oral argument. The appellant may save some of the allotted time for replying to the appellee's argument. The judges ask such questions as they deem useful. The three judges who hear the oral argument confer immediately after the argument and determine how the case should be decided. One of the judges writes the opinion for the court. If a case has unique importance, all of the judges in the circuit may hear the oral argument and participate in the decision making.

If the losing party determines that some controlling fact or legal issue has been overlooked by the appellate court, the losing party may file a motion for a rehearing. The motion must state the reasons why a rehearing is necessary. If the court is convinced by the written motion that a rehearing is justified, a rehearing is ordered. However, more often than not, motions for rehearing are denied without explanation. If the court does grant a rehearing, that does not mean that the court will have another oral argument. A second oral argument is extremely rare.

The United States Supreme Court is the highest federal appellate court. Most cases appealed to the Supreme Court come from the circuit courts of appeals. Subject to a few exceptions, parties do not have a right to appeal to the Court. A party initiates an appeal to the Supreme Court by petitioning the Court for a writ of certiorari. If the Supreme Court concludes that the case and issues are important, it issues a writ of certiorari to the lower court, requiring the lower court to transmit the record to the Supreme Court for review. At least four of the nine Supreme Court justices must vote in favor of granting the petition; otherwise, the petition is disallowed.

Once an appellate court has decided a rule of law, it should be followed by all courts in that jurisdiction. However, appellate courts have inherent power to overrule their own prior decisions by propounding new rules of law. The stability of our legal system depends upon the reluctance of appellate courts to change rules of law once decided. The principle is referred to as stare decisis. Most changes in the law should come through the legislative process.

If the appellant was entitled to judgment as a matter of law, the appellate court may reverse the trial court's judgment and order judgment for the appellant. In that event, the litigation is put to an end. Or, the appellate court may determine that an error was committed, but the appellant is not entitled to judgment on the present state of the record. The appellate court may remand the case to the trial court for a new trial. A new trial may be ordered on all issues or on certain specified issues.

Appellate courts have broad discretion in determining what costs should be awarded to the parties in connection with the appeal. The appellate court's decision specifies what costs, if any, are allowed and to whom the costs are awarded. Costs are not always awarded to the prevailing party.

A party may ask an appellate court for a writ of mandamus to require the trial judge to do a particular act, or seek a writ of prohibition to prohibit the trial judge from doing a particular act. A party uses these appeal procedures while the case is still in the district court. These writs are obtained to keep the judge from causing irreparable harm to a party.

KEY TERMS

appellant	dissent
appellee	concurring opinion
notice of appeal	vacate
cost bond	reversed
supersedeas bond	remand
amicus curiae	writ of mandamus
en banc hearing	writ of prohibition
majority opinion	

REVIEW QUESTIONS

1. What two circumstances must exist to successfully prosecute an appeal?
2. How does the appellant initiate an appeal?
3. What is the time limit for appealing?
4. What are the principal parts of an appellant's brief?
5. What are the principal limitations on an appellant's reply brief?
6. What are the grounds for filing an amicus curiae brief?
7. How does a party initiate an appeal to the United States Supreme Court from a circuit court of appeal's decision?
8. How does the United States Supreme Court decide whether it will review a case?
9. What is the purpose of obtaining a writ of prohibition?
10. How does a remand differ from a reversal?

SETTLEMENTS, RELEASES, AND DISMISSALS

Many more claims are settled than are tried and reduced to a judgment. When the parties are able to agree upon a settlement of their controversy without a court determination, they avoid uncertainty, gain economies, and secure a disposition that they know they can tolerate, if not embrace. Parties to a dispute implement and formalize their settlement by making a settlement agreement. The settlement agreement has the effect of releasing the claimant's claim. Therefore, a written settlement agreement is often called a release. The settlement agreement permanently concludes the dispute. The alternative is to proceed with litigation, but the civil justice system cannot guarantee a remedy or resolution that will satisfy all the parties. Indeed, a court-mandated solution may not satisfy any of the parties. Furthermore, there is no way of knowing what the court's resolution will be before the verdict is rendered or the appeal is concluded. The goal of the civil justice system is to provide a resolution that comports with society's standards of what is fair and reasonable, not a remedy that will satisfy the parties. Parties have good reason to choose to settle their dispute, even if the settlement may be somewhat unsatisfactory. If a lawsuit is already pending when the parties arrive at a settlement agreement, court rules provide the means for the parties to dismiss their suit.

A paralegal may be asked to prepare a release for the client. Although a lawyer must decide which kind of release to use, a paralegal may draft the release and suggest the relevant provisions.

SETTLEMENTS AND RELEASES

A settlement agreement and release is a contract. Since the effect of a settlement agreement is to release a cause of action, the written settlement agreement is customarily referred to as a release. A release states the terms and conditions of the parties' negotiated settlement. A release is enforceable like any contract.

A settlement agreement is not binding upon a minor unless the guardian obtains court approval of the agreement. Consequently, any party who must deal with a minor ordinarily insists upon negotiating through a guardian and having court approval of their agreement to settle.

A settlement agreement may provide for entry of a judgment that establishes the parties' rights and obligations between them. A party who pays money to settle a disputed claim is said to have "bought her or his peace." Settlement agreements are used to resolve contract disputes and claims that arise from alleged torts. A paralegal may prepare and examine releases for the client's use, but the release and any stipulation for dismissal must be approved by the responsible lawyer before they are executed.

The law favors voluntary settlements. Everyone benefits from an early, reasonable settlement. The parties avoid the expense, delay, and inconvenience of litigation. The government and community avoid the cost of providing a court for the trial. The parties have the opportunity to make a commitment with which they can live. If they go to trial, the plaintiff may recover nothing, leaving him or her in a desperate financial condition, or a large verdict in favor of the plaintiff might force the defendant to go into bankruptcy, so neither party benefits. A wise settlement is a better resolution, even if neither party is particularly happy with the terms of the settlement. Indeed, it is often said that if neither party is happy with the settlement, it is probably a good settlement.

Because the law favors settlements, the parties are encouraged to conduct settlement negotiations. Nothing the opposing parties or lawyers say to each other in the course of settlement negotiations may be used against them at trial. However, information and statements that are discoverable through other means are not protected from use at trial. For example, if the defendant says in negotiations that he came upon some photographs that tend to support the plaintiff's claim, the plaintiff could demand discovery of photographs. On the other hand, if the defendant offers to pay $10,000 for a settlement, the plaintiff cannot use that offer as evidence that the defendant recognizes he may have some responsibility for the occurrence. Similarly, if the defendant stated during the settlement negotiations that he went through the stop sign, then at trial the plaintiff could seek to prove the fact of the violation and that the defendant admitted the violation. But suppose the defendant were to say, "For purposes of settlement, let us assume that I went through the stop sign; still, your demand is too high.'' In that context, the statement made in negotiations could not be brought out at trial. Statements made during settlement negotiations are not absolutely privileged. The rules of evidence merely deem such statements as irrelevant to the civil suit. Therefore, some discretion must be used during settlement negotiations.

When the parties settle their dispute, they may establish their own criteria, terms, and conditions for concluding the dispute. They avoid expending time and money on litigation procedures. A party may elect to settle because the party knows that her or his evidence is weak or perhaps because the party cannot prove an essential element of her or his cause of action or defense. For example, a party may elect to settle because a key witness has died. The reason a party settles may be totally unrelated to the merits of the case or the state of the evidence. For example, a party may settle because she feels that a trial would be too strenuous. Or parties may settle their dispute on a handshake because they are friends and their friendship is worth more to them than winning money damages in a lawsuit. Friendship or even past friendship is not a consideration in determining or proving legal rights and obligations in court.

The parties to a settlement agreement must have a meeting of the minds concerning the terms and conditions of their agreement. A meeting of the minds comes about through a process of offers, counteroffers, and acceptance. The process is commonly referred to as settlement negotiations. The importance of a meeting of the minds is highlighted in personal injury cases where the claimant settles for a relatively modest amount but subsequently discovers that he or she has injuries that were not known at the time of the settlement. Or the claimant may subsequently discover unknown consequences of a known injury. Either way, the claimant did not consider the problem when he or she executed a full and final release. Was there a meeting of the minds? Suppose a young claimant's leg is broken in an automobile accident. The leg heals straight, strong, and without any loss of motion, and the claimant settles for a modest amount of damages. Two years after the accident, it is discovered that the injury damaged the bone so that it cannot grow anymore. Consequently, when the claimant obtains his full growth, his injured leg is two inches shorter than the other leg. Should the "modest" settlement be set aside?

Because a claimant may have injuries that the claimant and his or her doctors do not know about or because there may be unanticipated consequences of known injuries, most full and final releases in personal injury cases provide that the claimant releases his or her claims for all injuries, whether known or unknown. On that basis, there is a meeting of the minds as to what is being released. The parties may agree to settle their dispute on the basis that the claimant is releasing only known injuries. Then neither party really gambles. However, for many reasons, the defendant or the defendant's liability insurer may refuse to settle unless the claimant gives a full and final release. Suppose, in the preceding example, the case had gone to trial rather than being settled. The plaintiff's evidence would not have disclosed the fact that the broken bone could not grow anymore, so the plaintiff would not have been compensated for that problem. The problem of unknown injuries and unknown consequences of known injuries points out the importance of not settling personal injury cases too soon.

A settlement agreement must be voluntary and not the result of duress or undue influence. If a party threatens to inflict personal injury or property damage, that is an example of duress that would vitiate (invalidate) a settlement agreement. On the other hand, a party's desperate need for money or compelling desire to end the dispute, or another party's threat to end settlement negotiations, is not an act of duress that would give grounds for avoiding a settlement agreement.

The terms of a settlement agreement must provide for an exchange of consideration. The consideration given for a release must be clearly stated. The most common consideration for a settlement agreement is payment of money. The second most common form of consideration is a promise to do something or to refrain from doing something. A promise of performance is consideration that will support a settlement contract, provided the promisor is not already under a legal compulsion to do what she or he has promised. In that event, the promisor has really given nothing of value for the statement. An agreement between two litigants to mutually release each other from any and all liability is a valid agreement. The two promises constitute valid consideration, one for the other. However, the release of a claim is not valid consideration if the pretended claim is totally false. The consideration must actually be paid or exchanged for the contract to be effective. A mere recital of payment is not effective. If the consideration has no value, the release is unenforceable for lack of consideration.

Settlement agreements do not have to be in writing. However, as a practical matter, they should be reduced to a writing so that no subsequent disagreement arises over the terms, scope, and limits of the settlement. This general rule has one significant exception. The statute of frauds requires that all contracts that, by their terms, are not to be performed within one year from the date on which they are made, must be in written form and signed by the parties. Structured settlements, which provide for periodic payments on a settlement, often fall into that category, so they must be reduced to a writing and signed.

A release should identify the parties, the transaction or occurrence that gave rise to the claim, the type of injury or damage claimed, the consideration given for the release, and any special conditions or limitations that are part of the agreement. If the claim is for money, the money is ordinarily paid at the time the release is signed by the claimant. The released party need not sign the release. However, if the agreement provides for a mutual release, then both parties must sign. It is customary to have the claimant's signature witnessed and notarized even though no rule or law requires those formalities. If the parties to a settlement agreement have a subsequent disagreement about the terms and conditions of the agreement, a court would look to the writing to determine the parties' intent. If the court were to find the written release to be ambiguous, the court could receive parol evidence concerning the parties' intent, including evidence of the parties' negotiations.

Historically, the common law looked upon a release as having a single purpose and effect: to release the claimant's claim. Therefore, the ancient common law gave a broad and decisive effect to releases. A release barred all claims arising from the specified transaction or occurrence. It also released all persons who might have been liable to the claimant. The law now permits releases to be as broad as the parties want them to be, or to have a very narrow, specific, and limited effect. Many different release forms have been devised to apply to various settling situations.

■ GENERAL RELEASES

A **general release** is a very broad release. The claimant agrees to release not only all claims arising from a particular transaction or occurrence, but all claims he or she might then have against the persons released. A general release may release not only the person who pays the consideration for the release, but everyone else in the world who might be liable for the harm sustained by the claimant as a result of the particular transaction or occurrence. A party may have good reasons for insisting upon a general release. For example, the dispute between the parties may have arisen from a long-time business relationship that is now at an end, and the parties may want to ensure that they have settled all matters between them—even problems they do not know about but that could arise from their past dealings. A general release is intended to put an end to all claims the claimant may have against the released party for all transactions and occurrences between them as of the date of the release. If an action is pending, the plaintiff is required to stipulate to a dismissal of the action.

A **full and final release** releases only the party who has paid consideration for the release, and applies only to the particular transaction or occurrence. The release must identify the transaction or occurrence by type, time, place, and claimed loss. The release protects not only the party who paid consideration, but everyone else who might be liable to the claimant. A full and final release may provide the settling defendant with another benefit. Any tortfeasor who did not pay her or his fair share for the release is liable for contribution to the party who bought the release. The settling defendant may bring an action against any joint tortfeasor who has concurrent liability to the claimant. A full and final release is a predicate for the settling defendant's action to obtain contribution. It is customary to attach the release to the complaint as an exhibit to show that the settling defendant is the proper person to bring the contribution action. The release shows that the nonsettling tortfeasors are fully protected against any future claims by the claimant. The purchaser of a release must be able to prove that she or he settled the claim under a legal compulsion (not as a volunteer), and paid more than her or his share. When the released party contemplates bringing an action against a third person for contribution, it is customary to add the word *assignment* to the title of the release: full and final release and assignment. Technically, however, it is not an assignment of a cause of action.

A settling tortfeasor may insist on obtaining a full and final release of all claims arising from the occurrence in question because by obtaining a release of *everyone*, the settling party prevents the claimant from making a claim against others who, in turn, might bring a claim against the settling party for contribution. A full and final release provides a defense to everyone against any claim by the plaintiff arising from the transaction or occurrence identified in the release.

The parties may combine the features of a general release and of a full and final release into one agreement

Exhibit 25.1 illustrates a typical general release.

RELEASE OF ALL CLAIMS

FOR AND IN CONSIDERATION of the payment to me/us at this time of the sum of _____ dollars ($ _____), the receipt of which is hereby acknowledged, I/we, being of lawful age, do hereby release, acquit, and forever discharge _____ of and from any and all actions, causes of action, claims, demands, damages, costs, loss of services, expenses, and compensation, on account of, or in any way growing out of, any and all known and unknown personal injuries, developed or undeveloped, and property damage resulting or to result from the accident that occurred on or about the _____ day of _____ , 19 _____ , at or near _____ .

I/we hereby declare and represent that the injuries sustained may be permanent and progressive and that recovery therefrom is uncertain and indefinite, and in making this release and agreement it is understood and agreed that I/we rely wholly upon my/our own judgment, belief, and knowledge of the nature, extent, and duration of said injuries, and that I/we have not been influenced to any extent whatever in making this release by any representations or statements regarding said injuries, or regarding any other matters, made by the persons, firms, or corporations who are hereby released, or by any person or persons representing him or them, or by any physician or surgeon by him or them employed.

I/we clearly understand that I/we are releasing _____ and that this release includes all injuries now known to me/us and also all injuries now unknown, and I/we clearly understand that this release also includes all disabilities or results which may develop in the future from injuries now known or unknown to me/us.

It is further understood and agreed that this settlement is the compromise of a doubtful and disputed claim, and that the payment is not to be construed as an admission of liability on the part of _____ , by whom liability is expressly denied.

This release contains the ENTIRE AGREEMENT between the parties hereto, and the terms of this release are contractual and not a mere recital.

I/we further state that I/we have carefully read the foregoing release and know the contents thereof, and I/we sign the same as my/our own free act.

WITNESS _____ hand and seal this _____ day of _____ , 19 _____ . In presence of

CAUTION! READ BEFORE SIGNING

_____
_____   _____ (Seal)
_____   _____ (Seal)
_____

■ PARTIAL RELEASES

The general release was consistent with the historic common-law concept that a release must put an end to the parties' controversy. **Partial releases** were considered to be an anathema to the law. It was felt that partial releases led to uncertainty and did not actually terminate litigation, so they were disallowed. Historically, if an agreement purported to be a partial release, a court would refuse to enforce it or would give it the effect of a full and final release. Since the mid-1900s, courts have come to accept and enforce partial settlements in tort actions. With the advent of comparative fault, in which parties' tortious conduct can be allocated in percentages on the basis of causation, partial releases have become common. Many tort claims would not be settled if partial settlements and partial releases were not possible. Furthermore, experience has shown that when one facet of a dispute is settled, the rest of the case is more likely to settle. Having a portion of a dispute settled is better than not having any settlement. However, experience has also shown that creative partial settlements frequently lead to uncertainties concerning their scope and effect. Nevertheless, the modern view is that partial settlements are valid, provided no secrecy surrounds the settlement and the partial settlement does not prejudice the rights of persons who do not participate in the settlement agreements. Partial releases are seldom, if ever, used in disputes arising from contracts.

The parties must consider the effect the partial release will have upon the settling party's joint liability with joint tortfeasors or concurrent tortfeasors or both. Joint and concurrent tortfeasors are liable individually for the entire amount of the claimant's damages. Joint liability means the claimant may sue one or more of the wrongdoers separately for all the claimant's damages, or the claimant may sue all of them in one action, with each tortfeasor being fully responsible for the entire loss. When a claimant releases one settling tortfeasor from all liability and agrees to indemnify the settling tortfeasor against any contribution claims made by the nonsettling parties, the joint obligation or joint liability between the settling tortfeasor and the nonsettling tortfeasors is destroyed. In short, the claimant must look solely to the resources of the nonsettling tortfeasors for any additional recovery. Therefore, if a claim involves two wrongdoers, only one of whom is financially able to pay a judgment, it may not be wise for the claimant to enter into a partial release.

When the case goes to trial against the nonsettling defendants, at the beginning of the trial the court tells the jury about the partial settlement, but the jury is not told about the amount of the settlement. At the end of the trial the court instructs the jurors that they must determine whether the settling defendant was negligent and what percentage of causal negligence should be attributed to that defendant when determining the percentage of causal negligence to be attributed to the plaintiff and remaining defendants. The court may state this as follows:

> [Name of settling defendant] is no longer a party to this lawsuit, because [name of settling defendant] and plaintiff have entered into a settlement agreement. You are not to concern yourselves with the reasons for the settlement agreement. You are not to draw any conclusions from the fact of settlement or from the fact that other defendants remain in the lawsuit. The settlement agreement between plaintiff and [name of settling defendant] should in no way influence your judgment about the alleged negligence of the remaining defendants and plaintiff.
>
> Even though [name of settling defendant] is no longer a party to this lawsuit, you will still be asked to determine whether [name of settling defendant] was negligent and whether that negligence was a direct cause of the accident. This is to ensure that the apportionment of negligence you make is fair and accurate.

A partial release that releases one of several tortfeasors in effect releases a percentage or fraction of causal fault. A partial release cannot be used to discharge one of two defendants when one of the two defendants is only vicariously liable. A full and final release of an agent's liability necessarily releases the principal if the principal did not commit any separate wrongful act. For example, if the plaintiff brings an action against the driver and the owner of an automobile, and the plaintiff settles with the driver, there can be no residual liability against the owner. The claim against the owner is extinguished by a full and final settlement with the driver. There is no separate causal negligence on the part of the owner, at least in most cases. The example assumes that there is no claim that the vehicle was negligently maintained or defective so as to contribute to the accident. Similarly, if the plaintiff brings an action against the defendant and the defendant's employer, a settlement with the defendant will automatically release the employer.

■ PARTIAL SETTLEMENTS INVOLVING COMPARATIVE FAULT

Where the law of comparative fault applies, each settlement is for the percentage of causal fault attributable to the settling tortfeasor. For example, in an accident case involving two defendants, a settlement with defendant A discharges the percentage of causal negligence attributable to her. When the case goes to trial against the nonsettling defendant, the jury must determine the amount of the plaintiff's total money damages and the percentage of causal negligence attributable to *both* defendants. Suppose the verdict is in the amount of $20,000, and defendant A's causal negligence is set at 10 percent and defendant B's causal negligence is set at 90 percent. Defendant B receives a credit of 10 percent, or $2,000, against the amount of the verdict. Defendant A's $2,000 is deducted, and defendant B owes $18,000 to the plaintiff.

This kind of release has four basic elements:

1. The claimant releases a settling wrongdoer from the cause of action and discharges the part of the action that the wrongdoer was responsible for.

2. The claimant does not release his or her cause of action against the nonsettling wrongdoers.

3. The claimant agrees to pay for (indemnifies) any claims that are brought against the settling party by the nonsettling parties who are asking the settling party for a contribution.

4. The claimant agrees to satisfy any judgment obtained from the nonsettling party to the extent of the liability or fault of the settling party.

Partial settlements where comparative fault applies have some interesting ramifications. Suppose, in the preceding example, Defendant A paid $10,000 to obtain her release from the plaintiff. In light of the jury's verdict, which apportioned only 10 percent of the causal negligence to her, she paid $8,000 too much. Nevertheless, she is not entitled to a reimbursement of her overpayment. The plaintiff may retain the $10,000 collected from Defendant A and may recover an additional $18,000 from Defendant B, for a total recovery of $28,000. That is $8,000 more than the plaintiff's actual damages. The result may seem anomalous and unfair. The rationale for allowing it is that Defendant A bought her peace by voluntarily paying the $10,000, and the plaintiff took a calculated risk that the recovery from Defendant B might be considerably less than it was. If Defendant B were found to be only 30 percent at fault and the damages were set at $20,000, the plaintiff's recovery from Defendant B would be limited to $6,000. In that event, the settlement with Defendant A for $10,000 was a bad deal—or was it? Even though the verdict provided damages of $20,000, perhaps a total recovery of $16,000 is fair.

A settlement is somewhat of a gamble. The important consideration is that the settlement agreement be voluntary and not adversely affect the nonsettling defendant's rights. The nonsettling defendant does not have to pay more in damages than what she or he would have had to pay had the other defendant not settled. Furthermore, the nonsettling defendant should not obtain a windfall as a result of the settlement negotiated between the plaintiff and the settling defendant.

In the preceding example, if a jury found that the plaintiff was solely responsible for the accident and consequential injuries, the plaintiff would end up receiving the $10,000 from Defendant A. Note that because Defendant A settled the plaintiff's claim, Defendant A did not have to participate in the trial as a party. As a practical matter, the burden falls upon the nonsettling defendant to try to show that the settling defendant was negligent and caused the accident. The opportunity to settle with one party and shift the burden of proving negligence to the opponent provides another avenue of trial strategy.

■ PARTIAL SETTLEMENTS NOT INVOLVING COMPARATIVE FAULT

In states that do not have comparative fault, juries are not asked to determine percentages of causal negligence. Each defendant who is found liable is equally responsible with the other defendants. If there are two alleged tortfeasors, settlement with one discharges one-half of the recoverable damages—assuming that the jury determines the settling tortfeasor is partially liable. If there are three alleged tortfeasors, settlement with two discharges two-thirds of the recoverable damages. The claimant may give a partial release if the release expressly states that it is not to release anyone but the settling party. It is even a good idea to specifically identify the known tortfeasors who are not released by the settlement agreement. If the jury determines that the settling tortfeasor was solely responsible for the accident and injuries, the plaintiff will not obtain any compensation over and above the settlement.

The plaintiff and the defendant may enter into a partial settlement by which a part of the claim is resolved. The most common example is where the parties in an automobile accident case agree upon a settlement of the property damage claim, but litigate the personal injury claims.

■ PARTIAL RELEASES IN WORKERS' COMPENSATION CASES

Most employees who are injured in the course and scope of their employment receive workers' compensation benefits, which include payment of medical expenses, lost wages, and disability benefits. Even though the employee's injury occurred while he or she was working, it may have been caused by someone other than the employer. In that event, the injured employee has a right to receive workers' compensation payments *and* to pursue a common-law tort action against the tortfeasor. The most frequent causes of action are products liability actions and negligence actions. The employer who pays workers' compensation benefits is entitled, by law, to be reimbursed from any monetary recovery that the employee makes against the tortfeasor. If the employee neglects or refuses to pursue a claim against the tortfeasor, the employer may bring a subrogation action against the tortfeasor. Therefore, when an employee is injured, the injury may give the employee rights against the tortfeasor and create rights in favor of the employer against the tortfeasor. On occasion, the tortfeasor finds that he or she can settle with one but not the other. A special type of partial release is used in these cases, so that the tortfeasor may make a partial settlement.

A special workers' compensation release allows the employee who has received workers' compensation benefits to enter into a settlement with the tortfeasor without affecting the employer's subrogation rights. No monies are paid to the employer. The employer is left to pursue her or his own subrogation rights. The subrogation claim may be settled separately or go through a trial. The employee's partial settlement with the tortfeasor is valid, but it must not prejudice the employer's subrogation interests.

■ REVERSE SPECIAL WORKERS' COMPENSATION RELEASES

The tortfeasor may negotiate a full and final settlement of the employer's workers' compensation subrogation claim and leave open the plaintiff employee's claim. The form of the partial release is similar to that used to settle the employee's claim.

■ HIGH-LOW RELEASES

A **high-low release** is an agreement in which the settling wrongdoer guarantees a minimum amount to be paid to the plaintiff, and also puts an upper limit on his or her potential liability. In a multiparty situation, the agreement provides that if the verdict is against the plaintiff, the settling defendant will pay the guaranteed amount. If the plaintiff wins but receives a verdict for less than the guaranteed amount, the settling defendant will pay to the plaintiff an additional amount to make the recovery equal the guarantee. Also, the claimant agrees that if the plaintiff wins a verdict against the nonsettling tortfeasors that equals or exceeds the guaranteed amount, the plaintiff will pursue collection remedies only against the nonsettling defendants, and no payment will be required from the settling defendant.

A simplified version of a high-low release agreement can be used in cases involving only one tortfeasor. Here, the high-low agreement may provide that the claimant will receive a minimum guaranteed amount even if she or he loses the suit, and a maximum guaranteed amount if she or he wins on liability.

A high-low release agreement differs from an agreement that releases a percentage of causal fault in that no money is paid to the claimant at the time the settlement agreement is made. In addition, the settling party remains in the case throughout the trial. A high-low release can be advantageous when the claimant has a weak case, but the settling defendant risks a huge damage award if the claimant wins. Consequently, this type of settlement agreement helps to move cases along in a speedy fashion, reduces the likelihood of appeals, and permits the settling parties to avoid the risk of a disastrous outcome. On the other hand, a high-low release may mis-align the parties when there are multiple defendants, and distort the eventual outcome.

■ COVENANTS NOT TO SUE

A **covenant not to sue** is not a release. It is a device that allows the plaintiff and one of two or more tortfeasors to resolve their dispute without compromising the plaintiff's cause of action against the other tortfeasors. A covenant not to sue is a contract. The claimant agrees not to bring an action against the covenantee, or dismisses the pending action against the covenantee, but does not agree to release the claim or the covenantee. A covenant not to sue merely precludes the claimant from pursuing the claim against the covenantee. Since the cause of action remains in tact, the claimant may prosecute the claim against any other person who has liability to the claimant for the occurrence and injury. The person or party who pays for a covenant not to sue is not protected against a claim for contribution by a party who is held to be liable to the claimant. Suppose the claimant is a passenger in her husband's automobile when they collide with an automobile driven by the defendant. The husband driver has only $10,000 of liability insurance, and no assets. The claimant covenants not to sue her husband, and his insurer pays its policy limits for a covenant not to sue. The claimant can maintain an action against the other driver for the full amount of her claim. The other driver can bring a third-party action against the husband to obtain contribution for any sums he has to pay the claimant, but if the husband has no more insurance and no assets, the contribution action is not worth very much. In this way, the "deep pockets" defendant may be maneuvered into paying more in a settlement or judgment than could be obtained if a partial release were used. There is some question about the fairness of the device.

An example of a covenant not to sue appears in exhibit 25.2.

■ LOAN RECEIPT AGREEMENTS

A **loan receipt agreement** is a contract by which a tortfeasor, or his or her insurer, agrees to "loan" the claimant a specified sum of money, and the claimant agrees not to pursue his or her claim against the lender. Both believe that another party has substantial liability, and the claimant agrees to pursue the claim against that other party. The claimant agrees that if he or she recovers over a certain amount from the other party, he or she will repay all or part of the loan. If the claimant recovers little or nothing from the other party, the loan need not be repaid.

A loan receipt agreement may be used by a defendant's liability insurer, which makes an interest-free loan to its insured, who in turn pays the money to the plaintiff for a full and final release of the insured's percentage of causal negligence. As part of the agreement, the insured promises to prosecute an action for contribution against another joint tortfeasor. The insurer may agree to pay all the expenses incurred in the prosecution of the action for contribution. The loan to the claimant shall be repaid out of any proceeds the claimant obtains in the action against the joint tortfeasor.

COVENANT NOT TO SUE

KNOW ALL PEOPLE BY THESE PRESENTS, that Daniel Trost, Paul Trost, and Thomas E. Trost, hereinafter referred to as plaintiffs, for and in consideration of the sum of four thousand dollars and no cents ($4,000.00), the receipt of which is hereby acknowledged, do hereby covenant and expressly agree with The Griff Company and Mutual Insurance Company, their successors and assigns (all of whom are hereafter referred to as "Settling Parties"), not to further prosecute the suit for damages by plaintiffs pending against The Griff Company in the _____ District Court, County of _____ , State of _____ , and agree to execute a stipulation for dismissal with prejudice in said action insofar as The Griff Company is concerned.

Plaintiffs further covenant and expressly agree with the Settling Parties to forever refrain from instituting any other action or making any other demand or claims of any kind against said settling parties for damages sustained by them as a result of an accident which occurred on June 22, 19 ___ , in the village of _____ , _____ .

The aforesaid consideration is not intended as full compensation for damages claimed by plaintiffs arising from said accident. However, by this covenant, plaintiffs do hereby credit and satisfy that portion of the total amount of their damages from said accident which has been caused by the negligence, if any, of such Settling Parties hereto as may hereafter be determined to be the case in the further trial or other disposition of this or any other action. Plaintiffs do hereby release and discharge that fraction and portion and percentage of their total cause of action and claim for damages against all parties resulting from said accident which shall hereafter, by further trial or other disposition of this or any other action, be determined to be the sum of the portions or fractions or percentages of causal negligence for which any or all of the Settling Parties hereto are found to be liable.

By this settling agreement the Settling Parties are hereby discharged of their liability for contribution with respect to the claim for damages of plaintiffs resulting from said accident.

Plaintiffs reserve to themselves the balance of the whole cause of action which they may have against Lloyd Koesling as a result of said accident. This covenant is not entered into nor in any way intended to release any claim or cause of action by plaintiffs against Lloyd Koesling as a result of said accident.

Plaintiffs specifically agree to hold the Settling Parties harmless and specifically agree to indemnify them from any claim, demand, or cause of action by Lloyd Koesling for apportionment by way of contribution, whether such claim for contribution is alleged to arise by reason of judgment, settlement, or otherwise.

Plaintiffs will effect compliance with the provision of the last paragraph by settling and compromising any recovery which they might later obtain from Lloyd Koesling, whether or not arising from judgment, so that such recovery does not exceed the amount determined by application to total damages of plaintiffs of that proportion or fraction or percentage of causal negligence for which Lloyd Koesling may be found to be or considered to be liable and thereby eliminating any claim by Lloyd Koesling and his subrogees, insurers, assigns, or successors for equalizing contributions from the Settling Parties.

The Settling Parties in whose favor this covenant not to sue is executed, reserve and retain all claims and causes of action which they or any of them might have against others and, including without limiting the generality of the foregoing, any claim for contribution which they might have against Lloyd Koesling.

The payment of the consideration for this covenant is not to be construed as an admission, on the part of any of the Settling Parties, of any liability whatsoever in consequence of said accident, to plaintiffs or to any other party.

—*Continued*

■ **EXHIBIT 25.2**

Covenant Not to Sue, *Continued*

—Continued

This covenant is intended to release any claim for contribution against the Settling Parties in connection with said accident in the same manner and mode as the covenant and/or release before the court in the case of *Pierringer v. Hoger*, 21 Wis. 2d 182, 124 N.W.2d 106 (1963).

IN WITNESS WHEREOF I have hereunto set my hand and seal this _____ day of May, 19 ___ .

In presence of

_____

_____

_____
Daniel Trost

_____
Paul Trost

_____
Thomas E. Trost

STATE OF _____

COUNTY OF _____

} /s/

On this _____ day of May 19 ___ , before me personally appeared _____ to me known to be the persons described herein, and who executed the foregoing instrument and _____ acknowledged that _____ voluntarily executed the same.

_____
Notary Public

My term expires _____ , 19 ___ .

The reason for the loan is to keep the liability insurer from becoming the real party in interest for prosecuting the contribution action. In other words, the loan receipt device allows the first defendant (insurer) to prosecute an action for contribution in the name of the claimant. At times, that may seem to be the best trial strategy.

Loan receipt agreements can take many different forms and may be used in conjunction with other release agreements such as a release of a percentage of causal negligence. A loan receipt agreement is advantageous where the claimant and the settling tortfeasor are able to agree on the value of the claimant's claim, but feel a second tortfeasor is substantially responsible for the damage. If a loan receipt agreement is used alone, and not in conjunction with another release agreement, the lender is not protected against claims brought by other tortfeasors for contribution. On the other hand, the loan receipt device is ordinarily used only where the lender has paid most, if not all, the claimant's damages.

■ MARY CARTER AGREEMENTS

A **Mary Carter agreement** (from *Booth vs. Mary Carter Paint Co.*, 202 So.2d 8 [Fla. Dist. Ct. App. 1967]) is similar to the high-low and loan receipt agreements, with some important differences. A Mary Carter agreement is a secret or semisecret agreement between the claimant and one or more, but not all, of the tortfeasors. It provides that the settling party must remain in the lawsuit. In addition, the settling party can benefit from a verdict or judgment that is favorable to the claimant.

A Mary Carter release is made up of three elements:

1. A guarantee clause provides that the claimant will receive a guaranteed sum of money from the settling party even if the claimant loses or receives a recovery less than the guaranteed settlement amount. The claimant agrees to collect the amount of any verdict from a nonsettling tortfeasor. (In this situation, the settling party hopes the verdict will be larger than the amount she or he has guaranteed to pay.)

2. The settling party agrees to remain in the lawsuit until a judgment is reached or the claimant consents to its dismissal.

3. The settling party agrees to keep his or her agreement secret. In essence, the terms of the agreement are hidden from the knowledge of the court, the jury, and the nonsettling parties.

The third element, of secrecy, is the most complained-about aspect of Mary Carter agreements. Many people believe that such secrecy permits the claimant and the settling party to work together to the harm of the nonsettling parties. Element 2, requiring the settling parties to remain in the lawsuit, is a matter of concern to many commentators. It is felt that such arrangements pervert the adversarial system and amount to a fraud on the court.

In light of the secrecy attached to Mary Carter agreements, some state courts have held that they are illegal. However, it is usually permissible for settling parties to remain in the lawsuit as long the arrangements are not kept secret and the settlement agreement does not pervert the adversarial system.

■ CONSENT JUDGMENT AGAINST LIABILITY INSURER

A stipulated consent judgment is a unique settlement agreement. It is used only when a liability insurer has denied coverage to its insured or denied that the tortfeasor is an insured. The insurer's denial of coverage raises a coverage dispute. Too often, it is useless for the plaintiff to pursue a claim against the tortfeasor unless an insurance policy will pay the claim. The claimant may find it advantageous to work out an arrangement with the tortfeasor that protects the tortfeasor and at the same time allows the claimant to assume the right to manage the claim for insurance coverage. In this situation, a tortfeasor may escape personal liability by agreeing to allow the claimant to take a **consent judgment** against the tortfeasor. A consent judgment is not a default judgment. It establishes the defendant's liability to the claimant, and perhaps the amount of the plaintiff's damages. However, the agreement provides that the claimant may collect the judgment only from the proceeds of the liability insurance policy in question. After the consent judgment is entered, the claimant may bring a garnishment action against the liability insurer to establish that the policy does provide coverage for the claim.

At times, a stipulated consent judgment becomes a very practical means of proceeding for the plaintiff and the defendant. Suppose the plaintiff is a six year old who is injured while the defendant is baby-sitting with her. The defendant's personal liability insurer denies coverage on the grounds that the occurrence comes within the business exclusion found in most homeowner's insurance policies. The plaintiff's lawyer believes that the facts of the accident do not invoke the business exclusion. The defendant has no asset other than the insurance policy, to pay the plaintiff's claim. A stipulated consent judgment eliminates the necessity of a trial to establish the defendant's liability. With a judgment on the books against the defendant, the plaintiff may institute a garnishment action against the defendant's insurer. The defendant is then referred to as a judgment debtor. The claimant could bring an action on the policy and force the garnishee insurer to prove that its exclusion applies. The insurer has a right to challenge the reasonableness of the amount of the settlement in the garnishment action.

The consent judgment benefits the insurer by precluding the insured from prosecuting a bad faith action against the insurer for not settling the claim. Since the consent judgment protects the insured from any claim against her or his personal assets, the insured cannot be harmed by the insurer's refusal to settle the claim for the insured. Another benefit to the insurer is that if the plaintiff prevails on the insurance coverage issue, the insurer has avoided the expense of defending the insured in the tort action and the cost of the insured's attorneys' fees for a declaratory judgment action to determine coverage.[1] Also, the insurer benefits because the amount of the judgment creditor's recovery cannot exceed the amount of the insurance policy, so the insurer cannot be held liable for an excess verdict.

A consent judgment has some negative consequences for the insured, even though technically it is not enforceable against the insured. Some title insurance companies and mortgage companies do not appreciate the niceties of a consent judgment. They see the consent judgment as a cloud against the insured's title to any real estate the insured may own. Consequently, the insured should take steps to have the judgment book show that the judgment is satisfied as soon as the coverage issue is determined. Indeed, the terms of the agreement leading to the consent judgment should specify who will take the necessary action to obtain a satisfaction or cancellation of the consent judgment.

Unless the insurer has denied coverage, an insured violates the liability insurance policy's cooperation clause by entering into a stipulated judgment. A violation of the cooperation clause gives the insurer another coverage defense.

■ STRUCTURED SETTLEMENTS

Structured settlements are relatively new. They evolved from the need to provide periodic payments over a long period of time to individuals who might not be able to manage and/or conserve a large settlement. Structured settlements allow the tortfeasor to pay a lump sum of money to a bank or insurance company, which can issue to the claimant a customized annuity

---

1. In most states, when a liability insurance company brings an action to determine whether its policy covers the claim brought against its insured, the company is required to pay the costs and attorneys' fees its insured incurs, if the court determines that the policy does provide coverage.

that will provide scheduled benefits over a period of years or over the claimant's lifetime. Because the company that issues the annuity has the right to use or invest the money over the same period of time, the company can add significantly to the initial payment from the tortfeasor. Consequently, a settlement funded in the amount of fifty thousand dollars may result in payments over the claimant's lifetime totaling several hundred thousand dollars. In addition, the money the claimant receives is not subject to any income tax.

The structured settlement annuity must be purchased by the defendant, and the claimant must not be able to control the trustee's handling or investment of the funds. Otherwise, the settlement would lose its tax advantages: it would be the same as the claimant obtaining an award and proceeding to invest the money, and the interest earned on the *claimant's* monies is taxable as ordinary income. Customarily, a structured settlement is accompanied by the payment of additional monies used to cover past medical expenses, past lost wages, attorneys' fees, and litigation expenses. Despite the many benefits of structured settlements, most personal injury claims are still settled with a single lump sum payment.

■ SETTLEMENTS OF WRONGFUL DEATH ACTIONS

A wrongful death action must be prosecuted by a trustee appointed by the court. The trustee represents the decedent's heirs and next of kin. The trustee must apply for the office. When appointed, the trustee must provide a bond guaranteeing performance of his or her responsibilities. The trustee must act to represent the best interests of all persons who have an interest in the claim. If the representative is able to negotiate a settlement that he or she believes to be in everyone's best interests, the proposed settlement must be submitted to the court for approval. The court will then order how the money damages are to be allocated to the survivors. The court discharges the trustee only after a distribution of the settlement proceeds has been made.

■ MINORS' SETTLEMENTS

All states have laws that authorize parents and guardians to prosecute claims on behalf of their minor children. But the parents are not permitted to settle a child's claim without court approval. The statutes provide that no settlement or compromise of the action is valid unless it is approved by a judge of the court in which the action is pending. Most district courts have specific procedures for obtaining court approval of **minors' settlements.** If the procedures established by statute and court rules are followed, a release executed by a guardian on behalf of a minor is fully binding and enforceable against the minor. Though a minor cannot be bound by a release that she or he signed, the release may become valid and binding if it is ratified once the minor gains legal capacity.

■ RESCISSION OR CANCELLATION OF RELEASES

A release is merely a contract that settles the dispute between parties. A release may be rescinded (broken) if it was induced by fraud or if a mutual mistake was made concerning a significant term or condition of the release. Proving a mutual mistake requires challenging the language contained in the written release. Therefore, to avoid the release or to obtain reformation of the release, the claimant must present proof that is clear and convincing. Fraud in the inducement of the release is predicated upon conduct and statements that precede execution of the release and have nothing to do with the terms and conditions as set forth in the written document. Therefore, it can be proved by a mere preponderance of the evidence. The elements necessary to prove fraud are the same elements that apply to a cause of action in fraud.

With regard to a claim of mutual mistake, courts consider several circumstances in determining whether a release should be avoided:

1. The length of time between the injury and the settlement. (It is more likely that the parties did not really understand or appreciate the extent of the loss and the significance of the release if the settlement was made quickly.)

2. The amount of time that elapsed between the settlement and the attempt to avoid the settlement. (The longer the delay, the less sympathetic the courts are to the claim of mistake.)

3. The presence or absence of independent medical advice of the plaintiff's own choice before and at the time of settlement. (If the plaintiff did not have competent medical advice concerning the nature, extent, and effect of his or her injuries, the claim of mistake is probably well-founded.)

4. The presence or absence of legal counsel of the plaintiff's own choice before and at the time of settlement. (If the plaintiff had the advice of a lawyer concerning the terms of the release and concerning the settlement value, it is very difficult to claim a mistake.)

5. The language of the release itself.

6. The adequacy of the consideration paid for the release in light of the nature and extent of the injuries or other loss, and the chances of the settling party's being found liable for the accident.

7. The general competence of the releaser. The plaintiff's education and experience may be considered by the court.

8. Whether the injury claimed by the releaser was a known injury at the time the release was signed or a consequence flowing from an unknown injury.

Generally, only mistakes of fact permit avoidance. However, where a claimant is not represented by an attorney, and the tortfeasor's liability insurer undertakes to advise the claimant of her or his rights, a "fiduciary" type relationship may be established. Such a relationship could convert a mistake of law into a mistake of fact. Hence, the settlement between the parties may be voidable.

A release may also be avoided because of fraud, but such situations present difficult problems of proof for the claimant. Basically, the claimant must show that the person who procured the release made a material misrepresentation with the intent that the claimant would act upon that representation. In addition, the claimant must show that he or she did act in reliance upon the representation and consequently suffered damages.

■ OFFER OF JUDGMENT

In almost every case that goes to trial, the parties have conducted some settlement negotiations, but the negotiations were unsuccessful. Therefore, the parties have been forced to incur the expense of a trial. The prevailing party will be allowed to tax costs against the losing party. The defendant who is clearly liable to the plaintiff, but cannot reach a settlement with the plaintiff because the plaintiff's demands are excessive, is at a real disadvantage. Rule 68 provides some help. The rule allows the defendant to make a formal offer in writing to let judgment be taken against her or him for a specified amount. The **offer of judgment** must be made at least ten days before trial and must include an agreement to pay the plaintiff's taxable costs that have accrued to the date of the offer. An offer of judgment may be served by mail in accordance with Rule 5. The plaintiff has ten days in which to accept the offer of judgment. If service was by mail, the plaintiff has an additional three days in which to accept. If the offer of judgment is not accepted within the time limit, it is considered rejected. More time may be granted by the offeror. There is no limit on the number of offers of judgment the defendant may make.

An offer of judgment precludes the offeree from taxing costs against the offeror, unless the offeree obtains a judgment that is more favorable than the offer. Furthermore, the offeror may tax his or her costs against the offeree. An offer of judgment is not an offer to make an immediate payment of money. Therefore, even if the defendant does not have enough money to pay the judgment, he or she may still make the offer of judgment. As with settlement negotiations in general, neither the plaintiff nor the defendant may inform the jury about the offer of judgment.

If the offeree accepts the offer of judgment, either party may file the offer and acceptance with the clerk of court, along with the proofs of service. The clerk is authorized to enter judgment as provided in the offer of judgment. The lawsuit is concluded by the judgment. An offer of judgment cannot be made unless a civil action has already been commenced and is pending.

■ CONFESSION OF JUDGMENT

If the person against whom a claim is made recognizes the obligation but has no money or other means by which to satisfy the obligation, the laws of all states provide a method by which that person may make a **confession of judgment.** No lawsuit or other legal proceeding is needed. The obligor simply executes the necessary affidavits and forms, which authorize the clerk of court to enter a judgment pursuant to the parties' agreement.

A confession of judgment is binding only upon the parties to the agreement. It would not be binding upon the confessor's partners, spouse, heirs, assignees, or liability insurance company. The judgment remains a legally enforceable obligation for ten years, more or less, depending upon the laws of the particular state. The laws of most states impose some strict formalities to confessions of judgment, including the requirement that they be notarized by two witnesses. The confessor must be an adult for the confession to be valid.

DISMISSALS

A lawsuit may be concluded by entry of judgment or by a dismissal. If the parties' rights and obligations have been adjudicated by the court, they are propounded by the court's judgment. The judgment is prepared by the clerk of court pursuant to an order of the court and is made part of the clerk's permanent records. Judgments are discussed in greater detail in chapter 22.

A lawsuit may be terminated before a judgment is entered. Such a termination is called a dismissal. Three types of dismissals are used: court-ordered involuntary, voluntary unilateral, and stipulated. The procedures are controlled by Rule 41.

■ COURT-ORDERED DISMISSALS

If the plaintiff's case has a fatal defect, the court must order the case dismissed. For example, if the defendant were to prevail on any of the motions authorized by Rule 12, the court would enter an order dismissing the plaintiff's case. The court may also order a dismissal as a sanction where the plaintiff fails to comply with a valid court order, such as an order to permit discovery pursuant to Rule 37. A court may dismiss the plaintiff's case if the plaintiff has been dilatory in prosecuting the action. A court may order an involuntary dismissal if the plaintiff's evidence fails to prove a prima facie case of liability against the defendant. Courts may order involuntary dismissals on many other bases as well.

The effect of an order for dismissal is that the case is put to an end. Ordinarily, the dismissal does not result in entry of a judgment. However, if the plaintiff decides to appeal the court's decision to dismiss, the losing party will probably arrange to have judgment entered against herself or himself so that she or he can appeal from the judgment. A court order for dismissal is without prejudice, unless it specifically states that it is *with prejudice*. If the dismissal is without prejudice, the plaintiff can bring the lawsuit again and try to avoid the problem that led to a dismissal the first time. If the dismissal is with prejudice, the suit cannot be brought again; the case is res judicata.

■ VOLUNTARY DISMISSAL ON NOTICE

The plaintiff may voluntarily dismiss his or her claim. Rule 41(a)(1) imposes the following requirements:

> [A]n action may be dismissed by the plaintiff without order of the court (i) by filing a notice of dismissal at any time before service by the adverse party of an answer or of a motion for summary judgment, whichever first occurs, or (ii) by filing a stipulation of dismissal signed by all the parties who have ap-

peared in the action. Unless otherwise stated in the notice of dismissal or stipulation, the dismissal is without prejudice, except that a notice of dismissal operates as an adjudication upon the merits when filed by a plaintiff who has once dismissed in any court of the United States or of any state an action based on or including the same claim.

Though it is not expressly stated in the rule, the plaintiff should serve a copy of the **voluntary dismissal** upon the defendant. Many state courts allow the plaintiff to voluntarily dismiss upon notice at any time before the case is alerted for trial.

■ STIPULATED DISMISSAL

Parties are able to stipulate to a dismissal at any time on any terms. The **stipulated dismissal** may be the result of a settlement agreement and release, but not necessarily. A stipulated dismissal usually provides that all parties waive the right to recover costs from each other. A stipulated dismissal may be with or without prejudice. It should be very specific as to whether it is with or without prejudice.

Rule 41 provides, in part, as follows:

> [A]n action may be dismissed by the plaintiff without order of court by filing a stipulation of dismissal signed by all parties who have appeared in the action. Unless otherwise stated . . . in the stipulation, the dismissal is without prejudice.

If the parties fail to be specific, the rule presumes that the stipulation is without prejudice. Even though the rule specifies that the stipulation is to be signed by the parties, the rule is understood to authorize the parties' lawyers to sign the stipulation on behalf of the parties. Exhibit 25.3 illustrates a stipulation for dismissal.

The terms and conditions of the stipulated dismissal may be whatever the parties agree upon. If the parties have negotiated a settlement of their

■ EXHIBIT 25.3
Stipulation
for Dismissal

STATE OF MINNESOTA   DISTRICT COURT
COUNTY OF _____   _____ JUDICIAL DISTRICT

Georgia Watson,   Plaintiff, ⎱   STIPULATION FOR
        vs.   ⎰   DISMISSAL
Alvin Johanson,   Defendant. ⎰

The above-entitled action, having been fully compromised and settled,

NOW THEREFORE, it is stipulated and agreed, by and between the parties hereto, through their respective counsel, that said action may be and hereby is dismissed with prejudice and on the merits, but without further costs to any of the parties.

IT IS FURTHER STIPULATED AND AGREED that either party, without notice to the other, may cause judgment of dismissal with prejudice and on the merits to be entered herein.

_____
Attorney for Plaintiff

controversy and they stipulate to dismiss the case, the terms and conditions of the settlement need not be stated in dismissal.

SUMMARY

When the parties are able to agree upon a satisfactory resolution of their controversy without a court determination, they avoid uncertainty, gain economies, and obtain a disposition that they know they can live with, if not embrace. The effect of a settlement agreement is to release a cause of action. A release acts as a bar to the claim.

A release is a contract. It must comport with all the requirements of making a contract and is subject to all the defenses that apply to contracts.

A settlement agreement is not binding upon a minor unless a guardian obtains court approval of the agreement. Consequently, any party who must deal with a minor ordinarily insists upon negotiating through a guardian and having court approval of the agreement to settle.

A party who pays money to settle a disputed claim is said to have "bought her or his peace." Settlement agreements are used to resolve contract disputes and claims that arise from torts. A settlement agreement may provide for entry of a judgment that establishes the parties' rights and obligations between them.

The law favors settlements and settlement negotiations. Statements made in the course of settlement negotiations are deemed not to be relevant evidence and cannot be used against a party at trial. However, the information disclosed in settlement negotiations is not protected against discovery or use at trial. Therefore, some discretion must be used during settlement negotiations.

When the parties settle their dispute, they may establish their own criteria, terms, and conditions for concluding the dispute. They avoid expending time and money on litigation. They may have reasons for settling that have nothing to do with the merits of the claim or defenses.

The parties to a settlement agreement must have a meeting of the minds concerning the terms and conditions of their agreement. A meeting of the minds comes about through a process of offers, counteroffers, and acceptance. The process is commonly referred to as settlement negotiations.

A settlement must be voluntary and not the result of duress or undue influence. If a party threatens to inflict personal injury or property damage, that is an example of duress that would vitiate a settlement agreement. However, a party's desperate need for money or compelling desire to end the dispute, or another party's threat to end settlement negotiations, is not duress that would be a basis for avoiding a settlement agreement.

The terms of a settlement agreement must include an exchange of consideration. The consideration given for a release must be clearly stated. The most common forms of consideration are payment of money, and mutual promises to do something or to refrain from doing something. A promise of performance is consideration that will support a settlement contract, provided the promisor is not already under a legal compulsion to do what he or she has promised. Two promises constitute valid consideration, one for the other. The consideration must actually be paid or exchanged for the contract to be effective. A mere recital of payment is not effective. If the purported consideration has no value, the release is unenforceable for lack of consideration.

Settlement agreements do not have to be in writing. However, as a practical matter, they should be reduced to a writing so that no subsequent disagreement arises over the terms, scope, and limits of the settlement. The statute of frauds requires that all contracts that, by their terms, are not to be performed within one year from the date on which they are made, must be in writing and signed.

A release must identify the parties, the transaction or occurrence, the type of injury or damage claimed, the consideration, and any special conditions or limitations that are part of the settlement agreement. If the claim is for money, the money is ordinarily paid at the time the release is signed by the claimant. The party who is released need not sign the release. However, if the settlement agreement provides for a mutual release, both parties must sign. It is customary to have the claimant's signature witnessed and notarized. If the parties to a settlement agreement have a subsequent disagreement about the terms and conditions of the settlement agreement, a court will look to the writing to determine the parties' intent. If the court were to conclude that the written release is ambiguous, the court could receive parol evidence concerning the parties' intent, including evidence of the parties' negotiations.

In a general release the claimant agrees to release any and all claims that the claimant might then have against the person or persons released. A general release is calculated to put an end to all claims the claimant may have against the released party for all transactions and occurrences between them as of the date of the release.

A full and final release differs from a general release in that it applies only to a particular transaction or occurrence. The release should identify the transaction or occurrence by type, time, place, and claimed loss. The release protects not only the party who paid consideration for it, but anyone else who might be liable to the claimant.

A full and final release allows the settling party to prosecute an action against any other tortfeasor who did not pay for the release, because a full and final release protects all tortfeasors from being sued by the claimant. However, the tortfeasor remains liable to the tortfeasor who paid more than her or his fair share. The tortfeasor who seeks contribution from another tortfeasor must be able to show that she or he settled the claim under a legal compulsion (not as a volunteer), and paid more than her or his share. When the released party contemplates bringing an action against a third person for contribution, it is customary to add the word *assignment* to the title of the release: full and final release and assignment. Technically, however, it is not an assignment of a cause of action.

A tortfeasor may insist on obtaining a full and final release of all claims because by doing so, the settling party prevents the claimant from making a claim against others who, in turn, might bring a claim against the settling party for contribution.

Parties may combine the features of a general release and of a full and final release into one agreement.

Parties may enter into a settlement agreement that provides for only a partial release. A partial release may release only one of several causes of action or one of several tortfeasors or one of several claims or any combination of these. Partial releases are very common in jurisdictions that apply comparative fault in tort actions. When a case commences trial against a nonsettling defendant, the court tells the jury about the partial settlement, but the jury is not told about the amount of the settlement and is directed not to speculate about the reasons for the settlement. At the end of the trial, the court instructs the jurors that they must determine whether the settling defendant was negligent (at fault) and what percentage of causal negligence should be attributed to that defendant when determining the percentage of causal negligence to be attributed to the plaintiff and remaining defendants.

A partial release that releases one of several tortfeasors releases a percentage or fraction of the parties' combined causal negligence (fault). A partial release cannot be used to discharge one of two defendants when one of the two defendants is only vicariously liable. A full and final release of an agent's liability necessarily releases the principal if the principal did not commit any separate wrongful act.

The basic elements of a partial release that releases one of several tortfeasors are that (1) the claimant releases a settling wrongdoer from the action and discharges the part of the cause of action that the wrongdoer was responsible for; (2) the claimant reserves his or her cause of action against the nonsettling wrongdoers; (3) the claimant agrees to indemnify the settling tortfeasor from any claims that are brought against the settling party by the nonsettling parties for a contribution; and (4) the claimant agrees to satisfy any judgment obtained from the nonsettling party to the extent it includes any of the liability of the settling party. A partial settlement is somewhat of a gamble. The important consideration is that the settlement agreement be voluntary and not adversely affect the nonsettling defendant's rights.

In states that do not have comparative fault, juries are not asked to determine percentages of causal negligence. Each defendant who is found liable is liable equally with the other defendants. If there are two alleged tortfeasors, settlement with one discharges one-half of the recoverable damages—assuming that the jury determines the settling tortfeasor is partially liable. If there are three alleged tortfeasors, settlement with two discharges two-thirds of the recoverable damages. The claimant may give a partial release if the release expressly states that it is not to release anyone by the settling party.

A special workers' compensation release allows the employee who has received workers' compensation benefits to enter into a settlement with the tortfeasor without affecting the employer's subrogation rights. No monies are paid to the employer. The employer is left to pursue her or his own subrogation rights. The subrogation claim may be settled separately or go through a trial. The employee's partial settlement with the tortfeasor is valid, but it must not prejudice the employer's subrogation interests.

A tortfeasor may negotiate a settlement of the employer's workers' compensation subrogation claim and leave open the plaintiff employee's claim. The form of the partial release is similar to that used to settle the employee's claim.

A high-low release is an agreement in which the settling wrongdoer guarantees a minimum amount to be paid to the plaintiff, and also puts an upper limit on his or her potential liability. If the plaintiff wins but receives a verdict for less than the guaranteed amount, the settling defendant will pay to the plaintiff an additional amount to make the recovery equal the guarantee. Also, the claimant agrees that if the plaintiff wins a verdict against the nonsettling tortfeasors that equals or exceeds the guaranteed amount, the plaintiff will pursue collection remedies only against the nonsettling defendants, and no payment will be required from the settling defendant.

A covenant not to sue is not a release. It is a device that allows the plaintiff and one of two or more tortfeasors to resolve their dispute without compromising the plaintiff's cause of action against other tortfeasors. A covenant not to sue is a contract. The claimant agrees not to bring an action against the covenantee, or dismisses the pending action against the covenantee, but does not agree to release the claim or the covenantee. A covenant not to sue merely precludes the claimant form pursuing the claim against the covenantee. Since the cause of action remains in tact, the claimant may prosecute the claim against any other person who has liability to the claimant for the occurrence and injury.

A loan receipt agreement is a contract by which a tortfeasor, or her or his insurer, agrees to "loan" the claimant a specified sum of money, and the claimant agrees not to pursue her or his claim against the lender. Both believe that another party has substantial liability, and the claimant agrees to pursue the claim against that other party. The claimant agrees that if she or he recovers over a certain amount from the other party, she or he will repay all or part of the loan. If the claimant recovers little or nothing from the other party, the loan need not be repaid. Loan receipt agreements can take many different forms and may be used in conjunction with the other release agreements such as a release of a percentage of causal negligence.

A Mary Carter agreement is a secret or semisecret agreement between the claimant and one or more, but not all, of the tortfeasors. It provides that the settling party must remain in the lawsuit. In addition, the settling party can benefit from a verdict or judgment that is favorable to the claimant. These secret agreements are invalid in many states.

A stipulated consent judgment is used only when a liability insurer has denied coverage to its insured or denied that the tortfeasor is an insured. The insurer's denial of coverage raises a coverage dispute. The claimant may find it advantageous to work out an arrangement with the tortfeasor that protects the tortfeasor and at the same time allows the claimant to assume the right to manage the claim for insurance coverage. In this situation, a tortfeasor may escape personal liability by agreeing to allow the claimant to take a consent judgment against the tortfeasor. The judgment establishes the defendant's liability to the claimant, and perhaps the amount of the plaintiff's damage. However, the agreement provides that the claimant may collect the judgment only from the proceeds of the liability insurance policy in question. After the consent judgment is entered, the claimant may bring a garnishment action against the liability insurer to establish that the policy does provide coverage for the claim. The insurer benefits from a consent judgment because the judgment creditor cannot recover more than the amount of the insurance policy, so the insurer cannot be held liable for an excess verdict. An insured violates a liability policy's cooperation clause by entering into a stipulation for a consent judgment, unless the insurer has denied coverage. An insured's violation of the cooperation clause gives an insurer grounds for withdrawing coverage.

Structured settlements allow a tortfeasor to pay a lump sum of money to a bank or insurance company that provides scheduled benefits to the claimant over a period of years or over the claimant's lifetime. Because the company that issues the annuity has the right to use or invest the money over the same period of time, the company can add significantly to the initial payment from the tortfeasor. Consequently, a settlement funded in the amount of fifty thousand dollars may result in payments over the claimant's lifetime totaling several hundred thousand dollars. In addition, the money the claimant receives is not subject to any income tax. The structured settlement annuity must be purchased by the defendant, and the claimant must not be able to control the trustee's handling or investment of the funds; otherwise, the settlement would lose its tax advantages.

A wrongful death action must be prosecuted by a trustee appointed by the court. When a trustee settles the claim with a tortfeasor, the trustee must apply to the court for approval of the settlement. The court then determines how to allocate the proceeds to the decedent's heirs and next of kin. The court will not discharge the trustee until the settlement proceeds have been distributed.

Parents are not permitted to settle their children's claims without court approval. Most trial courts have specific procedures for obtaining court approval of minors' settlements. If the procedures provided by law are followed, a release executed by a guardian on behalf of a minor is fully binding and enforceable against the minor. Although a minor's release that is not court-approved cannot bind a minor, the release may become binding if it is ratified once the minor gains legal capacity.

A release may be rescinded (broken) if it was induced by fraud or if a mutual mistake was made concerning a significant term or condition of the release. The elements necessary to prove fraud are the same elements that apply to a cause of action in fraud.

Rule 68 allows a defendant to make a formal offer in writing to let judgment be taken against him or her for a specified amount. The offer of judgment must be made at least ten days before trial and must include an agreement to pay the plaintiff's taxable costs that have accrued to the date of the offer. The plaintiff has at least ten days in which to accept the offer of judgment. If the offer of judgment is not accepted within the time limit, it is considered rejected. More time may be granted by the offeror. There is no limit on the number of offers of judgment the defendant may make. An offer of judgment precludes the offeree from taxing costs against the offeror, unless the offeree obtains a judgment that is more favorable than the offer. Furthermore, the offeror may tax his or her costs against the offeree. Neither the plaintiff nor the defendant may inform the jury about the offer of judgment.

The person against whom a claim is made may avoid a lawsuit by confessing judgment. To confess judgment the obligor must execute the necessary affidavits and forms, which authorize the clerk of court to enter a judgment pursuant to the parties' agreement. Of course, a confession of judgment is binding only upon the person who confessed to the agreement. The judgment remains a legally enforceable obligation for as long as provided by the laws of the state in which the judgment is filed.

A lawsuit may be terminated before a judgment is entered. Such a termination is called a dismissal. Three basic types of dismissals are used:

court-ordered involuntary, voluntary unilateral, and stipulated. The procedures are controlled by Rule 41. If a dismissal is without prejudice, the plaintiff can bring the lawsuit again and try to avoid the problem that led to dismissal the first time. If the dismissal is without prejudice, the suit cannot be brought again; the case is res judicata.

KEY TERMS

general release	consent judgment
full and final release	structured settlement
partial releases	minors' settlements
high-low release	offer of judgment
covenant not to sue	confession of judgment
loan receipt agreement	voluntary dismissal
Mary Carter agreement	stipulated dismissal

REVIEW QUESTIONS

1. What are some of the advantages the parties obtain by settling their case before trial?

2. Why should a settlement agreement and release be reduced to writing?

3. When is court approval of a settlement agreement necessary to make the agreement effective?

4. How does a covenant not to sue differ from a release?

5. Why are releases favored by the law?

6. In a comparative fault state, what kind of a release would a claimant propose for settling the claim against one defendant when several defendants are jointly liable?

7. If the parties' stipulation for a voluntary dismissal fails to state whether the dismissal is with prejudice, what effect will a court give to the dismissal?

8. What advantages may the defendant obtain by making an offer of judgment to the plaintiff?

9. Under what circumstances might the claimant and the tortfeasor agree that the tortfeasor should stipulate that a consent judgment may be entered against him or her?

10. Why would parties consider entering into a high-low agreement?

ARBITRATION AND MEDIATION

■ CHARACTERISTICS OF ADR METHODS

Arbitration and mediation are alternatives to civil litigation for resolving disputes. The underlying concepts are as old as civilization. Parties arbitrate a dispute when they contract (agree) to submit the matter (dispute) to one or more **arbitrators** (persons who will decide the matter for them). The presumption is that the arbitrators will act independently, fairly, and objectively. An arbitration has no basis unless the parties agree to it. The agreement to arbitrate must have the elements of a contract in order to be binding upon the parties. A contract to arbitrate does not have to be in writing, but it must involve an offer; an acceptance; a meeting of the minds on the essential terms; and an exchange of consideration—usually mutual promises. The parties' contract to arbitrate may provide for **binding arbitration** or **nonbinding arbitration.**

When parties mediate a dispute they merely agree to have a third person act as a neutral guide and facilitate their negotiations. The parties retain control over the result. The parties arrive at an agreement of their own making. The mediator's role is to counsel, advise, and push toward a wise resolution. It may be a compromise or a new quid pro quo undertaking. The parties must have faith that the mediator is empathetic to both sides. A mediator facilitates the parties' communications. A mediator may keep the parties separated to prevent them from creating barriers to the negotiations. A mediator may bring some special quality to the process by being a respected expert in the field, jurist, or government official. Suppose two merchants in a small town have a dispute and both happen to have the same banker. They might agree to meet with the banker to obtain her advice about how they should resolve the problem. The banker would be a mediator, a facilitator. She would probably try very hard to not to show favoritism. Her objective would be to persuade the parties to make a wise settlement that maintains harmony in the community. A wise settlement is one that the parties can accept for the foreseeable future.

Unlike a dispute in civil litigation, one in arbitration or mediation does not have to be based upon a claim of the type that courts will handle. Arbitrators do not have to be judges or even learned in the law. Persons who present evidence and make arguments to arbitrators need not be lawyers. Therefore, a paralegal may handle any aspect of an arbitration proceeding, including acting as an arbitrator, presenting evidence, and arguing for an award in favor of a client. Furthermore, a paralegal may represent a party as an advocate in negotiations that use a mediator. The Uniform Arbitration Act,[1] section 6, expressly provides that any party has a right to be represented by an attorney at law. Nevertheless, even states that have adopted the Uniform Act do not exclude non-lawyers from participation.

At least forty states have adopted the Uniform Arbitration Act. The remaining states have statutes that are variations on the act. This act provides rules for conducting arbitration proceedings and defines the role of the civil justice system to support arbitration.

Courts are encouraging arbitration and mediation as methods of alternative dispute resolution. This is an interesting development because the common law found arbitration agreements to be contrary to public policy, since such agreements might deprive a party of legal rights. Historically, courts were reluctant to enforce contracts to arbitrate. Today, many courts use arbitration as an ancillary procedure to complement their handling of cases. Parties are even encouraged to stipulate to binding arbitration and to use binding arbitration instead of a trial. Arbitration is often cheaper, quicker, and more private than civil litigation. Arbitration usually produces reasonable results, albeit not the results a court would order.

Usually arbitration is a voluntary undertaking. However, many states have enacted statutes that mandate arbitration of certain types of disputes, such as no-fault automobile insurance claims, underinsured motorist claims, and uninsured motorists claims. An arbitrator cannot handle probate matters, divorce, adoption, child custody, or real estate title issues because the public has an interest in the proper disposition of such matters. A contract to arbitrate an illegal contract dispute is unenforceable. For example, if the parties agreed to arbitrate a dispute over a gambling debt and then one reneged, the reneger could not be compelled to arbitrate.

◼ TERMS AND DEFINITIONS

A dispute that is placed into arbitration is often called the **matter.** The party who makes the claim for arbitration is usually referred to as the **petitioner.** The arbitrator or arbitrators may be referred to as the **arbitration tribunal.** The defending party is commonly described as the respondent. The tribunal's decision is usually described as the **arbitration award.** The contract to arbitrate is often called the arbitration agreement.

◼ ARBITRATION

The purpose of civil litigation is to resolve disputes correctly—according to established rules of law and legal standards. The primary objective of

1. The Uniform Arbitration Act is a model code prepared by legal scholars. It has been adopted in many states subject to various modifications.

arbitration is simply to obtain a reasonable resolution. To that end, the arbitration tribunal determines the facts without being constrained by rules of evidence. The tribunal makes an award without the limitations of legal causes of action, legal measures of damages, legal remedies, legal precedent, or rules of law. Although the parties may expect that the tribunal will follow the law, the arbitrators' misunderstanding of the law or misapplication of the law is not grounds for setting aside an award that results from that misunderstanding. The goal is to bring the dispute to a conclusion on an evenhanded basis, consistent with the parties' scope of submission. (The scope of submission is the parties' prescription to the tribunal designating the extent and limits of the tribunal's authority.) Consequently, neither party has a right to appeal an arbitration award to a higher authority, except when the tribunal has exceeded its authority or engaged in fraud, or the prevailing party perpetrated a fraud. Court decisions are more predictable than arbitration awards, and less dependent upon the predilections of the arbitrator. Parties should think about these ramifications when they consider whether to submit to arbitration. Also, the arbitrators often charge substantial fees for their services.

The law does not require parties to arbitrate. Parties can be forced to arbitrate only if they previously entered into a contract to do so—the law will enforce such a contract as it does any other contract. A contract to arbitrate may be made before or after the dispute arises. The parties may contract to binding arbitration or to make the arbitration award merely advisory. An advisory award is non-binding. It may or may not be accepted by both parties. A non-binding award does have value. The award tells the parties whether their positions are reasonable. The award may help the parties to agree upon a compromise settlement.

The law does not require contracts to arbitrate to be in writing. However, in states that have adopted the Uniform Arbitration Act, written contracts to arbitrate are construed in light of that act. Therefore, if the contract to arbitrate has failed to provide guidance on how to manage some aspect of the arbitration, the arbitrators or the court may look to the Uniform Arbitration Act to supplement the contract or to help construe the contract. Agreements to arbitrate commonly incorporate by reference the provisions of the Uniform Arbitration Act.

Many organizations encourage their members to resolve differences through arbitration. For example, many lawyers' associations encourage their members to submit fee disputes to arbitration. Automobile manufacturers ask dissatisfied customers to arbitrate disputes concerning the merchantability of the product and concerning repair costs. Agreements to arbitrate are often included in employment, construction, insurance, collective bargaining, and real estate sales contracts.

Where the parties have a contract to arbitrate, but the plaintiff elects to commence a civil suit regardless, the civil action will be allowed unless the defendant raises the right to arbitrate as an affirmative defense. If the right to arbitrate is shown, the court will dismiss the civil action.

Scope of Submission

A contract to arbitrate must define the **scope of submission.** The scope of the parties' submission identifies the scope of the arbitrators' authority. The arbitrators' authority is similar in concept to a court's jurisdiction over the parties and over the subject matter. The scope of submission should clearly identify the transaction or occurrence to which the agreement applies. It should identify the problem that has arisen or that is anticipated. It should instruct the arbitration tribunal concerning the relief or remedy that it may award and provide whatever standards or measures the parties want the tribunal to apply. The parties may agree upon amendments to the scope of submission, and the tribunal is bound by the parties' amendments.

If a dispute arises over whether the parties have a contract to arbitrate, either party may take the issue to a court that has jurisdiction over the parties, and ask the court to decide whether a contract was made. If the parties agree that they have a contract to arbitrate, but dispute the scope of the arbitrators' authority or the scope of submission, either party may apply to a court to determine the scope. Otherwise, an arbitration tribunal would have absolute authority, and courts cannot permit that. Consider the situation where the XYZ Corporation sells many drill presses to the Star Tool Company, and the two firms have a contract to arbitrate any dispute that arises between them concerning the quality and performance of the product. At one point, Star Tool buys some machine parts from a corporation that is a subsidiary of XYZ, and alleges that most of the parts are defective. Star Tool demands to arbitrate the matter in accordance with the arbitration agreement; Star Tool believes that the agreement made by XYZ applies to its subsidiary, and did business with the subsidiary on that assumption. The Uniform Arbitration Act, section 2, provides that Star Tool may make a motion to a court having jurisdiction over the subsidiary corporation, for an order compelling the subsidiary corporation to submit to arbitration. When Star Tool makes the motion, the subsidiary denies the existence of an agreement to arbitrate. Therefore, the court must have a trial to determine the existence of the agreement or its application to the subsidiary.

The Uniform Arbitration Act provides that the court shall determine the issue in a *summary* manner. In other words, the case shall be accelerated on the trial calendar for an early determination. The court should allow the parties to conduct some discovery if reasonably needed. The court should limit the amount of discovery to prevent any delay and to keep costs low. Discovery should be limited to the existence of the contract to arbitrate. The court has authority to enjoin an arbitrator from proceeding with the arbitration pending the court's determination. The only issue for the court, at that point, is whether a binding agreement to arbitrate exists. The subsidiary corporation cannot argue to the court that the court should deny arbitration on the grounds that Star Tool's claim lacks merit.

Suppose that instead of asking for arbitration, Star Tool sues the subsidiary corporation for money damages, claiming a breach of contract because the parts were defective, and the subsidiary corporation defends against the suit by alleging that the parties must arbitrate under the agreement with XYZ. The allegation of the right to arbitrate will be raised in the subsidiary corporation's answer as an affirmative defense. Either party will have the right to move the court to determine the issue of arbitrability in a summary fashion, as a separate matter. If the court concludes that the contract with XYZ applies, the court will order the parties to arbitrate and to stay (put on hold) or dismiss the civil action. If the court concludes that no contract to arbitrate exists, the civil action will proceed and the affirmative defense will be stricken.

Arbitration Procedures

The contract to arbitrate should state how many arbitrators the tribunal shall have. The tribunal may be composed of just one arbitrator or many; the most common numbers are one or three. When more than one arbitrator sits on the tribunal, a mere majority may make the award, unless the contract to arbitrate requires unanimity or more than a majority.

The contract should state how the arbitrators are to be selected. The most common method is for each party to nominate one arbitrator, and the two nominees select a third person, who is often called the neutral arbitrator. The Uniform Arbitration Act, section 3, provides that where the parties cannot agree on the selection of an arbitrator or arbitrators, the court may appoint the tribunal for them. The court must construe the parties' agreement and follow it in making the selection. If the agreement fails to specify a method of appointment or is unintelligible or cannot be followed, the court may appoint one or more arbitrators for the parties. Suppose a contract between a school district and the local teachers' union provides for arbitration of a wage dispute, and that each party may nominate one arbitrator and the two nominees must select another. If the two nominees cannot agree on a third, the parties may move a court to appoint the third.

The arbitration tribunal must provide a reasonable notice of the time and place of the hearing, so that all parties have an opportunity to be heard. To the extent that the scope of submission does not delineate how the hearing is to be conducted, the tribunal has broad authority to make its own rules. Unless state law specifically requires that they do so, arbitrators do not have to take an oath of office. Ordinarily, the proceedings are not recorded. Therefore, if any problem develops that requires court intervention, the problem has to be shown by way of affidavits from persons who were in attendance. Each party must be given an opportunity to present evidence to support that party's position and to challenge the opposing party's evidence. If the parties' scope of submission provides that neither side will present live testimony, the tribunal is not permitted to receive testimony. In that event, the evidence must be in the form of documents, like a motion for summary judgment. The tribunal is without authority to make an award until a full hearing has taken place.

Disadvantages and Advantages of Arbitration

When parties agree to arbitrate their dispute, they waive some protection and some benefits afforded by the civil justice system. The arbitration tribunal is not bound to follow rules of law. Therefore, if a party has based his or her position on some rule of law, the tribunal's election not to apply that rule is not grounds for avoiding the arbitration award. If a party seriously questions the truth of the opposing party's evidence, arbitration may offer less opportunity to challenge the evidence by cross-examination. Technical defenses have less appeal and application in arbitration. Arbitrators who have not had judicial experience tend to seek compromise solutions. The arbitration tribunal has no power to add another person as a party even if the participation of the other person is necessary to be able to conclude the whole controversy. Agreements to arbitrate seldom provide for discovery of the type authorized by court rules of civil procedure; discovery is one complication and expense that the parties ordinarily seek to avoid by agreeing to arbitrate.

A number of attributes make arbitration attractive as an alternative to civil litigation. The parties do not have to wait for the tribunal, because the tribunal is ready to proceed as soon as the parties are ready; the tribunal does not have other matters pending. Arbitration is less formal. Arbitration is less bound by rules of procedure, rules of evidence, and rules of law. Consequently, the parties' preparation for an arbitration hearing is less extensive and less involved. The parties' presentation of evidence is less cumbersome and less expensive. The parties may agree to submit their respective versions of the facts through affidavits, summaries, and experts' reports. They may elect to present their arguments in written form or orally. The parties may select remedies not afforded by courts.

Arbitration Hearing

The parties' agreement may describe the procedure for the hearing. However, to the extent that the agreement fails to specify some aspect of the procedure, the arbitrators control the procedure. In that context, the tribunal must select the time and place for the hearing. The notice of the hearing may be given by mail; the Uniform Arbitration Act requires certified mail. The arbitrators may order a postponement, continuances, or recesses as they deem appropriate. If the notice was proper, the arbitrators may proceed with the hearing and make an award even though a party fails to appear. That party is considered to be in default and waives her or his right to object to any aspect of the proceedings, except to the scope of submission and fraud.

The Uniform Arbitration Act, section 7, authorizes duly constituted arbitration tribunals to issue subpoenas to compel witnesses to attend the hearing. The subpoenas may be obtained from the local court upon due showing that the matter is pending. A subpoena must be served in the manner provided for by the court's rules of civil procedure, which will be similar to Rules 4 and 45 of the Federal Rules of Civil Procedure. The tribunal must be able to administer oaths to the witnesses. The evidence must be taken under oath. If a person fails to comply with a subpoena, the arbitration tribunal cannot discipline that person. The parties or the tribunal must apply to the court that issued the subpoena and ask the court to take action against the recalcitrant witness. Whenever a party serves a subpoena upon a person to attend an arbitration hearing or a deposition, the party must pay the person the witness fee and mileage authorized by statute.

Parties do not have a right to conduct discovery, in the absence of an express agreement allowing discovery. They cannot serve interrogatories or demand records or require inspections. They cannot compel another party to undergo an independent medical examination. If some *item* of discovery is necessary, the party must make a motion to the tribunal for leave to do the discovery. The discovery will be limited to the one inquiry and the one item. Parties do have the right to take the deposition of a witness for the purpose of presenting the witness's testimony in deposition form.

As a general rule, arbitrators do not take an oath. However, when arbitration is mandated by statute, as where some insurance claims must be arbitrated, the law may impose an oath such as the following:

> I will act in good faith and with integrity and fairness.
>
> I have disclosed to the parties prior to this hearing any interest or relationship likely to affect impartiality or which might create an appearance of partiality or bias.

This statement highlights the expectation parties have for their arbitrators.

The Uniform Arbitration Act provides that the arbitrators have authority to administer an oath to witnesses who appear before the tribunal. The oath is an important safeguard. A person who violates the oath is subject to criminal prosecution for perjury.

Parties who appear are entitled to present evidence. The party who has the burden of proof, usually the petitioner, must present his or her evidence first. The Uniform Arbitration Act expressly preserves the right of cross-examination in the manner of civil actions. The arbitrators have the authority to rule on objections to evidence. However, if the evidence offered is reasonably appropriate for the tribunal to consider, tribunals are prone to hear the evidence. Consequently, objections are sometimes a matter of posturing or for pointing out the weaknesses of the evidence. If the tribunal has more than one arbitrator, the tribunal must decide how it will handle and rule on objections. The respondent must wait until the petitioner rests, to present evidence. The petitioner has a right to present rebuttal evidence, and so does the respondent. When the parties complete their presentations, the tribunal declares that the matter is "submitted." Neither side may present evidence after the submission.

If more than one arbitrator sits on the tribunal, all arbitrators must attend the entire hearing. The reason is that the decision process requires all the arbitrators to hear the evidence and participate in the tribunal's deliberations. Their input is considered essential to the process. Their input and the opportunity to change the mind of other arbitrators is as important as their vote. Therefore, if one arbitrator of three is absent, the hearing cannot proceed. The parties could write a new contract to arbitrate, and choose to have one fewer arbitrator. Otherwise, the hearing is a nullity if even one arbitrator misses any part of the hearing.

Arbitration Award

The arbitration award is the tribunal's decision. It must be made within the time specified in the contract to arbitrate or, if no time is specified, within a reasonable time. The law does not impose a certain time period. The award may be unanimous or by a simple majority, unless the agreement to arbitrate provides otherwise. The award must be in writing, but it need not be stated in any particular form. The award need not state the reasons for the award. It need not be notarized. It must make clear the matters decided, and should reflect the authority by which it was made. This is important so that the award can be filed with a court and converted into a court judgment where that is possible. The award must be signed by all the arbitrators who concur in it. A dissenting arbitrator need not sign and is at liberty to submit a statement of dissent to the parties.

The award must comply with the scope of submission. It should be complete on its face. It should appear from the award that nothing remains to be decided. If the award is incomplete, it may nevertheless be enforced insofar as it is within the scope of submission, but an award that is substantively incomplete is voidable. If the award goes beyond the scope of submission, the part of the award that is within the scope of submission is binding and enforceable.

If the award requires the parties to take some action, the procedure should be made clear; an award should not leave the parties with any calculations to make. The award is binding on the parties and anyone who is in privity with the parties. The award need not be filed with any court, unless the prevailing party wants to use it as the basis for obtaining a court judgment.

If the tribunal fails to make the award within a reasonable time, the parties may apply to a court for an order compelling the tribunal to make the award. The court may order the tribunal to issue the award by a certain date. If the tribunal fails to make the award within the time provided by the arbitration agreement or within the time ordered by the court, a party may deliver an objection to the tribunal members. The objection has the effect of disqualifying the tribunal from making any award. The rationale for this rule is that after an unreasonable delay, the arbitrators have probably forgotten the evidence and arguments of the parties, so the delay has impaired the validity of the process. If a party fails to object to a delay until after the award is made, that party waives the right to object to the delay. A party may not wait to see if the award is favorable, and if it is not, then object.

The arbitrators may deliver the award in person or send it to the parties by certified mail (Uniform Arbitration Act, section 8). The award must be of the type authorized by the agreement to arbitrate. Suppose two companies agree to arbitrate a claimed patent infringement. The scope of the submission is for the tribunal to determine whether an infringement occurred and if so, what the petitioner's money damages are. The tribunal decides an infringement occurred and awards some minor amount of money damages, but also awards the infringing party a license to use the patent in the future. The tribunal's award exceeds its authority. Insofar as the tribunal acts outside its authority, the award is invalid and may be set aside by a court.

Modifications of an Arbitration Award

If one or both of the parties believe the award contains a clerical error, such as a misdescription or miscalculation, a party may apply to the tribunal for clarification. A party may apply for a modification of the award on the grounds that the tribunal has exceeded the scope of submission. To the extent that the tribunal has exceeded its authority, it should grant the modification. A party may ask the tribunal to reword the award where the language or form creates some collateral problem for the party, but the change in wording would not affect the substance of the award.

The application for modification must be made within twenty days after the award is delivered to the party. The party who applies for a modification must serve a copy of the application on the other party. Otherwise, the right to object is waived. If application for modification is duly made, the opposing party has a right to serve and deliver an objection to modification. The objection must be delivered to the tribunal within ten days.

The Uniform Arbitration Act, section 13, authorizes either party to apply to a court within ninety days of the delivery of the award to that party, for a correction or modification of the award on the same grounds as those used for applying to a tribunal. A party could resort to asking a court for the correction or modification where the arbitrators are no longer available or where the time for applying to the arbitrators has expired or where the arbitrators have refused to make the correction. Why would the arbitrators ever refuse to make corrections that should be made? They might use the refusal as leverage to force payment of their bill for services. A motion to correct or modify an award limits the court's authority to that of giving effect to the tribunal's intent. A court does not have authority to change the substance or effect of the award.

Vacating an Arbitration Award

Either or both parties have a right to move a court to vacate the arbitration award on the following grounds:

1. The award was procured by corruption, fraud, or other undue means.

2. An arbitrator appointed as a neutral was partial, or any of the arbitrators was corrupt, or misconduct prejudicing the rights of any party occurred.

3. The arbitrators exceeded their powers.

4. The arbitrators refused to postpone the hearing even though sufficient cause was shown to justify a postponement, or refused to hear evidence material to the controversy, or otherwise conducted the hearing contrary to provisions of the Uniform Arbitration Act so as to prejudice substantial rights of a party.

5. No arbitration agreement existed, *and* the issue was not adversely determined in proceedings under the Uniform Arbitration Act, section 2, and the party did not participate in the arbitration hearing without raising the objection.

A **motion to vacate the award** must be made within ninety days after the award is delivered to the party. If the award is delivered to the parties on different days, the time period differs accordingly. When the ground for vacating the award is fraud or corruption, the ninety-day period does not begin to run until the party discovers the fraud or corruption or has reason to know about it. A motion to vacate may be combined with a motion to modify the award. The motion must be served upon the opposing party in the manner in which the state court allows a summons and complaint to be served. In other words, the methods of service are those applicable in the state court and are similar to Rule 4 of the Federal Rules of Civil Procedure.

If a court vacates an award, the court shall order a new arbitration hearing before new arbitrators. The court does not usurp the parties' agreement to arbitrate. Instead, it acts to enforce the agreement. The new arbitrators must be chosen in the manner provided by the agreement to arbitrate. If no agreement existed, the court may appoint the new arbitrator or arbitrators, or direct how the new arbitrators shall be selected by the parties. For example, the court could prepare a list of five persons and order that the parties each take two strikes, leaving one person who will be their arbitrator.

Unless the scope of submission provides otherwise, the award may determine which party is to pay the arbitrators' fees and expenses. The award may divide the fees and expenses between the parties. However, the tribunal is not authorized to award attorneys' fees to either party (Uniform Arbitration Act, section 10).

Enforcement of an Arbitration Award

A tribunal's arbitration award is not, in itself, enforceable against a party. If a party refuses to comply voluntarily with the terms of the award, the prevailing party may move the court to confirm the award. A **motion to confirm the award** must state that the arbitration was duly conducted and the award duly made. The moving party must attach to the motion a copy of the arbitration agreement, a copy of the arbitration award, and a copy of any modifications or corrections. If no objection is made or the opposing party's objections are overruled, the court adopts the award and orders an entry of judgment in the same words or to the same effect as the arbitration award. The clerk of court enters the award upon the court's judgment book. At that point the prevailing party has a civil judgment that may be enforced like any other judgment. The motion to confirm the arbitration award must be served upon the opposing party in the same manner that a summons and complaint may be served upon a defendant.

Arbitrators' Judicial Immunity

Arbitration is a quasi-judicial undertaking. Arbitrators have to exercise judgment in deciding how the dispute should be resolved. They should not labor under the pressure that if they decide the matter in a certain way, they will be sued by a disgruntled party. Therefore, the law provides that arbitrators cannot be sued for malfeasance in the performance of their duties. They have no civil liability for alleged negligence or even fraud. Proof of fraud on the part of an arbitrator is a basis for having the award set aside, but will not subject the arbitrator to personal liability. However, an arbitrator who has committed fraud is not entitled to compensation for his or her services.

Arbitrators' Compensation

The agreement to arbitrate usually provides how the parties will pay the arbitrators for their service. If no agreement exists, the arbitrators may determine, as part of the award, how the parties shall pay the fees.

■ MEDIATION

Mediation is a voluntary arrangement in which the parties to a dispute select a mediator to help them negotiate a freewill settlement. The mediator has no power to require the parties to settle and no power to do anything that might force a settlement.

The parties may enter into a written contract to mediate. The purpose of the contract is to provide in advance an understanding about the purpose of the mediation, its limits, and how it will be conducted. For example, it is a good opportunity for the parties to agree on how the mediator will be paid. The contract may provide a method of declaring that the mediation is ended. A mediator may insist upon a written contract that acknowledges that the mediator has no personal liability or responsibility to obtain a certain result.

A mediator may play many roles in a mediation. The mediator may be a go-between who delivers messages between the parties. Sometimes a go-between is essential because the parties or their lawyers simply cannot communicate without being offensive or creating barriers. A mediator may have experience and wisdom concerning the matters that gave rise to the dispute. For example, two lawyers who are dissolving their partnership may have some disputes about dividing the business, clients, and so forth. They may look to a third lawyer who has had a similar experience and whom they both respect, to mediate their matter. They need someone who can share and advise. A mediator may serve as an expert and adviser. Suppose an architect and a contractor who are constructing a bridge have a dispute they want to resolve. They may need someone who can understand the problem from both perspectives, someone who can communicate with them, someone who can see the big picture and is able to propose creative alternative solutions. Sometimes the parties need to listen to someone for whom they have great respect but who will play the role of a devil's advocate without being offensive.

The mediator's job does not end when the parties "shake hands." The settlement agreement should be reduced to a writing. The written settlement agreement may require additional documents, such as a release or revision of an existing contract, or a confession or judgment, or whatever. The mediator should remain involved, or at least available, until the concluding documents are executed and filed. Questions may continue to arise. The parties may even end up disagreeing about the meaning or application of the settlement agreement.

Mediation has very little to do with legal concepts and even less to do with legal procedures. Nevertheless, there is the underlying presumption that the parties have a right to have their matter resolved according to the law. If the mediator has a good idea how the matter would be handled and resolved in a court of law, that insight might be useful in giving the parties direction for a settlement. But the mediator does not look to legal processes to determine the underlying facts. Instead, the mediator has to assume that each side has some basis for the position it takes. The mediator usually does not challenge a party's claim about the evidence that is available. Neither side presents any evidence in a mediation. The mediator may look to solutions not provided by the law to resolve a dispute. For example, sometimes the mediator can obtain for a party an apology that is worth more than the money a court could award.

When parties enter into mediation, they must be open to modifying their positions and receptive to suggestions, or they will waste their time trying to mediate. A party should not enter mediation with the idea that the other side will come around to her or his point of view, or that the mediator will end up being on her or his side.

Parties enter into mediation because some compromise is possible and each is willing to reexamine his or her position, listen to suggestions, and perhaps give up a little more than the party wants to give. The value of mediation is that the parties can pursue it as soon as the disagreement becomes manifest. The sooner a matter is mediated the better. The parties can avoid the expense of litigation. Even arbitration is more expensive and more time-consuming. The mediator should not let discussions become encumbered with details. If the parties need to conduct discovery and get evidence and prove facts before they can adjust their differences, mediation is not the course for them.

Anyone who expects to engage in mediation should study the principles and advice in *Getting to Yes (Negotiating Agreement without Giving In)*, 2nd ed., by Roger Fisher and William Ury (New York: Penguin Books USA, 1991).

SUMMARY

Arbitration and mediation are alternatives to civil litigation for resolving private disputes. They are commonly referred to as ADR. ADR is a shortcut to dispute resolution. It is generally faster and more economical. ADR is concerned more with obtaining a resolution that is reasonable than with obtaining a resolution that is correct on the facts and on the law. Mediation is most useful when the dispute is new and the parties have not spent time and effort to buttress their positions.

Paralegals may handle any aspect of the mediation and arbitration processes. A person does not have to be a lawyer to be an arbitrator or mediator, or to represent another person in these procedures.

When parties submit their dispute to arbitration, they give up control over the resolution. They give to the arbitrators the right to decide how the controversy should be resolved. The arbitrators are supposed to base their award on the evidence and the law. However, an arbitration award cannot be set aside merely because the arbitrators made a mistake about what the law is or how the law applies.

The parties' agreement to arbitrate must be contractual to be binding and enforceable. The contract may be made before or after the dispute arises.

Almost any dispute involving contract rights, property damage, or personal injury may be arbitrated. The parties' agreement determines the scope of arbitration and should address all matters of procedure that concern the parties. Most states have adopted the Uniform Arbitration Act. The act will direct how the arbitration is to be conducted insofar as the parties' agreement to arbitrate is silent on any question that arises.

The parties' agreement to arbitrate must define the scope of submission—that is, it should explain or define the matter that is to be arbitrated, how the arbitration is to be conducted, and what kind of award the arbitrators may make. The scope of submission determines the arbitrators' authority. A court of general jurisdiction that has jurisdiction over the parties will review an arbitration award to determine whether the arbitrators exceeded their authority. A court can set aside an arbitration award that was obtained through fraud of the prevailing party or tribunal.

Where the parties have agreed to arbitration but cannot agree on the selection of a tribunal, either party may apply to the court for appointment of arbitrators. If the agreement to arbitrate has prescribed a certain method for selecting arbitrators, the court should try to follow it. Otherwise, the court has broad discretion in selecting arbitrators for the parties.

Parties do not have a right to conduct discovery of the type provided by the Federal Rules of Civil Procedure. Parties may take depositions for the purpose of presenting the deponent's testimony in that form. Parties may obtain subpoenas from a court to compel witness to appear and testify at an arbitration hearing. The parties may agree to present some or all of their evidence in the form of documentation.

An arbitration tribunal is not required to follow rules of evidence. Nevertheless, a party may object to another party's evidence, and the tribunal decides for itself what evidence it should hear and consider.

A tribunal must make an award. The award must be in writing. The award need not explain the tribunal's rationale for the award. A binding arbitration award may be filed with a court of general jurisdiction and be confirmed and become the basis for a court judgment. The judgment may then be enforced like any court judgment.

A court may order corrections to an arbitration award in order to make the award comport with the arbitrators' manifest intent, as where a clerical error or an error in calculations has occurred.

A party may petition (move) a court of general jurisdiction to vacate an arbitration award on the grounds that:

1. The award was procured by a party's corruption, fraud, or other undue means.

2. An arbitrator appointed as a neutral was partial, or any of the arbitrators was corrupt, or misconduct prejudicing the rights of any party occurred.

3. The arbitrators exceeded their powers.

4. The arbitrators refused to postpone the hearing even though sufficient cause was shown to justify a postponement, or refused to hear evidence material to the controversy, or otherwise conducted the hearing contrary to provisions of the Uniform Arbitration Act so as to prejudice substantial rights of a party.

5. No arbitration agreement existed, *and* the issue was not adversely determined in proceedings under the Uniform Arbitration Act, section 2, and the party did not participate in the arbitration hearing without raising the objection.

A motion to vacate the arbitration award must be made within ninety days after the award is delivered to the party. A motion to vacate may be combined with a motion to modify the award. If a court vacates an award, the court shall order a new arbitration hearing before new arbitrators.

A tribunal's arbitration award is not, in itself, enforceable against a party. If a party refuses to voluntarily comply with the terms of the award, the prevailing party may move the court to confirm the award. If there is no objection, or the opposing party's objections are overruled, the court adopts the award and orders an entry of judgment in the same words or to the same effect as the arbitration award. The clerk of court enters the award in the court's judgment book. The judgment may be enforced as any other judgment. The motion to confirm the arbitration award must be served upon the opposing party in the same manner that a summons and complaint may be served upon a defendant.

Arbitrators have an immunity from civil suit even if they engage in a fraud in making their award. The defrauded party's only remedy is to have the award set aside. Arbitrators who engage in fraud are not entitled to payment for their services.

When parties mediate their dispute, they retain control over the resolution of the matter. The premise of mediation is that the parties are willing to compromise for the purpose of resolving the dispute. If a party is not willing to compromise, she or he should not enter into mediation.

A mediator has no power to force a settlement. A mediator must rely upon persuasion to bring the parties together. A mediator must be able to see beyond the immediate problems to look for creative solutions that meet the parties' real interests and needs. A mediator looks to the parties' positions in the dispute and tries to help the parties find a way of moving to a settlement, rather than making judgments about the parties' truthfulness or the persuasiveness of the evidence. A mediator is a facilitator. Mediators tend to deal in generalities. On the other hand, if either or both parties' positions are without basis in law or fact, a mediator probably cannot help the parties. Unless a mediator can reason with the parties, negotiating will be useless. The parties must respect the mediator and be willing to consider the mediator's suggestions.

If a mediator helps the parties to arrive at a settlement, the settlement should be reduced to writing and accepted by the parties before the mediator withdraws. The parties' settlement does not have to comport with legal remedies.

KEY TERMS

arbitrators	arbitration tribunal
binding arbitration	arbitration award
non-binding arbitration	scope of submission
matter	motion to vacate the award
petitioner	motion to confirm the award

REVIEW QUESTIONS

1. Why does an agreement to arbitrate have to meet the requirements of a contract in order to be enforceable?

2. If the parties include an arbitration agreement in their contract for the sale of property, is the arbitration agreement enforceable even though the parties did not know at that time what disputes might arise under their sales agreement? Why or why not?

3. What value is it to the parties to contract for nonbinding arbitration?

4. How does nonbinding arbitration differ from mediation?

5. Will a court force two parties to arbitrate if they agree that they do not want to arbitrate their dispute and instead want to have a trial?

6. If a dispute arises over the scope of submission in an arbitration agreement, who resolves the dispute?

7. How may an arbitration award be enforced against a party who refuses to abide by the award?

8. What are the advantages of arbitration over civil litigation?

9. What are the advantages of civil litigation over arbitration?

10. What are the limitations on a paralegal's involvement in arbitration?

A Personal Note

As you prepare to assume responsibilities that, historically, were reserved to lawyers, give some consideration to the attitude with which you will approach those responsibilities. A few suggestions may help you to avoid mistakes, embarrassment, and disappointment.

A paraprofessional career in law should be interesting, fulfilling, and, on occasion, exciting. You should be proud of your association with the legal profession and the judicial system. Conduct yourself as a professional person. Dress appropriately. Be courteous to all persons with whom you come into contact, especially when dealing with an adverse party or opposing lawyer. Be on time and keep appointments. Use a calendar to schedule your appointments and deadlines. Avoid creating time conflicts. Operate on the premise that by being timely, you will do the best job possible. Strive to develop a reputation for reliability and candor.

Recognize that each matter you handle is very important to someone, even though the work may seem routine to you. When you handle an assignment for a client, demonstrate the same interest and concern that you would want for your own important matters. Some matters you will handle will be very personal in nature. Treat all matters, whether of a business nature or otherwise, as confidential. Avoid the temptation to make "innocent" disclosures about the cases you are handling. Guard against making accidental disclosures.

Do not violate court rules or court orders or professional ethics. On occasion, some advantage may be gained by disregarding professional responsibilities—do not do so. Do not let anyone mislead you into a violation. No case, no client, no employer is important enough to justify sacrificing your own integrity and professional standing for his or her convenience. The adversary system works well because each party has the opportunity and responsibility for presenting her or his own case. The process would collapse overnight if it were not conducted by professionals in accordance with rules and standards that are based in fair play. Do not do anything to upset that delicate balance.

Continue your education by attending seminars and reading professional articles relative to your work. Ask questions about assignments. Determine how your tasks relate to the overall project. Learn from your mistakes, and do not become defensive because of past mistakes. Accept responsibility for what you have done, and for what you should have done but did not. Accept advice, corrections, and suggestions graciously. Usually there is more than one way to perform a task. Be agreeable if the lawyers you work with prefer a different method than you learned or prefer.

Be thoughtful and innovative, but be careful not to exceed your authority. Look for ways to work more effectively and more efficiently. Keep copies of documents you prepare. When you later work on similar assignments, they will help you to do the job better and faster. One of the surest ways to gain satisfaction, if not enjoyment, from your work is to strive for excellence. There is always satisfaction in doing a job well—whether or not anyone else happens to notice. Even a tedious task can be made more interesting by approaching it with the intent of doing it perfectly.

Lawyers and all who serve the judicial system depend upon effective communications, both oral and written. Strive to be precise in your statements and questions. Develop a concern for using words correctly. Be alert to the meaning of words you use in your correspondence and reports. Use the language of the profession; legal jargon will help you to be more precise in your thinking and effective in your communications. Organize your thoughts before you write your letters, reports, and memorandums. Make your reports while the information is still fresh and clear in your mind. Learn to use short, specific questions when you make inquiries of witnesses and clients.

As you work on assignments, try to keep in mind the whole picture and the ultimate objective. Strive to be objective in analyzing the facts. It is all too easy to become oversold on a client's claim or defense. Lawyers and paralegals must avoid deluding themselves about the client's cause while serving the client. A client is better served by objective advisers than by fervent "yes-persons." Do not compromise your integrity for any case or any person.

APPENDIXES

APPENDIX A

TIME TABLE FOR LAWYERS IN FEDERAL CIVIL CASES

This Time Table [Amended to February 1, 1994] indicates the time for each of the steps of a civil action as provided by the Federal Rules of Civil Procedure and the Federal Rules of Appellate Procedure. Certain steps governed by statute and by the 1990 Revised Rules of the Supreme Court are also listed. Usually the periods permitted or each of these steps may be enlarged by the court in its discretion. In some cases no enlargement is permitted. Civil Rule 6(b) and Appellate Rule 26(b) state when, and under what conditions, an enlargement may be allowed.

Service by mail is complete upon mailing (Civil Rule 5(b) and Appellate Rule 25(c)). Whenever a period of time is computed from the service of a notice or other paper, and the service is made by mail, 3 days are added to the prescribed period of time (Civil Rule 6(e) and Appellate Rule 26(c)). Variations which make impossible the application of any rigid limitation of time to all steps of the action are indicated in the Time Table. Citations to supporting authority are in the form "Civ.R. —" for the Rules of Civil Procedure; "App.R. —" for the Rules of Appellate Procedure; "28 U.S.C.A. § —" for statutes; and "1990 Revised Rules of the Supreme Court, Rule —".

ADMISSIONS

Requests for admissions, service of	On any other party after the parties have conferred pursuant to Civ.R. 26(f). Civ.R. 36(a).
Response to requested admissions	Answers or objections must be served within 30 days after service of the request, or such shorter or longer time as court may allow or as parties may agree to in writing. Civ.R. 36(a).

ALTERNATE jurors — The institution of the alternate juror has been abolished. Civ.R. 47, 1991 Advisory Committee note, subd. (b).

ANSWER — See, also, "Responsive Pleadings", this table.

To complaint — Service within 20 days after being served with summons and complaint unless a different time is prescribed in a federal statute. Civ.R. 12(a)(1)(A).

Service within 60 days after date request is sent for waiver of service of summons or within 90 days after that date if defendant was addressed outside any judicial district of the United States unless a different time is prescribed in a federal statute. Civ.R. 12(a)(1)(B).

Service within 60 days after service upon the United States Attorney, in action against the United States or an officer or agency thereof. Civ.R. 12(a).

	The time for responsive pleading is altered by service of Civ.R. 12 motions. See "Responsive Pleadings", this table.
To cross-claim	Service within 20 days after being served with cross-claim. Civ.R. 12(a)(2).
	60 days for United States. Civ.R. 12(a).
	The time for responsive pleading is altered by service of Civ.R. 12(a) motions, see "Responsive Pleadings", this table.
To third-party complaint	Service of reply within 20 days after service of answer or, if reply is ordered by a court, within 20 days after service of order. Civ.R. 12(a)(2).
	60 days for United States. Civ.R. 12(a)(3).
To notice of condemnation	Service within 20 days after service of notice. Civ.R. 71A(e).
Removed actions	20 days after receipt of pleading, or within 20 days after service of summons, or within 5 days after filing of removal petition, whichever is longest. Civ.R. 81(c).
Proceedings to cancel certificates of citizenship under 8 U.S.C.A. § 1451	60 days after service of petition. Civ.R. 81(a)(6).

**ANSWERS (or objections)
   to interrogatories
   to party**

Service within 30 days after service of the interrogatories. A shorter or longer time may be directed by the court, or agreed to. Civ.R. 33(b)(3).

APPEAL

   As of right

30 days from entry of judgment or order. App.R. 4(a)(1).

District court may extend for excusable neglect or good cause upon motion filed not later than 30 days after expiration of time prescribed by App.R. 4(a); no extension to exceed 30 days past prescribed time or 10 days from entry of order granting motion, whichever occurs later. App.R. 4(a)(5).

60 days in cases in which the United States or its officers, agencies are parties. App.R. 4(a)(1).

If any party makes a timely motion of a type specified below, time for appeal for all parties runs from entry of order disposing of last of such motion outstanding. App.R. 4(a)(4).

(1) motion for judgment under Civ.R. 50(b);

(2) motion under Civ.R. 52(b) to amend or make additional findings of fact, whether or not granting the motion would alter the judgment;

(3) motion under Civ.R. 59 to alter or amend judgment;

(4) motion under Civ.R. 54 for attorney's fees if time to appeal extended under Civ.R. 58;

(5) motion under Civ.R. 59 for new trial;

(6) motion for relief under Civ.R. 60 if motion served within 10 days after entry of judgment.

App.R. 4(a)(4).

By other parties, within 14 days of filing of first notice of appeal, or within the time otherwise prescribed by App.R. 4(a), which ever last expires. App.R. 4(a)(3).

By permission under 28 U.S.C.A. § 1292(b) (interlocutory orders)	10 days after entry of order including statement that controlling question of law is involved and appealable under 28 U.S.C.A. 1292(b); App.R. 5(a).
Bankruptcy	If a motion for rehearing under Bankruptcy Rule 8015 is filed in a district court or in a bankruptcy appellate panel, time for appeal to court of appeals runs from entry of order disposing of motion. App.R. 6(b)(2)(i).
Inmates	A notice of appeal is timely filed if deposited in the institution's internal mail system on or before the last day for filing. App.R. 4(c), 25(a).
Representation statement	Within 10 days after filing notice of appeal, unless court of appeals designates another time, attorney who filed notice shall file with the clerk of court of appeals a statement naming each party represented on appeal by that attorney. App.R. 12(b).
Entry of judgment or order, notice of	Lack of such notice by clerk not affect time to appeal or relieve or authorize court to relieve party for failure to appeal within time allowed, except as permitted in App.R. 4(a). Civ.R. 77(d).
Record (Appellant)	Within 10 days after filing notice of appeal: Appellant to place written order for transcript and file copy of order with clerk; if none to be ordered, file a certificate to that effect; unless entire transcript to be included, file a statement of issues and serve appellee a copy of order or certificate and of statement. App.R. 10(b).
Record (Appellee)	Within 10 days after service of appellant's order or certificate and statement, appellee to file and serve on appellant a designation of additional parts of transcript to be included. Unless within 10 days after designation appellant has ordered such parts and so notified appellee, appellee may within the following 10 days either order the parts or move in district court for order requiring appellant to do so. App.R. 10(b).
Record (costs)	At time of ordering, party to make satisfactory arrangements with reporter for payment of cost of transcript. App.R. 10(b)(4).
Record (Reporter)	If transcript cannot be completed within 30 days of receipt of order, report shall request extension of time from clerk of court of appeals. App.R. 11(b).
Stay of proceedings to enforce judgment	Effective when supersedeas bond is approved by court. Civ.R. 62(d).

Supersedeas bond may be given at or after time of filing notice of appeal or of procuring the order allowing appeal. Civ.R. 62(d).

Briefs

Appellant must file a brief within 40 days after the record is filed. Appellee must file a brief within 30 days after service of the appellant's brief. A reply brief must be filed within 14 days after service of appellee's brief and, except for good cause shown, at least 3 days before argument. A court of appeals may shorten the times allowed for briefs either by rule for all cases or by order for specific cases. App.R. 31(a).

Transcripts

See "Record", ante, this heading.

APPEAL from magistrate judge to district judge under 28 U.S.C.A. § 636(c)(4) and Civ.R. 73(d)

Notice of appeal

Filed with clerk of district court within 30 days of entry of judgment. Within 60 days if United States or officer or agency thereof is a party. Within 15 days after entry of an interlocutory decision or order. Civ.R. 74(a).

When timely notice is filed by a party, any other party may file notice within 14 days thereafter or within time otherwise prescribed by Civ.R. 74(a), whichever period last expires. Civ.R. 74(a).

Upon showing of excusable neglect, time for filing may be extended on motion filed not later than 20 days from expiration of time for filing. Civ.R. 74(a).

Running of time for filing terminated as to all parties by timely filing of any of the following motions with the magistrate judge by any party, and the full time for appeal from judgment entered commences to run anew from entry of any of the following orders:

(1) granting or denying motion for judgment under Civ.R. 50(b);

(2) granting or denying motion under Civ.R. 52(b) to amend or make additional findings of fact;

(3) granting or denying motion under Civ.R. 59 to alter or amend judgment;

(4) denying motion for new trial under Civ.R. 59. Civ.R. 74(a).

Joint statement of case

Parties may file in lieu of record within 10 days after filing of notice of appeal. Civ.R. 75(b)(1).

Transcript

Within 10 days after filing notice of appeal appellant to make arrangements for production. Unless entire transcript is to be included, description of parts appellant intends to present must be served on the appellee and filed by the appellant within the 10 day period. If appellee deems transcript of other pats to be necessary, designation of additional parts to be included must be

	served on the appellant and filed within 10 days after service of appellant's statement. Civ.R. 75(b)(2).
Statement in lieu of transcript	If no record is available for transcription, parties must file a statement of evidence in lieu of transcript within 10 days after filing of notice of appeal. Civ.R. 75(b)(3).
Briefs	Appellant to serve and file within 20 days after the filing of transcript, statement of case, or statement of evidence. Civ.R. 75(c)(1).
	Appellee to serve and file within 20 days after service of appellant's brief. Civ.R. 75(c)(2).
	Appellant may serve and file reply brief within 10 days after service of appellee's brief. Civ.R. 75(c)(3).
	If appellee files a cross-appeal, appellee may file a reply brief within 10 days after service of the reply brief of the appellant. Civ.R. 75(c)(4).
Stay of judgments	Decision of district judge stayed for 10 days during which term a party may petition for rehearing. Civ.R. 76(b).
APPEAL from magistrate judge under 28 U.S.C.A. § 636(c)(3)	Appeal to court of appeals in identical fashion as appeals from other judgments of district courts. App.R. 3.1.
APPEAL from district court to court of appeals under 28 U.S.C.A. § 636(c)(5)	Petition for leave to appeal filed with clear of the court of appeals within time provided by App.R. 4(a) for filing notice of appeal, with proof of service on all parties to action in district court. App.R. 5.1(a).
	Within 14 days after service of petition for leave to appeal, a party may file an answer or cross petition in opposition. App.R. 5.1(a).
APPEAL to Supreme Court	
Direct appeals	30 days after entry of interlocutory or final order, decree or judgment holding Act of Congress unconstitutional under circumstances provided by 28 U.S.C.A. §§ 1252, and 1253. 28 U.S.C.A. § 2101(a), as amended by May 24, 1949, c. 139, § 106, 63 Stat. 104. [28 U.S.C.A. § 1252 was repealed and 28 U.S.C.A. § 2101(a) was amended by Pub.L. 100–352, §§ 1, 5(b), June 27, 1988, 102 Stat. 662, 663, respectively. For effective date and applicability to cases, see section 7 of Pub.L. 100–352, set out as 28 U.S.C.A. § 1254 note.]
	30 days from interlocutory judgment, order, or decree in any other direct appeal authorized by law from decision of district court. 28 U.S.C.A. § 2101(b).
	60 days from final judgment, order, or decree in any other direct appeal authorized by law from decisions of district court. 28 U.S.C.A. § 2101(b).
Other appeals and certiorari	90 days after entry of judgment or decree; justice of Supreme Court for good cause shown may extend time for applying for

writ of certiorari for period not exceeding 60 days. 28 U.S.C.A. § 2101(c).

Briefs supporting certiorari	No separate brief supporting petition for certiorari will be received; see 1990 Revised Rules of the Supreme Court, Rule 14.3
Brief opposing certiorari	30 days after receipt of petition unless time is enlarged by Court or justice thereof or by the clerk; see 1990 Revised Rules of the Supreme Court, Rule 15.2.
Brief on merits on appeal or certiorari	By appellant or petitioner, within 45 days of the order noting or postponing probable jurisdiction or of the order granting the writ of certiorari; see 1990 Revised Rules of the Supreme Court, Rule 25.1.

By appellee or respondent, within 30 days after receipt of the brief filed by the appellant or petitioner; see 1990 Revised Rules of the Supreme Court, Rule 25.2.

Reply brief, if any, within 30 days after receipt of brief for appellee or respondent, or actually be received by clerk not later than one week before the date of oral argument, whichever is earlier. See 1990 Revised Rules of the Supreme Court, Rule 25.3.

ATTORNEYS' fees — See "Costs", this table.

BILL of particulars — Abolished. See Civ.R. 12(e), as amended in 1948. See, however, "More definite statement", this table.

CLASS actions — As soon as practicable after commencement court is to determine by order whether action is to be so maintained. Civ.R. 23(c)(1).

CLERICAL mistakes in judgments orders, or record — May be corrected at any time; but during pendency of appeal, may be corrected before appeal is docketed in the appellate court, and thereafter while appeal pending may be corrected with leave of appellate court. Civ.R. 60(a).

COMPLAINT — Filing commences action—must be served with summons. Civ.R. 3. Service of summons and complaint within 120 days after filing. Civ.R. 4(m).

COMPILATION of time — Exclude day of the act, event or default from which designated period of time begins to run. Include last day of the period so computed unless it is a Saturday, Sunday, or legal holiday, or, when act to be done is the filing of a paper in court, a day on which weather or other conditions have made the office of the clerk of the district court inaccessible, in which event period runs until end of the next day which is not one of the aforementioned days. Civ.R. 6(a).

Intermediate Saturdays, Sundays, and legal holidays are excluded if the period is less than 11 days Civ.R. 6(a).

Exclude day of the act, event, or default from which designated period of time begins to run. Include last day of the period so computed unless Saturday, Sunday, or legal holiday, or, when the act to be done is filing of paper in court, a day on which weather or other conditions have made office of clerk inaccessible, in which event period runs until end of next day which is not one of aforementioned days. App.R. 26(a).

Intermediate Saturdays, Sundays, and legal holidays are excluded if the period is less than 7 days. App.R. 26(a).

Service by mail is complete upon mailing. Civ.R. 5(b); App.R. 25(c).

Service by mail adds three days to a period of time which is computed from such service. Civ.R. 6(e); App.R. 26(c).

Legal holidays are defined by Civil Rule 6(a) and App.Rule 26(a).

Supreme Court matters—See 1990 Revised Rules of the Supreme Court, Rule 30.

CONDEMNATION of property

Answer to notice of condemnation

20 days after service of notice. Civ.R. 71A(e).

COSTS

Taxation on 1 day's notice. Motion to review taxation of costs 5 days after taxation. Civ.R. 54(d).

Failure to comply with request for waiver of service of summons and to return waiver within time allowed which must be at least 30 days from date request is sent or 60 days from that date for a defendant addressed outside any judicial district of the United States. Civ.R. 4(d).

Attorney's fees and related nontaxable expenses

Motion filed and served no later than 14 days after entry of judgment. Civ.R. 54(d)(2)(B).

CROSS APPEAL

Optional appeal from magistrate judge to district judge

Appellee may file reply brief within 10 days after service of reply brief of appellant. Civ.R. 75(c)(4).

Appellate rules

Within 14 days of filing of first notice of appeal or within the time otherwise prescribed by Civ.R. 4(a), whichever last expires. App.R. 4(a)(3).

Inmates

Within 14 days after date when first notice of appeal was filed. The 14 day period runs from date district court receives first notice of appeal. App.R. 4(c).

DEFAULT

Entry by clerk

No time stated. Civ.R. 55(b).

Entry by court	If party against whom default is sought has appeared, the party shall be served with written notice of application for default judgment at least 3 days prior to haring on such application. Civ.R. 55(b).

DEFENSES and objections, presentation of

By pleading	See "Answer", this table.
By motion	Motion shall be made before pleading if further pleading is permitted. Civ.R. 12(b).
At trial	Adverse party may assert at trial any defense in law or fact to claim for relief to which such party is not required to serve responsive pleading. Civ.R. 12(b).
Motion affects time for responsive pleading	Service of motion under Civ.R. 12 alters times for responsive pleading. See "Responsive Pleadings", this table.

DEMURRERS   Abolished. Civ.R. 7(c).

DEPOSITIONS   See, also, "Interrogatories", "Depositions on written questions", this table.

Notice of filing	Promptly. Civ.R. 30(f)(3) and Civ.R. 31(c).
Notice of taking	Reasonable notice to every party. Civ.R. 30(b).
Objections	As to admissibility, objection may be made at trial or hearing, but subject to Civ.R. 28(b) and 32(d)(3). Civ.R. 32(b).
	As to errors or irregularities in the notice, service promptly. Civ.R. 32(d)(1).
	As to disqualification of officer, objection made before deposition begins or as soon thereafter as disqualification becomes known or could be discovered. Civ.R. 32(d)(2).
	As to competency of witness or competency, relevancy, or materiality of testimony—not waived by failure to make such objection before or during deposition unless the ground might have been obviated or removed if presented at that time. Civ.R. 32(d)(3)(A).
	As to errors and irregularities at oral examination in manner of taking deposition, in the form of questions or answers, in the oath or affirmation, or in conduct of parties, and errors which might be obviated, removed, or cured if promptly presented—seasonable objection made at taking of deposition. Civ.R. 32(d)(3)(B).
	As to form of written questions submitted under Civ.R. 31—service within time allowed for serving succeeding cross or other questions and within 5 days after service of last questions authorized. Civ.R. 32(d)(3)(C).
	As to completion and return (transcription, signing, certification, sealing, etc.)—motion to suppress made with reasonable promptness after defect is or might have been ascertained. Civ.R. 32(d)(4).

Orders of protection	Subsequent to certification that movant has in good faith conferred or attempted to confer with other affected parties to resolve dispute without court action. Civ.R. 26(c).
Motion to terminate or limit examination	Any time during a deposition. Civ.R. 30(d)(3).
Perpetuate testimony pending appeal	Motion in district court upon same notice and service thereof as if action was pending in district court. Civ.R. 27(b).
Perpetuate testimony before action	Service of notice and petition 20 days before date of hearing. Civ.R. 27(a)(2).
Taking	Time specified in the notice of taking. Civ.R. 30(b)(1).
	Prior notice by a party to deponent and other parties to designate another method to record deponent's testimony in addition to method specified by person taking deposition. Civ.R. 30(b)(3).
Review of transcript or recording	Request by a party or deponent before completion of deposition. Deponent has 30 days after notice of availability of transcript or recording to review and to indicate changes. Civ.R. 30(e).
DEPOSITIONS on written questions	See, also, "Depositions", "Interrogatories", this table.
When taken	After parties have met and conferred to discuss their claims, defenses, and possibility of settlement and to develop a proposed discovery plan under Civ.R. 26(f). Civ.R. 26(d).
Cross questions	Service within 14 days after service of the notice and question. Court may enlarge or shorten time. Civ.R. 31(a)(4).
Redirect questions	Service within 7 days after being served with cross question. Court may enlarge or shorten time. Civ.R. 31(a)(4).
Recross questions	Service within 7 days after service of redirect questions. Court may enlarge or shorten time. Civ.R. 31(a)(4).
Notice of filing of deposition	Promptly. Civ.R. 31(c).
Objections to form	Service within the time allowed for serving the succeeding cross or other questions and within 5 days after service of last questions authorized. Civ.R. 32(d)(3)(C).
DISCOVERY	See, also, "Admissions", "Depositions", "Depositions on written questions", "Interrogatories," "Production of Documents", this table.
	Except in exempted actions or when otherwise ordered, as soon as practicable and at least 14 days before a scheduling conference is held or a scheduling order is due under Civ.R. 16(b), the parties shall meet to discuss their claims, defenses, and possibility of settlement, to make or arrange for disclosures, and to develop a proposed discovery plan. A written report outlining the plan is to be submitted to the court within 10 days after the meeting. Civ.R. 26(f); See, also, Civ.R. 26(d).

Without waiting for a discovery request and within 10 days after the Civ.R. 26(f) meeting of parties, a party must provide information specified in Civ.R. 26(a)(1). Disclosure of expert testimony under Civ.R. 26(a)(2), in absence of court direction or stipulation, is to be made at least 90 days before trial date or date case is ready for trial, or, if evidence intended as rebuttal of Civ.R. 26(a)(2)(B), within 30 days after disclosure of such evidence. Civ.R. 26(a)(2)(C). All disclosures are to be promptly filed with court. Civ.R. 26(a)(4).

Identification of witnesses, documents, exhibits, including summaries of other evidence, and designation of witnesses whose testimony will be by deposition with a transcript of pertinent testimony if deposition is not taken stenographically to be provided to other parties at least 30 days before trial unless otherwise directed by court. Within 14 days thereafter, unless otherwise specified by court, a party may file objections. Civ.R. 26(a)(3).

DISMISSAL for want of subject-matter jurisdiction	Any time. Civ.R. 12(h)(3).
DISMISSAL by plaintiff voluntarily without court order	Any time before service of answer or motion for summary judgment. Civ.R. 41(a)(1).
DISMISSAL of counter-claim, cross-claim or third-party claim, voluntary	Before service of responsive pleading, or if none, before introduction of evidence at trial or hearing. Civ.R. 41(c).
DISMISSAL without prejudice	Service of summons and complaint not made within 120 days after filing of complaint. Civ.R. 4(m).
DOCUMENTS, production of	See "Production of Documents", this table.
ENLARGEMENT of time generally	
Act required or allowed at or within specified time by civil Rule, notice thereunder, or court order	Court for cause shown may (1) with or without motion or notice order period enlarged if request therefor is made before expiration of period originally prescribed or as extended by previous order, or (2) upon motion made after expiration of the specified period permit act to be done where failure to act was result of excusable neglect; but court may not extend time for taking any action under Civ.R. 50(b) and (c)(2), 52(b), 59(b), (d) and (e), 60(b) and 74(a), except to extent and under conditions stated in them. Civ.R. 6(b).
Affidavits in opposition, service	Time may be extended by court. Civ.R. 12(d).
Hearing of motions and defenses	May be deferred until trial. Civ.R. 12(d).

Mail, service by	Adds three days to a period that is computed from time of service. Civ.R. 6(e); App.R. 26(c).
Injunction—temporary restraining order	May be extended 10 days by order of court or for a longer period by consent of party against whom order is directed. Civ.R. 65(b).
Response to request for admissions	Time may be enlarged or shortened by court or as the parties may agree in writing subject to Civ.R. 29. Civ.R. 36(a).
Optional appeal from magistrate judge to district judge	Upon showing of excusable neglect, time to file notice of appeal may be extended upon motion filed not later than 20 days from expiration of time for filing. Civ.R. 74(a).
Motion for judgment notwithstanding the verdict	No enlargement of the 10 day period except to the extent and under conditions stated in Civ.R. 50(b). Civ.R. 6(b).
Findings by the court, amendment of additional findings	No enlargement of the 10 day period except to the extent and under conditions stated in Civ.R. 52(b). Civ.R. 6(b).
Motion for new trial	No enlargement of the 10 day period except to the extent and under conditions stated in Civ.R. 59(b), (d), and (e). Civ.R. 6(b).
Motion for relief from judgment or order	No enlargement of the 1 year period except to the extent and under conditions stated in Civ.R. 60(b). Civ.R. 6(b).
Notice of appeal from magistrate judge to district judge	No enlargement of the 30 day period except to the extent and under conditions stated in Civ.R. 74(a). Civ.R. 6(b).
Appellate rules	Court for good cause shown may upon motion enlarge time prescribed by App.Rules or by its order for doing any act or may permit act to be done after expiration of such time; but court may not enlarge time for filing notice of appeal, petition for allowance, or petition for permission to appeal; nor may the court enlarge time prescribed by law for filing petition to enjoin, set aside, suspend, modify, enforce or otherwise review, or a notice of appeal from, an order of an administrative agency, board, commission or officer of the United States, except as specifically authorized by law. App.R. 26(b).
Supreme Court matters	See 1990 Revised Rules of the Supreme Court, Rule 30.
EXCEPTIONS for insufficiency of pleading	Abolished. Civ.R. 7(c).

EXECUTION

Stay	Automatically: No execution to issue, nor proceedings for enforcement to be taken, until expiration of 10 days after entry of judgment; exceptions—injunctions, receiverships, and patent accountings. Civ.R. 62(a).
	Stay according to state law. Civ.R. 62(f).
	Motion for new trial or for judgment. Civ.R. 62(b).
	Stay in favor of government. Civ.R. 62(e).

Supersedeas on appeal. Civ.R. 62(d).

Stay of judgment as to multiple claims or multiple parties. Civ.R. 62(h).

Stay of judgment pending appeal from magistrate judge to district judge. Civ.R. 74(c). Stay of decision of district judge for 10 days during which time a party may petition for rehearing. Civ.R. 76(b).

FILING papers

Complaint must be filed at commencement of action. Civ.R. 3.

Service of summons and complaint within 120 days after filing of complaint. Civ.R. 4(m).

All papers required to be filed must be filed with clerk unless the judge permits them to be filed with the judge. Civ.R. 5(e).

Local court rules may permit papers to be filed by facsimile or other electronic means if authorized by and consistent with standards of Judicial Conference of the United States, and clerk shall not refuse for filing any paper solely because it is not presented in proper form under Rules of Civil Procedure or any local rule or practice. Civ.R. 5(e).

All papers after the complaint required to be served upon a party, together with a certificate of service, shall be filed with the court within a reasonable time after service. Civ.R. 5(d).

FINDINGS
  Motion to amend

10 days after entry of judgment. Civ.R. 52(b). Exception from general rule relating to enlargement. Civ.R. 6(b).

FINDINGS of master

See "References and Referees", this table.

FOREIGN law

Reasonable written notice required of party intending to raise an issue concerning the law of a foreign country. Civ.R. 44.1.

HEARING of motions

Unless local conditions make it impracticable, district court shall establish regular times and places for hearing and disposition of motions requiring notice and haring; but judge may make orders for the advancement, conduct, and hearing of actions. Civ.R. 78.

Service of notice 5 days before time specified for hearing unless otherwise provided by these rules or order of court. Civ.R. 6(d).

Hearing of certain motions and defenses before trial on application of any party unless court orders deferral until trial. Civ.R. 12(d).

HOLIDAYS

New Year's Day, Birthday of Martin Luther King, Jr., Washington's Birthday, Memorial Day, Independence Day, Labor Day, Columbus Day, Veterans Day, Thanksgiving Day, Christmas Day, and any other day appointed as a holiday by the President or the

	Congress of the United States or by the state in which the district court is held. Civ.R. 6(a); App.R. 26(a).
	Exclusion in computation of time. Civ.R. 6(a); App.R. 26(a).
INJUNCTION (temporary restraining order granted without notice)	Order shall be indorsed with date and hour of issuance, filed forthwith in clerk's office, and entered of record. Civ.R. 65(b).
	Expiration within such time, not to exceed 10 days, as court fixes, unless within time so fixed the order is extended for like period or, with consent of party against whom order is directed, for longer period. Civ.R. 65(b).
	Motion for preliminary injunction shall be set down for hearing at earliest possible time—takes precedence of all matters except older ones of same character. Civ.R. 65(b).
	Motion for dissolution or modification on 2 days' notice or such shorter notice as court may prescribe; hear and determine motion as expeditiously as ends of justice require. Civ.R. 65(b).
INSTRUCTIONS	
Requests	At close of evidence or such earlier time as court directs. Civ.R. 51.
Objections	Before jury retires to consider verdict. Civ.R. 51.
INTERROGATORIES to parties	See, also, "Depositions", "Depositions on written questions", this table.
	Service after parties have met and conferred pursuant to Civ.R. 26(f). Civ.R. 33(a).
Answers or objections	Service within 30 days after service of the interrogatories. A shorter or longer time may be directed by the court or agreed to. Civ.R. 33(b)(3).
INTERVENTION	Upon timely application. Civ.R. 24(a), (b).
	Person desiring to intervene shall serve a motion to intervene upon the parties as provided in Civil Rule 5. Civ.R. 24(c).
JUDGMENT or order	
Alter or amend judgment, motion to	Shall be served not later than 10 days after entry of judgment. Civ.R. 59(e). Exception to general rule, relating to enlargement. Civ.R. 6(b).
Clerical mistakes	May be corrected any time; but during pendency of appeal, may be corrected before appeal is docketed in the appellate court, and thereafter while appeal pending may be corrected with leave of appellate court. Civ.R. 60(a).
Default	See "Default", this table.
Effectiveness	Judgment effective only when set forth on a separate document and when entered as provided in Civ.R. 79(a). Civ.R. 58.

Entry of judgment	Upon general verdict of jury or upon court decision that a party shall recover only a sum certain or costs or that all relief shall be denied, entry forthwith and without awaiting any direction by court (unless court otherwise orders). Upon court decision granting other relief or upon special verdict or general verdict accompanied by answers to interrogatories, entry upon prompt court approval of form. Entry shall not be delayed for taxing of costs. Civ.R. 58.
Entry, notice of	Immediately upon entry, clerk shall serve notice thereof by mail in manner provided in Civ.R. 5 and make note in docket of the mailing. Any party may in addition serve a notice of such entry in manner provided in Civ.R. 5 for service of papers. Civ.R. 77(d).
	Lack of notice of entry by clerk does not affect time to appeal or relieve or authorize court to relieve party for failure to appeal within time allowed, except as permitted by App.R. 4(a). Civ.R. 77(d).
Offer of judgment	Service more than 10 days before trial begins. Civ.R. 68.
	Acceptance, written notice of—service within 10 days after service of offer. Civ.R. 68.
On pleadings, motion for judgment	After pleadings are closed but within such time as not to delay the trial. Civ.R. 12(c).
Relief from, on ground stated in Rule 60(b)	Motion within a reasonable time and not more than 1 year after judgment, order, or proceeding entered or taken, for following grounds: (1) mistake, inadvertence, surprise, or excusable neglect; (2) newly discovered evidence; (3) fraud, misrepresentation, or other misconduct. Civ.R. 60(b). Exception from general rule relating to enlargement. Civ.R. 60(b).
	Motion within a reasonable time, for following grounds: (1) judgment void, (2) judgment satisfied, released, or discharged, (3) prior underlying judgment reversed or otherwise vacated, (4) no longer equitable that judgment have prospective application, (5) any other reason justifying relief. Civ.R. 60(b). Exception from general rule relating to enlargement. Civ.R. 6(b).
Renewal of motion for judgment after trial	Within 10 days after entry of judgment. Civ.R. 50(b). Exception from general rule relating to enlargement. Civ.R. 6(b).
Stay	See "Execution", this table.
Summary judgment	See "Summary Judgment", this table.
JURORS	The institution of the alternate juror has been abolished. Civ.R. 47, 1991 Advisory Committee note, subd. (b).
JURY trial	
Demand	Service any time after commencement of action and not later than 10 days after service of last pleading directed to the triable issue. Civ.R. 38(b).

	Adverse party may serve demand for jury trial within 10 days after service of first demand or such lesser time as court fixes. Civ.R. 38(c).
Removed actions	If at the time of removal all necessary pleadings have been served, demand for jury trial may be served:
	By petitioner, 10 days after the petition for removal is filed;
	By any other party, within 10 days after service on party of the notice of filing the petition. Civ.R. 81(c).
	Demand after removal not necessary in either of two instances: (1) prior to removal, party has made express demand in accordance with state law; (2) state law does not require express demands and court does not direct otherwise. Civ.R. 81(c).
LEGAL HOLIDAY	See "Holidays", this table.
MAGISTRATE JUDGES	
Trial by consent	Consent of parties to magistrate judge's authority to be exercised within period specified by local rule. Civ.R. 73(b).
Pretrial matters	Objections of parties to order disposing of matter not dispositive of claim or defense to be served and filed within 10 days after being served with copy of order. Civ.R. 72(a).
	Clerk to forthwith mail copies to all parties of recommendation of magistrate judge for disposition of matter dispositive of claim or defense of a party or prisoner petition. Specific written objections to recommended disposition may be served and filed within 10 days after service. Response to objections may be made within 10 days after being served with copy. Civ.R. 72(b).
MAIL	Service by mail adds 3 days to period computed from time of service. Civ.R. 6(e); App.R. 26(c).
MASTERS	See "References and Referees", this table.
MORE DEFINITE STATEMENT	
Furnished	Must be furnished within 10 days after notice of order or other time fixed by court or court may strike pleading. Civ.R. 12(e).
Motion for	Must be made before responsive pleading is interposed. Civ.R. 12(e).
MOTIONS, notices, and affidavits	See also, specific headings, this table.
In general	A written motion, supporting affidavits, and notice of hearing thereof—service not later than 5 days before time specified for hearing unless a different time is fixed by rule or by order of court. Civ.R. 6(d).

Opposing affidavits may be served not later than one day before hearing, unless court permits otherwise. Civ.R. 6(d).

Pleading, written motion, or other paper not signed by attorney or party shall be stricken unless omission of signature is corrected promptly after being called to attention of attorney or party. Civ.R. 11(a).

NEW TRIAL

Motion and affidavits

Motion shall be served not later than 10 days after entry of judgment. Civ.R. 59(b). Exception from general rule relating to enlargement. Civ.R. 6(b). If motion based on affidavits, they shall be served with motion. Civ.R. 59(c).

Opposing affidavits

Shall be served within 10 days of service of motion for new trial; period may be extended for additional period not exceeding 20 days either by court for good cause shown or by parties by written stipulation. Civ.R. 59(c).

Initiative court

Not later than 10 days after entry of judgment, court may order new trial for any reason for which it might have granted new trial on motion. Civ.R. 59(d). Exception to general rule relating to enlargement. Civ.R. 6(b).

After giving parties notice and opportunity to be heard, court may grant motion for new trial, timely served for reason not stated in the motion. Civ.R. 59(d). Exception to general rule relating to enlargement. Civ.R. 6(b).

Judgment as a matter of law

Party against whom judgment as a matter of law has been rendered may serve a motion for a new trial pursuant to Civ.R. 59 not later than 10 days after entry of the judgment. Civ.R. 50(c)(2).

OBJECTIONS to orders or rulings of court

At time ruling or order of court is made or sought; if party has no opportunity to object to ruling or order at time it is made, absence of objection does not thereafter prejudice the party. Civ.R. 46.

Pretrial matters referred to magistrate judge

Objections of parties to order disposing of matter not dispositive of claim or defense to be served and filed within 10 days after being served with copy of order. Civ.R. 72(a).

Specific written objections to recommended disposition of matter dispositive of claim or defense of a party or prisoner petition may be served or filed within 10 days after service. Response to objections may be made within 10 days after being served with copy. Civ.R. 72(b).

OFFER of judgment

Must be served more than 10 days before trial. Civ.R. 68.

Acceptance must be served within 10 days after service of offer. Civ.R. 68.

ORDERS

See Judgment or order.

PARTICULARS, Bill of	Abolished. Civ.R. 12(e), as amended in 1948. See, however, "More definite statement," this table.
PLEADINGS	
Amendment of	Once as matter of course before responsive pleading served or within 20 days if no response is permitted and action has not been placed on trial calendar. Civ.R. 15(a).
	By leave of court or written consent of adverse parties, at any time. Civ.R. 15(a).
	During trial or after judgment to conform to evidence or to raise issues not raised in pleadings, but tried by express or implied consent of parties. Civ.R. 15(b).
Supplemental	Upon motion of party—court may upon reasonable notice permit service of supplemental pleading setting forth transactions, etc., which have happened since date of pleading sought to be supplemented. Civ.R. 15(d).
	Adverse party plead to supplemental pleading—if court deems advisable, it shall so order, specifying time therefor. Civ.R. 15(d).
Averments of time	Such averments are material and shall be considered like all other averments of material matter. Civ.R. 9(f).
Judgment on, motion for	After pleadings are closed but within such time as not to delay the trial. Civ.R. 12(c).
Striking of matter from	Motion made before responding to a pleading or, if no responsive pleading permitted, within 20 days after service of pleading. Civ.R. 12(f).
	On court's own initiative at any time. Civ.R. 12(f).
Signing of	Pleading, written motion, or paper not signed by attorney or party shall be stricken unless omission of signature is corrected promptly after being called to attention of attorney or party. Civ.R. 11(a).
PLEAS	Abolished. Civ.R. 7(c).
PRETRIAL conferences	Scheduling order to issue as soon as practicable but in any event within 90 days after appearance of a defendant and with 120 days after complaint served on defendant. Civ.R. 16(b).
PROCESS	See "Summons", this table.
PRODUCTION of documents	
Request for, service of	Without leave of court or written stipulation, request may not be served before parties have met and conferred pursuant to Civ.R. 26(f). Civ.R. 34(b).
	May accompany notice of taking deposition. Civ.R. 30(b)(5).

Response to request	Within 30 days after service of the request. A shorter or longer time may be directed by court or agreed to. Civ.R. 34(b).
Time of inspection	The request shall specify a reasonable time. Civ.R. 34(b).
Subpoena	See "Subpoena", this table.

REFERENCES and Referees

Order of reference	When reference is made, clerk shall forthwith furnish master with copy of order. Civ.R. 53(d)(1).
Hearings before master	Time for beginning and closing the hearings, as fixed by order of reference. Civ.R. 53(c).
Meetings	First meeting of parties or attorneys to be held within 20 days after date of order of reference. Civ.R. 53(d)(1). Upon receipt of the order of reference, unless order otherwise provides, master shall forthwith set time and place for such meeting and notify parties or their attorneys. Civ.R. 53(d)(1). Speed—either party, on notice to parties and master, may apply to court for order requiring master to speed the proceedings and make report. Civ.R. 53(d)(1). Failure of party to appear at appointed time and place—master may proceed ex parte or adjourn to future day, giving notice to absent party of adjournment. Civ.R. 53(d)(1).
Report of master	Filing of, time as fixed in order of reference. Civ.R. 53(c). Master shall serve on all parties notice of the filing. Civ.R. 53(e)(1). Master, unless otherwise directed by the order of reference, shall serve a copy of the report on each party. Civ.R. 53(e)(1). Objections (in non-jury actions) may be served within 10 days after being served with notice of filing of report. Civ.R. 53(e)(2). Court action on report and objections thereto—application (in non-jury actions) for such action shall be by motion and upon notice as prescribed in Civ.R. 6(d). Civ.R. 53(e)(2). Speed—either party, on notice to parties and master, may apply to court for order requiring master to speed the proceedings and make report. Civ.R. 53(d)(1).

REMOVED actions

Answers and defenses	Within 20 days after the receipt through service or otherwise of a copy of the initial pleading setting forth the claim for relief upon which the action or proceeding is based, or within 20 days after the service of summons upon such initial pleading, then filed, or within 5 days after filing of the petition for removal, whichever period is longest. Civ.R. 81(c).
Demand for jury trial	Demand after removal not necessary in either of two instances: (1) prior to removal, party has made express demand in accordance

	with state law; (2) state law does not require express demands and court does not direct otherwise. Civ.R. 81(c).
Notice of removal	Within 30 days after receipt through service or otherwise of a copy of the initial pleading setting forth the claim for relief upon which the action or proceeding is based, or within 30 days after service of summons of such initial pleading has then been filed in court and is not required to be served on defendant, whichever period is shorter. 28 U.S.C.A. § 1446(b).
	If the case stated by the initial pleading is not removable, a notice of removal may be filed within 30 days after receipt by the defendant, through service or otherwise, of a coy of an amended pleading, motion, order or other paper form which it may first be ascertained that the case is one which is or has become removable. 28 U.S.C.A. § 1446(b).
	A case may not be removed on the basis of jurisdiction conferred by 28 U.S.C.A. 1332 more than one year after action's commencement. 28 U.S.C.A. § 1446(b).

REPLY

To answer or third-party answer	Only if ordered by court. Civ.R. 7(a). Service within 20 days after service of order, unless order otherwise directs. Civ.R. 12(a).
To counterclaim	Service within 20 days after service of answer.
	United States or agency or officer thereof shall serve reply within 60 days after service upon U.S. attorney. Civ.R. 12(a).
Alteration of time by service of Civ.R. 12 motion	See "Responsive pleadings", this table.

RESPONSIVE PLEADINGS

	See, also, "Answer," "Reply", this table.
To amended pleading	Within 10 days after service of amended pleading or within time remaining for response to original pleading, whichever is longer, unless court otherwise orders. Civ.R. 15(a).
To supplemental pleading	As ordered by court. Civ.R. 15(d).
Alteration of time by service of Civ.R. 12 motion	Service of motion permitted under Civ.R. 12 alters times for responsive pleadings as follows unless different time fixed by court:

(1) if court denies motion, service of responsive pleading within 10 days after notice of denial;

(2) if court postpones disposition until trial on merits, service of responsive pleading within 10 days after notice of postponement;

(3) if court grants motion for more definite statement, service of responsive pleading within 10 days after service of the more definite statement.

RESTRAINING order, temporary without notice	See "Injunction", this table.
RETURN	The court may allow a summons or proof of service to be amended. Civ.R. 4(a) & (*l*). The person effecting service shall make proof thereof to the court. Civ.R. 4(*l*).
SANCTIONS	Presentation to court of a pleading, written motion, or other paper is a certification under Civ.R. 11(b). If after notice and reasonable opportunity to respond, court determines that Civ.R. 11(b) was violated, sanctions may be imposed by a motion for sanctions which shall not be filed or presented to court unless, within 21 days after service of the motion, the challenged matter is not withdrawn or corrected. Civ.R. 11(c). Sanctions are inapplicable to discovery. Civ.R. 11(d).
SATURDAYS AND SUNDAYS	Exclusion in computation of time. Civ.R. 6(a); App.R. 26(a).
STAY or supersedeas	See "Appeal", "Execution", this table.
SUBPOENA	
Objection	Within 14 days after service of the subpoena or before the time specified for compliance if such time is less than 14 days after service, there be served upon the party or attorney designated in the subpoena written objection to inspection or copying of any or all of the designated materials or of the premises. Civ.R. 45(c)(2)(B).
Motion to compel production	If objection has been made, the party serving the subpoena may, upon notice to the person commanded to produce, move at any time for an order to compel the production. Civ.R. 45(c)(2)(B).
Motion to quash	The court by which a subpoena was issued shall quash or modify the subpoena on timely motion. Civ.R. 45(c)(3)(A).
Witnesses, documentary evidence, etc.	Subpoena specifies time for attendance and giving of testimony or to produce and permit inspection and copying of designated books, documents or tangible things in the possession, custody or control of that person, or to permit inspection of premises. Civ.R. 45(a)(1)(C).
SUBSTITUTION of parties	In cases of death, incompetency, or transfer of interest—motion for substitution, together with notice of hearing, served on parties as provided in Civ.R. 5 and upon persons not parties in manner provided in Civ.R. 4 for service of a summons. Civ.R. 25(a), (b), (c). Dismissal as to deceased party unless motion for substitution is made not later than 90 days after death is suggested upon the record. Civ.R. 25(a). Successor of public officer substituted automatically. Order of substitution may be entered at any time. Civ.R. 25(d).

SUMMARY JUDGMENT,
motion for

Claimant	May move at any time after expiration of 20 days from commencement of action or after service of motion for summary judgment by adverse party. Civ.R. 56(a).
Defending party	May move at any time. Civ.R. 56(b).
Service	Service of motion at least 20 days before time fixed for hearing. Civ.R. 56(c).
	Service of opposing affidavits prior to day of hearing. Civ.R. 56(c).

SUMMONS — Served with a copy of complaint. Civ.R. 4(c)(1). If not served within 120 days after filing complaint, court may dismiss action without prejudice, direct service be effected within a specified time, or extend time for service. Civ.R. 4(m).

The person effecting service shall make proof thereof to the court. Civ.R. 4(*l*).

Service by any nonparty at least 18, a U.S. marshal, deputy U.S. marshal, or other person or officer specially appointed. Civ.R. 4(c)(2).

SUPPLEMENTAL pleadings — See "Pleadings", this table.

SUPERSEDEAS or stay — See "Appeal", "Execution", this table.

TERM — The district courts deemed always open. Civ.R. 77(a).

Terms of court have been abolished. 28 U.S.C.A. §§ 138–141, as amended by Act of Oct. 16, 1963, Pub.L. 88—139, 77 Stat. 248.

THIRD-PARTY practice — Third-party plaintiff need not obtain leave if third-party plaintiff files third-party complaint not later than 10 days after serving the original answer. Otherwise, must obtain leave on motion upon notice to all parties to the action. Civ.R. 14(a).

VERDICT

Renewal of motion for judgment after trial	Within 10 days after entry of judgment, motion for judgment as a matter of law may be renewed by service and filing where motion made at the close of all the evidence is denied or for any reason is not granted. Civ.R. 50(b).
	Exception from general rule relating to enlargement. Civ.R. 6(b).
New trial where judgment as a matter of law rendered	Party against whom judgment as a matter of law has been rendered may served a motion for a new trial pursuant to Civ.R. 59 not later than 10 days after entry of the judgment. Civ.R. 50(c)(2).

Source: *Federal Rules of Civil Procedure, 1994–95 Educational Edition.* 1994. St. Paul, Minn: West Publishing Company.

APPENDIX B

HYPOTHETICAL CASE

■ FACTS

John Griffin is a lawyer. He is married and has two adult sons who live in his home. He owned several vehicles, which were used by members of the family. In 1985 he bought a used 1982 GMC pickup truck from a lien holder who obtained repossession. John contacted his insurance agent, Frederick Burns, and asked him to insure the pickup truck with one hundred thousand dollars of liability insurance. Burns is the owner and sole proprietor of the Burns Agency. The agency is not incorporated. Agent Burns placed the coverage with the Security Insurance Company. Security sent a policy to John. It contained the coverage he had requested. John's adult son, Carl Griffin became the principal driver of the GMC pickup. They treated the pickup as though it belonged to Carl. Carl bought the gasoline and paid for minor repairs. However, John paid for the insurance. In 1994, Carl decided he wanted a Chevrolet Camaro instead of the pickup truck. John agreed that Carl could sell the pickup if he could find a buyer, and he could use the proceeds to buy a used Camaro. A friend told Carl that Bradley Harper was looking for a pickup truck. Carl contacted Harper, and they were able to agree on a sale price of twenty-one hundred dollars. Carl told John about the buyer and the tentative terms for the sale. John agreed that it was a fair price. John could not find his certificate of title for the pickup, to give to the buyer. He was concerned that he might be liable for Harper's operation of the truck until he could transfer the certificate of title to Harper. He concluded that he would keep insurance on the pickup to protect himself.

John Griffin prepared a handwritten buy-sell agreement for the transaction. The buy-sell agreement provided as follows:

SALE OF MOTOR VEHICLE

Seller: 333 Bittersweet Ln.
        Mitchell, Iowa

Buyer: Bradley Harper
       Goodthunder, Minnesota

I, Bradley Harper, hereby purchase from M. John Griffin a 1982 GMC pickup, Sierra Classic 1500 Series, today, April 6, 1994, for Two Thousand One Hundred Dollars ($2,100.00). The purchaser has inspected the vehicle and is purchasing the vehicle "as is," without warranty.

The seller does not have the certificate of title as of today. The seller shall use his best efforts to obtain said title as soon as possible. Seller shall keep insurance on said vehicle until title is obtained.

Dated this 6th of April, 1994.

> M. John Griffin, Seller
> Bradley D. Harper, Purchaser

On April 6, 1994, Carl Griffin met with Harper at their friend's house. They went over the terms of the written proposal. They agreed that the proposal was correct. Both men signed the sale-of-motor-vehicle agreement on April 6, 1994. Harper paid the full purchase price in cash. Harper took possession of the pickup. He made some modifications to it, including the installation of a new radio. Harper operated it as his own vehicle. Carl used the proceeds of the sale to buy the Camaro. He bought the Camaro on April 10, 1994.

On April 10, 1994, Carl Griffin informed the Burns Agency that his father had sold the pickup and that they had purchased a Chevrolet Camaro to replace the pickup. Carl requested automobile insurance coverage for the Camaro. An insurance secretary at the Burns Agency completed the necessary documents to cancel the policy on the pickup and transfer the unearned premium on a new policy for the Camaro.

Although the buy-sell agreement provided that John Griffin would use his best efforts to locate and deliver to Harper the certificate of title, six months passed and he stopped looking for it. In the meantime, Harper expected John Griffin to "keep" insurance on the pickup for Harper's benefit. However, contrary to John's expectations, the insurance coverage on the pickup terminated by operation of law when ownership of the pickup passed to Harper. Although he is a practicing lawyer, John did not realize that his coverage terminated, and he made no effort to buy other insurance for Harper.

On October 17, 1994, Harper was driving the 1982 GMC pickup easterly on Hubbard County Road 13. County Road 13 is a two-lane secondary highway with one lane in each direction. Harper had a passenger whose name is James Patner. His address and age are unknown. Harper was driving about 55 mph, which is the speed limit. The weather was clear. The road was in good condition. Traffic was very sparse. Driving conditions were good in every respect. Harper came upon a 1981 Chevette driven by William Nordby. Nordby was born on February 9, 1922. He was seventy-two years of age. Nordby was also proceeding easterly on County Road 13; however, he was driving quite slowly. Harper had a good view down the road. He could see that there were no oncoming vehicles. The County Road 118 intersection was less than two hundred yards ahead. County Road 118 formed a T-intersection with County Road 13 entering on the north side. Harper did not see any turn signal on the Chevette. He decided to pass Nordby's Chevette. Harper moved into the westbound lane to pass. As Harper's pickup truck was just about to pass Nordby's Chevette, Nordby made a left-hand turn to go north on County Road 118. Harper applied his brakes and skidded forward. The front end of the pickup struck the left rear fender of Nordby's Chevette. The police subsequently measured seventy-eight feet of skid marks[1] left by Harper's pickup. The Chev-

---

1. An accident reconstructionist was erroneously told or assumed the skid marks were 121 feet in length.

ette spun counterclockwise and came to rest north of the intersection on the east shoulder of 118. The pickup came to rest at the northeast corner of the intersection, facing southeasterly.

The Hubbard County sheriff investigated. Harper told the sheriff that the Chevette made a sudden turn in front of him while he was attempting to pass. The Chevette did not signal for a left turn. He could not avoid hitting the Chevette. Nordby was unconscious at the scene. He was transported to a regional hospital by ambulance. He did regain consciousness, but he never left the hospital. His injuries led to his death on April 5, 1995. He was never questioned by anyone about how the accident occurred. Nordby was seventy-three years of age at the time of his death. His wife and his adult daughter, Laura Raskin, survived him. They incurred $100,000 in medical expenses for Nordby's care and $4,772 for funeral and burial expenses. The Chevette was not repairable. It had a fair market value of $7,500.

Harper sustained some minor cuts on his face and scalp. He suffered a neck and back sprain. He did not lose consciousness, but he started having recurring headaches and was irritable for months following the accident. He did not require hospitalization. He saw his family doctor four times over the following six months. He had twelve chiropractic treatments for his neck and back during the second month following the accident. His condition improved, but his chiropractor believes that Harper will have some permanent disability of his spine because of the accident. His medical expenses total $300. His chiropractic expenses total $375. All the expenses have been covered by Harper's medical insurance. The pickup truck could not be repaired and was considered to be a total loss.

Harper contacted John Griffin to find out with which insurance company he had arranged to insure the pickup truck, as provided by the April 6, 1994, buy-sell agreement. John had made no effort to buy insurance to cover Harper and the 1982 GMC pickup truck after the sale. He had mistakenly assumed that he still had coverage with Security Insurance because he had not asked the agent to cancel the coverage. John contacted his agent, Burns, and explained the circumstances to the agent. Burns verified that the coverage on the pickup truck had been transferred to the Camaro on April 10, 1994. Security Insurance had issued a notice of the change of the policy. It also sent monthly billings to John, showing coverage on a Camaro and no coverage for the pickup truck after April 1994. John contacted attorney Sharon Gleason to help him deal with the situation. In the meantime, John explained to Harper that he believed that Security Insurance provided coverage, but the company was denying coverage.

On July 29, 1995, the Hubbard County District Court appointed Raskin, daughter of Nordby, to be trustee for the heirs and next of kin of the decedent. She brought suit in Hubbard County District Court in an action entitled *Laura Raskin, as trustee for the heirs and next of kin of William Nordby v. Bradley Harper.* Since John Griffin did not own the pickup at the time of the accident and was not vicariously liable for Harper's operation of the pickup, no action was brought against him. The trustee alleged that Harper was negligent for driving at an excessive rate of speed, failed to maintain control over his pickup, improperly passed, and failed to keep a proper lookout. The trustee asked for money damages in the amount of four hundred thousand dollars.

Harper duly interposed an answer. He denied that he was negligent. He alleged that Nordby was negligent for failing to keep a proper lookout, failing to signal his turn, and failing to keep his vehicle under control.

Harper brought a third-party action against John Griffin to obtain indemnity for any money damages for which Harper might be liable to the trustee. The claim for indemnity was based upon John's breach of contract for failure to obtain or provide insurance on the pickup as provided in the sale-of-motor-vehicle agreement.

John Griffin duly interposed an answer. He did not deny that he made the agreement, but he denied that the agreement is enforceable as a contract. He contended that there was no separate consideration for the promise to "keep" insurance coverage on the pickup truck. The twenty-one hundred dollars Harper paid was the consideration that Harper agreed to pay for the pickup. John also contended there was no meeting of the minds concerning essential terms and conditions, such as the amount of coverage or the identity of the insurer or the types of coverage. He contended that, at most, he is liable for the minimum amount of coverage required by state law. He alleged all the affirmative defenses that Harper alleged as defenses to the trustee's action.

John Griffin commenced a fourth-party action against Agent Burns. He alleged that Agent Burns was negligent for "cancelling" John's Security Insurance automobile policy on the pickup truck without his express authority. Further, he alleged that Agent Burns was negligent for not informing him that he had canceled the coverage or transferred it to the Camaro. He alleged that if Burns had told him about the change of coverage to the Camaro, he would have gone elsewhere to obtain the coverage he expected to provide to Harper.

Burns duly interposed an answer to the fourth-party complaint. The fourth-party answer denied that he effectively "canceled" coverage, because the coverage had already terminated by reason of John Griffin's sale of the pickup to Harper. He alleged that Carl Griffin had actual or apparent authority to order cancellation of the coverage on the pickup truck and request coverage for the Camaro. Agent Burns contended that John Griffin could not have been damaged by Burns's "transfer" of the coverage to the Camaro as Carl requested, because John could not insure the pickup as his truck after he sold it. Agent Burns's answer alleged all the defenses that John had to Harper's third-party action and all the defenses that Harper had to the trustee's wrongful death action.

This hypothetical case is predicated upon three separate actions and one counterclaim. (1) the trustee's wrongful death action arose from an occurrence. It is an action in tort. The cause of action is based upon negligence. The plaintiff trustee must allege and prove that Harper was negligent and that his negligence caused or contributed to the October 17, 1994, accident and Nordby's subsequent death. The plaintiff trustee must prove the nature and extent of the heirs' and next of kin's damages. (2) Harper has a claim for breach of contract against John Griffin for failing to provide insurance in some amount on the pickup truck to cover the accident. To exercise this claim, Harper must prove that he had a valid contract with John, that John breached the contract, and that Harper sustained damages. (3) John claims a right of action in negligence against Agent Burns on the grounds that Burns wrongfully canceled the insurance policy. John must prove that he sustained a loss and that the loss (damage) was caused by a breach of a legal duty Burns owed to John. Specifically, John must establish that Agent Burns was negligent for canceling John's coverage on the pickup truck and that Agent Burns's negligence was the proximate cause of John's loss.

In dealing with such case, paralegals are not required to determine the parties' legal rights and obligations or to analyze legal issues. Instead, they help lawyers conduct the procedures that make the system work. Each party needs legal representation and assistance. Each party must be interviewed. The accident must be investigated. The actions must be commenced. An accident reconstructionist (expert witness) may be necessary. Discovery must be conducted. The claims must be prepared for trial. Consideration should be given to severing issues for separate trials.

■ ACCIDENT REPORT

PS-32003-06 (1-91)

STATE OF MINNESOTA – DEPARTMENT OF PUBLIC SAFETY
TRAFFIC ACCIDENT REPORT
(FOR POLICE USE ONLY AS REQUIRED BY STATUTE)   PAGE _____ OF _____

FOR DPS USE ONLY

LOCAL CASE NO 90-2135B

HIT-AND-RUN: ☐ ATTENDED ☐ UNATTENDED | PUB PROP: No | VEHICLES: 2 | KILLED: 0 | INJURED: 3 | $ MIN | | MONTH 10 | DATE 17 | YEAR 94 | DAY Mon | TIME 1:37 ☐ AM ☐ PM

ROUTE SYSTEM: CSAH | ROUTE NUMBER OR STREET NAME: County Rd # 13 | ☒ AT INTERSECTION ↓ OR | ☐ MI ☐ N ☐ E ☐ FT ☐ S ☐ W OF ↓
WITH

COUNTY NO 39 | ☐ CITY ☒ TWP Lincoln | INT ELEM | REFERENCE POINT _____ + _____ . _____ | ROUTE SYS CR | ROUTE #, STREET, CORP LIMIT, REF POINT OR FEATURE CR 118

UNIT 2: ☒ VEHICLE ☐ PEDESTRIAN ☐ BICYCLE

FACTOR 1 | DRIVER LICENSE NUMBER - 1 H 16037 B 1496 | STATE Mn | CLASS C | DRIVER LICENSE NUMBER - 2 N- 468 291 73 103 | STATE | CLASS C | FACTOR 1

FACTOR 2 | NAME (FIRST, MIDDLE, LAST) Bradley Harper | RSTRCTNS COMPLIED Yes | WTHDRWN | NAME (FIRST, MIDDLE, LAST) William Nordby | RSTRCTNS COMPLIED Yes | WTHDRWN | FACTOR 2

MNUVER | ADDRESS | DATE OF BIRTH 12|22|60 | ADDRESS Tower Apartments | DATE OF BIRTH 2|9|22 | MNUVER

PHYSCL | CITY, STATE, ZIP Goodthunder, Minnesota | CITY, STATE, ZIP Rochester, Minnesota | PHYSCL

RCOMND | ADDRESS CORRECT ☐ | SEX M | EJECT No | RSTRNT No | INJCOD | TO HOSP No ☐ AMBULANCE ☐ OTHER | ADDRESS CORRECT | SEX M | EJECT Yes | RSTRNT Yes | INJCOD | TO HOSP Yes ☒ AMBULANCE ☐ OTHER | RCOMND

VEHTYP | OWNER NAME John Griffin | OWNER NAME Same as above | VEHTYP

FIRE | ADDRESS 333 Bittersweet Lane | OCCUP | ADDRESS | OCCUP | FIRE

TOW | CITY, STATE, ZIP Mitchell, Iowa | PULLING UNIT No | DIRECT | CITY, STATE, ZIP | PULLING UNIT | DIRECT | TOW

DMGLOC | MAKE GMC | MODEL Pickup | YEAR 82 | COLOR Blk | SEQUENCE OF EVENTS | MAKE Chev | MODEL Chevette | YEAR 81 | COLOR Maroon | SEQUENCE OF EVENTS | DMGLOC

DMGSEV Total | PLATE # 372 BWG | STATE | YEAR | INSURANCE Security Ins. Co. | PLATE # 875 RTS | STATE | YEAR | INSURANCE Farmers | DMGSEV Total

INJURED PASSENGERS/WITNESSES

	UNIT	POSTN	AGE	SEX	EJECT	RSTRNT	INJCOD	TO HOSP	TRANSPORT
James Patner, Goodthunder		Front	22	M	No	No		No	☐ AMBULANCE ☐ OTHER
									☐ AMBULANCE ☐ OTHER
									☐ AMBULANCE ☐ OTHER
									☐ AMBULANCE ☐ OTHER

ACCTYP | OWNER OF OTHER DAMAGED PROPERTY AND/OR YELLOW TAG NUMBER(S) | AMBULANCE SERVICE(S) AND/OR STATE AMBULANCE RUN NUMBER(S)

FXDOBJ | ON BRIDGE | LOCATN | RDWORK | RDESGN | RDSURF | RDCHAR

NORTH

N ↑

CR 118

CR 13

DESCRIPTION, CHARGES PENDING, AND OR CITATIONS ISSUED

Driver of Vehicle #1 stated when he came over the hill, about a quarter mile from the intersection, he saw a vehicle ahead of him on the roadway also pointed east. As he came upon the vehicle, the vehicle appeared stopped, or going very slowly. Harper stated that he attempted to pass on the left. The vehicle turned left, & they collided. Both vehicles ended up in ditch in NE corner of intersection, Driver #2 unconscious.

DEVICE | WORKING | SPEED LIMIT 55 INTREL | WEATHER Clear | PHOTOS TAKEN No LIGHT | DIAGRAM

OFFICER RANK, NAME, BADGE #, AND AGENCY Gordon Smith   Badge # 22   Hubbard County | ☐ PATROL ☒ SHERIFF | ☐ LOCAL ☐ OTHER

■ MEMORANDUM

TO: File

FROM: Paralegal

SUBJECT: Accident Reconstructionist

The reconstructionist has formed the following opinions:

1. The Harper pickup laid down 121 feet of skid marks before entering the northeast ditch. The vehicle continued its skid in the ditch. The left-side skid marks start 46 feet west of the right-side skids.

2. The left-side skid marks start 10.6 feet north of the south edge of the traveled portion of, or totally within, the eastbound lane.

3. Harper's minimum speed prior to the initiation of braking was 51 mph. After allowing for energy absorption by the collision itself and skidding or braking off the roadway, the likely speed at the time of initiation of braking activity was in excess of the speed limit of 55 mph.

4. The roadway is generally flat and level to the west of the scene of the accident, with good visibility. Accordingly, there is no reason that Harper could not view the Nordby Chevette for approximately one-quarter mile and appropriately reduce his speed. It is apparent that he did not do so and was traveling at or above the speed limit at the point he initiated braking.

5. Harper gave a statement on 11/17/94 in which he stated that when he first saw the Nordby Chevette, both vehicles were in the eastbound lane. He stated that he did not feel at that point that he would be able to stop or avoid contact by remaining in his own lane and, accordingly, went into the left lane to avoid collision. This statement, together with the physical fact that Harper skidded 121 feet before going into the ditch, confirms the conclusion that Harper did not have his vehicle under control sufficiently so as to avoid collision with the Nordby Chevette. This was obviously a panic maneuver, due to a high rate of speed and lack of control.

■ TRANSCRIPT OF TELEPHONE INTERVIEW

Q: Mr. Harper, this is Diane Kaplan. I am an investigator for the Security Insurance Company. Your accident has been reported to us. Mr. Griffin says that you are insured under his policy with this company. May I discuss the accident with you?

A: I guess so.

Q: Good. This should only take a few minutes. This telephone conversation is being recorded. I need to make a record of what we say. Is that allright with you?

A: Do I have any choice? . . . What are we going to talk about?

Q: Well, this is November 7, 1994. I want to get your version of the accident you had with William Nordby on October 15th—

A: October 17.

Q: I'm sorry. You're right. Yes. I need to talk with you about how the accident happened. The company needs to have your version.

A: I understand. Do I need an attorney.

Q: Do you have a lawyer?

A: Not yet. But I have talked to a couple.

Q: I can't tell you what you should do. I can tell you that I have to have a statement if Security is going to help you with this accident. You do understand that a recorder is running.

A: Yeah.

Q: What?

A: Yes.

Q: OK. What is your address?

A: Goodthunder.

Q: That's Minnesota.

A: Yes.

Q: What is your birth date?

A: December 22, 1960.

Q: Are you married?

A: No, I'm single.

Q: What's your occupation?

A: I'm a student.

Q: What is your social security number?

A: 555-55-5555.

Q: Who is the title holder of the GMC pickup truck you were driving? Do you know?

A: John Griffin, I think.

Q: You were driving with his permission?

A: Yes. I bought it from him. He said he would keep the insurance on it until he could give me the title card.

Q: He did what?

A: He said he would keep the insurance on it.

Q: Why?

A: He put it in writing. I have the bill of sale.

Q: OK. What kind of condition was it in?

A: Good. Real good.

Q: Was there any physical damage on it before the accident?

A: Not that I know of.

Q: Well, where were you coming from?

A: We were coming from Goodthunder. We were on our way to Bob Johnson's place.

Q: Who is we? Did you have a passenger?

A: Yes. Jim Patner.

Q: Can you spell that for me?

A: P-a-t-n-e-r.

Q: And the other vehicle involved, do you know who owned it?

A: The guy who was driving, I suppose. Nordby. Bill Nordby.

Q: What kind of car was it?

A: A late-model Chevrolet, or Chevette.

Q: And how was the condition; any prior damage on it?

A: What prior damage?

Q: Hum?

A: You mean its condition?

Q: Yes.

A: It was totaled.

Q: No. I mean before the accident.

A: No idea.

Q: Were you wearing a seat belt?

A: No. Doesn't have any.

Q: I see. Are there any restrictions on your license.

A: Nope.

Q: Was you passenger wearing his seat belt?

A: Negative.

Q: Had you had any drugs or alcohol before the accident?

A: You mean that day?

Q: What time did the accident happen?

A: About one in the afternoon.

Q: Had you had anything that day?

A: No.

Q: The previous day.

A: I don't do drugs.

Q: Any alcohol?

A: Not that I remember.

Q: How were the weather conditions?

A: Sky was overcast. Maybe, slightly misting.

Q: And were—what road were you on, or street were you traveling on?

A: County Road 13, going east.

Q: What's the speed limit?

A: Fifty-five miles per hour.

Q: OK. I'm trying to picture this. I'm going to make a sketch here. You're going east on 13 at fifty-five miles per hour. Where was the other car? Could you place that for me?

A: Yeah, I'm going east. Nordby was also facing, going, east on 13. It's a '81 Chevette.

Q: OK. Was he ahead of you or behind you?

A: He is ahead, long way ahead when I first seen him.

Q: How many lanes for 13?

A: Two lanes, one each way. East, west.

Q: What about lane markers? Any dotted lines, anything like that?

A: To my recollect, I believe there is a centerline markings.

Q: Just the dotted type?

A: Yeah. I believe so.

Q: Describe the surface?

A: I can't recollect for sure. The surface is blacktop.

Q: How long had it been misting?

A: I'd say about, probably within an hour.

Q: And did—at the time of the accident, did you need, use, your windshield wipers?

A: No, that wasn't necessary.

Q: How about the lay of the road; is it straight or curved or what?

A: Thirteen is straight. A quarter mile from the [inaudible] of collision a rise in the road.

Q: OK.

A: Otherwise, it's flat and straight.

Q: In your own words, why don't you tell me what happened.

A: We—I viewed Mr. Nordby's car sitting—I believe I initially viewed him in the distance. I viewed the vehicle in a stationary position, facing east in the right-hand lane, sitting there off center more towards the right without brake lights or blinker indicators. And viewed the vehicle as stationary and proceeded to pass him. It looked like he was sitting there an—watching him as I went into the left-hand lane to pass towards him or around him, seen him make a physical move to turn left, at which time I tried to move further to go around him, laying on my horn and going for the brakes and braking.

Q: How far back do you figure you noticed him making his left-hand turn?

A: Oh, I would say—I would say, I didn't view him actually making the physical move until point-blank range. When I was actually, had just made the lane change.

Q: OK.

A: I had seen him stationary. I was in a position where I couldn't brake the vehicle without—and avoid hitting him by staying in the same lane. I also didn't view the ability to go around him on the right, as I was making my commitment turn left at that time. I immediately, after I went into the left lane to start to go there, I seen his head—turn—to the left, which at that time I come to the realization possibly not stay sitting there and was going to make some sort of action. I put on the horn. I would say . . . approximately twenty-five foot, thirty foot.

Q: What was he turning?

A: He proceeded to turn left.

Q: Was it on a side road, or was he going to make a U-turn?

A: That's total subjectory for me, 'cause we had impact before obviously he made a completion of what he was going to do.

Q: Was there an intersecting road?

A: There is a T-road there. There is a road to the left but no road to the right.

Q: OK.

A: It was a field driveway approach. There is a field driveway approach to your right.

Q: At this intersection, I mean, does it have a, you know ... You were on County Road 13. Does that intersecting road have a county name or any-thing? an identifier?

A: One eighteen, I believe.

Q: And how fast were you going?

A: I was going the speed limit. Fifty-five miles per hour.

Q: Did you have your lights on or ...?

A: I can't recollect if I did or didn't. I believe I probably did not.

Q: And then what happened?

A: I went for the brake. I put the brakes on and tried to maneuver further to the left, around into the far ditch, and was unsuccessful at that. We had impact in a matter of short—or period of incident reactionary time of a second or two. He made contact with us in the front passenger fender at about the front wheel, right above the front wheel, and brought us together side to side, and we went into the left-hand ditch beyond the intersection.

Q: OK. Then what happened?

A: I got out of the vehicle and viewed the individual in the vehicle, and the first vehicle arrived on the scene I flagged down, and immediately sent for an ambulance assistance, medical assistance, called at ... And we waited by Nordby's car until they arrived.

Q: And how about injuries in your vehicle? Were there any injuries on your—

A: Injury to the party in my vehicle?

Q: Right.

A: No. Nothing of significance.

Q: Nothing of significance, but you didn't feel any—

A: No, there were no injuries.

Q: And was your car—was the pickup truck you were driving drivable after the accident?

A: I guess that's within question. The vehicle—the engine ran. We did not drive it after the accident. It was towed from the accident scene and sub-sequently towed also. It hasn't been driven since. Whether it's movable by driving, it's questionable.

Q: And you say it was owned by John Griffin. Did you have permission to drive this car—or the pickup, I mean?

A: Yes, I did. We had a purchase agreement made on it.

Q: Could you tell me about the purchase agreement, like when it was made?

A: The first week of April, dated on, I would assume, was the 6th of April. I made an exchange of two thousand one hundred dollars with John's son,

Carl, and signed an agreement that was written up by John and signed by John.

Q: But you said it was with John's son, Carl. Was Carl titled owner of the vehicle, or do you know if John was?

A: No, I believe John is.

Q: And when did you expect—when were they going to produce the title for you?

A: As quickly as possible. I was expecting it thereafter. Purchase agreement says that he would use his best efforts to obtain title as soon as possible.

Q: Was there another agreement?

A: No, this was an ongoing agreement with conversation following this.

Q: And did you report this to your insurance agent, or anything, that you would be driving this vehicle?

A: Yes, I did, actually. It was brought up that I would possibly upon receiving transfer of vehicle, that I would be insuring that pickup. Possibly in the winter of this coming month or whenever I obtained the title to said vehicle.

Q: And . . .

A: The last time I believe I had conversation and renewal of my policy, that was brought up.

Q: Last time you had renewal. About April or so? Does that sound about—

A: No, this was discussed with my agent just briefly as a topic of my policy, which directions—I had insured a vehicle and had said possibly this standard policy hadn't held, that I would call and, depending upon which vehicle, I would add or delete.

Q: Was it going to be—oh, you didn't know exactly if you were going to sell?

A: Recollect when this was?

Q: Well, you did know if it was going to be a replacement vehicle or an additional vehicle?

A: Right.

Q: On the—

A: Depending on, of course, what I would be driving and would be liable if I would continue to carry additional insurance on the minivan, or if it was decided that that vehicle . . . Then I would insure other vehicle or one would be added.

Q: Did you do anything to the pickup after you got it?

A: Yeah, I put a new stereo in it.

Q: Where can the truck be viewed?

A: I got it at home, now.

Q: Let's see, after the accident, did the police investigate?

A: Yes, there was the Hubbard County sheriffs and, I think, state troopers.

Q: Did you talk with the police?

A: Yes, I did.

Q: And what did they say afterwards?

A: Not a whole lot.

Q: Did they issue any tickets?

A: No, no tickets were issued.

Q: The—Nordby, do you know where he was taken to?

A: I believe he was taken to Redeemers Hospital and then transferred.

Q: Were there any witnesses?

A: Not at the time. Some came later.

Q: Who do you think was at fault for the accident?

A: Well, I feel that I've done everything correct in my behalf, so I would say that William Nordby was at fault for not using blinkers or indicators. I didn't see any brake lights or anything of that sort, so . . .

Q: Is there anything else that you would like to add concerning the accident details?

A: I think I've described them just as comprehensive as I can.

Q: OK. Have you understood all of these questions?

A: Yes, I believe so.

Q: And to the best of your knowledge, the information given is true and correct?

A: Yes, it is.

Q: And you understand that this interview has been continuously recorded?

A: I understand that, yes.

Q: This is Diane Kaplan concluding the interview with Bradley Harper on November 7, 1994, at 2:30 P.M.

■ EXPERT'S DIAGRAM

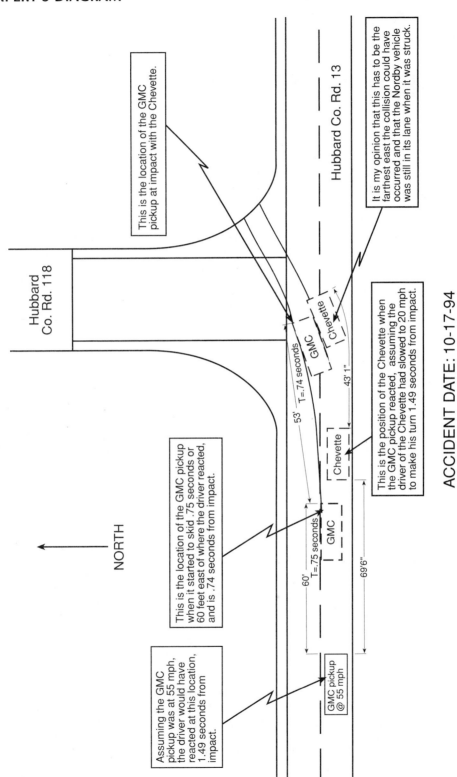

This is the location of the GMC pickup at impact with the Chevette.

It is my opinion that this has to be the farthest east the collision could have occurred and that the Nordby vehicle was still in its lane when it was struck.

Hubbard Co. Rd. 13

Hubbard Co. Rd. 118

This is the position of the Chevette when the GMC pickup reacted, assuming the driver of the Chevette had slowed to 20 mph to make his turn 1.49 seconds from impact.

This is the location of the GMC pickup when it started to skid .75 seconds or 60 feet east of where the driver reacted, and is .74 seconds from impact.

Chevette

GMC

Chevette

GMC

53'   T=.74 seconds

43' 1"

60'   T=.75 seconds

6'9'6"

NORTH

Assuming the GMC pickup was at 55 mph, the driver would have reacted at this location, 1.49 seconds from impact.

GMC pickup @ 55 mph

ACCIDENT DATE: 10-17-94

APPENDIX C

DEPOSITION TRANSCRIPT

The following is an actual discovery deposition. The deponent was a plaintiff in a personal injury action that resulted from an automobile accident. (Names, addresses, and dates have been changed to protect privacy.) The transcript illustrates the necessity of being persistent and detailed. Four major areas are covered, though the areas are not separated in any obvious manner: (1) the deponent's background, (2) the deponent's previous health and accidents, (3) the accident in question, and (4) the consequential injuries and expenses claimed by the deponent. Of particular interest is the deponent's obvious lack of preparation for the deposition. The transcript should be read in light of the various guidelines suggested for preparing a witness to testify. As an epilogue, the defendant's insurer was able to obtain a dismissal of the case with only a nominal settlement.

Duane Johnson, Plaintiff, vs. Clarence A. Souter, Defendant and Third-Party Plaintiff vs. Carolyn Jones, Third-Party Defendant.	DEPOSITION TRANSCRIPT

APPEARANCES

Ellen Clarke, Esq., appeared on behalf of the plaintiff.

John Fredricks, Esq., appeared on behalf of the defendant and third-party plaintiff.

Lang & Spencer, by Robert L. Lang, Esq., appeared on behalf of the third-party defendant.

DISCOVERY DEPOSITION OF DUANE JOHNSON, taken under the Federal Rules of Civil Procedure for the district courts, at 700 Titan Building, Detroit, Michigan, on August 13, 1994, before John R. Nash, a notary public, commencing at approximately 11:10 A.M.

DUANE JOHNSON,

plaintiff, called on behalf of the defendant and third-party plaintiff, having been first duly sworn, testified on his oath as follows:

EXAMINATION

By Mr. Fredricks:

Q: Will you state your full name, please?

A: Duane Anthony Johnson.

Q: What is your birth date?

A: One–twenty-two–seventy.

Q: Where were you born?

A: Kansas City, Kansas.

Q: Where?

A: Kansas City, Kansas.

Q: Where do you currently reside?

A: You mean in Detroit.

Q: Yes.

A: South Detroit

Q: What is your address?

A: 1530 East 40th and a Half-Street.

Q: East 40th and a Half?

A: Yes. South Detroit

Q: How long have you lived there?

A: About nine months?

Q: Are you married?

A: No, single.

Q: Have you ever been married?

A: No, I haven't.

Q: Do you live with anyone at that address?

A: Friend.

Q: Who?

A: Catherine Baker.

Q: What's the name again?

A: Catherine Baker.

Q: You say you are friends.

A: Well, just two-bedroom apartment.

Q: I mean you are not related in any way.

A: No.

Q: How long has she been there?

A: About a year or two. About a year.

Q: Where did you reside before moving to your current address?

A: 16th Avenue. I forgot that apartment number. It was on 20—26th and 16th Avenue.

Q: How long did you live at that address?

A: About two months, three months.

Q: Where do your parents reside?

A: At the present time, 4245 Park Avenue South.

Q: And your father's name is what?

A: Donald Johnson.

Q: Are you presently employed?

A: Part-time.

Q: Where do you work?

A: Hearns Auditorium.

Q: I'm having a hard time hearing you.

A: Hearns Auditorium. That's on the Detroit campus.

Q: What do you do there?

A: Work in the office. Office work.

Q: How long have you worked there?

A: This summer. Started this summer. Summer work. That's for Model City.

Q: Who is your immediate supervisor?

A: Henry Hyslop.

Q: Will you spell the last name?

A: H-y-l—H-y-s-l-o-p.

Q: Do you intend to continue working there indefinitely?

A: No. That's just summer work, you know.

Q: Will that job end then in September?

A: It ends this month sometime.

Q: What other jobs have you had since August of 1993?

A: I was working at Honeywell on an assembly line, I think that was in '93.

Q: You work at Honeywell where?

A: In Detroit, Honeywell.

Q: What kind of work did you do for Honeywell?

A: Was just small work, just on an assembly line–like thing. It wasn't no kind of strenuous work.

Q: For what period of time did you work there?

A: That was summer work too.

Q: What was your pay rate while at Honeywell?

A: Ten dollars.

Ms. Clarke: You are going to have to yell a little bit louder, because I'm having a little bit of trouble hearing you, too.

The Witness: About ten dollars an hour.

Q: [*By Mr. Fredricks*] Did you take an employment physical, exam—

A: No I didn't.

Q: —before going to work for Honeywell—

A: No.

Q: —while working at Honeywell?

A: No.

Q: Did you make out an application for that employment?

A: Yes, I did.

Q: And was there any inquiry about the status of your health or physical condition in that application?

A: No, there wasn't.

Q: Okay. What was your condition, your physical condition, when you made your application to work at Honeywell? Were you having any problems?

A: The application wasn't like that, you know, as far as your health. The application wasn't—you know, it didn't ask about your health, you know, your background, nothing like that.

Q: I'm asking you now—what was your condition when you made out that application?

A: Back trouble and neck.

Q: Back and leg trouble?

A: Back and neck.

Q: And neck. Anything else?

A: That was the most—main thing at that time.

Q: Did you have to make out an application for your work when you started working for Hearns Auditorium.

A: No.

Q: Have you had any other employment since August of 1993?

A: No. I was working—last year I was working at the Children's Theatre and—

Q: Where?

A: Detroit, South Detroit. That was at—at the Mann. No, not the Mann, it's on 3d Avenue, the Art Institute, Detroit Art Institute, and I was working for the Children's Theatre. That's combined together.

Q: How long did you work there?

A: That was summer work also.

Q: What was your pay rate at the time?

A: Ten dollars an hour.

Q: You worked forty hours a week, did you?

A: Yes.

Q: When you were at Honeywell, did you work forty hours a week?

A: Yes, it was.

Q: Did you work regularly at all of these jobs during the summer months? Did you work regularly, or did you have to miss a lot of time?

A: Well, I was getting hot pack treatments at Dr. Peterson's office.

Q: You mean after work?

A: Well, sometimes I have to go on work [time] because his office is only open in the afternoon.

Q: Other than the times you went for back treatments, did you have to miss any time from work?

A: Yes. A little sometimes, yes.

Q: Do you have a record of what time you missed from work?

A: At home when I started I did, yes.

Q: Do you have that with you?

A: I don't have it with me, no.

Q: What chiropractor were you seeing?

A: Dr. Peterson.

Q: Thomas Peterson?

A: Thomas Peterson.

Q: I understand he is a chiropractor?

A: I beg your pardon.

Q: Do you understand that he is a chiropractor?

A: He was my doctor, I don't know what he was.

Q: I thought you said you were seeing a chiropractor. Did I misunderstand?

Mr. Lang: [*Nods head*]

Ms. Clarke: Maybe he was talking about therapist. Were you talking about the guy that gave you the heat and all that stuff?

The Witness: I don't know his name.

Q: [*By Mr. Fredricks*] Bill Freeman?

A: Yes, something like that.

Q: William Freeman or something like that.

A: Yes, I believe so. You see, when I was going to Wahlstrom I was getting treatment too before I seen him.

Q: You completed high school?

A: Yes.

Q: What high school did you attend?

A: Central, Detroit Central.

Q: When were you graduated?

A: Ninety-three.

Q: Did you participate in sports in any school?

A: That was '92, I'm sorry. Sometimes, yes.

Q: What sports?

A: Basketball and just any—really any intramural thing. I didn't go out for—

Q: Were you ever injured in any sports?

A: No.

Q: Have you been involved in any other motor vehicle accidents other than the one of August 17, 1993?

A: No.

Q: At any time?

A: No.

Q: Have you ever been in a car when it has collided with another car, or object, or—

A: No. No.

Q: Even if you weren't hurt.

A: No.

Q: This is the only motor vehicle accident you have ever been in?

A: Yes it was.

Q: All right. Have you been injured in any other accidents of any kind at any time?

A: No, I haven't. Any other automobile accidents?

Q: No, no, any other accidents of any kind—

A: No.

Q: —at any time where you hurt yourself any way.

A: Well, I was just in an accident—

Q: All right.

A: —about two weeks ago, maybe a month ago.

Q: Where did the accident happen and—

A: On Traverse.

Q: What?

A: Traverse. Exact address I don't know. It was somewhere down Traverse Avenue.

Q: What happened?

A: Crossed the centerline.

Q: Was this automobile accident?

A: Yes.

Q: Oh. Well, you tell me, describe for me what—were you a driver?

A: Yes, I was.

Q: And what happened?

A: I was fixing a calendar watch and I was—the passenger was fixing my calendar watch, and she turned it—messed it up, and I looked down at it and went in the other lane.

Q: Was this a head-on type collision?

A: Yes.

Q: Did the police investigate?

A: Yes, they did.

Q: What time of the day did it happen?

A: In the afternoon, about twelve o'clock, one o'clock.

Q: It was daylight at that time?

A: Yes, it was.

Q: Who was your passenger?

A: Rebecca Parsons.

Q: Where doe she live?

A: Cleveland.

Q: Cleveland?

A: North Cleveland.

Q: Where in North Cleveland?

A: I forget the address.

Q: Will you get that for me or get it to your attorney?

Ms. Clarke: No, I'm not going to get—why don't you find out if he got hurt. If he got hurt, then I will get you what you want, but you are dinging around on a fender bender, I suspect, and if that's where you are going—

Q: [*By Mr. Fredricks*] Were you hurt at all in the accident?

A: Just stitches on my lip.

Q: You struck your face against something inside the car?

A: Yes.

Q: Where did you get the stitches?

A: In the lip and also chin.

Q: Lip and chin.

A: Yes.

Q: Any other injuries in the accident?

A: And teeth, my teeth.

Q: What happened to your teeth?

A: They were all out, just about. Oh, they are all loose, you know.

Q: Lower-front teeth were loosened?

A: Lower and upper.

Q: Any other injuries?

A: That was about all. I just hit the steering wheel.

Q: Have any headaches following the accident?

A: No.

Q: You haven't had any headaches since that accident a month ago?

A: No I haven't.

Q: What doctors did you go to, for example?

A: General Hospital.

Q: Where else?

A: That was it.

Q: All of the treatment you have received was at General Hospital?

A: Yes.

Q: Have you been to Dr. Thomas Peterson since that accident?

A: No.

Q: Earlier I asked you about my other automobile accidents—

A: Yes.

Q: —and you didn't mention this.

A: Well, I didn't—you know, I really forgot about the accident. It didn't, you know, mean nothing.

Q: All right. Now, you search your mind: are there any other automobile accidents?

A: No.

Q: Do you have a driver's license?

A: Yes, I do.

Q: What's the number on it? Would you get it out and check it for me? Now, have you been involved in any other accidents of any kind? I'm not referring—

A: You mean a passenger—no, I haven't, nothing.

Q: In no sports—you have never fallen down and hurt yourself, you have never burned yourself, you have never cut yourself, you have never had any other trouble?

A: No.

Q: All right. Have you been hospitalized at any time in your life other than for childbirth?

A: Just for asthma.

Q: When was that?

A: That was—I was born with it.

Q: When were you hospitalized for it?

A: I don't remember the exact date. Last year sometime. Two years before that. I stayed in the hospital with asthma.

Q: What hospital did you go to?

A: General Hospital.

Q: Have you ever made a claim against anyone for injuries other than this accident?

A: No.

Q: After completing high school you went to college.

A: Yes.

Q: What colleges have you attended?

A: Wahlstrom in Uhler, Michigan.

Q: What years did you attend?

A: Ninety-three, '94.

Q: Did you have a physical examination at that college?

A: Yes.

Q: Did you have any treatment for your back condition?

A: Yes, I did.

Q: What course of study did you pursue there? Liberal arts?

A: Liberal arts.

Q: All right. Did you complete one academic year at Wahlstrom?

A: It was more or less a program like for people who aren't capable of going to college but may, you know, learn something at college, you know, if they have the opportunity to go. Do you understand?

Q: Is there a name for that program?

A: It was called Demos.

Q: What?

A: Demos. D-e-m-o something. Demos. I don't know how to spell that.

Q: What month did you start then, September?

A: Yes.

Q: And—

A: Ninety-three, '94.

Q: What month did you complete the course?

A: I went the whole—full two years.

Q: Okay. Have you gone to another institution, college?

A: I'm going to the university at the present time.

Q: Well, you mean you have actually registered for class?

A: Yes.

Q: Will you be starting as a freshman?

A: Sophomore and junior, half and half now.

Q: Didn't you attend at Chicago?

A: No, I haven't. I seen it in the thing but I changed it. It was at Wahlstrom.

Q: I see. Did you live on campus when you were at Wahlstrom?

A: Yes, I did.

Q: Have you had your physical examination for the university?

A: Last year I did.

Q: When was that?

A: I don't know. It was at the beginning of the school year.

Q: Have you received any treatment for any physical condition or problems at the university health service?

A: No, I haven't.

Q: Or hospital?

A: No.

Q: All right. Now, referring to the accident of August 17th, 1993, that happened early on a Friday morning, didn't.

A: Friday morning?

Q: Thursday night or Friday morning.

A: Yes.

Q: Do you recall what time it happened?

A: No, I can't. It was—I think it was about one, one o'clock.

Q: Okay. It was dark out at the time, wasn't it?

A: Yes, it was.

Q: And would it be consistent with your recollection that it was about 1:35 in the morning?

A: Probably so.

Q: Who were you with that night?

A: Carolyn Jones. She was driving. And a Ruby Watts, another girl, was in the back seat.

Q: Who was the other girl?

A: Ruby Watts.

Q: Ruby what?

A: Watts, W-a-t-t-s.

Q: W-a-t-t-s? Where does she live?

A: I have no idea.

Q: Where were you going at the time?

A: Probably home.

Q: Probably?

A: Yes.

Q: Don't you remember?

A: It was probably my house. I'm pretty sure it was. See, I live about four blocks from the accident, and we were going in the direction. I believe we were. She was taking me home, I'm pretty sure.

Q: Where had you been?

A: Probably a dance or something. At a dance.

Q: Where?

A: Downtown. I forget the name of the club. I believe we went, you know, here and there. Let's see—

Q: Did you have anything—

A: No, no, no, this was a house party. I'm sorry. It was a house party, a get-together.

Q: Did you have anything alcoholic to drink?

A: No. They didn't have anything. I'm sure they didn't. No.

Q: How about Ms. Jones?

A: No, she doesn't drink.

Q: Were you dating that night? Was this a date with either of the two girls?

A: Well, I knew Carolyn from—we grew up together, just about. Well, we went to school together, high school, grade school. She just stopped and picked me up.

Q: All right. At the time of the accident, you were riding in a Buick automobile?

A: [*Nods head*]

Q: And you were traveling in an easterly direction on 38th Street.

A: Yes.

Q: And the other car was in a northerly direction on 2d Avenue.

A: Yes.

Q: Do you recall whether Ms. Jones put on her turn signals as she approached this intersection?

A: We were going straight. We were going straight.

Q: Did she put on her turn signals, or don't you know?

A: I'm sure she didn't. I'm sure she didn't, because wasn't no sense in turning, you know, that way.

Q: How far were you going to continue going straight ahead?

A: Oh, I would say we were going to my house, and I live about four blocks away on Park Avenue, and I believe it happened on 2d Avenue. Well, I was staying at 38th and Park at that time.

Q: Well, all right. What happened? How did the cars come together, do you know?

A: No. I was hit on my side, on the right side of the car.

Q: Did you see the Souter car at any time before the collision?

A: No.

Q: How fast was Ms. Jones driving?

A: I didn't look at the speedometer. We weren't speeding or in a rush to go anywhere, you know. She normally drives slow anyways, the speed limit.

Q: Did anyone say anything before the collision occurred? Any exclamations?

A: No. Just hit. Surprised everybody.

Q: How would you describe the collision?

A: Sudden. Just happened, you know. I didn't—you know, surprised me.

Q: All right. What happened to the car in which you were riding, the Buick, when the collision did occur?

A: Seemed like it just pushed the car around in a circle, seemed like. Seemed like it just went around, you know.

Q: Are you saying the car was pushed sideways?

A: Yes. Like when it hit, seemed like I was—seemed like pain was just in my body, and I was just in pain, you know, for a second or two, and the car was just moving around.

Q: What was its position when the car came to rest?

A: It was in this way [indicating], turned like that all the way around.

Q: Well, the car had been traveling east, easterly?

A: [Nods head]

Q: What way was it facing when it came to rest?

A: South. It might even have spun the whole time, you know, one whole time. Seemed like it was spinning a long time and sliding.

Q: Now, the other car stopped right at the point of impact, didn't it?

A: I—I thought it was down—across the intersection, I'm sure. I'm pretty sure it did.

Q: Did Ms. Jones's car come to a stop outside of the intersection? Did it continue through the intersection and—

A: It was knocked past the intersection. Spun down, you know, like, towards west, east, went down. Like it spun and sort of pushed it forward down the street in a way and spun it too. Seemed like it happened—it did happen like that. Then it came to a stop.

Q: East of the intersection.

A: Yes.

Q: Is that your testimony?

A: It went past the intersection, a little way past it, I think.

Q: So that would be east of the intersection?

A: Yes. Going towards the river, that's—yes, right.

Q: All right. So that we are clear on this, you say that the Jones car came to rest east of the east curb line of 2d Avenue.

A: It what? Pardon me.

Q: You say that the car came to rest east of the east curb line of 2d Avenue.

A: Yes.

Q: Okay. Now, what happened to you when the collision occurred?

A: As soon as it hit?

Q: Right.

A: Seemed like I was in pain, and seemed like I was—seemed like I was just in pain for a short time, about a second or two, and like everything had blacked out for a second or two as I was in pain.

Q: Well, did you strike yourself against anything in the car, against the windshield?

A: Against the door, that side door I believe, or probably in the corner.

Q: You what?

A: Or probably in the corner of the—not the windshield. You know, like towards—kitty-corner over.

Q: Do you remember that clearly?

A: It was—I know it was on the side, what I'm saying. It wasn't the windshield. I didn't hit the windshield at all.

Q: Did you have any accident markings on your person, any cuts, bruises, bumps?

A: Yes.

Q: What?

A: Legs—well, like everything was sore, but it was—you know, like—seemed like this side [*indicating*], and my legs were sore, like they were bruised and stuff.

Q: Well, Mr. Johnson, you have told me you were sore, but I want to know if there were any bumps or bruises, anything that someone else could see or feel.

A: I think it was just skinned, more or less.

Q: Skinned?

A: Skinned like.

Q: An abrasion?

A: Pardon.

Q: You mean an abrasion or rubbing of the skin?

A: Yes, abrasion.

Q: Where the skin wasn't actually broken, but it was just an abrasion of the skin, is that what you are saying?

A: Yes, I guess abrasion, I don't know. It was like—you know, it was skinned.

Q: And you are indicating that this was someplace on your right arm.

A: It was on my—down here [*indicating*] on my chin.

Q: Now you are indicating your right chin.

A: Yes. Seemed like most of the pain was up here. Seemed like I hit the door, but my legs was hurting too.

Q: You are now indicating your right arm near your right elbow.

A: Well, seemed like my whole side was hurting, and my leg somehow was hurting too.

Q: Now you are indicating your whole right side was hurting.

A: Yes. Seemed it was a lot—I really know exactly—all I remember is something like my legs were hurting, too.

Q: Both legs. Is that what you are telling us?

A: I really don't remember. Just seems like it was hurting. My legs, they didn't—I didn't write it down or nothing what was hurting. It was a long time ago, and I don't remember exactly what was scratched or nothing like this.

Q: All right. You didn't notice any pain in your back or your neck immediately following the accident, did you?

A: No.

Q: The police came and investigated, didn't they?

A: Yes.

Q: And what did you tell the police about your condition?

A: Nothing. When I was walking around I thought I was all right.

Q: Did you seek any medical examinations or treatments right after the accident?

A: No.

Q: Well, didn't you go to General Hospital?

A: Yes. Well, like they were—they were busy like always, and they just took my temperature and told me to leave and—I could leave.

Q: Well, now you must listen to my questions carefully. I asked you if you sought any medical examinations. Well, you did—

A: The doctor—yes, I did—

Q: You went to General Hospital.

A: Yes.

Q: All right.

A: But I mean—go ahead.

Q: But they didn't do anything for you other than take your temperature, is that what you say?

A: No. Right.

Q: When did you next seek any medical examinations or treatment?

A: About a month or two after.

Q: Who did you see?

A: Dr. Peterson.

Q: How did you happen to go to Dr. Peterson?

A: Well, he is the only doctor that I knew over North, and I believe Carolyn told me about him because she was going there too.

Q: Who?

A: Carolyn Jones, the driver of the car.

Q: Okay. Had you ever been to Peterson before?

A: No.

Q: When did you first have any symptoms of neck problems, pains or discomfort?

A: About a month or two after when I went to see Dr. Peterson.

Q: Okay. That's when you first really noticed any pain or problem in your neck.

A: Yes.

Q: Okay. All right. When did you first notice any pain or discomfort or any problem in your back?

A: About the time when I went to see him.

Ms. Clarke: You mean, you went for thirty days and you didn't have any trouble, and all of a sudden one day you had trouble with your back?

The Witness: Seemed like that.

Ms. Clarke: I don't believe that.

Mr. Fredricks: Pardon me.

Ms. Clarke: You mean, you didn't have any trouble the day of the accident or the day afterwards?

The Witness: No.

Mr. Lang: Objected to as leading and suggestive.

Mr. Fredricks: Ellen—

Ms. Clarke: Well, fantastic. I don't believe him.

Mr. Lang: Whether you believe him or not, that's what he said.

Ms. Clarke: I don't think he understands the question.

Mr. Lang: It's clear that he does.

The Witness: I mean, it didn't hurt just one month later. It was such a long time ago, like it—problems.

Ms. Clarke: Well, they are trapping you. The way you have answered these questions, that's the end of your lawsuit. That's basically what they have trapped you into here. Now, if you understand—

Mr. Fredricks: Now, that isn't true.

Ms. Clarke: That's true.

Mr. Fredricks: The word *trap* is not at all appropriate here, Ellen.

Ms. Clarke: Well, it is when it's obvious to me he doesn't understand your question, that's all.
   And if you understand what you are doing, then you can answer any way you want, but I want you to understand what you are saying here. That's why I'm here, to make sure you understand your questions.

The Witness: See, it was—

Mr. Fredricks: Let's see if we can't clarify this.

Ms. Clarke: Why don't you let him answer.

Q: [*By Mr. Fredricks*] About the time that you first had difficulties with your neck and low back is when you went to see Dr. Peterson. Whether that was a week after or a month after, that's when you started having difficulty, and you went to see him at that time because you did notice that you were having difficulty.

A: Well, let me say—like I probably had some pain first. It was a long time ago, and I don't exactly remember how—how many days or what it was when I went to see Dr. Peterson after the accident or nothing like this. Like the pain probably came a week after, and I probably didn't think nothing of it, you know—

Q: All right.

A: —and it was probably there. I mean if a pain is just there, you don't go the same day, you see. I mean this is the way I looked at it. And from the questions you asked, you know, it was probably a month when I seen a doctor, a month or two months after when I went to see him to—

Q: But I'm asking you not when you went to see Dr. Peterson but when you first became aware of any discomfort in your neck or back, and you have said it was about a month, and now—

A: I mean I seen Dr. Peterson about a month or two after.

Q: That's what you meant.

A: I really don't even know exactly how long that was, exactly.

Q: But now it is your recollection that it was about a week or more after the accident before you first had any difficulty with your neck or your back, is that correct?

A: It was probably a week or so after I had trouble with my back?

Q: Yes.

A: I don't know exactly the—I really don't know. It probably was a week when I first felt pain somewhere.

Q: Now, do you recall if you were doing something particular, you were engaged in some activity when you first noticed this back pain, where you were walking up a stairway, or lifting something, or driving a car, or—

A: I really don't remember.

Q: By the way, when you had this accident about a month ago, were you driving your own automobile?

A: No, I wasn't.

Q: Whose car were you driving?

A: The girl's car.

Q: Ruby's?

A: No.

Q: What was her name?

A: Rebecca Ann Parsons.

Q: Rebecca. It was her car.

A: Yes.

Q: Do you know who she had her insurance with?

A: No, I don't.

Q: Well, you must have talked with some insurance man—

A: Yes.

Q: —since the accident.

A: I don't remember his name though.

Q: Did he give you a card or—

A: He called on the phone.

Q: Okay.

Ellen, do you have a copy of that—did the police investigate that accident?

Ms. Clarke: No, but if you have an authorization you want signed at all, why don't you give them to him now and I will have him check them.

Mr. Lang: What was the name of the person you had the accident with?

The Witness: I beg your pardon.

Mr. Lang: What was the name of the person you had the accident with?

The Witness: The other person. I forget her name. She was an elderly lady.

Mr. Lang: Do you know where she lives?

The Witness: South Detroit.

Q: [*By Mr. Fredricks*] All right. When you first noticed this pain in your back, or when you first noticed pain in your neck, what did it feel like? Describe it for me.

A: Just seemed like a sharp pain.

Q: Where was it located?

A: It was just a pain all over, seemed like. Seemed like I was paralyzed maybe—if that's the right term to use. Seemed like it was just—I can't even explain it.

Q: All right. Was this pain localized at any particular place in your back?

Ms. Clarke: You better explain what localized means, you know.

Q: [*By Mr. Fredricks*] You know—

A: I don't know—I really couldn't tell you.

Q: Was the pain in your neck localized or at any particular spot in your back? Was it on one side or the other?

Ms. Clarke: What he is trying to say is what part of your neck—when you talk about your back, he wants to know whether it's in the middle of your back, or in the low back, or upper back. He wants to know what part of your neck or your back you are talking about.

The Witness: When I was going to say pain, it seems like a pain all over, I— you know, I didn't stop and think of where it was at, no, or nothing like this, because at the time I was being shook around at the same time.

Q: [*By Mr. Fredricks*] At the time you were being what?

A: At the time of the accident, you know. There was pain, and I was being shaken around at the same time, and I couldn't tell you exactly, you know, where the pain was. It was just a pain in the head all over.

Q: You have indicated that there was some period of time elapsed after the accident before—

A: Yes.

Q: —you became aware of pain in your neck and your back. Now I want to know when you did become aware of your neck pain or your back pain, where was it located?

A: Oh, you mean when I—after the accident.

Q: Yes.

A: Yes.

Q: It was a week or more after the accident, as I understand your testimony. Tell me what you felt.

A: It was in the lower back, pain in the lower back.

Q: All right. And was it on one side or the other? Was it on your left side or right side?

A: It was down the center of my back, the spinal cord.

Q: Right in the middle.

A: Yes.

Q: Was it below your belt?

A: It was down in the lower back.

Q: Below your belt line.

A: Lower part of my back.

Q: Was it below your belt line or above it?

A: Is this [*indicating*] below my belt line?

Q: This [*indicating*] is your belt.

A: Is this my belt [*indicating*], below my belt, or what?

Q: Yes, that's your—you have placed your hand well below your belt line.

A: That's where it was. That's where it was.

Q: All right, fine.

A: And my neck right here [*indicating*].

Q: Now, was there any particular activity, or were you doing something when you first noticed this pain in your low back?

A: I don't remember.

Q: All right. When you first noticed this pain in your low back, did it limit you in any way? Were your activities limited? Were your movements limited?

A: What do you mean, limited? What do you mean, was I limited? Could I walk?

Q: Did you have to go to bed because of the back pain, or did you have to stop swimming, or did you—is there anything that it did affect you in any way?

A: Like when it hurt, I just—well, it was—it would hurt. Like when I'm sitting at school. For instance, when I first notice it I was in school or sitting in the chair.

Q: All right.

A: And it was just uncomfortable to sit in a chair.

Q: All right. Now, this would have been at Wahlstrom.

A: Yes, it was—well, like—it couldn't have been, because I seen Dr. Peterson before I went to Wahlstrom, and he said—let's see—I don't now how—I seen Dr. Peterson before I went to Wahlstrom, I was getting therapy at the clinic before I went to Wahlstorm, and now that—when I noticed it how it acted. Then I couldn't tell, but like when I was at school when I was sitting down at the chair, I remember that, you know, because I was always turning and stuff.

Q: How does your low back feel right now?

A: Uncomfortable.

Q: Well, is there pain in it?

A: Just seemed like a slight—slight pain.

Q: Slight pain.

A: [*Nods head*]

Q: Does that keep you from doing anything?

A: No. I go—I still do what I do.

Q: How about your neck, how is that?

A: It's fair. It's all right.

Q: It's okay.

A: [*Nods head*]

Q: All right. You are not having any trouble with it now?

A: No.

Q: When is the last time you had any trouble with your neck?

A: I was in the hospital about last month or month—about two months ago, month and a half ago, for treatment.

Q: Which hospital?

A: Mt. Sinai.

Q: And you did have trouble with your neck at that time?

A: Yes. My neck and back.

Q: And is that Mr. William Freeman again who gave you therapy?

A: This was in the hospital.

Q: Yes. He worked at—or he—at least he did work at Mt. Sinai.

A: No, I was in traction, they put me in traction.

Q: All right. The heat packs and traction seemed to help.

A: It was all right. Like, after I got out of the hospital, well, last—about a week ago, I drove—well, rode down to Missouri, and it was uncomfortable sitting in the car.

Q: You were what?

A: It was uncomfortable sitting in the car, you know, long-distance. Like, you know, drove to Missouri.

Q: Where in Missouri?

A: Monroe.

Q: Monroe?

A: Monroe.

Q: What did you go to Missouri for?

A: To see some people.

Q: Who?

A: Some people, some friends.

Q: Who did you go to see?

A: Some friends.

Q: What's their names?

A: I forget their last name.

Q: Who did you go with?

A: Some friends. Friend of mine and his family. See, they were—I just went for the ride, just to go, just to go out of town, and it was their cousins and things.

Q: Whose car?

A: Their car.

Q: And what is their name?

A: Cross. Cross.

Q: First name.

A: I forget their first name, lady's first name. I went with a family and a friend of mine my age.

Q: And what's his name?

A: Brian Cross.

Q: What?

A: Brian Cross.

Does that make any difference who I go down there with?

Ms. Clarke: You tell him exactly what it was, that's all. You just tell him the truth, that's all I care about.

Q: [*By Mr. Fredricks*] Was it on that trip then—that was the last time you had any discomfort in your neck?

Ms. Clarke: I think he is talking about his back.

The Witness: My back. See, I—

Q: [*By Mr. Fredricks*] I thought you told me it was a month ago that you last had any problem with your low back.

A: No. It was my neck.

Q: Your neck.

A: My neck is pretty much better now, but my back I still have some pain. Like I feel a slight pain now in my lower back.

Q: All right.

A: And during the trip down to Monroe, Missouri, I felt discomfort in my back on the way down and on the way back, and—

Q: And what month did you make that trip, July of 1994?

A: It was this month.

Q: August of 1994.

A: Yes.

Q: Did you seek any treatment for your back?

A: After this?

Q: While on that trip.

A: No.

Q: Did you take—

A: I was just taking hot baths and stuff.

Q: I see.

A: And I got a massage a couple times.

Q: You did.

A: Well, from, you know, his mother. She rubbed it down with Ben-Gay and stuff like that.

Q: After the trip.

A: Well, when I went down, got down to Monroe.

Q: Did you say your mother?

A: No, this—the dude's mother massaged my back when I was down there.

Q: Okay.

A: Mrs. Cross massaged by back.

Q: Have you had any military service?

A: No.

Q: Have you had a physical exam for military service?

A: No. See, I was going to school and they must gave me a deferment for going to school.

Q: Do you have a military classification?

A: No, I don't.

Q: You don't have a military identification card or anything.

A: No.

Q: Have you ever been convicted of a crime?

A: No.

Q: Did you ever see or talk to this Souter after the night of the accident?

A: No.

Q: Did you talk to Mr. Souter at the scene of the accident?

A: No.

Q: Was there anyone in the car, Ms. Jones's car, besides you and Ruby?

A: No, just the three of us. Three of us.

Q: Do you have any plans to see Dr. Thomas Peterson again?

A: Well, I called him the other day, but he wasn't in, and I just wanted to talk to him because I haven't talked to him after I came out of the hospital. See, like, when I came out of the hospital, then I—he went into the hospital.

Q: He himself went in?

A: Yes. And, like, I sort of tried to avoid going over to—I have just been sitting in a hot bath, hot water.

Q: You can move your neck, and your back is all right now, as I understand your testimony.

A: Yes.

Q: And it's your low back at this moment, you have slight pain in your low back.

A: Yes.

Q: Does that get worse at times?

A: At night.

Q: At night.

A: Yes.

Q: What happens at night that causes your back to bother you?

A: Seems like there is a pain all down my back.

Q: Well, what are you doing, or what position causes your back problem?

A: I got a water bed, and it still hurts.

Q: You have a water bed?

A: Yes.

Q: How long have you had that?

A: About two months?

Q: Did it seem to help at all?

A: Not really. See, first I was sleeping on a mattress with a board up under, and that didn't seem to help it either.

Q: Did someone suggest that you try a water bed?

A: No.

Q: It was your own idea.

A: Yes.

Q: Does the water bed seem to hurt your back?

A: Not really. See, it hurts once in a while at night. It didn't hurt every night.

Q: I see. So usually your back feels better during the day than it does at night.

A: Sometimes I don't notice it during the day, sometimes I notice it during the day, sometimes at nights—

Q: What are you doing during the daytime that causes you to have back problems?

A: See, I sit down, I will be working in the office in Hearns Auditorium, and that's a lot of sitting, but I still walk around, you know, to—just to walk around, move my back around and stuff.

Q: The walking around seems to help.

A: Well, it's just moving around, if it—

Q: It does help.

A: It probably helps a little bit just get up and move around.

Q: Does it?

A: Yes, it does. But when I sit down again for about five minutes, half hour again, I can feel the pain again.

Q: The pain in your legs cleared up quite soon after the accident?

A: Seemed like that came back little bit later too, pain in the other side of the leg.

Q: Your legs don't bother you now.

A: Not right now, no.

Q: When is the last time either or your legs bothered you? Been a long time?

A: Yes. About when I was seeing Dr. Peterson, getting therapy along in that time. Not the last—it probably was the last one. I haven't seen him—

Q: For about a year?

A: No, it hasn't been that long. About three—three or four months.

Q: Have you taken any drugstore medicines or—

A: Prescriptions?

Q: Prescription medicines?

A: Yes.

Q: When is the last time?

A: About four months ago.

Q: What drugstore do you get your medicine at?

A: I didn't get the medicine, this girl got it for me. It was just pain pills.

Q: Ms. Jones?

A: Yes.

Q: The girl—

A: The one I'm staying with now, she went to the drugstore and got it. It was a pain pill though.

Q: Is it her prescription or yours?

A: Prescription Dr. Peterson wrote me.

Q: And when you had taken this medicine, why did you take it?

A: Why did I take it?

Q: Why?

A: For the pain.

Q: Where in?

A: My back pain.

Q: All right. Not your legs, not your neck, not for any headaches.

A: It was just—just a pain pill, Darvon. It's just for the pain. If you have pain in your leg, you know, supposed to knock it all out.

Q; The reason you have taken the Darvon is for you low back.

A: Yes, sir.

Q: All right. And that's all.

A: Yes, sir.

Q: Okay. You haven't had any particular problem with headaches following this accident, have you?

A: Yes.

Q: You have.

A: Yes.

Q: For what period of time did you have headaches?

A: Sometime I had it all evening. Well—

Q: I mean for—was it a month following the accident, two months, three months?

A: I couldn't—I couldn't tell you exactly. It's—it should be in Dr.—

Q: I'm not asking for an exact period of time, I'm asking for some—

A: I really couldn't tell you. It should be in Dr. Peterson's record, because I let him know when it happened.

Q: When is the last time you recall being bothered by a headache—long, long time ago, over a year ago?

A: I still have them. Well, like when I went on that rip I had headaches going on the way down, something like a migraine headache. I remember the last time I had a terrible headache. Then again it was three, four months ago I was getting headaches, a headache, too.

Q: When?

A: About two or three months ago I was getting a headache.

Q: Did you have headaches while you were at Wahlstrom College?

A: I believe—I believe so.

Q: You don't recall now.

A: I'm pretty sure I did, because I remember getting a headache, you know, once in a while, serious headache.

Q; Like once a week?

A: No. I couldn't say exactly when—once a week or every two weeks. It was just a headache, you know, have a—a bad headache, you know, pain, headache.

Q: How often?

A: How often? What do you mean, how often?

Q: How often, when you were in college at Wahlstrom, did you have a bad headache?

A: Well, I can't answer that, you know, too perfect.

Q: Do you have any photographs about the accident, connected with the accident?

A: Do I have any pictures?

Q: Yes.

A: No.

Q: Do you claim that you have lost any income as a result of the accident?

A: Work?

Q: [*Nods head*]

A: Well, working, and taking the bus over there.

Q: Pardon me.

A: Taking the bus over from wherever I was at, taking a bus over to Dr. Peterson's office. And going too from Wahlstrom I was getting treatment, I had to—

Q: All right. You are claiming that you have lost some income.

A: Income and schooling too.

Q: Well, I'm not concerned about school time, I'm concerned about income right now. Do you file a tax return?

A: Did I this past one?

Q: Yes. Have you filed a tax return at any time since the August—

A: Yes.

Q: —accident?

A: Yes.

Q: Federal tax returns? You have.

A: [*Nods head*]

Q: All right.
   Ellen, I will prepare authorizations for tax returns, and also an authorization for the accident report, and I will send them to you.

Ms. Clarke: Why don't you have him sign them now. Just sign any blank authorizations you have for any reason, because I would like to know about these things too. You can fill them in.
   While you are looking, my notes show you were at the hospital for four hours.

The Witness: At General?

Ms. Clarke: Yes.

The Witness: I was there a long time just sitting.

Ms. Clarke: My notes also show you saw a doctor the next day. Who did you see the next day?

The Witness: A doctor.

Ms. Clarke: Yes, that's what this shows.

The Witness: I don't know. If it was anybody, it was Dr. Peterson, but I don't remember. I didn't see nobody at General.

   [*Whereupon a discussion was had off the record.*]

Q: [*By Mr. Fredricks*] Have you ever had any injections in your neck or shoulders with a needle administered by any doctors?

A: No. No I haven't.

Q: Pardon me.

A: No, I haven't.

Q: Have you ever had any electromyogram tests where they put a needle in your muscles and—

A: Just in the head, scalp.

Q: You have had that in your scalp?

A: Yes.

Q: And when was that done?

A: When I went to the doctor.

Q: For what?

A: When I went to the hospital for Dr. Peterson, at Mt. Sinai Hospital.

Q: And was that soon after the accident then, or when?

A: No, this was recently when I just went to the hospital about two months ago, month and a half ago, for treatment, treatments in the hospital.

Q: That was at Mt. Sinai.

A: Yes, it was.

Q: And that's the only place you have had any such tests.

A: Yes.

Ms. Clarke: I notice there is a bill here for injection something into your neck muscles; what's that for?

The Witness: What is it? What is it?

Ms. Clarke: Did it in the hospital, apparently.

The Witness: Which hospital?

Ms. Clarke: June 21st. It says injection, superior angles. Apparently into your neck.

The Witness: That was at Mt. Sinai.

Ms. Clarke: Yes.

The Witness: That's what it was then, at Mt. Sinai.

Ms. Clarke: You just told him you never had any injections. I want to know what you are talking about.

The Witness: I just seen it in the head and up here [*indicating*], but I don't know what he stuck down here [*indicating*].

Q: [*By Mr. Fredricks*] Do you know what I mean by a hypodermic needle, where you get a—

A: Blood thing?

Q: Yes. Needle that goes into your arm and they inject something under the skin or into the muscle.

A: All I remember is when they put pins all in the head and stuff, and—

Q: You don't remember Dr. Peterson ever injecting any needles into your neck or back?

A: No, I don't.

Q: Okay.

A: That one right there—they might have put some up here [*indicating*], but I don't remember.

Q: Sometimes he doesn't do it, Ellen, and he records it in his records, so I'm not surprised.

Ms. Clarke: He charged twenty bucks for doing it.

Mr. Fredricks: Yes.

Ms. Clarke: I got to know, if he didn't do it, I want to know about it.

The Witness: Where was it I said those pins were at?

Ms. Clarke: I don't have to tell. We are asking you the questions. You were there, I wasn't.

The Witness: I had pins up here [*indicating*]. Probably if they had some here [*indicating*], you know, I didn't feel it too much.

Q: [*By Mr. Fredricks*] You never had any problems and any discomfort in your throat area of your neck, have you? You didn't ever develop any pain in the front portion of your neck, did you?

A: Not that I recall.

Q: Okay.

A: Well, it was just—

Q: Just in the back of the neck.

A: You mean as far as strep throat or anything like this?

Q: No, I mean following the accident. Any injury to the front portion of your neck?

A: No, I can't—if it was, it was slight. It was just—what Dr. Peterson said it was, I don't know if it was here—you mean did I feel pain exactly right here [*indicating*] somewhere up in here [*indicating*].

Q: Yes.

A: No.

Q: Have you had strep throat or some problem like that?

A: One time, long time ago.

Q: Dr. Peterson didn't treat you for that?

A: No.

Q: You have been treated with some physical therapy at Mt. Sinai Hospital, and traction.

A: Yes.

Q: Have you had therapy or traction anywhere else?

A: At his office, at his clinic, and at Wahlstrom, downtown clinic.

Q: What clinic downtown? Was that Kennan's?

A: No. This was in Uhler, Michigan.

Q: Oh. What clinic?

A: It was at the hospital, at the Uhler Hospital down in Uhler, Michigan.

Q: But you said there was a clinic downtown in Uhler.

A: I meant Uhler Hospital, and there is a clinic there.

Q: At the hospital.

A: I believe so, yes.

Q: You saw some private doctors in Uhler.

A: Yes.

Q: Do you remember their names?

A: No, I don't.

Mr. Fredricks: Do you have that, Ellen?

Ms. Clarke: No, except it's on the—I sent your adjuster the bill for some X rays down there, and I assume from that you can get a lead as to who ordered the X rays. I don't even know that.

Q: [*By Mr. Fredricks*] Right. At the present time you are engaging in all of the activities that you used to participate in and enjoy before this accident.

A: Yes.

Q: You are not claiming that you are now handicapped or prevented from doing things that you would otherwise do due to this accident?

A: Well, I—you know, I know my back is hurting, I won't be picking up something that's heavy or something. I try to use some common sense what to do and what not to do with my back.

Q: All right. But you can throw a softball and you can—

A: Yes.

Q: If you enjoyed ice skating, you would go ice skating, or if you bowled you would go bowling, and if you want to take a trip like to Missouri, you go ahead and do it.

A: Yes.

Q: Okay. Have you made any other trips—

A: No.

Q: —out of the state or out of town since?

A: Yes. Yes.

Q: Where?

A: San Antonio.

Q: Texas?

A: Yes.

Q: When?

A: Right after school was out.

Q: And what was the purpose for that trip?

A: Just going down to San Antonio, Texas.

Q: Did you make this trip by car?

A: Yes.

Q: Who did you go with?

A: Some friend of mine. It was three in the car.

Q: Well, who were the friends?

A: Some friends I went to school with.

Q: I'm interested in names.

A: They were no kin or nothing like—

Q: Pardon me.

A: They were no kin to me or nothing like that.

Q: All right. But what were their names? Was it Ms. Jones? Was it Ruby?

A: No.

Q: Who?

A: Cooley. Cooley. They are from out of town. They are from out of town, from Des Moines.

Q: Oh, okay. Anyone else or any other trips?

A: No.

Q: How long were you gone to San Antonio?

A: Just down and back.

Mr. Fredricks: I believe that's all the questions I have.

EXAMINATION

By Mr. Lang:

Q: Have you ever worn any kind of belt, or brace, or collar?

A: Yes. Like when I went for my—on the trip to Monroe I wore a back brace.

Q: Where did you get that?

A: At Mt. Sinai. Well, see, it was a traction belt and I just cut the things off of it and used it, just used it as a belt.

Q: How wide is that?

A: This wide [*indicating*].

Q: About six inches wide?

A: Yes.

Q: How many times have you been hospitalized since this accident of August of '93?

A: Just that once.

Q: And how long a time was that?

A: A week.

Q: Did the hospitalization help you?

A: Not really. Not really.

Q: How long have you lived in the Detroit area?

A: About eleven or twelve years.

Q: Did you have headaches before this accident?

A: Not that I can recall, no.

Q: You referred to migraine headaches; now, have you been bothered with migraine headaches?

A: Not like that. Not no headaches like this one. I used to have just plain headaches, you know, like cold headaches, but like these headaches is something else.

Q: How often do you get those?

A: Once in a while.

Q: How often is that? Once a month?

A: Once a month, twice a month. You know, it isn't—

Q: How long do they last?

A: A long time; about three or four hours.

Q: Do you take anything for them?

A: Yes.

Q: What do you take?

A: Aspirins.

Q: Does that relieve them?

A: No.

Mr. Lang: I have no further questions.

Ms. Clarke: We will waive the reading and signing and the notice of filing of the deposition.

* * *

STATE OF MICHIGAN ⎱   SS.
COUNTY OF WAYNE ⎰

Be it known that I took the deposition of Duane Johnson, pursuant to agreement of counsel; that I was then and there a notary public in and for said county and state; that I exercised the power of that office in taking said deposition; that by virtue thereof I was then and there authorized to administer an oath; that said witness, before testifying, was duly sworn to testify to the truth, the whole truth and nothing but the truth relative to the cause specified above; that the deposition is a true record of the testimony given by the witness; that the reading and signing of the deposition was waived by the witness and pursuant to agreement of counsel; that I am neither attorney or counsel for, nor related to or employed by, any of the parties to the action in which this deposition was taken, and further that I am not a relative or employee of any attorney or counsel employed by the parties hereto or financially interested in the action.

WITNESS MY HAND AND SEAL this 13th day of August, 1994.

_____

John R. Nash

Notary Public, Wayne County, Michigan
My Commission Expires November 25, 1997.

GLOSSARY

Abuse of process A cause of action in tort to recover money damages for personal injury caused by another person's willful misuse of the civil or criminal legal process. The tortfeasor must have intentionally used the legal process for an improper purpose.

Accident scene The situs of an accident before the conditions have changed, so that observations of the scene show the conditions as they were at the time of the accident.

Accord and satisfaction A type of release that arises from the parties' decision to replace their former agreement (contract) with a new agreement, called an accord, which, if fully performed, constitutes a satisfaction of the prior contract or obligation.

Action A claim that has been placed in suit. A lawsuit. Also called an action at law.

Actual bias A state of mind that prevents a venireman juror or witness from being impartial. A predisposition or preconceived opinion about the issues, parties, or type of case, that precludes a venireman from being fair. A witness who demonstrates an actual bias against a party may be cross-examined by that party as a hostile witness.

Ad damnum clause The "Wherefore" clause at the end of a civil complaint, in which the plaintiff specifies the relief or recovery the plaintiff wants from the defendant. The clause at the end of the defendant's answer, cross-claim, or counterclaim, that specifies the relief the defendant wants from the court.

Additur A court-ordered increase in the amount of money damages awarded to a party by a jury. A trial court has the authority to increase the amount of the award when the damages are manifestly inadequate. Usually the trial court gives the defendant the option of paying the additur, or going through a new trial where a new jury can determine the amount of damages. The trial court may order an additur even though no error of law or procedure explains the jury's inadequate award.

Adverse party A party whose interests in the outcome of the litigation conflicts with or opposes those of the other party. A party may cross-examine an adverse party. When adversity exists between parties, they cannot be required to share peremptory challenges in the jury selection.

Affidavit A written ex parte statement made under oath before an officer of the court or a notary public. An affiant (person who swears to an affidavit) is subject to prosecution for perjury for making a false statement under oath. Therefore, affidavits provide some assurance of truthfulness, but they lack the safeguard of a cross-examination.

Affidavit of identification An affidavit, usually prepared by an attorney or paralegal, to establish the identity of the judgment debtor so that the court may issue an order to the sheriff or marshal to seize the debtor's property to satisfy the judgment.

Affidavit of no response An affidavit, usually prepared by an attorney, to evidence that another party has failed to perform an act required by a court order or court rule. An affidavit commonly used to show that another party has not served a response to a request for admissions within the time allowed thereby establishing that the request is admitted as evidence.

Affirmative defense A defense to a cause of action, that bars all or part of the cause of action. An affirmative defense bars a cause of action even if the party proves the claim to which the defense is asserted. The defense must be pleaded by the party who asserts the defense, otherwise the defense is waived. The party who asserts the affirmative defense has the burden of proving the defense.

Agent A person or corporation that has authority to act for another person, who is usually called a principal, and to make legally binding commitments on behalf of the principal. The agent's authority may come from a contract, express or implied, between the principal and the agent, or it may be created by statute.

Alternate juror A person who is selected to sit on a jury to hear and decide a case, but who does not participate in the jury's deliberations unless one of the regular jurors becomes unavailable. If the alternate is not needed, he or she is usually excused when the parties have completed their final arguments and the court has instructed the jury on the law. The parties may stipulate to let an alternate juror deliberate and participate in the verdict.

Alternative dispute resolution (ADR) Any procedure or method for resolving disputes between persons that does not involve the courts. The primary methods of alternative dispute resolution are arbitration and mediation.

Amicus curiae Friend of the court. A nonparty may seek amicus curiae status in order to appear in a case for the limited purpose of presenting argument and authorities on a question of law that, when decided, may affect the nonparty in some way. The nonparty must first petition the court for leave to participate. The participation is limited to issues of law.

Appears When a party serves or files a pleading or motion. By appearing in an action, a person submits to the court's jurisdiction unless the appearance is limited to the purpose of challenging the court's jurisdiction.

Appellant An aggrieved party who appeals to a higher court to review the proceedings of the trial court's order or judgment on the grounds that the trial court committed an error of law or procedure that adversely affected the outcome.

Appellate court A court having jurisdiction to review the law as applied to a trial court's orders and judgments. The court's function is limited to reviewing the lower court's handling of the case.

Appellee A party against whom an appeal is taken. The party who seeks to sustain the trial court's order or judgment.

Arbitration A procedure by which parties submit their dispute to another person or tribunal for decision. The submission may be voluntary, or pursuant to a contract to arbitrate, or pursuant to a statute that requires arbitration.

Arbitration award The decision of an arbitration tribunal. The award may be binding or nonbinding on the parties, depending upon the agreement under which the arbitration is conducted.

Arbitration tribunal The person or persons appointed by parties to decide their dispute using an arbitration format. The arbitration tribunal may be composed of one or more persons, usually an odd number to avoid a tie vote. Members of an arbitration tribunal are called arbitrators.

Arbitrator *See* **Arbitration tribunal.**

Assault A cause of action in tort that allows the victim to recover money damages for personal injury, usually mental suffering, caused by an intentional threat of bodily harm or death even though no actual physical contact occurs. The threat may be made through acts or words that put the victim in fear of immediate bodily harm. However, words that are not accompanied by the apparent means of making good on the threat of bodily harm do not give rise to an action for assault. An assault may be accompanied by a battery.

Assignment A transfer of one's property or legal rights to another.

Assumption of risk An affirmative defense to an action in negligence and to some other tort actions. The defendant must show that the claimant voluntarily placed herself or himself in a position to incur a known risk of harm. Some courts recognize a difference between primary assumption of risk and secondary assumption of risk. A *primary assumption of risk* precludes the defendant from having any legal duty to the plaintiff. A *secondary assumption of risk* is treated as a form of contributory negligence or comparative negligence.

Attachment A proceeding by which a judgment debtor's property is seized to satisfy the debtor's legal obligation to the judgment creditor.

Attorney pro se A person who acts as his or her own attorney in a civil action.

Attorneys' work product A doctrine, predicated upon Rule 26 of the Federal Rules of Civil Procedure, that prevents one party from discovering what another party's attorneys have tried to do and have accomplished in preparation for trial. The work that attorneys have done for a client.

Battery An intentional, impermissible physical contact of an injurious nature, or a physical contact that is offensive to ordinary sensibilities. A battery gives rise to an action in tort for personal injury. The claimant must prove that the physical contact was intentional, although the claimant need not prove that an injury was specifically intended.

Binding arbitration Arbitration in which the parties must comply with the arbitration tribunal's award. The award may be filed with a court that has jurisdiction, for confirmation. The court will enter a judgment on the basis of the confirmed award. The judgment may be enforced in the same manner as any civil judgment.

Bill of particulars A common-law discovery document through which a party discloses in detail the facts and circumstances that were referred to in the party's pleading. The bill of particulars is usually prepared pursuant to a court order.

Breach of contract. A cause of action to recover money damages, flowing from a person's violation of the terms of a contract.

Burden of proof The duty of a party to present evidence to establish a claim, defense, or allegation. The burden of proof embodies two distinct concepts: One, it refers to the obligation to present sufficient evidence on all the elements of a claim or affirmative defense in order to establish a prima facie case. Two, it also refers to the degree to which a party may have to convince the court in order to establish a claim or defense. In most civil actions, the proponent must prove a claim by a fair preponderance of the evidence. Some claims and defenses in equity require proof by clear and convincing evidence. In criminal cases guilt must be proved beyond a reasonable doubt.

Calendar call   A procedure in which a court requires the attorneys who have cases pending to appear at a specified time and indicate whether their case is ready for trial. This procedure allows the court to schedule cases for trial at a reasonably convenient time.

Case-in-chief   The body of evidence a party presents to establish the party's claim or affirmative defenses before the party rests. The plaintiff's body of evidence must establish a prima facie case or the claim will be dismissed. The defendant's body of evidence must establish a prima facie defense or the defense will be dismissed. A party's case-in-chief does not include the party's rebuttal evidence.

Cause of action   A claim that is recognized by law and enforceable through the courts; a claim upon which a court may grant relief. A cause of action presumes that the defendant has breached a legal duty and in doing so directly caused the plaintiff to sustain an injury or property damage or other loss. A cause of action is the basis for obtaining legal redress.

Certiorari   A writ of review or inquiry. When a higher court grants certiorari in a case, it directs the lower court to deliver to the higher court its records and files concerning the case, so that the higher court can review the proceedings to determine whether some error in the proceedings may have affected the outcome.

Challenge for cause   A party's objection to a venireman on the grounds that the venireman's obvious or implied bias compels the court to excuse the venireman from serving as a juror in the particular case.

Champerty   An agreement between an attorney and a client by which the attorney pledges to bear the cost of the client's litigation in return for a portion of the expected recovery of money damages.

Circumstantial evidence   Indirect proof that depends upon the application of logic and common experience to infer the existence of a fact; evidence that is offered to prove facts that reasonably permit an inference of other material facts. For example, a person's fingerprints on a glass are circumstantial

evidence that the person handled the glass. The proof is by inference rather than by direct observation.

Claim   A demand for compensation or restitution for personal injury, property damage, or loss of profits. A claim may be made without actually starting a lawsuit or having a lawsuit pending. A mere claim may or may not be based upon a legal right. A claim may or may not qualify as a cause of action for which a court may provide relief. For a claim to be enforceable in court, it must be based upon a breach of a legal duty owed to the claimant.

Claimant   A person who asserts a claim against another person, whether or not a lawsuit has been commenced.

Clear and convincing   Creating a *firm* belief in the mind of the trier of fact. Clear and convincing proof is more than a fair preponderance of the evidence, which is the most common standard of proof applicable to civil actions, but less than beyond a reasonable doubt, which is the standard imposed upon the government in the prosecution of criminal cases.

Collateral estoppel   An affirmative defense that precludes the plaintiff from suing defendants not named in a prior case on the same cause of action, where the verdict against the plaintiff in the prior case held that the plaintiff either did not sustain a loss or was solely responsible for the loss. *See also* **Estoppel.**

Commencement of action   The date on which the plaintiff causes the action to begin against the defendant. In federal district courts, the action is ordinarily commenced at the time the plaintiff files the complaint with the clerk of court (see Rule 3).

Common law   A system of law that is based upon precedent, rather than a civil code of laws. The law is derived from court decisions that evolve into rules of law that are followed as precedent unless or until the court that established them decides to replace or modify them. Most states rely upon the common law to resolve disputes in civil litigation.

Comparative fault   An expanded concept of comparative negligence that includes strict liability in tort, breach of warranty, dramshop liability, and other causes of action not based upon intentional wrongful conduct. Liability is apportioned on the basis of the causal fault attributable to each party, including a plaintiff. In states that have comparative fault, a jury may be asked to compare one party's causal negligence with another party's liability and to apportion the causal fault on a percentage basis. The degree to which the breach of legal duty contributed to the loss, not the degree of culpability, is the basis for allocating damages. Indeed, comparative fault statutes include within their purview some torts that impose liability without fault, such as strict liability in tort.

Comparative negligence A legal doctrine that requires the fact finder (jury) in a negligence action to determine the percentage of causal negligence attributable to each person involved in the occurrence. A plaintiff's causal negligence does not necessarily bar the plaintiff from a recovery of compensatory money damages. If the plaintiff is found to be causally negligent, the amount of money damages recoverable is reduced by the amount of causal negligence. However, if the plaintiff is more causally negligent than the defendant, the laws of some states preclude the plaintiff from making any recovery against the defendant. If two or more defendants are found to be causally negligent, as between them, they must share the liability for money damages in proportion to their percentage of causal negligence; however, each defendant remains separately liable for all the claimant's damages.

Compensatory damages A sum of money that is awarded to a person to reimburse her or him for personal injury or property damage. Compensatory damages are not intended to penalize the person who must pay them; they are intended to make up for the plaintiff's loss.

Complicity An affirmative defense to a dramshop action. The liquor vendor can avoid liability to the plaintiff who was injured by an intoxicated person, if the vendor can prove that the plaintiff was complicit in the illegal sale of intoxicants to the intoxicated person. For example, complicity is established by showing that the plaintiff bought the intoxicants for the intoxicated person.

Compulsory counterclaim A defendant's claim against the plaintiff that arises from the same transaction or occurrence as the plaintiff's claim. If the defendant fails to assert the claim in a counterclaim, it is waived by operation of law. The Rules make the counterclaim compulsory to avoid multiple trials based on a single occurrence.

Conclusion A determination about a fact obtained by reasoning from evidence and other known facts. An inference drawn by the jury or judge from the entire body of evidence provided by the witnesses as to the ultimate question of fact.

Conclusion of law A determination that results when the court applies the law to a given set of facts. For example, if the facts show that a motorist violated a traffic light and the law provides that a traffic signal violation is negligence, the legal conclusion is

that the motorist was negligent. In an action decided by a judge without a jury, the judge must prepare a document that contains his or her findings of fact and conclusions of law. The conclusions of law determine the parties' rights and obligations and are the basis for the court's order for judgment.

Concurring opinions An appellate court opinion written by an appellate judge to explain why the judge agrees with the decision or result reached by the majority of judges as expressed in their opinion, but disagrees with the reasons given by the majority for their decision.

Confession of judgment A person's written admission, made under oath, that she or he is indebted to the person named, and that the person named is entitled to have the court enter a judgment in her or his favor for a specified amount of money. A confession of judgment may be made without having an action pending against the confessor. Confessions of judgment are strictly regulated by statute in most states.

Conflict of interest A situation in which a lawyer's duty to a client to act or refrain from acting is or may be harmful to the interests of another client or to the lawyer's own interests.

Consent Voluntary acquiescence. Consent is a complete affirmative defense to most tort actions. It may be expressed in words or acts, or implied from circumstances. For example, the act of kissing a person is a battery, unless the person who is kissed consents to the physical contact.

Consent judgment A judgment for which the parties to a civil lawsuit stipulate the terms and conditions. Occasionally a defendant may stipulate that the plaintiff may enter a judgment against the defendant for a specified amount of money, with the provision that the plaintiff may collect the money only from the defendant's liability insurance policy. In that event, the plaintiff, who becomes a judgment creditor without having to go through a trial, covenants not to execute against the defendant's personal assets, other than the insurance policy. The plaintiff assumes the burden of establishing that the claim is covered by the insurance policy.

Contingent Dependent upon something else. An obligation or duty may be contingent upon the occurrence of an event or performance of an act before it comes into being.

Contingent fee A fee for legal services based upon an agreed percentage of the monies actually recovered. If the client does not recover any money damages in the litigation, the lawyer is not entitled to any fee.

Contribution   A right or obligation between parties who are jointly liable to a third person, usually the plaintiff, for money damages recoverable in a civil action.

Contributory negligence   Negligence on the part of the plaintiff, that contributed to the accident and the plaintiff's injuries or other loss. Historically, contributory negligence provided the defendant with a complete defense to the plaintiff's action in negligence. The defense has been replaced in most states by the principles of comparative negligence and comparative fault.

Conversion   The wrongful exercise of control of ownership over another person's personal property. A conversion of personal property is tantamount to a theft of the property.

Cost bond   A bond that a party must provide to the court to guarantee payment of the adverse party's taxable costs and disbursements. An appellant may be required to provide a cost bond as a condition to prosecuting an appeal. Otherwise, some parties would appeal merely to delay payment of the judgment obtained against them.

Count   A separate statement of a claim within a complaint, counterclaim, or cross-claim. Counts may be used to state separate causes of action or to state claims arising from separate transactions or occurrences.

Counterclaim   A claim asserted by the defendant against the plaintiff to obtain compensation for a loss or damages suffered by the defendant, or the pleading in which such a claim is asserted. A counterclaim may be founded in tort or contract. It is attached to or made part of the defendant's answer.

Court of record   A court in which the judicial proceedings and acts are recorded and permanently retained.

Covenant not to sue   A type of settlement agreement in which the plaintiff agrees not to commence or maintain an action against the defendant but does not release the defendant from liability for the occurrence. A tortfeasor who obtains a covenant not to sue avoids defending against the plaintiff's claim, and the plaintiff preserves the right to pursue the claim against a joint tortfeasor.

Criminal   That which pertains to or is connected with the law of crimes or the administration of penal justice, or relates to or has the character of crime. Criminal justice and criminal procedures are quite distinct from civil justice and civil procedures.

Cross-claim   A claim by one defendant against one or more codefendants, arising from the same facts that support the plaintiff's claim against the defendants. An action to obtain relief in the form of indemnity or contribution from a codefendant.

Cross-examination   The examination of an adverse party or hostile witness in which the examiner may ask leading questions and may seek to limit answers by asking very narrow, circumscribed questions.

Cross-motions for summary judgment   Motions for summary judgment made by both adverse parties. The parties may assert or rely upon different grounds for their motions.

Curriculum vitae   A written description of a witness's background, education, training, associations, and publications.

Damages   (1) The injury, loss, or other harm to a person or property that is proximately caused by another person's breach of a legal duty. (2) An abbreviation of the term *money damages*, which is compensation for the injury, loss, or other harm caused by another person's breach of a legal duty. In contract actions, money damages are paid in compensation for the loss of the bargain.

Day certain   The date on which a trial has been ordered to begin. The court has cleared its calendar so that the case will definitely begin on that date. The parties must be ready to start the trial at the appointed time.

Declaratory judgment   A court decree that interprets and declares the parties' legal rights and obligations pursuant to a writing such as a contract, statute, deed, ordinance, or regulation. A court may issue a declaratory judgment even though the parties have not violated the alleged legal right or obligation. Most states have adopted the Uniform Declaratory Judgment Act, which determines when and how a declaratory judgment action may be prosecuted.

Declaratory judgment action   An action to obtain a declaratory judgment.

Defamation   The publication of a false statement, oral or written, that damages another person's reputation. *See also* **Libel** and **Slander.**

Demand for inspection   A written demand served by one party upon another party to schedule an inspection of any item of real or personal property that is in the control of the second party and relevant to the case. An action must be pending for a party to use the procedure. The demand may be made without first obtaining leave of the court. The procedure is prescribed by Rule 34.

Demand for jury   A request made by a party on his or her pleading or in a separate document entitled "Demand for Jury," by which the party notifies the court and other parties of a request for a trial by jury. The written demand for jury may specify only certain issues that the party wants tried to a jury; all other issues will then be tried to the court, unless another party serves a demand for jury on those issues.

Demonstrative evidence Physical or tangible evidence that can be brought to the courtroom and used to prove a fact or for illustrative purposes to help a witness explain testimony. Demonstrative evidence may have been created by the transaction or occurrence in question, or it may be specially prepared by a party for use at trial.

Deponent A person who gives testimony under oath in an affidavit in an oral deposition, in a written deposition, or in court. Although answers to interrogatories are similar to an affidavit, a party who signs answers to interrogatories is not usually referred to as a deponent.

Depose (1) To give testimony in an affidavit, in a deposition, or in court. (2) To take a person's deposition by asking the person questions (see Rule 30).

Deposition The *procedure* for taking a person's testimony and the *transcript* of a person's testimony. Lawyers commonly describe the interrogation process as taking the deponent's deposition. *Deposition* is synonymous with *testimony*. (1) A written deposition is a procedure established by Rule 31 of the Federal Rules of Civil Procedure. It enables a party to obtain written testimony of any party or witness for the purpose of discovering information or to preserve the testimony for use at trial. The deponent may be compelled to testify by serving a subpoena on the deponent. The right to cross-examine the deponent is preserved. (2) *See also* **Oral deposition.**

Deposition transcript A verbatim copy of an oral deposition, either typed or printed in a booklet form.

Directed verdict An order by the trial judge that dismisses a claim or an affirmative defense on the grounds that there is insufficient evidence to prove the claim or defense or that the claim or defense is conclusively established by the evidence so there is nothing for a jury to decide or resolve. The order leads directly to an entry of judgment in favor of the prevailing party. The judge *must* determine that a reasonable jury could decide the facts only one way, therefore the judge is able to apply the law to the facts to resolve the litigation.

Direct evidence Testimony about a fact by an eyewitness who observed the fact, or an exhibit that tends to prove the existence or nonexistence of the fact. The evidence depends upon the reliability of the witness or exhibit from which it comes. *See, for contrast,* **Circumstantial evidence.**

Direct examination The examination that a lawyer conducts of the lawyer's own client or client's witness. The form of the examination precludes leading questions and impeachment, unless the interrogator can show surprise.

Discovery deposition A deposition of a party or witness taken for the purpose of obtaining information and evidence relevant to the case.

Dismissal The termination of a lawsuit pursuant to Rule 41. The termination may be the voluntary act of the plaintiff or by stipulation of the parties or by court order.

Dismissal without prejudice A dismissal subject to the right of the claimant to bring the lawsuit again in the court or at a later date.

Dismissal with prejudice A dismissal that precludes the plaintiff from bringing the claim at a later date against the party who has obtained the dismissal.

Dispositive motion A motion that seeks a court order that would dismiss the plaintiff's claim or the defendant's counterclaim or the defendant's affirmative defenses.

Dissent An opinion filed by an appellate court judge who disagrees with the holding and reasoning of a majority of the judges whose opinion becomes the law of the case.

Diversity of citizenship A basis for providing jurisdiction of a civil lawsuit to a federal district court when the amount in controversy exceeds fifty thousand dollars. The plaintiff and the defendant must have their domiciles in different states at the time the action is commenced. The parties are not required to be residents of different states at the time of the transaction or occurrence that gave rise to the lawsuit.

Dramshop action A civil action against liquor vendors and in favor of persons, other than the inebriate, who suffer harm as the result of an illegal sale of intoxicants. A sale of intoxicants may be illegal because the customer was underage or obviously intoxicated.

Duress The threat of death, bodily harm, or damage to property. If a person was under duress at the time of making a contract, will, or other legal commitment, a court will set aside the legal obligation. Duress is an affirmative defense that must be pleaded and proved by the party who claims to have been under it.

Efficient intervening cause   A cause of an injury or loss that insulates or relieves the defendant from liability for negligence. An efficient intervening cause must have occurred after the defendant's original negligence; must not have been brought about the defendant's original negligence; must have actively worked to bring about a result that would not otherwise have followed from the original negligence; and must not have been reasonably foreseeable by the defendant. An efficient intervening cause relieves all prior negligent conduct of any liability for an accident. It is not a basis or grounds for allocating fault. Efficient intervening cause is often referred to as superseding cause.

En banc hearing   An appellate court hearing in which all the judges of the court participate.

Equity   (1) In its broadest and most general signification, the spirit and habit of fairness, justness, and right dealing that regulates the intercourse of persons—the rule of doing to all others as we desire them to do to us, or, as expressed by Justinian, "To live honestly, to harm nobody, to render to every man his due." *Equity* is, therefore, the synonym of *natural right* or *justice.* But, in this sense, its obligation is ethical rather than jural, and its discussion belongs to the sphere of morals. It is grounded in the precepts of the conscience, not in any sanction of positive law. (2) In a restricted sense, equal and impartial justice as between two persons whose rights or claims are in conflict; justice, that is, as ascertained by natural reason or ethical insight, but independent of the formulated body of law. This is not a technical meaning of the term *equity,* except insofar as courts that administer equity seek to discover it by these agencies, or apply it beyond the strict lines of positive law. (3) In a still more restricted sense, a system of jurisprudence, or branch of remedial justice, administered by certain tribunals, distinct from the common-law courts and empowered to decree equity in the sense listed last in definition 2. Here *equity* becomes a complex of well-settled and well-understood rules, principles, and precedents.

Estoppel   An affirmative defense that precludes the plaintiff from recovering money damages for a loss that resulted from the defendant's mistake where that mistake was induced by the plaintiff's wrongful conduct in the first place. Estoppel has its origin in equity. To be able to invoke the doctrine, a party must show that she or he would be damaged if the doctrine were not applied. The doctrine precludes a party from denying the truth of a statement upon which another person duly relied if the other person would be harmed by that denial. Estoppel may also arise from a party's conduct. It must be alleged as a cause of action or defense in order to be made an issue in a civil suit.

Evidence   Anything that tends to prove a fact, especially testimony and exhibits offered at a trial.

Excusable neglect   A party's failure to perform an order of the court or follow a rule that the court will allow the party to cure. The neglect must not be willful. Ordinarily, to be excusable, the conduct must not be more culpable than inadvertence, oversight, or mere carelessness.

Ex parte   On one side only; by or for one party; done for, on behalf of, or on the application of one party only. An ex parte judicial proceeding is one initiated on behalf of and for the benefit of one party, in which the opposing party does not participate and of which the opposing party receives no notice.

Ex parte motion   A motion made by one party without giving notice to another party. Ex parte motions are heard by the court with only one party in attendance. Ex parte motions are rarely made and are generally improper. However, a party may make an ex parte motion to increase the time period provided by an order or rule if he or she does so before the authorized period expires (see Rule 6(b)). An ex parte motion may be made whenever the opposing party is in default.

Expert opinion   An opinion of a person who has special education, training, and experience in a subject not ordinarily known or understood by laypersons. The opinion may be about the existence of facts or the effect of facts material to the parties' controversy. For an opinion to be admissible in evidence, the presiding judge must determine that the opinion would help the jury to better understand the evidence in the case. The opinion must have a foundation in the evidence presented by the parties. As part of the foundation, the party who offers expert opinion testimony must show that the expert has the education, training, and experience to be an expert. A judge has broad discretion in determining whether a witness's background is adequate to make the witness an expert in a particular field.

Expert witness   A person who has special education, training, and experience in a particular subject or field and whose opinions would help the jury to understand the evidence or facts relevant to the case.

Fact   A truth; something that happened; something that exists or did exist. A fact is an absolute, something certain, but the existence of a fact may be far from clear.

Fact brief   A brief that a lawyer prepared to determine whether he or she has all the necessary evidence to prove the client's case and refute the adverse party's claims. The fact brief identifies the remaining issues, the facts to be proved, the evidence available with which to prove contested facts, the method of presenting the evidence, the use of evidence to defeat or contradict the opposing party's evidence, and the use of rules and procedures to defeat the opposing party's claims and defenses.

Fact finder   The person or persons who resolve disputed facts and the ultimate questions of fact from the evidence presented by the parties. When the trial is by jury, the jury is the fact finder. When there is no jury, the judge is the fact finder.

Fiduciary   A person or corporation that has assumed a special relationship with another person or another person's property, such as a trustee, administrator, executor, lawyer, or guardian. The fiduciary must exercise the highest degree of care to maintain and preserve the right or property within her or his charge. A fiduciary must place the interests of that charge ahead of her or his own. A lawyer is a fiduciary concerning any secrets, documents, and money given to her or him by the client for safekeeping during the professional relationship. A lawyer is not a fiduciary in the handling of the client's litigation.

Final argument   The argument or summation that each party's lawyer may make at the end of the trial The arguments are made after all the parties have rested but before the judge instructs the jury on the law. The arguments may be used to remind the jury what evidence was presented, why certain evidence should be believed or not believed, what the evidence proves or fails to prove, how the law applies to the facts of the case, and how the jury should answer the questions in the verdict form.

Findings of fact   A determination of facts made by the trial court from the evidence produced in a trial. The trial court applies the law to those facts to reach its conclusions of law.

Foundation   A body of evidence that tends to establish either that a witness is competent to testify on a certain matter or that other evidence is relevant, thus making the testimony or evidence potentially admissible and usable in the case. Foundation is a legal requirement for a witness to testify, for a witness to qualify as an expert, or to show that evidence is relevant. Foundation is lacking when an exhibit is offered without proof concerning its source or authenticity.

Fraud   An intentional misrepresentation of a material fact upon which another person reasonably relies to his or her detriment. Fraud is a cause of action in tort and may be used as an affirmative defense. A statement of mere opinion is not usually actionable. However, if a false statement is rendered by an expert concerning a matter within the scope of his or her expertise, it may be actionable as fraud or negligent misrepresentation.

Frivolous   Not supported by facts, or contrary to law. Any party who prosecutes a frivolous claim or defense is subject to sanctions and disciplinary action. The sanctions may include the assessment of costs, an order striking the party's pleadings, or even an award of judgment in favor of the opposing party. The lawyer or the party or both could even be held in contempt of court (see Rule 11).

Full and final release   A release that discharges from liability not only the party who paid consideration for it, but anyone else who might be liable to the claimant. The release applies only to the particular transaction or occurrence. It must identify the transaction or occurrence by type, time and place, and losses claimed. A full and final release is a predicate for settling the defendant's action to obtain contribution.

Fundamental error   *See* **Plain error.**

Garnishment   A procedure by which a judgment creditor may attach property or money that is in the hands of a third person and belongs to the judgment debtor. The judgment creditor serves upon the custodian (garnishee) a garnishment summons that requires the custodian to disclose what property she or he has that belongs to the judgment debtor and to hold it until further order.

Garnishment disclosure   A document served and filed by a garnishee in which the garnishee discloses whether he or she is holding any money or property and the amount or particular items held.

General jurisdictions   The authority of a court to adjudicate all controversies that may be brought before it within the legal bounds of rights and remedies, as opposed to special or limited jurisdiction, which covers only a particular class of cases, or cases where the amount in controversy is below a prescribed sum, or which is subject to specific exceptions.

General release   A release in which the claimant discharges all claims of any kind against the person or persons who obtained the release. A general release discharges all claims the claimant has from the transaction or occurrence in question. It discharges all persons who might be liable for the injury or other loss the claimant may have sustained. It is intended to put an end to all claims the claimant may have against the released parties for all transactions and occurrences between them as of the date of the release. If an action is pending, the plaintiff is required to stipulate to a dismissal of the action; nothing remains to be litigated.

General verdict   A verdict in which the jury simply finds in favor of the plaintiff by specifying an amount of money damages, or finds for the defendant. The jury does not have to make any specific findings.

General verdict with interrogatories   A general verdict in which the jury finds for the plaintiff or defendant, and, in addition, must answer specific questions about the facts of the case. The judge decides what questions to ask and how to word the questions. The answers may help the court or parties decide whether an appeal would be useful or would help resolve some collateral problems raised by the case (see rule 49(b)).

Genuine   Actually being what it purports to be, as in the case of a document.

Good cause   Some basis in fact and law; substantial compliance with a legal requirement or legal standard. A party may be required to show good cause in order to obtain an independent medical examination of an adverse party. The requirement is to show a substantial reason for the medical examination.

Grand jury   A jury of inquiry that is summoned and returned by the sheriff to each session of the criminal courts, and whose duty is to receive complaints and accusations in criminal cases, hear the evidence adduced on the part of the state, and find bills of indictment in cases where it is satisfied a trial ought to be held. The jury issues an indictment if it determines there is good reason to believe that a crime has been committed and the accused is the perpetrator.

Grounds   A basis or foundation for a claim, motion, cause of action, or allegation.

Guardian ad litem   A guardian appointed by a court to help a minor to prosecute or defend a lawsuit in which the minor is a party. The minor may be the plaintiff or defendant. The guardian may or may not be a parent. A lawyer who represents a minor could *not* act as the guardian ad litem. A guardian ad litem has ultimate responsibility for making decisions about settlement and whether the action should be maintained or dismissed.

Hearsay   Evidence proceeding not from the personal knowledge of the witness, but from the mere repetition of what the witness has heard others say. That which does not derive its value solely from the creditability of the witness, but rests mainly on the

veracity and competency of other persons. The very nature of hearsay evidence shows its weakness, and it is received at trial only in limited situations owing to necessity. Hearsay evidence is competent to prove a fact and will be received by the court in the absence of an objection.

High-low settlement   An agreement between parties to settle their dispute by payment and acceptance of a sum of money within an agreed range, leaving to the court or tribunal the award of money damages. The parties commit to be bound by the amount of the award if it is within the agreed range. If the award is for more than provided in the agreement, the parties settle for the high amount provided by the agreement. If the award is for less than provided in the agreement, the parties settle for the low amount provided by the agreement. The high-low agreement reduces the risk of an excessively high or low award.

Hostile witness   A witness who has demonstrated animosity toward one of the parties. If the court declares a witness to be hostile toward a party, that party may cross-examine the witness even if that party called the witness to the stand to testify.

Hung jury   A jury whose members have concluded that they cannot reach an agreement on the facts so they cannot return a verdict. When the judge is satisfied that the jury cannot reach a verdict, the judge must declare a mistrial.

Hypothetical question   A question put to a witness that asks the witness to assume specified facts and render an opinion on the basis of those facts. The evidence must provide some basis for the assumed facts; otherwise, the question would be irrelevant and disallowed. The witness is not asked or required to validate the assumed facts.

Illustrative evidence   Evidence that does not, in itself, have probative value, but that helps a witness to explain her or his testimony. For example, a photograph or drawing that depicts the location of an accident may help a witness to explain what the witness observed. Illustrative evidence is received at trial solely as an aid for the witness. The jury may not be allowed to take a piece of illustrative evidence to its deliberations, because the exhibit's only value is to help the witness describe or explain her or his testimony; it is not, in itself, evidence of anything.

Impeachment   The casting of doubt on the credibility of a witness or exhibits by showing inconsistencies in what the witness says or in the use of the exhibits. A witness may also be impeached by showing that the witness has been convicted of a crime of a type that indicates the witness is willing to disregard the obligations of the oath.

Impeachment evidence   Evidence offered solely to cast doubt on other evidence received by the court and that will not, in itself, support a verdict. Prior inconsistent statements of a party may be both impeachment evidence and substantive evidence.

Implied bias   Bias that is assumed to exist because of the relationship that the witness or venire member has with a party.

Incompetent   Lacking the capacity, fitness, qualifications, or ability to act.

Indemnity   Total reimbursement for a loss. Insurance is a contract providing indemnity.

Independent medical examination   A medical examination of a party to an action conducted by a physician selected by an adverse party for the purpose of evaluating the party's physical, mental, or blood condition. The medical examination is not in itself an adversary proceeding. The physician is expected to follow professional practices and procedures in conducting the examination and in making an evaluation. The right to the examination is prescribed by Rule 35. In some jurisdictions this type of examination is referred to as an adverse medical examination.

Injunction   A court order that prohibits a party from engaging in a specified activity. A prohibitive writ issued by a court of equity against a defendant, forbidding the defendant to do some act the defendant is threatening or attempting to commit or restraining the defendant in the continuance thereof. A court may enjoin a defendant's conduct where the harm to the plaintiff cannot be adequately redressed by an action at law with money damages.

Insufficiency of process   A failure to follow the procedures prescribed by law for serving process on another party.

Integrated bar   A state bar association that controls the right to practice law. All lawyers in the state must belong to the bar association.

Interrogatory   A written question to another party to a civil action that must be answered under oath (see Rule 33).

Invasion of privacy   A cause of action in tort for personal injury for wrongful publishing a person's likeness or private information about the person in a manner that is outrageous. The right to privacy is subject to the public's right to matters that have news value and are legitimately of public interest.

Irrelevant   Not related or not applicable to the matter in issue. Not tending to prove or disprove a material fact or issue.

Joint liability   A condition in which two or more parties are concurrently liable to a claimant for the claimant's entire loss. Joint liability may arise from contract or tort. Tortfeasors may acquire joint liability by acting in concert for a joint purpose, or merely because their wrongful acts happen to be concurrent and contribute to an indivisible loss.

Judge's minutes   The notes a judge keeps concerning the evidence and proceedings in a trial.

Judgment   (1) A court's ultimate determination of the parties' rights and obligations concerning a particular matter. (2) The official decision of a court of justice upon the respective rights and claims of the parties. (3) The clerk of court's record of the court's declaration of the parties' rights and obligations in a particular action.

Judgment book   The public record containing civil judgment.

Judgment creditor   The party who has obtained a judgment in his or her favor against another party for a sum of money.

Judgment debtor   A person against whom a judgment has been entered declaring her or him to be indebted to the judgment creditor named in the judgment.

Judicial notice   A rule of evidence by which a court may recognize a fact that is capable of being known or determined to a certainty by consulting indisputable sources. For example, a court may take judicial notice that Christmas falls on December 25, that water freezes at zero degrees centigrade, that there are 5,280 feet in a mile.

Jurisdiction   The power and authority of a court. A court's jurisdiction depends upon the court's following due process of law. Jurisdiction may be limited to a specific territory or to certain types of actions or to certain types of controversies or certain classes of parties. A court's jurisdiction is necessarily limited by the authority of the body that created the court.

Jury demand   A notice on a pleading or separate statement served and filed by a party, indicating that the party wants a trial by jury.

Law of the case   The law according to which the parties tried their case without objection, so that the rules of law are considered controlling even though they might not be correct.

Leading question   A question that suggests the answer the interrogator wants to receive.

Legal duty   A duty that the law imposes upon a person to act or refrain from acting. The breach of a legal duty gives rise to a cause of action against the violator for compensation for any injury or damage caused by the breach. The legal duty may arise by contract or by operation of the common law or by statute.

Letters rogatory A formal, written communication sent by a court in which an action is pending, to a court or judge of a foreign country or state, requesting that the testimony of a witness who resides within the latter's jurisdiction be taken under that court's direction and transmitted to the first court for use in the pending action. Letters rogatory is a means of obtaining jurisdiction over a witness for the purpose of obtaining the witness's deposition. The court to whom the request is directed will have to use its subpoena power.

Liability A legal obligation to make restitution or pay compensation. Liability may be contingent or absolute.

Libel A cause of action in tort for injury to a person's reputation caused by the publication of a false statement in writing.

Loan receipt agreement A contract by which a tortfeasor, or the tortfeasor's insurer, agrees to "loan" the claimant a specified sum of money and the claimant agrees not to pursue his or her claim against the lender, but both believe that another party has substantial liability and the claimant agrees to pursue the claim against that other party. The claimant agrees that if he or she recovers over a certain amount from the other party, he or she will repay all or part of the loan. If the claimant recovers little or nothing from the other party, the loan need not be repaid.

Loss-of-bargain measure of damages The amount of money a party duly expected to receive as a profit from the adverse party's full performance of the parties' contract.

Maintenance The practice of advancing monies to a litigant on the basis that the "loan" will be paid out of the verdict or settlement.

Majority opinion The opinion written or signed by a majority of the judges on an appellate court, when one or more other judges on the court file a separate dissent or concurring opinion.

Malicious prosecution A cause of action in tort to recover money damages for personal injury caused by the defendant's intentional wrongful use of criminal court proceedings, without justification, for an improper purpose.

Malpractice Negligence committed by a person while rendering professional services.

Mandamus An order or writ that is issued by a court of superior jurisdiction and is directed to a governmental officer or to an inferior court, commanding the performance of a particular act. The

basis for the writ is that the officer or judge has a duty to perform the act and has neglected or refused to do it. A writ of mandamus may direct a lower court to restore to the complainant legal rights or privileges of which she or he has been illegally deprived.

Mary Carter agreement A secret agreement between parties to settle the case between them but to continue prosecution of the case against another party.

Material Important; more-or-less necessary; going to the merits; having to do with matters of substance, as distinguished from mere form. In a civil action, evidence is material if it relates to the issues raised by the pleadings.

Material fact A fact that directly relates to an issue in the case.

Matter The subject of a civil action or arbitration.

Measure of damages The basis for assessing the monetary value of an injury, loss, or compensable harm. The rules of law by which courts determine the basis of compensation for various kinds of injuries and losses.

Mediation A dispute resolution procedure in which an intermediary facilitates communication between the parties, helps the parties overcome barriers in the negotiation process, and identifies the parties' real interests and needs so that they can make their own agreement. A mediator does not have authority to impose a solution on the parties.

Memorandum of interview An investigator's memorandum of his or her interview with a witness. The memorandum contains the same information that would be in a witness statement, but the memorandum is not signed. A memorandum of interview would be work product and generally not discoverable, whereas many jurisdictions allow discovery of witness statements.

Minor's settlement A settlement that must be approved by the court to be binding upon the minor. The minor's parent or guardian must petition the court to approve the settlement and must show that the settlement is fair to the minor. In the absence of court approval, the settlement is not binding until the minor reaches majority plus one year. If the minor has not objected to the settlement by that time, it is automatically ratified and binding.

Misrepresentation A false statement or representation concerning a fact, that may give rise to a cause of action for fraud or negligent misrepresentation.

Mistrial (1) A trial that has been aborted because of some defect in the proceedings that prevents it from being valid or fair. (2) The presiding judge's determination and order that cancel a trial, usually allowing the case to be tried again.

Money damages A sum of money awarded to a claimant in compensation for injury, loss, or other harm. *See also* **Damages.**

Motion An application to a court for a ruling or order concerning a matter of procedure or law. The term *motion* is generally employed with reference to all such applications, whether written or oral.

Motion for directed verdict *See* **Motion for judgment as a matter of law.**

Motion for judgment as a matter of law A dispositive motion that asks the court to apply the substantive law to the facts before the court and make the ultimate determination that the moving party is entitled to have the judgment entered in her or his favor. The moving party must convince the judge that reasonable minds could not differ on the import of the facts, so all the court need do is apply the law to the facts clearly established by the evidence. The motion may be made by the defendant when the plaintiff rests, or by the plaintiff when the defendant rests. Either party or both parties may make or renew the motion when both parties have rested. The motion may be limited to a particular issue. The motion is authorized by Rule 50. In many jurisdictions this motion is called a motion for a directed verdict.

Motion for more definite statement A motion that is made by a defendant, usually before the answer is due, for an order requiring the plaintiff to state the claim or cause of action with more clarity and more detail.

Motion in limine A motion made at the beginning of a trial, for the purpose of obtaining an order allowing or disallowing certain evidence. A motion in limine may be used to resolve some procedural issue. It may not be used to obtain a ruling on the application of the substantive law to the case, such as a motion for summary judgment.

Motion to confirm award A motion made in a court of general jurisdiction, to have the court approve an arbitration award and convert the award into a civil judgment that can be enforced against the losing party.

Motion to vacate award A motion made in a court of general jurisdiction, to set aside or void an arbitration award. The motion must show that the award was procured through fraud or corruption or that the arbitration tribunal exceeded the scope of its authority.

Mutual mistake A basis for reforming a written contact. Where people have a meeting of minds concerning the terms and conditions of a contract that they reduce to writing, but the written contract fails to express their mutual intent, the written contract may be reformed to comport with their intent. The party who wishes to reform the written contract must prove that both parties agreed on the terms, but they made a mutual mistake in expressing the terms in the writing. In most jurisdictions the mutual mistake must be proved by clear and convincing evidence.

Negative evidence Evidence that tends to negate or disprove the existence of an alleged fact, such as testimony by a witness that the train did not sound a whistle at the crossing. The foundation for such evidence requires a showing that, for example, the witness would have heard the whistle if it had been sounded.

Negative statement A signed or recorded witness statement relating that the witness does not have any knowledge about the transaction or occurrence. A statement that is obtained to make sure the potential witness does not have information or evidence that is adverse to the client's position. The purpose of such a statement is to eliminate the potential witness as a threat to the client's case.

Negligence A failure to exercise the degree of care that a person of ordinary prudence would exercise under the same circumstances. A person may be negligent toward another person or toward himself or herself. All persons owe the legal duty to conduct themselves with reasonable care so as not to injure another person or another person's property. A person does not have a duty to act to protect another person from harm caused by a third person or force of nature, unless the person has a *special relationship* recognized by law that imposes upon that person a duty to act and protect. The special relation may be based upon requirements in the common law, a statute, or a contract.

Negligence per se An act or omission that is declared by statute to be wrongful and therefore is treated by the courts as negligence as a matter of law, without any reference to the reasonable person standard and without any reference to the foreseeability of harm that the act or omission may cause. For example, the violation of a statute that prohibits the sale of firearms to minors could be the basis for a court to hold that a vendor's sale to a minor constitutes negligence per se; the sale could be negligent even if the vendor believed that the buyer was an adult and that the firearm would be used properly. The illegal sale would subject the vendor to strict liability. The victim would have to be a person within the class of persons intended to be protected by the statute.

Negligent misrepresentation A statement made as a fact when the person making it does not know whether it is true or not true, and has reason to know that the person to whom it is made may rely upon it. A negligent misrepresentation may be made in writing or orally.

Nonbinding arbitration Arbitration in which the tribunal's award is only advisory. A nonbinding award may be accepted, rejected, or modified by the parties. In no event may it be confirmed by a court order. The parties' scope of submission should state whether the award is binding or nonbinding.

Note of issue A document used in civil litigation in many state courts, by which a party demands a jury trial or court trial. The document identifies all the parties and their attorneys. It must be served upon all the parties and filed with the court to be effective. A note of issue places the case on the active trial calendar. Federal courts do not use notes of issue; instead, the demand for jury must be made upon the pleadings or in a jury demand. In federal court, cases are automatically moved along for trial once they are filed.

Notice of appeal A notice that the appellant files with the district court to start the appeal process. The notice must be served upon all other parties. In federal courts, the notice must be served and filed within thirty days after entry of the judgment from which the appeal is taken. Upon receiving the notice of appeal, the district court clerk must send the file to the clerk of the appellate court. The district court loses jurisdiction over the case once the appeal has been commenced.

Notice of deposition A notice that one party serves upon all other parties, scheduling the deposition of a person who may have knowledge, information, or evidence relevant to the case. The person to be deposed may be a party or an independent witness (see Rule 30(b)(1)).

Notice of motion A notice that accompanies a motion and sets the time and place at which the motion will be heard by the court.

Notice of withdrawal A notice filed with the court and served upon all other parties, stating that the attorney for a party has withdrawn or will withdraw from the case. The notice of withdrawal ordinarily informs the court and parties where and who notices may be served upon that party after the date of withdrawal.

Nuisance A cause of action in tort to recover money damages for the unreasonable interference of an occupant's use or enjoyment of real property. The harm must be substantial. It does not matter whether the interference is negligent or intentional. The claimant must show that the harm greatly outweighs the utility of the defendant's conduct. The claimant may seek money damages and injunctive relief.

Obviously intoxicated Objectively manifesting signs of intoxication through personal conduct. Obvious intoxication is an ultimate question of fact and predicate for civil liability in a dramshop action. A liquor vendor may be liable in money damages caused by a patron to whom an alcoholic beverage was supplied while the patron was obviously intoxicated. The intoxicated person's inebriation must have been a contributing factor in causing harm to the claimant.

Offer of judgment A procedure authorized by Rule 68, by which a party may offer to let judgment be taken against him or her in a specified amount, together with accrued costs. If the officer is accepted, judgment may be entered forthwith according to the terms of the offer. If the offer is not accepted and the offeree fails to obtain a judgment that is more favorable, the offeror is entitled to recover the offeror's costs. The offeree is precluded from recovering costs even though otherwise the offeree would have been considered the prevailing party. If the offeree obtains a more favorable judgment by trying the case, the offer is without effect. The offer of judgment must be made at least ten days before the trial begins.

Offer of proof A procedure that may be used at trial to put in the record evidence that the trial judge disallowed. The offer of proof may be made by having the witness testify, out of the hearing of the jury, about the matters excluded by the judge's ruling. In some courts an offer of proof is sufficient if the attorney who offered the evidence merely states in the record what the evidence would have shown.

Opening statement A lawyer's statement to a jury made at the beginning of a trial, in which the lawyer outlines the evidence that she or he expects to present on behalf of the client. The opening statement is not supposed to be an argument. Lawyers are not supposed to argue the effect of the evidence or the application of the law to the facts.

Opinion A written statement by an appellate court, containing the court's decision and the reasons or analysis by which the court reached its decision. An opinion differs from a mere conclusion in that an opinion requires application of the witness's experience to form the judgment, whereas a conclusion is reasoned from facts. Where a witness makes logical deduction from the evidence, the result is nothing more than a conclusion. As a general rule, the jury is supposed to make its own conclusions from the evidence without hearing conclusions of the witnesses. *See also* **Expert opinion.**

Oral deposition A procedure, established by Rule 30 of the Federal Rules of Civil Procedure, that enables any party to obtain the testimony of any other party or witness for the purpose of obtaining information and evidence or to preserve the testimony for use at trial. The deponent may be compelled, under penalty of law, to testify. The procedure requires the deponent to testify under oath. It preserves the right of interested parties to cross-examine the deponent. The deponent and parties have a right to be represented by counsel. A party may arrange for his or her own deposition to preserve testimony.

Order for judgment A trial court's order directing the clerk or administrator to enter a judgment in the judgment book, including the terms of the judgment.

Ordinary comparative negligence Comparative negligence in which the plaintiff's claim is barred if the claimant's causal negligence is more than the defendant's causal negligence.

Original jurisdiction The court in which an action may properly be commenced. A trial court has original jurisdiction. An appellate court does not have original jurisdiction.

Out-of-pocket damages The measure of damages allowed to the victim of a fraud. The out-of-pocket damages measure includes the victim's actual expenses and losses, but does not allow recovery for loss of the bargain, profits, or expectancies. It is to be distinguished from the loss-of-bargain measure of damages.

Overrule A court order that denies a party's objection to another party's evidence or acts committed in prosecuting an action.

Parol evidence Evidence that would have the effect of changing or modifying the terms of a written contract. Parol evidence may be written or oral.

Partial release A contract that releases fewer than all the persons against whom a claim has been asserted or that releases only a part of a claim, expressly reserving the releasor's right to pursue other aspects of the claim.

Partial settlement A settlement that resolves only part of the claim arising from a transaction or occurrence.

Party A natural person, corporation, or other legal entity that is the plaintiff or defendant in a civil action.

Peremptory challenge By law and court rule, the right of each party to a civil action to remove a specified number of jurors, usually two or three, from the panel during the voir dire examination, without explanation or justification.

Permissive counterclaim A counterclaim that does not arise from the transaction or occurrence that is the subject of the plaintiff's complaint but that may be prosecuted in the same action.

Person In law, a natural person or a legal entity such as a corporation, unless otherwise defined.

Personal jurisdiction A court's jurisdiction or authority over a person, obtained through due process.

Personal property Tangible property that is not real estate. The term *personal property* does not include personal property that has been incorporated into a structure as a fixture in the structure.

Petition A formal request made in writing to a court that asks the court to take some specific action concerning a matter that affects the petitioner. A petition ordinarily recites the relevant facts, the nature of the petitioner's concern, and the action the petitioner requests.

Petit jury A jury that tries the facts in a civil action.

Plain error Very basic error that goes to the heart of the case. Plain error may be noted for the first time in a posttrial motion for an appeal. An appellate court will consider plain error in an appeal even though no objection was made during the trial. By characterizing the error in this manner, an appellate court acquires some discretion to decide whether or not to deal with the problem. If the court concludes that a serious miscarriage of justice occurred, it may call the error plain error or fundamental error and use that characterization as a basis for setting aside the lower court's judgment even though the error was overlooked during the trial stage.

Polling the jury A trial procedure in which the judge asks each juror whether the juror agrees to the verdict after it has been read in open court.

Prejudicial error Error that has adversely affected the outcome of the case for one of the parties.

Preponderance of evidence The greater weight of the evidence as determined by its persuasiveness. Preponderance of evidence does not mean the greater number of witnesses or exhibits. It should cause the trier of fact to believe that a disputed fact is more likely true than not true.

Preserving evidence Following procedures to make sure that evidence that may be needed is kept available. The preservation of evidence requires the exercise of forethought and anticipation of problems or events that could cause the loss of evidence. If a witness may not be available when the case reaches trial, the witness's evidence may be preserved by taking an oral deposition, deposition on written questions, affidavit, recorded statement, or signed statement—in descending value of usefulness and persuasiveness. The method by which evidence should be preserved depends upon its importance, the degree of possibility that it may not be available, and the cost of preserving it.

Pretrial conference A conference ordered by the court for the purpose of expediting a disposition of the case by securing admissions, securing stipulations, and narrowing the issues; establishing a plan for managing and moving the litigation toward trial and avoiding unnecessary delay; determining the state of preparedness of the parties and encouraging full preparation; and helping the parties to avoid unnecessary expense. The court may consider any aspect of the case in a pretrial conference (see Rule 16).

Pretrial order The order that a court issues following a pretrial conference that embodies the court's rulings and plan for managing the progression of the case to trial.

Prima facie case A case in which a party presents sufficient evidence to establish all the elements of the cause of action or evidence that supports all the elements of an affirmative defense. The evidence must be sufficient to support a verdict or finding on a legal issue. A prima facie case may exist even though the evidence is in conflict or disputed. A court does not consider the credibility or persuasiveness of the party's evidence in determining whether a party has presented a prima facie case.

Prima facie evidence of negligence Sufficient evidence to establish all the elements of an action in negligence. Evidence of a violation of a statute is sufficient to establish a prima facie case of negligence unless the opposing party offers evidence that tends to excuse or justify the violation.

Prima facie negligence An act or omission that is, on its face, negligent. Proof of an act or omission that is specifically prohibited by law establishes that the applicable standard of due care has been violated. In the absence of some compelling excuse or justification, the fact finder (jury) must find that the conduct was negligent. The party against whom the claim of prima facie negligence is asserted may be permitted to explain and justify the violation, whereas an act or omission that is negligent per se may not be explained or justified.

Privileged communication A communication that is protected by law from disclosure. A court will not require a party to a privileged communication to disclose it to another party, another person, or even the court. A party may waive the privilege.

Privity A relationship between persons that gives rise to some mutuality of interest. The privity between an assignee and an assignor imposes the obligations of one upon the other. The relationship between contracting parties is described as the privity of contract and is the basis for establishing legal rights and obligations between them.

Procedural law The rules of law that govern the conduct of a legal procedure or process, as distinguished from the law that determines the parties' substantive rights. Procedural rules govern the manner in which the substantive rights will be determined and enforced.

Products liability The liability that the manufacturer, vendor, or bailor for hire may have for supplying a product that is defective or is unreasonably dangerous for use. The liability may arise from a defect in the product or in the design of the product or from a failure to provide adequate instructions concerning the product's use or to provide warning concerning inherent dangers in its use.

Proponents A party who makes some demand or request on another party or who actively seeks some action by a court.

Protective order An order that limits the demands one party may make upon the protected party. Protective orders are most commonly used in discovery procedures (see Rule 26(c)).

Proximate cause A cause that has a direct and substantial part in bringing about an occurrence, injury, loss, or harm for which a party seeks a remedy in court.

Punitive damages Money damages awarded to a plaintiff in a civil action to punish the defendant for willfully committing a wrongful act that injured the plaintiff or damaged the plaintiff's property. Punitive damages are recoverable in addition to compensatory damages. In determining the amount of punitive damages, the jury may consider the nature of the wrongful act, the seriousness of the plaintiff's harm, and the financial condition of the defendant. Some courts take into consideration whether the defendant has already been subjected to punitive damages to other plaintiffs for the same occurrence.

Pure comparative negligence The plaintiff may recover money damages from a defendant who was causally negligent, regardless of the fact that the plaintiff may have been much more negligent than the defendant. However, the plaintiff's damages are reduced by his or her percentage of causal negligence.

Qualified admission An admission, made in response to a Rule 36 request for admissions, that is limited or qualified by the respondent.

Qualified denial A denial, made in response to a Rule 36 request for admissions, that explains something or provides some information notwithstanding the party's denial.

Quotient verdict A verdict for money damages arrived at by having each juror selecting an amount, adding the amounts, and dividing the total by the number of jurors. The jurors then agree on the quotient amount as the amount for the verdict. A quotient verdict is improper because the jurors avoid discussing reasons for their differences and rely on the wrong basis for compromise.

Real party in interest A party who actually owns the cause of action and who is directly affected by the outcome of the litigation.

Real property Land, and structures that are appurtenant to the land.

Reasonable certainty A high degree of probability that the opinion is correct or the expectation will materialize.

Reasonable inquiry An inquiry or investigation that a reasonably prudent person would make to ascertain facts in light of the potential harm and the difficulties of making the inquiry or investigation. A person may have a duty to make a reasonable inquiry where that person has a duty to know facts so that he or she can act with due care to protect himself or herself or another person or property.

Reasonable probability More than a 50 percent chance that the opinion is correct or the expectation will materialize.

Rebuttal evidence Evidence that a party offers to contradict or refute evidence previously offered by another party.

Recorded statement A witness statement that is a verbatim record of the witness's words made by an electronic means, shorthand, or other means.

Redeem To regain possession of something by payment of an obligation, or to repurchase the item.

Release A contract by which a person releases a legal claim or right against another person. A release is usually made in writing.

Relevant evidence Evidence that tends to establish or negate a controverted fact (see Rule 401). Evidence must be relevant to be received in a trial.

Remand To send back. An appellate court remands a case for a new trial or further consideration if it finds that the trial court committed an error that may have affected the outcome of the case.

Remedial measure A party's conduct to correct some danger or problem after an injury or damage has occurred. Evidence of remedial measures is not admissible, as a public policy to encourage persons to make repairs and corrections without fear that the improvement will be used as evidence against them (see Rule 407).

Remittitur A court-ordered reduction in the amount of money damages awarded to a party by a jury. A trial court has the authority to reduce the award when the damages are manifestly excessive and apparently made as the result of prejudice or passion. The trial court may order a remittitur even though no error of law or procedure explains the jury's excessive award. Usually the trial court gives the plaintiff the option of accepting the remittitur, or having a new trial where a new jury can determine the amount of damages.

Replevin An action at law to recover a specific item of property that the defendant wrongfully took or wrongfully retained.

Request for admission A party's formal written demand to another party to admit the existence of a particular fact or the genuineness of a particular document (see Rule 36).

Res ipsa loquitur A legal doctrine by which one party may establish an inference of negligence on the part of another party. The inference of negligence comes from a showing that the accident in question was caused by an instrumentality that was in the exclusive control of the defendant; that the accident was not caused by any act of the plaintiff or some third person; and that the accident is of a kind that ordinarily does not occur in the absence of negligence.

Res judicata A matter adjudged; a thing judicially acted upon or decided; a thing or matter settled by judgment. Res judicata is a legal doctrine that precludes a plaintiff from relitigating the same claim against the same defendant once the cause of action has been determined on its merits.

Respondent (1) The party against whom an appeal is taken; also called an appellee. (2) A party who must answer or respond to some formal demand in the litigation process.

Rests When a party formally announces that he or she has no more evidence to offer in support of a claim or defense. At that point the opposing party may proceed with the presentation of evidence in rebuttal.

Restitution The restoration of property or a legal right that was wrongfully taken, or the provision of its equivalent.

Reverse To overthrow, set aside, or invalidate. An appellate court reverses a lower court when the appellate court changes the outcome without ordering a new trial or other proceedings.

Sanction   A penalty a court imposes upon a party who fails to comply with the court's order or rules.

Scheduling conference   A court-ordered conference convened to create a schedule that will keep the case moving toward trial and meet the needs of the case and of the parties (see Rule 16(b)).

Scheduling order   An order containing the schedule that is the product of a scheduling conference (see Rule 16(b)).

Scope of submission   In an arbitration, the parties' agreement concerning the issues that the arbitrators may resolve and other limitations on the process or award.

Self-help   An action conducted outside the court system to obtain revenge or payment for an injury; for example, the taking of another person's property because that person has damaged the actor's property.

Sequestration   An exclusion of witnesses from a trial or hearing for the purpose of preventing them from hearing other witnesses and being influenced by them.

Settlement   An agreement between parties that results in a resolution of their dispute. Settlement agreements are usually made on the basis of a compromise between parties and arrived at without a judicial order or decree. Where money is paid as a result of a settlement agreement, the sum is often also referred to as the settlement. A jury verdict or arbitration award is *not* a settlement.

Slander   A cause of action in tort for injury to a person's reputation caused by the publication of a false statement made orally.

Sound discretion   The power to make a decision based on knowledge and experience. The presiding judge has a great deal of discretion, or latitude, in certain matters concerning the admissibility of evidence and trial procedures. The judge's decision concerning such matters will not be disturbed by an appellate court, even if the appellate court disagrees with the trial court's handling, unless the ruling was palpably unfair. An appellate court would have to find that the trial court judge clearly abused her or his discretion before finding that the trial court's actions constituted error that would require a new trial.

Special damages   Out-of-pocket expenses that a party has incurred because of another party's wrongful conduct. In a personal injury action, the plaintiff's medical expenses, loss of past income, and property damage are items of special damages. They must be listed in the complaint, although the dollar amount may be omitted. In a breach-of-contract action, the amount of lost profits and consequential expenses should be stated. The defendant needs to know about special damages at the outset; consequently, special damages must be specifically alleged in the parties' pleadings (see rule 9(g)).

Special verdict   The jury's answer to specific questions of fact that the court submits to the jury. A special verdict does not require the jury to apply rules of law to the determined facts for the purpose of deciding which party is entitled to the court's judgment. Instead, the court must apply the rules of law to the facts, as determined by the special verdict, in order to determine which party is entitled to judgment and to decide the terms of the judgment (Rule 49(a)).

Specific performance   A remedy provided by a court that equity powers. A remedy in which a court orders a party to perform a contract obligation because an award of money damages would be inadequate or because the measure of damages is without a basis in law.

Splitting a cause of action   Dividing one cause of action or claim into two or more lawsuits. A party who splits a cause of action is bound by the result in the first trial and is barred from prosecuting the second part of the claim. Courts have a strong policy favoring the total resolution of a dispute in one action.

Stare decisis   The doctrine of abiding by, or adhering to, decided cases. The principle that precedent should be followed unless and until compelling reasons occur to change the rule of law.

Statement of case   An administrative document that some courts require parties to file to help the court manage the case. The statement of case may require information about the party, the party's evidence, witnesses, insurance, theory of the facts, theory of the law, and preparedness. Federal district courts do not use statements of case.

Statute of frauds   A body of law that precludes certain types of contracts from being enforceable unless the contracts are in writing and are signed by the person to be bound.

Statute of limitations   A statute that limits the time during which a lawsuit may be brought against a person. The time period provided by a statute of limitations usually begins to run at the time the cause of action accrues. The running of the statute may be tolled by a party's minority or other legal disability. The statute of limitations does not begin to run against an action based upon fraud until the person discovers the fraud or reasonably should have discovered it.

Statute of repose A statute that has the effect of barring a claim because the act that gave rise to the claim took place many years ago, and even if the injury is recent, the actor should not be held accountable at such a late date.

Stipulated dismissal A dismissal of a court action by agreement of the parties (see Rule 41(a)).

Stipulation An agreement voluntarily entered into between the parties, concerning some aspect of their litigation. An agreement between the parties that the court will recognize and accept to facilitate judicial proceedings. Stipulations may go to matters of procedure or to substantive rights.

Stipulation of facts A stipulation by which the parties express their agreement that a fact or a body of facts is true and may be relied upon by the court. The most common uses for a stipulation of facts are to facilitate a trial and to support a motion for summary judgment.

Strict liability in tort A cause of action that is available in products cases. Liability of the defendant is not based upon fault. Manufacturers and vendors of products are held strictly liable in tort for injuries caused by defective products. In such cases it is not necessary to show that the manufacturer or vendor was negligent or breached an express warranty. A product is considered to be defective if it is unreasonably dangerous when used in the ordinary, foreseeable manner.

Structured settlement A type of settlement that allows the settling party to buy an annuity for the benefit of the claimant. The settling party pays a lump sum of money to a bank or insurance company, which provides scheduled benefits to the claimant over a period of years or over the claimant's lifetime. Because the company that issues the annuity has the right to use or invest the money over the same period of time, the company can add significantly to the initial payment from the tortfeasor. The annuity payments are structured to provide financial protection to the claimant and prevent other persons from having access to the funds. The claimant does not earn interest on the funds, so the claimant avoids a tax obligation. Nevertheless, the annuity has a total value to the claimant that exceeds the amount the settling party pays for it.

Sua sponte Voluntarily, as when a court takes some action or step without request by a party. When a court makes an order without either party

having made a motion to obtain the order, the court has acted sua sponte.

Subject matter jurisdiction Jurisdiction over the type and subject of a case. A court must have jurisdiction over the subject of the litigation to be able to render an enforceable judgment. The parties cannot invest the court with jurisdiction over the subject matter.

Subject to objection Controlled by the rules of governing objections. Evidence or procedure that is in violation of a court rule or standard is subject to an objection. If the objection is not made, the evidence may be received or the procedure used, and the party who failed to object cannot later complain.

Subpoena (1) A process commanding a party, witness, or deponent to set aside all pretenses and excuses, and appear before a designated court or magistrate at a specified time and place to testify. Failure to comply places the person under penalty by the court. A subpoena may be used in connection with motions, trials, and depositions. (2) A document that the court causes to be served upon a person and that requires the person to appear before the court for the purposes of the particular case.

Subpoena duces tecum A subpoena that directs a witness to bring and present specified documents or things to be reviewed when the witness testifies at court or in a deposition.

Subrogation The substitution of one person in the place of another to make a claim or prosecute a cause of action. The subrogee acquires subrogation rights of the subrogor by paying the subrogor's loss under legal compulsion. The subrogee cannot acquire any greater rights than were possessed by the subrogor. For example, where a fire insurance company pays its insured for damage to property because of a fire, the insurer acquires the rights of its insured to bring a claim against the tortfeasor who caused the fire and loss. The insurance contract compels the insurer to pay the loss to the insured, so the insurer is not a volunteer in paying the loss. The insurer is limited to recovering damages in the amount it paid to its insured and is subject to any defenses the tortfeasor had against the insured.

Substantive evidence Evidence that will support a judgment that determines the parties' rights and obligations. Evidence adduced for the purpose of proving a fact in issue, as opposed to evidence given for the purpose of merely discrediting a witness.

Substantive law Law that creates, defines, and regulates legal rights between persons. Substantive law is distinguished from remedial and procedural law that prescribes the means for enforcing substantive legal rights or obtaining redress for the invasion of substantive rights.

Summary judgment A procedure by a which a party may avoid a trial by showing the court that the material facts are not in dispute. The procedure allows the court to apply the law to the undisputed facts and order entry of a judgment for a party. The procedure is initiated by a written motion filed with the court and served upon all the other parties. A summary judgment may be dispositive of the entire action or resolve only part of the dispute. The motion deals with the parties' substantive rights and decides an issue or case on its merits (see Rule 56).

Summons A court mandate that informs a person that a civil action has been commenced against him or her and requires that person to appear in the case and defend; otherwise, the plaintiff is entitled to obtain by default a judgment for the relief specified in the complaint. The summons must be served with the complaint, except when service is by publication (see Rule 4).

Supersedeas bond A bond that the appellant must file with the court to ensure that the judgment the appellee has been granted will be paid if the appellant does not obtain a modification of that judgment.

Superseding cause *See* **Efficient intervening cause.**

Supplemental complaint A complaint that alleges a new, additional claim that arose from a transaction or occurrence that took place after the initial complaint was filed.

Supplementary proceedings Legal proceedings that a judgment creditor may use to discover what property the judgment debtor has with which to pay the judgment (see Rule 69(a)).

Sustained Accepted or admitted. A party's objection to another party's evidence or conduct is sustained when it is accepted by the court and is allowed.

Taxable costs Costs of litigation that a prevailing party is entitled to recover from the losing party. The recoverable costs are set by statute and court rules.

Territorial jurisdiction The geographic area in which a court may function is determined by the political boundaries. With some few exceptions, courts have no authority beyond their territorial limits.

Third-party action An action brought by a defendant against a person other than the plaintiff, to recover money damages as contribution or indemnity to the obligation, if any, that the defendant has to the plaintiff. The defendant cannot seek damages for her or his own loss in a third-party action (see Rule 14).

Tort A private or civil wrong that causes injury to person or damage to property. A wrong independent of contract. A violation of a duty imposed by general law or otherwise upon all persons involved in a given transaction or occurrence. The violation must involve some duty owed to the plaintiff, and generally must arise by operation of law and not by mere agreement of the parties.

Tortfeasor A person who commits any kind of a tort. For example, a person who was negligent and caused an accident, or a person who committed a battery against another person, may be called tortfeasor.

Transaction An act between two or more persons in which their legal relations are changed by their agreement or by operation of law concerning some identified, specific undertaking. The most common examples of transactions are the making of contacts, the sale of property, the making of loans, and the like. A transaction is never an accidental occurrence.

Transitory cause of action A cause of action that follows the defendant and therefore may be commenced in any jurisdiction where the defendant can be found.

Trespass A cause of action in tort to recover money damages for damage to real estate resulting from a wrongful entry upon the land. A trespass occurs whenever the entry is made without consent of the possessor or without legal authority. An entry without consent of the occupant makes the trespasser liable for nominal damages even if no actual damage can be shown. The law affirms the possessor's right to exclusive, peaceful occupancy.

Trial brief A brief that a party prepares for the court, to supply authorities concerning contested points of law and to help the court identify and frame issues.

Trial de novo A second trial that is a new trial in all respects. A trial de novo is totally unaffected by rulings or determinations made in the first trial.

Trial notebook A notebook that a lawyer prepares for her or his own use as a reference for handling the case in trial. It may contain an abbreviated fact brief in which the issues are identified and evidence is listed to support the client's version of the facts. The notebook is not prepared for the court or the other party to see. A trial notebook usually outlines the lawyer's trial strategy, lists important points concerning the substantive law and procedure, and lists authorities the lawyer may cite during the trial. Paralegals may provide significant input to the preparation of a trial brief, particularly in identifying the remaining disputed facts and marshaling the evidence around the facts.

Ultimate facts The conclusion of fact made by the jury from all the evidence. The conclusions that are dispositive of the claims and defenses of the parties. The facts to which the rules of law are applied so that a judgment can be rendered by the court. For example, in a negligence action, the ultimate questions of fact are whether the defendant was negligent, whether the defendant's negligence was a proximate cause of the harm, and what amount of compensation the plaintiff is entitled to.

Ultrahazardous activity Activity that gives rise to strict liability in tort for money damages, because the activity is inappropriate to the place where it is conducted and necessarily involves a risk of serious harm to others or their property, and the risk cannot be eliminated by exercising the utmost care. Blasting tasks and pile driving are examples of ultrahazardous activities that give rise to strict liability in tort.

Unfair prejudice The unacceptable consequences of some procedure or improper evidence that a party has wrongly injected into the case. Almost anything a party does in the furtherance of his or her case is in some way prejudicial to the opposing party, but only certain wrongful conduct or improper evidence is unfairly harmful to the opposing party.

Unilateral mistake A mistake concerning the terms or effect of a contract, made by just one of the parties.

Vacate judgment To declare that the judgment is of no force and effect; that it is void.

Venireman A person who has been selected to undergo questioning to determine whether she or he may qualify to sit on a petit jury.

Venue The judicial district in which an action is brought for trial and that is to furnish the panel of jurors.

Verdict The jury's decision based upon its determination of the facts and its application of the law to those facts.

Voidable Capable of being voided. A contract is voidable when the contract's purpose is not contrary to law but is technically defective owing to the wrongful conduct or inadvertence of one of the contracting parties. The party or parties to the contract who did comply with all legal requirements have the option of enforcing the contract or avoid it. A contract that is void cannot be enforced by any party.

Voir dire (1) The preliminary examination of jurors in which competency, interest, and so forth are

tested. (2) A preliminary examination of a witness to determine whether the witness is competent to testify.

Voluntary dismissal A dismissal of a cause of action or an action, given by a party without being subject to a court order (see Rule 41(a)(1)).

Waiver An intentional, voluntary giving up of a legal right. A waiver may be expressed in writing or orally, or implied from circumstances.

Work product A doctrine that protects from discovery the impressions, mental processes, legal theories, and strategies that a party and the party's attorney formulated while preparing to prosecute or defend a civil action. The doctrine has been expanded to include the party's indemnitor or liability insurer. The doctrine is separate from but complements the attorney-client privilege against disclosure of their communications. It has express support in Rule 26(b) of the Federal Rules of Civil Procedure.

Writ A written precept issued by a court and addressed to a person or officer of the government, that commands the person to do something as described in the writ. A type of court order.

Writ of certiorari A writ issued by a superior court to a lower court, that requires the lower court to transmit its record to the superior court so that the superior court can inspect the proceedings and determine whether any irregularities occurred. If the superior court determines that there was some error that ought to be addressed, it will authorize the petitioning party to appeal.

Write of execution (1) A writ that directs the sheriff or marshal to seize certain property that belongs to the named judgment debtor and to hold or sell the property for the benefit of the judgment creditor. (2) Any writ that puts into force the court's judgment.

Writ of prohibition A writ issued by an appellate court and directed to a judge in a trial court, ordering the judge not to enforce an order already issued. A party may seek a writ of prohibition as an interim appeal to prevent the trial court from causing irreparable harm, as where a trial court has wrongly ordered a party to disclose privileged information.

Written response to demand for inspection A written response that must be served within thirty of any demand for inspection. The written response must acknowledge the request and agreement to the terms of inspection as expressed in the demand. If the respondent objects to any of the terms in the demand, the objections must be stated and reasons must be given for each objection (see Rule 34(b)).

Wrongful death action An action at law, created by statute, that permits the heirs and next of kin to recover money damages from a tortfeasor for the pecuniary losses resulting from the decedent's death. The elements of the cause of action are established by statute in each state. State statutes also declare what pecuniary losses are compensable and the limitation, if any, on the total amount of damages recoverable.

Geographical Boundaries of
United States Courts of Appeals and United States District Courts

LEGEND

— Circuit Boundaries

— State Boundaries

······ District Boundaries

D.C. CIRCUIT
Washington, D.C.

FEDERAL CIRCUIT
Washington, D.C.

INDEX